# Who Decides?

A volume in
*Research and Theory in Educational Administration*
Arnold B. Danzig and William R. Black, *Series Editors*

# Research and Theory in Educational Administration

Arnold B. Danzig and William R. Black, *Series Editors*

# Who Decides?

## Power, Disability, and Educational Leadership

*edited by*

## Catherine A. O'Brien
*Gallaudet University*

## William R. Black
*University of South Florida*

## Arnold B. Danzig
*San José State University*

INFORMATION AGE PUBLISHING, INC.
Charlotte, NC • www.infoagepub.com

**Library of Congress Cataloging-in-Publication Data**

A CIP record for this book is available from the Library of Congress
http://www.loc.gov

ISBN: 978-1-64802-911-0 (Paperback)
978-1-64802-912-7 (Hardcover)
978-1-64802-913-4 (E-Book)

Printed in the United States of America

# CONTENTS

## SECTION I
### INTRODUCTION

## SECTION II
### LEADERSHIP AND DIS/ABILITY: ONTOLOGY, EPISTEMOLOGY, AND INTERSECTIONALITIES

# SECTION III

## EDUCATIONAL LEADERS AND DISABILITY: POLICIES IN PRACTICE

# SECTION IV

## EXPERIENCE AND POWER IN SCHOOLS

# SECTION V

## ADVOCACY, LEVERAGE, AND THE PREPARATION
## OF SCHOOL LEADERS

# SECTION VI

## AFTERWORD

# SECTION I

INTRODUCTION

# CHAPTER 1

# INTRODUCTION

**Catherine A. O'Brien**
*Gallaudet University*

**William R. Black**
*University of South Florida*

**Arnold B. Danzig**
*San José State University*

**Adam Rea**
*University of South Florida*

*We all have different gifts, so we all have different ways of saying
to the world who we are*

—Rogers, 1994, p. 7

We were on the cusp of a pandemic and the realization of the dangers of the coronavirus (COVID-19) when the editor's call for chapter proposals was first announced and chapters were accepted. Along with our contributors, we found ourselves scrambling to work from home and homeschool children while caring for loved ones and grieving the loss of family and friends. Schools, universities, businesses, churches, and social outlets shuttered and

*Who Decides?*, pages 3–25
Copyright © 2022 by Information Age Publishing
www.infoagepub.com
All rights of reproduction in any form reserved.

everyone remained home, navigating life through Zoom and loneliness. The pandemic has changed us through the past year and a half, as many of us struggled and persevered. Despite these challenges, this volume came to be, through sheer persistence.

Drs. O'Brien, Black, and Danzig are pleased to be able to bring the *Who Decides? Power, Dis/Ability, and Education Administration* volume to you. The book came about through a casual conversation that started at the World Educational Leadership symposium held in Zug, Switzerland in September, 2018. Catherine, Bill, and Arnie met after Arnie and Bill's presentation on their recently published edited book on leadership preparation policy and practice. Titled *Who Controls the Preparation of School Leaders?* (Danzig & Black, 2019), the book was the first volume published under their editorship of the Research and Theory in Educational Administration book series with Information Age Publishing (IAP). During our conversation we discussed possibilities for a new volume, engaging topics related to special education policy and practice, disabilities, dis/able, school leaders, and school leadership preparation. We also briefly discussed our familiarity with children and adults identified with disabilities or who were differently abled. Further, we also noted that we had not seen an edited book that comprehensively focused on many of these topics.

During UCEA in November of 2018 we met again during breakfast and discussed "becoming" involved with disabilities and disability studies. One of Bill's doctoral students, Juliana Capel, also joined us at that meeting. During the meeting we told stories of how we had become involved with disabilities, special education, advocacy, protests, fighting for rights, policy change advocacy, and struggling with the education system in various ways. Ultimately, we began to see parallels in our stories both as theory and as powerful narratives of parents, children, students, educators, and scholars with disabilities or who are differently abled to describe their experiences at home, in school, and in the workplace.

We discussed the unacceptability of the all too common practice of school administrators, principals, and other experts or professionals, standing by as parents and students do the hard work of advocating for needs and services (see Almager & Valle, 2021). Catherine also noted the many lawsuits that have occurred in the United States due to these practices (i.e., San Antonio, Texas 2019 regarding a deaf[1] student and Blue Springs, Missouri 2017 regarding bullying of a student with a speech disability). The act of school leaders stepping aside and letting parents and individuals with disabilities do the advocacy work around policy, agency, and access, and not taking the responsibility for the heavy lifting on these issues is a concern we shared. In these preliminary conversations, the purpose of the edited volume evolved and resulted in the call for chapter proposals. We noted that special education administration is a complex discipline and that this field was not particularly active or even taught as part of required administrator preparation programs. By contrast, the fields of disability studies and critical disability studies, as well as special education policy analysis were quite rich and provided multiple new avenues for generative and intersecting strands of inquiry and narrative insight.

When we announced the *Who Decides?* volume, we were excited but unsure of the number of proposal submissions we would receive. In the beginning, the proposals and emails of excitement about the edited volume started to slowly emerge and by the time we arrived at our deadline for proposals, we saw that there was a huge appetite for this work. We received 70 chapter proposal submissions with several authors asking if they could submit both a theoretical chapter as well as a more narratively oriented chapter. Through the number of submissions that we received, we saw there was a need and a thirst for work to be published. Further, we saw that our contributors were diverse in the fields they represented, as they were scholars and parents with children with disabilities, scholars who had disabilities or were differently abled, special education scholars, school leadership scholars, school leaders, teachers, policy scholars, activists, and advocates.

One editor, a tenured faculty member in higher education, was also forced to advocate for herself as she navigated her doctoral program and attended professional conferences. She often stood alone to advocate, teach, re-teach, while pushing knowledge, research, and legal frameworks to gain access to the noisy but lonely field of educational leadership. We also noted the importance of various approaches within the higher education field; these faculty need both specific technical knowledge, introspection, advocacy, and emotional knowledge to produce the change and access that is needed. In this volume we saw this evidence come from the authors' narratives, the policy savvy, the fighters, and the despairing and exhausted academics who are disabled or differently abled.

## POLICY, DIS/ABILITY, AND EDUCATIONAL LEADERSHIP

Over the last quarter century, educational leadership as a field has developed a broad strand of research that engages issues of social justice, equity, and diversity. This development includes the work of many scholars who advocate for a variety of equity-oriented leadership preparation approaches. Critical scholarship in education administration and educational policy is concerned with questions of power and in various ways asks questions around who gets to decide. In line with this broader critical tradition of inquiry, this volume interrogates policies, research, and personnel preparation practices which constitute interactions, discourses, and institutions that construct and perpetuate deficit thinking and frameworks for understanding ability and disability within the disciplinary field of education leadership.

Many policies have impacted the education of children with differing abilities/disabilities in the United States (see Yell, 2018). Further, special education broadly is the most litigated field within the U.S. education system (Yell, 2016, 2019). In 1975, Congress enacted the Education for All Handicapped Children Act (EAHCA, which is known as Public Law 94-142) to support states and localities in protecting the rights and meeting the individual needs of children with disabilities (Howard, 2004; Yell, 2006; Ysseldyke & Algozzine, 2006). The 1974 law PL 94-142, a landmark legislation, is currently enacted as the Individuals With Disabilities Education Act (IDEA). IDEA was amended in 1997 and reauthorized in 2004 (Howard, 2004; Yell, 2006; Ysseldyke & Algozzine, 2006). IDEA was again amended in 2015 through Public Law 114-95, to include the Every Student Succeeds Act (IDEA, 2015). However, IDEA has not been reauthorized since 2004.

Under IDEA, there are two legally recognized rights of children with disabilities: (a) the right to a free and appropriate public education (FAPE) and (b) the right to be educated "to the maximum extent appropriate" in the general education classroom (Wright, 1999, p. 11). Students with disabilities have the right to an appropriate public education but not the most appropriate education (Yell, 2006). Challenging this notion is the most recent Supreme Court decision, March 22, 2017, to unanimously reverse the lower court's decision on how students with disabilities are educated—*Endrew F. v. Douglas County School District*. As Justice Roberts stated, "When all is said and done, a student offered an educational program providing 'merely more than de minimis' progress from year to year can hardly be said to have been offered an education at all" (Supreme Court of the United States, 2016, p. 14). To date, the recent Supreme Court decision has not changed policy nor has it impacted or changed how special education access is provided or services are delivered. More importantly, it has not changed the way academic success is measured for students with disabilities. Therefore, the onus is now on school districts, the principal, and school leaders and not the special educators, to ensure that all students in special education are given access to the curriculum *and* the support needed to achieve academically in the educational setting.

When discussing schools and how schools manage students with disabilities, Temple Grandin (2006) stated, "In special education, there's too much emphasis placed on the deficit and not enough on the strength" (p. 231). It is important to note that school leaders often navigate or balance school, district, state, and federal requirements with those in charge of assessing/determining abilities, academic access, and ethical commitments towards a more inclusive and just set of practices. Coming to engage the simple question in our title—"Who Decides?"—implies a broad historical understanding of the nature of ability and constructs associated with disability; it also implies consideration of the ontological and epistemological concerns used to make these determinations, which serve to advantage and disadvantage certain children, youth, and educators in schools.

The ontological and epistemological challenges to disability norms and special education practices through disability studies, critical disability studies (CDS), and DisCrit intersectional theoretical frameworks are critical for school leaders to understand the underpinnings of special education and to understand what it means to give access to an education. According to Liasidou (2014), disability and race/ethnicity have been intertwined in history, with both strands providing genetic "traits" that were used as points of exploitation by society in order to scrutinize and discriminate against certain members of society (p. 725). However, "unlike other sources of social disadvantage such as race and gender, disability has been excluded from discussions concerning unequal and discriminatory treatment" (Liasidou, 2014, p. 724). Additionally, Liasidou (2014) suggests that "able-bodiedness has a precarious ontological status, unlike whiteness that constitutes a perennial and immutable ontological entity" (p. 729), and that disability is a "potential ontological status" (p. 729). Not only does DisCrit highlight how normative identity is constructed, but it pushes us to consider the social and cultural norms of educational leadership research and preparation for practice. DisCrit is a framework that allows for the critical investigation of "the ways in which race, racism, dis/ability and ableism are built into the interactions, procedures, discourses, and institutions of education" (Annamma et al., 2013, p. 7).

## GUIDING QUESTIONS FOR THE VOLUME AND CONTRIBUTORS

For this volume, we discussed what questions we wanted to ask and what questions our contributors could ponder as they created their full proposals and eventual chapters. These questions emerged through our editorial discussions and through discussions with our contributors. After much thought the following six questions emerged:

1. How might we build theory in educational administration through research on institutional normalization of ability as a central organizing concept in school governance?
2. Drawing on the tenets of critical disability studies, how might we best challenge marginalizing practices associated with disability and special education?

3. How do school administrators best learn to work with differently abled students and their families?
4. What purposeful programs are available for school leaders that provide opportunities to engage with students often identified for special education?
5. What are the implications of the legal and policy architecture around special education, disability studies, and personal perspectives from the field for the preparation of future school administrators and professional development of current teachers and administrators?
6. What are generative pathways for future scholarship on disability studies for education leaders?

The volume seeks to provide a more nuanced view of what it means to be "able" or what it means to be differently abled in ways that others overlook. We ask who decides how to organize schools around criteria of ability and/or disability and what that implies for leadership in schools. The book is decidedly interdisciplinary as the chapters draw from multiple disciplines including special education, cultural studies, disability studies, education and Americans with Disabilities Act policies, organizational leadership, school–community relationships, critical theory, leadership development and preparation, identity theory, and the multiple intersectionalities housed therein. These chapters illustrate many important dilemmas and tensions, including:

- Tensions between critical disability studies' ethic of critique and embrace of subjectivism and the pragmatist stances, often centered in educational leadership research and practice, particularly as it relates to special education policy and practice.
- Criticism of the shortcomings of education systems and leaders while recognizing ways educational leaders are trying to do the best that they can, in an imperfect system.
- Support for leadership preparation and developing the leadership needed to make changes while navigating policies that marginalize the populations they are intended to serve.

The volume is organized around four themes: (a) Leadership and Dis/Ability: Ontology, Epistemology, and Intersectionalities; (b) Educational Leaders and Disability: Policies in Practice; (c) Experience and Power in Schools; (d) Advocacy, Leverage, and the Preparation of School Leaders. Intertwined within each theme are chapters which explore conceptual arguments, present empirical research, and narratives that bring personal experiences to the discussion of disability and the multiple ways in which disability shapes experiences in schools. In some instances, these perspectives explored the experiences and challenges that our colleagues have faced in schools. Other times, these conversations involved stories of parents talking about how they negotiated and advocated to improve their children's experiences in schools or their own experiences in academia.

## THE POWER OF NARRATIVES: REFLECTIONS FROM THE VOLUME EDITORS

The original thinking behind this volume (and chapter) was to focus attention on concepts, theories, and empirical research at the intersection of disability studies and educational leadership. The editors (Drs. O'Brien, Black, and Danzig) also wanted to provide narratives to reveal the many ways that dis/ability is experienced in the personal and professional lives of the editors and chapter authors. For O'Brien, this conversation concerned her own experiences navigating education systems and the workplace as an undergraduate and graduate student and now as a university professor. For Black, this discussion meant talking through the imperfect and sometimes marginalizing systems that he experienced as a parent, while teaching the future administrators who work in the educational systems he supports and critiques. For Danzig, this conversation focused on family, with special attention to his daughter, Sidney. We also added our colleague Adam Rea's learning as he listened to our editorial conversations while assisting in the preparation of the volume. Our hope is that this introductory chapter extends the effort to build community by sharing some of the editors' experiences with dis/ability, highlighting issues that are considered by the chapter authors. In addition, the chapter (and volume) crafts an overall narrative that connects these examples of the ways dis/ability is experienced with the conceptual and scholarly literature. We hope that the resulting understanding will help current and future educational and organizational leaders rethink current practices that may be counterproductive.

In the first reflection listed below, O'Brien shares her experiences in school and in the work/professional environment as being the first and only Deaf person within the group, social settings, classrooms, and workplaces. Black opens his narrative by questioning whether he can ever truly speak for his "nonverbal" son while also recognizing his duty to speak and advocate. He then narrates the struggles and duality of his two son's experiences with e-learning during COVID-19 (one in "gifted" and the other starting high school on alternative curriculum with few supports). The third narrative begins with Danzig's wife, Lori, sharing her lament on community and getting needed support for their daughter. Danzig then reflects on his experiences as a father, husband, professor and the learning that resulted from his experiences raising Sidney. The fourth narrative is written by Adam Rea.

## STANDING OUT, NEVER REALLY BELONGING: MEMBERSHIP HAS ITS PRIVILEGES—O'BRIEN REFLECTS

Research has shown that students having a sense of belonging in academic settings is critical for academic success and student retention (Treece, 2021; Vaccaro, Daly-Cano, & Newman, 2015; VandeKamp, 2013). Students with disabilities have many hurdles to overcome to gain peer acceptance and membership within educational settings. Though there are many political policies to support students in academic settings (e.g., ADA, IDEA, Section 504 of the Rehabilitation Act), students have long struggled toward acceptance and membership in educational settings.

Growing up, I was labeled as a low-income student with a disability who was homeless with little chance of success. Schooling, in general, was a place where I stood out but never really belonged nor did anyone try to understand who I was or what I needed or what knowledge I possessed. I was the only deaf student in the school and did not know any deaf peers or deaf adults in school or in the community. In an oral after-school program, I learned how to act hearing, to go along with the group, however, in school I was never a member of the group. I learned to fake it when not understanding, and how to laugh when I had no idea why everyone was laughing, and to agree to go along when I had no clue where I was going. I sat in the front of the class to understand and read everything I could get my hands on. These skills were my coping skills. I continued to resiliently push myself to learn and not rely on anyone to teach me. Many of the teachers were not interested in teaching me nor wanted to know what I knew nor wanted to know what my interests were, they just wanted me to comply. During this time the school and public library became my place of comfort as the librarians were always nice and left me alone to read. The public librarian gave me books; she gave me an occasional sandwich but always had cookies and there was a working water fountain. The libraries were always a peaceful, warm, dry, and clean place to be.

When beginning my undergraduate degree program, I was told that I was the first deaf student that attended the university. Further, when I inquired about supports such as a note taker or interpreter I was told there was no funding for this. Access to classes and the coursework was not granted.

During my first week, I was told not to tell anyone that I could not hear, to hide it. Then I began to realize that hiding my inability to hear was not effective as faculty and staff thought I was not trying or that I was aloof. So I began the daunting task of informing my professors. In one class the professor asked me to drop the class. When I refused to drop the class the professor began to give oral quizzes while walking around a table. I could not speech read the professor in this manner and I subsequently failed all of the quizzes which lowered my grade substantially. While in a theater class, we were assigned to watch a play in action and critique the play. With all of the actors moving about, it was impossible to understand (speech read) them so I went to the library and read the script of the play several times hoping it would help me to speech read the actors and write my critique. I attended the play three times, however, my efforts proved to be useless as my critique was given a failing grade. Situations like these plagued my undergraduate experiences. I was not given a notetaker for my classes until my third year.

I really did not feel as though I belonged and felt alone during my undergraduate years. I was often made fun of by my peers and sometimes by my instructors but acted like I didn't know it. I thought if I responded to their comments or negative gestures, it would make matters worse, so I stayed silent as I did not have a support system. After graduating, I thought I would never go back to school as I was exhausted from the experience.

Years later the Americans With Disabilities Act was passed. It was then I was presented an opportunity to complete a master's degree in special education and applied for a federal grant. During this time, I was once again told that I was the first deaf student to be accepted into the program. When I inquired about access for my classes, I was told what services I needed to have access to the classroom. I was never consulted about what I felt I needed, so they assigned interpreters to my classes. I did not have a notetaker as an interpreter was provided. However, I did not know sign language and the interpreters were useless until I became brave enough to ask the interpreters to please enunciate the words in English as they signed. Then one interpreter told me that I needed to learn sign language, but still complied with my request to enunciate the spoken words as they signed so I could speech read. The interpreters still continued to sign, however, I was clueless about where to learn or if there were other deaf students like me. I completed my degree with a perfect grade point average but connections with hearing peers and the academic and personal communities were limited. I was a Deaf person in a hearing world and I realized I was not perceived as a member.

After completing my master's degree in special education, my school principal, Rolan J. Werner, PhD, encouraged me to apply for the school leadership preparation program offered in collaborative partnership between the school district, University of Missouri, and the Wallace Foundation. He was a positive support of my work within the school and school district. I was again the only deaf educator teaching in general education and special education hired by the district during this time. At his request, I applied to the program and was accepted. This was an 18-month education specialist degreed program. My experiences in this program reflected the same experiences in education. My peers questioned my ability to lead a school because I was deaf. My academic abilities were respected; however, my "disability" was reflected mainly within the group and extended to the district level.

For example, after a particularly long day in class, I stepped out into the hallway during a break. I noticed a group of four people chatting down the hallway. Their conversation caught my eye as one person said the word "deaf" in conversation. So, I walked in their direction and on man stated, "they even have a deaf woman in this group. They are taking anyone to lead schools." I promptly walked up to the group, introduced myself, and explained that I was a part of the leadership preparation program. While shaking their offered hands I explained that I was the deaf woman they were talking about. They immediately dispersed. When explaining this experience to one of the professors, she stated that she was aware of the gossip. I never felt like I was a member of this group with my peers. No matter how hard I worked and supported others, I was never truly accepted.

Earning my doctorate was different than the other educational experiences. My peers at first were uncomfortable with me. One peer told me that I was "lucky" I was accepted into the doctoral program. He then went on to explain his perception of affirmative action. When I told him I was admitted due to my work and educational background and applied through the same channels as he did, he was surprised. However, during the second semester, my peers started inviting me for social and work events. The camaraderie that I felt with this group was like nothing I had felt before. In one classroom experience a professor demanded that the American Sign Language (ASL) interpreter sit in the hallway at the door while he was teaching. My peers in the class became very upset and met with me during the class break asking how they could support me. I asked that one group of two peers write down everything the professor said and the other group write everything he wrote on the board. Then I promised to compile all the notes and email a complete set of notes to each before the next morning. This was a lot of work, but I kept my promise, and they did as well. When the professor refused to call on me to ask questions, I created my questions before class and asked them to ask the professor and document his response. We did this for the entire semester, and we were all successful in passing the class earning among the highest grades in the class. This specific group of students and I maintained contact and socialized often. Although peers in my doctoral program were very supportive and engaging we worked hard, leaned on each other, attended academic conferences together, and graduated together.

From this time on, my academic and professional experiences have been mixed. In some ways, I know I have peer support and in other ways, I struggle to become a member of the various academic, professional, and educational groups. However, I believe my positive inner resiliency, can-do attitude, and work ethic have served me well and that I am an outlier when considering research regarding belonging. Unfortunately, not everyone has this energy within them. I believe educators and administrators can support or push out student in educational setting due to their behaviors and lack of knowledge either intentionally or unintentionally. I believe the same is true for peers in professional settings. Through the work put forth within this book, through our authors, and those who will read this volume, I am hopeful for positive changes all of you will make for students and peers!

I am truly grateful for those who have supported me along the way. The professional peers who have continued to extend membership and instill a sense of belonging are some of the most amazing professionals nationally and internationally who actually "walk the talk." I am indebted to my co-editors for this volume who willingly and consistently ensured peer membership and have given and assured that I have access through our work together and in conference presentations. I am proud and grateful for our work together.

## LOVE AND ADVOCACY—BLACK QUESTIONS HIMSELF

Black asks, "Should I ever speak or write for someone else? What if I don't?"

How do I speak for someone else? What are the parameters of responsibility to speak out and be present for and with a child who does not speak? How might I overreach in love and advocacy?

In the spring, our kids went to school online immediately after spring break. It became quickly obvious to me how distinct the adjustment to the new pandemic seemed to be for my colleagues with children—as meetings seemed continually tethered to the care of children. I recall one meeting when I had to leave a zoom call to jump into the pool after Gaby—a rather awkward and prolonged "Excuse me, I will be back." Clearly, commitments had to somehow be curtailed, and so I began to consider which meetings were essential and what I could commit to doing. I began to realize that the time I had to speak with friends or colleagues tended to be when I was driving the car with Gaby—otherwise I had little time. Jessica and I alternated schedules working and caregiving. While the weather in Florida was still good in the spring, I worked outside on the patio away from the bustle of the household. I was asked to consider applying for a chair position and it became clear that this was not the year to consider this role—with children (and even more so with the physical and developmental care that Gaby required) and the time and energy to devote to my relationships and physical health, I felt that it was not a possibility for me. In my teaching, I immediately went to asynchronous instruction. Many of my students had their own parenting responsibilities as well and we could all benefit from more flexibility in scheduling—I found that there was no need to directly translate my activities to a synchronous version of my class. I cut assignments—just thinking about the workload for my students who were also pivoting to online instructions.

After what seemed to be weekly and then monthly updates on potential school reopenings in the spring, David's third grade school year was finally finished online. David's teachers generally navigated the online environment with competency, courage, and commitment to success. In general, we did not feel that he lost that much instruction. Given the course of the pandemic, we knew he would go back to school online in the fall. In particular, his gifted education teachers for math and science have been very good and timely in their responses and fourth grade has seen relatively strong instruction. As relatively strong as his pedagogical experience has been, institutional divergences and marginalizations have literally been brought home during the pandemic. The range of capacity and commitments to the gifted range of exceptional education David experiences and the experience we have had with Gaby during this time, who is in the "lowest" access points curriculum in exceptional education (Gabriel). Back in the spring, Gaby had been attending a school run by ABA therapists—it was expensive and not particularly effective, but was safe and he had a one-on-one aide, paid by insurance and a voucher. During middle school, we had been trying alternative approaches. As he had only a few months left and there was little contact between the "teacher" (noncredentialed) who barely reached out to us, he had little to no instruction in the spring. He did have some billable therapy online which did not work. I got very upset considering that maybe we had not made the right decision to keep him there earlier, but the hustle and bustle of large schools is very difficult for him (and us) with as many loud noises as there are. So in the spring, we had already known we were transitioning him back to the public school system for the fall and just felt like we did not have many options but to do a modified homeschooling experience. Instructional time was very limited and it required one of us as parents to be fully one-on-one with him—so it cannot be for more than perhaps an hour and a half a day—both for him and for us. So, we rotated our in-home supports—Jessica, myself, and his grandparents during the day. I remember now how corrupt the system seemed, not out of intent, but out of outcome. The voucher system in Florida requires parents to sign a check over to the school quarterly. Gaby was supposed to go to the school through July and transition. As there was little happening educationally, we clearly saw limits of the voucher system accountability and refused to sign the check for the voucher. It seemed completely unethical and we did not want to bill insurance for ABA therapy that was online and ineffective (for which we, as parents, had to do the work). To make the weird even stranger, we had an IEP meeting online for the fall admission to the high school. In order to hold the IEP meeting per district protocols, he needed to be in the system, so he was enrolled in a middle school in April on paper but he did not attend. His ABA school had reopened and immediately reopened with a therapist who tested positive for COVID. Sending Gabby to ABA was no longer an option. So we started limited externally supported education and fully supported parenting education at home in March and continue to do so to this day. Given these dynamics, I began a new ritual of taking Gaby for a walk most days of the week at a park at the very end of our neighborhood. These walks benefitted Gaby, myself, and the family.

In June, David attended a summer online camp and did well at first, however, the second iteration of the camp was less satisfying. We did laps and played in the pool and we knew that the summer would not bring camp or other activities that we had enjoyed before. David also kept cycling a bit with me, this was something he had begun to do late at age nine. He also completed some school work that Jessica oversaw. In many ways he was waiting... waiting for the summer to end.

Gaby did some therapy work online. We lost the therapist who was working with Gaby and who had built some knowledge of him. She transitions as a supervisor, as always happens with therapists with any experience, they seem to become supervisors quickly. We jumped in the pool at home and at my mom's home regularly. One of the gifts of the pandemic has become the ability to listen to stories from my mom and my in-laws. During times in the pool with Gaby, I got to hear about my mom's friends from San Antonio who were the only two women to graduate from the University of Texas Law School. One went on to run Planned Parenthood in San Antonio for many years. I also heard about her time on the Grand Jury in New Orleans, (which I knew about as a child), and the corruption and overt racism in the system. We got to hear my in-laws stories of immigration from Ecuador and life in Chicago, these stories were part of the pandemic pedagogy for David.

As we prepared to return to school, David's fourth grade teachers reached out to him and held multiple orientations the 2 weeks before school. He was able to get the same great teacher he had in second grade for language arts and social studies, and then had two gifted teachers who sent very detailed instructions to the 15 students in their charge. The effort and organization of the school has been good in spite of the many challenges. He was excited as the semester started and in general has continued to learn. The accumulation of time online and continued challenges of our space has led him to be "tired." The greater challenges have begun to be around activity and motivation to go do activities outside.

The differences with Gaby have been striking and fraught with uncertainty and stress. Consider your child starting high school. Gaby was starting high school as a ninth grader in a segregated classroom setting where modified standards (access points curriculum) were being used. After multiple phone calls and emails, we reached the weekend before school was to begin with no information about who his teacher was or how to access school material online. We received a phone call the Sunday before class was to begin on Monday from this primary teacher. Despite Gaby being a higher funded student, she was going to begin the year with a student enrollment of 35. Gaby has class with his teacher from 9:00–10:00 a.m., while David has class from 7:40 a.m.–2:00 p.m. Gaby has intermittent speech therapy at school that we concluded is not worth attending. His math and science teacher in the afternoon would be pulled for other duties and would not plan for class (again recognizing the charade of what some online learning can be like for people like Gaby). It got to the point that I just said that Gaby will not be attending school in the afternoon—it was not appropriate and the teacher was inconsistent. Even with that, Gaby made the first 9 weeks honor roll.

The differences in the school experiences are huge. Jessica and I try not to interfere with class, but we need to provide complete support for Gaby to engage for the 1 hour (and then 15 minutes one-on-one in the afternoon) so we are present. We try to stay in the background in order to respect the teaching spaces that we now inhabit. But, I still had to call out the speech therapist for racist assumptions. Yet, his morning teacher is dedicated and has found a way to connect with Gaby. We are no longer certain that the institution we call school still exists. And still, we get more from the school, which means more work from us. Where might that extra time come from?

Given all these challenges, I was hoping maybe we could find an in-person alternative for Gaby, if it was careful. Then one of the most depressing days for me was when the Florida governor moved the state to Phase 3 in the fall—reopening of bars and restaurants at nearly full capacity. I was starting to think maybe we could invite a caregiver to the home or see some other people as the positivity rate was declining. But the move to Phase 3 meant we would inevitably see rises in cases. Shortly thereafter, even more of my students (largely teachers in schools) were put in quarantine and several had tested positive. So, we decided that we are not moving Gaby and this year will be what it has been.

During these last 10 months, as I considered my role and responsibility as a parent, I did so in light of broader patterns of interest and behavior. I engage in an inner dialogue around legacies of self-interest (I want my family and my economic health) as individual rather than collective choice (just wear a damn mask and stay away from others). As I took on a leadership role in a national organization, I considered social and political pollution, including anti-blackness, and the politicized reduction of risk of the pandemic with both leading to deaths. I find myself no longer harboring the detritus of delusions around the exceptionality of higher education as an ethical space as universities expose their material interests. I currently find myself in a battle to try and save the University of South Florida College of Education from extinction, which is the only public university in a diverse region of 3 million.

## DANZIG'S WIFE LORI'S LAMENT

Her parents have loved and cherished their daughter Sidney from the very day she was conceived. She was planned for. She had good prenatal care. Her parents didn't drink, or smoke, or take drugs.

Two days before she was born her mother knew something was terribly wrong. No one listened or no one cared. They went to the emergency room.

"Something is terribly wrong," said the mother. "My baby isn't moving." The medical staff hooked her up to a fetal monitor and then sent her home.

Two days later, the beautiful Sidney was born, meconium stained and placed under an oxygen hood. "Do you want to see your baby?" the nurse said. "Oh, yes!" said her mother. An hour later and no baby. Her mother thought, "She's dead." Another nurse came in. "Do you want to see your baby?" "Yes, yes!" said the very anxious mother. An hour later and no baby. Nurse number three said, "Don't you want to see your baby?" Sidney's mother cried, "Of course I want to see my baby!" "Well get up and go see her!" said the nurse. Sidney's mother got up and walked down the long hall to the nursery, dripping blood down her legs until she got to the nursery. There was the beautiful Sidney lying on her little front, her head under an oxygen hood, so still, so very, very still. Sidney's parents knew she was going to die. The hospital released her. "She's just fine," said her physician, "but I want to see her in a few days for a weight check and to measure her head." They took the beautiful, motionless Sidney home and loved her. Every few weeks the physician would measure her head, then check her weight. And always he would say: "She's just fine." None of Sidney's parents' friends had their baby's heads measured so often, if at all. Her parents knew she was dying.

At 6 months of age, Sidney's parents took her back to the doctor and said, "Something is terribly wrong with our baby. Our baby is dying." The physician said, "All baby's are different." Sidney's parents took the beautiful Sidney and left the town of Denial, a small town in Northern Arizona, and went to the Tucson Medical Center. The doctor said, "Your baby has a small head, she is profoundly retarded, she will probably be able to enjoy music and bright colors. Do you want us to take her now?" Sidney's parents loved her and wanted to keep her home with them as long as possible. So they put the beautiful Sidney in the car and drove back to the town of Denial.

The whole town of Denial supported Sidney's family. Or did they. Her physician said, "There is no way of telling…this could just be mild." Sidney's parent's went through several long hard years in the town of Denial. They were told this could be just mild, yet at 2 years old, no preschool would take her. She wasn't toilet trained and she couldn't feed herself. The advocacy people kept telling them they had rights. "But our child has rights!" exclaimed the beautiful Sidney's parents. "If she is not toilet trained and cannot feed herself, she cannot go to preschool," said the preschool directors. Sidney's parents were told of an integrated preschool for handicapped children. "It is not our job to feed her." You feed her, we teach her colors," said the preschool teacher. "But she has to be fed every 2 hours. She doesn't know how to eat, she can't drink, she already has crystals in her urine. Her parents pleaded—"If you don't feed her, she will starve to death." "I'm sorry, it's not our job to feed your daughter," said the director and the bureaucrats agreed. Was it that they weren't listening or was it that they didn't care?

It's been six long years now of loving Sidney. There really wasn't much time for love. Most of the time was spent holding, rocking, calming, cleaning up vomit, changing and washing clothes...doing all the things the bureaucrats said to do. Taking her to doctors and wheelchair clinics and therapists and evaluations. Her 16 year old brother started flunking in high school and is unlikely to get his degree. Sidney's 5 year old sister makes herself vomit so that she can get a crumb of attention. Sidney's 3 year old sister bangs her head on the floor and has actually knocked her eye out of alignment. Sidney's mother is so tired she slurs her words and has a tremor in her hands. She feels she is going to die. Sidney's father loves his wife and family, but feels helpless to help them. He wonders whether it is time to save himself and leave the family.

Sidney's mother knows she has rights. Or does she? She calls an institution, which takes care of children like Sidney. She sees it as the perfect choice for her family. It is well lit, it is public, many people walk through daily. It is open, not even the bathroom doors are closed, and any abuse would be detected easily in such a setting. Sidney gets to ride horses (with support). There is a swimming pool. She goes to school every day. She is well cared for. The staff always dressed her in pretty clothes, pretty hair bows, and even jewelry. Although Sidney doesn't recognize her family, they can visit her anytime, 24 hours a day, without prior notice. This was Sidney's parents' choice.

The State says they have no choice, Sidney cannot stay there. Sidney must leave. The State threatens with phone calls and letters. "Institutions are warehouses for children." "It is filthy," they say. They send reports on the death of other children, on incidents of questionable practices. The State has a foster home waiting in the wings to take Sidney away, should her parents decide not to take her back. Sidney's parents did not choose a foster home. They chose the best placement for their daughter's medical condition, and the best place to keep their family intact.

We are on appeal. It doesn't look good. Did we ever have any rights? Does Sidney have any rights? Does the State really own Sidney? Did they own her the second she was born? Are we bad parents? Could someone else have done a better job? After 6 years of giving up our lives, our sleep, and each other, were we really just dupes for the State, taking care of *their* Sidney for free? Is all the propaganda of integration and home- and community-based care, really what is best for our children. Or is it political propaganda to lower the level of service children will get? At one time we believed it and fought for it, but now we see, only too late, that the "Emperor has no clothes."

## DANZIG REFLECTS ON DIS/ABILITY AND CAREER: SCRATCH A THEORY AND FIND A PERSONAL STORY

In the concluding chapter, I share some key events in our daughter's life that have to do with Sidney's education and care. In many cases the family's priorities—for preschool, feeding program, integrated classroom, residential care—all reveal a major disconnect between programs and education policies on the one hand and the parents priority on safety and care. These experiences have helped me to grow—as a man, as a husband, and as a professor; it has also led me to think about the underlying theoretical critique of schooling and the way that change happens in the world. The experiences have also helped me face my own complicity, when I stayed quiet and failed to engage in the conflict that might have led to needed change, or when I decided to seek alternative options outside of the system because it was easier than fighting the system.

I finished my doctoral studies in 1981 and accepted my first professional appointment as a tenure track assistant professor in the Fall of 1982. My dissertation focused on the writing of the sociolinguist Basil Bernstein and the ways in which his work had been misinterpreted by social scientists and misapplied in schools. My earliest professional publications were based on my dissertation and looked at how language structures the ways in which people experience reality, which I called a "bewitchment" perspective (Danzig, 1985, 1986, 1992, 1994). Before my daughter Sidney was born, I prioritized theory and theoretical concerns. In 1984, my daughter Sidney was born with microcephaly, a chronic condition associated with lack of brain growth. After her birth, my wife and I were basically told that she would be able to hear sounds and maybe see colors, but not to expect much else over her life course. Microcephaly is one of the conditions that has also been associated with the Zika virus, but in 1984, no one had ever heard of Zika and microcephaly was often confused with hydrocephalus (buildup of fluids in the brain cavities), which is usually managed through surgery and placement of a shunt to drain excess fluids.

Sidney's birth was the beginning of a decades long learning process to negotiate, advocate, and provide for her care. During these years, many agencies, organizations, and institutions—public, private, and nonprofit—contributed to her care. I would like to think that these interactions, on behalf of Sidney and for my family's well-being, have served a larger purpose to reform the system so that other people would not have to fight the same battles that we fought. When advocating for Sidney, we often said that what Sidney needed was also needed by many other children and that the conflict experienced would have larger benefits for other children. For example, I took Sidney to the Children's Rehabilitation Clinic to be fitted for a wheelchair. The clinic provided only a base model that was painted black and I wanted a pink Barbie wheelchair. My beautiful daughter Sidney deserved something special, and I was willing to pay the difference in cost. When I strongly objected and refused to leave, the police were called and I was escorted from the building. Did the conflict make a difference for Sidney or for other children? Not at that time, but many years later Sidney got her Barbie wheelchair. And maybe, other children got to pick the color of their choice as well.

A more important advocacy had to do with residential care. The state took a philosophical position that no child should be placed in a residential care setting. Side effects of caring for Sidney and additional costs on the family were not part of the state's policy and philosophy of least restrictive environment. After many conversations and being accused of having a personality disorder (I refused to "agree to disagree"), we sued the state of Colorado for the needed assessment required for placement in a nursing home. It took the better part of a year, but in the end, Sidney was allowed to live close to our home and attend the same neighborhood public school that our other two daughters attended. Did this advocacy and legal case help other families? Maybe, as we put a few holes in the state's policy that blocked a child's placement in a nursing home. I am not sure, however, that many other parents would have chosen this option. But it worked well for us and maybe, provided space and opportunities for other parents to articulate their particular needs for safe and stable settings.

As a father, I also became concerned with my son's participation in school. As an adolescent who did not quite fit into the mainstream, and with lots of unsupervised time, the academic and school challenges that he experienced came to the surface. He failed all his classes in eighth grade though he got promoted to high school. We attended many meetings with teachers and principals on his behalf, trying hard to get schools to recognize his talents and also see how his alienation and disaffection for traditional learning in classes could be addressed. While we argued for the needs of many children that didn't fit in the traditional school model, we were not successful in these negotiations. We were not able to negotiate an appropriate classroom setting or considerations from school authorities for his needs. We also became more frustrated with trying to change others' thinking or practices and instead looked for work-arounds and alternatives. I also used these experiences in my publications on the experiences of adolescents, particularly as it related to school-to-work policies, as he had dropped out of high school (Danzig & Vandegrift, 1994, 1995). Our son's challenges of negotiating and finding needed services continue to the present day, with limited responsiveness of the medical community for diagnosis of a multitude of health issues and even less coordination among medical, social, legal, and employment providers.

Our third daughter was equally frustrated by her public school experience and in the end we sent her to boarding school to get through high school. I attribute some of the challenges related to her need for stability and the time we spent on caring for Sidney. At the same time, my daughter has always been her own person. At birth, she held her eyes tightly shut as the nurses tried to put the required drops in her eyes. At 11, she refused to put a functional device in her mouth that the dentist claimed was needed to straighten her teeth and correct an overbite. When told they might have to break her jaw when she was 18 she said "Fine, I'll face that future when it happens. But that thing is not going in my mouth for 12 hours a day." In eighth grade, she told me that she was going to steal the golf cart at her local junior high school because they left the keys in the ignition. When I told her she would get suspended, she didn't care. As a responsible parent, I called the principal and asked him to remove the keys. To my chagrin, when he called 2 weeks later telling me that he was going to suspend my daughter for a week for stealing the golf cart, I thought it was unfair, as I had told him it would happen. Two months later, I got a letter from the superintendent saying that the policy of leaving keys in the golf carts had been changed. Fast forward 20 years, she is a special education teacher and pregnant with our first grandchild. So maybe we did ok.

Does advocating for one's family, engaging in conflict, fighting the system, make a difference? I would like to think yes, but it ultimately doesn't matter. I continue to fight for the things that I think are right, not only for my children or family, but for all children and families. I hope that we put holes in the walls of some of the least friendly and most damaging policies and practices: stigmatizing labels, unfriendly or dangerous classroom and placement options, hidden authority for decision-making, low priority on parent participation, dismissive professional discourse that ignores the wishes of those closest to the person involved. We try to navigate a balance between managing the immediate needs of our child and family and the long term goal of changing the system for the better.

Now, as a professor engaged in teaching current and future school leaders, I also view the importance of narrative and stories to focus on learning from experience. Stories help build community based on the lived experiences of the many people that are part of the education systems, provider, and end user. The stories in this chapter, and in the volume, provide a context for understanding the values of school leaders and the unconscious biases and tacit knowledge that they bring to their actions (Danzig, 1997a, 1997b; 1999a, 1999b; Danzig & Wright, 2007). Stories limit isolation and promote community in preparation programs and during the professional development of school leaders. These stories highlight the human concerns found among the people who work in schools as well as the people that are served by schools. They provide needed context for understanding how schools work and how to navigate the complex policies and systems intended to provide needed help and services.

I was both surprised and honored to receive an invitation to be a part of this volume; surprised because studying the experiences of students with disabilities was not my area of expertise, honored because this work afforded me the opportunity to do so. My background in academia has focused on American and European history and educational law and policy implementation, with some brief work with English language learners. Being a part of this team has afforded me the chance to expand my intellectual horizons and gain insight into a field about which I had previously known little. Policy makers can benefit from this work in many of the same ways that I did. They can come to understand that disability intersects with students in a variety of ways. Standardized procedures, it seems, do not always have their desired organizational elects. Despite what appears to be genuine efforts by educators and policy makers, many students with disabilities struggle throughout their time in school, facing systems and individuals often incapable (or sometimes unwilling) of doing them justice. Those daily struggles directly relate to the emotions that parents of these students face on a regular basis. Feelings of powerlessness, of anger, and of sadness too often result from observing their children in school. Educators need to be cognizant of these situations and do their utmost to accommodate special needs, whenever and wherever they can. Policy makers should be equally aware, and communicate regularly with educators and local community members with flexibility and proper funding in mind.

As I write this narrative near the end of our work, I am reminded that my academic inexperience regarding this topic directly connects to my lived (in) experiences as a student and then as a high school teacher. My next door neighbor growing up had a version of what we would call autism today, though I never remember that term being applied. He and I would often play video games in his home, he was 2 years younger than I and our other interactions were limited. I liked playing sports and he did not, and video games were never really my passion. My neighbor had various aides throughout school, though I believe mostly because his parents made sure he attended one of the best school districts in our hometown. I was diagnosed with attention deficit hyperactivity disorder (ADHD) late in elementary school, however, minus my daily ritalin pill for 4 years, I know of no effort made by my school system to accommodate the uniqueness of my ADHD needs. I remember school as a mostly frustrating experience; I was almost constantly in some form of trouble. I am not sure how he remembers school today.

Eleven years after moving to Florida I started teaching social studies in a public high school. I know that several of my students had various diagnosed learning disabilities, but short of complying with their individualized education plans (IEPs), the school seemed to pay little attention. I had no pedagogical training prior to becoming a teacher, as both my bachelor's and master's degrees were in American history, and my ability to differentiate instruction was limited. I did the best I could for my students during those 3 years, and at a minimum, I hope that they knew I was genuinely invested in their success. These experiences, both studying and teaching, have caused me to think about my neighbor, more so during the time working on this book. I wonder how his life would have been different if he had been born in 2005 instead of 1985? Perhaps a great deal I think, or perhaps not much at all. My thoughts then turn to myself. How did I really behave as a young student? Was I really such a problem? Was an ADHD diagnosis helpful, or accurate, or fair? Did the pills (given to calm me and help me focus) stunt my growth? How might my childhood have been different if I had been born in 2003 instead of 1983? Hard to say, I imagine. I wonder too, how well I served my students. Did I do right by them? Could I have done more? Was I too strict? Was I suffciently accommodating? The questions above are diffcult for me to answer and, frankly, now a topic for the past. I do hope, however, that as you read the material in this book you ask yourselves these types of questions. What has been your role in shaping the lives of the people around you? Have you helped the people who needed it most? What can you do, now, to contribute to the betterment of your fellow human beings? What can you do to make the world a kinder, more inclusive place? I imagine a great deal.

We chose these narratives to introduce the first chapter for multiple reasons. These descriptions are what Weick (1979, 1995) called stories of sensemaking and they include issues related to conflict, power, struggle, domination, and hegemony. We hope that they will highlight for the reader the powerful examples of dis/ability presented in this volume and in the world. Our narratives also share a sense of community with the chapters written by the volume's authors and the descriptions of the experiences of people identified with dis/abilities. We believe that the combination of conceptual and empirical chapters paired with narrative chapters will illustrate some of the many challenges faced by those that experience dis/ability themselves and those that advocate for needed care, educational, and community services. While drawing from the personal, it is also our hope that the volume will help readers generalize from the specific episodes in which dis/ability is experienced to a set of explanations that informs the work of: (a) educational and other system providers, (b) the leadership within these systems, and (c) those responsible for policy and governance of these systems. We do not intend these generalizations to ignore the personal; however, we also think that attention to the structures in which these systems operate is needed to improve the systems and make them more accountable to users and stakeholders. This effort draws nicely from the very title of the Information Age Publishing Series Research and Theory in Educational Administration to which this volume belongs.

Finally, we think that the chapters illustrate the interactions that connect the personal and organizational, and which infuse both users and providers with identities, capabilities, and mission. Ultimately, it is our belief that the experiences of dis/ability that are explored will inform educational leaders, university professors in leadership and education preparation programs, policy makers, and future researchers charged with defining, implementing, and measuring new practices. And by extension, we hope that the information, knowledge, and contextual details will help to craft better roadmaps for navigating the many interactions and destinations experienced around dis/ability.

## NOTE

1. In this volume, when deaf is referred to the disability the "d" is lower case; when Deaf is referred to the culture the "D" is upper case

## REFERENCES

Annamma, S. A, Connor, D. J., & Ferri, B. A. (2013). Dis/ability critical race studies (DisCrit): Theorizing at the intersections of race and dis/ability. *Race, Ethnicity & Education 16,* 1–31. https://doi.org/10.1080/13613324.2012.730511

Danzig, A. (1985). The British sociology of education: Some implications for the education of minorities in the U.S. *CORE: An International Journal of Educational Research, 93,* 1–33.

Danzig, A. (1986). Slamming the door on minority opportunities in education. *Urban Educator, 8*(1), 59–67.

Danzig, A. (1992). Basil Bernstein's sociology of language applied to education: Deficits, differences, and bewitchment. *Journal of Education Policy, 7*(3), 285–300.

Danzig, A. (1994). Social class and professionalism: Removing barriers for integrating services to children and families. *Sociological Abstracts, 42/7,* Abstract No. 94S30311.

Danzig, A. (1997a). Leadership stories: What novices learn by crafting the stories of experienced administrators. *Journal of Educational Administration, 35*(2), 122–137.

Danzig, A. (1997b). Building leadership capacity through narrative. *Educational Leadership and Administration, 9,* 49–59.

Danzig, A. (1999a). How might leadership be taught? The use of story and narrative to teach leadership. *International Journal of Leadership in Education: Theory and Practice, 2*(2), 117–131.

Danzig, A. (1999b). The use of stories in the preparation of educational leaders. *International Studies in Educational Administration, 27*(1), 11–19.

Danzig, A. (2007). How aspiring school leaders draw from cultural and family stories in the Navajo school administrators preparation program: The relevance of personal knowledge to learner-centered leadership. In D. C. Thompson & F. E. Crampton (Eds.), *Fostering compassion and understanding across borders: An international dialogue on the future of educational leadership.* University Council for Educational Administration.

Danzig, A. (2012). Don't ask, don't tell, don't pay: Services for children with severe and chronic disabilities. In M. Strax, C. Strax, & B. Cooper (Eds.), *Kids in the middle: The micro politics of special education* (pp. 123–140). Rowman & Littlefield.

Danzig, A., & Black, W. R. (Eds.). (2019). *Who controls the preparation of education administrators?* Information Age Publishing.

Education for All Handicapped Children Act, Public Law 94-142 (2015). https://www.govtrack.us/congress/bills/94/s6

Grandin, T. (2006). *Autism spectrum disorders: Identification, education, and treatment.* Lawrence Erlbaum Associates.

Howard, P. (2004) The least restrictive environment: How to tell. *Journal of Law and Education, 33*(2), 167–180.

Individuals With Disabilities Education Act, *20 U.S.C.§ 1400* (2015).

Liasidou, A. (2014). The cross-fertilization of critical race theory and Disability Studies: Points of convergence/divergence and some education policy implications. *Disability and Society, 29*(5), 724–737. https://doi.org/10.1080/0968 7599.2013.844104

Rogers, F. (1994). *You are special: Neighborly words of wisdom from Mr. Rogers.* Penguin Random House.

Supreme Court of the United States. (2016). *Syllabus: Endrew F., a minor, by and through his parents and next friends, Joesph F. et al v Douglas County School District RE-1.* Ceriorari to the United States Courts of Appeals for the Tenth Circuit No. 15–827. Argued January 11, 2017–Decided March 22, 2017. https://www.supremecourt.gov/opinions/16pdf/15-827_0pm1.pdf

Wright, E. (1999). Full inclusion of children with disabilities in the regular classroom: Is it the only answer? *Social Work in Education, 21*(1), 11–22.

Yell, M. (2006). *The law and special education: Includes the IDEA Improvement Act* (2nd ed.). Prentice Hall.

Yell, M. (2016). *The law and special education: Includes the IDEA Improvement Act* (4th ed.). Prentice Hall.

Yell, M. (2018). *The law and special education* (5th ed.). Pearson.

Ysseldyke, J. E., & Algozzine, B. (2006). *The legal foundations of Special Education: A practical guide for every teacher.* Corwin Press.

# SECTION II

## LEADERSHIP AND DIS/ABILITY: ONTOLOGY, EPISTEMOLOGY, AND INTERSECTIONALITIES

The assumptions that we hold about the nature of the world around us deeply inform professional practice. The ways in which knowledge and power are inextricably linked to each other deeply informs assumptions that guide how each of us comes to know what we know and enact leadership. Taken together, the narrative and conceptual contributions of the 5 chapters in this section surface ontological and epistemological assumptions underpinning dis/ability, schooling, and leadership. They raise questions such as: "Is dis/ability a historical concept socially constructed to be deconstructed or might elements of what is considered dis/ability be visible and scientifically measurable?"; "In what ways does dis/ability always connect to intersecting identities?" and "In what ways are language, race, and ableism in relationship with one another?"

Sedgwick opens the section with an insightful and emotive narrative titled "Red Is the Most Beautiful Color: Reflections From a Non-Speaking Autistic Educator of Non-Speaking Autistic Students." The chapter is based on his personal experiences and time as an educator working with dis/abled youth. By using a compositional ethnographic approach, Sedgwick provides the reader with a "collage of memories and emotions woven together" to provide insight into the world that dis/abled students and educators inhabit. This effort exists, among other things, to demonstrate how a variety of theories of dis/abled education manifest in professional practice.

"Ability and Belonging: Contested Ontology and Epistemology That Shape School Practice" is the second chapter of the section. In the chapter, Bornstein and Manaseri ask leaders to examine (a) how they describe a student who deserves to be included, and (b) what they will accept as truthful ways of knowing what students themselves know and can do. They argue that deeply entrenched ways of knowing and examining the world, specifically ableism and racism, centrally inform the ways schools are organized. Seeking to help leaders avoid oppressive complicity, Bornstein and Manaseri aim to first inform a debate on the ontology of disability in educational settings, destabilizing the assumption that belonging is predicated on racialized normalcy. Secondly, the authors seek to challenge the educational system's epistemological assumptions about disability, in which school structures and policies promote a racialized normalcy as truth. Thirdly, they consider educational responses to disability through administrative decision-making in practice and policy. Ultimately, the chapter deepens discussion on the question of who belongs in school and what counts as truthful knowledge through the engagement theories of normalization, DisCrit, and transformative leadership.

Autoethnography has and continues to play a role in the movement for social justice in education by providing a window into people's personal experiences to others in revealing and insightful ways. Gerald's chapter, "On Being Annoying: Neurodivergence and Mood Disorders as a Black Face in a White Space" provides an autoethnographic account of educational experiences in elementary school, high school, and college as a neurodivergent Black youth in predominantly privileged White spaces. The chapter describes what he characterizes as mild and undiagnosed learning difficulties that "fortunately" resulted in him only being labeled as "annoying." Engaging in a close conversation with the work of other authors to build his narrative, Gerald provides a rich description of neurodivergence and how disability profoundly shaped his experiences at school and over his life. He argues that school's primary responsibility should be to ensure that marginalized students feel "loved and cared for." He implores teachers and leaders from all backgrounds to consider the importance of his narrative and provide care for all those children and students that have been thought of as "annoying."

The chapter by Wright, Lawyer and Bart details the importance of intersectional analysis to understanding marginalizations that have been experienced by the Deaf community in the Western world. In "Decision-Making in the Era of Post-Modern Audism: Examining the Post Colonizing Normate," Wright and colleagues provide detailed examples of how this marginalization is experienced in various educational institutions, especially in higher education. Using document analysis and contemporary statistical reports, the authors illustrate a variety of policies that colonized the deaf body through a Eurocentric cultural lens. The chapter provides an analysis of the historical foundations of the Deaf President Now protests from the Milan Conference (1880) to the present. Wright and colleagues describe the rise of Audism and its enduring effects on discourse applied to Deaf people, as well as how Deaf critical theory (Deaf Crit) was used by a variety of academics to unpack and deconstruct many audist norms. The authors conclude that now, more than 4 decades after the DPN protests, post-modern audism (PMA) should replace the Deaf critical theory (DeafCrit) lens. In their view, PMA provides better explanations of realities faced in the Deaf community and should be adopted in future scholarly research and analyses of institutional practices.

The realities of the Deaf community and other students with disabilities is not, of course, limited to the United States. Collins et al. argue for increased utilization of disability critical race studies as a tool for the analysis of educational policy in Quebec in the following chapter, "Shedding Light on Disability and Race in a North American Linguistic Majority Context: A DisCrit Analysis of Special Education in Quebec." The authors demonstrate how Quebec's unique cultural and linguistic history, in both modern-day Canada and former imperial British North America, have shaped marginalizing practices around disability, race, and special education in Quebec. In particular, the chapter explains how the priority of language in Quebec has precluded a parallel concern for the significance of race and disability, as education policy in Quebec officially emphasizes a "raceless" society in favor of one based on language and cultural distinctions. As an alternative, the authors use DisCrit to argue that concepts related to culture, ableism, and race are needed to understand and promote a more inclusive set of special education practices in Quebec. Collins and colleagues argue that ignoring race in the study of special education and the application of disability labels ignores important on-the-ground realities of how children are identified and labeled for special education services and how students of color experience schooling.

CHAPTER 2

# RED IS THE MOST BEAUTIFUL COLOR

## Reflections From a Nonspeaking Autistic Educator of Nonspeaking Autistic Students

**Marrok Sedgwick**
*University of Illinois at Chicago*

"That looks fun," I tell the boy sitting next to me in a cubicle, praising a forbidden act. He's running his fingers repeatedly through crayons that fill a bin. A rainbow of waxy cylinders dance and flow with his fingers. I turn around and check that I'm not being watched by the classroom teacher or any of the full-time paraprofessionals. I am just a substitute, and if I'm caught, they might not let me come back.

By the time I have met them, my students have already been issued their dis/ability labels (Annamma, 2018). Dis/ability is not a replacement for the word disability, but rather calls attention to the cultural process of being disabled, and the political identity of disability (Moore, 2018). As a substitute, I am not generally privy to specific diagnoses, but as an autistic person

*Who Decides?*, pages 31–52
Copyright © 2022 by Information Age Publishing
www.infoagepub.com

myself, it's easy for me to pick out the students whose bodies speak my native body language. Some of the classrooms expressly define themselves as autism-only learning environments. Others have students with a range of intellectual, developmental, and/or other disabilities. I work almost exclusively in most restrictive environments (MREs) where the primary work of students, who are segregated from nondisabled peers, is that of rehabilitation of their bodies (Kurth et al., 2015) from deviant to normate (Garland-Thomson, 1997).

I watch as the boy runs his fingers through the crayons over and over and over again. I'll call him Kyle (a pseudonym). I watch Kyle's hands because they are far more expressive than his face. Autistic faces are riddled with a fakery that comes from our teachers (Kyle's special education teachers, my drama teachers) telling us the "right" way to show our emotions. The "rightness" of these expressions falls apart when research asks whether we (autistic people) can understand each other (we can). Empirical evidence confirms what autistic adults have been screaming all along: We don't have a communication deficit, we simply communicate in a different body language (Crompton, Fletcher-Watson et al., 2020). Kyle's hands are a shimmering spectacle in my synesthesia, telling me he's anxious, but working on it. (But take care, this movement isn't tied to anxiety for all autistic people.) Fluttering fingers through a rainbow of wax cylinders is self-care. His anxiety makes sense. He doesn't know me, and now he's stuck in a cubicle with me.

I watch for a while, enjoying the colors rolling around, and letting my grapheme-color synesthesia match his every move. Then, I ask him, "What's your favorite color?"

He keeps running his fingers through the crayons. Maybe he is so enraptured that he didn't hear what I said. Maybe he just doesn't care. Maybe he needs more time to process my question and his answer. I'm in no hurry, and there's no reason why, because I have asked the question, he should be required to respond (see Freire, 2004). I wait and watch.

After a time, he reaches over to his talker (a tablet with icon-to-speech software installed), flips through some menus, and says, "red."

"I like red, too," I respond.

He returns to running his fingers through the crayons. We sit together, getting acquainted in a way more natural to our bodies than a handshake or small talk.

Technically, when a student engages in "target behaviors" (such as repeatedly and tirelessly running his fingers through a bin of crayons instead of, say, doing something more "socially appropriate" like drawing with them), I am supposed to make a note in his binder. It holds a chart for tally marks. When Kyle got mad that another student stole his juice at lunch, how many times did he bang his fist on the table? Have our interventions helped him contain his impulses? How autistic is he today? Schools like

Kyle's engage in a process of *hyper-surveillance* (Annamma, 2018). They track every wanted and unwanted movement first on paper at the back of a student's binder, and then in a software that converts weeks worth of behavior into graphs. These graphs are used to reify labels, through a process of *hyper-labeling* (Annamma, 2018) that ensures that everything dis/abled students do can be categorized as a product of their disability, or a product of their rehabilitation.

Kyle stops suddenly, moves his talker closer to him, flipping through menus.

"Beautiful," he says.

I'm surprised the word beautiful is loaded into his talker (usually they only contain words for basic needs and scripted classroom conversations). I am not surprised that my patience has been rewarded with the assertion that red is the most beautiful color.

For 4 years, I worked in various learning environments that either centered, or at least included, youth with intellectual and/or developmental disabilities. The majority of these learning environments were either public schools (where I was a substitute teacher or substitute paraprofessional), with a short stint working as a full-time paraprofessional at a specialized nonpublic, nonprofit school for youth with disabilities, and some day camps. Over the course of that same 4 years, I became nonspeaking (by which I mean that a disability caused me to lose my ability to produce spoken language without the aid of technology). I was born multiply-disabled, including autistic, but was never a special education student. I had heard things were bad in special education from other disabled adults, and believed them. But until I saw it first hand, I didn't really understand.

The deficit model (Dinishak, 2016) frames disabled students as lacking desirable traits. Disabled students receive interventions (speech therapy, occupational therapy, applied behavior analysis, etc.), while their nondisabled (or, perhaps more accurately, non-labeled) peers learn from curricula. The difference between intervention and curriculum is more than a matter of semantics. Interventions identify deficits and attempt to rehabilitate them. A curriculum teaches something academic. This chapter moves against the deficit model, presenting disabled students instead as agential actors on a sociopolitical stage scrambling to engage in self-determination within systems that are designed to stifle them (Williams, 2018).

The epistemic wisdom for survival and social transformation that disabled adults have developed as central to the disability rights movement (Charlton, 2000) and the disability justice movement (Piepzna-Samarasinha, 2018) are notably missing from learning environments that serve students with disabilities, leading to reduced educational opportunity and dehistoricized understandings of disability. This troubles me greatly. I work to make evident the transformative value in welcoming disability as a political identity (Putnam, 2005) in classrooms, and disabled educators as vital to the creation of innovative, equitable learning environments for students with disabilities.

This chapter is echolalic mythology: a collection of stories from my time working with disabled youth that I repeat to myself and others over and over. They are not anecdotes about single moments, nor are they ethnographic composite narratives. They are a collage of memories and emotions woven together to try to make meaning out of a confusing and often painful world. Through repetition, I try to clumsily dream of something less confusing, and less painful. I share them here to make evident how theory is interwoven in practice, and how I navigate multiple epistemologies (Bang & Medin, 2010) in the special education classroom.

## WHAT ARE YOU WORKING FOR?

Before I became nonspeaking, and before I needed crutches to run, I was bright-eyed and bushy-tailed and looking for a place to use my bachelor of science to benefit my community members. I had read from autistic elders like Mel Baggs (may her memory be a shield), Amy Sequenzia (i.e., Sequenzia, 2015), Kassiane Asasumasu (i.e., Asasumasu, 2013), and Julia Bascom that there was this thing called applied behavior analysis (ABA), and that it was wrong. I believed them. I also believed my degree in decision science, a subfield of psychology, could help me unsettle ABA. This is how I found myself working in an ABA school.

The interview process set the mood. I arrive at the school, a small building with the hallmark bright green paint and ADA compliant sidewalks that tell me it is a recent construction. To the right of the building is a heavy iron fence surrounding a small playground with a swing set and a track. Students are followed by adults wearing green polo shirts that reflect the building's paint. The architecture is wood, paint, and human form. I enter the front door and sign in at the front desk.

"I'm here for a job interview," I explain.

"Great, I'll let Karen know."

I sit down in one of the chairs that line the wall. A teenager walks past, staring at the ground as he goes, followed closely by a paraprofessional in a green shirt. The para holds a binder and pencil, making notes as they walk past. I am struck by the young man's gait. It has a slight bounce to it, which doesn't move into his shoulders. I am struck not because it is strange, but because it is familiar, like peering through a looking glass.

Karen, from human resources, and a man whose name I can't remember, collect me and take me into a conference room down the hall. We sit down across from each other.

"Do you have any experience working with people with autism?"

I am prepared for this question. "Not in a school setting. One of my best friends is on the spectrum, and talking with her is what inspired me to want to work in special education." None of this is a lie, but it is carefully swapping in language that I am assuming this school will appreciate ("on the spectrum" and "inspired"). My answer seems to pass muster. I am clasping my hands in my lap, squeezing as tightly as I can to remain still. I add that my degree in a subfield of psychology has given me a solid understanding of how brains work, which will come in handy here.

"The students here are different from other students. This is what you call a most restrictive environment, which means we accept students from other schools who are unable to support them due to the students' behavioral needs."

I smile and nod. In this moment, I think I know what I'm getting into. (I don't.) I feel well prepared. I have read up on "complex behavioral needs." I did this by diving deep into the autistic pride corners of Tumblr and WordPress and devoured all the words I could find that described why other autistic people do things that get them stuck in schools like this one.

The man is a blur in my memory. I remember liking his shirt. It seemed too nice and starched for someone working at a school (where every inch of you is at risk of being splashed with paint or a sneeze). It was white with thin, dark blue horizontal and vertical lines making a lot of squares.

Karen and the man glance at each other.

"For example, a student might rip off your shirt. Some people find that really embarrassing."

"Okay," I say with a shrug, keeping a smile plastered on my face.

"You will be exposed to every body fluid," Karen adds. "Have you ever helped someone use the restroom? Will that bother you? Some of our students still wear diapers."

"That doesn't bother me." Words come out of my mouth but I am focusing on squeezing my hands under the table.

The interview goes on like this, in which Karen offers increasingly "disgusting" or "scary" things that kids at the school have done. I am unafraid, not disgusted, and keep telling her so. Finally:

"Do you still want to work at this school?" she asks.

"Yes," I say, staring at her cheekbone, which I know she will think is eye contact. Neurotypicals can never tell the difference if I'm looking at their cheekbone or their eyes. It's almost never their eyes. If I work here, I can teach kids this survival skill.

"Great, next we will give you a tour of the school," says the man with the square-covered shirt. I assume I've passed the first test.

The school, they tell me, was designed especially for them. There are classrooms at each of the four corners, a front lobby, a back staff room, and a central rectangular hall that encircles a conference room and the staff bathrooms. There are large round mirrors hanging from the ceiling at each of the four turns in the hallway. We walk around it as they point out these features. I am doing my damndest not to burst out laughing because I have clearly walked into an architectural panopticon (Foucault, 1977) and this horrifies and amazes me. This school has been built from the ground up to maximize the adults' ability to control the students. My glee at catching atrocity in the act is immediately replaced. They take me into the first class-room, and I look around. Cubicles line the walls.

"We use the Morgan model," Karen tells me. "Are you familiar with that from your psychology classes?" (I should add that this school is not the Morgan Center for Autism in San Jose, California, which I have never visited, but which most of the schools I have worked for tried to copy.)

"No." I explain, "None of my faculty studied autism."

Karen and the man, who is mostly quiet, take me through the class-rooms, pointing to students and describing what we are looking at. "You can see the paraprofessionals working with Yancey are wearing arm shields. That's because he bites. Janey is really sweet and compliant most of the time, but you can see when her para isn't looking she starts to flap again. And over in the back corner, you can see Samuel in a protective hold. We do that when…" I am no longer in a school, being interviewed by HR. I have stepped off the map into a surreal modern freak show in which youth who have not provided assent are being showcased, and an "expert" tells me how to interpret the "acts" before me.

The disabled people in these rooms have not carefully designed and rehearsed their acts with me in mind, nor do they have control over their representation, like many freak show performers did (Chemers, 2008). The goal of this freak show is, of course, to showcase all the "horrible" things that autistic kids do, to overwhelm me, and test me for weakness. Later, this attitude is reflected when I substitute at other schools. Every time I work for a new classroom for the first time, someone asks me, "Did we scare you off?" This is, of course, a completely fucked up way to frame children. While Karen showcases the students' alleged badness, I am reminded of the primacy effect in psychology (Digirolamo & Hintzman, 1997). She is planting seeds of disgust, fear, and pity as an initial interpretation of autistic children's ways of being. Her tour is setting dehumanization as the norm.

Karen is also a nondisabled person taking control of disabled peoples' narratives, framing everything we see from her nondisabled perspective. She is talking about us, without us, in direct conflict with what disabled activists have been demanding for decades (Charlton, 2000). I am filled with rage as they take me around to each classroom, inviting me to gaze at students, painting everything the students do as troublesome, pathological. I keep my smile plastered on my face like a shield.

I stand in a doorway, watching Janey flapping her hands in front of her face, her mouth open, as a deep forest green erupts in my synesthesia. Sparks of yellow and brown and purple flick off the swirling green that I can sense in my mind's eye, responsive to Janey's hands. A shock punches through my rage as I realize: I understand this body language. I can see her humanity bright and clear not despite this thing that ABA wants to stop, but because of it. I can see her distress and her struggle to process that distress and I glance around the room at other students and see their emotions again and again with a clarity that I have never felt in my entire life. I do not know it, but what I am experiencing is the interpersonal rapport that comes from neurotype-matching (Crompton, Sharp et al., 2020). Their body language is native to my body.

I pass every step of the interview and I get the job.

I sit a few feet back from the scene that unfolds, taking notes diligently. I face a table with two people on the opposite side. Nearest to me is the experienced paraprofessional who I am shadowing this afternoon. She sits at a table with a token board, a set of tokens, and a binder with tables she is tasked to fill with check marks. Beyond the binder and token board, farther along the table, is a set of objects: an empty water bottle, a cardboard book (the kind for toddlers), and a pencil. This is where the teenage boy sits, looking down at the object set. To his left, the table touches the walls of the cubicle in which he learns.

"What are you working for?" my co-worker asks, pointing to the top of the token board, where that phrase is typed.

The teen, Rahul, chooses one from a set of special tokens showing the rewards on offer. He picks "hot tamale" and places it on a Velcro tab in the top right of the token board.

My co-worker repeats in a well-practiced singsong voice, "Great, you're working for a hot tamale!"

She points to the token, which has the hot tamale logo on it, when she says the words hot tamale. Rahul must now complete the task before him correctly 10 times. Every time he completes it correctly, my co-worker will add a generic token (printed with airplanes on them, because Rahul likes airplanes) to the token board on waiting velcro tabs. If he fills the token board, he gets his hot tamale. If he exhibits a target behavior (a behavior that is targeted in his IEP as something his family or teachers have decided to "extinguish"), one or more tokens may be removed from the token board, requiring him to do extra work to earn his treat. All of this, according to the board certified behavior analysts who run the morning trainings, is to use extrinsic rewards to develop motivation for learning.

My co-worker removes a laminated flashcard from Rahul's binder. She quickly flashes it in my direction so I know what she's doing. It reads "book" in large black letters without any picture or icon.

She places the flashcard on the table in front of Rahul, who is flapping his hands above his head.

"Quiet hands!" she says.

Rahul drops his hands to the table in front of him, clasping them together the way some people do to pray. I wonder what kind of cognitive load that hard-won stillness requires, and how spending that cognitive energy on stillness might negatively impact Rahul's learning.

The paraprofessional reaches her index finger up near his face, catching his gaze, then moves it down to touch the card.

"Show me book!" she says excitedly. She takes his hand in hers, forms it into a clasping shape, slides the flashcard into his grip, and places it near the book. This earns him singsong praise: "Very smart! Great work!" and the first token on his token board.

My co-worker sets the flashcard to the side, shuffles the water bottle, book, and pencil to different positions, and asks Rahul to quiet his flapping hands again. The pattern repeats, again and again, despite empirical evidence that repetition and drilling may, in fact, hinder the learning of autistic people (Harris et al., 2015). After a couple rounds of hand-over-hand prompting, she tries touching his elbow instead. As his token board nears full—and the prize hot tamale grows ever more tangibly in reach, she tries without any physical prompts at all, having (in the behaviorist model) provided a good deal of appropriate responses (placing the card near the book) to the stimulus "book," spoken and written on the card. Rahul quiets his hands on command, awaiting the next instruction.

"Show me book!" She sings.

Rahul reaches out with his right hand, left hand waiting at the edge of the table. He picks up the card and is about to place it near the water bottle in front of him. My co-worker deftly reaches out and grabs his hand, forcing him to place the card near the book. This is called errorless learning, I learned earlier that morning, and it is central to ABA. "Very smart! You're doing sooooooo great, working for your hot tamale!" The goal is always to praise the student for doing the right thing (and guide them to do that right thing), and never to tell them they've done something wrong.

Later, I learn about Manu Kapur's research, which suggests that making mistakes can be a valuable learning experience. Kapur (2008) found that students who failed to solve a complex problem on the first attempt later did better than those who did not experience that *productive failure*. While these situations are not analogous (Kapur's work with Newtonian kinematics is a different sort of task than pointing to a flashcard), it suggests to me that learning is far more complex than operant conditioning, and the errorless learning of ABA may be diminishing opportunities to learn.

For now, Rahul earns his token. He has two more to go to earn the hot tamale.

On the next round, he moves the flashcard to the book on his own. This results in an eruption of praise, the application of both remaining tokens to the token board, and the promised hot tamale.

My co-worker pulls a clear, plastic tackle box—the kind my dad uses to store fishing flies in—from a shelf on the cubicle behind her, and removes one-half of a hot tamale. The smell of a dozen different sweet treats wafts sickeningly out of the tackle box. Each square is filled with something different—cookies cut into quarters, M&Ms, beheaded Sour Patch Kids.... She holds the partial candy out to Rahul, who makes a deep sound like "hmmmm" while gently picking it up. He eats his reward.

My co-worker marks down tallies in Rahul's binder, then clears the token board of its tokens exuberantly, crack! craaaack! goes the Velcro. The sound still sends a shiver down my spine.

A new flashcard is drawn from the binder. Again the question: "What are you working for?" The cycle repeats.

I survived as a paraprofessional at that school for not quite 10 school days. During that time, my job was to go to trainings, shadow experienced paraprofessionals, input data, and clean (first thing in the morning, last thing in the afternoon, and any time a kid threw up or had an accident). If I had stayed longer than that 2 weeks, I would slowly be faded into working one-on-one with students, and managing one student's IEP file, under the supervision of the credentialed teacher. I remember the richness and complex personhood (Gordon, 2008) of every one of my students there. I miss them.

The ABA model I have described above implies that there is a right answer to everything, and that right answer is known by the instructor (credentialed teacher, paraprofessional, etc). The students must arrive at that right answer via errorless operant conditioning. And so, students must permit the instructors to physically manipulate their bodies to successfully condition the correct answers. They cannot refuse to be touched. This model places overwhelming power with the instructor. Students do resist in a myriad of ways (discussed below), but the central goal of this power structure is to demand and enforce compliance. This power imbalance, and ABA writ large, may be harming students who survive it, by producing learned helplessness, psychological damage, and increasing their risk for sexual violence (Jones, 2015; Sandoval-Norton & Shkedy, 2019).

Patti Berne (a disability justice movement founder) asserted that even if all a person can manage to do is be in the room, lying on a couch to the side of the action, their presence is not only participation, but it is a vital contribution (Berne et al., 2020). Here, she rejects power structures that place some peoples' bodies as in need of change. This welcome is not trite or naive. It is an assertion of disabled peoples' bodily autonomy, and a demand to welcome us as we are. I see this epistemic wisdom as necessary for the design of more hopeful, more loving learning environments. The order "quiet hands" (and behavior modification writ large) is a euphemism for "shut up," which is antithetical to hope and love.

## DO IT THE RIGHT WAY

We walk together, students, paraprofessionals, and teacher, down the sidewalk, bunched into pairs. I'm at one of my new jobs as a substitute (I signed up with multiple districts), hoping that public schools would be kinder, and use alternatives to ABA. Adults keep our eyes on our assigned student, as we walk down the street to the public library, making sure no one walks into the street.

A student in front of me veers off the sidewalk, slamming into a large bush. Her paraprofessional barks:

"Do it the right way!"

He reaches out and guides her out of the bush, and I have to stop as he returns her to the spot on the sidewalk where she veered off course. He walks her past the bush again, hand on her shoulder, stopping her from trying to walk into the bush again. He praises her for walking past "the right way."

I think of my own embodied explorations of my surroundings as a kid, feeling the textures and scents of the natural world by brushing up against bushes, and stroking the trunks of trees. I learned that pushing hard through the sagebrush on the side of the hill near my parents' house would release a sharp, fresh scent. I treasure my time spent in the chaparral forests in my yard with my dog. I can now hypothesize that the physical and emotional sensations of the chaparral forest were *internalized* because they became the smell of home, of me-and-my-dog-together, and therefore became a part of my identity, contributing to the *intrinsic motivation* to learn the natural history of the land in which I lived (Deci et al., 1991). Thousands of miles away and decades later, the thought of *artemisia californica* burns yellow and green and brown in my synesthesia. It makes me homesick not only for the sensory experiences of Central Coast California, but for the narratives (biology, geology, history) attached to those experiences.

I think of Mel Baggs (of blessed memory), whose short film *In My Language* translates the exploration embedded in stimming. In her own words: "It's about being in a constant conversation with every aspect of my environment" (Baggs, 2007, 3:39). Touching and smelling and moving with everything that shares this world with us is a research method, an epistemological move. Academics do sensory ethnography (Pink, 2009). Autistic students are given IEPs.

Stimming into the bush is *inquiry learning* (to read more about *inquiry learning* see Minstrell & Van Zee, 2000). It is full-body scientific observation and sensory exploration. Extinguishing this innate research method is also extinguishing and limiting students' opportunities to learn. Here in Illinois, the CRONCH! of leaves under my feet releases a smell of blue and dark green and deep brown, and I want to learn: With whom do I share my new home? The world is rich with enticing textures that want to teach us.

## PLAYING TOGETHER

There is an old myth that autistic people do not play, that somehow manages to persist here and there.

I am sitting in a cubicle with a small girl. There is a table between us, and I sit on a stool in the opening to the cubicle. She cannot escape (that's the design feature). The girl, Nicki, is standing at the table, bouncing up and down on the balls of her feet. Her eyes are bright as she reaches for the tablet on the computer and opens a game. She glances at me. While it is true that autistic people usually find direct eye contact painful, we do catch peoples' gazes when they're looking elsewhere. She grabs mine for a second, looking to see if I will take the tablet away from her and hold it hostage until she does some work.

Most of the activities in this classroom are ABA-based, and I leave them on the shelves. I let her do her thing. I can learn more about her if I watch how she engages with her world. She starts playing the game, smiling and making excited noises. When she makes an excited hum, I catch myself repeating it back to her. She looks at me when I do this, bouncing with joy. I didn't do it on purpose—it was just echolalia. But as the epistemic wisdom of autistic people (Bascom, 2012) and empirical evidence (Sterponi & Shankey, 2014) suggest, echolalia is communicative, and can be incredibly playful.

Again, Nicki makes a loud humming sound, and a deeper humming sound erupts from my own lungs. At first I am nervous, because stimming at work always feels dangerous (I am not "out" as autistic at work). But, it just happens. And then I notice, my echolalic response to Nicki's excited humming is building a connection between us. Nonautistic people do a similar thing. A kid plays a game and giggles, their parent or teacher laughs and asks, "What's so funny?" Nicki and I are making a connection.

I catch on to this connection building. It becomes a conversation, and one she escalates. She slides the tablet towards me and moves around the table next to me, rocking into me, as we hum at each other over the game. She reaches and grabs my forefinger. Her tiny fingers wrap around my finger and a burst of bright yellow flashes across my synesthesia. She pulls my finger towards the tablet and I let her use my finger to play the game. We carry on like this, as she prompts me to play the game, and we hum at each other.

Suddenly, the classroom teacher is standing with us. It's time to switch students.

The next student is Derrick, surly and always in motion. He climbs on me, standing on my knees to peer over the edge of the cubicle. I don't fight him. I need to know what he wants, or what he's interested in. He's squinting his eyes. He climbs down and runs out of the cubicle. I follow. Derrick runs to the wall where the light switch is and starts flipping all the lights on and off. There are four different switches. I think he is playing, and notice he's squinting up.

The classroom teacher is reaching out and grabbing Derrick away, leading him back to the cubicle. Derrick lunges against his captor, clearly upset. This is not a gentle taking of the hand to cross the street. This is a cupping of the shoulders to assert the calm, firm pressure of "you must comply." We re-enter the cubicle, and the classroom teacher walks away.

Derrick's on his feet again, rushing for the light switch. He gets there before me, flicks all the lights off, and turns away. He's not playing in a joyful sense, I realize. He's playing in an experimental sense, trying to find the right combination of switches up and down to turn off the fluorescent lighting. Something about them is bothering him.

Our 15 minutes together is over, and it's time to switch students.

It's time for recess, and I follow the student I'm paired with now to the playground. He and another student play with a castle. The castle has a dragon, and when one of the boys pulls a lever, it snaps its jaws. I wait for my moment—just when the dragon jaws snap shut, I stick my hand in, and make a fake gasp. One of the boys opens his mouth in a gasp, too, eyes wide looking up at me. The other boy (who can speak) announces, "I'll save yoooooouuuuu!" He peels the jaws of the dragon open and my hand is saved. I want to cry with joy at how adorable these kids are, and I hum my absolute pleasure at their light. I've worked here enough, and so the students know me well enough, that this noise relieves the worried boy.

In their play, I see skills and learning and empathy. Nicki shares with me the game she is playing. Derrick advocates for his bodily needs, and experiments with his environment towards a well-defined goal. The boys on the playground express worry (imaginary and real) at my hand's predicament, "caught" in a dragon's mouth. They are empathetic. All of these things happen in MREs.

I see a grave danger. Nicki takes my forefinger and directs me what to touch on the tablet screen in order to progress through her game. Now, she is small and cute and can get away with grabbing. She is grabbing my finger for a friendly reason, and this is evident in our peaceful interaction. Her grab for my forefinger is not spontaneous, or a result of her disability. It is a learned behavior.

In ABA contexts, hand-over-hand prompting is an established norm. As described above, physical prompting is a key practice. Nicki has learned that if you want to teach someone to do something, you reach out and grab them.

Derrick has learned if someone does something you don't like, you push them away. Our students learn by our example (Vossoughi et al., 2020). What happens when they are no longer small and cute, and try to physically manipulate others? It is not just that prompting models physical assault. It is the message that strict compliance from authority figures is inescapable. It is the way that *hyperlabeling* (Annamma, 2018) will lead these behaviors to be listed as symptoms of disability (not imitation of adults). It is the way that *hyperpunishment* (Annamma, 2018) will siphon these students further and further away from their peers and community, even though the adults who taught them through example are paid and praised for the same behavior. The only difference is that the kids are assumed to be deficient, and the adults are not.

## HOW TO BE A SMART, GOOD STUDENT

"It's really sad," the classroom teacher says to me, looking across the classroom. "He'll have these conversations with you that make it seem like he's just a normal kid, but he just can't learn."

This is an aside. The teacher has just outlined a task he'd like me to do with the student in question. Another day, I saw him reading a book. The classroom teacher noticed me looking and explained, "He reads but doesn't really understand much." I never saw Brett with a book again after that.

I wonder whether anyone has offered Brett audiobooks. I wonder why this teacher equated textual literacy with the ability to learn. Brett was constantly reading and writing his world in the Freirean sense: he would criticize practices he noticed in the classroom. He would yell at anyone who misgendered me.

Our students listen to what we say, develop their own conclusions about it, and then respond. That is reading and writing the world in the Freirean sense. It is learning and using what they learned to try to shape the world around them.

When I told him I was leaving, and would not be back again, I promised him: "I'm not leaving because I don't enjoy working with you. I'm leaving to go to school so I can try to make special education better."

His shoulders slumped, and I worried he was about to freak out. Instead he just replied, "Good. It needs to be better."

When I was in first grade, I remember being pulled out of class. It sticks out in my mind because it was a deviation from my routine, and that was scary. I went with a few other students from my class to a room where students from other classrooms were, and we were invited to do art. Just as I started to feel comfortable, my teacher was in the room, pulling me away again. As we walked across the playground, she turned to me and said, "You don't need to go there. On the day we did the testing, you must have just had a bad day." I believe that was some form of special education program, because my friend who stayed that day was ultimately shifted deeper and deeper into the special education programs, until by high school she disappeared to a special school.

When I was in third grade, I was labeled "gifted." There were two exams to determine this categorization. I did not pass the first test, but I came close. My teacher called me to her desk, and told me "On the day we did the testing, you must have just had a bad day." She insisted that I be allowed to take the second test. She succeeded, and I passed it.

Smartness belonged to me. It does not always. Brett's alleged inability to learn, even if his teacher simply misspoke and didn't mean Brett couldn't learn anything, is not a reflection of Brett's cognition. Smartness is not a biological, neurological fact—it is a construct defined by White, nondisabled, capitalist norms that cannot be understood without an understanding of both racism and ableism (Leonardo & Broderick, 2011). The students determined to have it are given curricula. I was put in the gifted program at my elementary school, and therefore placed in more challenging classes in middle school, until I started failing maths and sciences in high school (when my disabilities caught up to me). The students who don't succeed are given interventions. They put wooden cylinders through holes in the lids of jars, memorize their parents' phone numbers for "maths," and learn "life skills" like washing the PE uniforms of the nondisabled students.

When Maya, who has an intellectual disability, sits on the floor in front of the door of the classroom and refuses to get up, she is "having a behavior." Due to her disability, she lacks the smartness (in the eyes of her teachers) to be conceived of as intentionally blocking the movement of others in protest. I learned from reading the extensive blogs of Mel Baggs and Amy Sequenzia that drawing a line between intelligent and not intelligent is inherently ableist.

When I look at Maya sitting on the floor, hands gripping her ankles tightly in defiance, I feel a burst of pride. It doesn't matter to me if she knows about the 504 Sit-In, when disabled activists held a 3-week-long sit-in strike to press for antidiscrimination legal protections (see, e.g., Schweik, 2011). It also doesn't matter to me whether she is trying to make some broader demand beyond, "I don't want to go back to my cubicle." I see a kid who has read something in her world that she doesn't support, and has decided to do something about it.

I sit down beside her, set my talker on the floor, and hold my hands over the keyboard. I want to tell her about the legacy she has inherited by birth.

Another paraprofessional rushes over, and grabs Maya's criss-crossed legs.

"Don't do that!" I say. I wish my talker could give a sharp tone.

"This is what they said we have to do, to get her up. Otherwise she'll stay there all day."

Still seated, I type a slow, monotone rant about consent, about manhandling kids, but the woman keeps pulling and untwisting Maya's limbs. She keeps repeating it's what she was told must be done. Maya struggles silently against her captor. My co-worker prevails, forcing Maya into a chair.

Goodness is also property (Broderick & Leonardo, 2016). Maya isn't practicing civil disobedience, she's exhibiting a "target behavior" that must not be tolerated, because she lacks the goodness and smartness for her sit-in to be read in any positive, intelligent light. In first grade, I paid attention, didn't argue with my teacher, and never sat in the doorway and refused to get up. Being "good" is perceived as smartness, and this leads some students, especially White nondisabled students, to be offered educational opportunities not offered to other students (Broderick & Leonardo, 2016).

The students who have the least smartness and the least goodness are placed in the most restrictive schools. ABA is designed to produce self-policing. Self-policing is Foucault's biopower and is ubiquitous in carceral institutions that seek to control disabled people (Erevelles, 2014) and our unruly bodies (Erevelles, 2005). It doesn't matter how "nice" your "modern" ABA is, or how many smiles you see on children's faces. (I wear my smile like a shield.) ABA is inseparable from violence and oppression because it enforces assimilation to nondisabled norms.

The carceral logics (Ben-Moshe, 2020) of special education that devalue resistance and overvalue goodness and smartness (both of which are inherently racist, ableist constructs) prepare students to be compliant subjects of congregate care. Special education produces carceral subjects who cannot survive outside of imprisonment.

## HELPING

I let kids play with my talker. They type their names, their favorite things, or letters that do not form words that I can recognize, but may be *invented spelling* (e.g., see Treiman, 2017) Nicki leaves me many saved phrases: gifts that I cherish, such as, "frdcecedbz." Can you make out what it means?

A kid points to my elbow canes, leaning in a corner. I hand them to him, and show him where to put his arms. He lights up: He has become quadrupedal, and runs around the classroom growling like a dinosaur (usually he crawls on his hands and knees).

Kids reach out to feel my hearing aids sitting in my ears.

My co-workers always come running over to "rescue" me. It is very hard for many of them to break from their vision that disabled people need help (especially from other disabled people, who may be considered dangerous).

Nicki uses her talker to tell me she wants a snack.

Her teacher runs over, saying, "What do you want?"

Nicki touches the icon for "Cheese."

"Say it to me," he encourages gently.

Nicki struggles to mouth the word for a bit.

"You have to learn to speak in order to communicate," he adds.

Nicki turns and looks me right in the eye as I stand next to her, my talker held in my hand.

I shake my head "no" very subtly, worried if I say the words in my heart ("Bullshit; I can't talk and I'm living my best life"), I might get fired.

Dr. Joy Ladin (see Ladin, 2013), poet and professor, told me in an email conversation that she defines inclusion as having three parts: (a) people miss you when you're gone, (b) people value your wisdom, and (c) people recognize your contributions to the community. Inclusion, then, becomes about love, respect, and equity. To me, this formulation of inclusion defies any formulation of disability that positions us as needing help. I am not saying that we do not need support for many tasks that nondisabled people take for granted. I am saying that interdependence should be approached with the same creativity, equity, and enthusiasm that a well-balanced theater ensemble or design team uses. When disabled people are positioned as the objects of help, and others as the providers of that help, it creates a power imbalance that cannot, under Dr. Ladin's definition, ever be inclusion.

## COMPLIANCE AND RESISTANCE

I have mixed emotions about the time I have spent with young people with intellectual and developmental disabilities. Even the worst day with them (the days when children are harmed) are somehow better than the best days without them. But the harm is ever present, insidious, and haunts me whether I'm awake or asleep. My PTSD will not permit me to throw away the manuals from the ABA school I worked for. I can't imagine how much worse it is for the kids who live that reality every day and cannot walk away like I did.

It is against the rules for me to look, but I can't help it. I've been working in this ABA school for a week now. It has a different kind of soundscape than most places I've been. Even though I am hard of hearing, the voices of students leap into my ears, and I pretend I am not disturbed. The voices are full of pain and anger and fear and defiance as they scream or cry. If I show how disturbed I am, my at-will employment might end. If I break the rules and look at a student while she's screaming and am caught, I might "reinforce" the screaming. And then my at-will employment might end. But the paraprofessional I'm shadowing right now is 5 steps ahead of me, her gaze due north, and I turn to the west just in time to see the antecedent to the scream.

Harry is always followed by two paraprofessionals, because it is in his behavior intervention plan (BIP). Both are full-grown men. Harry is 10 and tiny. Harry is leading his entourage towards his desk. One of the full-grown men asks him to sit down. Harry turns around and looks up at the man. He reaches out his small hand and pushes the man. Understand, he did not push the man hard. The man does not budge. He calmly looks down at the place on his belly that Harry has pushed against and lets out a big sigh.

What happens next is violent, and I will not describe it because it is not my story to tell. Suffice it to say, I witness a combination of physical and mechanical restraints, all used completely within the prescribed limitations of California State and Federal laws. I also witness Harry's screaming, red face, wet with tears. This image is seared into my memory so harshly there are no colors in my synesthesia.

This is the moment when I don't quite realize how deeply I love these kids. It is the moment I realize I cannot work at this school. It is the moment when I lose my bright eyes and bushy tail, and forget for a long time how to dream.

Every method of restraint is a pre-approved, well-practiced ritual that (when I was asked one day to input Harry's data into a spreadsheet) I discovered he lives through several times a day. The Number 117 stands out in my memory. I can't remember the time scale it represented. Was it for the school year so far? The academic quarter? This is Puar's (2017) right to maim: These students are so dis/abled that the state grants people the right to traumatize them. Sometimes there are accidents and children are suffocated to death (Morrar, 2018).

When Harry pushed his para, the para's sigh was an essay. It told me this is a ritual they go through constantly. Harry, who cannot speak, and who did not appear to have a talker or other technology for saying "No," used the only communication available to him, and the one used against him. But because pushing is a "target behavior," if Harry pushes, then he must be pushed back (to his seat). If Harry's gesture was honored as communication, and his autonomy and self determination respected and encouraged, the para might instead have tried to figure out why Harry did not want to go to his desk, and then things probably would not have escalated. Mona Delahooke (2019) and other psychologists have many alternatives to offer that do not escalate people in crisis, and yet the carceral logic of compliance and control prevails.

Some professionals in the ABA world might read this chapter and think the schools where I worked must be doing ABA wrong. That if my co-workers had done the ABA right, then the students never would have escalated. All I can say is that those schools were highly respected as pillars of modern, "humane" ABA. No one looked wistfully back at Ivar Lovaas's lab, where children were hit and shocked with electricity (Grant, 1965). These schools accepted the students who were sorted out of environments where no one was willing to restrain them. Anyone who thinks ABA can be done without restraint is simply ignoring the fact that kids who fight back just get sent along to a different school, a group home, or potentially even jails and prisons, more willing to do the dirty deed. Imagine how the insidious racialization of Black, Indigenous, and Brown students as "dangerous" plays into this school to prison pipeline.

If we name their "target behaviors" civil disobedience, what does that make us?

## ALL MY DREAMS ARE NIGHTMARES, BUT WHEN I LOOK AT MY STUDENTS, I FEEL HOPE

I look back on these experiences and think: We have so much power over children's lives. With that power in mind, I echololically chant: May our youth have the strength and resilience to survive what we do to them, and the generosity to tell us. May we have the humility to hear them, no matter how they tell us, and do *teshuvah* (to do right by them next time).

I have been complicit in all of the above. I have watched people do terrible things to children, and been silent, telling myself it was because I did not want to be banned from the room. I have drawn tally marks in binders and responded poorly to students in crisis. I felt I had to comply as the price of admission to be with these students. This does not mean that I have not also resisted, but it feels important to acknowledge my complicity. We are all complicit in this inherently oppressive system, and until we acknowledge that, we cannot work toward something better.

One of my autistic elders (of blessed memory), who was a speech pathologist, remarked to me once on his guilt at his complicity. He responded by changing what he did. When I met him, he worked for an ABA-free school that only serves students who other schools put in MREs. That school honors their complex personhood (Gordon, 2008) by supporting the students to become fully integrated into their communities, instead of hiding them away until they meet impossible standards of normalcy.

The longer I worked as a substitute, the more emboldened I became. When staff did things I disapproved of, I would wait for them to walk away, and then turn the volume of my talker down to mutter to a kid, "You did not deserve to be treated like that. I am sorry." Then, I started to confront my co-workers. "What you are doing is mean."

"This is what I was told to do," they'd retort, reminding me of Milgram's (1974) experiments investigating how far people would go to harm another person if an authority figure told them to.

The ABA environment demands perfect compliance from all involved, especially the instructors. The ABA practitioner must be ready at all moments to redirect a student. It is incredibly exhausting. Many of the students express visible distress, or struggle against their instructors. Fellow substitutes would walk out in the middle of the day. One classroom had a new teacher every year that I worked there. ABA burns people out. Environments that center control and compliance negatively affect students' motivation, as do environments wherein teachers assume students are externally motivated (Deci et al., 1991). So why burn ourselves out constructing them? There are already many empirically-based alternatives to ABA (some are referenced in Agran et al., 2014), and many more yet to be created.

I dream a forbidden dream in which everyone gets so fed up with the burn out, they stage a mass sit-in strike. The paraprofessionals and teachers show up to school, and the students attend as usual. But instead of doing business-as-usual (ABA), they demand that districts implement something less painful, less carceral, and through their collective struggle for liberation from the oppressive paradigm, seek out empowering things to do instead, such as what Annamma (2018) proposes. Dr. Annamma proposes a pedagogy of resistance founded on love, that centers students' struggles against racism and ableism.

I am inviting you to read our world in a way that builds solidarity between educators/administrators and disabled students and that pushes for (special) education to welcome multiple epistemologies (Bang & Medin, 2010). I am invested as an activist in epistemologies from disability cultures, such as autistic culture (Bascom, 2012) and disability justice culture (Sins Invalid, 2019); as a learning scientist in epistemologies from cognitive psychology, anthropology, and DisCrit (Connor et al., 2016); and as an educator in epistemologies from critical pedagogy (Freire, 1970). I believe that these things can coexist in learning environments and lead to richer, more hopeful futures for disabled youth than the ones we offer at this writing. But what excites me the most is discovering and supporting disabled youths' own epistemic moves, which necessarily grow out of their resistance, their love, and their dreams. I want to know, if we (adults) stop pretending that we know best, what will they teach us?

## REFERENCES

Agran, M., Brown, F., Hughes, C., Quirk, C., & Ryndak, D. L. (2014). *Equity and full participation for individuals with severe disabilities: A vision for the future.* Paul H. Brookes Publishing Company.

Annamma, S. A. (2018). *The pedagogy of pathologization: Dis/abled girls of color in the school-prison nexus.* Routledge.

Asasumasu, K. (2013, October 4). *If you don't use your words you won't be indistinguishable* [Blog post]. Radical Neurodivergence Speaking. https://timetolisten.blogspot.com/2013/10/if-you-dont-use-your-words-you-wont-be.html

Baggs, M. (2007, January 15) *In my language* [Video]. YouTube. https://www.youtube.com/watch?v=JnylM1hI2jc

Bang, M., & Medin, D. (2010). Cultural processes in science education: Supporting the navigation of multiple epistemologies. *Science Education, 94*(6) 1008–1026.

Bascom, J. (Ed.). (2012). *Loud hands: Autistic people speaking.* The Autistic Self Advocacy Network.

Ben-Moshe, L. (2020). *Decarcerating disability: Deinstitutionalization and prison abolition.* University of Minnesota Press.

Berne, P., Brown, L. X. Z., & Piepzna-Samarasinha, L. L. (2020, April 2). *Organizing in a time of social distancing: The wisdom of disability justice organizers* [Zoom panel presentation]. JOIN for Justice, the Jewish Organizing Institute and Network, Boston, MA.

Broderick, A., & Leonardo, Z. (2016). What a good boy: The deployment and distribution of "goodness" as ideological property in schools. In D. Connor, B. Ferri, & S. Annamma (Eds.), *DisCrit: Disability studies and critical race theory in education* (pp. 55–67). Teachers College Press.

Charlton, J. I. (2000). *Nothing about us without us: Disability oppression and empowerment.* University of California Press.

Chemers, M. M. (2008). *Staging stigma: A critical examination of the American freak show.* Palgrave Macmillan.

Connor, D., Ferri, B., & Annamma, S. (Eds.). (2016). *DisCrit: Disability studies and critical race theory in education.* Teachers College Press.

Crompton, C. J., Fletcher-Watson, S., & Ropar, D. (2020, September 24). *Autistic peer to peer information transfer is highly effective.* https://doi.org/10.31219/osf .io/j4knx

Crompton, C. J., Sharp, M., Axbey, H., Fletcher-Watson, S., Flynn, E. G., & Ropar, D. (2020). Neurotype-matching, but not being autistic, influences self and observer ratings of interpersonal rapport. *Frontiers in Psychology, 11.* https:// doi.org/10.3389/fpsyg.2020.586171

Deci, E. L., Vallerand, R. J., Pelletier, L. G., & Ryan, R. M. (1991). Motivation and education: The self-determination perspective. *Educational Psychologist, 26,* 325–346.

Delahooke, M. (2019). *Beyond behaviors: Using brain science and compassion to understand and solve children's behavioral challenges.* PESI Publishing & Media.

Digirolamo, G. J., & Hintzman, D. L. (1997). First impressions are lasting impressions: A primacy effect in memory for repetitions. *Psychonomic Bulletin & Review 4,* 121–124. https://doi.org/10.3758/BF03210784

Dinishak, J. (2016). "The deficit view and its critics." *Disability Studies Quarterly, 36*(4). https://dsq-sds.org/article/view/5236/4475

Erevelles, N. (2005). Educating unruly bodies: Critical pedagogy, disability studies, and the politics of schooling. *Educational Theory, 50,* 25–47. https://doi .org/10.1111/j.1741-5446.2000.00025.x

Erevelles, N. (2014). Crippin' Jim Crow: Disability, dis-location, and the school-to -prison pipeline. *Disability Incarcerated.* Palgrave Macmillan US.

Foucault, M. (1977). *Discipline and punish: The birth of the prison.* Pantheon Books.

Freire, P. (1970). *Pedagogy of the oppressed.* Continuum.

Freire, P. (2004). *Pedagogy of indignation.* Paradigm Press.

Garland-Thomson, R. (1997). *Extraordinary bodies: Figuring physical disability in American culture and literature.* Columbia University Press.

Gordon, A. (2008). *Ghostly matters: Haunting and the sociological imagination.* University of Minnesota Press.

Grant, A. (1965, May 7). Screams, slaps & love: A surprising, shocking treatment helps far-gone mental cripples. *Life Magazine,* 90–96.

Harris, H., Israeli, D., Minshew, N. J., Bonneh, Y., Heeger, D. J., Behrmann, M., & Sagi, D. (2015). Perceptual learning in autism: Over-specificity and possible remedies. *Nature Neuroscience, 18,* 1574–1576. https://doi.org/10.1038/nn.4129

Jones, S. R. (2015). ABA—Applied Behavior Analysis. In M. Sutton (Ed.), *The real experts: Readings for parents of autistic children* (pp. 50–59). Autonomous Press.

Kapur, M. 2008. Productive failure. *Cognition and Instruction, 26*(3), 379–424. https://doi.org/10.1080/07370000802212669

Kurth, J., Morningstar, M., & Kozleski, E. (2015). The persistence of highly restrictive special education placements for students with low-incidence disabilities. *Research and Practice for Persons With Severe Disabilities, 39*(3), 227–239. https://doi.org/10.1177/1540796914555580

Ladin, J. (2013). *Through the Door of Life: A Jewish Journey between Genders.* University of Wisconsin Press.

Leonardo, Z., & Broderick, A. A. (2011). Smartness as property: A critical exploration of intersections between Whiteness and disability studies. *Teachers College Record, 113*(10), 2206–2232.

Milgram, S. (1974). *Obedience to authority: An experimental view.* Harper & Row.

Minstrell, J., & Van Zee, E. H. (2000). *Inquiring into inquiry learning and teaching in science.* American Association for the Advancement of Science. https://www.aaas.org/resources/inquiring-inquiry-learning-and-teaching-science

Moore, L. F., Jr. (2018, September 22). *Creating criminals out of disabled girls of color: Interview with Dr. Subini Annamma* [Interview with Dr. Subini Annamma]. National Black Disability Coalition. https://blackdisability.org/nbdc.info/2018/09/22/creating-criminals-out-disabled-girls-color/

Morrar, S. (2018, December 7). School where student with autism collapsed and later died violated restraint rules, California regulators find. *The Sacramento Bee.* https://www.sacbee.com/latest-news/article222799470.html

Piepzna-Samarasinha, L. L. (2018). *Care work: Dreaming disability justice.* Arsenal Pulp Press.

Pink, S. (2009). *Doing Sensory Ethnography.* SAGE Publications.

Puar, J. (2017). *The right to maim: Debility, capacity, disability.* Duke University Press.

Putnam, M. (2005). Conceptualizing disability. Developing a framework for political disability identity. *Journal of Disability Policy Studies, 16*(3), 188–198. https://doi.org/10.1177/10442073050160030601

Sandoval-Norton, A. H., & Shkedy, G. (2019). How much compliance is too much compliance: Is long-term ABA therapy abuse? *Cogent Psychology, 6*(1), Article 1641258. https://doi.org/10.1080/23311908.2019.1641258

Schweik, S. M. (2011). Lomax's matrix: Disability, solidarity, and the Black power of 504. *Disability Studies Quarterly, 31*(1). https://dsq-sds.org/article/view/1371/1539

Sequenzia, A. (2015, February 11). *My thoughts on ABA.* Autistic Women and Nonbinary Network. https://awnnetwork.org/my-thoughts-on-aba/

Sins Invalid. (2019). *Skin, tooth, and bone: The basis of movement is our people a disability justice primer* (2nd ed.) [Digital version]. https://www.sinsinvalid.org/disability-justice-primer

Sterponi, L., & Shankey, J. (2014). Rethinking echolalia: Repetition as interactional resource in the communication of a child with autism. *Journal of Child Language, 41*(2), 275–304. https://doi.org/10.1017/S0305000912000682

Treiman, R. (2017). Learning to spell words: Findings, theories, and issues. *Scientific Studies of Reading, 21*(4), 265–276. https://doi.org/10.1080/10888438.2017.1296449

Williams, R. (2018). Autonomously autistic. *Canadian Journal of Disability Studies, 7*(2), 60–82. https://doi.org/10.15353/cjds.v7i2.423

CHAPTER 3

# ABILITY AND BELONGING

## Contested Ontology and Epistemology That Shape School Practice

**Joshua Bornstein**
*Fairleigh Dickinson University*

**Holly Manaseri**
*University of Hawai'i at Mānoa*

Educational leaders can have a great deal of influence on the policies, practices, structures, and discourses that govern how inclusive their schools will be. We begin from the premise that serving leaders and aspiring leaders who may read this volume do not question whether or not schools should be inclusive. However, we want to push that assumption by asking leaders to examine (a) how they describe a student who deserves to be included and (b) what they will accept as truthful ways of knowing what students themselves know and can do. The policies, structures, and practices even of inclusive schooling are predicated on normative cognitive and emotional standards for students. We regard those norms as deeply entrenched in

*Who Decides?*, pages 53–67

Copyright © 2022 by Information Age Publishing

www.infoagepub.com

**53**

ableism and racism, and consider it a moral imperative for leaders to disrupt them (Bornstein & Manaseri, 2018).

This chapter is an attempt to make those predicates explicit, especially when they are implicit in policy, structure, and practice. We offer this analysis so that leaders can avoid making their schools complicit in oppression. The roots of all three words—implicit, explicit, and complicit—are from the Latin for "folding together." Hence, we aim to lay them open so that leaders can build afresh with more clarity.

The moral imperative that animates deconstructing normalcy is about inclusion but is more fundamentally about justice. The ontology of who belongs in school and the epistemology of what counts as truthful knowledge in those determinations are fundamental matters for school leaders and teacher leaders who seek to build schools of moral integrity. If "justice is what love looks like in public" (West, 2017), then loving and just schools should strive to build structures, policies, and practices that are rooted in the principle that all students belong simply because they exist, not just because they approximate some construction of being normal. This is the work for all in K–12 school settings as leadership is distributed across a school and not contained just to official roles designated under school administrators. Such schools must also philosophically and functionally embrace ways of knowing students that the students, their families, and their cultures can validate.

This chapter has three aims. The first aim is to inform a debate on the ontology of disability in educational settings, destabilizing the assumption that belonging is predicated on racialized normalcy. The second aim is to challenge the educational system's epistemological assumptions about disability, in which school structures and policies prove that racialized normalcy is a true way to know students. The third aim is to consider educational responses to disability through administrative decision-making in practice and policy. We expect this chapter to deepen a discussion on DisCrit in educational leadership that has recently been gaining momentum in the leadership for social justice literature (Bornstein & Manaseri, 2018; Capper & Roth, 2017; DeMatthews, 2020; Kozleski et al., 2020). Capper and Roth (2017) noted an alarming gap in the literature in both theory and practice for DisCrit intersectional analysis of racism and ableism. We began to fill that gap with a special issue of *Review of Disability Studies* (Manaseri & Bornstein, 2018) devoted to applying disability studies to leadership preparation and our own exploration of Disability Studies in Education (DSE) and DisCrit in that effort (Bornstein & Manaseri, 2018). More recently, DeMatthews (2020) has laid out a framework for applying DisCrit to leadership practices, but DeMatthews' (2020) analysis relies more on pulling apart the intersectional nature of classification and discipline data, rather than striking at how ableism is used to rationalize those disproportionate outcomes.

## ONTOLOGY OF BEING AND BELONGING

In this section, we analyze how school policies, structures, and practices such as discipline (Losen & Gillespie, 2012), multi-tiered systems of support (MTSS; Bornstein, 2017), and special education (Harry & Klingner, 2014; Skiba et al., 2008) implement normative Whiteness as ableist/racist rationales as the fundamental means to know students and decide how to include and exclude them. Schools operate with the implicit belief that human differences in academic performance and behavior distribute along a bell curve (Fendler & Muzaffar, 2008), even if they do not always go to the extreme of believing the pseudoscience (Herrnstein & Murray, 1996) that this bell curve rationalizes hierarchical racial classification.

Overwhelmingly, schools prioritize normalcy as the essential way to know and place students. Synonyms for norm and normal abound in formal and informal descriptions of students. Consider how deeply the words norm, normal, average, ordinary are woven into school vernacular, as are their variants above—or below—average, extraordinary, and so forth. These designations have institutional significance because they become the fundamental logic for stratification structures such as tracking (honors, general, and remedial), levels on standardized testing reports (1 through 4), and tiers on the pyramidal structure of MTSS (universal, targeted, and intensive). Thus, the way that students resemble normalcy is not only a deep-seated school identity, but also the criterion for enrolling them in the basic systems with which a school manages curriculum, schedules, and support. From Foucault (1991), this is the concept of governmentality, the way an identity inscribes an individual into relationships of power, particularly whether people are the subjects who act or the objects who are acted upon. The discourse of inclusion and exclusion exemplifies governmentality.

Consequently, normalcy is powerful. Normalcy is key to belonging in classrooms. We talk about "general education" classrooms and a host of spin-off spaces in which "exceptional" students learn, for example. The simple euphemism of "exceptional" students supports normalcy as the preferred identity. Normal students learn in the regular classroom with regular teachers, and exceptional students learn elsewhere with specialists. The exceptional students may stay in the regular classroom, but likely at a segregated space within that room and still under the tutelage of teachers with special credentials. This is an insidious logic because while "exceptional" implies "superlative" in the same way that "special" does, the marker inordinately applies to students with disabilities who are regarded as less competent than their peers, yet allows the adults to feel better about themselves because they have avoided pejorative labels. This self-soothing logic shores up complicity because it avoids the implication of malicious segregation.

Indeed, the right to belong because one approximates normalcy has deep roots in U.S. struggles to be included in the citizenry. Baynton (2001) points out that most movements for civil rights in the United States—including abolishing slavery and Jim Crow segregation, gaining women's suffrage, and immigrant rights—have argued that they should win inclusion because the excluded group was just as normal as the dominant group. Indeed, they were fighting implicitly ableist logic for exclusion each time. African Americans were held to be psychologically unable to handle the responsibility of citizenship or economic self-determination. Women likewise were deemed to be too hysterical—a psychological state rooted in the reproductive system—to exercise independent judgment. Immigrants were similarly regarded as biologically predisposed to laziness, criminality, and infectious disease. When Baynton (2001) wrote this historical analysis nearly 20 years ago, readers could be excused for expecting that those explicit justifications for inequality were relics. However, President Trump's ascendancy clearly emboldened many activists, politicians, and citizens to resurrect them.

Indigenous scholar Hollie Mackey (2018) offered a different provocation on the ontology of belonging. Normalcy has no role in an Indigenous concept of belonging:

> Indigenous people consider all to be fully participating members of the community regardless of ability, each contributing as intended by the creator, mediated through natural, relational forces. This is a direct reflection of Indigenous ontology that does not seek to establish one objective truth, but recognizes multiple realities exist in relation to one's orientation towards the truth. (p. 6)

Not only does this reframing obviate the need for considering normalcy, but it also emphasizes relationship as a key precept of belonging. In other words, whereas Eurocentric ontology makes belonging contingent on normalcy, Indigenous ontology makes belonging a central component of existence itself. We exist by virtue of being in relationship to each other.

White supremacy is implicit in conventional dynamics of inclusion and exclusion. The power to define who can be in a space or use it implies the power of ownership. Harris (1995) defined Whiteness as property in the context of law. School owns the classroom, and demonstrates that authority by delineating who may be there and the rationale for the inclusion or exclusion. Conventionally, students being smart and good are each regarded as common-sense indicators for belonging in the classroom. Those qualities are synonymous with White expressions of cognition and compliance (Bornstein, 2015; Broderick & Leonardo, 2016; Leonardo & Broderick, 2011). Leonardo and Broderick (2011) build on Baglieri et al.'s (2010) notion of the "normative center" that implicates the inclusion/exclusion discourse of racism and ableism:

> In terms of race, the category, white, cannot exist without its denigrated other, such as Black or people of color generally; in terms of ability, constructs such as smartness only function by disparaging in both discursive and material ways their complement, those deemed to be uneducable and disposable. In both cases, the privileged group is provided with honor, investment, and capital, whereas the marginalized segment is dishonored and dispossessed. (Leonardo & Broderick, 2011, p. 2209)

Therefore, Whiteness as property operates on several levels. In terms of ontology, at an individual student level some students possess the requisite and preferred intellectual and behavioral traits, which are the traits typically demonstrated by White people. Organizationally, that identity is essential to the discourse of rights, needs, and resources at the heart of MTSS and special education.

> Students expected to perform comfortably at or above the benchmark are diagnosed as "safe" and left to succeed; students expected to perform just below the target but believed to have the "ability" to make the improvements necessary to push them over the benchmark are diagnosed as 'suitable for treatment' and targeted for intervention. (Saltmarsh & Youdell, 2004, p. 11)

Multi-tiered systems of support (Jimerson et al., 2007) are a salient example of this discourse. MTSS is the most recent iteration of a triage model that has its origins in public health (Merrell & Buchanan, 2006). In the MTSS pyramid, students are conventionally placed on the escalating tiers of deficit relative to normalcy.

To begin, it is worth deconstructing the ontological assumption built into the phrase "identifying a student." Educators use it as a way to make a student known as eligible for a given program that supplements, supplants, or supports conventional instruction. It is hardly controversial language. Linguistically, "identifying" is to give a student a new identity. That is ontological work. The identity becomes how the student is known. Brantlinger (2006) brings to our attention the idea of "fixing" students with these abnormal identities, both in the sense of (a) rectifying something wrong with them and (b) fastening a stigma to them.

In this way, the MTSS functions as a "hunt for disability" (Baker, 2002), predicated on finding disability as a logic for efficient school functioning. Leaders may see this system in artifacts such as the MTSS data wall that maps out the student body as a whole. Labels or pyramids will often adorn the wall, with student names arranged in color-coded tiers: green = Tier I, yellow = Tier II, red = Tier III. The traffic symbolism of that system is also obvious, signaling the need for the school's overall control authority and the heightened danger to normal school operations produced by the upper tiers.

Whiteness as property (Harris, 1995) is closely aligned with this argument. Possession encompasses the exclusive right to use something or someplace. Having a White identity entitles students to belong in school and to use what school offers (Harris, 1995). Annamma et al. (2014) engage DisCrit to extend that discourse to the intersection of racism and ableism in conferring which students belong and have a right to school's essential functions:

> Whiteness and ability bestow profits to those that claim those statuses and disadvantages those who are unable to access... Once individuals or groups of students are positioned as less desirable, they are barred access to 1) curriculum that is engaging and accurate; 2) pedagogy that is responsive and ingenuous; and 3) relationships that are authentic and hopeful. (p. 72)

Educators will be familiar with the common use of labeling. We hear references to the "special ed" kids, the "inclusion" kids, or perhaps the "Tier I," "Tier II," or "Tier III" kids in faculty rooms, data review meetings, and any number of other forums. Furthermore, the identity derives from systems set up by the institution. This is Foucault's (1991) governmentality as it operates in school. Students' identities are derived from their place in the power structure of the institution rather than from their innate humanity.

When a school asks who belongs where in its structure, it is speaking ontologically. Triage ascribes value to the different identities, privileging Tier I as the safe, normal, ideal state. Students belong in Tier I not simply because they attend the school, but because they match certain ideal characteristics. As those characteristics are associated with Whiteness (Baglieri et al., 2010; Bornstein, 2015; Leonardo & Broderick, 2011), this system enshrines Whiteness as supreme, leading us to designate it and analogous structures as White supremacist.

We argue that belonging applies to all students simply because they exist, not because their identity approximates ableist, racist norms (Baynton, 2001; Danforth & Naraian, 2015). We mean educational "belonging" in two conventional senses: inclusion and possession. First, students belong in that they should be included in the groups (classes) and places (school buildings and classrooms) of education. Second, students properly possess all the "profits" of schooling. Indeed, this ownership provides the basis for students' legal due process protections both in special education and discipline (Cambron-McCabe et al., 2014).

Leaders can use these two definitions of belonging as a North star to guide their schools as they navigate the often convoluted and treacherous ableist and racist practices and structures that undermine students' rights (Annamma et al., 2014). We offer this metaphor of the North star because it suggests remaining oriented to the truth, which can be challenging in the many practices that schools use to justify exclusion and marginalization as valid responses to a student's condition.

## EPISTEMOLOGIES THAT VALIDATE EXCLUSION

Two questions about students' ability guide instructional decisions in school: (a) What do our students know? and (b) How do we know that they know it? Epistemology tells us how we know we have a true answer to either of those questions. To that end, what we know about ability discursively constructs what we think we know about disability. This section provides a critical analysis of traditional epistemologies that pervade concepts of disability. We address how ableism is the epistemological basis of deciding what our students should know, and therefore how we can trust what we know about our students' cognition. Furthermore, understanding these epistemologies helps explain the ontologies of includable and excludable students in the previous section. We argue that ableism encodes White norms for intellectual, social, and emotional expression. In addition, this section we examine how this code informs and justifies exclusion and segregation.

Simply put, curricular and instructional priorities of what knowledge is worth teaching and learning determine how to place and support students for the most effective education. Arranging the curriculum in a hierarchy conventionally drives class assignments in a parallel hierarchy of student ability to meet the curriculum. Smart students meet intellectually challenging curriculum, while other students are likewise placed and supported to meet the curriculum at their own appropriate levels. Our critique lies in interrogating the ableist and racist epistemological assumptions that go into judging the suitability of those matches of students, curriculum, support, and placement.

Beginning in 1948, a group of educators undertook the task of classifying education goals and objectives. The intent was to develop a classification system for three domains: the cognitive, the affective, and the psychomotor. Work on the cognitive domain was completed in the 1950s and is commonly referred to as Bloom's taxonomy of the cognitive domain (Bloom et al., 1956). The major idea of the taxonomy is that educational objectives represent high priority knowledge and can be arranged in a hierarchy from simple to complex. The levels are understood to be successive, so that one level must be mastered before the next level can be reached. The original levels by Bloom et al. (1956) were ordered as follows: knowledge, comprehension, application, analysis, synthesis, and evaluation. Anderson et al. (2001) published a revised edition of Bloom's taxonomy, suggesting that in the cognitive domain, creation appears as a higher-order process as compared to evaluation. This model has become a mainstay of the American school and has served as a mechanism for exclusion in several key ways.

This fundamental epistemological assumption drives many instructional decisions, and placement decisions thereafter, about where and by whom different levels of learning are appropriate. We concur with Kompa's (2017) critique that decontextualizing Bloom's taxonomy by ignoring the historical and social construction of knowledge and learning (Bandura, 2001, 2006) is oppressive and dangerous:

> Knowledge creation and relating thinking skills do not exist as *a priori* phenomena, but they are evoked and engaged by people. Knowledge is a foremost social construct while learning is facilitated by social processes. In this light, Bloom's taxonomy does not take into consideration the social relation of persons in the creation of knowledge. This includes crucial aspects such as the motivation to acquire knowledge, reiterative and diverse cycles of research, dynamics of open inquiry, the validation of related arguments or the ongoing refinement of concepts within teams. (Kompa, 2017, para. 9)

Bloom's taxonomy tells us nothing about the role that learners play in knowledge acquisition and creation, including a learner's intellectual values, the psychological effects of learning experiences, individual differences in cognitive processing, or the communicative processes involved in research and development. Bloom's taxonomy does not explain how people collaboratively create, manage, and modify knowledge, and especially how they do so while navigating persistently ableist and racist schools.

In our work with school leadership candidates, we found that the structural framework of schools made far more sense to them when they appreciated the structures' epistemological foundations (Bornstein & Manaseri, 2018). Leaders then recognized how institutionalized ableist assumptions shone through everyday decisions on assessment and instruction, school placement, and curriculum design. Not only did excavating ableist epistemology make school conventions clearer, it also made clear where transformative leaders could effectively disrupt oppressive power (Bornstein & Manaseri, 2018).

## IMPLICATIONS OF CRITICAL PERSPECTIVES FOR EDUCATIONAL LEADERSHIP

Next, we turn our attention to informing the development of more sophisticated methodologies and strategies for studying the epistemology of ability, belonging, and community. There has been little attempt to create a specific methodology of epistemological processes on which our understanding of impairments and disability has been founded (Hayhoe, 2012;

Pfeiffer, 2002). Historically, critical scholarship in educational administration has seen some significant moments through the work of Bates (1983), Callahan (1962), Evers and Lakomski (1991, 1996, 2000), Foster (1986), Greenfield and Ribbins (1993), and Smyth (1989). Leadership for social justice has been explored by scholars looking to investigate how schools and leaders' practices have, often despite good intentions, resulted in inequitable and sometimes discriminatory outcomes for students of a variety of backgrounds (Blackmore, 2006; Marshall & Ward, 2004; Normore, 2008; Shields, 2018; Theoharis, 2007).

In terms of critical perspectives of and within educational leadership, such approaches entail interrogations of the power structures of education, critical examinations of knowledge production and intellectual resources used to understand and promote leadership, and a concern for social justice (Niesche & Gowlett, 2019). The field continues to evolve with scholarship in disability studies influencing educational leadership in preparation (Bornstein & Manaseri, 2018; DeMatthews, 2020; Pazey & Cole, 2012; Theoharis & Causton-Theoharis, 2008).

We propose an intensification of scholarship with theoretical framings of DisCrit at its core combined with practical application to the field focusing on in-service school leadership. As scholars teaching in school leadership preparation, we are acutely aware of the limitations on the influence of leadership epistemological development given the constraints of an abbreviated and compressed timeline of most leadership preparation programs varying from 27–36 credit hours of graduate study. Many accelerated programs place leadership candidates into internships concurrent to coursework and still others have candidates in roles as acting building or district leaders while they are addressing requirements for their certification. We therefore look to mine the gap between leadership preparation and in-service leadership and offer a lens for leadership development that is reflective through a recursive process. We extend Shields' (2018) transformative leadership framework with DisCrit to argue that leaders must deconstruct destructive ideologies and practices at the same time that they attempt to build empowering ones.

Shields (2018) offers a critical approach to transformative leadership, provoking leaders across the nation to rise against the inequities within their institutions. Shields argues that leaders must adopt a transformative leadership approach; a critical, socially aware, and equity-driven method. That method highlights the harmful effect that homogeneity and its normalization can have on intellectual communities, including the othering and exclusion that result from this perpetuation of elitism and privilege.

Shields' (2018) tenets for transformative leadership present a helpful matrix for laying out how to apply the anti-racist and anti-ableist ontological and epistemological reframing we have discussed above. Into those tenets, we also weave Mackey's (2015) Indigenous ethical framework that foregrounds relationship as a primary condition of being, and the epistemological principle that "despite differences, all belief systems are valued and allowed without forcing those systems on others" (p. 167). Table 3.1 outlines leadership practices that would enact this version of transformative leadership.

**TABLE 3.1   Anti-Racist and Anti-Ableist Epistemology and Ontology in Transformative Leadership**

| Shield's Framework | Leadership in Action |
| --- | --- |
| Tenet 1: Deep and Equitable Change | Initiate audits and reviews of policies, practices, and structures that assume White and ableist precepts of normalcy. |
| | Gain democratic buy-in for the notion that all students belong in this school and in their classrooms simply because they exist, not because they approximate normative expectations. |
| Tenet 2: The Necessity of New Knowledge | Convene stakeholders to redefine what school expects of its students and teachers, with thorough acceptance of the variety of cultures present in the school community. |
| Tenet 3: Address the Inequitable Distribution of Power | Explicitly replace the historic bias toward medicalized analysis in decision-making teams and processes by encouraging multiple valid realities about students: teacher-, family-, and community-based epistemic knowledge. |
| Tenet 4: Balancing Private and Public Good | Disrupt any argument that atypical students somehow detract from the learning of typical students in inclusive classrooms. Promote the benefits of differentiated instruction and universal design for learning. |
| | Likewise, replace exclusionary discipline practices with restorative justice that emphasize healing relationships that may have been injured. |
| Tenet 5: A Focus on Emancipation, Democracy, Equity, and Justice | Incorporate into school mission the principle that full citizenship in the school is accorded to every student simply because they are enrolled at the school. Students' rights to an education are not compromised when the students differ from White and ableist norms. Further emphasize that excluding some students harms the relationships of all, and thereby diminishes their role in the school community. |
| Tenet 6: An Emphasis on Interdependence, Interconnectedness, and Global Awareness | Highlight interdependent restorative practices, such as problem-solving UDL dilemmas. Support teachers to make difficult decisions that emphasize interdependence but may compromise conventional school achievement practices. |
| Tenet 7: Balance Critique and Promise | Emphasize the promise of UDL, while critiquing exclusionary conventions. Audit curriculum for funds of knowledge (Moll et al., 2005) approach to cultural responsiveness. |
| Tenet 8: Exhibit Moral Courage | Explicitly invite the difficult conversations among stakeholders. Trust decision-makers to solve problems collaboratively as they achieve full inclusion, especially where conventional practices, policies, and structures may be compromised. |
| | Demonstrate the self-awareness to critique one's own practice and assumptions. |

Our DisCrit amendment to Shields' (2018) framework brings leaders back to unpacking the ontological and epistemological assumptions in oppressive structures. For example, with a DisCrit analysis, balancing and private good as in Tenet 4 means not only deconstructing the notion that meeting the needs of some students will detract from the needs of others, it also means challenging the conventional ableist rationale of whose rights should be protected—whose entitlements govern that space—as also inherently racist. Likewise, if DisCrit thinking informs the curriculum and system audits we ascribe to Tenets 1 and 7, then they should interrogate how any justifications for differentiating among students by their ability may be encoding Whiteness. As a third example, in the wake of 2020's global pandemic and the reignited movement for racial justice, the guiding principles of Tenet 6 must emphasize how deeply educational and health equity are entwined. When schools may scramble to address "learning loss" (a pandemic-inspired incarnation of the achievement gap) with targeted and segregated compensatory programs, leaders who embrace a DisCrit analysis will invite their communities to challenge ableism embedded in that alarm. Furthermore, these transformative leaders will also challenge the degree to which ableist assumptions of learning loss prioritize what White students know and can do in schools already constructed to privilege their culture, and thereby sanitize and concretize institutional racism.

## CONCLUSIONS

We intend to push transformative leaders beyond diversity and inclusion as sufficient remedies for institutional ableism and racism. We oppose neither diversity nor inclusion. However, leaders need to be able to deconstruct the logic for exclusion in order to effectively build inclusion. When ableism is the motivating logic for creating segregated spaces, we invite leaders to challenge the truth value (epistemology) alongside the identity construction (ontology) embedded therein. For example, educators may analyze racial disproportionality in disability classification as an unfortunate necessity of a priori neutral and rational decisions about curriculum and instructions, and similarly apparently neutral diagnoses of students' needs. A DisCrit-informed leader must lead their schools to recognize that all the grounding of those assumptions are ableist and racist because they are predicated on White norms and the preservation of normalcy as an instructional imperative. The pain in those conversations comes in challenging educators to deal with the racist and ableist impact of their benevolent intentions.

Thus, embracing diversity and inclusion is about more than bringing many stakeholders to the table in personnel, curriculum, and decision-making. It is about disrupting all those instances when belonging has been predicated on being normal or approximating being normal, which has also tacitly meant being or approximating being White. Leaders will need the courage to challenge the apparent racial neutrality and positivist rationalization of data protocols and curricular and instructional hierarchies, noting that the hierarchies themselves are ableist.

As of this writing, we are in the midst of schools responding to 2020's twin cataclysms of COVID-19 pandemic and the reinvigorated movement for racial justice. In the first phase, injustice and inequity were more clearly exposed for all to see. What was implicit had become explicit for many. Progressive educators were likely well aware of these dynamics prior to 2020 but may have pushed like Sisyphus against them. Transformative leaders who exhibited Shields' (2018) traits may well have found more hospitable conditions with a broadly awakened sense of the need for connection, justice, resilience, and courage. For so many, there was a powerful sense that returning to business as usual was not an acceptable option.

Yet as schools have attempted to reopen with a wide variety of options, we see some retrenchment to customary practices and policies. Like the Stockholm syndrome, battered communities and schools may settle for oppressive circumstances just because they are familiar. The routinely implicit ableism and racism have some cracks in it, however, as a broader swath of our communities now have tacitly acknowledged systemic injustice. Complicity is more obviously on the line at such a moment. The choice is clearer to expose and disrupt or to leave in place the veils that hide the oppressive norm. We hope that the tools offered here are genuinely encouraging for educational leaders as they are persuaded to realize this moment's potential to advance justice.

# REFERENCES

Anderson, L. W., Krathwohl, D. R., Airasian, P. W., Cruikshank, K. A., Mayer, R. E., Pintrich, P. R., Raths, J., & Wittrock, M. C. (2001). *A taxonomy for learning, teaching, and assessing: A revision of Bloom's taxonomy of educational objectives.* Pearson.

Annamma, S., Morrison, D., & Jackson, D. (2014). Disproportionality fills in the gaps: Connections between achievement, discipline and special education in the school-to-prison pipeline. *Berkeley Review of Education, 5*(1).

Baglieri, S., Valle, J. W., Connor, D. J., & Gallagher, D. J. (2010). Disability studies in education. *Remedial and Special Education, 32*(4), 267–278. https://doi .org/10.1177/0741932510362200

Baker, B. M. (2002). The hunt for disability: The new eugenics and the normalization of school children. *Teachers College Record, 104*(4), 663–703.

Bandura, A. (2001). Social cognitive theory: An agentic perspective [Article]. *Annual Review of Psychology, 52*(1), 1. https://doi.org/10.1146/annurev.psych.52.1.1

Bandura, A. (2006). Toward a psychology of human agency. *Perspectives on Psychological Science, 1*(2), 164–180. https://doi.org/10.1111/j.1745-6916.2006.00011.x

Bates, R. (1983). *Educational administration and the management of knowledge.* Deakin University Press.

Baynton, D. C. (2001). Disability and the justification of inequality in American history. In P. K. Longmore & L. Umansky (Eds.), *The new disability history: American perspectives* (pp. 33–57). New York University Press.

Blackmore, J. (2006). Deconstructing diversity discourses in the field of educational management and leadership. *Educational Management Administration & Leadership, 34*(2), 181–199.

Bloom, B., Englehart, M. F., Hill, W., & Krathwohl, D. (1956). *Taxonomy of educational objectives: The classification of educational goals. Handbook I: Cognitive domain.* Longmans, Green.

Bornstein, J. (2015). "If they're on Tier I, there are really no concerns that we can see:" PBIS medicalizes compliant behavior. *Journal of Ethnographic and Qualitative Research, 9*, 247–267.

Bornstein, J. (2017). Can PBIS build justice rather than merely restore order? In N. Okilwa, M. A. Khalifa, & F. M. Briscoe (Eds.), *The school to prison pipeline: The role of culture and discipline in school* (pp. 135–167). Emerald Group. https://doi.org/10.1108/s2051-231720160000004008

Bornstein, J., & Manaseri, H. (2018). Disability studies and educational leadership preparation: The moral imperative. *Review of Disability Studies: An International Journal, 14*(3), 6–21.

Brantlinger, E. A. (2006). *Who benefits from special education?: Remediating (fixing) other people's children.* Lawrence Erlbaum Associates.

Broderick, A. A., & Leonardo, Z. (2016). What a good boy: The deployment and distribution of goodness as ideological property in schools. In D. J. Connor, B. A. Ferri, & S. A. Annamma (Eds.), *DisCrit: Disability studies and critical race theory in education* (pp. 55–70). Teachers College Press.

Callahan, R. E. (1962). *Education and the cult of efficiency.* University of Chicago Press.

Cambron-McCabe, N. H., McCarthy, M. M., & Eckes, S. (2014). *Legal rights of teachers and students* (Third edition. ed.). Pearson.

Capper, C. A., & Roth, H. (2017, November 15–19). *Implications of disability studies theories for equity leadership across identities.* University Council for Educational Administration Annual Convention, Denver, CO.

Danforth, S., & Naraian, S. (2015). This new field of inclusive education: Beginning a dialogue on conceptual foundations. *Intellectual and Developmental Disabilities, 53*(1), 70–85. https://doi.org/10.1352/1934-9556-53.1.70

DeMatthews, D. (2020). Addressing racism and ableism in schools: A DisCrit leadership framework for principals. *The Clearing House: A Journal of Educational Strategies, Issues and Ideas, 93*(1), 27–34. https://doi.org/10.1080/00098655.2019.1690419

Evers, C. W., & Lakomski, G. (1991). *Knowing educational administration: Contemporary methodological controversies in educational research.* Pergamon Press.

Evers, C. W., & Lakomski, G. (1996). *Exploring educational administration.* Elsevier.

Evers, C. W., & Lakomski, G. (2000). *Doing educational administration.* Elsevier.

Fendler, L., & Muzaffar, I. (2008). The history of the bell curve: Sorting and the idea of normal. *Educational Theory, 58*(1), 63–82. https://doi.org/10.1111/j.1741-5446.2007.0276.x

Foster, W. (1986). *Paradigms and promises.* Prometheus Books.

Foucault, M. (1991). Governmentality. In G. Burchell, C. Gordon, & P. Miller (Eds.), *The Foucault effect: Studies in governmentality* (pp. 87–104). University of Chicago Press.

Greenfield, T., & Ribbins, P. (1993). *Greenfield on educational administration: Towards a humane science.* Routledge.

Harris, C. I. (1995). Whiteness as property. In K. Crenshaw, N. Gotanda, G. Peller, & K. Thomas (Eds.), *Critical race theory: The key writings that formed the movement.* The New Press.

Harry, B., & Klingner, J. K. (2014). *Why are so many minority students in special education? Understanding race & disability in schools* (2nd ed.). Teachers College Press.

Hayhoe, S. (2012). *Grounded theory and disability studies: An investigation into legacies of blindness.* Cambria Press.

Herrnstein, R. J., & Murray, C. A. (1996). *The bell curve: Intelligence and class structure in American life.* Simon & Schuster.

Jimerson, S. R., Burns, M. K., & VanDerHeyden, A. M. (2007). *Handbook of response to intervention: The science and practice of assessment and intervention.* Springer.

Kompa, J. S. (2017, February 7). *Why it is time to retire Bloom's taxonomy.* Joana Stella Kompa: Digital Education & Social Change Blog. https://joanakompa.com/2017/02/07/why-it-is-time-to-retire-blooms-taxonomy/

Kozleski, E. B., Stepaniuk, I., & Proffitt, W. A. (2020). Leading through a critical lens: The application of DisCrit in framing, implementing, and improving equity-driven, educational systems for all students. *Journal of Educational Administration, 58*(5), 489–505. https://doi.org/10.1108/JEA-12-2019-0220

Leonardo, Z., & Broderick, A. A. (2011). Smartness as property: A critical exploration of intersectons between Whiteness and disability studies. *Teachers College Record, 113*(10), 2206–2232.

Losen, D. J., & Gillespie, J. (2012, August 7). *Opportunities suspended: The disparate impact of disciplinary exclusion from school.* https://www.civilrightsproject.ucla.edu/resources/projects/center-for-civil-rights-remedies/school-to-prison-folder/federal-reports/upcoming-ccrr-research/?searchterm=opportunities%20suspended

Mackey, H. (2015). Educational administration in Indian Country: The peculiar position of Indigenous languages, tribal self-determination, and federal policy. In A. Normore, P. Ehrensal, P. First, & M. Torres (Eds.), *Legal frontiers in education: Complex issues for leaders, policymakers and policy implementers* (pp. 167–181). Emerald Group Publishing Limited.

Mackey, H. (2018). Toward an indigenous leadership paradigm for dismantling ableism. *Review of Disability Studies: An International Journal, 14*(3), 1–12.

Manaseri, H., & Bornstein, J. (2018). Dismantling ableism: The moral imperative for school leaders. *Review of Disability Studies: An International Journal, 14*(3), 4–63.

Marshall, C., & Ward, M. (2004). "Yes, but...": Education leaders discuss social justice. *Journal of School Leadership, 14*(3), 530–563.

Merrell, K. W., & Buchanan, R. (2006). Intervention selection in school-based practice: Using public health models to enhance systems capacity of schools. *School Psychology Review, 35*(2), 167–180.

Moll, L. C., Amanti, C., Neff, D., & González, N. (2005). Funds of knowledge for teaching: Using a qualitative approach to connect homes and classrooms. In N. González, L. C. Moll, & C. Amanti (Eds.), *Funds of knowledge: Theorizing practices in households, communities, and classrooms* (pp. 71–88). Lawrence Erlbaum Associates.

Niesche, R., & Gowlett, C. (2019). Critical perspectives in educational leadership: A new 'theory turn'? In *Social, critical and political theories for educational leadership* (pp. 17–34). Springer.

Normore, A. H. (2008). *Leadership for social justice: Promoting equity and excellence through inquiry and reflective practice.* Information Age Publishing.

Pazey, B. L., & Cole, H. A. (2012). The role of special education training in the development of socially just leaders: Building an equity consciousness in educational leadership programs. *Educational Administration Quarterly, 49*(2), 243–271. https://doi.org/10.1177/0013161x12463934

Pfeiffer, D. (2002). The philosophical foundations of disability studies. *Disability Studies Quarterly, 22*(2). http://dx.doi.org/10.18061/dsq.v22i2.341

Saltmarsh, S., & Youdell, D. (2004). 'Special sport' for misfits and losers: educational triage and the constitution of schooled subjectivities. *International Journal of Inclusive Education, 8*(4), 353–371. https://doi.org/10.1080/13603 11042000259148

Shields, C. M. (2018). *Transformative leadership in education: Equitable and socially just change in an uncertain and complex world* (2nd ed.). Routledge.

Skiba, R. J., Simmons, A. S., Gibb, A. C., Rausch, M. K., Cuadrado, J., & Chung, C.-G. (2008). Achieving equity in special education: History, status, and current challenges. *Exceptional Children, 74*(3), 264–288.

Smyth, J. (1989). *Critical perspectives on educational leadership.* Routledge Falmer.

Theoharis, G. (2007). Social justice educational leaders and resistance: Toward a theory of social justice leadership. *Educational Administration Quarterly, 43*(2), 221–258. https://doi.org/10.1177/0013161X06293717

Theoharis, G., & Causton-Theoharis, J. N. (2008). Oppressors or emancipators: Critical dispositions for preparing inclusive school leaders. *Equity & Excellence in Education, 41*(2), 230–246. https://doi.org/10.1080/10665680801973714

West, C. (2017). *Spiritual blackout, imperial meltdown, prophetic fightback* [Video]. Askwith Lecture Series, Cambridge, MA. https://youtu.be/7wCIWFlrYak.

# CHAPTER 4

# ON BEING ANNOYING

## Neurodivergence and Mood Disorders as a Black Face in a White Space

**JPB Gerald**
*CUNY–Hunter College*

I want to begin by telling you about three boys. All attended the same exclusive, expensive private school. All had parents with relatively high incomes. All deliberately obstructed instruction in their classroom, yet two were protected, and one was corrected and rejected. None were given a public diagnosis, yet only one was pathologized. Their names were David, Ben, and Justin.

David,[1] who was White, was older than the other two by a year. His father worked in financial services and his mother was a homemaker, and they lived within walking distance of the school; they also owned a beach house. Well-liked by his peers, he began to challenge his teachers' authority in middle school, refusing to follow directions and relishing the opportunity to be sent to administrators' offices when he had become too disruptive. There was also a public, performative kindness to him, and a generosity of spirit for those he favored. He handed out treats for Christmas in a Santa

---

*Who Decides?*, pages 69–89
Copyright © 2022 by Information Age Publishing
www.infoagepub.com
All rights of reproduction in any form reserved.

hat and frequently invited classmates over on the last day of school. He also resolutely refused to engage with any curriculum he found unpleasant, boring, or, most importantly, offensive. He and his family negotiated a personal allowance for him not to have to read or discuss books with subjects such as LGBTQ rights and relationships, this all despite attending a nominally progressive and artsy school. He was gleeful in his misogyny, his homophobia, and his racism, although he would never admit to such things. He caused considerable turmoil in his classes, but he nonetheless remained inside the school's social embrace.

Ben, who was also White, was school royalty. His family also lived near the school, and they owned a mountain home. His parents were both prominent school employees, and many of his teachers were close family friends. He demonstrated poor focus, frequently forgot his school materials, and rarely completed his homework on time. He fell asleep in class and completed the bare minimum of what was required of him, unless he felt inspired, in which case he often produced something exemplary, particularly when it came to technology or creative writing. He inherited his father's eccentricity, which is a kind way of saying he had little use for societal or personal boundaries. He wasn't much of a disruption in class, but required considerable extra coaching from his teachers; he retained enough social capital to be one of his grade's speakers at their graduation.

Justin was Black. His grade featured five Black students (out of 78), a sharp contrast to the city at the time, and to public schools. Justin's parents had high incomes, but no generational wealth or vacation homes. He lived far from school, traveling long enough each day that several other parents wouldn't let their children visit him at his mother's house, even though the neighborhood was perfectly safe, albeit a little too Black.[2] Justin was a precocious child, so he skipped first grade and was suddenly an extremely small, 6-year-old second grader. From that point on, he tried desperately to be welcomed by his peers and his teachers, yet there was always something that didn't quite click. He spoke too fast or stared too long. He spun in circles to get attention. He couldn't relax or feel comfortable socially, so he looked to his peers for modeling and tried to mimic the people who seemed not to have any restrictions. People like David and Ben.

Ben disliked David, and vice versa. But Justin sought desperately to impress both of them, going out of his way to join in on David's class-disrupting schemes, and asking his mother to let him stay overnight at Ben's house, since he knew the school scion didn't have any rules at home. At some point, Justin nearly ceased to exist as his own person, adopting a fluid persona attempting to impress the greatest number of people and almost always failing. This was reflected in his report cards, as he was told he spoke out of turn in class and that he needed to learn to be less disruptive. Like Ben, he frequently forgot his homework or avoided it if it was too difficult and then fell behind. The other kids weren't outwardly cruel but made little effort to include him socially, and the harder he tried, the more they seemed to pull away. A few teachers remembered him as the shy child who'd once been obsessed with subway trains, but everyone else just thought he was annoying, and told him as much. It never occurred to him that he might have been neurodivergent, partially because these words weren't used at the time, and partially because that sort of label was only for kids like the classmate who was always folding himself into a pretzel shape. He wasn't like that, and *that* kid deserved to be teased. He was like everyone else. He was like Ben and David. He *was* special, like his parents said, but he wasn't *special*. He was just annoying, like they all told him. And he carried that belief with him everywhere he went, until it fractured him into unstable pieces and left him deeply anxious and depressed, prone to lashing out at the people who showed him kindness. Only after natural maturation, extensive academic study, and effective professional help was he able to see that. Whether or not the same was true of David and Ben, he had always struggled socially and had difficulty connecting with his peers for perfectly understandable reasons that weren't actually his fault, even if he was indeed responsible for the poor choices he made in reaction.

Would a diagnosis have helped him feel more supported in school, or would it have led to even more isolation? Would the legal protection of a label have afforded him the same social status in school as David and Ben, or would it have harmed him even further? And what was the impact of an idiosyncratic independent institution in full denial of its racism, let alone an ableism that it couldn't have even named? In this autoethnographic narrative (Ellis, 2004), I will explore how the racialized nature of dis/ability diagnosis can lead to students like Justin not quite falling through the cracks, but being pushed into the margins at the same time they are constantly in the spotlight. Though we ultimately lived a materially comfortable life, I intend to make clear the power of pathologization, even for a student who met all accepted metrics of intelligence.

I hope this narrative sheds light on an identity that is rarely showcased, that of a Black student at a predominantly White independent school with a mild but undiagnosed dis/ability, who wanted only to be like everyone else instead of understanding that, no matter how hard he tried, he was always going to be different, and that that difference was seen as fundamentally annoying.

## AUTOETHNOGRAPHIC COUNTERNARRATIVES

This chapter exists in close conversation with the work of Hernandez-Saca and Cannon (2019), albeit with a few key differences. Whereas in their article, they ask, "How does being labeled with a special education dis/ability category, as Black and Brown people, impact emotional, affective, and spiritual development in and around schools?" (p. 245), I seek to understand the impact of having a divergent brain while never coming close to being diagnosed, in the specific context of an exclusive independent school, and a very singular independent school at that (see "Educational Context" below). Hernandez-Saca and Cannon refer to their reportage as *autoethnographic critical reflective counternarrative vignettes* (p. 254); their work emerged from more than 4 years of documented conversations, whereas mine descends from personal experience. We are working toward similar goals, just with different paths. For my part, I hope to tell a story rarely told and place my experience among the literature, so that educators with students like me, or with students like the one that my young son may someday become, can make different and better choices.

There is a particular power, for marginalized groups, and especially so for racialized scholars, in employing autoethnography in sharing our stories and reconstructing the narratives that have otherwise been forced upon us. One can look at a few recent articles for examples of racialized scholars seizing control of their externally-imposed narratives (e.g., Hughes, 2019; Kim, 2019), as well as Black scholars seeking to problematize the Whiteness of teacher preparation (e.g., Ohito, 2016). In other words, autoethnography is a vital tool in challenging the status quo, and that is my aim with this work. There is no discipline untouched by racism, and dis/ability studies is surely counted among this number, with the construction and oppression of dis/ability tracking neatly alongside our country's inborn anti-Blackness (Nielsen, 2012). As the citation of influential scholarship often requires basing one's work on those who might have excluded us at the time their work was completed, following an autoethnographic path as an emerging scholar serves as an attempt at addressing these issues.

This chapter will provide further evidence of the harmful ways in which dis/ability is constructed for students of color through the lens of my specific story, and will counter the assumption that these multiple marginalizations cease to matter for racialized students who are not working class or poor. My own mistaken and unspoken assumption was that it was possible to achieve my way out of any oppression I might face, an externally-imposed belief in a just, meritocratic system. But as Godfrey et al. (2019) found, an adherence to such an ideology can correlate with negative outcomes for marginalized students. We do not, in fact, live in a just world, and so by believing the lie that we do, when I struggled and was criticized for it by my institution, I took all of the blame upon myself and allowed it to fester. Accordingly, this narrative seeks to investigate the ways in which the pathologization of students categorized as both Black and neurodivergent can leave lasting scars, even for individuals who are somewhat protected by class and by not having a formal label affixed to them. This narrative is designed to demonstrate the unshakable power of both racism and ableism, even in a school that claimed to cherish its students' idiosyncrasies.

## EDUCATIONAL CONTEXT

I attended the same institution for 14 years, from the beginning of pre-school to the end of high school. It was, and remains, a school known for producing successful (White) artists, musicians, fashion designers, actors, and writers, and in the past decade has become more expensive than many 4-year colleges, though it was hardly cheap in my era. The school, which is in Brooklyn, is a private institution that allowed entry for toddlers based on a version of an IQ test; it refuses to mandate uniforms, and eschews letter grades, class ranks, valedictorians, and traditional rites of passage such as prom and homecoming. The school barely had athletic teams and rented time on a field a few miles away for baseball, softball, and track. They encouraged their students to be emotive, creative, and expressive. In other words, it was not only unusual in its status as an independent school, it considered itself independent even from the traditions of other independent schools. At least in my years, they had no separate classes for students classified as dis/abled, nor any separation for students whose first language was not English, though truthfully, I do not know if they have ever accepted anyone in the latter category.[3]

Many people sent their kids to this school to keep them out of the city's public school system, but also as a way to thumb their nose at older, more conventional independent schools, the type of schools where students wore blazers. As a bonus, the school was known for an exceptional track record with Ivy League and Ivy-adjacent universities. To gain acceptance to this school was to stamp your educational passport to success while also maintaining your nonconformity. These days, it warrants a mention in the tabloids when a famous actor's offspring is rejected from the school.

We students looked down our noses at traditional private schools while, without saying as much, we didn't even think about the city's public schools. We were very proud of ourselves and we were certain we were better than schools that eagerly participated in oppression. The racism I experienced and which I will detail in my vignettes was never of the more direct sort, but closer to the *liberal racism* described by Zamudio and Rios (2006), in which Whites attempt to distance themselves from racism but "deny the existence of the structural disadvantage of people of color" (p. 488). We held group assemblies and town halls when important societal events occurred (e.g., the stalemate after the 2000 presidential election) and prided ourselves on our willingness to probe deeper than other institutions, but the school's superiority complex was never challenged, and indeed was bolstered by our administration, an ideology I fully bought into.

We had approximately 80 students per grade, the vast majority of whom were White. In the years after I entered high school, we began to accept low-income Black and Latinx students via New York's Prep for Prep program, which only increased these grades' racialized population from "a handful" to "two handfuls" but improved our self-image immeasurably. Before these students arrived, race was almost never discussed except during the traditional units on the American Civil War and civil rights. My classmates, aside from David, and my teachers, with a few exceptions I will mention below, never mentioned my race in any way, resting comfortably on what Annamma et al. (2016) call *color-evasiveness*, a term that more accurately conveys the conscious choice to avoid race than does *color-blindness*, while also removing the ableism of the latter term. My school would certainly have believed it was *post-racial* while that term was popular in recent years (Bonilla-Silva, 2015), but all of these methods of avoiding the truth are not neutral acts. As Picower (2009) writes, "These tools are not simply a passive resistance to but much more of an active protection of their hegemonic stories and White supremacy" (p. 205). For all our supposed complexity and nuance, our single annual "non-White" literature reading[4] focused vaguely on the exoticized culture depicted in the novels, with the stories framed as distinctly alien from our own lives, and the connection between the racism explicitly depicted by the authors and the realities of the present day absent from any discussion.[5] I would not say that these patterns were particularly egregious for a school in the 1990s, but that it both contradicted our self-professed boundary-busting progressivism and reified the ways in which Whiteness was an ever-present, silent factor in the school's pedagogy. The context was reminiscent of what Dr. King (1967/2010) once referred to as *comfortable vanity*, ideological safety disguised as boldness and risk-taking. It is not exactly revolutionary to upset the apple cart if a school is doing so on behalf of other wealthy White students, and their Whiteness was accordingly positioned as the norm against which appropriate behavior was measured. The school believed it was operating outside of the dominant system by insisting upon a very narrow, very White, and very wealthy version of weirdness, remaining situated quite comfortably within what Voulgarides (2018) refers to as "false notions of meritocracy" (p. 4). The institution embraced those who were potentially struggling with behavioral issues but within expected cultural and racial norms while viewing those who were otherwise similar but outside of the dominant group as in desperate need of correction.

Indeed, there were certainly students who, in retrospect, had emotional or behavioral challenges during my time, and a few with visible mobility issues, the latter of whom were, thankfully, treated with kindness by the entire community. Most commonly, neurodivergent students struggled to connect with others, and although they were not excluded from any instruction, they were heavily ostracized socially. Our school had a self-image of rejecting the status quo, so there was a bit of an unstated assumption among the students that if you were so off-putting as to stand out in a negative way, you deserved to be bullied. In a way, with our refusal to award letter grades and our avoidance of class rankings and other traditional institutional trappings, we believed that we were more civilized than schools rife with explicit meritocratic ideologies and hierarchies.[6] As with our inability to avoid the pitfalls of Whiteness and racism, we were not immune to the implicit belief that social injustice, and in this case bullying, was justly deserved as a result of personal failure (Mijs, 2014). We did have a slightly more forgiving definition of acceptable behavior than most schools, and harsh discipline was rare, but for those who were unable to fit within our marginally expanded construction of normalcy, the social results were severe. None of the students categorized as fully deserving of the bullying they received for their visible neurodivergence stayed at the school long enough to graduate with the rest of us.[7]

I watched this teasing, I watched these boys cry, I laughed alongside the rest of the other kids, and I internalized the need not to be seen as different enough to be deserving of their scorn. Unfortunately, because of my external and internal differences, I was unable to avoid a milder version of the same fate. I don't expect these descriptions to be particularly shocking; much worse occurs within school walls. I describe my context in this way not to suggest it was an overtly cruel or physically violent place but to contradict both the school's own self-description as well as the general sense that these types of marginalizations occur less often in supposedly safe independent schools. The academic research on students with my particular background and experience at exclusive independent schools is scant,[8] and the discussions featured in nonacademic articles about gifted and talented programs (Pirtle, 2019), about segregation and private schools (Barnum, 2019), and about special education in private schools (Tucker, n.d.), are all missing a piece of the story I aim to share, though they are all valuable work.

More recently, the school has created affinity groups for marginalized students, and introduced a director of diversity,[9] whom I have spoken with, and who has begun the necessary work countering the aforementioned liberal racism endemic to the institution.[10] Though I am not hopeful that the school will ever be fully safe for Black students, I expect, at the least, that fewer students are being teased mercilessly for dis/abilities they were unable to hide. But the particular contours of my marginalization are somewhat difficult to define, and in order to do so, I need to share the ways in which my identity diverged from the norm.

## IDENTITY

From the beginning, I was told I was smart, a label that is itself a form of social stratification (Leonardo & Broderick, 2011). My parents speak of all the precocious things I used to do, such as flipping through the newspaper at age four to look up movie times when they didn't want to take me to see *Teenage Mutant Ninja Turtles*, or memorizing the New York City subway map when I was home sick with scarlet fever. What most of the stories about the toddler version of me have in common is that I had (and still have) an exceptional long-term memory, especially for facts and figures, the sort of thing that eventually translated into success at trivia, but at the time meant I flew through the books assigned to me and was doing long division in kindergarten.[11] Eventually, my parents and the school agreed that I should skip first grade, and so I was a 6-year-old second grader who was also very small for his age. My problems, such as they were, started to develop after that, because I was simply unable to relax and play along easily with my classmates, and I became more concerned with impressing them and fitting in than anything else, all of which must have seemed normal to everyone around me, and is probably fairly common for children who are new to a group. My party-trick memory wasn't enough to sustain me as a student once I had to actually put work in, though, and I began to falter in fourth grade.

I am, to this day, dreadfully poor at concentrating on tasks in which I am not particularly interested. If I can find my way "in," I can focus on something for hours or days, but by middle school, there were a lot of topics in which I had zero interest, to the point that I knew I'd really have to work to accomplish them, and since I was far more concerned with getting my classmates to accept me, I tried to amass social capital by turning myself into a popular class clown. Unfortunately, I was only guessing at how other people would react, so I was merely loud instead of funny. No one laughed, which meant that I tried harder and harder, and fell farther behind on my schoolwork, which embarrassed me, so I lied to my parents until I got so overwhelmed that I started skipping classes. The work wasn't actually that hard, and I didn't realize I had an attention problem at the time because I excelled at a few classes that I enjoyed and where I could rely on memorization. Consequently, this cycle continued for years. I frequently lost assignments into the black hole of my backpack, spilled my yogurt onto my worksheet and hid it because I was ashamed,[12] and had (and still have) truly illegible handwriting. I would struggle with several aspects of executive function, ignore the issues until there was some sort of minor disaster, and then see the annoyance on the faces of my classmates and my teachers when I needed to be rescued.

Looking back, I had no complex thoughts about being a Black face in a White space until I was in high school. I had been at the same school since before my working memory began, and it was all just "school" to me. I didn't think I was different, either internally or externally, and I had a rather severe deficit mindset about myself and why I seemed to have several dozen acquaintances but not very many close friends. "If I just try harder," I told myself, "it will turn around."

To my parents, I performed and insisted upon the image of a very bright child who was rather accident prone, who always maintained that everything was fine, and who started crying when things overwhelmed me. In other words, if they made any mistakes, it was only that they loved and trusted a child who was clearly capable of completing his assigned work, and none of us were privy to the analysis I have now done to reframe my story more accurately. Indeed, they were often upset that my report cards came home with the notes that I talked out of turn, believing it an unfair statement they often brought up at their teacher conferences.[13] Ultimately, if anything harmed me, it was the institution and the era. In the early 1990s, and especially if you had tested as having a high IQ, there was no way I would be screened for a diagnosis so long as I was merely an annoyance who scored well on standardized tests. The best remedy was to write me up in my report cards and allow the social structure of the school to set me straight.

Should I have been diagnosed? Based on the years of work I did as an adult to try to untangle my own brain, as well as the official evaluation I undertook at age 35, I have a mild form of attention deficit/hyperactivity disorder (ADHD), combined type, and it has impacted me in academic, professional, and personal situations. I still lose things frequently and have to expend considerable effort to focus on topics or even conversations in which I am not naturally interested, I tend to look away from people when I'm talking, and I come off as either overly friendly or distant. I'm old enough now to know how off-putting this can be, and so I tend to opt for "distant" if I need to choose, because it's safer. I have damaged friendships and professional relationships through my poor understanding of social cues. Even my wife barely has enough patience to put up with me on a daily basis.

I'm deeply fortunate to have met my wife, because for decades I assumed I would never marry. People sometimes found me superficially charming when I adopted a boisterous class-clown public persona, but once I dropped the façade, they often lost interest. My social struggles from my neurodivergence resulted in rather extreme anxiety and occasional lapses into depression, and these mental health issues and the constant isolation I felt led to anger that mostly tore at me internally but occasionally spilled out onto the people who bothered to show me kindness. All the time that I tried desperately to connect with people but mostly failed, I assumed it was just because I was annoying, and I did whatever I could to make my real personality smaller and smaller until I barely existed behind a variety of memorized public-facing tics and behaviors. Through all of it, I never told anyone what was going on, because I knew they'd just make fun of me.

So, again, should I have been diagnosed? My school did offer extra testing time to a few (White) students, but testing wasn't an area in which I struggled, and of course, having internalized an ableism that I didn't realize impacted me, a diagnosis would have been embarrassing and shameful, a contradiction to my self-image as the special, precocious child if I was really just *special.* Though I didn't understand this at the time, I existed as what Kendi (2017) might have called a *Black exhibit,* unheard but extremely visible all at once, and I may well have been transformed into an object of pity if saddled with a dis/ability label. It might have given me peace of mind as my adult diagnosis eventually did, but I may well have been more explicitly scorned. Or, worse, I could have experienced the detrimental outcomes of students who are both Black and dis/abled (Erevelles & Minear, 2010; Frederick & Shifrer, 2019). I was of course operating on the false assumption that racism wasn't a factor, but to be Black and dis/abled would have been a social death sentence, and perhaps an academic one as well. Ultimately, I never had to make the choice, because I was certain I was just an annoying kid who deserved the isolation he felt on a daily basis, and I kept it all to myself as I tried again and again to prove I was just like everyone else.

## COUNTERNARRATIVE VIGNETTES

These vignettes have been chosen to exemplify the ways in which my school, my teachers, and my classmates pathologized me as "annoying," how I responded to this externally-imposed identity in reckless and counterproductive ways, and what the results of my desperate attempts to escape this marginalization were. My hope is that the reader will see echoes of aforementioned literature, particularly Picower's (2009) notion of the hidden ways that White educators maintain hegemony, Kendi's (2017) concept of *Black exhibits* who are only visible as threats and fascinations but never allowed an inner life, and most importantly, Hernandez-Saca and Cannon's (2019) work on counternarratives, built to construct a new version of the story that my school and my society had always told to me, for me, and about me. The vignettes shared here are necessarily a reconstruction of my experience; I didn't keep a diary and this was long before my entire life was available for perusal on the internet, though I have some old yearbooks in which my contemporaneous opinion of myself matches what I share below. I chose these stories because they are among the handful for which I can clearly remember the dates, parties involved, and the emotional experience, even if I only came to fully understand my own context as an adult. Each of these brief stories was firmly lodged in my brain, for decades, as evidence for why I deserved my own marginalization, but I seek, here, to rebuild these vignettes with intentionality and in defiance of the identity that was forced onto me by dominant groups.

## 1. Institutional Identity Codification

In sixth grade, I dropped a pencil on the floor in my history class. As was my habit whenever I did something clumsy, I made a big show of crawling around after it, desperately seeking the attention of my classmates for my supposed hilarity. My classmates did their level best to ignore the tiny boy on the floor, but my history teacher shouted out, "To irk!" You see, in our class, we kept a running list of new vocabulary words, with no connection to the material or any particular aim other than to increase our linguistic knowledge, and these words were written on the board whenever they crossed our teacher's mind, with the instruction being that we were to look up their definitions in a dictionary before the next class. I had never heard the word "irk" before that afternoon, and since I didn't do much of my homework when I was 10, I only learned the meaning in the next class, but I somehow knew exactly what he meant when he said it, because the proclamation was accompanied by a look I seemed to elicit in many of my teachers and classmates for reasons I didn't fully understand at the time. I knew that I irked people, and I was told as much repeatedly. Mr. McDowd, a beloved teacher who passed away in recent years, was a mostly kind man who lacked patience for tomfoolery. His assessment carried considerable weight at our institution, and deservedly so, as he possessed more wisdom than most. In his eyes, and through his intentional if impromptu actions, I was codified as a student who was both intelligent and worthy of scorn for my behavior. At the time, the institutional narrative convinced me that the annoyance was my own fault, but now I can see that my identity was a challenge for the environment and for the educators who were meant to guide and support me, and that it was easier to classify me as the definition of irksome than to show me the care I genuinely deserved.

## 2. An Invisible Panic

In seventh grade, I had the latest in my ongoing cycles of falling behind in my schoolwork, lying to my teachers and parents, and then becoming overwhelmed. This time, however, instead of repeatedly skipping a single math class like I had in fourth grade,[14] I simply did not go to school to face the music. I was riding the subway to school alone by then, having indeed memorized the map years earlier, so instead of getting off at the normal stop, I just rode around looking at stations I had never been to and using my lunch money to stop at McDonald's. I did this for 3 days, returning home each day around the same time as I otherwise would have. Again, my parents' only mistake was trusting me, but they had no reason to know I hadn't attended any classes because the school didn't call home until I'd missed three entire days. Teachers at this school were lax about attendance for everyone, sure, but there was no real way not to notice that your only Black student who spends every class cracking grating jokes is suddenly absent. Maybe they assumed I got sick, but I didn't miss a single day of school for sickness between 6th and 12th grade. I enjoyed my sojourn until I got in well-earned trouble at home, and my teachers were deeply annoyed when I finally showed up on Thursday, having done none of my homework. I suppose I can't prove it, but I suspect, had Ben or David suddenly not attended more than 3 days of class, great concern would have been shown for what grave occurrence might have caused this disruption. When they finally called home, they told my parents I had missed "a lot of classes," and the trouble I got in at home was because they assumed I'd simply started cutting class again. The school never actually noticed I'd missed the entire 3 days. At the time, I thought it was great that the school wasn't paying much attention to me, and that all I had to deal with was several annoyed teachers when I got back to class. I think now that it's a little bit unnerving how few people at the school expressed concern about my disappearance, especially considering that I was very small for 11, and this basically confirmed to me that, no matter the punishment, I had made the right decision to skip school. The narrative I was sold was what the school told my parents, that I was a kid who sometimes did silly things like cut class, and I knew it was right for my teachers to be annoyed I was behind in my work, and for none to ask if, after suddenly being out for half a week, anything was wrong, or why a person who was clearly capable of what was assigned wasn't completing any of it. I only started doing my homework diligently in ninth grade when the head of the high school, who seemed to understand me to some extent, suggested I start reading "classic" novels in my spare time to improve my verbal test scores. It took just the one conversation to change my trajectory, and the assumption I was capable and not just a nuisance to be dealt with. I see my attention-seeking now as an attempt to gain control of my own narrative, and these brief consultations with this administrator allowed me to feel a rare agency about myself and my abilities. I didn't understand at the time why so few at the school had been able to understand what I needed, but I know now they were unable to see past the pathologization they had placed upon me.

## 3. A Reckless Attempt to Change the Story

In 11th grade, more desperate than ever to find my way inside of the social scene, I engineered a plan to attend a big school party with Ben, knowing as I did that he did not have any sort of curfew or restrictions. This would be my chance to prove I was just like everyone else, and by this point, that meant that I wasn't barred from the parties and the rampant wealthy-child substance abuse my classmates enjoyed. I couldn't just follow along though, because as an individual with deeply internalized deficiencies, I had to go far over the top to match up with my classmates, drinking directly from liquor bottles I was handed despite literally never having had more than a beer before. I woke up in the emergency room attached to machinery, having suffered alcohol poisoning and shattered my parents' trust.[15] The upsetting part of the story wasn't the hospitalization, though, but the fact that it turned out that my gamble had been successful. My plan had worked. When I got back to school first thing Monday morning, the story had already spread to the entire school[16] and people were talking about me with excitement. All of a sudden I wasn't just that annoying kid anymore.[17] At the time I was ecstatic, no matter how much trouble I was in at home, and having learned absolutely nothing from this lesson, I resorted to this, what I might call, *performative excess* in many future social situations, though I managed never to have alcohol poisoning again. In retrospect, I would say that, by seriously endangering myself, I had temporarily erased my identity as a nuisance, brought myself as close to their version of Whiteness and carefree wealth as possible, and for most of the rest of high school, although I still rarely attended social events, people were a little less annoyed by me. I was never going to be normal, never White or neurotypical, but alcohol poisoning was as close as I would ever get. My grandmother told me, when I came home from the hospital that day, that I didn't need to do what everyone else was doing just because they were doing it. I wish I had listened to her.

## 4. A Threat Realized

In 12th grade, as we all applied to colleges, several of my classmates sought me out to have conversations about affirmative action, and by "conversations" I mean they wanted me to validate their opinion that it was unfair to them. It seemed like I got cornered every week by some White classmate who wanted me to agree with him[18] that it was oppressive, or that if it was going to exist it should be based entirely on socioeconomic status.[19] Though I can't say I classified these conversations as examples of racism at the time, it was at moments like this, when incredible effort was expended to dismiss the reality of racism directly to the face of a racialized person, that I could feel most distinctly that something was deeply wrong. Sadly, I was still more interested in social acceptance than the truth. I couldn't go back to being annoying by pushing back on their claims, after all, so I usually just nodded and let them feel good about themselves. It was interesting that after having succeeded in the most dangerous of ways in making myself visible, my Blackness became salient, both to me and to others. Indeed, as if the entire institution had started to resent me, suddenly, I had a teacher compare me to a "hoodlum" when she saw me on the street, and another teacher make certain to explain how Black and White people walked differently, after which everyone in the classroom quickly turned to look at me while I tried to disappear. I had by this point found a way to adapt to my attention issues by furiously completing all of my homework as early as possible[20] but I was suddenly very explicitly Black when I became a threat to their future. The funny thing was, I actually *was* a threat to them, because by arbitrary college admissions standards, I was fully deserving of acceptance at the top schools and not all of my classmates were. I really didn't work very hard to do well on standardized tests, while many of my classmates were tutored and intellectually massaged for years. I sat down and consumed vocabulary for a few weeks, my skills boosted by the novels I'd read on the administrator's suggestion, and then I aced the SATs and most of my other exams. I applied to the school that Ben's father recommended I attend, and I got in early decision. Despite all my issues, I had made it exactly where everyone wanted me to be. I was precisely as skilled as my parents had always expected. Deep down, however, I was unable to recognize that all of those racist conversations had been successful in convincing me that I hadn't really earned my place at the Ivy that had accepted me. I carried such intense self-doubt about my race into college[21] that I was far more focused on the social scene than my academics, and I started annoying a whole new group of wealthy, White classmates. It took me years to escape the cycle of performative excess and desperation for social acceptance, and through all of it, through college and much of my early adulthood, I fought the fear of being pathologized as annoying, and I usually lost the battle.

I gather some readers might be thinking that no matter how unpleasant some of these experiences may have been in the moment, the fact remains that I went to one "elite" school after another, for which my parents were largely able to pay, and although I needed support as an adult, I came out "okay." And it's true that, aside from some brief moments in my 20s, I have not spent most of my life existing in precarity. Rather than this representing the story of a privileged kid who just didn't fit in, though, my goal here is to counteract the common notion that merely bringing in a Black face or a neurodivergent brain will resolve the racism and ableism of an institution, even an institution vocally proud of its liberal nature. If schools do not take the necessary steps to dismantle the racism at their core but nonetheless import more racialized students, a hierarchy that prevents them from even noticing the ways in which they might need to support a pathologized student, they are doing nothing but setting these students up for a particular sort of trauma, and, even worse, sending them the message that they ought to be grateful for the opportunity to be traumatized. Much ink has been spilled on the problems found in public schools, to the point where, especially given the era, it made perfect sense to send your bright Black boy to such a place if you could afford it. Yet so few of these schools have done the work necessary to be truly safe and supportive to anyone other than their ideal student, and this neglectfulness leaves lasting scars.

## CONCLUSION

My wife encouraged me to get help about a year into our marriage. I was on a roller coaster of volatile self-loathing and public chest-pounding and it was unsustainable and deeply corrosive. I was reluctant to attend, thinking it would just confirm my beliefs that I was the problem in our marriage and in my life, and I resisted until I had no other choice. It took time with three different professionals and almost as many setbacks as breakthroughs, but eventually I came to see that the problem wasn't just me, but the environment to which I had been exposed. I cycled through several possible explanations for my issues, many different causes for my behavior, until I landed firmly on what may have been the simplest of all possible reasons.

Williams (1987) called it *spirit murder*, the way that hostile spaces can squeeze the life out of marginalized people even without harming them physically. For anyone outside of the norm, the pressure to match the dominant values can hollow you out without even informing you it's doing so. I had no idea what had happened to me until years later. Shalaby (2017) writes of several Black children classified as dis/abled and labeled as "troublemakers," who are somehow very loud yet invisible to their institutions. Yoon (2019) classified emotional and behavioral dis/abilities as manifestations of *haunted trauma*, a reaction to the treatment marginalized and racialized learners have received for generations rather than a true deficit that requires fixing. These days, my struggles would most likely fall under "other health issues," according to the 13 categories of IDEA, which usually places ADHD there (U.S. Department of Education, 2006). Yet, considering the existence of disproportionality, and the stories told by Shalaby and others, if I had struggled at a different school, there was a strong chance I might well have acted out in class, and then been labeled "emotionally disturbed," with all the baggage that might have followed.

In truth, as difficult as it was, I was fortunate that the only label I got was "annoying," and that my condition, even undiagnosed, was mild enough to mostly swallow, even if it nearly choked me. Indeed, I was capable of pretending to be someone I wasn't, more so than many of the students in Shalaby's book, whose conditions, both neurological and socioeconomic, were more severe than mine, but that desperate pantomime, that futile attempt to be seen the same as the White kids who didn't struggle with social connections, left me feeling isolated, somehow both a juicy target for my peers and an afterthought for many of the educators who didn't worry about me because they believed I just wasn't trying hard enough. In some ways, they weren't wrong; I wasn't trying hard enough at my schoolwork because I was trying way too hard every time I looked around the room and tried to figure out how to make people accept me.

The part that upsets me the most, though, is how wrong I was about myself. I spent more than a decade believing I was annoyance incarnate, yet every classmate I've encountered at reunions or around New York has been happy to see me. That doesn't mean I didn't annoy them at the time, just that I am not inherently a problem the way I always felt that I was. The lesson I take away from this new information is that pathologization, no matter the flavor of oppression, is a one-way street, which leaves no imprint or memory on the dominant group but carves deep wounds into the targets. And when that pathologization is institutional rather than merely interpersonal, there is little escape, and your identity will either fight back or slink away to avoid being seen.

My experience being racialized and neurodivergent—keenly aware of the former but oblivious to the latter—has brought me a community as an adult and forced me to view my adolescence through a wholly different lens. I wonder, if I were in middle school now, if I would have been identified as such and given support, or if I still would have been seen as both smart and annoying and little else. I have found a way to work within my brain that I am comfortable with, but I might have found it decades ago if they had known what to look for. I suppose it didn't really matter to them, though; I graduated and served as another notch on their college acceptance belt and they can take credit for it.

At my school, a bright sunbeam of an institution that still has yearly puppet parades, I had fallen into a crevasse without anyone realizing it. I was Black, but not the type of Black that fit the expectations of White liberals. For however many years, I attempted to scrub away the distance between me and the rest of my classmates, kids I had known since preschool in some cases, putting myself in danger in the process, only succeeding on rare occasions when I abandoned all of the valuable lessons I had learned from my loving family. On the other hand, I wasn't poor, like some of the students who followed years after me, and who were able to build their own community amongst themselves. I wasn't the same as my classmates, but I wasn't distant enough to be regarded with paternalistic pity, and so I just became a confounding nuisance. And when you're annoying, when you don't quite fit into any box even at a school proud of its refusal to follow conventions, then they miss the ways in which you really do need support.

Do I know for certain that David and Ben had the same sort of afflictions as I did? Well, in David's case, no. I think he was just a person who wasn't raised to respect very many people in social categories beneath him and that I was the Black friend he could point to as a shield for his racism, but the manifestation of his antisocial behavior was extremely disruptive in the classroom, especially when the teachers were female. Nevertheless, he was embraced by his peers and rarely challenged on his choices. As for Ben, he very clearly had focus issues and some boundary issues undoubtedly encouraged by his status as a school scion. I mention Ben and David not to present myself as saintly but to point out that, although our behavior was broadly similar in the classroom, our positionality and perspectives were, and are, quite different. I am certain they remember me fondly and they are welcome to continue to view me that way while I reconstruct my own view of myself.

I hesitate to diagnose either of them, because that isn't the point. I have come to understand that, far from being pathological, my behavior, though certainly disruptive, was almost a natural response to the environment around me, one that had rarely provided me with the tools and support I needed. Now, if David and Ben "had" anything, it was Whiteness and maleness and wealth and all sorts of things that ensured a smoothly plowed path in front of them. We all react to the world in which we live, and I was living in a world that rejected one part of my identity so strongly, and so disingenuously, that it never bothered to see the other part that was in need of support, patience, and love, to the point that it took me 15 years to uncover the truth for myself. In fact, though some might call my behavior "maladaptive," I understand now that I lacked the tools to make better choices and that my school simply let me down. Overall, I experienced what I might classify as the forced exhibitionism of racialized students at predominantly White institutions and I tried to corral the scrutiny by acting out in ways that never quite aligned with my majoritized peers, which just got me pathologized as an irritant.

Truth be told, I was the lucky one. I struggled, yes, and I felt pain and isolation, anxiety and depression I blamed on myself for far too long, but I still made it out. I did indeed go to that Ivy, and graduate, and get another degree, and get married, and have a son, for whom I want nothing more than to protect from this facet of Whiteness, especially if he is neurodivergent like me. My story could have been so much worse, and it was still this much of a challenge. The only conclusion I can draw is that racism is monumentally powerful, whether exhibited in the way most White Americans understand it, as "explicit behavioral racist acts" (Zamudio & Rios, 2006, p. 485), or hidden behind smiles and performative warmth, with educators falling prey to what I refer to as the *altruistic shield* (Gerald, 2020), a belief that the inherent social good of one's work exempts one from the perpetuation of racism. I have no doubt that almost everyone at my school felt they were helping me and all of the other marginalized students they had, but I also have no doubt that they were, like most educators, so steeped in Whiteness that they were not equipped to see the full humanity of students outside of the norm, even if their norm was slightly off-kilter and festooned with bright colors. Ultimately, there's no remedy for the deficit mindset inherent to Whiteness other than a direct commitment to a dismantling of educational White supremacy that is also deeply engaged with the realities of ableism and its intersection with racism, and within that engagement needs to be a nuanced understanding of how to support students with every type of dis/ability, as well as the mood disorders that can follow swiftly behind them.

Even at a school more expensive than most universities, my experience was fraught with the impacts of my multiple marginalizations and my intense reaction to these differences having led to my pathologization as an annoyance. I suspect, however, that this was somewhat inevitable for someone with my identity, and that I'll always have to take special care to calibrate my behavior so as not to push people away from me. The issue wasn't whether or not I was actually annoying. No, the issue, and the concern I am left with in recounting my experience, is that even at *that* school, perhaps the very best sort of school for a person like me, I came to believe that my behavior meant that I was a problem, that my identity needed to be eliminated, and, ultimately, my school rarely saw me well enough to try and stop me from doing so. I am deeply grateful that I failed, and that I have found my way to a truce with myself. It shouldn't have taken so much time, effort, and money to reach a measure of peace, though.

My son is too young for any of this to matter to him yet, but if his brain works anything like mine does, people will be urging me to send him to a school like the one I went to. I have considered this deeply, and gone back and forth, but the conclusion I have come to after reliving the stories above is that, if he attends a school where he is perhaps a bit bored, then, as an educator myself, I can supplement his learning fairly easily, and challenge whatever harmful version of American history he is given. But if we send him to an independent school that hasn't done the work on racism, no matter how liberal it claims to be, and they pathologize him too, I do not have the skills to fix that damage, and I will have spent a lot of money on unnecessary trauma. He will not be attending an independent school.

In my view, a school's primary task is to make their marginalized students feel loved and cared for, and as educators, if we ever find ourselves thinking that the kid on the floor is annoying, even if they really get on our last nerve, instead of broadcasting our disdain to the classroom, maybe we should just talk to them and make sure they know that they're not as much of a problem as they believe that they are. An institution that lets its marginalized students believe they are annoying has failed in its covenant. So if you, as an academic, a teacher, an administrator, or a parent, come across any "annoying" kids from marginalized groups, do whatever you can to see them, hear them, and love them.

## NOTES

1. All names are pseudonyms, aside from "Justin," which is the author's name.
2. It has since been fully gentrified.
3. Certainly there were wealthy students from European countries, but none who struggled in English.
4. Usually something like *To Kill a Mockingbird*, which was itself written by a White author.
5. One English teacher, exceptional in every way, taught us Morrison and Hurston.
6. As opposed to ours, which were merely implicit.
7. It might be worth pointing out here that this was several years before the most progressive versions of the IDEA were passed, and the school was not legally obligated to provide these supports to the same extent as public institutions (Office of Innovation and Improvement, 2004).
8. Perhaps because there are so few of us that a large sample would be difficult to find.
9. Thankfully, they are not White.
10. Although stories of students' racism remain far from infrequent, and an Instagram account called "Blackat[the school's name]" suggests that what I experienced was mild.
11. Which I most assuredly cannot do now.
12. Until the liquid rotted and I needed a new backpack.
13. Though that didn't stop the note from being included.
14. And hiding in the bathroom for 45 minutes.
15. Ben, who hadn't had any less to drink than I had, was, as expected, not punished in the slightest when his father showed up.
16. This was long before social media.
17. "You're a real drinker now," a senior named Callie said.
18. It was always a "him."
19. This is the reason why I still bristle at White peers who insist that all oppression is class based.
20. Which remains my process during my current doctoral studies.
21. And no real habits for managing my neurodivergence.

## REFERENCES

Annamma, S., Jackson, D., & Morrison, M. (2016). Conceptualizing color-evasiveness: Using dis/ability critical race theory to expand a color-blind racial ideology in education and society. *Race Ethnicity and Education*, 20(2), 147–162. https://doi.org/10.1080/13613324.2016.1248837

Barnum, M. (2019, September 30). *Worried about school segregation? Don't forget private schools.* Chalkbeat. https://chalkbeat.org/posts/us/2019/09/30/private-school-segregation-research/

Bonilla-Silva, E. (2015). The structure of racism in color-blind, "post-racial" America. *American Behavioral Scientist, 59,* 1358–1376. https://doi.org/10.1177/0002764215586826

Ellis, C. (2004). *The ethnographic I: A methodological novel about autoethnography.* AltaMira.

Erevelles, N., & Minear, A. (2010). Unspeakable offenses: Untangling race and disability in discourses on intersectionality. *Journal of Literary and Cultural Disability Studies, 4*(2), 127–146. https://doi.org/10.3828/jlcds.2010.11

Frederick, A., & Shifrer, D. (2019). Race and disability: From analogy to intersectionality. *Sociology of Race and Ethnicity, 5*(2), 200–214. https://doi.org/10.1177/2332649218783480

Gerald, J. (2020). Combatting the altruistic shield in English language teaching. *NYS TESOL Journal, 7*(1), 22–25.

Godfrey, E., Santos, C., & Burson, E. (2019). For better or worse? System-justifying beliefs in sixth-grade predict trajectories of self-esteem and behavior across early adolescence. *Child Development, 90*(1), 180–195. https://doi.org/10.1111/cdev.12854

Hernandez-Saca, D., & Cannon, M. (2019). Interrogating disability epistemologies: Towards collective dis/ability intersectional emotional, affective and spiritual autoethnographies for healing. *International Journal of Qualitative Studies in Education, 32*(3), 243–262. https://doi.org/10.1080/09518398.2019.1576944

Hughes, S. (2019). My skin is unqualified: An autoethnography of Black scholar-activism for predominantly White education. *International Journal of Qualitative Studies in Education, 33*(2), 151–165. https://doi.org/10.1080/09518398.2019.1681552

Kendi, I. X. (2017). *Stamped from the beginning: The definitive history of racist ideas in America.* Bold Type Books.

Kim, H. J. (2019). 'Where are you from? Your English is so good': A Korean female scholar's autoethnography of academic imperialism in U.S. higher education. *International Journal of Qualitative Studies in Education, 33*(5), 491–507. https://doi.org/10.1080/09518398.2019.1681551

King, M., King, C. (Foreword), & Harding, V. (Introduction). (2010). *Where do we go from here: Chaos or community?* Beacon Press. (Original work published in 1968)

Leonardo, Z., & Broderick, A. (2011). Smartness as property: A critical exploration of intersections between Whiteness and disability studies. *Teachers College Record, 113*(10), 2206–2232.

Mijs, J. (2014). The unfulfillable promise of meritocracy: Three lessons and their implications for justice in education. *Social Justice Research, 29*(1), 13–34. https://doi.org/10.1007/s11211-014-0228-0

Nielsen, K. (2012). *A disability history of the United States.* Beacon Press.

Office of Innovation and Improvement. (2004). *Provisions related to children with disabilities enrolled by their parents in private schools.* U.S. Department of Education.

Ohito, E. (2016). Thinking through the flesh: A critical autoethnography of racial body politics in urban teacher education. *Race, Ethnicity, and Education, 22*(2), 250–268. https://doi.org/10.1080/13613324.2017.1294568

Picower, B. (2009). The unexamined Whiteness of teaching: How White teachers maintain and enact dominant racial ideologies. *Race, Ethnicity, and Education, 12*(2), 197–215. https://doi.org/10.1080/13613320902995475

Pirtle, W. (2019, April 23). The other segregation. *The Atlantic*. https://www.theatlantic .com/education/archive/2019/04/gifted-and-talented-programs-separate -students-race/587614/

Shalaby, C. (2017). *Troublemakers: Lessons in freedom from young children at school*. The New Press.

Tucker, G. C. (n.d.). *6 things to know about private schools and special education*. Understood. https://www.understood.org/en/school-learning/choosing-starting-school/ finding-right-school/6-things-to-know-about-private-schools-and-special -education

U.S. Department of Education. (2006). *Sec 300.8 Child With a Disability*. Individuals With Disabilities Education Act. https://sites.ed.gov/idea/regs/b/a/300.8

Voulgarides, C. K. (2018). *Does compliance matter in special education? IDEA and the hidden inequities of practice*. Teachers College Press.

Williams, P. (1987). Spirit-murdering the messenger: The discourse of fingerpointing as the law's response to racism. *University of Miami Law Review, 42*(1). https://repository.law.miami.edu/umlr/vol42/iss1/8/

Yoon, I. H. (2019). Haunted trauma narratives of inclusion, race, and disability in a school community. *Educational Studies, 55*(4), 420–435. https://doi.org/10 .1080/00131946.2019.1629926

Zamudio, M., & Rios, F. (2006). From traditional to liberal racism: Living racism in the everyday. *Sociological Perspectives, 49*(4), 483–501. https://doi.org/10 .1525/sop.2006.49.4.483

CHAPTER 5

# DECISION-MAKING IN THE ERA OF POSTMODERN AUDISM

## Examining the Colonizing Normate

**S. J. Wright**
*Rochester Institute of Technology*

**Gloshanda Lawyer**
*Independent Scholar*

**E. H. Bart IV**
*Independent Scholar*

Who decide(d)s whether the identity of a Deaf[1] person is a disability or a cultural identity? Who decide(d)s that spoken English is inherently superior to signed languages? Who decide(d)s what Deaf bodies are normative within the Deaf communities? Historically, much of the research and theorizing upon Deaf bodies has occurred through the etic perspectives

*Who Decides?*, pages 91–121
Copyright © 2022 by Information Age Publishing
www.infoagepub.com

of White, hearing individuals whereas emic perspectives by and for Deaf individuals have been largely missing from the literature (Cue et al., 2019; Lawyer, 2018; Wright, 2020). In large part, this can be attributed to the pervasive presence of audism in which Deaf people have for centuries been regarded as inferior, in want of rehabilitation, linguistically deprived, and colonized by the ideals of oralism and ableism (Ladd, 2003; Lane, 1999). The ability of Deaf individuals to obtain doctoral degrees in the United States has historically been a challenge reserved only for those who have the most privilege, which is tempered by proximity to normative practices, who then go on to succeed (Garberoglio et al., 2019). In other words, only those who were able to successfully navigate the hearing world with an ability to speak, an ability to master the English language, particularly that of the academic register, while presenting as White and relatively abled, have been among the first to receive doctoral degrees and thereby, allowed into academic discourse. Although remarkable, those precious few are simply not enough to amass a robust body of research that shifts the status quo of Deaf Studies, Deaf Education, and literacy away from the body of decades of etic perspectives. However, in the last decade, we have seen the number of Deaf scholars increase significantly, allowing for emic perspectives to challenge the status quo. New, emic perspectives give organic accounts of experiential phenomena, and shift meaning-making through the diversity of Deaf bodies. This shift thereby allows Deaf communities to articulate our own multiple epistemologies, interpret our own being-in-the-world, challenge the dominance of ableism, colonialism, and audism, while carrying the torch of our predecessors who have opened the doors into academia.

This chapter explores the broad topics of ableism, audism, racism, and colonization as they apply to the Deaf community. Particularly, this chapter sharply examines the persistence of über-ableism and supremacy of White Deaf individuals in positions of power, the institutions that continue to enshrine them through comfortable degrees of proximity to the White hearing normate, and legal frameworks that masquerade as the great equalizer, resulting in an unchallenged single-identity approach in the U.S. Deaf context. We do this through exploring the colonization of Deaf bodies, particularly Deaf people of color, unpacking the notion of dis/ability, critically examining normative practices that occur *within* the Deaf communities, and demonstrate the gaps in diverse representation of Deaf people. We argue that first-wave Deaf critical theory (DeafCrit) is no longer sufficient nor reflective of the current state of multiple Deaf communities, where we posit that postmodern audism (PMA) as built by Deaf scholars is the appropriate multiple-identity approach.

In order to demonstrate how we understand PMA as an emic, multiple-identity lens approach to the current plurality of Deaf communities, it is necessary to understand a few monumental moments in history that are helpful in understanding what constitutes three major themes in this chapter: proximity to the normate, audism, and linguicism as an element of audism. We begin this chapter with a brief visit to the 1988 Deaf President Now protest, followed by a brief analysis of the Milan Conference (1880), in order to set the stage for critical discourse in the rest of this chapter.

## THE WAKE OF DEAF PRESIDENT NOW

Since its founding in 1864, for 124 years Gallaudet University—the only university in the world specifically designed to meet the needs of Deaf and hard of hearing students (Gallaudet, 2020b)—had been served by White hearing presidents. In 1988, the notorious Deaf President Now (DPN) protest led to the downfall of a stronghold by hearing leadership and ushered in I. King Jordan, the university's first Deaf president (Christiansen & Barnartt, 2003). The DPN protests began on March 6, 1988 as news of the appointment of Zisner, a hearing president who had no American Sign Language (ASL) skills, and had no experience in Deaf education was selected over qualified Deaf candidates. The news quickly gained traction across campus and was picked up by major news networks across the United States. Protesters spanning the likes of Gallaudet students, alumni, faculty, and the Deaf community from all over the country took to the streets, eventually marching on to Capitol Hill. By Monday, March 7th, the university was shuttered and students boycotted classes, blocked the entries to campus with school buses, and formed human chains to prevent administrators from entering campus buildings. This monumental protest sparked the cry "Deaf president now!" chanted in ASL, and this became the rallying cry of the protest.

From the heat of battle, the "Gallaudet Four" of the DPN protest was formed: Bridgetta Bourne, Jerry Covell, Greg Hlibok, and Tim Rarus (Christiansen & Barnartt, 2003; Gallaudet, 2020b). The Gallaudet Four became the face of the protest, handling media interactions and public demonstrations, and they were key players in the development of the infamous four demands made to Gallaudet's board of trustees. These four demands were: (a) Zinser must resign and a Deaf president must be selected; (b) Spilman, the university's board Chairperson who was also hearing, must resign from the board; (c) Deaf people must constitute a 51% majority on the board; and (d) there must be no reprisals against any of the protestors (Christiansen & Barnartt, 2003; Gallaudet, 2020b). While all four demands were met, the DPN protests also succeeded in installing an international platform for Deaf peoples' battle cry for equity and chartering the course of social change parallel to the brewing momentum behind the Americans With Disabilities Act (ADA, 1990).

In the wake of three decades, we can see that DPN set significant precedents, but it was constrained due to cultural and historical factors beyond the scope of the DPN organizers. The protests focused squarely on the installation of Deaf people in leadership roles, while the president and the board of trustees at the time consisted of primarily hearing individuals. What the protests did not have the opportunity to articulate were the reasons why the system had allowed hearing people to maintain power for more than a century. The protests, and the publicized narratives that came out of those protests, solidified the idea of Deaf as an identity to be proud of, but did not unpack the totality of what it means to be Deaf. Despite establishing precedent, the binary of Deaf/Hearing was perpetuated, largely because the unified front concealed the diversity of the various communities that form the "Deaf community." DPN was the first time many hearing people in the United States and around the world were exposed to the battle cry that Deaf people did not consider themselves inferior to hearing people despite being regarded as such. In order to understand the impetus which led to DPN as a watershed moment in Deaf history, it is essential to examine the caustic nature of audism, the ushering in of legal protections masquerading as equity, and proximity to the hearing normate through the lenses of racism and ableism. The sinister forces of audism are responsible for Gallaudet University's 124-year history led by hearing individuals who often had little or no working knowledge of Deaf education, little or no knowledge of signed languages, and lacked the epistemological knowledge essential to being-in-the-world as a culturally Deaf individual. These historical events represent the power dynamics between Deaf and hearing communities in miniature. The following sections further unpack the monoliths of racism and audism, followed by the essence of equity, and conclude with the call to dismantle single-identity lenses that uphold the White, Deaf body in favor of those who are most hearing-like as a matter of proximity.

## POSTMODERN AUDISM

Broadly defined, *audism* is the belief that speaking and hearing are superior, and the purest form of ability (Bauman, 2004; Humphries, 1977). The term was first penned (although it is disputed who actually coined the term socially) by Humphries (1977). Audism is a 140-year normalization of ableism and the belief that to speak and hear is superior to the alternative. Although audism has existed much longer (see Van Cleve & Crouch, 1989 for a brief historical overview of attitudes towards the Deaf), we begin in 1880 for reasons that will become apparent. In 1880, an international conference of educators for the deaf met in Italy. Now known as the Milan Conference, the predominantly hearing assembly banned the use of sign language in the instruction of deaf pupils (Moores, 2010). The aftermath of decisions made in 1880 has relegated the Deaf body to a form of second-class citizenship, and it manifested outwardly as audism, especially as it was demonstrated in DPN. Furthermore, the ripple effects of this proclamation led to the mass expulsion of deaf educators from schools for the deaf under the premise that deaf people are not competent enough to educate deaf children and sign languages lead to the mental atrophy of deaf people. It was at this moment in history that audism was given a perceptible, malevolent form (Moores, 2010; Van Cleve & Crouch, 1989). From this point forward, Alexander Graham Bell rose into prominence as one of the greatest opponents to signed languages in the last century and a half, touting oralism in the place of signed languages as a method by which deaf people could be saved (R. A. Edwards, 2012; Van Cleve & Crouch, 1989). This movement birthed the valorization of spoken language over signed languages, cementing the deaf body to second-class citizenship following the Milan Conference; it continues to do so.

It is important to understand this second-class citizenship status within a frame of colonization because colonized/colonizer is not a binary nor is it a static status (Lawyer, 2018). Therefore, those 140 years had several effects: (a) indoctrinating generations of Deaf individuals into believing they could not assume leadership positions; (b) indoctrinating those in power into paternalistic roles when concerning administration of deaf spaces; (c) creating groups of Deaf leaders who felt that their only gateway into administrative positions would be to assume qualities of the dominant, normative group; and (d) continuing to deny access to leadership positions to those who are the most marginalized within the Deaf community. This resulted in the vying for power over Deaf spaces, even as more (multiply-marginalized) Deaf people gained higher degrees of education.

Based on the origins of audism post-Milan, and the ripple effects we have discussed up until this point, the effects upon deaf bodies have been overt. The former status quo of deaf being-in-the-world functions largely from a state of dysconscious audism (Gertz, 2003) in which deaf and hearing bodies are separated by a literal sound barrier. We argue that the aftermath of DPN is not the golden age for the Deaf community, but rather it inspired the beginnings of DeafCrit, focusing on the validity of the Eurocentric Deaf body (Whiteness), which currently informs PMA. PMA makes exceptions for deaf bodies in certain spaces, *so long* as they exhibit characteristics of the hearing normate, as we can see through the events of DPN. This era of audism operates in a more covert fashion where colonialism still reigns, but also in more sophisticated ways, which has the duality of both avowing and disavowing deaf bodies, in addition to accepting on one hand the existence of signed languages and on the other hand, denying the right to signed languages, perpetuating linguicism and language deprivation (Hall, 2017; Hall et al.,

2017; Humphries et al., 2012, 2017; Skutnabb-Kangas, 2016). PMA moves away from the us vs. them binary, the hearing vs. Deaf binary, which has been the focus of early DeafCrit work in establishing the centrality of the Deaf body as distinct from but equal to hearing bodies. PMA acknowledges that while Deaf bodies have legal and theoretical equality, the shift moves to address intersectionality and encompass multiple epistemologies of Deaf bodies that further unpack the worldhood of being Deaf. Seemingly, this could be considered second-wave Deaf studies, as we argue where junior scholars such as ourselves attempt to push the boundaries of Deaf studies to incorporate these intersectional and epistemological understandings and bring to light hidden hierarchical systems within the community, we continually expand the challenge of ahistoricism. For example, while dysconscious audism (Gertz, 2008), an important element of first-wave DeafCrit, can address the Deaf community on an individual basis, it has difficulty when extended to schools, organizations, and other Deaf cultural institutions. We define PMA through the threading together of our individual scholarship which involves the colonization of Deaf bodies, the proximity of hearing power, the notion of dis/ability, and the challenges to the status quo of DeafCrit. In order to understand our argument towards PMA as the current status quo, it is essential to provide background on how we understand and interpret colonialism as it applies to the Deaf community.

## UNPACKING COLONIALISM

Colonization can be described as the processes that condition individuals within a society into their superordinated and subordinated positions, and all the mechanisms that are used to construct this stratification as normal and innate, keeping it largely elusive particularly to those who have dominant or superordinated positions (Lawyer, 2018). Colonization encompasses all forms of oppression and violence that manifest as racism, anti-blackness, audism, linguicism, ableism, classism, heteronormativity, and others. The history of Deaf education in the United States is teeming with examples of how racism, audism, and ableism have worked in tandem against Deaf communities. For example, consider the decimation of Deaf education in the aftermath of Milan: In the years between 1882 to 1919, the percentage of Deaf students taught using sign language went from over 92% to 20% (Van Cleve & Crouch, 1989). Similarly, and significantly, the percentage of Deaf teachers of Deaf students in schools for the Deaf went from a peak of 41% to a low of 21% by the 1920s (Baynton, 1996). Also worth noting is that although sign language dropped in White Deaf schools, it was still quite vibrant in Black Deaf schools. However, when Deaf schools became integrated, signing Black Deaf teachers were quickly retired from their positions, even though they had the potential to revitalize sign language and Deaf culture within the Deaf schools. This is a clear example of how racism prohibited the U.S. Deaf communities' rebound from post-Milan language policies (Baynton, 1996; Lawyer, 2018; McCaskill, 2010; Moges, 2020). Additionally, teachers who had the ability to speak were favored over teachers who did not have the ability to speak (Van Cleve & Crouch, 1989) and this favored normate continues to this day. According to a survey conducted by Simms et al. (2008), employment results show similar percentages, namely that 22% of teachers of the Deaf and 14.5% of administrators are Deaf themselves. Conversely, the majority of educational authorities in the field of Deaf education are White and hearing. Simms et al. (2008), in a survey of schools serving Deaf students, found that 88.3% of administrators in these schools are White, and approximately 85% of Deaf education personnel are hearing.

A primary manifestation of colonization in Deaf education is evident: audism. Audism exists at the intersections of ableism, racism, and linguicism. For the colonized, the proximity to ability is clear: Hearing people, and by logical extension, White Deaf people who can speak, are in the current climate of Deaf education, which reflects the nexus of oppression inherent in the colonization of the Deaf community. Linguicism, generally defined as beliefs and systemic practices that confer (or deny) power to groups based on the language(s) they use (Skutnabb-Kangas, 2016; see also Reagan, 2011), is demonstrated in the denial of the use of the natural sign language of the U.S. Deaf community, American Sign Language. Educators who are able to use the spoken language of English are favored, despite the resurgence of ASL as a pedagogical strategy (Humphries, 2013; Nover & Andrews, 1998; Prinz & Strong, 1998; Simms & Thumann, 2007; Wilbur, 2000). The danger in this proximity is the perpetuation of the dichotomous images of the colonizer and colonized: hearing as abled, and Deaf as disabled and the reification of the hearing hegemony (Davis, 1995, McRuer, 2005; Memmi, 1991). Through a disability studies and critical race theory (DisCrit) lens, the images of the hearing person and the Deaf person are socially constructed. The superordinated group must maintain this imagery, constructing aspirational versions of the abled hearing person upon which Deaf students can model themselves. Furthermore, casting hearing people in authority roles creates the concomitant Deaf normate (Wright, 2020) interrogated in this chapter. Here is particularly where we depart and challenge DeafCrit because in theory and praxis, DeafCrit only draws comparisons to the experience of being negatively racialized and does not account for the experiences of racism and audism for Black, Indigenous, and people of color (BIPOC) Deaf community members, for example.

## THE PRICE OF PROXIMITY

Deaf*ness* in and of itself is the medical perspective of the loss or lack of hearing, but does not define the culture nor the worldhood of *being* Deaf, as is the topic of much scholarly inquiry into Deaf studies within the past 5 years (see Lawyer, 2018; Wright, 2017, 2020). Individuals who identify as culturally Deaf experience varying degrees of trauma—most notably related to language deprivation and oppression at the expense of ableism (Hall, 2017; Lawyer, 2018; Wright, 2020). Such trauma often manifests itself in the forms of literacy inequity, socialization atrophy, and the insidious struggle to access worldly capital necessary for survival in a capitalist society such as the United States. These experiences are not to be discounted, as they form the topography of being-in-the world which translates to Deaf epistemology. In other words, Deaf epistemology attempts to describe how we Deaf people relate to, understand, interpret, and experience our own consciousness both collectively and individually (Cue et al., 2019; Hauser et al., 2010; Holcomb, 2010). When institutions perpetually enshrine White, "Deaf/Hearing" individuals into positions of leadership within Deaf education, it sends an unequivocal message that a single degree of proximity is acceptable. Such actions effectively exclude multiple narratives and intersectionalities that spell out the deaf experience in all of its permutations. Single-lens identity of equating Deaf to deaf, deaf to a little hard of hearing/very hard of hearing are dangerous in tandem with perpetuating White supremacy within the Deaf community. Proximity to the normate shuns those Deaf individuals who viscerally and inherently understand the topography of Deaf epistemology, especially BIPOC Deaf.

## THE PROBLEM WITH DEAFCRIT

First, it is important to begin with a broad definition of what constitutes DeafCrit, before delving into the finer points that define it. DeafCrit has its roots in the civil rights movements of the 1960s, where it was patterned after minority groups such as Black, Latinx, and women (Gertz, 2003). Similar to minority groups of the civil rights movements, leaders of the Deaf community noticed parallels between the bilingual/bicultural characteristics of the Latino rights movement, and began to adopt similar principles during the background of ASL research in the 70s which gave it academic linguistic legitimacy for Deaf people (Gertz, 2003). During that time, academics began to identify the shapes of various forms of oppression with "isms": Black people use "racism," women use "sexism," and it would naturally occur that Deaf people would use the term "audism" to express our unique oppression (Bauman, 2004; Gertz, 2003). Through the use of critical race theory, the formalized notion that the experiences of minorities can be expressed as a central theory lent credence to a similar parallel as to how Deaf people could theorize and apply similar principles to the lived experiences of Deaf people (Gertz, 2003).

DeafCrit starts with the premise that audism is pervasive, permanent, and exists in the interest of self-preservation (Gertz, 2003; Lane, 1999). DeafCrit has four central tenets which suggest that (a) *becoming* d/Deaf is a journey; (b) it *rejects* audism, ahistoricism, and the label of disability; (c) it *embraces* ASL as a true and bona fide language; and (d) it *defines* itself as a culture (Gertz, 2008; Ladd, 2003). At face value, it seems that DeafCrit embraces the Deaf body as worthy of equality, embraces ASL as a language that belongs in the international community, and is a natural process in which deaf people become Deaf, and in itself, creates a culture based on perceived norms and linguistic values.

Early scholars of Deaf studies have used these underpinnings to demonstrate lived experiences that work as theorems rooted in critical race theory. Examples beyond that of audism are *surdescence*—the process of becoming Deaf (Gertz, 2003), which derives from the concept of *Nigrescence* (Cross, 1995)—the process of developing a healthy Black identity. In essence, surdescence examines how—as 95% of Deaf individuals are born to hearing parents (Mitchell & Karchmer, 2004)—deaf individuals navigate a journey towards becoming culturally and linguistically Deaf (Gertz, 2003; Wright, 2017). However, much of the early work in Deaf studies and thereby, DeafCrit, focuses on legitimizing the Deaf body as a cultural and linguistic minority, moving away from the disabled binary that is the focus of much of the medical and public view of Deaf bodies (Wright, 2017; 2020). After Jordan's presidency in the wake of DPN, Deaf studies has recently begun to explore the intersectionality of the lived experiences of Deaf people as noted in the wave of young authors producing scholarship, including the authors of this chapter. It is only now that we begin to understand that focusing on "Deafness" alone naturally lends itself to proximity to hearing bodies. At this point in time, we begin to examine what is meant by Deaf bodies—particularly those who are among the most marginalized—BIPOC Deaf, DeafBlind, DeafDisabled, and DeafQueer (Wright, 2020). Here, we are interested in expanding the boundaries of DeafCrit to become more inclusive by filling in gaps that have been lost in the focus on proximity.

However, the problematic gaps of DeafCrit are what it does not include—particularly that of BIPOC Deaf, Queer Deaf bodies, sociolinguistic modalities of ASL such as ProTactile ASL (PTASL) in the DeafBlind community—and it nearly expresses itself as a culture of conversion (Bechter, 2008, Wright; 2020). Wright (2020) asserts that DeafCrit functions as a "panopticon" (p. 15) in which the "epistemologies of sighted, Deaf of Deaf, White, cisgender, heterosexual hold guard over other permutations of Deaf bodies..." (p. 15). In other words, where the Deaf community is concerned, DeafCrit shuns the notions of disability, race, and sexual orientation, relegating the intersectionality of Deaf bodies to an inferior status. The foundation of Deaf-Crit largely focuses on single-identity, White, linguistically-endowed, abled individuals while ignoring the simple concept of intersectionality (Wright, 2017, 2020). First-wave DeafCrit bases its Eurocentric underpinnings on that of Black American identity development (Nigrescence), while seemingly rejecting that DeafCrit is whitewashed as it does not formally introduce the multiple oppressions of race, disability, sexuality, and queerness where the White deaf body is an unmarked identity and the deaf bodies of BIPOC, LGBTQIA, and DeafDisabled are essentially disavowed identities. Underpinning DeafCrit on Black American identity development is a form of anti-Blackness, which allows White deaf bodies to come into power as über-abled in the guise of proximity while shifting disavowed identities as ultra-disabled. In the same manner that DeafCrit seeks to illuminate hearingness and its problematic nature because any theory developed within hearing circles cannot sufficiently circumscribe hearingness, DeafCrit cannot sufficiently illuminate the unmarked identity of White, abled, Deaf people without critical insight by non-White Deaf scholars.

The epistemological knowledge of Deaf being-in-the-world simply cannot fit in one neat paradigm of epistemology, as it appears to consist of multiple epistemological loci—which conflicts with the spirit of epistemological research in and of itself (Cue et al., 2019). Further, while DeafCrit engages in this ideology, Deaf people effectively don the colonizer's coat in deciding which bodies are desirable and which are deviant, actions derived from centuries of oppression at the hands of ableism and audism (Lawyer, 2018; Wright 2020). This perpetuates the constructivist notion of disability as an imagineered construct wherein the corollary highlights the über-abled while simultaneously delineating the ultra-disabled (Vehmas & Watson 2016; Wright, 2020). First-wave DeafCrit presupposes that a single epistemological model applies to all, whereas junior scholars in the era of PMA are demonstrating that the nascent concept of a Deaf ecology may very well exist, as it theorizes a Deaf ecological systems model which purports to delineate that all pervasive power structures and systems have biological and social implications upon Deaf bodies that are vastly diverse, not singular in space and time (Cue, 2020).

Within this ecology in the period of PMA, we see the emergence of specific epistemological standpoints such as Deaf LatCrit (García-Fernandez, 2020) and Black Deaf Gain (Moges, 2020). Deaf LatCrit challenges the spaces where Deaf individuals who identify as Latinx are routinely rejected based on their plurality of linguistic knowledge or rather, the lack of access to cultural signed and spoken languages in the face of White supremacy while articulating the epistemological locus of what it *means* to be Deaf Latinx. In parallel, Deaf Gain reframes Deaf bodies as positively contributing to the biodiversity of the human race, where the benefits of Deaf culture and ways of being benefit the public at large (Bauman & Muray, 2009). Black Deaf Gain revisits (White) Deaf Gain from the objective ontology of the Black Deaf experience. In doing so, Black Deaf Gain, through the Deaf LatCrit framework, becomes a critical tool that more appropriately analyzes the Black Deaf experience, particularly in Deaf education.

For all the scholarly merit of PMA, the central question of Deaf/ness as a disability or a culture still remains elusive. Early DeafCrit is quick to establish that the condition of being Deaf, along with the rich heritage of ASL, frames itself as a culture, not a disability (Gertz, 2008; Wright, 2020). More recently, there has been closer examination as to how Deaf individuals in the United States continually masquerade as both disabled *and* as members of a sociolinguistic culture depending on the turn of the prism that is fortified by the ADA (1990), Section 504 (1973), and Individuals With Disabilities Education Act (IDEA, 1990; Lawyer, 2018; Wright, 2017). PMA attempts to reconcile this with the threading together of multiple-identity lenses, as is the focus of much of the scholarly work of the authors of this piece. Particularly, we argue that deaf people are simultaneously members of a sociolinguistic culture and a disabled group by a contract of adherence with legal frameworks that afford us access to a hearing society (Lawyer, 2018; Wright, 2017). In other words, we champion our collective identities as members of distinct Deaf communities while at the same time, if we want to access the hearing world vis-a-vis sign language interpreters, closed captioning, PTASL, or any such modification, we must mark and disavow our cultural identities as "disabled" in time and space, recognizing both the social constructedness of disability and the very real access barriers a hearing, sighted world presents.

## (DE)CONSTRUCTING DIS/ABILITY

We cannot analyze the historic implications of audism and the U.S. Deaf populations without examining how, through colonization, being Deaf has been socially constructed within disability. In the context of the United States, *disability* has been an often-changing conceptualization used as a weapon against those who are considered less desirable in our society. This has been a primary agenda of colonization. In the past, LGBTQ populations, BIPOC, and poor individuals were all considered *disabled* because they were rejected from the dominant social norm (Seldon, 1999). In the more recent decades, neurodivergent individuals and individuals with varying physical and communicative abilities have been relegated into the category of disability. There has been little acknowledgement by dominant society regarding how these constructions of disability have shifted in ways that continue to cater to capitalism. In other words, a nondisabled body/mind is one that is able to contribute in a capitalist society and therefore, deserves to be granted rights to full humanity (Lawyer, 2018).

It is important to analyze disability from this historical context as it reinforces that disability can impact any population at any time. Additionally, it is often the case that societal marginalization through different and multiple forms of oppression results in disability (Crenshaw, 2017). Disability is often a result of trauma and systemic oppression in marginalized communities which are often unnamed. For example in indigenous reservation communities, mainstream media focuses on high rates of addiction and suicide without naming that these are the results of historic material deprivation by the U.S. government, toxic land environments due to oil pipelines, and waste dumping. Yet, suicide rates and addiction often are unnamed when we think about disability whereas legally and historically, *disability* has been framed in ways that benefit White individuals. Both factors are of particular importance for the following reasons: (a) Deaf individuals with other marginalized identities (LGBTQIA, immigrant, users of other languages, other apparent or nonapparent disabilities) are often further disabled due to having their participation and access to society limited; (b) multiply-marginalized Deaf individuals have a qualitatively different experience than members of the community who are afforded dominant group access and privileges vis-a-vis proximity to White, hearing normates; and (c) identity politics through various forms of oppression also exist in the U.S. Deaf communities.

A brief example that highlights these reasons can be found in the case of Douglas McCray, a Black Deaf man who sued the city of Dothan, Alabama (Leagle, n.d.c). McCray was assaulted during questioning by police regarding car damage, and he claimed violations of his civil rights as a Black person and as a Deaf person. The court's opinion notes there is not enough evidence to support the claim that he was treated differently because he was Black. However, in the same opinion, they state he was not treated differently because of his "hearing impairment" yet both factors contributed to the escalation of the situation between the Black Deaf man and White police officers. A second example parallels the narrow legal boundaries in which the Black female plaintiffs in *DeGraffenreid v. General Motors* (1976) found themselves constrained as noted in Crenshaw's (1989) landmark writing on intersectionality. Both the Black women and the Black Deaf man in their respective cases were discriminated against and the court sought to parse out and adjudge according to each singular identity facet, which dooms the lawsuits to failure due to lack of compelling evidence of discrimination against either facet. This reflects the prevailing desire to compartmentalize multiply-layered identities and leave the full treatment of such people unexamined. This desire plays out in K–12 schooling, higher education, and in educational leadership.

We have invoked Foucault's (2004) panopticon, but we must remember that one core element is to separate the subject apart from others, isolating that individual. Current educational law dealing with Deaf people and other disabled people has the effect of divorcing the student from the community to which they have ties. Consider the current law regulating students with disabilities: the IDEA, so named in 1990. At its core is the labeling of a student as an individual, considered distinct from other students with similar disabilities. Starting with Section 504 (1973) and continuing to today's IDEA, the legal standard of examining cases regarding Deaf people and other people with disabilities has invariably been on an individual basis. *Strathie v. Department of Transportation* (1984; Dewey, 2016), in which a Deaf man sued to be permitted to drive interstate commercially, set a precedent of examining only the circumstances surrounding the individual in the case rather than considering the disability community to which the person may be affiliated. When Strathie's lawyers focused only on the particulars of Strathie's case, they missed an opportunity to show that all Deaf people are capable of being commercial drivers. The focus on Strathie's use of accommodations (i.e., his hearing aids) maintained the hegemonic focus on the idea that driving requires the sense of hearing, despite a body of evidence showing Deaf drivers on average are safer than hearing drivers.

The concept of a disabled student in isolation was fossilized in 1982 in *Hendrick Hudson Board of Education v Rowley* (Schley, 2016) in which the U.S. Supreme Court examined the then new IDEA law and set the standard of what a free and appropriate public education (FAPE) means in the context of IDEA. The Rowleys, two Deaf parents of a young Deaf child, sued to have sign language interpreters included in Rowley's individualized education plan (IEP). Her school balked, stating that the student was making adequate progress, which satisfied IDEA requirements, particularly that of a FAPE. The court agreed with the school board, stating that in Rowley's particular circumstances, she was performing well in school without access to her home language, ASL. The court did not consider Rowley's whole life, noting that sign language was one of her primary languages, as well as the language of the community to which she belonged, which clearly can be interpreted as a result of linguicism. Rowley was simply a student with a disability, to be considered in isolation from other factors. Her right to communication access was not a consideration (Eckert & Rowley, 2013), and the decision rendered enabled linguicism to continue in the education of Deaf children. So long as a deaf child is able to use the majority language, spoken English, to make academic progress, that child ostensibly does not have the right to their linguistic heritage of ASL.

The Supreme Court considered one other challenge to IDEA recently, in the 2017 case of *Endrew F. v. Douglas County School District* (Leagle, n.d.a). Endrew F., a student with multiple disabilities, struggled in school and his parents were dissatisfied with the IEP goals set for him and transferred him to a school that specialized in education of students like him. The question at hand was whether the original school violated the FAPE requirement of IDEA. The court altered their standard for FAPE, to suggest that rather than simply making progress (which could and had led to the development of goals that merely aimed for the minimum), students were to make adequate progress based on their individual circumstances. The delineating framework of individualism continues in the case through the court's rejection of *amicus curiae* briefs submitted by Down Syndrome and autism advocacy groups (Leagle, n.d.b). The court stated the briefs had no bearing on the specific individual circumstances of Endrew F., while in the very same response, noted that the educational strategies outlined could benefit students with Down Syndrome and autism, which precisely described Endrew F.

With the preceding examples, we can see the legal panopticon developed to isolate disabled people and prevent a view of these people as belonging to communities. Crucially, the Deaf community historically has very little input on laws that regulate our bodies, a point made by Bryan and Emery (2014) in their examination of legal theory filtered through Deaf perspectives. This lack of input is not by happenstance; it is a product of colonization.

Laws designed to help disabled people, such as IDEA and the Americans With Disabilities Act, constitute a larger welfare program purportedly intended to support the disability community. One must not forget what Freire (2013) stated of welfare programs, that they were

> instruments of manipulation ultimately serv[ing] the end of conquest. They act as an anesthetic, distracting the oppressed from the true cause of their problems and from the concrete solutions of these problems. They splinter the oppressed into groups of individuals hoping to get more benefits for themselves. (p. 152)

Thus, we see how the colonization of educational laws disaggregates Deaf people and disabled people, achieving the same ends as the legal system which ignores the intersectionality of people with multiple identities.

Disability has been situated in various ways depending on the context. In academic contexts, it has been historically treated as an afterthought or siloed into specialized fields such as special education and disability studies which has necessitated the development of theories such as DeafCrit, and DisCrit ,and fields such as critical disability studies. In the professional context, disability has been treated as a burden. Lawyer (2018) found that most BIPOC Deaf upon entering their careers were often leaving positions and transitioning into other fields because their employers felt requesting interpreters and making other accommodations were a financial burden as well as a personal inconvenience to hearing colleagues. In the professional world, ADA is the law that provides for accommodations in the workplace; yet those are often the minimum standard for public businesses and organizations, placing responsibility on the Deaf employee to establish the need for accommodations. This often positions disability in a deficit view. Within social movements, disability has historically been erased in favor of the movement of the moment. For example, in regards to the civil rights movements of the 1960s, most of the leaders were themselves disabled either from birth or as a result of the injustices they were fighting against (Thompson, 2018). Black feminists such as Audre Lorde were also disabled activists, yet she was often only referred to in regards to her Blackness. Therefore, disability is considered something to overcome or not worth mentioning, falling secondary to race when the movements are fighting against racism. This is often evident in the lack of accommodations for disabled individuals within these groups (e.g., no interpreters, not hosting events in accessible buildings, not providing captioning or transcripts, no video or image descriptions, etc.). This is a function of colonization (Lawyer, 2018) which prevents us from recognizing how social constructions such as race and disability are mutually sustaining (Lewis, 2020).

From a critical theory standpoint, DeafCrit also situates disability as undesirable and something to be rejected as part of accepting Deaf identity, which we see from Deaf individuals born to Deaf parents also referred to as DOD or "the Deaf Elite" (Wright, 2017, 2020). DeafCrit does not take into account that DeafBlind and DeafDisabled individuals also comprise the Deaf community. Furthermore, within DeafCrit sign language is uplifted at the expense of the multiple ways Deaf, DeafBlind, DeafDisabled, and Hard of Hearing individuals from diverse linguistic backgrounds communicate in addition to sign language. In many ways, DeafCrit essentializes the U.S. Deaf community and perpetuates historic tropes of groups attempting to distance themselves from the disability label (Lawyer, 2018). Although DeafCrit claims to be modeled after critical race theory (CRT), it completely ignores race and structural systems that impact racialized Deaf bodies. The hyperfocus on the Deaf experience in a hearing society is not unwarranted; however, the theory is left largely incomplete when it erases the disabled/disabling and racialized experiences of Deaf populations. Therefore, we argue we must look beyond DeafCrit when critiquing Deaf education, especially to consider the layered impact of disability, race, and the context of educational leadership.

Though there have been individuals pushing for acknowledgement and analysis of dis/ability and race even before contemporary critical theories (Annamma et al., 2016a), the field of Disability studies in education was the first to fully explore the social construction of disability and how it relates to education (Bell, 2011). Pushing the envelope further, *Disability Studies and Critical Race Theory in Education* (DisCrit; Annamma et al., 2016b) challenges how disability studies in education have largely ignored the social construction of race and how it intersects and sustains the construction of disability. This is an important lens for the U.S. Deaf population because instead of examining the Deaf identity, it examines how Deaf people are enabled or dis/abled in society within different social and educational contexts. DisCrit framework "theorizes about the ways in which race, racism, dis/ability, and ableism are built into the interactions, procedures, discourses, and institutions of education . . . which affect students of color with dis/abilities qualitatively differently than White students with dis/abilities (Annamma et al., 2016b, p. 14). DisCrit also recognizes the "historical, social, political, and economic interests of limiting access to educational equity to students of color with dis/abilities on both macro and microlevels" (Annamma et al., 2016a, p. 15).

The shadowed spaces of audism take on a new light with the most recent Black Lives Matter movements happening across the United States. Now the protests have expanded beyond addressing police violence against (disabled) people of color and into the daily experiences of violence that BIPOCs face in various social institutions. One such experience is the treatment of BIPOC students in the educational system. In 2020, the Texas Education Agency, after investigating the records of Frisco Independent School District, reported that Black students, especially those in special education, were punished at a disproportionate rate compared to other students (D'Annunzio, 2020). This matches a national trend, as noted in Peguero and Shekarkhar (2011) and MacSuga-Gage et al. (2020). For instance, in the school year 2017–2018, 65% of Black or African American students with disabilities were removed from educational environments for disciplinary reasons, compared to 26% of White students with disabilities (Office of Special Education Programs, 2020). Peguero and Shekarkhar (2011) found an increased tendency for Latinx students to be disciplined over White students, and the researchers have located multiple factors such as gender and generational status (e.g., third generation Latinx students are more likely to be disciplined than first generation Latinx students). MacSuga-Gage et al. (2020), studying the use of corporal punishment in the states that allow it (mostly in the Southern United States), found that Black students were more likely to be punished than White students, and this risk lowered when there were more Black students in the student body. Additionally, Black students with disabilities in elementary schools also had a higher risk of being punished. MacSuga-Gage et al. assert that their research indicates the power of implicit bias that influences how school personnel treat BIPOC students, in addition with those with disabilities.

Simson (2014) addressed the significance of implicit bias in his analysis of school discipline with critical race theory. Implicit bias shows the expectations of the person holding such a bias and how this is tied to the assumption of normative behavior. Deviance from such normative behavior triggers negative reactions, and consequently decisions regarding the application of discipline. Deviancy in racial expectations of behavior (i.e., White behavior) in addition to deviancy in expectations of physical or mental ability (i.e., abled behavior) results in negative perceptions. These expectations (in terms of race and ability) are either enshrined in school conduct rules (e.g., hairstyle and dress codes), or unwritten hegemonic norms. BIPOC students and students with disabilities, in order to avoid undue punishment, have to learn how not to be deviant. This lesson remains with students who graduate high school and pursue professional degrees and contributes to their conceptions of normativity.

Postmodern audism highlights two essential points: (a) there is a discord between what Deaf elites who are White, DOD, heterosexual, and über-abled individuals (Wright, 2020) conceptualize as justice and equity and what BIPOC Deaf, DeafBlind, and Deaf Disabled people conceptualize as justice and equity; and (b) for the longest time Deaf elites have been able to convince BIPOC Deaf , DeafBlind, and DeafDisabled people to accept Deaf elite visions of justice or force into silence those who do not. The Deaf elite vision of justice repeatedly shows itself to aim for access to White, hearing, middle to upper class, male, cisgender, and heterosexual systems and norms. In pursuit of that type of access, Deaf elites have further marginalized and oppressed BIPOC Deaf, DeafBlind, and DeafDisabled community members (Lawyer, 2018; Wright, 2020).

## BYPRODUCT OF COLONIZATION:
## PROXIMITIES OF ABILITIES

The primary colonialist impulses of hearing educators in the United States can be seen in the push to deprive Deaf students of their common language, ASL, through the influence of Horace Mann, Samuel Gridley Howe, and Alexander Graham Bell (R. A. Edwards, 2012; Van Cleve & Crouch, 1989). R. A. Edwards (2012) notes that Mann believed Deaf students had to be educated in the use of spoken English in order to share the same norms valued by hearing people. This creates a proximity in the ability to use the dominant language, spoken (and written) English. Deaf people with the ability to speak English are then deemed as sharing the same citizenship as hearing people, setting up a crucial aspect of the normate that can achieve leadership within a colonized institution. The lack of Deaf leaders in education recalls Freire's (2013) work in *Pedagogy of the Oppressed*.

Freire, building on concepts articulated by Memmi (1991), showed that oppression (i.e., colonization) could be maintained by Othering the subjects (the colonized) into objects without agency. If representation were to show the colonized as subjects with their own agency rather than defective objects (which creates a normate), the rationalization for oppression is diminished, both to the subjects and the oppressors. By setting up systemic audism within Deaf education, which then forces the Deaf community to accept and desire proximity of ability, hearing authorities perpetuate their grip on their cottage industry of educating (re/habilitating) the Deaf. This has pervasive influences within the U.S. Deaf communities.

Graduates of Deaf education are instilled with the colonizers' values, with the idea of a normate (hearing) and a Deaf normate that emulates the primary template of hearing normativity. Even though the majority of graduates are hearing, about 18% of graduates who become teachers are Deaf, and out of that group, less than 3% are BIPOC and Deaf (Andrews & Jordan, 1993; Simms et al., 2008). One has to wonder about the effects of colonization on this small group of graduates. DeafCrit is able to interrogate this consequence of colonization up to a certain extent. Earlier, we mentioned how Gertz (2008) coined a term that describes the results of colonization of Deaf minds: *dysconscious audism* and its relationship to PMA. Here, in closer detail, dysconscious audism is a form of impaired consciousness, preventing the development of a healthy Deaf identity and full acceptance of core Deaf community values. Persons with such an impaired consciousness may articulate a sense of possessing a Deaf identity and a pride in possessing this identity, which is often undercut by contradictory views that elevate the hearing ideal to the detriment of a Deaf identity. Gertz outlines examples of dysconscious audism, and the effects thereof, notably in passively accepting hearing dominance and problems in fully accepting ASL and Deaf studies. As seen in Freire (2013), this impaired consciousness is a desirable outcome as it prevents the Deaf object from engaging in society as an agent. Without a strong sense of self as an agent, as opposed to a passive object, members of an oppressed group have difficulty confronting the oppressor's narrative. Eckert and Rowley (2013) note how proximity of ability appears in audism, citing evidence of how Deaf people who could speak English were accorded more rights than those who could not speak. By becoming more like the normate, Deaf people become less capable of disrupting the dominant narrative, and less willing to do so out of fear of affecting their elevated status.

As per colonization strategy, education is infected with systemic racism, sexism, and classism, and in the case of Deaf schools, systemic audism. Schools segregated Deaf students on tracks based on the use of spoken language. When oralism took precedence in Deaf education, tracks formed in which all students were taught orally, and those who "failed" to achieve success with spoken English would then be put in classes where manual fingerspelling was used (Baynton, 1996; R. A. Edwards, 2012). These *oral failures* were seen as intellectually inferior for they could not learn and utilize spoken English. When signing came back in favor, it returned in bastardized forms of signed English, or chained to spoken English in the case of simultaneous communication (Czubek & Snoddon, 2016). The underlying sentiment, the dysconsciously audist thought, was that being able to use English, whether spoken or signed, was more desirable than being skilled in ASL, supporting the desirability to emulate the colonizer's normate.

In higher education we see the heavy hand of audism backed up with institutional force. Lane (1999) first expanded the definition of audism beyond Humphries's original 1977 definition to include how institutions instill and perpetuate audism. Bauman (2004) clarified the effect of audism by noting it created a system of advantage based on the ability to hear. Eckert and Rowley (2013) distilled the previously cited definitions to this: "a structural system of exploitative advantage that focuses on and perpetuates the subordination of Deaf Communities of origin, language, and culture" (p. 106). In 1891, when Gallaudet College established a "normal school" in which teachers would be trained, restrictions were established: only hearing candidates were accepted and they were taught the oral method of Deaf education (Winefield, 1987). Although today these restrictions are no longer in place, one can see how this established systemic audism which prompted the desire of proximity of ability. If only hearing people can become teachers of the deaf, then their young Deaf students will be placed in the duality Freire (2013) discusses, in which the Deaf students need to be like their hearing teachers, which means they need to be like their oppressors.

The proximity of the ability to hear, or at least use a language, is connected to the ability to think and reason. The hierarchy is thus, a Deaf person who could speak English was more capable than a Deaf person who could sign in English—that is, use English word order and indicate towards English words through initialized signs and fingerspelling, and a Deaf person who could sign in English (which means one could *think* in English) was more capable than a Deaf person who signed in ASL. Thus, we have the creation of Deafnormativity geared through proximity of ability to use the colonizer's language. The stratification of the Deaf community is evident through the use of DeafCrit, but a survey of the history of Deaf education reveals a glaring lack of examination in other forms of proximity, such as race and other elements (Lawyer, 2018; Wright, 2020).

Deaf schools, just the same as other schools in the United States, were segregated along racial lines (Van Cleve & Crouch, 1989), and the most visible outcome of this segregation was the birth of Black ASL (McCaskill et al., 2011). The physical segregation between Black Deaf children and White Deaf children led to linguistic segregation as both groups contributed to the growth of their versions of ASL. McCaskill et al. (2011) notes that her ASL was suppressed in favor of standard ASL (which in actuality is White ASL, only unmarked). In the same way Black hearing people had to conform to the normate of White America, Black Deaf people had to code switch between Black ASL and White ASL. DeafCrit does little to examine the racist attitudes inoculated into White Deaf students when attending segregated schools. Not only were state schools segregated, but Gallaudet itself did not admit Black students until 1951 (Gallaudet, 2020a). The National Association of the Deaf (NAD), founded in 1880 as purportedly a civil rights organization, barred Black members in the years between 1925 and 1953 (Burch, 2002). Gallaudet and the NAD are incubators of leaders within the Deaf community, and the racism that pervaded these institutions only served to create Deaf normates. One disquieting trend in Simms et al. (2008) is the decrease in Black Deaf teachers and increase in White Deaf teachers—6.9% decrease and 5% increase respectively—between the years 1993 and 2004. Aside from the obvious question of how racism plays out in this shift in hiring practices, we can suggest this is the result of two different things.

First, this shift away from hiring Black Deaf teachers towards more White Deaf teachers is an indicator of how the normate is an essential part of the hiring practices of educational institutions. A hearing-run institution may be willing to hire Deaf people, which diverge from the standard (hearing) normate; but not too much. Hiring a White Deaf person still lies within a zone of comfort whereas hiring a BIPOC Deaf person diverges too much from the normate. This may point to why the Deaf community has developed such a Deaf normate. In the struggle to get recognition and representation, the Deaf community may have decided the best chance to get Deaf leaders into positions of power is to align closely enough to the normate to become enfranchised. This same tactical strategy has appeared in other minority battles such as women's suffrage and Black rights; the minority within the minority are pushed aside in favor of more favorable candidates of leadership. Second, the decrease in Black Deaf and increase in White Deaf may point toward the "intellectual oppression" that Simms et al. (2008) discuss; that is the stifling of growth and development of BIPOC Deaf people in education and the resultant small pool of qualified BIPOC candidates to go on to work at schools. In either case, White Deaf people are complicit in the systemic racism that has led to these hiring trends in the same way that hearing people are complicit in the systemic audism that has kept Deaf people from becoming teachers of their fellow Deaf sisters and brothers.

Secondly, schools are segregated based on ability. Beyond the audist categorization of Deaf based on their ability to hear and speak, we have the categorization of children based on their ability to see. DeafBlind students rarely are taught in the same classes as sighted Deaf students, often placed in isolated rooms or in segregated classrooms with DeafBlind students of color, or hearing students of color, as was common practice in the Deep South up until 1971 (Wright, 2017). Again, the effects of this segregation can be found in the conception of DeafCrit which chooses not to interrogate the treatment of the DeafBlind by the larger Deaf community. To sighted Deaf people, the DeafBlind are manifestations of the sighted Deaf elite's worst nightmare and thereby cast out as undesirable, deviant bodies (Wright, 2020), the untouchables in the caste system of the Deaf community. DeafCrit cannot process the obvious disability contained in DeafBlind persons because being deaf cannot be a disability, for in DeafCrit and the larger Deaf community, the state of being deaf is taken not as disability but as difference (Sherry 2004; Wright, 2020). However, being blind is codified as a disability, and a Deaf person who is also blind is disabled, despite the rejection of deaf-as-disability. As DisCrit pointedly states, disability is socially constructed and in a DisCrit view, DeafBlind are disabled by Deaf people as much as they are disabled by hearing, because their disablers share a common ability—being blind is deviant, being sighted is the normate. To Deaf people, a person who is both deaf and blind cannot carry on a conversation using standard ASL, and their cultural perspectives diverge from the Deaf normate (Wright, 2017, 2020). The permutation of DeafBlind bodies necessitates accommodations such that individuals can participate fully in the Deaf community, mirroring the need for sighted Deaf people to obtain accommodations to participate fully in the mainstream hearing society.

No matter how well a sighted Deaf person can emulate the hearing normate, assimilation is impossible to achieve. Memmi (1991) notes, if the colonized can fully assimilate to become the colonizer, then the distinctions that separate the colonizer from the colonized vanishes, which results in the loss of supremacy. This too can be applied towards the view of Deaf elites. If there is no distinction between a Deaf elite and a DeafBlind person, Deaf elites lose their superiority, therefore the normate cannot entertain resemblance to anything but the ideal, which is a byproduct of colonization.

The pressures of colonization have created a Deaf normate (Wright, 2020). As noted throughout this chapter, the axes of this normate align with the axes of the hearing normate. Any deviation from these axes makes it much more difficult for a Deaf person to be elevated into a position of authority. Such a normate would be White, abled as well as Deaf, potentially DOD with ASL being that person's first language and English as a strong second language; in essence, a "Vanilla Deaf" person (Lawyer, 2018; Wright, 2020). One might argue given the reclamation of the term capital-D-Deaf and the subsequent growth of Deaf studies and its critical theory, DeafCrit, how can the Deaf normate be anything but an opposition to the hearing normate? One only has to look at DeafCrit, which in fact champions the hegemony of the hearing normate. Produced by Deaf elites, who have spent their formative years in colonized institutions and learned their lessons well,

DeafCrit perpetuates the ableist binary of abled and disabled and circum-scribes the intersectional experience of BIPOC who are Deaf outside of the walls of its panopticon. The guards in the central tower of this institution are hidden away because of how much they resemble the hearing normate. Deafnormativity, as articulated in Wright (2020), may resolve the issue of why the BIPOC Deaf community feel disconnected from the goals and values of the presumptive Deaf community. One aspect that seems to go by uninter-rogated is the privilege of Whiteness. Player (2020) posits that White Deaf people also possess a certain privilege borne out of their race, something he labels as White Deaf privilege. So too should Whiteness be considered as part of Deafnormativity. Though Whiteness has gone by unmarked in earlier iterations of critical theory related to Deaf people and the Deaf commu-nity, Whiteness is a real and present element, as noted by Niyongabo (2020) when remarking on Gallaudet's leadership and the perceived inaction with regards to racial tensions on the Gallaudet campus. The fact that the major-ity of administration are Deaf, like the members of the National Black Deaf Advocates, does not offset their Whiteness; it is part and parcel of their Deaf identities and as such, they pass through the halls of the panopticon of Deaf-Crit without challenge. When placed in the panopticon of DeafCrit, which hides away Whiteness and ability in rigid cells, Wright (2020) questions how to address issues facing administrators who are Deaf which become much more difficult because key elements and experiences are missing. As in the creation of a hearing normate, the privileges of being White, abled, middle-class or better, male, and so forth, all support the journey of a Deaf person in becoming that normate. The proximities of abilities for a White, abled, male, Deaf person are much closer to the hearing hegemony regardless of that person's Deaf identity or language use, compared to the BIPOC Deaf. These proximities cannot be interrogated if they are not seen as elements within DeafCrit. The systemic racism in the Deaf world and current Deaf leadership cannot be addressed with DeafCrit. Further, both DeafBlind and DeafDisabled confront the question of ability and disability. The Deaf com-munity, and DeafCrit, can excuse the physical ability to hear as not neces-sarily being a disability, but cannot expand further to include those without vision, or mobility, or neurotypical cognition. This reveals that the normate Deaf view of disability is exactly the same as the normate hearing view of dis-ability. A significant indicator in the Deaf identity normate is strong ASL skill (Lawyer, 2018; Wright, 2016, 2020). If one grew up signing English only due to lack of exposure to ASL until adulthood, one would see such a Deaf per-son struggling to enter the Deaf world due to proximity of ability. Through no fault of their own, that Deaf person happens to be in proximity to hear-ing people, and conversely is not in proximity to the Deaf normate, and risks rejection or denigration of their developing Deaf identity. To prevent this unfair judgment of Deaf people who compare unfavorably to the Deaf normate, DeafCrit needs to transform its current panopticon model and open up the arenas of race and ability to truly examine what constitutes the development of a healthy Deaf identity.

## THE DANGERS OF PROXIMITY

Consider Deaf studies' role in this perpetuation of the normate. We are seeing increased calls for more input from the Black Deaf community, the Indigenous Deaf community, and other marginalized communities. Why has this not been part of Deaf studies all along? Because the Deaf people who have been setting the agenda are the White and abled Deaf people. Going back to DPN, we can see the leadership as consisting of the so-called elite Deaf (which usually means White and abled Deaf) within the Gallaudet Four, for example. This group of Deaf elites often go on to become the vanguard of Deaf academics (Wright, 2020).

These Deaf elites set research questions that interest and apply specifically to themselves, disregarding differences in race and other experiential factors that appear inapplicable to themselves, which in itself generates a form of anti-blackness (Lawyer, 2018). Furthermore, these Deaf academics are the ones that mentor young and upcoming Deaf people. A lack of representation is one chilling effect on young BIPOC Deaf, in addition to other challenges such as limited support systems and reduced social capital (Cawthon et al., 2016). These young people lack mentors who have experienced life as they do. Lynn et al. (2020) highlight the problems Deaf scholars face in mentoring, calling for mentoring services that take into consideration linguistic and cultural competency (i.e., access to information through ASL and understanding the values of Deaf culture). Already a minority within a minority (e.g., Black Deaf children account for approximately 16% of U.S. Deaf education students, and Hispanic students comprise about 22% [Andrews et al., 2004]), this small percentage leads to a lower number of minorities within the fields of Deaf studies and Deaf education, which in turn results in fewer mentors available to assist the next generation of Deaf protégés. This small number of available mentors harms the Deaf world by allowing the epistemologies of Deaf elites to go unchallenged.

Take the current debate on whether or not ProTactile ASL (PT-ASL) is a language of its own, descended from ASL, or simply a dialect of ASL, or just ASL in a different modality. The few DeafBlind who have earned their bona fide chops in the academic world are more inclined to consider PT-ASL as potentially being a complete language while sighted Deaf vary in their opinions (T. Edwards, 2014; Wright, 2016, 2020). Just as Hearing epistemologies have been challenged by Deaf researchers (Cue et al., 2019;

Hauser et al., 2010; Holcomb, 2010), we need more DeafBlind research-ers to challenge sighted Deaf stances on visual and tactile sign language. Another example of a gap in Deaf studies that needs emic researchers—In-digenous Deaf people. DeafCrit has made much of the intrinsic audism and linguicism in hearing people and their societies in America and elsewhere. But what are the attitudes towards signed languages and multilingualism in a group of people who have historically valued knowing more than one language, as well as having signed languages as part of the heritage for both hearing and Deaf members alike? Indigenous Deaf people would be able to shed more light on whether hearingness automatically carries within it the seed of audism and linguicism, contributing to our understanding of the relationship between hearingness and audism, something that DeafCrit espouses to explore.

Instability is currently inherent in the Deaf community: instability of language, ability, and identity. All Deaf people are compared in terms of proximity of ability, to hearing people, especially the hearing normate, and to other Deaf people, especially the Deaf normate. Those who are in close proximity of the normates in both worlds are not fully aware of the exis-tence of these normates; however, those who are far from these normates are keenly conscious of the normates' existence. As Memmi (1991) and Freire (2013) put it, the oppressed forever tries to transform into the op-pressor but will never achieve this assimilation in a system of colonization.

## NEXT STEPS

This chapter, like the series in which it is published, begins with asking, "Who decides?" Through the analysis of first-wave DeafCrit, and the argu-ment towards PMA, we have laid out the case for a multiple-identity lens as a critical tenet worthy of merit in order to better address the issues of aud-ism, colonialism, power of proximity, dis/ability, and ultimately that of the White, Deaf normate. With the formation of PMA, the resounding answer to the question of "Who decides?" is that "We, members of the Deaf com-munities, decide." We decide in this new era of collective consciousness in which we explore multiplicity through PMA and recognize that the trauma of our history through colonization and audism have allowed White Deaf elites to dictate the status quo of a singular Deaf community. Through emic perspectives of intersectionality, the recognition of and the continuous exploration of multiple epistemologies, we continue to strive for a more organic and inclusive approach to understanding our collective conscious-ness, while simultaneously recognizing the various intersections that incor-porate multiple communities under the umbrella of the Deaf community.

Allowing Deaf people who do not fit the current normate in the Deaf community will require some sacrifice. As already requested, hearing people need to step aside, recognizing that they do not have the full set of tools needed to teach and manage the affairs of the Deaf community. This same request will need to be asked of the White abled Deaf leaders. From the demographics cited earlier, there is no question that being White and abled is a huge boon for Deaf leadership. As our hearing allies have done, White and abled Deaf leaders will need to recognize their duty to make room for DeafBlind, DeafDisabled, Deaf LGBTQ, and BIPOC Deaf leaders. Simms et al. (2008) observed something they call "apartheid" and an "intellectual oppression" in academia, a phenomenon in which Deaf people from minority populations face steeper challenges navigating through higher education and eventually graduating with advanced degrees and obtaining jobs in their chosen professions. As noted earlier, Simms et al. (2008) outlined the corralling effect of Deaf education, which inevitably leads to higher failure rates in academics. Opportunities are closed off to these students, echoing the concerns of researchers observing minorities in the workplace (Growe & Montgomery, 1999; Jean-Marie, 2013). Just as White, abled Deaf individuals have succeeded as we have shown through the analysis of first-wave DeafCrit, so too must we serve as allies to marginalized members of the Deaf communities.

The watershed moment of DPN opened up opportunities for the majority within the Deaf community. The floodgates need to be opened again to allow the same opportunities for the Othered members of the Deaf community. This has to be done with deliberate intent by those who make decisions that impact the lives of all Deaf people across the United States, from the Deaf leaders already given positions of power, to the Deaf who *also* are BIPOC, to the DeafBlind, the DeafDisabled, and Deaf LGBTQ. We push for more access to academic discourse, bringing Othered Deaf people in from the margins. As we can see in our shift from first-wave DeafCrit to PMA, our critical analysis based on our scholarly work as emic researchers takes root in the tradition of the standpoint theory (Hekman, 1997), in which light is cast towards normative practices from those who are most marginalized. When we look from the outside in, we are able to reveal what was once concealed: those power structures and hierarchies which hold power over other bodies, casting some as the "decider" and the rest as subjugates. In this new landscape of emic questioning, we are excited at the prospect of marginalized hands entering the field of academic discourse, as a great many unknowns remain yet to be discovered, so the Deaf communities can continue to, and perpetually decide for ourselves.

## NOTE

1. In this chapter, the use of D/deaf shifts with intent. Deaf, when it appears capitalized, refers to individuals who identify as culturally Deaf in the context of the United States and communicate in American Sign Language (ASL). The lowercase deaf refers to individuals who do not identify as culturally deaf.

## REFERENCES

Americans With Disabilities Act of 1990, 42 U.S.C. § 1201 et seq. (1990). https://www.ada.gov

Andrews, J. F., & Jordan, D. L. (1993). Minority and minority-deaf professional: How many and where are they? *American Annals of the Deaf*, 138(5), 388–396. https://doi.org/10.1353/aad.2012.0340

Andrews, J. F., Leigh, I. W., & Weiner, M. T. (2004). *Deaf people: Evolving perspectives from psychology, education and sociology*. Pearson.

Annamma, S. A., Connor, D. J., & Ferri, B. A. (2016a). Introduction: A truncated genealogy of DisCrit. In D. J. Connor, B. A. Ferri, & S. A. Annamma (Eds), *Disability studies and critical race theory in education* (pp. 1–32). Teachers College Press.

Annamma, S. A., Connor, D. J., & Ferri, B. A. (2016b). Dis/ability critical race studies (DisCrit): Theorizing at the intersections of race and dis/ability. In D. J. Connor, B. A. Ferri, & S. A. Annamma (Eds.), *DisCrit: Disability studies and critical race theory in education* (pp. 9–32). Teachers College Press.

Bauman, H. L. (2004). Audism: Exploring the metaphysics of oppression. *Journal of deaf studies and deaf education*, 9(2), 239–246. https://doi.org/10.1093/deafed/enh025

Baynton, D. C. (1996). *Forbidden signs: American culture and the campaign against sign language*. University of Chicago Press.

Bechter, F. (2008). The deaf convert culture and its lessons for deaf theory. In H. L. Bauman (Ed.), *Open your eyes: Deaf studies talking* (pp. 60–79). University of Minnesota Press.

Bell, C. M. (2011). Introduction. In C. M. Bell (Ed.), *Blackness and disability: Critical examinations and cultural interventions* (pp. 1–7). Michigan State University Press.

Bryan, A., & Emery, S. (2014). The case for deaf legal theory through the lens of deaf gain. In H. D. L. Bauman & J. J. Murray (Eds.), *Deaf gain: Raising the stakes for human diversity* (pp. 37–61). University of Minnesota Press.

Burch, S. (2002). *Signs of resistance: American Deaf cultural history, 1900 to World War I*. New York University Press.

Cawthon, S. W., Johnson, P. M., Garberoglio, C. L., & Schoffstall, S. J. (2016). Role models as facilitators of social capital for deaf individuals: A research synthesis. *American Annals of the Deaf*, 161(2), 115–127. https://doi.org/10.1353/aad.2016.0021

Christiansen, J. B., & Barnartt, S. N. (2003). *Deaf president now!: The 1988 revolution at Gallaudet University*. Gallaudet University Press.

Crenshaw, K. (1989). Demarginalizing the intersection of race and sex: A Black feminist critique of antidiscrimination doctrine, feminist theory and antiracist politics. *University of Chicago Legal Forum, 1989*(1), 139–167.

Crenshaw, K. W. (2017). *On intersectionality: Essential writings.* The New Press.

Cross, W. E., Jr. (1995). The psychology of nigrescence: Revising the Cross model. In J. G. Ponterotto, J. M. Casas, L. A. Suzuki, & C. M. Alexander (Eds.), *Handbook of multicultural counseling* (pp. 93–122). SAGE Publications.

Cue, K. R. (2020). Hegemonic deaf and hearing cultures in the United States: A deaf ecological systems perspective (Order No. 27993623). ProQuest Dissertations & Theses Global.

Cue, K. R., Pudans-Smith, K. K., Wolsey, J.-L. A., Wright, S. J., & Clark, M. D. (2019). The odyssey of deaf epistemology: A search for meaning-making. *American Annals of the Deaf, 164*(3), 395–422. https://doi.org/10.1353/aad.2019.0017

Czubek, T., & Snoddon, K. (2016). Bilingualism, philosophy and models of. In G. Gertz & P. Boudreault (Eds.), *The sage deaf studies encyclopedia* (pp. 80–82). SAGE Publications. https://www.doi.org/10.4135/9781483346489.n28

D'Annunzio, F. (2020, December 16). Frisco ISD revising practices after TEA finding of disproportionate discipline among Black students, other groups. *Community Impact Newspaper.* https://communityimpact.com/dallas-fort-worth/frisco/education/2020/12/15/after-a-tea-finding-of-disproportionate-discipline-among-black-students-frisco-isd-revises-policies/

Davis, L. J. (1995). *Enforcing normalcy: Disability, deafness, and the body.* Verso.

DeGraffenreid v. GENERAL MOTORS ASSEMBLY DIV., ETC., 413 F. Supp. 142 (E.D. Mo. 1976). https://law.justia.com/cases/federal/district-courts/FSupp/413/142/1660699/

Dewey, J. (2016). Strathie v. department of transportation. In G. Gertz & P. Boudreault (Eds.), *The SAGE deaf studies encyclopedia* (pp. 929–930). SAGE Publications.

Eckert, R. C., & Rowley, A. J. (2013). Audism: A theory and practice of audiocentric privilege. *Humanity & Society, 37*(2), 101–130. https://doi.org/10.1177/0160597613481731

Edwards, R. A. (2012). *Words made flesh: Nineteenth-century deaf education and the growth of deaf culture.* NYU Press.

Edwards, T. (2014). From compensation to integration: Effects of the pro-tactile movement on the sublexical structure of Tactile American Sign Language. *Journal of Pragmatics, 69,* 22–41. https://doi.org/10.1016/j.pragma.2014.05.005

Endrew F. v. Douglas County School District RE–1, 580 U.S. ___ (2017). https://supreme.justia.com/cases/federal/us/580/15-827/

Foucault, M. (2004). Discipline and Punish. In J. Rivkin & M. Ryan (Eds.). *Literary theory: An anthology* (2nd ed., pp. 549–566). Blackwell.

Freire, P. (2013). *Pedagogy of the oppressed* (M. B. Ramos, Trans.). Bloomsbury Publishing USA. (Original work published 1970).

Gallaudet. (2020a). *Historical timeline.* https://www.gallaudet.edu/about/history-and-traditions/historical-timeline

Gallaudet. (2020b). *History behind DPN.* https://www.gallaudet.edu/about/history-and-traditions/deaf-president-now/the-issues/history-behind-dpn

Garberoglio, C. L., Palmer, J. L., Cawthon, S. W., & Sales, A. (2019). *Deaf people and educational attainment in the United States: 2019.* National Deaf Center on Postsecondary Outcomes. https://www.nationaldeafcenter.org/sites/default/files/Deaf%20People%20and%20Educational%20Attainment%20in%20the%20United%20States_%202019.pdf

García-Fernández, C. (2020). Intersectionality and autoethnography: DeafBlind, DeafDisabled, Deaf and Hard of Hearing-Latinx children are the future. *Journal Committed to Social Change on Race and Ethnicity, 6*(1), 41–67. https://doi.org/10.15763/issn.2642-2387.2020.6.1.40-67

Gertz, E. N. (2003). *Dysconscious audism and critical Deaf studies: Deaf crit's analysis of unconscious internalization of hegemony within the Deaf community* [Unpublished doctoral dissertation]. University of California Los Angeles, CA.

Gertz, E. N. (2008). *Dysconscious audism: A theoretical proposition.* In H. L. Bauman (Ed.), *Open your eyes: Deaf studies talking* (pp. 219–234). University of Minnesota Press.

Growe, R., & Montgomery, P. (1999). Women and the leadership paradigm: Bridging the gender gap. *National Forum of Educational Administration and Supervision Journal, 1E*(4), 38–46.

Hall, W. C. (2017). What you don't know can hurt you: The risk of language deprivation by impairing sign language development in deaf children. *Maternal and child health journal, 21*(5), 961–965. https://doi.org/10.1007/s10995-017-2287-y

Hall, W. C., Levin, L. L., & Anderson, M. L. (2017). Language deprivation syndrome: A possible neurodevelopmental disorder with sociocultural origins. *Social Psychiatry and Psychiatric Epidemiology, 52*(6), 761–776. https://doi.org/10.1007/s00127-017-1351-7

Hauser, P. C., O'Hearn, A., McKee, M., Steider, A., & Thew, D. (2010). Deaf epistemology: Deafhood and deafness. *American Annals of the Deaf, 154*(5), 486–492. https://doi.org/10.1353/aad.0.0120

Hekman, S. (1997). Truth and method: Feminist standpoint theory revisited. *Signs: Journal of Women in Culture and Society, 22*(2), 341–365.

Holcomb, T. K. (2010). Deaf epistemology: The deaf way of knowing. *American Annals of the Deaf, 154*(5), 471–478. https://doi.org/10.1353/aad.0.0116

Humphries, T. (1977). *Communicating across cultures (deaf/hearing) and language learning* [Unpublished doctoral dissertation]. Union Graduate School, The Union Institute and Universities.

Humphries, T. (2013). Schooling in American Sign Language: A paradigm shift from a deficit model to a bilingual model in Deaf education . *Berkeley Review of Education, 4*(1), 7–33. https://doi.org/10.5070/B84110031

Humphries, T., Kushalnagar, P., Mathur, G., Napoli, D. J., Padden, C., Rathmann, C., & Smith, S. (2012). Language acquisition for deaf children: Reducing the harms of zero tolerance to the use of alternative approaches. *Harm Reduction Journal, 9*(16), 1–9. https://doi.org/10.1186/1477-7517-9-16

Humphries, T., Kushalnagar, P., Mathur, G., Napoli, D. J., Padden, C., Rathmann, C., & Smith, S. (2017). Discourses of prejudice in the professions: The case of sign languages. *Journal of Medical Ethics, 43*(9), 648–652. https://doi.org/10.1136/medethics-2015-103242

Individuals With Disabilities Education Act. Public Law 105-17 U.S.C. § 1400 et seq. (1990). https://sites.ed.gov/idea/e

Jean-Marie, G. (2013). The subtlety of age, gender, and race barriers: A case study of early career African American female principals. *Journal of School Leadership, 23*(4), 615–639.

Ladd, P. (2003). *Understanding Deaf culture: In search of Deafhood.* Multilingual Matters.

Lane, H. (1999). *The mask of benevolence* (2nd ed.). DawnSign Press.

Lawyer, G. (2018). *Removing the colonizer's coat in Deaf education: Exploring the curriculum of colonization and the field of Deaf education* [Unpublished doctoral dissertation]. University of Tennessee-Knoxville, Knoxville, TN.

Leagle. (n.d.a). *Endrew F. v. Douglas County School District RE-1: No. 15-827.* https://www.leagle.com/decision/insco20170322f98

Leagle. (n.d.b). *Endrew F. ex rel. Joseph F. v. Douglas County School District RE 1: Civil action no. 12-cv-02620-LTB.* https://www.leagle.com/decision/infdco2017 1117b66

Leagle. (n.d.c). *McCray v. City of Dothan.* https://www.leagle.com/decision/200114 29169fsupp2d126011303

Lewis, T. L. (2020, August 17). *Why I don't use "anti-Black ableism" (& language longings).* https://www.talilalewis.com/blog/why-i-dont-use-anti-black-ableism

Lynn, M. A., Butcher, E., Cuculick, J. A., Barnett, S., Martina, C. A., Smith, S. R., Pollard, R. Q., Jr., & Simpson-Haidaris, P. J. (2020). A review of mentoring deaf and hard-of-hearing scholars. *Mentoring & Tutoring: Partnership in Learning.* https://doi.org/10.1080/13611267.2020.1749350

MacSuga-Gage, A. S., Gage, N. A., Katsiyannis, A., Hirsch, S. E., & Kisner, H. (2020). Disproportionate corporal punishment of students with disabilities and Black and Hispanic students. *Journal of Disability Policy Studies, 32*(3). https://doi.org/10.1177/1044207320949960

McCaskill, C. (2010). *Deaf culture and race* [presentation]. Gallaudet University NCORE. Washington, DC.

McCaskill, C., Lucas, C., Bayley, R., & Hill, J. (2011). *The hidden treasure of Black ASL: Its history and structure.* Gallaudet University Press.

McRuer, R. (2005). Crip eye for the normate guy: Queer theory and the disciplining of disability studies. *PMLA, 120*(2), 586–592. https://www.jstor.org/stable/25486189

Memmi, A. (1991). *The colonizer and the colonized* (H. Greenfeld, Trans.). Beacon Press. (Original work published 1965)

Mitchell, R. E., & Karchmer, M. A. (2004). Chasing the mythical ten percent: Parental hearing status of deaf and hard of hearing students in the United States. *Sign Language Studies, 4*(2), 138–163. https://doi.org/10.1353/sls.2004.0005

Moges, R. T. (2020). "From White Deaf people's adversity to Black Deaf gain": A proposal for a new lens of Black Deaf educational history. *Journal Committed to Social Change on Race and Ethnicity, 6*(1) 69–99. https://doi.org/10.15763/issn.2642-2387.2020.6.1.68-99

Moores, D. F. (2010). Partners in progress: The 21st International Congress on Education of the Deaf and the Repudiation of the 1880 Congress of Milan. *American Annals of the Deaf, 155*(3), 309–310. https://doi.org/10.1353/aad.2010.0016

Niyongabo, I. (2020, June 16). *NBDA open letter to Gallaudet University Board of Trustees, June 2020*. National Black Deaf Advocates. https://www.nbda.org/news/nbda-open-letter-to-gallaudet-university-board-of-trustees-june-2020

Nover, S., & Andrews, J. (1998). *Critical pedagogy in Deaf education: Bilingual methodology and staff development* (USDLC Star Schools Project Report 1). New Mexico School for the Deaf.

Office of Special Education Programs. (n.d.). *OSEP Fast Facts: Black or African American Children with Disabilities*. IDEA. https://sites.ed.gov/idea/osep-fast-facts-black-or-african-american-children-with-disabilities-20/

Peguero, A., & Shekarkhar, Z. (2011). Latino/a student misbehavior and school punishment. *Hispanic Journal of Behavioral Sciences, 33*(1), 54–70. https://doi.org/10.1177/0739986310388021

Player, D. A. (2020, May 27). *Dear White deaf people*. https://Whitedeafprivilege.wordpress.com/2020/05/27/dear-White-deaf-people/

Prinz, P., & Strong, M. (1998). ASL proficiency and English literacy within a bilingual deaf education model of instruction. *Topics in Language Disorders, 18*(4), 47–60. https://doi.org/10.1097/00011363-199808000-00006

Reagan, T. (2011). Ideological barriers to American Sign Language: Unpacking linguistic resistance. *Sign Language Studies, 11*(4), 606–636. https://doi.org/10.1353/sls.2011.0006

Schley, S. (2016). Hendrick Hudson Board of Education v. Rowley. In G. Gertz & P. Boudreault (Eds.), *The SAGE deaf studies encyclopedia* (pp. 471–472). SAGE Publications.

Section 504 of the Rehabilitation Act of 1973, 29 U.S.C. § 794 (1973). https://www.hhs.gov/civil-rights/for-individuals/disability/laws-guidance/index.html

Seldon, S. (1999). *Inheriting shame: The story of eugenics and racism in America*. Teachers College Press.

Sherry, M. (2004). "Overlaps and contradictions between queer theory and disability studies." *Disability & Society, 19*(7), 769–783. https://doi.org/10.1080/0968759042000284231

Simms, L., Rusher, M., Andrews, J. F., & Coryell, J. (2008). Apartheid in Deaf education: Examining workforce diversity. *American Annals of the Deaf, 153*(4), 384–395. https://doi.org/10.1353/aad.0.0060

Simms, L., & Thumann, H. (2007). In search of a new, linguistically and culturally sensitive paradigm in Deaf education. *American Annals of the Deaf, 152*(3), 302–311. https://doi.org/10.1353/aad.2007.0031

Simson, D. (2014). Exclusion, punishment, racism and our schools: A critical race theory perspective on school discipline. *University of California Los Angeles Law Review, 61*(2), 506–563. https://ssrn.com/abstract=2129117

Skutnabb-Kangas, T. (2016). Linguicism. In G. Gertz & P. Boudreault (Eds.), *The SAGE deaf studies encyclopedia* (pp. 583–586). SAGE Publications. https://www.doi.org/10.4135/9781483346489.n188

Strathie v. Department of Transp., Com. of Pa., 547 F. Supp. 1367 (E.D. Pa. 1982). https://law.justia.com/cases/federal/district-courts/FSupp/547/1367/1478845/

Thompson, V. (2018, March 16). *The overlooked history of Black disabled people.* Rewire News Group. https://rewirenewsgroup.com/article/2018/03/16/overlooked -history-black-disabled-people/

U.S. Reports: Hendrick Hudson Dist. Bd. of Ed. v. Rowley, 458 U.S. 176 (1982). https://www.loc.gov/item/usrep458176/

Van Cleve, J. V., & Crouch, B. A. (1989). *A place of their own: Creating the deaf community in America.* Gallaudet University Press.

Vehmas, S., & Watson, N. (2016). Exploring normativity in disability studies. *Disability & Society, 31*(1), 1–16. https://doi.org/10.1080/09687599.2015.1120657

Wilbur, R. B. (2000). The use of ASL to support the development of English and literacy. *Journal of Deaf Studies and Deaf Education, 5*(1), 81–104. https://doi .org/10.1093/deafed/5.1.81

Winefield, R. (1987). *Never the twain shall meet.* Gallaudet University Press.

Wright, S. J. (2016). Diversity: Deaf studies and disability. In G. Gertz & P. Boudreault (Eds.), *The SAGE deaf studies encyclopedia* (pp. 305–390). SAGE Publications.

Wright, S. J. (2017). *From Deaf to Deaf-Blind: A phenomenological study of the lived experiences of Deaf-Blind individuals in the deep south* (Order No. 10654904) [Doctoral dissertation, Gallaudet University]. ProQuest Dissertations and Theses Global.

Wright, S. J. (2020). Deafnormativity: Who belongs in deaf culture? *Disability & Society, 36*(8), 1221–1239. https://doi.org/10.1080/09687599.2020.1787818

CHAPTER 6

# SHEDDING LIGHT ON DISABILITY AND RACE IN A NORTH AMERICAN LINGUISTIC MINORITY CONTEXT

## A DisCrit Analysis of Special Education in Quebec

**Tya Collins**
*Université de Montréal*

**Corina Borri-Anadon**
*Université du Québec à Trois-Rivières*

**Marie-Odile Magnan**
*Université de Montréal*

Educational equity for all students is a major preoccupation for scholars and government bodies at local, national, and global levels. In spite of international movements to ensure universal access and equal opportunities for all (United Nations Educational, Scientific, and Cultural Organization [UNESCO], 2015), various marginalized groups continue to face disturbing school experiences and outcomes. In addition to economic, environmental, and geographical factors, many children and youth are regularly restricted or denied access to equal chances in education (Hébert & Abdi, 2013). In particular, students who are designated disabled or racialized[1] are at increased vulnerability to socio-academic challenges and injustices. Despite the social denouncement of disability perceived as tragedy (Oliver & Barnes, 2012) and the scientific refutation of race as a biological phenomenon, predominant societal views remain largely grounded in historical ableism and racism (Leonardo, 2013). The prevalence of these issues, and more specifically, the disproportionate representation of racialized youth in special education as an international phenomenon (Cooc & Kiru, 2018; Waitoller et al., 2010), implies wider-scale systemic and structural problems that are crucial to investigate.

In Quebec, students designated with special needs experience academic lag, lower success rates (Ministère de l'Éducation [MEQ], 1999), and persistently higher dropout rates (Ministère de l'éducation et de l'enseignement supérieur [MEES], 2017; MEQ, 2003). Congruent with international findings, Indigenous and other racialized groups are disproportionately represented among this population (Regroupement des centres d'amitié autochtones du Québec [RCAAQ], 2020). However, unlike the sociopolitical context of the United States where "disability has been [relatively] excluded from discussions concerning unequal and discriminatory treatment" (Liasidou, 2014, p. 724), in Quebecois educational research, policy, and administration, both disability designation and racialization tend to be overshadowed by issues related to linguistic and cultural integration. The section that ensues will bring to light some historical underpinnings of this particularity, followed by the theoretical anchors that address this analytical gap. Next, an overall portrait of students at the intersections of disability and race will be presented, and finally, the implications for school policy, governance, and leadership will be discussed.

## HISTORICAL OVERVIEW OF QUÉBEC'S SOCIOPOLITICAL CONTEXT: FROM *"LES N\*GRES BLANCS"* TO A RACELESS SOCIETY

Indigenous groups have lived in the territory known in today's Western terms as Quebec for thousands of years. They formed complex political, economic, cultural, social, and educational systems long before their first contact with groups non-Indigenous to the land, such as the first settlers from France (Oliver, 2010). While these French newcomers colonized the Indigenous through violent and genocidal means, these settlers were in turn conquered by their British co-colonizers in 1763. These events set the stage for political upset and contention between these two "founding nations" that still persist today.

Two centuries of Anglo rule and domination over the Indigenous land occupants and French settlers followed until the 1960s, which marked the beginning of the rise of French nationalism. French settlers would distance themselves from "French Canadian" identity and assert themselves as *Quebecois* (Potvin, 2010). While the indigenous communities remained marginalized both at provincial[2] and federal levels, the Quebecois took their place as the demographic, linguistic, and sociological majority, and established their political power and influence over their own development and governance.

Their unique location as a majority at a provincial level, but as a linguistic minority on a national level has consequences for minoritized groups,[3] most notably (though not exclusively) from immigrant backgrounds. Since the 1970s their integration and education has been a cause for concern for the Quebecois partly due to the overall omnipresence of the English language in the economic and communication domains and potent Anglo-Canadian and American influences in cultural spheres (Thésée & Carr, 2016a). Before 1977, despite political efforts, new immigrants were largely integrated into Quebec society through English-speaking institutions (Gagné & Chamberland, 1999). To counter this current, while ensuring the sustainability of the French language, the Quebec government adopted the Charter of the French Language (Bill 101), delineating French as the one and only official language of Quebec. This legislation rendered French-language instruction mandatory by law for the public schooling of new immigrants, therefore ensuring a French cultural and linguistic based integration process. Similarly, an intercultural model was adopted which established a "moral contract" between immigrants and the host society, made up of rights and duties. It promoted cultural assimilation through integration in the French-speaking majority culture, while recognizing intercultural exchange and making "reasonable accommodations" (Potvin, 2010; Satzewich & Liodakis, 2013). In addition, it established a sort of distinction from the multicultural approach to diversity adopted by the rest of Canada. In fact, Canadian multiculturalism provoked a sense of indignation among certain Quebecois as its aim was perceived as an attempt to obscure Quebec's national reality by relegating Francophones to the status of ethnic minority like "any other group" (McRoberts, 1997, p. 135).

Hence, while Quebec formally welcomes ethnic, cultural, and linguistic diversity in its institutions, it continues to perceive a sense of insecurity and injustice within Canada (Thésée & Carr, 2016a). Antithetically, its peripheralized settler colonial history marked by racism, slavery, and genocide bears witness to the marginalization of Indigenous and racialized groups, while obscuring racial hierarchies through dominant national discourses surrounding language, culture, integration, and acculturation (Austin, 2010; Haque & Patrick, 2015). Interestingly, the Quebecois, who once (falsely) equated their own struggles for liberation and social justice to those of African Americans, suggesting that they occupied the social position of "*les n\*gres blancs d'Amérique*"[1] (Austin, 2010; Vallières, 1968), have now shifted to a dominant narrative that denies the existence of race and inevitably, the existence of racism. Racism has thus become "a thing of the past," while explanations for problematic social relationships stemming from unassimilable cultural differences are preferred by the French-speaking, White majority group (Howard, 2020).

Consequently, while concepts surrounding race and racism have been focal points in educational research in other parts of Canada and the United States (Brathwaite, 2010; Dei, 1996; Ladson-Billings & Tate, 1995; Leonardo, 2013), they have been by and large invisibilized in Quebec, in favor of an analysis based on culture (Thésée & Carr, 2016b). We argue that positioning the educational experiences of racialized youth in an arena overwhelmingly surrounding culture and integration has created an overemphasis on sociodemographic factors in explaining the educational trajectories of nonsettler groups. As a result, sociopolitical and historical dimensions related to social power relations, race, ability, racism, and ableism have been eclipsed. It is from this vantage point that we suggest the importance and utility of mobilizing a disability critical race studies (DisCrit) analysis in the educational context of Quebec.

## DISABILITY CRITICAL RACE STUDIES IN EDUCATION

DisCrit addresses the interrelationship of disability and race, how they are socially constructed, and the associated consequences for people who are simultaneously designated disabled and racialized (Annamma et al., 2013). It is a branch of critical race theory that grew out of the emanating need to make space for disability in intersectional analysis. Thus, while disability and race are foregrounded in DisCrit, "classic" dimensions of identity such as gender, class, immigration status, and so forth also maintain a sound bearing within the framework. The analytical focus is placed on the contextual dimensions of the dualities between ability and disability, Whiteness and non-Whiteness, and normalcy and abnormalcy. DisCrit considers how the social construction of these dimensions happens concurrently, how they come to be defined as natural deviants, and how they work in tandem to maintain systems of oppression (Adams & Erevelles, 2016).

Therefore, DisCrit's dual analysis of disability and race acknowledges how these dimensions lead to a process of othering and minoritizing individuals and groups. As such, biological explanations of both disability and race are rejected, while foregrounding the oppressive consequences of these same identifiers in order to reveal how ableism and racism operate as normalizing processes in society. DisCrit has been used in a variety of ways to investigate the operation of macro- and micro-level issues of racism and ableism. For example, Collins (2016) analyzed how 17-year-old Trayvon Martin was positioned as dangerous, deviant, and criminal, during legal proceedings in Florida, resulting in a non-guilty verdict for the White man who fatally shot him; Fenton (2016) investigated how norms emanating from eugenics and pseudoscience are reproduced and maintained by amalgamating race and disability with criminality; and Kozleski (2016) examined how data structures reify the social construction of difference.

In education, DisCrit theorizes how the above-mentioned dualities are embedded into institutional procedures and discourses, and how students who are subjected to these processes are affected in their everyday lives (Annamma et al., 2013). Specifically, boundaries of normalcy are investigated in terms of how they are constructed, who is involved, how they change over time, and their impact on students, systems, and society (Annamma et al., 2013). Furthermore, a critique of historical and contemporary factions is advanced, namely regarding the medical model of disabilities, the within-child deficit view, and the pathologization and criminalization of racialized youth (Adams & Erevelles, 2016). With regard to special education, DisCrit has been deployed, for example, to understand the experiences of African American students (Banks, 2017) and Black middle-class families in Britain (Gillborn et al., 2016) within placement processes, as well as to examine to what extent racialized students leave special education programs for reintegration into "regular" settings (Garcia, 2017). Given that special education disproportionality is a particularly salient issue in terms of the educational success of racialized youth, an overview of the research concerning this topic will be presented from a DisCrit perspective in the next section, followed by a presentation of the specific case of Quebec.

## THE DISPROPORTIONATE REPRESENTATION OF RACIALIZED STUDENTS IN SPECIAL EDUCATION

Disproportionality in special education involves identification rates of specific social groups that are proportionally higher or lower than expected based on their overall representation in the student body (Gabel et al., 2009). It is a "complex phenomenon that provides the opportunity to examine educational inequities for particular groups of students that are shaped by macro and micro forces" (Waitoller et al., 2010, p. 29), which can take the form of underrepresentation or overrepresentation. Underrepresentation occurs when specific social groups receive special educational services at a notably inferior proportion than their representation in the overall school population. It becomes a concern when a lack of access to special education services for students, who may legitimately require them, is observed. Scholars suggest sociocultural factors leading to misunderstanding student needs and structural barriers (ineffective instruction, insufficient resources) as possible explanations for the underrepresentation of racialized groups (Cooc & Kiru, 2018; Strand et al., 2006). On the other hand, overrepresentation refers to the representation of certain social groups in special education, in excess of their proportional enrollment in the general school population. Racialized groups tend to be simultaneously under and overrepresented: They are underrepresented in low incidence[5] categories (Brown & Parekh, 2010; Sullivan & Bal, 2013) and overrepresented in high incidence categories such as behavioral disorders, intellectual impairments, and emotional disturbance (Shifrer et al., 2011; Wagner et al., 2005). Despite the lack of consensus among scholars regarding the causes of special education overrepresentation, a number of plausible explanations have been advanced pertaining to socioeconomic factors (Shifrer et al., 2011) and problematic institutional processes and practices (Ahram et al., 2011; Harry & Klingner, 2014). Both raise questions regarding unequal social power relations.

Most researchers across the globe who have investigated special education disproportionality have employed documentary analysis methods to compare trends at various levels of operation (comparisons by country, region, school board, district, etc.). Findings reveal an overrepresentation in special education of the following groups by geographical region:

- Serbian, Italian, and Portuguese students in Germany (Gabel et al., 2009);
- Māori students in New Zealand (Gabel et al., 2009);
- Indigenous students in Australia (Graham, 2012);
- Pakistani, Bangladeshi, and Black-Caribbean students in England (Strand & Lindsay, 2009); and
- Romani students in the Czech Republic and Sweden (Berhanu, 2008; Cashman, 2016).

In the United States, the special education disproportionality debate has been ongoing ever since developmental disability educator Lloyd Dunn raised the flag in 1968. He argued that special education labeling, and placement in segregated settings of disadvantaged and "minority" youth, was unjustifiable (Dunn, 1968). Over 50 years later, much of disproportionality research is intended to contribute to the debate on whether it in fact exists for racially and ethnically minoritized groups, especially when accounting for individual and contextual sociodemographic factors. Certain researchers confirm overrepresentation (Shifrer et al., 2011; Sullivan & Bal, 2013), while others focus on underrepresentation (Hibel et al., 2010; Morgan et al., 2015).

Though not documented as extensively as in the United States, Canadian research also confirms the overrepresentation of racialized groups in special education, specifically for Indigenous and Black students. In British Columbia, Indigenous students are overrepresented in all special education categories, except the *gifted* category (Mattson & Caffrey, 2001). In Ontario, while the overall proportion of Black students in the general student population is 14%, descriptive analyses among one of the largest school boards in the province ($N = 259,958$) reveal that they represent 36% of students with behavioral problems; 33% of those with mild intellectual disabilities; 30% of those with developmental disabilities; and 24% of students with language impairments (Brown & Parekh, 2010).

Recalling Quebec's raceless sociopolitical stance, there is little to no provincial race-based data available in special education, especially concerning Indigenous youth. Framed from an approach based on culture, Quebec confirms the special education overrepresentation of certain minoritized groups in its public education system according to their regions of origin as immigrants. In a study involving a high school cohort between 1998–2000, the higher special education identification rates of three groups were revealed: those from Central and South America (30.4%), South Asia (32.1%), as well as the Caribbean and sub-Saharan Africa (37.4%) (McAndrew, Ledent, & Murdoch, 2011). These immigrant groups, which can also be considered racialized groups, receive special education designations at a rate that is at least 10% higher than that of the general population (McAndrew, Balde, et al., 2015). Among these subgroups, it was determined that Black students have the most concerning portrait (those from the Caribbean and sub-Saharan Africa). In fact, researchers classify first-generation[6] immigrant, Creole-speaking boys from disadvantaged neighborhoods, designated as having a disability as the most "at-risk" student group for high school non-completion in Quebec (McAndrew, Balde, et al., 2015).

From a DisCrit perspective, the overrepresentation of racialized students in special education is an indicator of how social constructions of race and disability manifest through labeling when student learning and behavior do not coincide with normalized notions stemming from the White middle class. Mendoza et al. (2016) posited that such reductive notions of learning not only disregard student funds of knowledge (knowledge gained from family, peer groups, and cultural backgrounds over time) and critical thinking, but can also produce an overreliance on social norms at the genesis of special education placement. In fact, Thomas and Loxley (2007), suggest that special education has become the de facto intervention for students whom teachers find difficult to teach. However, because special education is heavily anchored in settler colonialism, it is accepted as a legitimate intervention based on "the enduring belief that impairment and disability are empirical facts" (Reid & Knight, 2006, p. 19). There is a contradiction between the goals of special education and the medical model on which it is founded. While the purpose of special education is to provide equal opportunities for all, its operations are grounded not only in a deficit perspective, which focuses on fixing individuals to adapt and assimilate to dominant cultural norms, but also on ideologies that reproduce social inequalities in schools such as meritocracy and educational opportunity. These ideologies are particularly salient in special education processes, which operate as cryptic forces of oppression masked through seemingly well-intended practices and policies to "help" those in need. In the next sections, the special education implications for racialized youth in Quebec will be discussed, guided by the tenets of DisCrit.

## A DISCRIT ANALYSIS OF QUEBECOIS SPECIAL EDUCATION

As mentioned above, Quebec's unique sociopolitical and linguistic position in North America incites a finer investigation of how disability and race operate in educational contexts. In order to achieve this, three DisCrit tenets will be used as they appear in the seminal text entitled *Dis/ability Critical Race Studies (DisCrit): Theorizing at the Intersections of Race and Dis/Ability* authored by Annamma et al. (2013, p. 11): (a) "DisCrit considers legal and historical aspects of dis/ability and race and how both have been used separately and together to deny the rights of some citizens" (Tenet 5); (b) "DisCrit values multidimensional identities and troubles singular notions of identity such as race or dis/ability or class or gender or sexuality, and so on" (Tenet 2); and (c) "DisCrit focuses on ways that the forces of racism and ableism circulate interdependently, often in neutralized and invisible ways, to uphold notions of normalcy" (Tenet 1).

### The Legal and Historical Use of Race and Disability to Deny Some Citizens Their Rights (Tenet 5)

A primary objective of DisCrit is to smoke out hidden forms of domination and oppression in day-to-day life with recognition of how the rights of disabled and racialized people have been denied and violated throughout history, and how the law has operated in favor of such injustices. The history of slavery in Quebec and Canada has been largely the object of concealment (Cooper, 2007) and tends to be mostly associated to its perceived racist American neighbors to the south. However, despite Quebec's general posture of slavery-denial or downplay, it is documented that over a 200-year period, Indigenous people and Africans abducted by colonial human traffickers were subjected to forced unpaid labor in oppressive, humiliating, and inhumane conditions (Cooper 2007; Maynard, 2017).

A relatively less disputed example of the mass violation of human rights in Canadian history lies in the institution of residential schools intended to assimilate Indigenous children into settler colonial culture. For over a century since the early 1830s, more than 150,000 Indigenous children were forcibly uprooted from their families and communities to be placed in educational institutions run by religious authorities in collaboration with settler colonial governments, where they were prevented from speaking their languages and living according to their culture (Milloy, 2017). The survivors of these institutions, in large numbers, bear witness to enduring physical, emotional, sexual, psychological, and spiritual abuse. The aftermath of these horrors continues to afflict these communities through various forms of intergenerational trauma (Truth and Reconciliation Commission of Canada [TRCC], 2015). Approximately 11 of these schools are recorded to have been in operation in Quebec, although similar unofficial endeavors had been undertaken since 1608 (TRCC, 2015). An analysis of education in Quebec is thus incomplete and misleading when we fail to recognize the settler colonial principles in which it is grounded, and how it has propagated the inferiority of those configured as "Other." Although the education system has evolved over time, these principles did not suddenly evaporate when slavery was abolished or when the last residential school closed in the 1990s.

Moreover, Erevelles (1996) posited that "the ideology of disability is essential to the capitalist enterprise because it is able to regulate and control the unequal distribution of surplus through invoking biological difference as the 'natural' cause of all inequality" (p. 526). Therefore, the ideology of disability became a justification of social and economic inequalities while setting the foundation for the construction of other forms of difference. This neoliberal approach to disability, which associates it with deficiency and difficulty inherent to individuals, is divergent from predominant Indigenous views. For many Indigenous communities, the concept of disability does not exist as an individual condition, and in many cases, there is no word in traditional languages to designate it (Lovern, 2017; Senier, 2013). Historically, individuals deemed "disabled" by Western standards would be valued in Indigenous communities (Pengra & Godfrey, 2001; Senier, 2013). In other words, the difference would be acknowledged as an experience that would benefit the whole community (Ineese-Nash, 2020) rather than demeaned and corrected. However, according to Kress (2017), this posture seems to have been largely overridden by dominant Western influences, like many other aspects of Indigenous culture, as a result of assimilationist practices.

Further, discourses of disability have historically been intricately linked to a racial hierarchy and the justification of dehumanizing practices such as those mentioned above. The scientific endeavor of intelligence testing, with the goal of proving the inferior acumen of racialized groups, is an infamous example of how disability has been historically racialized (Du Bois, 1920; Skiba et al., 2008). Similarly, in the 19th century United States, a mental illness called *drapetomania* was scientifically fabricated to label enslaved people seeking freedom as defective (Artiles & Trent, 1994; Myers, 2014), illustrating how racism had validated disability and vice versa. According to Wolbring (2008), ableism is arguably one of the most significant "isms," as it can give rise to other "isms" (racism, sexism, ...) by justifying dominance based on ability and the ideology of normalcy. Some possible implications for racialized students are harmful misdiagnoses or *missed diagnoses* based on settler colonial norms. Their overrepresentation in special education (McAndrew & Ledent, 2008) and constricted access to mental health services (Thomson et al., 2015) may serve as indicators. These multilayered notions of identity that can be construed as inferior, deviant, or defective, in conjunction with multilayered forms of oppression, point to the necessity of an intersectional framework to better understand the experiences of racialized students who are designated as disabled.

## The Intersections of Disability, Race, and Language (Tenet 2)

The specificities of the Quebecois sociopolitical and linguistic context serve as a backdrop for how its social issues are framed in education, and how students who are simultaneously racialized and disabled are affected. The tensions between federalism and nationalism, English and French, and Canadian multiculturalism and Quebecois interculturalism play a key role in structuring social relationships. The consequences for those configured as "Them" are manifold for Indigenous groups. The presence and precedence of the settler-colonial Quebecois majority leads to their social erasure as they are positioned as "ethnic minorities," while the possibilities of a nation-to-nation relationship are hindered (Bouchard, 2011). For both Indigenous and other racialized groups, the overemphasis on cultural integration occurs to the detriment of social power relations. It is for reasons such as this, that DisCrit advances multidimensional identities rather than singular notions. Centralizing the singular notion of culture makes it possible to dismiss the concept of race and the existence of racism. In fact, studies in Quebec analyzing the socio-educational integration processes of immigrant students are rich and numerous (e.g., Kanouté et al., 2016; McAndrew, 2015), whereas those specifically addressing race are very few.

In the single statistical study that specifically investigated the educational portrait of Black students (McAndrew & Ledent, 2008), students whose mother tongue was either French or English were not counted since language (having a mother tongue other than French or English) was a key variable for defining the target group. Moreover, the student region of origin (Caribbean and sub-Saharan Africa) was used to infer that the students belonged to a Black racial group, thereby excluding Black students from any other countries and erasing the existence of long-standing, Black-Quebecois communities, whose history in Quebec can be linked beyond an immigrant generational status, to being taken hostage in the slave trade, or fugitivity from it, among others (Gay, 2004; Williams, 1989). As highlighted by Thésée and Carr (2016b), black skin acts as a peremptory social marker of non-belonging configured as "Other": newcomers, Quebec-born immigrants, and those from long-standing generations remain challenged alike in the construction of a racial identity in Quebec society.

Therefore, by overemphasizing culture and integration, the understanding of the educational experiences of racialized students stays rooted in a perspective that implies culture as an obstacle to academic success and social participation, or even as a possible reason for overrepresentation in special education, while eclipsing sociopolitical and historical dimensions related to social power relations, race, and racism. Similarly, the effects of racism are attributed to the culture of racialized youth, most often categorized as "immigrant" or "ethnocultural minority," rather than the processes of school segregation, marginalization, exclusion, medicalization, and ableism. Such a positioning essentializes culture and consequently essentializes race. To deny, trivialize, avoid, neglect, or reject racialization as a determinant sociological construct in socio-educational experiences, is to reinforce racism both in terms of the dynamics involved and the effects produced (Thésée & Carr, 2016b). Along the same lines, just as singular notions of identity should be troubled, so should singular ways of conceptualizing disability, which will be elaborated in the next section.

## The Camouflaged Circulation and Interdependence of Ableism and Racism (Tenet 1)

Tenet 1 of DisCrit makes it possible to foreground the reciprocity between ableism and racism and how they are insidiously embedded in educational policies and practices. As discussed previously, educational policies in Quebec have surrounded notions of human rights, integration and adaptation to differences. These policies are grounded in a medical model, which assumes that disabilities are intrinsic to individuals, and emphasizes physical and/or mental deficits that need to be corrected, treated, or accommodated. It also anchors the categorical approach at the heart of special education placement processes in Quebec, which entails pre-established standards for normalcy, and the identification, categorization, and "normalization" of students deemed deviant from these standards. While it is officially applied in order to make services available to students "in difficulty," which are intended to help them succeed, it also plays a role in making students vulnerable to stereotypes and prejudices, as well as their long-lasting effects (Commission des droits de la personne et des droits de la jeunesse [CDPDJ], 2018).

Similarly, the terminology used to refer to students involved in special education processes is equally problematic. Two predominant terms are employed: (a) *élèves handicapés ou en difficulté d'adaptation ou d'apprentissage,* which officially translates to "students with handicaps,[7] social maladjustments or learning difficulties," and more recently, (b) *élèves à besoins particuliers,* meaning "students with special needs." While the latter may appear more inclusive than the former, both terms imply deficiency and reinforce the categorization and normalization of students designated with special needs, even more so for those who are not from a settler Quebecois background (Bauer et al., 2019). Modifying the terminology to designate difference, while maintaining the ableist and racist structure it is founded on creates an illusion of its acceptance. Yet, these designations not only individualize school success, but also fail to recognize school and social inequalities that contribute to the social construction of difficulties, in order to maintain the norms of the able-bodied, French, White, middle- and upper-class.

Further, institutional practices can be viewed as the management component of a social power system that is grounded in structural and systemic racism and ableism. In schools, oppression can be perpetuated "through system-wide social policies managed primarily through bureaucracies" (Collins, 2009, p. 302). Special education itself is a prime example of a highly bureaucratic system and its organization in Quebec is no exception. This can be illustrated by its preordained standards of achievement and normalcy; its categorical approach which influences funding for services— and also happens to contradict its individualized approach to special needs; and the ambiguity that is allowed to permeate referrals, assessments, and conditions necessary to access services (Borri-Anadon, 2016; CDPDJ, 2018).

Researchers in Quebec and the United States have suggested that some assessment practices are susceptible to identifying cultural notions that run countercurrent to dominant norms, rather than the actual difficulties or deficiencies they are intended for (Borri et al., 2018; Harry & Klingner, 2014). Although the medical approach has advanced the rights of students with disabilities, as well as greater access to regular classroom instruction and opportunity for socialization for certain students (Kalubi et al., 2015), the clear overreliance on diagnosis and categorization compromises the core values related to the celebration of diversity, equity, and human rights that Quebecois educational policies claim to value (CDPDJ, 2018). These types of diagnoses and categorization processes imply a causal relationship between students designated as having special needs and their deviance from the "norm," as well as the need to correct, treat, or accommodate an assumed deficit rather than "being open to others and valuing diversity" (MEES, 2017, p. 47). This is made evident, in part, through the pressure perceived by speech therapists in Quebec to provide recommendations that lead to the access of adapted services for students via a difficulty code attribution (Borri-Anadon, 2014). Similarly, the most recent educational government policy (MEES, 2017) advances that

> in a pluralistic society such as ours, schools must act as agents of social cohesion by fostering a feeling of belonging to the community and teaching students how to live together. [...] They must likewise prevent exclusion, which jeopardizes the future of too many young people. (p. 25)

The problematic use of French-only tools and standardized tests, as well as the unilingual practices of speech-language therapists responsible for assessing students from immigrant backgrounds have also been brought to light (Borri-Anadon et al., 2018; Borri-Anadon et al., 2021). These tests and practices that are perceived by their administrators as allowing for assessments based on facts and ensuring validity, can be qualified as ableist and racist from a DisCrit point of view. Not only do they reinforce a medical approach, but they are based on social, historical, political, economic, and cultural conventions, stemming from categorization processes within unequal social relationships. Ableism circulates in such relationships by revering productivity, competence, and success, while positioning anything countercurrent to these values as "abnormal" (Wolbring, 2008). This posture adopted by assessment professionals acts as an obstacle to the recognition of other dimensions that may play a part in student performance such as culture and second (or more) language acquisition (Borri-Anadon et al., 2018). Measuring the aptitudes of students from diverse linguistic and immigrant backgrounds based exclusively on supposedly objective norms without accounting for any funds of knowledge from their own cultural experiences or aptitudes in their mother tongues constitutes another racist practice that is reinforced by ableism as they are placed at a distance from French Quebecois normalcy. These same test results that are deemed scientifically valid can also be used to justify disparities between settler Quebecois students and nonsettlers despite the fact that "a number of observers and experts from the education sector asserted that the processes for evaluating and categorizing students as [special needs] could be tainted by racial profiling" (CDPDJ, 2011, p. 65).

Further, while the integration of all students in regular classrooms with their peers is standard policy, there is an increased likelihood for racialized students to be placed in nonintegrated settings (McAndrew & Ledent, 2008). These types of placements result in lack of exposure to rich and stimulating learning experiences, and compromised opportunities for social interaction (Connor, 2006; Underwood, 2012). DisCrit is particularly concerned with this form of exclusion and segregation. These dislocating practices (Adams & Erevelles, 2016) conceal dominant ideologies that enable deficit-perspectives and cultural biases in referrals, assessment, and identification to pass as normal everyday practice carried out by well-intended practitioners.

Moreover, such placements seem to inadvertently trigger the enactment of zero-tolerance policies (the execution of rigid and unforgiving codes of conduct), particularly when students in such settings are designated labels such as *behavioral problems* or *emotional disturbances* (Cassidy & Jackson, 2005). A report issued by the *Commission des droits de la personne et des droits de la jeunesse* (CDPDJ, 2011) brought to light the over-policing, racial profiling, and enforcement of zero-tolerance policies toward Black students in Quebec schools. These manifest in the form of heightened surveillance in common spaces where students congregate, or during activities that are popular among Black students such as sporting or musical events. Swift and excessive punishment such as suspensions and expulsions without reasonable recourse to less permanent, restitutive, or meaningful alternatives were also revealed. These types of practices that are all linked, can be further associated with increased criminalization (Adams & Erevelles, 2016) and engagement with the justice system (Meiners, 2010). The interdependence between racism and ableism as well as their insidious nature can be illustrated through the previously discussed overrepresentation of racialized students in special education in conjunction with dislocating practices such as school segregation and the enforcement of zero tolerance policies. From a DisCrit lens, these types of practices consist of an ableist approach, which penalizes students for behaviors beyond their control, which are deemed unacceptable or deviant from school norms. Moreover, unlike the situation in the United States where intricate inquiries are mandated by law prior to enforcing exclusionary disciplinary measures (albeit notable application challenges; Alnaim, 2018), no such protective measures exist for students in Quebec.

## IMPLICATIONS FOR SCHOOL POLICY, GOVERNANCE, AND LEADERSHIP

Despite the evolving orientations and actions undertaken in Quebec to welcome diversity and foster equitable and inclusive conditions in its schools, the socio-educational situations of the racialized students we have highlighted indicate that there is still much work to be done. In fact, since the movement to democratize the Quebecois school system in the 1960s, inequalities have remained persistent or worsened. Within the current context of the COVID-19 pandemic, these inequalities are being exacerbated by measures enforced to contain the virus, notably concerning those at the intersections of disability and a minoritized status (Russo et al., 2020). Decisions taken by authorities amidst this unpredictable health crisis to massively invest in increasing nonintegrated classes for students who are "in difficulty" or who are "gifted," rather than the possible aftermath of the unequal access to resources experienced by students from disadvantaged backgrounds during the mandatory quarantine periods, particularly raise concerns (Fortier, 2020).

Along the same lines, in what appears to be a cultural assertion of Quebecois polity, the newly elected political party has recently passed a law (Bill 21) which prohibits state employees (including school personnel) from wearing ostentatious religious symbols (National Assembly of Quebec, 2019), under the premise of affirming state secularism. Many citizens and human rights collectives have denounced and challenged this law as legitimizing discrimination as well as religious and racial profiling. Further, in light of long-standing recommendations made by various organizations (e.g., CDPDJ, 2011, 2019) and actions taken by community members, student groups, and activists against systemic racism and discrimination, the government has expressed a denial of its existence. When protestors in Quebec organized in solidarity with African Americans in the wake of the graphic murder of George Floyd by police officers, to call attention to the similar position of Black people in Quebecois society, the government doubled down on its position, framing racism as an individual issue rather than systemic (Loewen, 2020). Only a few months following this incident, the heinous degradation and racial abuse of 37-year-old Atikamekw woman, Joyce Echaquan, at the hands of settler Quebecois hospital staff was Facebook live-streamed minutes before her death. The Premier of the province condemned the actions of the specific individuals involved, relentlessly emphasizing that "this does not mean that Quebec is racist" (Godin, 2020, n.p.).

The individualization of issues that are systemic in nature is particularly salient with regards to how diversity is broached in Quebecois schools. The predominant positioning of students from nonsettler backgrounds as cultural, ethnic, linguistic, or religious minorities (including Indigenous students), and the challenges related to their integration emphasizes inter-individual and inter-group differences, to the detriment of the oppressive processes that construct them (Borri-Anadon, Prud'homme, et al., 2018). Similarly, when it comes to students designated with disabilities, the categorical approach previously highlighted reflects an overemphasis on student differences based on school norms established by settler Quebecois. Diversity and disability are therefore conceived as differences that are fixed and additive rather than socially constructed and intersectional.

A DisCrit approach would thus require educational authorities and administrators in Quebec to move beyond a posture of "welcoming and celebrating diversity" in light of individual differences, to one that explicitly addresses ableism and racism, as an additional means of fostering inclusion in schools. This may start by acknowledging all parts of Quebec's settler colonial past, which have structured and upheld its current unequal social relations, not only those that make it possible to portray its "founders" and their descendants as *exalted subjects* (Thobani, 2007). In the same vein, the contributions and voices of those that are typically configured as "Them" or "Other" in Quebecois dominant discourse, should move from a marginalized position to one that is centered in all aspects of formal education including pedagogy, curriculum, governance, and policy. As highlighted by Kozleski and colleagues (2020):

> Once at the table, those who have not been served by educational systems and the policies that drive them may challenge the presiding policy agenda by poking at its vulnerabilities and providing solutions to those vulnerabilities through story telling about the ways things are and ought to be from their perspectives. These stories set up a counter-narrative that shakes faith in current initiatives and also proposes a new vision for how things ought to be. ("Centering Marginalized Perspectives" section, para. 2)

The intolerance, ignorance, and difficulty that exist when it comes to centering marginalized perspectives for dominant groups, and the need for this concept to be developed in Quebec can be illustrated through a highly sensationalized debate in 2020 concerning the use of racial slurs in academic contexts. Following a complaint made by Black university students regarding the use of the n-word by a White professor and her consequential suspension, a petition was penned by nearly 600 settler-Quebecois academics in defense of their colleague (Chapuis & Gauthier, 2020). The petition, which gained wide public support, including that of the prime minister of Quebec, condemned the faculty dean's abuse of power, as well as the infringement of rights to academic freedom and freedom of expression. The actual experiences and perspectives of the Black students concerned were either minimalized, discredited, or omitted. The covert forms of ableism were also present as the petition accused the students of being incapable of making distinctions between the constituents of racism and a university education and making reasonable judgments on what qualifies as racist (Chapuis & Gauthier, 2020). The petition also dictated what in fact does qualify as racism, and how to combat it.

Beyond the important voices of nondominant groups, other recommendations have been put forth such as promoting honest, professional, and critical action, guided by the goals of equity, inclusion, and social justice; encouraging contributions from the entire educational community (Larochelle-Audet et al., 2020); making race-based data available concerning the special needs student population and their placements; as well as making intercultural and antiracism training compulsory for all personnel that serve ethnic and racialized students (CDPDJ, 2011). We would add that racism and ableism are not only local or individual issues and training should not be limited to establishments with racialized populations, but made mandatory for all schools.

Finally, we bring specific attention to administrators' roles in administering disciplinary responses and surveillance towards racialized students. Their tendency to employ zero-tolerance policies without reasonably examining the root and context of perceived negative behaviors (Williams et al., 2013) seems to reinforce a cycle, as students with high numbers of suspensions are at increased risk of special education identification and vice versa (Sullivan & Bal, 2013). At the foundation of DisCrit is its call to action through resistance, activism, and building solidarity with students "to explicitly reject the continued focus on behavior and classroom management; conversations about managing students and classrooms are predicated on the notion of fixing something in students" (Annamma & Morrison, 2018, p. 76). Administrators are therefore called upon to critically reflect on institutionally embedded disciplinary measures that are aimed at correction and punishment, which derive from norms that position "goodness," attentiveness or compliance as equivalent to "smartness," thus operating as a mechanism that disables students (Broderick & Leonardo, 2016).

## CONCLUSION

The aim of this chapter was to bring to light, through a DisCrit lens, how schooling and special education in Quebec are grounded in settler colonial principles, which have propagated the inferiority of those configured as "Other;" how racist and ableist ideologies of normalcy continue to be bolstered in camouflaged ways through historical and contemporary factions; how the predominant discourse of Quebec as a raceless society and the stable prevalence of the medical model of disabilities in education can harm racialized students; as well as to discuss the implications for school policy, governance, and leadership.

In alignment with the intersectional posture of DisCrit, by focusing on racism and ableism in this work, we do not minimize other factors that affect school success. We simply offer a different approach in response to academic challenges and injustices experienced by racialized students that have persisted for centuries. Nor do we discount the work done by others in Quebecois educational research who have made significant headway in understanding the educational success of immigrant students from a culturalist approach. However, a more complete portrait contributes to this understanding and reveals important systemic and structural obstacles to educational success and social justice that are otherwise obscured. Canada and Quebec champion themselves as pro-diversity and equality-driven societies, partially based on the outstanding academic portrait among immigrants, that is quasi unprecedented internationally. However, this portrait does not apply to all immigrants, notably those who are racialized. Furthermore, this stellar state of affairs can be widely attributed to selective neoliberal immigration policies, aimed at welcoming only skilled and educated immigrants, which are fundamentally ableist and racist.

With this in mind, we acknowledge that our work here will not "change the world" despite the evidence we have presented that indicates it is urgently needed. The notion that research must necessarily culminate in recommendations for best practices and policy seems to us premature, when fundamental long-standing and ongoing inequalities are not even acknowledged by those who hold power and influence the very structure of our education system. We do believe, however, that whenever, and wherever possible, school actors, on all levels (especially students), must continue to have critical conversations that involve critiquing and challenging power and privilege issues in education and society, in order to produce transformation. This entails promoting and prioritizing embodied, reflexive, and multiple ways-of-knowing, not only those that are considered abstruse and objective; challenging dominant ideologies that influence processes and practices that marginalize individuals or groups based on race, gender, class, ability, sexual orientation and so forth; and promoting activism and empowerment to instigate transformative change, such as moving beyond a one-size-fits-all model that has pervaded the education system for far too long (Kozleski et al., 2020).

## AUTHOR NOTE

We have no known conflict of interest to disclose.

Correspondence concerning this chapter should be addressed to Tya Collins, Université de Montréal, tya.collins@umontreal.ca

## NOTES

1. We consider both disability designation and racialization as processes stemming from unequal social power relations resulting in assigned identities of disability and race rather than biological facts.
2. Geographically, Canada consists of 10 provinces and 3 territories. Under federal governance, the provinces are allocated legislative authorities (distinct or shared at the federal level) in specific domains such as education, health, immigration, and so forth.
3. In this chapter, we use the term *minority* as a statistical reference to a group lower in numbers than the overall population, as defined by the Canadian Official Languages Act (1991). In contrast, the term *minoritized* refers to a process involving unequal social power relations through which individuals are "rendered minorities in particular situations and institutional environments that sustain an overrepresentation of whiteness" (Harper, 2013, p. 207).
4. Can be translated to "the white *negroes* or *n\*ggers* of America." In Quebec, certain scholars perceive appropriate circumstances for the use of the n-word, which will be elaborated in the discussion section.
5. Low incidence implies that students are identified in these categories at low rates. These rates can differ according to context. In Quebec, low incidence categories include mild to severe motor impairments, organic impairments, visual impairments, hearing impairments, wherein a diagnosis is required by a general practitioner or medical specialist (MELS, 2007).
6. Immigrants born outside of Quebec (first-generation) as opposed to children born in Quebec whose parents were born abroad (second-generation).
7. The term *handicap* in French does not carry the same pejorative connotation as it does English. It reflects a situational approach (Fougeyrollas, 2002) which emphasizes the social production of disability and the contextual nature of the difficulties experienced (Barral & Roussel, 2002).

## REFERENCES

Adams, D. L., & Erevelles, N. (2016). DisCrit, dis/respectability, and carceral logics. In D. J. Connor, B. A. Ferri, & S. A. Annamma (Eds.), *DisCrit: Disability studies and critical race theory in education* (pp. 131–144). Teachers College Press.

Ahram, R., Fergus, E., & Noguera, P. (2011). Addressing racial/ethnic disproportionality in special education: Case studies of suburban school districts. *Teachers College Record, 113*(10), 2233–2266

Alnaim, M. (2018). The impact of zero tolerance policy on children with disabilities. *World Journal of Education, 8*(1), 1–5.

Annamma, S. A., Connor, D., & Ferri, B. (2013). Dis/ability critical race studies (DisCrit): Theorizing at the intersections of race and dis/ability. *Race Ethnicity and Education, 16*(1), 1–31.

Annamma, S., & Morrison, D. (2018). DisCrit classroom ecology: Using praxis to dismantle dysfunctional education ecologies. *Teaching and Teacher Education, 73,* 70–80.

Artiles, A. J., & Trent, S. C. (1994). Overrepresentation of Minority Students in Special Education: A Continuing Debate. *Journal of Special Education, 27*(4), 410–437.

Austin, D. (2010). Narratives of power: Historical mythologies in contemporary Quebec and Canada. *Race & class, 52*(1), 19–32.

Banks, J. (2017). "These people are never going to stop labeling me": Educational experiences of African American male students labeled with learning disabilities. *Equity & Excellence in Education, 50*(1), 96–107.

Barral, C., & Roussel, P. (2002). De la CIH [classification international du handicap] à la CIF [classification international du fonctionnement]: Le processus de révision [From ICD (International Classification of Disability) to ICF (International Classification of Functioning): The review process. *Handicap, revue des sciences humaines et sociales,* 94–95, 1–23.

Bauer, S., Borri-Anadon, C., & Laffranchini Ngoenha, M. (2019). Les élèves issus de l'immigration sont-ils des élèves à besoins éducatifs particuliers? [Are students from immigrant backgrounds students with special educational needs?] *Revue hybride de l'éducation, 3*(1), 17–38.

Berhanu, G. (2008). Ethnic minority pupils in swedish schools: Some trends in over-representation of minority pupils in special educational programmes. *International Journal of Special Education, 23*(3), 17–29.

Borri-Anadon, C. (2014). *Pratiques évaluatives des orthophonistes à l'égard des élèves issus de minorités culturelles: Une recherche interprétative-critique* [Assessment practices of speech therapists with regard to students from cultural minorities: An interpretative-critical research project ] [PhD dissertation]. Université du Québec à Montréal Montréal.

Borri-Anadon, C., Collins, T., & Boisvert, M. (2018). Pratiques d'évaluation en contexte pluriethnique et plurilingue: Démarche d'accompagnement d'orthophonistes scolaires [Assessment practices in multi-ethnic and multi-lingual contexts: A support process for school speech therapists]. *Recherche Formation, 3,* 45–56.

Borri-Anadon, C., Lemaire, E., & Boisvert, M. (2021). Les enjeux de l'évaluation des besoins des élèves en contexte de [The challenges of assessing student needs in a context of diversity]. In M. Potvin, M.-O. Magnan, & J. Larochelle-Audet (Eds.). *La diversité ethnoculturelle, religieuse et linguistique en éducation: théorie et pratique* (2e édition) [Ethnocultural, religious and linguistic diversity in education: theory and practice (2nd editions)] (pp. 292–303). Fides Éducation.

Borri-Anadon, C., Prud'homme, L., Ouellet, K., et Boisvert, M. (2018). La formation à l'enseignement dans une perspective inclusive: De l'hégémonie du cloisonnement à une approche holistique. In C. Borri-Anadon, G. Gonçalves, S. Hirsch, & J. Queiroz Odinino (Eds), *La formation des éducateurs en contexte de diversité: Une perspective comparative Québec-Brésil* [Educator training in a diversity context: A comparative Quebec-Brazil perspective] (pp. 206–224). Deep Education Press.

Bouchard, G. (2011). What is interculturalism? *McGill Law Journal, 56*(2), 395–468.

Broderick, A., & Leonardo, Z. (2016). What is a good boy: The deployment and distribution of "goodness" as ideological property in schools. In D. Connor, B. Ferri, S. A. Annamma (Eds.), *DisCrit: Critical conversations across race, class, & dis/ability* (pp. 55–69). Teachers College Press.

Brathwaite, O. (2010). The role of school curriculum to obliterate anti-Black racism. *Our Schools, Our Selves, 19*(3), 305–326.

Brown, R., & Parekh, G. (2010). *Special education: Structural overview and student demographics, research report.* Research and Information Services, Toronto District School Board. https://www.tdsb.on.ca/Portals/research/docs/reports/SpecEdStructuralOverviewStudentDemo.pdf

Cashman, L. (2016). New label no progress: Institutional racism and the persistent segregation of Romani students. *Race Ethnicity and Education, 20*(5), 1–14.

Cassidy, W., & Jackson, M. (2005). The need for equality in education: An intersectionality examination of labeling and zero tolerance practices. *McGill Journal of Education, 40*(3), 445.

Chapuis, M., & Gauthier, M. (2020, October 20). Enseigner dans le champ miné de l'arbitraire [Teaching in the minefield of arbitrariness]. *Le Devoir.* https://www.ledevoir.com/opinion/idees/588101/enseigner-dans-le-champ-mine-de-l-arbitraire#

Collins, K. M. (2016). A DisCrit perspective on The State of Florida v. George Zimmerman: Racism, ableism, and youth out of place in community and school. In D. J. Connor, B. A. Ferri, & S. A. Annamma (Eds.), *DisCrit: Disability studies and critical race theory in education* (pp. 183–201). Teachers College Press.

Collins, P. H. (2009). *Black feminist thought: Knowledge, consciousness, and the politics of empowerment* (2nd ed.). Routledge.

Commission des droits de la personne et des droits de la jeunesse. (2011). *Profilage racial et discrimination systémique des jeunes racisés* [Racial profiling and systemic discrimination of racialized youth]. https://www.cdpdj.qc.ca/publications/Profilage_rapport_FR.pdf

Commission des droits de la personne et des droits de la jeunesse. (2018). *Le respect des droits des élèves HDAA et l'organisation des services éducatifs dans le réseau scolaire québécois: Une étude systémique* [A systemic study into the rights of students with special needs and organization of educational serivces within the Québec school system]. http://www.cdpdj.qc.ca/Publications/etude_inclusion_EHDAA.pdf

Commission des droits de la personne et des droits de la jeunesse. (2019). *Mémoire à l'office de consultation publique de Montréal dans le cadre de la consultation publique sur le racisme et la discrimination systémiques* [Advisory for the office de consultation publique de Montréal as part of the public consultation on systemic racism and discrimination]. https://www.cdpdj.qc.ca/Publications/memoire_OCPM_racisme-systemique.pdf

Connor, D. J. (2006). Michael's story: "I get into so much trouble just by walking": Narrative knowing and life at the intersections of learning disability, race, and class. *Equity & Excellence in Education, 39*(2), 154–165.

Cooc, N., & Kiru, E. W. (2018). Disproportionality in special education: A synthesis of international research and trends. *The Journal of Special Education, 52*(3), 163–173.

Cooper, A. (2007). *The hanging of Angelique: The untold story of Canadian slavery and the burning of Old Montreal.* HarperCollins.

Dei, G. J. S. (1996). *Anti-racism Education: Theory and Practice.* Fernwood Publishing.

Du Bois, W. E. B. (1920). Race intelligence. *The Crisis, 20*(3).

Dunn, L. M. (1968). Special education for the mildly retarded: Is much of it justifiable? *Exceptional children, 35*(1), 5–22.

Erevelles, N. (1996). Disability and the dialectics of difference. *Disability & Society, 11*(4), 519–538.

Fenton, Z. E. (2016). Disability does not discriminate: Toward a theory of multiple identity through coalition. In D. J. Connor, B. A. Ferri, & S. A. Annamma (Eds.), *DisCrit: Disability studies and critical race theory in education* (pp. 203–212). Teachers College Press.

Fortier, M. (2020, June 19). Québec veut des classes pour les élèves doués [Quebec wants classes for gifted students]. *Le Devoir.* https://www.ledevoir.com/societe/education/581139/education-quebec-veut-des-classes-pour-les-eleves-doues#

Fougeyrollas, P. (2002). L'évolution conceptuelle internationale dans le champ du handicap: Enjeux sociopolitiques et contributions québécoises [International conceptual evolution in the field of disability: Sociopolitical issues and Quebec contributions]. *Perspectives interdisciplinaires sur le travail et la santé, 4*(2).

Gabel, S. L., Curcic, S., Powell, J. J. W., Khader, K., & Albee, L. (2009). Migration and ethnic group disproportionality in special education: An exploratory study. *Disability & Society, 24*(5), 625–639. https://doi.org/10.1080/09687590903011063

Gagné, M., & Chamberland, C. (1999). L'évolution des politiques d'intégration et d'immigration au Québec [The evolution of integration and immigration policies in Quebec]. In M. Mc Andrew, D. André-Clément, & C. Coryse (Eds.), *Les politiques d'immigration et d'intégration au Canada et en France: Analyses comparées et perspectives de recherche, Actes du séminaire* [Immigration and integration policies in Canada and France: Comparative analyzes and research perspectives, Proceedings of the Seminar], Montréal, 20, 71–89.

Garcia, A. (2017). *Exit from special education: Part of the continuum of services or just a pipe dream? A study on the characteristics of students who exit special education* [PhD dissertation, California State University].

Gay, D. (2004). Portrait d'une communauté: Les Noirs du Québec, 1629–1900 [Portrait of a community: Blacks from Quebec, 1629–1900]. *Cap-aux-Diamants: La revue d'histoire du Québec, 79*, 10–12.

Gillborn, D., Rollock, N., Vincent, C., & Ball, S. (2016). The Black middle classes, education, racism, and dis/ability. In D. J. Connor, B. A. Ferri, & S. A. Annamma (Eds.), *DisCrit: Disability studies and critical race theory in education* (pp. 35–54). Teachers College Press.

Godin, M. (2020, October 9). She was racially abused by hospital staff as she lay dying. Now a Canadian Indigenous woman's death is forcing a reckoning on racism. *Time.* https://time.com/5898422/joyce-echaquan-indigenous-protests-canada/

Graham, L. (2012). Disproportionate over-representation of Indigenous students in New South Wales government special schools. *Cambridge Journal of Education, 42*(2), 163.

Haque, E., & Patrick, D. (2015). Indigenous languages and the racial hierarchisation of language policy in Canada. *Journal of Multilingual and Multicultural Development, 36*(1), 27–41.

Harper, S. R. (2013). Am I my brother's teacher? Black undergraduates, racial socialization, and peer pedagogies in predominantly White postsecondary contexts. *Review of Research in Education, 37*, 183–211. https://doi.org/10.3102/0091732X12471300

Harry, B., & Klingner, J. K. (2014). *Why are so many minority students in special education? Understanding race and disability in schools* (2nd ed.). Teachers College Press.

Hébert, Y., & Abdi, A. A. (2013). *Critical perspectives on international education.* Sense Publishers.

Hibel, J., Farkas, G., & Morgan, P. L. (2010). Who is placed into special education? *Sociology of education, 83*(4), 312–332.

Howard, P. S. S. (2020). Have you ever seen a real, live racist? In L. Kowalchuk & C. Levine-Rasky (Eds), *We resist: Defending the common good in hostile times* (pp. 38–47). McGill-Queen's University Press.

Ineese-Nash, N. (2020). Disability as a Colonial construct: The missing discourse of culture in conceptualizations of disabled Indigenous children. *Canadian Journal of Disability Studies, 9*(3), 28–51.

Kalubi, J., Chatenoud, C., Guillemette, S., Larivée, S., & Leroux, J. (2015). *Portrait de la situation des EHDAA au Québec (2000–2013): Une analyse multidimensionnelle des caractéristiques, besoins, réseaux de soutien et pistes d'innovation* [Portrait of the situation of students with special needs in Quebec (2000–2013): A multidimensional analysis of characteristics, needs, support networks and avenues for innovation]. Université de Sherbrooke.

Kanouté, F., Gosselin-Gagné, J., Guennouni, R., & Girard, C. (2016). Points de vue d'élèves issus de l'immigration sur leur vécu à l'école en contexte scolaire montréalais défavorisé [Perspectives of students from immigrant backgrounds on their experiences at school in a Montreal underprivileged context]. *Alterstice, Revue internationale de la recherche interculturelle, 6*(1), 13–26.

Kozleski, E. B. (2016). Reifying Categories: Measurement in search of understanding. In D. Connor, B. Ferri, & S. Annamma (Eds.), *DisCrit: Disability studies and critical race theory in education* (pp. 101–116). Teachers College Press.

Kozleski, E. B., Stepaniuk, I., & Proffitt, W. (2020). Leading through a critical lens: The application of DisCrit in framing, implementing and improving equity driven, educational systems for all students. *Journal of Educational Administration, 58*(5). https://doi.org/10.1108/JEA-12-2019-0220

Kress, M. M. (2017). Reclaiming disability through pimatisiwin: Indigenous ethics, spatial justice, and gentle teaching. In *Ethics, equity, and inclusive education* (pp. 23–57). Emerald Publishing Limited.

Ladson-Billings, G., & Tate, W. F. (1995). Toward a critical race theory of education. *Teachers College Record, 97*(1), 47–68.

Larochelle-Audet, J., Magnan, M. O., Doré, E., Potvin, M., St-Vincent, L. A., Gélinas-Proulx, A., & Amboulé Abath, A. (2020). *Diriger et agir pour l'équité, l'inclusion et la justice sociale: Boîte à outils pour les directions d'établissement d'enseignement* [Leading and acting for equity, inclusion and social justice: A toolkit for school administrators]. Observatoire sur la formation à la diversité et l'équité.

Leonardo, Z. (2013). *Race frameworks: A multidimensional theory of racism and education*. Teachers College Press.

Liasidou, A. (2014). The cross-fertilization of critical race theory and disability studies: Points of convergence/divergence and some education policy implications. *Disability & Society, 29*(5), 724–737.

Loewen, C. (2020, June 2). *As premier denies systemic racism, Black Quebecers point to their lived experience.* CBC News. https://www.cbc.ca/news/canada/montreal/systemic-racism-police-brutality-quebec-1.5594071

Lovern, L. L. (2017). Indigenous perspectives on difference: A case for inclusion. *Journal of Literary & Cultural Disability Studies, 11*(3), 303–320.

Mattson, L., & Caffrey, L. (2001). *Barriers to equal education for Aboriginal learners: A review of the literature* [Report]. British Columbia Human Rights Commission.

Maynard, R. (2017). *Policing Black lives: State violence in Canada from slavery to the present.* Fernwood Publishing.

McAndrew, M., Balde, A., Bakhshaei, M., Tardif-Grenier, K., Armand, F., Guyon, S.,…, Rousseau, C. (2015). *La réussite éducative des élèves issus de l'immigration: Dix ans de recherche et d'intervention au Québec* [The educational success of students from immigrant backgrounds: Ten years of research and intervention in Quebec]. Les Presses de l'Université de Montréal.

McAndrew, M., & Ledent, J. (2008). *La réussite scolaire des jeunes noirs au secondaire québécois: Rapport de recherche* [The academic success of Black youth in secondary school Quebec: Research report]. Chaire en relations ethniques, Université de Montréal.

McAndrew, M., Ledent J., & Murdoch, J. (2011). *La réussite scolaire des jeunes québécois issus de l'immigration au secondaire: Rapport de recherche* [The academic success of young Quebecers from immigrant backgrounds in high school]. Ministère de l'Éducation, du Loisir et du Sport/Groupe de recherche Immigration, Équité et Scolarisation.

McRoberts, K. (1997). *Misconceiving Canada: The struggle for national unity.* Oxford University Press.

Meiners, E. R. (2010). *Right to be hostile: Schools, prisons, and the making of public enemies.* Routledge.

Mendoza, E., Paguyo, C., & Gutierrez, K. (2016). Understanding the intersection of race and dis/ability: Common sense notions of learning and culture. In D. J. Connor, B. A. Ferri, & S. A. Annamma (Eds.), *DisCrit: Disability studies and critical race theory in education* (pp. 71–86). Teachers College Press.

Milloy, J. S. (2017). *A national crime: The Canadian government and the residential school system, 1879 to 1986.* University of Manitoba Press.

Ministère de l'éducation et de l'enseignement supérieur, Gouvernement du Québec. (2017). *Politique de la réussite éducative: Le plaisir d'apprendre, la chance de réussir* [Educational success policy: The pleasure of learning, the chance to succeed]. Gouvernement du Québec.

Ministère de l'Éducation du Québec, Gouvernement du Québec. (1999). *Une école adaptée à tous ses élèves. Prendre le virage du succès. Politique de l'adaptation scolaire.*

[gouvernement éd.] [A school adapted to all its students. Take the turn of success. Special education policy]. Gouvernement du Québec.

Ministère de l'éducation, Gouvernement du Québec. (2003). *Les difficultés d'apprentissage à l'école: Cadre de référence pour guider l'intervention* [Learning difficulties at school: A Reference framework to guide intervention]. Gouvernement du Québec.

Morgan, P. L., Farkas, G., Hillemeier, M. M., Mattison, R., Maczuga, S., Li, H., & Cook, M. (2015). Minorities are disproportionately underrepresented in special education: Longitudinal evidence across five disability conditions. *Educational Researcher, 44*(5), 278–292.

Myers, B. E., II (2014). *"Drapetomania" rebellion, defiance and free Black insanity in the Antebellum United States* [Doctoral Thesis, University of California]. UCLA Electronic Theses and Dissertations. https://escholarship.org/content/qt-9dc055h5/qt9dc055h5.pdf?t=nk49cg

National Assembly of Quebec. (2019). Bill 21, An Act respecting the laicity of the State. Québec, QC: National Assembly of Quebec. http://www.assnat.qc.ca/en/travaux-parlementaires/projets-loi/projet-loi-21-42-1.html

Oliver, M., & Barnes, C. (2012). *The new politics of disablement.* Palgrave Macmillan.

Oliver, T. (2010). *A brief history of effects of colonialism on First Nations in Canada.* Simon Fraser University.

Pengra, L. M., & Godfrey, J. G. (2001). Different boundaries, different barriers: Disability studies and Lakota culture. *Disability Studies Quarterly, 21*(3), 36–53.

Potvin, M. (2010). Interethnic relations and racism in Quebec. In C. Kirkey, R. Jarrett, & S. Gervais (Dir.), *Quebec questions: Québec studies for the 21st century* (pp. 267–286). Oxford University Press.

Reid, K. D., & Knight, M. G. (2006). Disability justifies exclusion of minority students: A critical history grounded in disability studies. *Educational Researcher, 35*(6), 18–23.

Regroupement des centres d'amitié autochtones du Québec. (2020). *Comprendre et soutenir les transitions scolaires harmonieuses chez les jeunes autochtones en milieu urbain* [Understanding and supporting smooth school transitions for urban indigenous youth]. http://www.rcaaq.info/wp-content/uploads/2020/02/Transitions-scolaires-harmonieuses_Janvier2020_FR.pdf

Russo, K., Magnan, M. O., & Soares, R. (2020). A pandemia que amplia as desigualdades: A COVID-19 e o sistema educativo de Quebec/Canadá [The pandemic that widens inequalities: COVID-19 and the Quebec/Canada education system]. *Práxis Educativa, 15*, 1–28.

Satzewich, V., & Liodakis, N. (2013). *"Race" and ethnicity in Canada: A critical introduction* (3rd ed.). Oxford University Press.

Senier, S. (2013). "Traditionally, disability was not seen as such" writing and healing in the work of Mohegan medicine people. *Journal of Literary & Cultural Disability Studies, 7*(2), 213–229.

Shifrer, D., Muller, C., & Callahan, R. (2011). Disproportionality and learning disabilities: Parsing apart race, socioeconomic status, and language. *Journal of Learning Disabilities, 44*(3), 246–257.

Skiba, R. J., Simmons, A. B., Ritter, S., Gibb, A. C., Rausch, M. K., Cuadrado, J., & Chung, C. G. (2008). Achieving equity in special education: History, status, and current challenges. *Exceptional Children, 74*(3), 264–288.

Strand, S., & Lindsay, G. (2009). Evidence of ethnic disproportionality in special education in an English population. *The Journal of Special Education, 43*(3), 174–190.

Strand, S., Lindsay, G., & Pather, S. (2006). *Special educational needs and ethnicity: Issues of over- and under-representation.* Department for Education and Skills.

Sullivan, A. L., & Bal, A. (2013). Disproportionality in special education: Effects of individual and school variables on disability risk. *Exceptional Children, 79*(4), 475–494.

Thésée, G., & Carr, P. R. (2016a). Triple whammy, and a fragile minority within a fragile majority: School, family and society, and the education of Black, francophone youth in Montreal. In A. Ibrahim & A. Abdi (Eds.), *The education of African Canadian children: Critical perspectives* (pp. 131–144). McGill-Queen's University Press.

Thésée, G., & Carr, P. (2016b). The words to say it: Acculturation or racialization? Critical anti-racist theory (CART) in the study of the schooling experience of Canadian Black youth within francophone contexts. *Comparative and International Education, 45*(1), 1–17.

Thobani, S. (2007). *Exalted subjects: Studies in the making of race and nation in Canada.* University of Toronto Press.

Thomson, M. S., Chaze, F., George, U., & Guruge, S. (2015). Improving immigrant populations' access to mental health services in Canada: A review of barriers and recommendations. *Journal of immigrant and minority health, 17*(6), 1895–1905.

Thomas, G., & Loxley, A. (2007). *Deconstructing special education and constructing inclusion* (2nd ed.). McGraw-Hill Education.

Truth and Reconciliation Commission of Canada. (2015). *Truth and reconciliation commission of Canada.* House of Commons.

Underwood, K. (2012). A case study of exclusion on the basis of behaviour (and experiences of migration and racialisation). *International Journal of Inclusive Education, 16*(3), 313–329.

United Nations Educational, Scientific and Cultural Organization. (2015). *Education 2030: Equity and quality with a lifelong learning perspective.* UNESCO.

Vallières, P. (1968). *Nègres blancs d'Amérique: Autobiographie précoce d'un terroriste québécois* [White Negroes of America: Early autobiography of a Quebec terrorist]. Maspéro/Parti pris.

Wagner, M., Kutash, K., Duchnowski, A. J., Epstein, M. H., & Sumi, W. C. (2005). The children and youth we serve a national picture of the characteristics of students with emotional disturbances receiving special education. *Journal of Emotional and behavioral Disorders, 13*(2), 79–96.

Waitoller, F. R., Artiles, A. J., & Cheney, D. A. (2010). The Miner's Canary: A review of overrepresentation research and explanations. *The Journal of Special Education, 44*(1), 29–49. https://doi.org/10.1177/0022466908329226

Williams, D. W. (1989). *Blacks in Montreal, 1628–1986: An urban demography.* Éditions Yvon Blais Inc.

Williams, J. L., Pazey, B., Shelby, L., & Yates, J. R. (2013). The enemy among us: Do school administrators perceive students with disabilities as a threat? *NASSP Bulletin, 97*(2), 139–165.

Wolbring, G. (2008). The politics of ableism. *Development, 51*(2), 252–258.

# SECTION III

## EDUCATIONAL LEADERS AND DISABILITY: POLICIES IN PRACTICE

In many substantive ways, framing and incentivizing educational practices around dis/ability have been framed and incentivized by federal and state level educational policies. In order to help us ponder the question in the book title (*Who Decides?*), the chapters in this section illuminate various foundational dimensions of special educational policies, analyze effects of enacted policies, and provide personal and practitioner narrative insight into lived policy experiences.

Murdick and Wood open this section by providing an important historical analysis of special education policy in the United States in their chapter, *Special Education Services: Historical Underpinnings for Educational Administrators.* Murdick and Wood take readers through an exploration of varying attitudes towards special education in the West—from the Middle Ages and Renaissance to the modern day. Drawing on philosophers such as Locke and Rousseau, as well as language provided in important U.S. Supreme Court cases, Murdick and Wood explain how historical foundations, legal precedents, and early special education policy considerations shape contemporary special education policy and practice. Their chapter illustrates ways in which knowledge of the past can help inform current education policy deliberations around special education services and move schools toward more equitable practices in the future.

Special Education services are often located within the individual education plan (IEP). In "What Is an IEP? A Special Education Teacher's Reflection on IEP Narrative and Practices," Mehta shares vignettes based on her personal experiences working as a public elementary special education teacher in suburban Georgia. The vignettes highlight the internal conflicts and challenges she encountered during a single year. Following each vignette, she examines the narratives and practices evidenced in the IEP process, focusing on IEP's normalized routines and language that promotes deficit perspectives on students' abilities. Specifically, she addresses (a) the deficit-oriented discourses in the IEP, (b) ways accountability policies reinforce deficit perspectives, (c) the lack of culturally sustaining practices in IEPs, and (d) the need for student engagement in the IEP process. Lastly, she discusses how educators can move towards strength-based practices within the frameworks of community of practice and person-centered planning.

Educational leaders charged with improving both practice for students identified with a dis/ability typically have an awareness of the Individuals With Disability Education Act (IDEA). In "Leadership, Equity, and the Individuals with Disabilities Education Act," Voulgarides delineates the principal components of the IDEA. The chapter provides important background information and a clear summary of the civil rights and social justice foundations of IDEA (2015). Voulgarides argues that the Act's original intent and tenets change when put into action by school leaders and educators. As a result, the current protections built into IDEA and its component provisions do not meet the legislation's original civil rights and social justice intent. Voulgarides suggests that while the Act continues to have the potential to promote positive outcomes, significant concerns related to equitable special education outcomes endure. Local efforts to implement IDEA guidelines are often insufficient and lacking in cultural appropriateness. She describes *zones of mediation*, where inertial, technical, normative and political forces are applied in special education settings. The chapter concludes by discussing ways in which educators can move past simply observing and implementing the law's requirements and towards the law's spirit and intent.

We next turn to a personal narrative related to navigating special education policies in Bradshaw's "Narrative of an Older Sibling With a Younger Brother With a Developmental Disability." Bradshaw deals directly with how families navigate many of the potential minefields in her narrative of her life as an older sibling to a younger sibling with a developmental disability. She highlights connections between specific experiences she experienced and theoretical perspectives from literature on disability critical race theory (DisCrit), intersectionality, funds of knowledge (FoK), and related practices of inclusion and empowerment. The chapter provides insights into an older sibling's sense-making of the intersection of complex policies in practice shaping the life of a younger brother with a developmental disability. In her narrative, Bradshaw delineates how practices, instruction, and school climate as a special education student may have contributed to shaping her brother's sense of self-efficacy.

Policies in practice are critically examined in the next chapter, Yoon's "Multi-Tiered Marginalization by Race, Gender, Disability, and Poverty in a

Diverse School: Implementing PBIS With Pedagogies of Pathologization and Pushout." Yoon posits that disproportionalities in special education placements and exclusionary discipline exemplify the ways in which the implementation of "progressive" special education policy is counterproductive and harmful, especially for disabled Black, Indigenous, and students of color (BISOC). Yoon's research, which utilizes ethnographic observation methods, describes ways in which educators at one elementary school used surveillance, labeling, and punishment in the implementation of positive behavioral interventions and supports (PBIS) in ways that support the school–prison nexus. Yoon argues that PBIS practices function as pedagogies of pathologization that criminalize BISOC with disabilities in patterns of practice that on the surface may not appear harmful: catching students being good, asserting responsibility rhetoric, and using token economies to trade goods for goodness. She discusses implications of these patterns and illustrates the carceral logics that PBIS perpetuates about BISOC through the use of disability labels, particularly as the labels relate to behavior and emotion.

Some of the struggles experienced by BISOC students in Yoon's study relate to unexamined institutionalized conceptions of "normal." Jones and Jones present a critical disability case study in which they identify conceptions of normality ensnared in enrollment and disenrollment decisions made by private preschool leaders in publicly funded prekindergarten programs. In "Re(imagining) Educational Markets: A Critical Disability Case Study of a Preschool Marketplace," Jones and Jones argue that through policy enactments and various organizational practices of the private preschool leaders in the study, child(ren) and parent(s) were (re)constructed as a consumer of and a commodity in the local preschool education market. In response to those dynamics, Jones and Jones advocate for the creation of a potential site for resistance to marginalizing practices that normalize ableist constructions in school choice programs. For some leaders in their study, spirituality offered an inclusionary counter-discourse to the exclusion of children with disabilities widely accepted and utilized within the local market. The chapter (re)imagines early education for all children and families through a "leadership within" framework for school leaders and a democratic experimentalism market framework.

Conceptions of commoditization can diffuse into families through exertions of time, emotional energy, and money. The ways in which families operate when supporting a child with particular special needs can vary greatly. In the next chapter, "Seeing the Able: Disability Through the Eyes of a Younger Sister," Greer details her experiences as a younger sibling of an older brother who experienced seizures and underwent experimental surgery. Greer's narrative profiles a family that experienced a paradigm shift due to an unexpected and challenging disability. As a child who moved from being the recipient of attention and care to a provider, Greer explains how medical conditions can dramatically alter a family dynamic, a childhood, and broader educational experiences and outcomes.

In concluding Section III, McFadden and Whitaker review findings from a 2015 Arizona study that surveyed 224 parents and guardians and 634 high school students with disabilities across 17 school districts. "Stuck in a Poor Post-School Outcomes Loop for Students With Significant Disabilities: What We Can Learn From Arizona" provides an overview of students' experiences at school and describes how these experiences help or hinder students and parents ability to prepare for life beyond high school. McFadden and Whitaker found that Arizona's education system and other state and local education systems of student support suffer from overall lowered expectations for youth with disabilities, because of the generally ableist attitudes exhibited in the academic setting. These low expectations contribute to students' low levels of confidence and performance and eventually to poor post-school outcomes. In contrast, the authors' analysis suggests that districts, charter schools, private schools, providers, and businesses that have been actively working to overcome barriers faced by students with significant disabilities tend to have leadership structures that reflect a strong belief in students' "abilities" beyond the academic context. The collective goal and definition of success, they argue, should be to build academic, vocational education, socialization, and employment skills and opportunities among all students; not just for those who are deemed "able."

# CHAPTER 7

# SPECIAL EDUCATION SERVICES

## Historical Underpinnings for Educational Administrators

**Nikki L. Murdick**
*Saint Louis University*

**Jo Nell Wood**
*Saint Louis University*

Educational administrators serve as leaders in educational systems in the provision of educational services for children with disabilities. They serve on the evaluation and IEP teams, provide support for teachers and other educational personnel in their development of educational programs, serve as the sounding board for parents and other advocacy groups, and allocate the funding required for the provision of services throughout the school system. Therefore, leaders must be knowledgeable about the historical background of the development of special education services in schools and their ethical and legal underpinnings. Without this knowledge, educational leaders may not

*Who Decides?*, pages 153–181
Copyright © 2022 by Information Age Publishing
www.infoagepub.com
All rights of reproduction in any form reserved.

be effective in providing appropriate supports and instructional leadership for their staff and students or understand the reasons for the legal rights and individualized programs provided in general education settings to ensure a least restrictive environment. As Kauffman (1999) posited to educators, "As a group of professionals, we are woefully ignorant of our past" (p. 244).

If leaders are to provide appropriate services to all students in schools, they must learn the history of services for students with disabilities. They need to know what services, if any, were provided to these students and what changes have occurred to lead to the schools of today in serving students with special needs. According to Esteves and Rao (2008), when educational leaders—such as principals, superintendents, and directors—begin to plan ways to improve the services they provide to students with disabilities within their districts, they should consider and reflect on the following questions:

- What can be learned from the history of special education?
- Are the actions and decisions of general education and special education teachers reflective of the philosophy employed in my building?
- What underlying factors might be affecting negative views from members of the community, principals, and teachers?
- What are teachers doing to differentiate instruction for all learners and how can I support their efforts? (p. 3)

This chapter will focus on providing a background for administrators to review when answering the first question posed by Esteves and Rao.

In today's educational milieu, parents expect the public schools to provide special education services. But, as Guidara (n.d.) noted, special education services have not always been provided in schools for children with special needs. Less than a century ago, the lack of services provided to such children was the norm, rather than the exception. Individuals with disabilities of all ages have been present throughout history, whether they have been included in the educational system or not ("The history of special," 2020). For this chapter, the definition of special education (sometimes called special needs education) is "the education of children who differ socially, mentally, or physically from the average to such an extent that they require modification of usual school practices" (Tikkanen, 2013, para. 1).

## EARLY HISTORY OF SPECIAL EDUCATION SERVICE DELIVERY (PRE-1950s)

"Although special education is a relatively new concept, students with disabilities have been present in every era and society" ("The history of special," 2020). Early Greek and Roman societies idealized physical perfection and any physical defects were regarded as undesirable. In fact, both Plato and Aristotle called for infanticide stating that no deformed child should be allowed to live (Minnesota Governor's Council on Developmental Disabilities, n.d.; Tremblay, 2007). Western religious beliefs played an important role in the view of disability and the subsequent provision or lack of services. As described in the New Testament, Jesus encouraged showing kindness to those with afflictions (Luke 9:46). Because of Jesus' teachings, a gradual change in attitude about people with disabilities began to occur.

The Middle Ages, from approximately 400 to 1400 AD, has been called the Era of Ridicule when those with disabilities were often seen as deviant and ridiculed for their physical and intellectual differences (Wolfensberger, 1975). Following the crusades (1100–1300 AD), religious institutions were the main agents of support and care for people with disabilities. With the advent of the Renaissance period in the 1300s, the focus shifted from attitudes of indifference and custodial care to cultural attitudes of humane treatment of those with disabilities. This change in attitude combined with an increased emphasis on science, led to an expanded understanding of disability (Tremblay, 2007).

Even with this cultural shift, religious leaders such as Martin Luther (1483–1546) and John Calvin (1509–1564) considered people with disabilities, especially those with mental retardation, not to be "of God's chosen people to be saved" (State of Alaska, 2019, "Panel 2"). However, in the latter 1500s, Queen Elizabeth I of England passed a series of laws, known as the Elizabethan Poor Laws, requiring basic care of the poor, including those with disabilities (State of Alaska, 2019). During the 16th and 17th centuries, the concept of rationalism with an expanded study of human nature began. One of those who had a major impact during this time was John Locke, who posited the idea that all learning comes through experiences and that our minds are actual *tabula rasa* or blank slates on which what one experiences and learns is written (Minnesota Governor's Council on Developmental Disabilities [MNDDC], n.d.). It was at this time that what is known as the medical model emerged with its beliefs that disability is not a result of God's punishment but is based on a biological or medical issue. As a result, "persons with disabilities assumed the ongoing role of patients, needing to be cured" (State of Alaska, 2019, "Panel 4").

The history of special education as we think of it is considered to have its beginning during the 1700s. It was during this time that Jean Jacques Rousseau (1712–1778) published his ideas of the "noble savage" and also that education for all children should be based on the involvement of the senses. His work provided the impetus for later educators such as L'Epée, Seguin, and Itard (MNDDC, n.d.; Tremblay, 2007). Abbé Charles L'Epée (1712–1789) pioneered his ideas of how to teach students with disabilities in the school he founded in Paris for students with disabilities. Jean-Marc Itard (1774–1838) was one of the most influential teachers at that time as he believed that all children could be educated, that is, the "blank slate" described by John Locke in 1789. Based on this belief, Itard began his famous study of "Victor, the Wild Boy of Aveyron," publishing a book in 1805 explaining his efforts to educate Victor (Humphrey & Humphrey, Trans., 1962). Although Itard did not consider his work with Victor a success, it resulted in the development of many different methods for teaching individuals with severe sensory and intellectual disabilities. From the studies of Seguin (1812–1880), a student of Itard's methods, the idea evolved that mental disorders were "caused by a weakness of the nervous system, and could be cured through a process of motor and sensory training" (State of Alaska, 2019, "Panel 6") which was the precursor to the positive reinforcement and modeling that is used in today's schools.

During the early 19th century, efforts by such people as Thomas Gallaudet (1787–1851) and Samuel Howe (1801–1876) moved forward the issues of educating students with special needs (Winzer, 2009). By the late 1800s, public school education had become established in the United States with many of the states including education in their state constitutions. Education, although seen as a requisite factor in a democracy, is not included in the federal constitution; it is considered the responsibility of state government and was incorporated into state constitutions (Yell et al., 1998). Most state constitutions were not written to include children with disabilities in their educational systems. The exception was the inclusion of the development of state-supported institutions focused on preparing individuals for vocations or with providing safe environments for those who it was believed could not benefit from any form of educational or vocational training. Spaulding and Pratt (2015) noted:

> Special education as a discipline emerged not as an off-shoot of general education or as an expression of charitable compassion, but to quench the philosophical pursuits of the French Enlightenment, to satisfy the empirical inquiries of the content positive event of this era's temporary medical community, and to serve the economic interests of an industrializing society. (p. 95)

It was during this same period, following the Revolutionary War, that soldiers with injuries needed assistance. This need resulted in the first pension law enacted by the Continental Congress on August 26, 1776 to assist individuals with disabilities ("Pensions Enacted by Congress for American Revolutionary War Veterans," n.d.). This Act, amended numerous times, was the forerunner to other disability rights legislation that would be enacted in the late 1900s.

By the early 1900s, the number of students in schools had increased as compulsory education laws were enacted, although students with disabilities often received exemptions for attending school (Winzer, 2009). This was a time when educators believed the best placement for individuals with disabilities was in a segregated setting such as an institution or a separate school. The major thought was that children with disabilities did not learn in the same manner as "normal" children and should be supported in a setting where they could be taught more appropriately and protected from ridicule by other students. As a result, state legislators supported the development of state institutions for those children and adults with disabilities who had been excluded from public schools (Murdick et al., 2014). School administrators did not see their role as purveyors of education for children with disabilities nor were they required to develop and implement educational programs for them. In fact, "most children with disabilities were excluded from public schools, and many children with more significant disabilities received no education at all" (Crockett, 2011, p. 353). During these 200 years from the enactment of the legislation providing pensions for war veterans until the enactment of special education legislation in the 1900s,

> little was done to advance the rights of its disabled students. In fact, over 4.5 million children were denied adequate schooling before legislation to ensure equal educational opportunities for special education children began in the early 1970s. This was a dark period in special education. (All Star Staff, 2018, para. 4)

This view held by educators and educational administrators about the education and educational placement of children with disabilities began to change in the middle of the 20th century with the changes occurring around the world, both philosophically and sociologically (Winzer, 2009).

## Deinstitutionalization and the Normalization Movement

During the 1960s and 1970s, there was a significant movement to address issues related to the integration of people with disabilities. Concerns began to arise that the current placement of children and adults with severe disabilities in institutions was not appropriate as these places had begun to function less as training sites and more as custodial placements for lifelong care (Thompson & Wehmeyer, 2008). As a result, many institutions became seriously overcrowded and both the public and professionals became concerned that "many institutions were not providing the level of services, or quality of life, that should be available to all individuals" (Murdick et al., 2014, p. 3). This concern was brought to the forefront of public awareness with the publication of Blatt and Kaplan's 1974 seminal exposé, *Christmas in Purgatory*; Rivera's (1972) exposé, *Willowbrook*; and American Association on Mental Deficiency's (now the American Association on Intellectual and

Development Disability [AAIDD]) national study on the status of institutions for individuals with disabilities in 1971 (Vitello & Soskin, 1985).

The response to consider alternatives to institutionalization was the emergence of the concept of deinstitutionalization with the accompanying philosophy of normalization. Deinstitutionalization was the term used for the belief and the process by which individuals should be moved out of institutions and into the community where they could receive services in a more "normal" setting. The philosophy supporting and underpinning deinstitutionalization was normalization. The normalization movement was first espoused in the Scandinavian countries and emphasized the notion that individuals with disabilities should have experiences as well as "normalized" living arrangements similar to their nondisabled peers. This concept was first introduced into the United States through the works of Bank-Mikkelson (1976) and Nirje (1969) and later expanded and clarified by Wolfensberger in his seminal works on normalization and its successor, the concept of "social role valorization" (SRV; Murdick et al., 2014; Wolfensberger, 1972, 1983). Wolfensberger saw SRV as a way to change the perceptions of the value in the social roles played by people with disabilities. He posited that by enhancing their social role value, those with disabilities would be more valued and included in society (Thomas, 2017).

As a result of the normalization, deinstitutionalization, and SRV movements of the 1960s and 1970s, there was a move in the public school system to review the appropriateness of segregated classes and special education as a system (Winzer, 2009). These concerns focused on issues related to bias in the identification and evaluation of minority students with disabilities as well as concerns that segregated classes were not efficacious and were perpetuating stigmas related to persons with disabilities. Therefore, parents and special education professionals began to advocate for changes in the special education system (Crockett, 2011).

## Parent Advocacy and a "Bill of Rights" for Individuals With Disabilities

With the changing social arena, parents became frustrated with the lack of educational opportunities for their children with disabilities in public tax-funded schools (Murdick et al., 2014). This frustration led to the organization of parents into local support groups which eventually combined into national organizations such as The Arc, formerly known as the National Association for Retarded Children (ARC). The expansion of the various parent organizations in conjunction with disability advocacy groups (e.g., the International League of Societies for the Mentally Handicapped, the American Association on Mental Retardation, and Joint Commission on Mental Health of Children) began the push for a national conversation related to the rights of individuals with disabilities (Osgood, 2005). An international movement to address the issues of persons with disabilities culminated in the 1975 enactment of the "Declaration on the Rights of Disabled Persons" (United Nations General Assembly, 1975). The 13 rights emphasized the idea that people with disabilities should be afforded the same rights as all other individuals.

In addition, parents began to look to the U.S. court system to redress what they saw as a denial of their children's rights for educational opportunity. As Forte Law Group (2017) outlined, "Prior to the foundational disability rights cases being decided, exclusion of students with disabilities was the rule across the United States" (p. 2). Parents, in their move to address this exclusion, based their reasoning on the seminal civil rights case, *Brown v. Board of Education* (1954), expanding its focus to an additional "class" of people, those with disabilities, by insisting students with disabilities should be accorded the same rights as those students without disabilities in the public school system (Yell et al., 1998). The following statement from the *Brown* decision was used as the basis for future legislation in special education:

> In these days, it is doubtful that any child may reasonably be expected to succeed in life if he is denied the opportunity of an education. Such an opportunity, where the state has undertaken to provide it, is a right which must be made available to all on equal terms. (*Brown v. Board of Education of Topeka, Kansas*, 1954, p. 493)

## Early Special Education Litigation and Legislation

Early litigation in special education used *Brown* as support for their push to have schools provide services for all children including those with disabilities. *Hobson v. Hansen* (1967) was the first major case raising questions about placement in special education and the issue of physical exclusion from school. This federal court case was filed on the charge that the educational system deprived Blacks and the poor of their right to equal educational opportunities. In the *Hobson* decision, Judge Wright sought to remedy the resegregation or de facto segregation enforced by educational policies, including that of tracking and optional-transfer zones. The court ruled using "biased" assessment results to group students into "tracks" was unconstitutional because it discriminated against them by mislabeling them and placing them in segregated classes that had a significantly different curriculum from that provided to students in regular classes (Justia U.S. Law, 2020; Murdick et al., 2014). Although this case did not focus specifically on students with disabilities, it introduced the idea that segregation of students based on some unalterable characteristic may violate their right to an appropriate education.

In 1972, another landmark decision for the field of special education was heard in the case of *PARC v. Commonwealth of Pennsylvania*. In this case, the federal court decided that children with mental disabilities must be provided a free and appropriate public education. This case was based on two basic clauses included in the U.S. Constitution—due process and equal protection. This case illustrated the difference in the legal view of disability and society's view at the time that children with disabilities were unable to learn or fit in with their mainstream peers (Friend & Bursuck, 2012). This case and subsequent cases eventually paved the way for changes in society's viewpoint and the passage of further legislation that protects the rights of students with disabilities (Yell et al., 1998).

The case of *Mills v. Board of Education of DC* (1972) is very similar to that of *PARC* except it expands the class of individuals from those with mental retardation to "exceptional," which included students who had received the labels of behavior problems, intellectual disability (mental retardation), emotional disturbance or hyperactivity. The litigation addressed the issue of exclusion from education settings without the constitutional right of due process, which denied them the opportunity for an education (Murdick et al., 2014). The *Mills* case, like the *PARC* case, served as an important precedent in future federal decisions pertaining to students with disabilities (Yell et al., 1998). In addition, this case introduced the terminology and concept of sufficient funds because students with disabilities were still being denied a public education based on lack of funding. The result of the *Mills* decision was that schools could no longer deny education based on funding issues (Gargiulo & Bouck, 2019).

An additional case that provided the basis for requirements in later special education legislation was that of *Diana v. State Board of Education* (1970). This case addressed the use of standardized tests to identify, classify, and place students in segregated school settings. Diana was a California student who was Spanish-speaking and placed in a class for students with mild mental retardation based on her low score on an IQ test given to her in English. There was another issue with the tests: They had been standardized on a White, native-born American population. Because the court addressed bias in testing, all students in the state of California being considered for special education placement had to be tested in their primary language, and those currently labeled as having an intellectual disability as a result of this testing were to be retested (School Psychological Resource, n.d.). Based on this litigation, "unbiased" testing was included in the later enactment of the Individuals with Disabilities Education Act (Murdick et al., 2014).

The concept of testing bias was expanded and clarified in *Larry P. v. Riles* (1972, 1974, 1979, 1984). The plaintiffs in this case were African American students who were either placed in, or being considered for placement in, classes for children with mental retardation. The issue, as in the *Diana* case, concerned the use of standardized intelligence tests. At issue was the possible bias of the tests and the resulting disproportionate placement of minority groups in segregated classes as evidence of discrimination (UCLA Mental Health Project, n.d.). The courts agreed with the plaintiff's argument, and in their decision, held that students of minority groups being considered for special education services could not be placed until unbiased assessments were developed. In addition, the State of California was required to retest all students in special education programs and subsequently provide them with any requisite compensatory education (Murdick et al., 2014).

In summary, these early pieces of litigation focused on the rights of individuals with disabilities and were the impetus for the move toward the expansion of special education services and the enactment of legislation to support that expansion. The early cases addressed issues focused on the use of segregated classes based on possibly biased testing (*Hobson v. Hansen*, 1967), denial of educational services for children with intellectual disabilities (*PARC v. Commonwealth of Pennsylvania*, 1972), exclusion from school without due process (*Mills v. Board of Education of DC*, 1972), placement in segregated classes based on language and cultural bias (*Diana v. State Board of Education*, 1970), and use of IQ tests with minority groups leading to bias and disproportionality in special education placements (*Larry P. v. Riles*, 1972, 1974, 1979, 1984). Both *PARC* and *Mills* used the *Brown* decision as the basis for their cases "by using the due process clause of the 14th Amendment to provide parents of children with disabilities specific rights to challenge and strike down state law that denied their children the right to a public education" (Forte Law Group, 2017, p. 3). However, Martin et al. (1996) insisted that "many of the laws had loopholes (such as applying only to children "who could benefit from education") or were simply not enforced by state officials" (p. 28). As a result of this lack of oversight, enforcement, and funding, frustrated parents and disability advocates began to look to the federal arena for resolution of this national problem.

## SPECIAL EDUCATION SERVICE DELIVERY DURING THE CIVIL RIGHTS ERA (1950s THROUGH THE 1970s)

### Philosophical Change Supported by Civil Rights for All

Exclusion of students with disabilities had its roots in the philosophy of exclusion (Esteves & Rao, 2008), which can be traced to 1893 when the Massachusetts Supreme Court upheld the decision in *Watson v. City of Cambridge*. In the *Watson* decision the exclusion of a student with intellectual and physical disabilities was based solely on his disabilities (Smith, 2004). This case was followed by *Beattie v. Board of Education of Antigo* in 1919 which upheld the exclusion of a student with normal intellect who was unable to physically care for himself (Yell et al., 1998). Even though compulsory education laws were put in place in 1918, students with disabilities were often excluded from public schools based on court decisions such as those described above. "Even as recently as 1958 and 1969, the courts upheld legislation that excluded students whom school officials judged would not benefit from public education or who might be disruptive to other students" (Yell et al., 1998, p. 220).

All Star Staff (2018) indicated that "special education came into existence almost exclusively within the last 50 years" (p. 1). While the civil rights movement began with the issue of segregation of minority individuals, it transcended race and spread its efforts to include individuals with handicapping conditions. The landmark case of *Brown v. Board of Education* (1954), although it addressed racial segregation, significantly influenced special education. The decision that individuals were segregated on the basis of race violated equal educational opportunity and opened the door to a growing understanding that all people had a right to a public education. While the Supreme Court decision outlined the right, there remained the issue of schools being able to choose whether or not to participate in special education incentive programs until the mid-1960s (Smith, 2004). In 1961, U.S. President Kennedy appointed a President's Panel on Mental Retardation (Montgomery, 2003). On February 5, 1963, he said: "We must promote—to the best of our ability and by all possible and appropriate means—the mental and physical health of all our citizens" (John F. Kennedy and People with Intellectual Disabilities, n.d.). After the decision in *Brown,* parents of children with special needs started to file lawsuits against school districts for excluding and segregating their children. Their arguments were that by excluding these children the schools were discriminating against them because of their disabilities (Wright, n.d.b).

During the 1960s and 1970s, societal perceptions of disability once again changed due to myriad factors including medical advances related to disability, and advocacy efforts to change public attitudes (Spaulding & Pratt, 2015). In addition, Skiba et al. (2008) found it is important to remember "special education was borne out of, and owes a debt to, the civil rights movement" (p. 264). Without litigation such as *Brown* and the civil rights movement that emphasized the rights of persons who are different from the norm, the subsequent expansion of services for students with disabilities was unlikely to have happened. As Murdick et al. (2014) wrote, "The result of these political advocacy and judicial actions was an awareness of a need for civil rights legislation for persons with disabilities" (p. 15).

According to Winzer (2009), "The United States has a long history of placing great faith in law and legislation as the palliative to discrimination and prejudice" (p. 115). Thus, during the 1960s, there were several new laws that emphasized education for students with disabilities and provided funding to schools for their provision of such services. In fact, "during the 1960s and the early 1970s there was a pervasive national concern with the rights of the individual who had previously been disenfranchised by the government" (Murdick et al., 2014, p. 8). One of the first significant instances of federal involvement in the education of students with disabilities occurred in 1958 with the enactment of the Expansion of Teaching in the Education of Mentally Retarded Children Act (Yell et al., 1998). This law focused on the provision of federal funds for the training of teachers for students with mental retardation. Then in 1965, the Elementary and Secondary Education Act (ESEA) was passed, which provided schools with monies from the federal government to address various categories of children in the schools who had specialized educational needs. In 1966, an amendment to the ESEA, Title VI, set aside funds earmarked for students with disabilities (Yell & Katsiyannis, 2004). Thus, as the country moved into the 1970s there was a change both in the philosophy and implementation of educational services for students with disabilities.

## Early Legislation Including the Rehabilitation Act and the DD Act

In the early 1970s, with the aforementioned litigative and legislative action, parent advocacy, and philosophical belief changes, the federal government began to consider how to address the civil rights of persons with disabilities. The Rehabilitation Act of 1973 was an attempt to provide civil rights legislation for persons with disabilities. It included a section known as Section 504 that stated:

> [No] otherwise qualified individual with a disability in the United States... shall, solely by reason of her or his disability, be excluded from the participation, be denied the benefits of, or be subjected to discrimination under any program or activity receiving Federal financial assistance or under any program or activity conducted by an Executive agency or by the United States Postal Service. (29 U.S.C. § 794)

Although this piece of legislation addressed the issue of services for those with disabilities, no funding was allotted to address the issue of program delivery in the schools. In addition, it only extended the rights to those individuals who were in programs currently supported by federal funds. Two years later, in 1975, another piece of legislation known as the Developmental Disabilities Assistance and Bill of Rights Act (DD Act) was enacted to implement the recommendations of the President's Panel on Mental Retardation originally appointed by John F. Kennedy in 1961 (Montgomery,

2003; Murdick et al., 2014). This act did contain funding, but only for "the development of research centers, university-affiliated facilities, and community facilities" (Murdick et al., 2014, p. 14). This act did not address school issues, only the expansion of knowledge and services for individuals with disabilities, specifically those with mental retardation. School administrators were faced with parent advocacy, societal beliefs in the rights of students with disabilities, and legislation and litigation at both the state and national level that called for schools to provide appropriate services for all children in their schools.

## ERA OF INCLUSION FOR STUDENTS WITH DISABILITIES (1970s THROUGH 2000s)

### Philosophy of Educational Equity and Inclusive Programs

During the past century, the advocacy movement and its accompanying litigation and legislation have focused on the issue of educational equity. Educational equity is defined as "a measure of achievement, fairness, and opportunity in education" ("Educational Equity," 2020, para. 1). The concept of educational equity can be linked back to the *Brown* decision that one's educational opportunity can be correlated with future quality of life. Although the terms equity and equality are sometimes used interchangeably, the two terms are not the same (see Sayed & Soudien, 2003 for a more in-depth discussion of the controversy over exclusion and inclusion). According to Rise (2022):

> If fairness is the goal, equality and equity are two processes through which we can achieve it. Equality simply means everyone is treated the same exact way, regardless of need or any other individual difference. Equity, on the other hand, means everyone is provided with what they need to succeed. (p. 1)

Ainscow et al. (2013) indicated that movement of school systems to address the needs of children with disabilities has been "a step-by-step movement from exclusion to special education provision, through to an emphasis on integration and finally to the idea of inclusive education" (p. 4). Both litigation and legislation throughout the 1900s focused on how best to educate students with disabilities. This service delivery focus has changed depending on what perspective or model is used to view individuals with disabilities and subsequent school options. The three main perspectives being used are the deficit model, the social constructivist view, and the ecological perspective.

## Deficit Model

The deficit model of special education views the person with the disability from a bi-directional viewpoint—normality vs. abnormality. Thus, the focus of education should be to provide the student with a disability, that is, abnormality, the means or skills to function more normally in the educational milieu (Boroson, 2017; Dudley-Marling & Burns, 2014). In this model, it is the responsibility of teachers and administrators to identify the student's disability, prepare lessons to address the identified deficits in the learning profile, and identify the appropriate environment where the individual can be successful and be closest to "normal" peers.

## Social Constructivist View

Dudley-Marling and Burns (2014) posited the view that "disability is a social construction" (p. 23). In this viewpoint, individual differences should not be considered as deficiencies, nor should they be denied or overlooked but they should be seen as only one aspect of the individual. Thus, in the social constructionist view of inclusion, the regular classroom would be the default setting, not the aspirational setting (Brantlinger, 1997; Dudley-Marling & Burns, 2014). This change in viewpoint looks at schooling and the inclusion of special education students through a different lens, that of individual competence. Thus, it becomes the responsibility of the teachers and administrators to provide educational opportunities for students with disabilities in age-appropriate classrooms (National Center on Inclusive Education, 2011).

## Ecological Perspective

This perspective focuses on the interactions of students with disabilities, their peers without disabilities, and their teachers within the general education classroom instead of focusing on educational outcomes. Thus, this perspective views education from a more holistic view of the "classroom ecosystem in order to identify the conditions and supports necessary for inclusion to improve outcomes for all students (Gilmour, 2018, p. 15). There is concern that viewing special education issues from this viewpoint may result in conflicts between policy makers, school personnel, and parents that can lead to litigation (Gilmour, 2018).

The differing views on what constitutes an appropriate classroom and curriculum for students with disabilities is a continuing controversy (see Brantlinger, 1997 for an early review of the controversy). The move toward inclusion has resulted in litigation focusing on issues related to all aspects of education for students with disabilities. Legislation to ensure students with disabilities receive an appropriate education has also been enacted. With that in mind, a brief review of the more recent legislation and litigation is provided.

# Legislation Including IDEA and Its Successors

ESEA of 1965 (P.L. 89-10) was the basis for legislation that has impacted schools throughout the United States. This act was considered the original commitment of the federal government to intervene to improve the educational opportunities for "disadvantaged" students in the nation's schools. This legislation was amended later in 1965 and again in 1966 to expand the funding to children with disabilities and in 1970 became the ESEA Amendments of 1970 (P.L. 92-230), which consolidated various grant programs funding services for children with disabilities and was renamed the Education of the Handicapped Act of 1970 or EHA. This piece of legislation was followed by the Education of the Handicapped Act Amendments of 1974 (P.L. 93-380), which directed states to develop plans for how they were going to provide educational opportunities for children with disabilities.

Public Law 94-142, the Education for All Handicapped Children Act (EAHCA; 1975), is considered by advocates and special educators to be the culmination of the advocacy and litigation that occurred in the 1960s and 1970s (United States Department of Education, 2007). They also describe it as the legal manifestation of the philosophical move toward equity in the provision of educational opportunities for children with disabilities. This can be seen in its stated purpose:

1. To ensure that all children with disabilities have available to them a free, appropriate public education that includes special education and related services designed to meet their unique needs;
2. To ensure that the rights of children with disabilities and their parents are protected;
3. To assist States and localities to provide for the education of all children with disabilities; and
4. To assess and ensure the effectiveness of efforts to educate those children. (34 C.F.R. § 300.1)

This legislation includes eight parts which contain the basic information required for educators to provide educational services for the children with disabilities in their districts. In addition, these parts can be seen as legal manifestations of six basic principles that arose during the push for equity in education for all children. These six principles are (a) zero reject, which is affirmed through the requirement that all children are entitled to receive a free appropriate public education (FAPE); (b) nondiscriminatory assessment, which is based on the belief that any testing should be racially or culturally nondiscriminatory; (c) procedural due process, which supports the previous two principles by requiring that safeguards are included to guarantee the rights of children with disabilities and their parents; (d) parental participation, which is an essential principle to ensure that parent advocacy is included in the provision of educational services; (e) least restrictive environment (LRE), which is a result of the belief that children learn best in the "normal" school environment; and (f) the individualized education program (IEP), which is a required principle that ensures that all children receive an education that is appropriate to their unique needs (Murdick et al., 2014).

Over the past almost 50 years since this original piece of legislation, P.L. 94-142 or EAHCA was enacted, it has been reauthorized and amended to meet the changing educational scene and the evolving philosophical belief system. The most important of these amendments are considered to be the Individuals With Disabilities Education Act of 1990 or IDEA (P.L. 101-476), which had its name changed to reflect the use of "people first" language; the IDEA of 1997, which focused on improving educational results through access to the general curriculum (Villa & Thousand, 2003) and promoting school safety; and the IDEA of 2005 (P.L. 108-446), which focused on the alignment of IDEA requirements with the requirements of the No Child Left Behind Act of 2001 (P.L. 107-110). The No Child Left Behind Act (NCLB) act was considered to be a significant move by the federal government. The purpose of NCLB was to ensure "that all children have a fair, equal, and significant opportunity to obtain a high-quality education and reach, at a minimum, proficiency on challenging State academic achievement standards and state academic assessments" (20 U.S.C. § 1001). This far-reaching piece of legislation incorporated the philosophical move for educational equity to all children, not just those with disabilities.

## Litigation Today: The Continued Search for Educational Equity

Throughout the history of special education, the courts have clarified issues that have arisen in the interpretation and implementation of legislative mandates. Education, since it is not listed in the U.S. Constitution, is considered to be a form of equity law, that is, it deals with issues affecting the individual's rights to due process and equal protection (Murdick et al., 2014). At both the state and federal level, courts require the individuals bringing a lawsuit to exhaust all remedies prior to initiating a court action, such as completion of mediation, due process, and so forth. The appeals then proceed through the system with the final decision being made at the U.S. Supreme Court, if the court decides to hear the case. There is no appeal from a decision by the U.S. Supreme Court except by a subsequent ruling by the court or an amendment to the U.S. Constitution. Decisions made by the U.S. Supreme Court become the law for all courts in the United States (Arons, 2020).

The first special education case to reach the Supreme Court was *Board of Education v. Rowley* (1982). This case addressed the issue of what is "appropriate" when considering the FAPE required by IDEA. According to the court, an appropriate education was one in which the student was provided the basic opportunity to receive an education to meet the unique needs of each child with a disability (Arons, 2020). The court devised a two-part test for schools to use to decide this issue. The *Rowley* test, as it was known, asked two questions: (a) "Had the procedures set forth by the state and IDEA been followed"?; and (b) "Was the IEP developed according to the procedures and reasonably calculated to enable the child to receive educational benefits?" The *Rowley* case was followed by cases that addressed issues related to clarifying what related services are and why they are essential (*Irving Independent Sch. Dist. V. Amber Tatro,* 1984), the parent's right to be reimbursed for private school expenditures if the IEP is inadequate or inappropriate (*Burlington Sch. Committee v. Mass. Bd. of Ed.,* 1985), and development of standards ("stay-put" requirement) to address when a school could expel or suspend students as a result of aspects of their disability (*Honig v. Doe,* 1988). Additional cases were heard related to parents' rights to receive reimbursement for private educational placement (*Florence County School District Four v. Shannon Carter,* 1993), the definition of "prevailing party" for the allocation of attorney's fees (*Buckhannon v. West Virginia Dept. of Health and Human Resources,* 2001), the identification of who has the burden of proof in a due process proceeding (*Schaffer v. Weast,* 2005), the delineation of what are reasonable attorneys' fees (*Arlington v. Murphy,* 2006), and whether parents have rights under IDEA for themselves (*Jacob Winkelman v. Parma City School District,* 2007).

After a 10-year hiatus, the U.S. Supreme Court heard two significant special education cases focused on the issues of the requirement of use of the exhaustion doctrine (*Fry v. Napoleon Comm. Sch. Dist.,* 2017) and the concept of educational benefit when developing an IEP (*Endrew v. Douglas County Sch. Dist.,* 2017). In the *Fry* case, the parents of Elena, a child with cerebral palsy who used a service dog to assist her in attending and benefiting from her education, filed suit in federal court. They stated, the school district did not allow her the use of a support dog in all aspects of her schooling under the auspices of the Americans With Disabilities Act (ADA) and Section 504 of the Rehabilitation Act (Wright & Wright, n.d.c). The Supreme Court ruling, known as a Holding, was:

> Exhaustion of the administrative procedures established by the Individuals with Disabilities Education Act is unnecessary when the gravamen of the plaintiff's suit is something other than the denial of the IDEA's core guarantee of a "free appropriate public education." (SCOTUSblog, 2017)

Therefore, this decision may be read as the gravity of a child's educational needs may override the procedural requirements of the exhaustion of remedies before filing in federal court is required.

The case that has made the most impact is that of *Endrew v. Douglas County* (2017). The court in this case expanded the discussion of what is appropriate, first considered in the *Rowley* case, and stated it was "clarifying that a different standard needs to be used when children with disabilities are not fully mainstreamed" (Wright, n.d.a, para. 9). The court addressed the arguments related to an IEP providing "some" educational benefit, known as the *de minimis* standard, versus an IEP providing "meaningful" educational benefit. This decision returns to the issue of what exactly satisfies the requirements for the development and implementation of an appropriate IEP (Wright & Wright, n.d.a, n.d.b). Justice Roberts in his decision did not overturn the *Rowley* test but expanded it to clarify the second question as to the appropriateness of the IEP (Yell & Bateman, 2017) and rejected the *de minimis* standard that had been the rule since 1982 (Howe, 2017). As the Bazelon Center for Mental Health Law (2017) in their *amicus brief* stated, "*Endrew* rejects the 'bigotry of low expectations' that marked prior interpretations of *Rowley*. It requires that schools provide special education that is designed to help students with disabilities become academically proficient and advance from grade to grade" (p. 3).

For school administrators and all members of the IEP team, the *Endrew* ruling brought a momentous change in the development of the IEP. As the Council of Parent Attorneys and Advocates (COPAA; 2017) presented, "each child needs to have the opportunity to learn, receive meaningful benefit, and meet challenging objectives under his or her Individualized Education Program, commensurate with the student's unique abilities" (para. 1). When the decision in *Endrew* is linked with the requirements under the Every Student Succeeds Act of 2015 (ESSA), administrators need to become cognizant of the ethical and legal requirements for the provision of services for students with disabilities. Currently, under ESSA, states are to prepare the education plans for their schools within a framework provided by the federal government. The law offers parents a chance to weigh in on these plans; this is important if the child is to receive appropriate special education services. Each state plan must include a description of the academic standards, annual testing, school accountability, goals for academic achievement, plans for supporting and improving struggling schools, and state and local report cards. There are several more requirements for states and school districts, but these are the ones that most directly affect children with learning and thinking differences. As state and local administrators begin to develop and implement their plans, they should remember the words of Esteves and Rao (2008): "Whereas integration was the prominent theme in decades past, today we are accountable for education that is meaningful, formative, results-oriented and individualized for *all* students, not just those with diagnosed disabilities" (p. 2).

As a result of the philosophical changes, the continuing litigation to ensure the rights of children with disabilities, and the enactment of federal and state legislation, educational leaders must be aware of their role in this fast-changing environment. As Harpell and Andrews (2010) wrote, "It is of paramount importance that educational leaders make every effort to generate and maintain the values of inclusive education and humanitarian philosophy in teachers. The attitudes administrators present are critical to the success of inclusive classrooms" (p. 202).

## Importance of Leadership for Students With Special Needs

Research has demonstrated that effective principals are the critical ingredients for successful schools (Leithwood et al., 2004). Goor et al. (1997) found, though, that principals had increased demands placed on them to lead schools to meet the needs of a diversifying student population, including students with special needs. These demands have continued to increase and as Harpell and Andrews (2010) noted, without strong, knowledgeable leadership in schools, the supports needed will not be provided, maintained, or evaluated for appropriate institutionalization in the schoolhouse.

Instructional leadership has been studied in public education for decades, but not many studies have addressed the administrator practices used to ensure that students with disabilities receive a free, appropriate, public education (FAPE; Bays & Crockett, 2007). One of the greatest challenges for instructional leaders is ensuring that students with disabilities are provided FAPE in the least restrictive environment. As Edwards (2012) explained:

> Paradoxically, the only constant in these school leaders' ever increasing responsibilities is that of change—change in the physical environment, change in the curriculum, change in staff, change in the type of special needs students emerging, and significant change in the budgets meant to serve this special population. It is critical that all school leaders and other special education stakeholders must become the primary catalysts in their respective roles in order for these changes to become both positive and lasting. (p. vi)

Leaders must realize that inclusion of students with disabilities is more than just placing a student with disabilities in the regular classroom; it requires the leader to develop a school culture embracing diversity (DiPaola et al., 2004; DiPaola & Walther-Thomas, 2003; Walther-Thomas et al., 2002). This type of inclusion requires a culture led by the vision and practices of the school administrator (DiPaola et al., 2004). The leader must create a setting where students with disabilities are valued and have the opportunity to socialize, be challenged, and where disabilities are not seen as an excuse to set lower expectations. Principals are encouraged to "focus on fundamental instructional issues, demonstrate strong support for special education, and provide ongoing professional development" (DiPaola et al., 2004, p. 3). The instructional leader should demonstrate expertise in curriculum delivery, ensure teachers have the instructional materials and resources needed, facilitate evidence-based intervention practices, and offer strategies and methods for teachers to meet the needs of all students in the classroom (Loiacono & Palumbo, 2011). These instructional leaders must maintain a focus on instructional improvement which includes an explicit responsibility to consider the needs of students with disabilities. According to Bays and Crockett (2007), many of the recent reform initiatives created a situation where special education is a major concern. "School principals," according to Katsiyannis (1994), "are responsible for ensuring the appropriate education of all students, including those with disabilities" (p. 6). According to Gersten et al. (2001) these leaders are able to affect "virtually all critical aspects of (special education) teachers' working conditions" (p. 557). Thus, the leaders need the abilities to ensure appropriate provision of special education programs and services (Katsiyannis, 1994). To do this, instructional leaders have to acquire an understanding of the requirements of NCLB (2001) and IDEA (2004) as well as the ability to understand and recognize good instructional practice, provide classroom and personnel resources necessary for meeting students' needs, and have a working knowledge of how to use data in coordination with progress monitoring to evaluate program effectiveness (DiPaola et al., 2004). According to DiPaola et al. (2004), "If school... goals are to be realized, effective leaders must be prepared to address diverse learning needs" (p. 8). To meet school goals, DiPaola et al. outlined school leadership practices which could improve special education services. These practices include:

1. promote an inclusive school culture,
2. provide instructional leadership,
3. model collaborative leadership,
4. administer organizational processes, and
5. build and maintain positive relations with teachers, families, and the community. (p. 8)

In addition to DiPaola et al.'s (2004) list, Crockett (2002) proposed that school leaders need five additional skills to create a successful inclusive school environment. These leadership skills include the leader (a) demonstrating ethical practices where the school leader advocates for opportunities for all students, (b) considering issues of individualized needs and specific instructional techniques to meet student needs, (c) applying legal equity by acquiring the knowledge to ensure compliance with all legal requirements and developing policies and practices aligned with legal mandates, (d) supervising and evaluating both general and individualized instructional programs, and (e) developing meaningful collaborative partnerships with various stakeholders while practicing listening to those advocating on behalf of students with disabilities. Researchers have insisted that these are components that should be evident in the school culture and that culture resides in the leader's vision and practices (DiPaola et al., 2004; Frick et al., 2013).

To assist instructional leaders responsible for the education of students with special needs, the Council for Exceptional Children (CEC) began developing draft standards for educational leaders in May of 2019 and released the updated Standards in 2020. CEC is considered to be the premier professional organization for all professionals involved in the education of children with disabilities. They have developed standards that outline guidelines for the initial preparation of teachers along with advanced standards for administrators. These standards were intended to be used as guidelines that reflected current demands for ensuring inclusive practices and accountability for school leaders:

Standard 1: Vision, Mission, and Direction Setting

Standard 2: Implementation of Pollicy, Legal and Ethical Practices for Special Education Programs and Services

Standard 3: Organizational Leadership and Management for Special Education

Standard 4: Program Oversight, Improvement, and Instructional Leadership for Special Education

Standard 5: Human and Fiscal Management of Special Education Programs and Services

Standard 6: Collabooration and Communication with Special Education Stakeholders

Standard 7: Equity and Cultural Responsiveness (CEC, 2022)

These CEC standards span the practices required by effective instructional leaders in today's inclusive schools (see "CEC Administrator of Special Education Professional Leadership Standards" for a complete description of each standard and its subcategories, CEC, 2022). The CEC standards include the factors Fullan (2009) cited as the work of school leaders for all students to assist leaders in being accountable. The continually rising accountability to ensure programs are developed, implemented, and monitored to meet the needs of all learners has become the central focus of the work of educational administrators (Leithwood et al., 2008). These skills are needed for general education leaders as they see their ever-changing role as instructional leaders. As Crockett (2002) indicated, there is a need for leaders to broaden their knowledge to include skills used for ensuring the meeting of all student needs. As the role of the special education administrator evolves, these leaders must utilize leadership practices in the development and implementation of effective, inclusive educational programs and services to ensure that students with disabilities receive high quality instruction to meet the same learning standards as their nondisabled peers (Fullan, 2009). The influence of education reforms on school leadership in general, and on the roles of general and special education leaders continues to shift their responsibilities.

## SUMMARY

### Where Are We Going? A Change in Philosophy?

Special education services in the schools, as this overview has described, is a relatively recent development that has looked at what works for students at the margins of education. As Kauffman (1999) noted, "We have considerable capacity for self-correction and finding order where others see disorder" (p. 253). Over the past few years, schools have seen more and more students educated in the general education classroom, often referred to as "inclusive education" (Smith, 1998; Whitten & Rodriguez-Campos, 2003). However, as Portelli and Koneeny (2018) stated:

> Despite the fact that inclusion is a relatively recent concept that developed within contemporary education theory and practice, the achievement of inclusion has been a fundamental component of the teaching experience for educators and policy makers. (p. 133)

Odom and Diamond (1998) reported the word "inclusion" could be found in the 1990s and focused on improving existing initiatives of integrating children with disabilities into regular education classrooms. Even with belief that inclusion could provide equality of opportunity, there has been resistance based on differing views of disability and education (Slee, 2009). Despite this resistance, inclusive education has become a global movement and continues to create policy shifts around the world (e.g., see the Salamanca Declaration prepared by UNESCO, 1994).

While there may be some who dispute the full inclusion idea, inclusive education promises social justice based on the redistribution of access and social good. As Kozleski et al. (2014) said:

Inclusive education is not about relocation of people in the mainstream. Inclusive education presses us to consider the ontology of special and regular; presses us to resist such a bifurcation as redundant in democratic education. Expansion and contraction within local activity systems intersect with racial, class, caste, sexuality and gender identities, knowledge systems, culture, ethnicities, and abilities. (p. 231)

This is a time of unprecedented change and uncharted territory in education (Gangone, n.d.). Administrators need to be prepared to address the issues and challenges that have arisen, including those from the COVID-19 pandemic. O'Leary (2019) identified five possible areas that may impact special education in the future: technology, trauma-informed teaching, homelessness and poverty, twice exceptional students, and parental support. Three of these areas may significantly impact not only the education of special education students but that of all students during this time when schools are impacted by the pandemic. These significant areas are technology, including the availability of equipment and remote services at a time when schools may not be able to be in session (Brenner, 2020); trauma-informed teaching as students, teachers, and staff respond to the fears and realities in a time of pandemic; and homelessness and poverty as the realities of the economy and loss of jobs impact students and their families. Hill (2020) insisted:

No one yet knows what the long-term impact will be on special-ed students. Some teachers and researchers predict a major backslide in learning, that students will return to school having significantly regressed. This phenomenon already happens, in special-education students particularly, over winter and summer breaks—what's sometimes called the "summer slide"—and the longer students are out, the more likely they are to fall behind. Researchers are already starting to see a "melt" of skills among students in general, which portends even greater losses among those with disabilities. (para. 13)

Mitchell (2020) addressed concerns related to the possibility of disagreements between parents and schools over their child's education resulting in due process hearings and litigation. So far this fear that parents will sue unless a comparable education is provided to their children has not been of consequence as lawsuits have been filed in only three states (Mitchell, 2020). Administrators need to remember "the obligation to provide a free appropriate public education doesn't go away just because we've transitioned to remote learning" (Okungu, 2020, para. 16).

As administrators navigate through the changes in schooling related to the pandemic, they must consider how to provide educational services for all students including equitable and appropriate services for their students with special needs. Although the government has provided states and districts with the option to extend timelines and to conduct hearings via video (Diamont, 2020), this is considered to be temporary and not a change in the law's requirements. According to the Council of Administrators of Special Education (CASE; 2020), during these trying times administrators should keep in mind four priorities. The first is to focus on the safety, health, and welfare of the students and staff members in the school and/or district. To do this, the Center for Disease Control and Prevention (CDC) and state guidance documents should be followed as school opening is reviewed, and plans should be developed to assist all students and faculty in terms of mental health issues that may arise from both long-distance learning and the possibility of opening school during a pandemic (CASE, 2020). Secondly, it is essential to deliver FAPE to the special education students as reasonably as possible, providing as many services as possible via remote learning, and continuing to provide individualized services to students with disabilities in the district (CASE, 2020). The third priority is to document all decisions and efforts made to provide appropriate services to the students in the school district, which will assist if litigation occurs in the future. According to CASE, it is imperative to "make sure documentation is focused, consistent, detailed and demonstrates a good faith effort to provide good services" (CASE, 2020, Slide 4). And lastly, remember special education and "IDEA wasn't built for this" (CASE, 2020, Slide 5). Education for all students will certainly look different in the future, and the needs seen today will not disappear after the pandemic ends (Jones, 2020). This is especially true as "officials are acknowledging again that services for students with disabilities may not look the same as they used to, but…with collaboration, parents and educators can work to meet children's needs" (Diamont, 2020, para. 4).

## REFERENCES

Ainscow, M., Dyson, A., & Weiner, S. (2013). *From exclusion to inclusion: Ways of responding to students with special educational needs.* CfBT Education Trust.

All Star Staff. (2018, March 6). *A brief history of special education in the United States.* https://www.alleducationschools.com/blog/history-of-special-education/

Arlington v. Murphy, 548 U.S. 49 (2006).

Arons, L. J. (2020). *Landmark cases in special education law.* https://specialeducation lawyernj.com/special-education-law/landmark-cases-in-special-education-law/

Baank-Mikkelson, N. E. (1976). Denmark. In R. B. Kugel & A. Shearer (Eds.), *Changing patterns in residential services for the mentally retarded* (rev. ed.). President's Committee on Mental Retardation.

Bays, D., & Crockett, J. (2007). Investigating instructional leadership for special education. *Exceptionality, 15*(3), 143–161.

Bazelon Center for Mental Health Law. (2017). *Bazelon center applauds Supreme Court's decision in Endrew F.* http://www.bazelon.org/wp-content/uploads/2017/04/Endrew-announcement.pdf

Beattie v. Board of Education, 172 N.W. 153 (Wis. 1919)

Blatt, B., & Kaplan, F. (1974). *Christmas in purgatory: A photographic essay on mental retardation.* Human Policy Press.

Board of Education v. Rowley, 458 U.S. 176 (1982).

Boroson, B. (2017). Inclusive education: Lessons from history. *Educational Leadership, 74*(7), 18–23.

Brantlinger, E. (1997). Using ideology: Cases of nonrecognition of the politics of research and practice in special education. *Review of Educational Research, 67*(4), 425–459.

Brenner, K. (2020, April 10). Coronavirus compounds challenges for special education. *The Marin Independent Journal.* https://www.govtech.com/public-safety/Coronavirus-Compounds-Challenges-for-Special-Education.html

Brown v. Board of Education, 347 U.S. 483 (1954).

Buckhannon v. West Virginia Dept. of Health and Human Resources, 532 U.S. 598, 121, S.Ct. 1835 (2001).

Burlington Sch. Committee v. Mass. Bd. of Ed., 471 U.S. 359 (1985).

Council for Exceptional Children. (2022). *Administrator of special education professional leadership standards.* https://www.cec.sped.org/Standards/advanced-administrator-special-education-professional-leadership-standards

Council of Administrators of Special Education. (2022, May). *Navigating the COVID-19 pandemic for special education administrators, April 24.* https://casecec.org/covid-19

Council of Parent Attorneys and Advocates. (2017). *Practical applications of Endrew F. USSC decision.* https://www.copaa.org/page/Endrew

Crockett, J. B. (2002). Special education's role in preparing responsive leaders for inclusive schools. *Remedial and Special Education, 23,*189–199.

Crockett, J. B. (2011). Conceptual models for leading and administrating special education. In J. M. Kauffman & D. P. Hallahan (Eds.), *Handbook of special education* (pp. 351–362). SAGE Publications.

Developmental Disabilities Assistance and Bill of Rights Act, 42 U.S.C. § 6000 *et seq.* (1975).

Diamont, M. (2020, June 23). *Ed Department issues new guidance on special education during pandemic.* Disability Scoop. https://www.disabilityscoop.com/2020/06/23/ed-department-new-guidance-special-education-pandemic/28517/

Diana v. State Board of Education, Civ. Act No. C-70-37 RFP (N.D. Cal. 1970) further order (1973) (unpublished opinion).

DiPoala, M., Tschannen-Moran, M., & Walther-Thomas, C. (2004). School principals and special education: Creating the context for academic success. *Focus on Exceptional Children, 37*(4), 1–8.

DiPaola, M. F., & Walther-Thomas, C. (2003). *Principals and special education: The critical role of school leaders* (COPPSE Document No. IB-7). University of Florida, Center on Personnel Studies in Special Education.

Dudley-Marling, C., & Burns, M. B. (2014). Two perspectives on inclusion in the United States. *Global Education Review, 1*(1), 14–31.

Education for All Handicapped Children Act, 20 U.S.C. § 1400 et seq. (1975).

Education of the Handicapped Act, 20 U.S.C. § 1471 et seq. (1970).

Education of the Handicapped Act Amendments, 20 U.S.C. § 1400 (1974).

Educational equity. (2020). In *Wikipedia.* https://en.wikipedia.org/wiki/Educational _equity

Edwards, B. S. (2012). *The impact of educational leadership decisions on the delivery of special education services in school districts* (Publication No. 3536256) [Doctoral dissertation, American International College]. ProQuest Dissertations Publishing. https://www.proquest.com/docview/1314782178

Elementary and Secondary Education Act, 20 U.S.C. 2701 et seq. (1965).

Elementary and Secondary Education Act Amendments, 20 U.S.C. 2701 et seq. (1966).

Elementary and Secondary Education Act Amendments, 20 U.S.C. § 2701 et seq. (1970).

Endrew F. v. Douglas County School District RE-1, 580 U.S. _____ (2017).

Esteves, K. J., & Rao, S. (2008). The evolution of special education. *Scholarship and Professional Work – Education. 72.* https://digitalcommons.butler.edu/cgi/viewcontent.cgi?article=1074&context=coe_papers

Every Student Succeeds Act, 20 U.S.C. 28 *et seq.* (2015).

Florence County School District Four v. Carter, 510 U.S. 7 (1993).

Forte Law Group. (2017, October 4). *History of special education: Important landmark cases.* http://www.fortelawgroup.com/history-special-education-important -landmark-cases/

Frick, W. C., Faircloth, S. C., & Little, K. S. (2013). Responding to the collective and individual "best interests of students": Revisiting the tension between administrative practice and ethical imperatives in special education leadership. *Educational Administration Quarterly, 49*(2), 207–242.

Friend, M., & Bursuck, W. D. (2012). *Including students with special needs: A practical guide for classroom teachers* (6th ed.). Pearson.

Fry v. Napoleon Comm. Sch. Dist., 137 S. Ct. 743 (2017).

Fullan, M. (2009). Large-scale reform comes of age. *Journal of Educational Change, 10,* 101–113.

Gangone, L. M. (n.d.). *Special education equity in the era of COVID-19.* Thought Leadership. https://aacte.org/2020/04/special-education-equity-in-the-era-of-covid-19/

Gargiulo, R. A., & Bouck, E. C. (2019). *Special education in contemporary society* (7th ed.). SAGE Publishing.

Gersten, R., Keating, T., Yovanoff, P., & Hamiss, M. K. (2001). Working in special education: Factors that enhance special educators' intent to stay. *Exceptional Students, 67,* 549–453.

Gilmour, A. (2018). Has inclusion gone too far? Weighing its effects on students with disabilities, their peers and teachers. *EducationNext, 18*(4). https://www.educationnext.org/has-inclusion-gone-too-far-weighing-effects-students-with-disabilities-peers-teachers/

Goor, M. B., Schwenn, J. O., & Boyer, L. (1997). Preparing principals for leadership in special education. *Intervention in School and Clinic, 32*(3), 133–141.

Guidara, A. (n.d.). *The history of special education in the late 1800s to mid-1900s: A look through Beverly Schools.* https://primaryresearch.org/the-history-of-special -education-in-the-late-1800s-to-mid-1900s-a-look-through-beverly-schools/

Harpell, J. V., & Andrews, J. J. W. (2010). Administrative leadership in the age of inclusion: Promoting best practices and teacher empowerment. *The Journal of Educational Thought, 44*(2), 189–210.

Hill, F. (2020, April 18). The pandemic is a crisis for students with special needs. *The Atlantic.* https://www.theatlantic.com/education/archive/2020/04/special -education-goes-remote-covid-19-pandemic/610231/

Hobson v. Hansen, 269 F. Supp. 401 (D.D.C. 1967), *aff'd sub nom,* Smuck v. Hobson, 408 F.2d 175 (D.C. Cir. 1969).

Honig v. Doe, 484 U.S. 305 (1988).

Howe, A. (2017). *Opinion analysis: Court's decision rejecting low bar for students with disabilities, under the spotlight.* SCOTUSblog. https://www.scotusblog .com/2017/03/opinion-analysis-courts-decision-rejecting-low-bar-students -disabilities-spotlight/

Individuals With Disabilities Education Act, 20 U.S.C. § 1400 et seq. (1990).

Individuals With Disabilities Education Act Amendments, 20 U.S.C. § 1400 et seq. (1997).

Individuals With Disabilities Education Improvement Act, 20 U.S.C. § 1400 et seq. (2004).

Individuals with Disabilities Education Act, 20 U.S.C. § 601 et seq. (2005).

Irving Independent Sch, Dist. v. Amber Tatro, 468 U.S. 883 (1984).

Itard, J-M-G. (1962). *The wild boy of Aveyron* (l'enfant sauvage) (M. Humphrey & G. Humphrey, Trans.). Prentice Hall. (Original work published in 1805)

Jacob Winkelman v. Parma City School District, 550 U.S. 516 (2007).

John F. Kennedy and People With Intellectual Disabilities (n.d.) https://www.jfklibrary .org/learn/about-jfk/jfk-in-history/john-f-kennedy-and-people-with-intellectual -disabilities

Jones, C. (2020, April 7). *Disability rights groups, school administrators spar over possible changes to special education laws.* EdSource._https://edsource.org/2020/ disability-rights-groups-school-administrators-spar-over-possible-changes-to -special-education-laws/628376

Justia U.S. Law. (2020). *Hobson v. Hansen.* https://law.justia.com/cases/federal/ district-courts/FSupp/269/401/1800940/

Katsiyannis, A. (1994). Individuals with disabilities: The school principal and 504. *NASSP, 78*(565), 6–10.

Kauffman, J. M. (1999). Commentary: Today's special education and its messages for tomorrow. *The Journal of Special Education, 32*(4), 244–254.

Kozleski, E. B., Artiles, A., & Waitoller, F. (2014). Equity in inclusive education: A cultural historical comparative perspective. In L Florian (Ed.), *The SAGE handbook of special education* (pp. 231–249). SAGE Publications.

Larry P. v. Riles, 343 F. Supp. 1306 (N.D. Cal. 1972), aff'd 502 F.2d 963 (9th Cir. 1974), further proceedings, 495 F. Supp. 926 (N.D. Cal. 1979), aff'd in part, rev'd in part, 793 F.2d 969 (9th Cir. 1984).

Leithwood, K., Harris, A., & Hopkins, D. (2008). Seven strong claims about successful school leadership. *School Leadership and Management, 28*(1), 27–42.

Leithwood, K., Seashore Louis, K., Anderson, S., & Wahlstrom, K. (2004). *How leadership influences student learning*. Center for Applied Research and Educational Improvement: Ontario Institute for Studies in Education.

Loiacono, A., & Palumbo, A. (2011). Principals who understand applied behavior analysis perceived they are better able to support educators who teach students with autism. *International Journal of Special Education, 26*(3), 212.

Martin, E. W., Martin, R., & Terman, D. L. (1996). The legislative and litigation history of special education. *The Future of Children, 6*(1), 25–39. http://www.jstor.org/stable/1602492

Mills v. Board of Education of the District of Columbia, 348 F. Supp. 866 (D.D.C. 1972).

Minnesota Governor's Council on Developmental Disabilities. (n.d.). *Parallels in time: A history of developmental disability*. https://mn.gov/mnddc/parallels/one/3.html

Mitchell, C. (2020, July 13). *A few parents have sued over special education during COVID-19. Will more follow?* EducationWeek. https://blogs.edweek.org/edweek/speced/2020/07/special_education_and_lawsuits.html

Montgomery, D. (2003). *Gifted and talented children with special educational needs.* David Fulton Publisher.

Murdick, N. L., Gartin, B. C., Fowler, G., & Crabtree, T. (2014). *Special education law* (3rd ed.). Pearson.

National Center on Inclusive Education. (2011). *Rationale for and research on inclusive education.* https://iod.unh.edu/sites/default/files/media/InclusiveEd/research_document_long.pdf

Nirje, B. (1969). The normalization principle and its human management implications. In R. W. Kugel & W. Wolfensberger (Eds.), *Changing patterns in residential services for the mentally retarded.* President's Committee on Mental Retardation.

No Child Left Behind Act, 20 U.S.C. § 6301 *et seq.* (2001).

Odom, S. I., & Diamond, K. E. (1998). Inclusion of young children with special needs in early childhood education: The research base. *Early Childhood Research Quarterly, 13*(1), 3–25.

Okungu, J. (2020, May 2). *Coronavirus creates fresh challenges for special education.* Fox Business. https://www.foxbusiness.com/lifestyle/virus-pandemic-poses-unique-threat-to-special-education

O'Leary, W. (2019, April 12). *Five current trending issues in special education.* Edmentum Blog. https://blog.edmentum.com/five-current-trending-issues-special-education

Osgood, R. L. (2005). *The history of inclusion in the United States.* Gallaudet University Press.

PARC v. Commonwealth of Pennsylvania, 343 F. Supp. 297 (E.D. Pa. 1972).

Pensions Enacted by Congress for American Revolutionary War Veterans. (n.d.). https://sites.rootsweb.com/~fayfamily/pensions.html

Portelli, J. P., & Koneeny, P. (2018). Inclusive education: Beyond popular discourses. *International Journal of Emotional Education, 10*(1), 133–144.

Rehabilitation Act, 29 U.S.C. § 794 *et seq.* (1973).

RISE. (2022). *RISE activity: Visualizing equality vs. equity.* https://risetowin.org/what-we-do/educate/resource-module/equality-vs-equity/index.htm

Rivera, G. (1972). *Willowbrook: A report on how it is and why it doesn't have to be that way.* Random House.

Sayed, Y., & Soudien, C. (2003). (Re)framing education exclusion and inclusion discourses: Limits and possibilities. *IDS Bulletin, 34*(1), 9–19.

Schaffer v. Weast, 546 U.S. 49 (2005).

School Psychological Resource. (n.d.). *Legal briefs: Diana v. CA Board of Education.* https://sites.google.com/site/schoolpsychquickreference/legal-briefs/diana-v-ca-state-board-of-education

Scotusblog. (2017). *Fry v Napoleon Community Schools.* SCOTUSBlog. https://www.scotusblog.com/case-files/cases/fry-v-napoleon-community-schools/

Skiba, R. J., Simmons, A. B., Ritter, S., Gibb, A. C., Rausch, M. K., Cuadrado, J., & Chung, C.-G. (2008). Achieving equity in special education: History, status, and current challenges. *Exceptional Children, 74*(3), 264–288.

Slee, R. (2009). The inclusion paradox: The cultural politics of difference. In M. Apple, W. Au, & L. A. Gandin (Eds.), *The Routledge international handbook of critical education* (pp. 177–189). Routledge.

Smith, J. D. (1998). *Inclusion: Schools for all students.* Wadsworth Publishing Company.

Smith, J. D. (2004). The historical contexts of special education. In A. McCray Sorrells, H. Rieth, & P. T. Sindelar (Eds.), *Critical issues in special education* (pp. 1–14). Pearson Education.

Spaulding, L. S., & Pratt, S. M. (2015). A review and analysis of the history of special education and disability advocacy in the United States. *American Educational History Journal, 42*(1), 91–100.

State of Alaska, Governor's Council on Disabilities & Special Education. (2019). *Disability history exhibit.* http://dhss.alaska.gov/gcdse/Pages/history/html_content_main.aspx

The history of special education in the United States. (2000, June 26). *Special Education News.* https://specialednews.com/the-history-of-special-education-in-the-united-states/

Thomas, S. (2017, April). *Social role valorisation.* https://wolfwolfensberger.com/life-s-work/social-role-valorisation

Thompson, J. R., & Wehmeyer, M. L. (2008). Historical and legal issues in developmental disabilities. In H. P. Parette & G. R. Peterson-Karlan (Eds.), *Research-based practices in developmental disabilities* (2nd ed., pp. 13–42). Pro-Ed.

Tikkanen, A. (2013). Special education. In *Encyclopedia Britannica.* https://www.britannica.com/topic/special-education

Tremblay, P. (2007). *Special needs education basis: Historical and conceptual approach.* UNESCO.

UCLA Mental Health Project. (n.d.). *Controversy over assessment: The changing sociopolitical climate.* http://smhp.psych.ucla.edu/conted2/abc3.htm

United Nations Educational, Scientific and Cultural Organization. (1994). *The Salamanca statement and framework for action on special needs education.* https://unesdoc.unesco.org/ark:/48223/pf0000098427

United Nations General Assembly. (1975). *Declaration on the rights of disabled persons.* https://www.ohchr.org/EN/ProfessionalInterest/Pages/RightsOfDisabledPersons.aspx

United States Department of Education. (2007). *History: Twenty-Five Years of Progress in Educating Children With Disabilities Through IDEA.* https://files.eric.ed.gov/fulltext/ED556111.pdf

Villa, R. A., & Thousand, J. S. (2003). Making inclusive education work. *Educational Leadership, 61*(2), 19–23.

Vitello, S. J., & Soskin, R. M. (1985). *Mental retardation: Its social and legal context.* Prentice Hall.

Walther-Thomas, C. S., DiPaola, M. F., & Butler, A. J. (2002). *A national study of endorsement requirements for principals: No wonder they don't understand special education.* In M. F. DiPaola & C. Walther-Thomas (2003), *Principals and special education.* University of Florida, Center on Personnel Studies in Special Education.

Watson v. City of Cambridge, 157 Mass. 561 (Mass. 1893).

Whitten, E., & Rodriguez-Campos, L. (2003). Trends in the special education teaching force: Do they reflect legislative mandates and legal requirements? *Educational Horizons, 81,* 138–145.

Winzer, M. A. (2009). *From integration to inclusion: A history of special education in the 20th century.* Gallaudet University Press.

Wolfensberger, W. (1972). *The principle of normalization in human services.* National Institute on Mental Retardation.

Wolfensberger, W. (1975). *The origin and nature of our institutional models.* Human Policy Press.

Wolfensberger, W. (1983). Social role valorization: A proposed new term for the principle of normalization. *Mental Retardation, 21,* 234–239.

Wright, P. (n.d.a). *Endrew v. Douglas County: IDEA demands more: Inclusion & progress in regular curriculum; IEP 'tailored to unique needs.'* https://www.wrightslaw.com/law/art/endrew.douglas.scotus.analysis.htm

Wright, P. (n.d.b). *The history of special education law in the United States.* https://www.wrightslaw.com/law/art/history.spec.ed.law.htm

Wright, P., & Wright, P. (n.d.a). Educational benefit: "Merely more than 'de minimis' or 'meaningful'?" *Wrightslaw.* https://www.wrightslaw.com/law/art/endrew.douglas.benefit.fape.htm

Wright, P., & Wright, P. (n.d.b). Endrew F. v. Douglas Sch. Dist. RE-1. *Wrightslaw.* https://www.wrightslaw.com/law/caselaw/2015/10th.endrew.douglas.benefit.fape.pdf

Wright, P., & Wright, P. (n.d.c). Fry v. Napoleon Community Schools. *Wrightslaw.* https://www.wrightslaw.com/law/caselaw/2017/ussupct.fry.napoleon.15-497.pdf

Yell, M. L., & Bateman, D. F. (2017). *Endrew F. v. Douglas County School District (2017): FAPE and the U.S. supreme court. TEACHING Exceptional Children, 50*(1), 7–15.

Yell, M. L., & Katsiyannis, A. (2004). Placing students with disabilities in inclusive settings: Legal guidelines and preferred practices. *Preventing School Failure: Alternative Education for Children and Youth, 49*(1), 28–35.

Yell, M. L., Rogers, D., & Rogers, E. L. (1998). The legal history of special education: What a long, strange trip it's been! *Remedial and Special Education, 19*(4), 219–228. https://doi.org/10.1177/074193259801900405

CHAPTER 8

# WHAT IS IN AN IEP?

## A Special Education Teacher's Reflection on IEP Narratives and Practices

**Eleanor X. Mehta**
*University of Georgia*

I am a special education teacher
Asian American girl
   can do everything
Yes, I know what I am doing
   except
    I don't
Still learning
   questioning
    trying
to teach
   what I don't know.

As an Asian American special education teacher, I have taught in public elementary schools in a suburban town in the southern region of the United States for many years. The schools were situated in primarily White

*Who Decides?*, pages 183–201
Copyright © 2022 by Information Age Publishing
www.infoagepub.com
All rights of reproduction in any form reserved.

middle-class neighborhoods, and many of my students were students of color. In this chapter, I share four autobiographical vignettes based on my personal experiences working in this context through the individualized education plan (IEP) process. The IEP is a well-established framework within No Child Left Behind (2002) and Individuals With Disabilities Education Act (2004) for educators to provide services and supports for students with disabilities. My student, Peter,[1] was a fifth grader on my caseload. Peter was an African American boy with autism. He came from a single parent household and has been attending the school since third grade. The vignettes highlight the internal conflicts and challenges I encountered as I worked with Peter and his mom, Ms. Jones. Following each vignette, I examine the narratives and practices throughout the IEP process and how they often promote a deficit perspective on students' abilities. Specifically, I address (a) the deficit-oriented discourses in the IEP, (b) accountability policies reinforcing deficit perspectives, (c) the lack of culturally sustaining practices, and (d) the need for student engagement in the IEP process. Finally, I discuss how we can move forward towards strength-based practices within the frameworks of community of practice and person-centered planning.

## VIGNETTE 1: AM I MAKING A DIFFERENCE?

It was a typical day at Main Street Elementary. As the dismissal announcement started, I sat down at my desk, anticipating two more hours of paperwork before I could head home. I opened Peter's IEP draft on my laptop and started adding data to his "Present Levels of Performance," including his school-wide assessment, testing scores, grades, and data from his current IEP goals. As I gathered all the information I needed, my mind flashed back to the first time when I met Peter during Sneak Preview. Peter walked in first with his mom, Ms. Jones, following. As I walked towards her and introduced myself, Peter was already busy looking at my bulletin board with a number of colorful posters and the words "dream big" spanning across the board. Ms. Jones called him over, told him that I would be his fifth-grade teacher. I greeted Peter with a big smile and enthusiasm. Peter glanced at me and grinned back, showing a beautiful smile through his brown skin. Without saying a word, he turned away to look at the bulletin board again.

I blinked as I tried to pull my focus back to the screen. Under the first section of the IEP on "Impact of the Disability," a short statement read, "Peter meets eligibility for autism; demonstrates communication, social, and fine motor delays that interfere with his learning. His weakness in the area of working memory affects his ability to attend to and retain information." Underneath was the next section on "Present Level of Performance and Educational Needs," where I needed to update on Peter's progress. I stared blankly at the numbers in Peter's grade report. Peter's assessment scores showed that he was significantly behind grade-level performance in reading, language arts, and math. His academic records told the same story. I was well aware of Peter's needs. Since the first day on the job, I had heard about Peter. Other teachers told me that Peter was known for having breakdowns and eloping the classroom. They often struggled to engage Peter in the general education classroom setting. There were questions about his current placement setting in the co-teaching classroom, and suggestions to increase his time spent in a special education classroom.

I stared at the numbers again, hoping somehow, they could show me a way forward.

Peter was an enigma to me.

As much as I was aware of his needs, after 4 months of teaching, I still wasn't sure whether I "knew" Peter and what he really needed. There were glimpses of his abilities when Peter showed me his well-organized drawings during his break time, yet Peter was often frustrated by the work that was required of him—especially math. After consistent support from the IEP team, Peter made little progress on the IEP goals proposed. I couldn't help but wonder, "Is what I'm doing actually making a difference?" Well into my fourth year as a special education teacher, I knew how to differentiate my teaching and how to write an IEP, but was I making a difference? For Peter, I was quite uncertain.

## DEFICIT-ORIENTED DISCOURSES

My experiences with Peter have shown me that the deficit-oriented discourses in the IEP process bring harm to the student and impedes the IEP team to move towards collaborative practices. The present level of performance (PLOP) of the student is an important section in the IEP document. Once the present level is established and conveyed to the IEP team, the team can discuss and determine appropriate educational goals and services the student would receive the following school year. Therefore, PLOP lays the foundation to later discussions in the IEP meeting. The PLOP section uses a number of grades, standardized testing results and other quantitative data to demonstrate the competency of the student in different academic subjects (Individualized Education Programs, 2019). In addition, PLOP also uses teacher observations on specific skills and behaviors to describe the students' needs and areas that are in need of improvement. Even though students' progress is also shared in PLOP, when it is compared to the standardized scores used in grade level testing, the challenges often seem insurmountable. Like my experience in writing Peter's IEP, this comparison to their "typical" peers can be demoralizing for students, parents, and educators. It "conceptualizes children as an exception to a standardized norm" and focuses on the limitations of students' functioning (Boyd et al., 2015, p. 1539).

Cultural critic bell hooks (2003) reflects on how shaming plays a role "in maintaining social subordination" regardless of one's access to resources (p. 93). I find this dynamic playing out in the IEP process. Students with disabilities are shamed for being a deviant from the norm when their scores are constantly compared to the grade level average, even though the lower test scores were used to qualify them to receive special education. The deficit-oriented narrative reinforces the idea that students with disabilities will never be able to succeed like their peers. Studies have shown the importance of self-efficacy to improve learning outcomes for students with disabilities (Decker & Buggey, 2014; Mostafa, 2018). However, if the IEP team does not believe that students can succeed, how can they develop and support students' self-efficacy?

In addressing the relations among language, power, and politics, French sociologist Pierre Bourdieu (1977) argues that "language is not only an instrument of communication...but an instrument of power" (p. 648). The language used in an IEP often "frames children as passive and powerless through the use of the passive voice" (Boyd et al., 2015, p. 1546). In a passive voice, the action is done to the subject of the sentence. Examples include "the student was tested in September" or "the student was given adapted paper to practice handwriting and motor skills." The passive voice "positions children as the recipient" of the services within the IEP, rather than the individual who will achieve his or her own goals (Boyd et al., 2015, p. 1546). As it did in Peter's IEP from the start, the language also foregrounds disability and reduce[s] children's identities to a disorder or condition (Boyd et al., 2015; Runswick-Cole and Hodge, 2009). As a special education teacher, I struggled to frame Peter's identity in the context of the IEP. I knew what the IEP could speak about Peter was grossly insufficient, yet the way I viewed Peter was also affected by how the IEP document is "actualized in practice" (Boyd et al., 2015, p. 1549). In other words, I knew Peter was more than his deficits, yet the deficits were all that I could see.

What we need desperately, is a strength-based model for IEP. Both the psychology and disability field have shifted from deficit-based models to strengths-based approaches in recent years (Niemiec et al., 2017). The strengths-based approaches seek to understand the competencies of people with disabilities, including character strengths and personal talents, and use them to guide supports planning (Niemiec et al., 2017; Buntinx & Schalock, 2010). To build a strength-based model for IEP, students' strengths need to be considered throughout the IEP process. Inclusive special education researchers Elder et al. (2018) suggest that person-centered planning can help "establish a powerful, strength-based foundation for an IEP"

(p. 132). They connect the questions asked in the McGill Action Planning System (MAPs) process to the process of IEP planning (Vandercook et al., 1989). Specifically, they demonstrate ways in which MAPs can help the IEP team to identify the strengths of students and how they can contribute to the classroom community. The current IEP practices, driven by data collection and progress monitoring, often do not provide IEP teams the complete picture of students' abilities and their individualities. The question is, if we don't really know our students, how do we know what is best for them? By whose standards are we making decisions and who will they really benefit?

## VIGNETTE 2: DON'T WATCH ME

It's late in the spring. As students in my resource math classroom sat down with a laptop, a piece of scratch paper, a pencil, and a desk divider, I gave them a few directions on the assessment they were about to take. It's that time of the year again—a week of school-wide assessment monitoring students' progress in math and reading skills. It's also my least favorite time of the year. I did not like proctoring, especially proctoring my own students. Today, they are taking the assessment in math.

I walked around the room and came by Peter's desk. He has just logged in. He looked at me and then looked away.

"Don't watch me." He whispered.

I bent down by his desk. "Peter, remember Ms. Mehta wants to see how much math you learned since last year, ok? Make sure you read every question carefully."

"Ok."

I walked away uneasily. I knew Peter did not like testing. With most of the testing nowadays on the computer, Peter often clicked through the answers just to get over the ordeal. Though he had accommodations such as frequent breaks and read-aloud test questions, it did not reduce his distaste in testing. I couldn't blame Peter. Time and time again, his math progress has been shown at the bottom 1%. Who wants to take a test only to fail it again? Personally, I also dreaded getting the reports. The reports frequently showed that many of my students have grown very little and they made me question whether I have taught at all. Of course, sharing these reports with parents and colleagues during the IEP process also meant I will be reminding everyone else that again, my students are "low."

"I'm done." Peter raised his hand and looked at me.

I looked at the clock, it's been hardly 15 minutes. "Are you sure?"

"Yes!"

"You can take a break. Remember everyone else is still testing." I handed Peter a clipboard with a piece of drawing paper and some colored pencils.

Peter was the first one to finish, but clearly, he's had enough of sitting down and staying quiet. He jumped out of his seat and laid down on the carpet by the window, rolling around and giggling. I walked by and gave him a visual reminder to stay quiet. Peter sat up and started drawing.

As I continued to walk around and monitor other students, frustration started to set in. What would Peter's score be this time? What a waste of time! I walked back to my desk, a notification just popped up on my laptop telling me a student has finished the test and a report was generated. I clicked on the report, and a bar graph appeared, showing no progress of the student between fall and spring. It was Peter's report.

"Ms. Mehta, look!" Peter was holding up his drawing.

I walked over. To my surprise, Peter's drawing was filled with fractions—pizza fractions that he learned about in class earlier this week. I remembered that Peter enjoyed that lesson. He got to cut the paper pizza into equal pieces and write unit fractions on each of them. We also played a game where he shared the pizza with his classmate Tyler by dividing the pizza into different fraction parts.

"I love your drawing, Peter! Look at all the fractions you wrote down on the pizza. Are you sharing the pizza with me?"

"Yes. I'm sharing the pizza with you and Tyler."

I smiled. "Thanks, friend! I would love it, yum!"

Peter went back to coloring his pizza, looking quite content. The morning sun casted a gentle shadow around him. I walked away. For a second, a sense of contentment also came over me.

## ACCOUNTABILITY POLICY THROUGH TESTING

As shown through the vignette, standardized testing often had a negative impact on Peter's learning. The tests not only took away instructional time, but also drained Peter's energy to stay focused the rest of the day. Peter did not care about the tests, neither did the tests assess accurately what he knew. Yet, the IEP team continued to use standardized testing scores as the basis for Peter's strengths and weaknesses to plan for IEP goals. To understand this focus on standardized testing in the IEP, we must take a look at the history of testing in the U.S. education system and how accountability policy has influenced the IEP process over time.

Standardized testing was first introduced to the education system during WWI, when educators started adapting tests used by the army for recruitment and placement of soldiers (Smyth, 2008). In 1957, the Soviet Union launched Sputnik I, and the incident sparked great fear that the United States was falling behind in scientific research compared to the Soviet Union (Turgut, 2013). Policy makers called for educational reform, and in 1958, the National Defense Education Act (NDEA) was passed to promote knowledge in science, math, and foreign languages (Jolly, 2009). This was the first time the federal government was directly involved in educational reform (Turgut, 2013). The subsequent legislations, including "A Nation at Risk" (NAR) in 1983 and "No Child Left Behind" (NCLB) in 2001, followed a similar narrative that our education system has fallen behind in comparison to other countries (Turgut, 2013).

When IDEA was amended in 2004, it aligned itself with NCLB and caused "an unprecedented shift in special education policy" (Jones, 2010, p. 36). Prior to IDEA (2004), IEP goals and objectives were written based on students' specific strengths and weaknesses (Jones, 2010). However, after IDEA (2004), there was a policy shift in special education to be accountable for "the academic performance of students with disabilities on state standards-based tests" (Skrtic et al., 2005, p. ix). This policy shift towards accountability set the stage for future policies that would drive me as a special education teacher to constantly juggle between the individual needs of my students and the need to teach the curriculum.

Since NCLB required schools to demonstrate "adequate yearly progress" (AYP), standardized testing was created in each state to assess students' yearly progress (Mooney et al., 2004). Test results were divided into different categories, "including minority groups, students with disabilities, economically disadvantaged students, and students with limited English proficiency" (Mooney et al., 2004, p. 242). The requirements of AYP are often the same for students with disabilities as for students without disabilities, with the exception of students who have alternative testing provisions due to significant cognitive delays (Thompson & Thurlow, 2003). Essentially, schools are judged based on "the scores all students make on high stakes testing" (Jones, 2010, p. 38). Peter's scores, for example, would affect the overall scores of the grade level AYP at the school. Even though alternative assessment is available, it is only used among 2% of the population of students with disabilities (Jones, 2010).

Following the launching of the Common Core State Standards (CCSS) in 2009, Standards-Based Reform and the accountability movement continued to affect both the curriculum and assessments in special education. It forced students with disabilities to conform to "general education curriculum and the general education standards-based testing" (Jones, 2010, p. 38), leaving little room for the IEP to be truly individualized. In many ways, accountability policies reinforce and reify deficit perspectives on students with disabilities. Since CCSS and standardized testing are never designed for students with disabilities, they fall short of what those students really need. Jones (2010) expresses this concern among educators:

> There is much concern among educators about the special needs students who are being held accountable for their progress in the general education

curriculum, as are their teachers, principals, and schools when it was known previously that they probably could not accomplish the general education academic standards. Is this appropriate education for students with disabilities or for students from low socioeconomic environments who are all functioning below grade level? (pp. 36–37)

Waitoller and King Thorius (2016) propose that culturally sustaining special education practices should require assessments to be "ongoing and flexible in how information is presented and ways students may perform"; they should also be "informed by students' cultural repertoires, identities, and out-of-school practices to widen what is assessed" (p. 383). For Peter, the ongoing assessment of his IEP goals was more flexible than the grade level standardized testing. Even so, the IEP team was hesitant to provide greater flexibility on how Peter's progress should be assessed, for fear that he will not be prepared for standardized testing. As a result, these standardized assessments are used as "pedagogical tools of exclusion" which "sort students into ability profiles" (Waitoller & King Thorius, 2016, p. 383). The only path towards inclusion is to master these assessments, despite the possibility that students with disabilities may never be able to do so.

## VIGNETTE 3: THERE'S NO WAY AROUND IT

It was near the end of another school day at Main Street Elementary. I greeted Ms. Jones at the front entrance and walked her through the quiet hallways to the conference room. The rest of the IEP team has already settled down around the long oval shaped desk in the middle of the room. After some friendly chatting, I passed out the IEP draft. I started the meeting with introductions and the statement of parental rights, followed by a summary of Peter's current educational performance. Then, I proceeded to the next section of the IEP on parental concerns.

"Ms. Jones, could you share with us any concerns you have for Peter?"

"Well, I understand his challenges you know—but I want him to catch up and be successful at school." She paused. "I'm glad Peter has improved in terms of behavior this year, but I'm still concerned that he won't be ready for middle school." Ms. Jones spoke in a calm voice, but there was worry in her eyes, "I saw Peter has not mastered the multiplication facts. I'm worried about that."

I knew Ms. Jones for about 4 months now. I would call home often afterschool to talk about Peter's progress. From our conversations, I came to know that she was a single mom, working a full-time job, and raising three kids. Ms. Jones was always responsive and supportive. Under her calm and collected demeanor, however, I knew it must not be easy to walk in her shoes.

I nodded. "Yes, Peter has really improved in behavior this year. He has also made progress in many of his IEP goals. We will definitely prepare Peter for the middle school transition." I looked towards Ms. Jones, choosing my words carefully, "For the math goal, I am thinking about adjusting it. As you know from the psychological, Peter's not strong in long term memory. What if we change his goal to master 1 to 10-digit multiplication using a multiplication chart?"

Ms. Jones paused for a second, then shook her head. "I know memory is not Peter's strength, but this is a skill that he needs for testing, right? I feel like there's no way around it. He needs this skill in order to catch up."

I nodded mechanically. I understood where Ms. Jones was coming from, yet internally I was conflicted. I pictured Peter repeating the same goal of multiplication facts day after day, until he drew funny faces all over the worksheet out of frustration. "There's no way around it." Ms. Jones' words echoed in my head.

## ACCOUNTABILITY POLICY FRAMING IEP DISCOURSES

The flow of the conversation in this IEP meeting is not unique to Ms. Jones. As part of the first section in an IEP, parents are asked to share about their concerns for their child. This often guides parents' responses towards concerns rather than, for example, a strengths-based discussion of their children and celebration of the progress they have made. Even though Ms. Jones was happy about Peter's progress in behavior, it was overshadowed by her concerns that Peter would not be ready for middle school. Ms. Jones' concerns were certainly valid, and it was important for the team to address them. However, the IEP also needs to support parents to "reframe the conversation from 'concerns' to expressions of their children's strengths, preferences, and interests, as well as sharing insights from home" (Kurth et al., 2019, pp. 494–495). The IEP team can then use the information to identify the students' competencies and find appropriate support for students to achieve their learning goals (Niemiec et al., 2017).

In our discussion of IEP goals in the meeting, a deficit perspective was also present and reified by accountability policies. When the IEP was written based on standardized testing scores and common core standards, the conversation shifted from centering around how Peter could demonstrate individual growth, to how much he could "catch up" to his grade-level peers. The structure of various psychological and academic standardized tests "create a social context that demands conformity" (Kliewer et al., 2015, p. 7). In the Special Education Rules Implementation Manual (2019) given by Georgia Department of Education, it states that "IEP annual goals are written to address an individual child's needs/deficits in order to enable that child to be involved in and make progress in grade level standards" (p. 8). Again, the passive voice and the language of exceptionality is problematic for the framing of the purpose of IEP goals (Boyd et al., 2015). It asks children to continuously measure up to the grade level standards while previously casting doubts on whether they "possess the agency, ability, or ambition to do so" (Boyd et al., 2015, p. 1549).

Going back to the concerns shared by Ms. Jones about Peter's academic progress and readiness for middle school, it seemed that there were underlying issues behind her concerns that were worth exploring deeper, such as the purpose of an education in Peter's life, the gatekeeping function of certain academic standards in the context of testing, and whether setting IEP objectives based on these academic standards support or impede Peter's learning and life goals. However, the IEP meeting does not provide such a space for in-depth collaborative exploration. As Black and Montalvo (2017) have observed, the IEP focuses more on compliance and the needs of the individual "rather than collective advocacy" (p. 9). To truly address Ms. Jones' concerns requires the IEP team to get to know one another, walk in each other's shoes and share their knowledge not just in an IEP meeting once a year, but throughout their relationship building. Therefore, Black and Montalvo propose a new vision for the IEP to be "a democratic space for relational development" (p. 10), in which the focus is placed on building the network of service providers, neighbors, siblings, and parents around the child, and deepening "their knowledge and expertise in this area by interacting on an ongoing basis" as trust is built (Wenger et al., 2002, p. 4).

## TOWARDS A STRENGTH-BASED PERSPECTIVE: CULTURALLY SUSTAINING PRACTICES

To build on Black and Montalvo's (2017) relational framework for the IEP, we need to address the lack of culturally sustaining practices in the IEP process. Developing a relational network requires all stakeholders to recognize the humanness of each member of the team. Students' identity in the IEP document can often be reduced to their disability, instead of being recognized in all aspects of who they are. The IEP document does not "account for other complexities of individual identity, such as race, class, gender, or sexuality," and it does not "attend to the intersectionality of other forms of oppression" (Boyd et al., 2015, p. 1546). In Peter's case, he was an African American boy from a single parent household, attending a public school in a primarily White middle-class suburban neighborhood. As an Asian American teacher, I struggled to interrogate ways "normalcy" and "Whiteness" were constructed within the school culture (Waitoller & King Thorius,

2016). In the U.S. context, Whiteness exists in relations to other racialized identities, such as Blackness and Asianness. It is "a set of values, norms and forms of cultural capital" that are valuable and respectable, in relation to other ways of being that are devalued (Garner, 2007, p. 62). Peter's challenging behaviors, such as refusal to follow a teacher's directive and leaving the designated area without permission, had always been a focus in his IEP, as they did not conform to the norms within the school culture. His behaviors conforming to the norm was seen as a marker for progress and success. However, was it progress at all if by focusing on conformity, we took away Peter's individuality in the process?

As educators in special education, it is important to acknowledge "the relationship between racism and ableism as one of interlocking forms of exclusion" in order to move towards culturally sustaining practices and a strength-based perspective (Waitoller & King Thorius, 2016, p. 371). The deficit perspective not only exists within special education, but also pervades U.S. schools among students of color and their families. It positions students of color to be "at fault for poor academic performance" because they do not have the "normative cultural knowledge and skills" (Yosso, 2005, p. 75). However, the discourse of "exceptionality" foregrounds disability and "minimize[s] the importance of alternative aspects of identity" (Boyd et al., 2015, p. 1546). Considering the students' identity in all aspects is crucial for the IEP team to critically examine how "power and privilege shape and block learning opportunities at the intersection of raced/abled identities" and to support students and families in culturally sustaining ways (Waitoller & King Thorius, 2016, p. 376).

By using the concept of cultural wealth, Tara Yosso (2005) argues that schools should begin "with the perspective that Communities of Color are places with multiple strengths" instead of deficits (p. 82). She also points out the need for educators to acknowledge the cultural wealth among communities of color such as aspirational, social, navigational, linguistic, resistant and familial capitals. Similarly, the strength-based perspective of cultural wealth is applicable for disability communities. Positioned in the intersection of race and disability, the cultural wealth Peter's family embodied often went unnoticed and unvalued. The fact that Peter showed up to school day after day, facing numerous challenges in and outside of the classroom, demonstrated his aspirational capital to hope and dream beyond the present obstacles. The resilience Peter's mom had navigating through the IEP process and advocating for her child as a single working mother, was tremendous. As educators in special education, to recognize and value the cultural wealth embodied by our students and their communities is the first step towards a strength-based perspective.

## VIGNETTE 4: CAN'T WAIT TO MEET HIM

It was a pleasant afternoon in early May. The trees outside of my classroom window shook gently in the breeze, their bright green leaves signified new beginnings. I sat down at a large rectangular table with everyone on Peter's IEP team. This was the last meeting of the year for Peter, and we have invited the middle school special education teacher, Mrs. Wilson, to discuss Peter's placement in the coming year.

"Hello everyone, before we start, I would like to share with you some of Peter's reflections on his time at Main Street Elementary." I passed around a collection of Peter's writings and drawings. Some of the writings are typed, some handwritten. The room fell silent. Everyone was instantly absorbed by Peter's work. Peter was quite a prolific drawer. Under "My Favorite Memory at Main Street," he drew colorful cars built from Legos and wrote in detail about his favorite memory of "playing Legos with my friend Carson." Under "How I Feel about Middle School," Peter drew a map of the cafeteria and an arrow pointing to where he would be standing in the lunch line. Lunch was certainly one of the highlights of Peter's day at Main Street. Under the picture, Peter wrote, "Pizza is the best food in the world. If you don't like pizza, you are missing a lot of good food. One day, I want to share my pizza with friends in middle school."

"This is amazing." Mrs. Wilson looked up from Peter's writing, "I love seeing his personality coming through. Can't wait to meet him!"

Ms. Jones smiled, "Peter's very excited about middle school. Of course, we are anxious about the change, but he's looking forward to it. He's come a long way." Mrs. Jones turned and nodded at me. "Thank you for all your hard work."

Smiling back, I found myself in an unexpected moment of joy.

The rest of the meeting went on as usual. Parent concerns were shared, Peter's present levels of performance were discussed, and his new IEP goals were drafted. Two hours later, the meeting came to a close. As I said goodbyes to everyone, Ms. Jones walked up to me.

"Thank you for everything you've done for Peter this year, Ms. Mehta."

"Of course, I loved having Peter! I will miss him next year for sure." I nodded, smiling as I waved goodbye to Ms. Jones. Her affirmation gave me a sense of assurance.

The room became quiet again, the afternoon sun hung low through the trees. I sat down as I gathered all the papers. It had not been an easy year for Peter, and the road ahead was still full of challenges. Well, I have done what I could. I thought to myself.

Suddenly, a piece of paper with Peter's drawing caught my eye. It was part of a writing piece he wrote about school. Under "What I Find Challenging," Peter wrote in big letters, "MATH." Beside it, he drew cards with multiplication equations on them, still waiting to be solved. I took a deep breath. What would Peter think about his IEP? Would anything be different if he was here in the meeting? I looked around the empty room. The sense of peace I felt had somehow vanished.

## REIMAGINE THE IEP: COMMUNITY OF PRACTICE AND PERSON-CENTERED PLANNING

As I ran into the limitations of the IEP as a special education teacher, I questioned whether there could be an alternative, a reimagined IEP that was truly inclusive. Kathleen Mortier (2020), a researcher in inclusive education, speaks of the community of practice "as an alternative theoretical framework of knowledge" that addresses "some of the persistent barriers to inclusive education" (p. 329). Mortier proposes that the community of practice can be "an in-between space in which team members can embrace doubt, curiosity, and subjectivity to develop local knowledge" to creatively solve problems and build trusting partnerships (p. 334). To build upon this understanding of community of practice, I believe students with disability should be the center of their communities, so that the IEP process will not only empower parents and educators, but also students themselves.

Even as I attempted to present Peter's perspective in the IEP meeting, Peter was not an active participant in his own IEP process. The power of Peter's voice had long been overlooked. In my attempt to make it heard, I also realized that Peter's voice was embraced because it was planned and controlled through the sharing of his work. According to Anderson and Keys (2019), the IEP process "is subject to power imbalances brought into the IEP meeting by individuals and maintained by the system" (p. 325). We may, in theory, believe in student empowerment, but in practice, the student is excluded, and their perspectives not valued (Anderson & Keys, 2019).

Even though the IEP meeting allows the student with disability to participate, the student's participation is certainly not required (Special Education Rules Implementation Manual, 2019). The role and place of students with disability in the IEP meeting is often ignored, when IEP goals are developed and given to students without their input. These practices frame students with disability as passive and "minimize their importance as independent individuals," implying "disability as inherent" (Boyd et al., 2015, p. 1547). It is paradoxical that even though the IEP is written for the student with disability, the student is not involved in the process. As adults without autism, we were placed in a position to decide on Peter's educational goals without knowing or considering his lived experiences. Peter's subsequent "problematic" behaviors might only be a result of these decisions that did not value his voice and input.

What would it take for Peter to be in the center of the community of practice? Kliewer et al. (2015) suggest that parents and teachers need to suspend "deeply held ideologies of deficit" in order to engage the student in new contexts (p. 9). For Peter, the IEP team not only needs to recognize his right to participate, but also presume his competence to participate in an IEP meeting. "The process toward ultimately and genuinely presuming competence requires perseverance on the part of team members, an openness to the possibility of learning something new and of being surprised by and about the individual and one's self" (Kliewer et al., 2015, pp. 9–10). This means that the IEP team needs to continually reflect on how they center the student in their practice and be willing to adjust and solve problems creatively. Research shows that when students with disabilities are involved from the start of the IEP planning process, they are likely to be more successful in their educational outcome (Bui et al., 2010). Therefore, student engagement should not be a supplemental piece to the IEP process, but a fundamental principle.

Our discussion points back to person-centered planning (PCP). PCP has often been used during transition planning involving youth and adults with disabilities (Miner & Bates, 1997; Menchetti & Garcia, 2003). However, it is not widely implemented among elementary school students. "By placing the person with the disability in a leadership role in plan development, and by responding to a person's unique preferences, strengths, and needs," PCP can support the community of practice to frame individualized goals that are "appropriate, familiar and motivating" (Trainor, 2007, p. 93). Furthermore, PCP's emphasis on individualization and community collaboration, together with its flexibility in implementation, all create spaces for culturally responsive special education practices (Kalyanpur & Harry, 1999; Trainor, 2007). Special education scholars Maureen Keyes and Laura Owens-Johnson (2003) share a few suggestions in conducting IEP using PCP strategies:

1. Begin every IEP meeting by describing the strengths, gifts, and talents of the student by sharing an example or two of how the student's life has touched others' lives.
2. Increase student levels of responsibility for developing and implementing their plans.
3. Develop a checklist to use at the IEP meeting so everyone understands the interrelatedness among goals, dreams, needs, nightmares, and plans. Illustrate on paper the necessary links with resources—personnel and financial—especially as these relate to transition.

4. Involve peers and members from the individual's community (when mutually agreed upon) to demonstrate the value in interdependence for all team members. Encourage the student to invite friends, family members, or others in his or her circle of support, especially those who are not paid. (p. 151)

In addition to these suggestions, it is important for education professionals to understand the cultural values and beliefs of the students and their communities (Trainor, 2007; Bui & Turnbull, 2003). In their research on PCP among Asian American communities, Bui and Turnbull recommend education professionals to adjust their practices to the Asian American context. Their recommendations include (a) establishing a relationship with the student's family, (b) arranging meeting logistics according to the needs of the family, and (c) communicating during the meeting with awareness of cultural differences. These recommendations echo Black and Montalvo's (2017) vision of a relational IEP, and they can also guide other communities to adjust PCP based on culturally sustaining practices. Furthermore, if schools truly want to go beyond the existing IEP framework, school leaders need to recognize the need for special education teachers and service providers to explore and experiment in "what they do not know." This requires spaces to be created for the IEP team to collaborate and resources provided for the special education teacher to organize and foster collaboration. Simply staying in compliance should not be the end goal of the IEP, but it should serve as a guiding framework for an inclusive, relational, and culturally sustaining community.

## CONCLUSION

> Hold fast to dreams
> For if dreams die
> Life is a broken-winged bird
> That cannot fly.
> Hold fast to dreams
> For when dreams go
> Life is a barren field
> Frozen with snow.
> —*Dreams* by Langston Hughes (1995, p. 32)

When I was teaching, I rarely allowed myself to stop and dream. My work was defined by constraints of time and resources. In March 2020, when the COVID-19 pandemic interrupted schools and learning, I found myself facing both a challenge and an opportunity. I stopped focusing on things like data collection and progress reports and turned my attention to the needs of my students, their families, and my colleagues. We reached out and took care of each other physically and emotionally. In surprising but also unsurprising ways, we made things work. What the IEP once was, as a place of exclusion, somehow became a place of belonging.

It was also around the same time that I started reflecting. I created the autobiographic vignettes in this chapter as a means of inquiry (Ambler, 2012). Peter and his mom are composite characters I constructed to explore ideas related to the IEP process from my experience teaching special education in public elementary schools. Apart from my own recollections, I also used anecdotal notes that I have taken throughout my teaching career. As Graue and Walsh (1998) describe in the use of vignettes in research with children in context, in writing these vignettes, my hope is that they will not only be illuminative for me to conceptualize the issues within the IEP process, but it will also allow the reader to enter into the lived experiences of students, teachers, and parents.

What would my freedom dream be for the IEP? First, I believe change is possible. Once I did not believe it, as I was confined in my classroom with piles of paperwork awaiting me. Now, I dare to believe. I believe the IEP can be a space where students' strengths, gifts, and talents are celebrated, and where their individualities are seen. I believe the IEP can be a community where ideas and creative solutions are shared, and where students find their voices and are heard. If we allow each other to reach out, to care and love, and to dream, I believe we will find ourselves in the process, transformed.

## NOTE

1. All names of people and places in this chapter are pseudonyms.

## REFERENCES

Ambler, T. (2012). Autobiographical vignettes: A medium for teachers' professional learning through self-study and reflection. *Teacher Development, 16*(2), 181–197. https://doi.org/10.1080/13664530.2012.679864

Anderson, A. J., & Keys, C. B. (2019). Social inequality within the IEP meeting: Three factors that disempower students. *Journal of Prevention & Intervention in the Community, 47*(4), 325–342. https://doi.org/10.1080/10852352.2019.1617381

Black, W. R., & Montalvo, J. (2017). The individual education plan: From individual needs to meaningful relationships. *TASH Connections, 42*(1), 8–13.

Bourdieu, P. (1977). *Outline of a theory of practice.* Cambridge University Press.

Boyd, V. A., Ng, S. L., & Schryer, C. F. (2015). Deconstructing language practices: Discursive constructions of children in individual education plan resource documents. *Disability & Society, 30*(10), 1537–1553. https://doi.org/10.1080/09687599.2015.1113161

Bui, X., Quirk, C., Almazan, S., & Valenti, M. (2010). Inclusive education research and practice. *Maryland Coalition for Inclusive Education*, 1–14.

Bui, Y. N., & Turnbull, A. (2003). East meets West: Analysis of person-centered planning in the context of Asian American values. *Education and Training in Mental Retardation and Developmental Disabilities, 38*, 18–31.

Buntinx, W. H., & Schalock, R. L. (2010). Models of disability, quality of life, and individualized supports: Implications for professional practice in intellectual disability. *Journal of Policy and Practice in Intellectual Disabilities, 7*(4), 283–294. https://doi.org/10.1111/j.1741-1130.2010.00278.x

Decker, M. M., & Buggey, T. (2014). Using video self- and peer modeling to facilitate reading fluency in children with learning disabilities. *Journal of Learning Disabilities, 47*(2), 167–177. https://doi.org/10.1177/0022219412450618

Elder, B. C., Rood, C. E., & Damiani, M. L. (2018). Writing strength-based IEPs for students with disabilities in inclusive classrooms. *International Journal of Whole Schooling, 14*(1), 116–155.

Garner, S. (2007). *Whiteness: An introduction.* Routledge.

Graue, M. E., & Walsh, D. J. (1998). *Studying children in context: Theories, methods, and ethics.* SAGE Publications.

hooks, b. (2003). *Teaching community: A pedagogy of hope.* Psychology Press.

Hughes, L. (1995). Dreams. In *Collected poems of Langston Hughes* (p. 32). Knopf.

Individualized Education Programs, 34 C.F.R. §§ 300.320-300.323 (2019)

Individuals With Disabilities Education Act, 20 U.S.C. § 1400 (2004)

Jolly, J. L. (2009). The National Defense Education Act, Current STEM Initiative, and the Gifted. *Gifted Child Today, 32*(2), 50–53.

Jones, C. J. (2010). *Curriculum development for students with mild disabilities: Academic and social skills for RTI planning and inclusion IEPs.* Charles C. Thomas Publisher.

Kalyanpur, M., & Harry, B. (1999). *Culture in special education: Building reciprocal family–professional relationships.* Brookes.

Keyes, M. W., & Owens-Johnson, L. (2003). Developing person-centered IEPs. *Intervention in School and Clinic, 38*(3), 145–152. https://doi.org/10.1177/10534512030380030301

Kliewer, C., Biklen, D., & Petersen, A. (2015). At the end of intellectual disability. *Harvard Educational Review, 85*(1), 1–28. https://doi.org/10.17763/haer.85.1.j260u3gv2402v576

Kurth, J. A., McQueston, J. A., Ruppar, A. L., Toews, S. G., Johnston, R., & McCabe, K. M. (2019). A description of parent input in IEP development through analysis IEP documents. *Intellectual and Developmental Disabilities, 57*(6), 485–498. https://doi.org/10.1352/1934-9556-57.6.485

Menchetti, B. M., & Garcia, L. A. (2003). Personal and employment outcomes of person-centered career planning. *Education and Training in Developmental Disabilities, 38*, 145–156.

Miner, C. A., & Bates, P. E. (1997). The effect of person centered planning activities on the IEP/transition planning process. *Education and Training in Mental Retardation and Developmental Disabilities, 32*(2), 105–112.

Mooney, P., Denny, R. K., & Gunter, P. L. (2004). The impact of NCLB and the reauthorization of IDEA on academic instruction of students with emotional or behavioral disorders. *Behavioral Disorders, 29*(3), 237–246. https://doi .org/10.1177/019874290402900307

Mortier, K. (2020). Communities of practice: A conceptual framework for inclusion of students with significant disabilities. *International Journal of Inclusive Education, 24*(3), 329–340. https://doi.org/10.1080/13603116.2018.1461261

Mostafa, A. A. (2018). Academic procrastination, self-efficacy beliefs, and academic achievement among middle school first year students with learning disabilities. *International Journal of Psycho-Educational Sciences, 7*(2), 87–93.

Niemiec, R. M., Shogren, K. A., & Wehmeyer, M. L. (2017). Character strengths and intellectual and developmental disability: A strengths-based approach from positive psychology. *Education and Training in Autism and Developmental Disabilities, 52*, 13–25.

No Child Left Behind Act of 2001, 20 U.S.C. § 6319 (2002).

Runswick-Cole, K., & Hodge, N. (2009). Needs or rights? A challenge to the discourse of special education. *British Journal of Special Education, 36*(4), 198–203. https://doi.org/10.1111/j.1467-8578.2009.00438.x

Skrtic, T. M., Harris, K. R., & Shriner, J. G. (2005). *Special education policy and practice: Accountability, instruction, and social challenges.* Love Pub. Co.

Smyth, T. S. (2008). Who is No Child Left Behind leaving behind? *The Clearing House: A Journal of Educational Strategies, Issues and Ideas, 81*(3), 133–137.

Special Education Rules Implementation Manual. (2019, January 16). Georgia Department of Education. https://www.gadoe.org/Curriculum-Instruction-and-Assessment/Special-Education-Services/Documents/Implementation%20 Manual%202018-19/IEP%2012-14-20.pdf

Thompson, S., & Thurlow, M. (2003). *2003 State special education outcomes: Marching on.* University of Minnesota, National Center on Educational Outcomes.

Trainor, A. A. (2007). Person-centered planning in two culturally distinct communities: Responding to divergent needs and preferences. *Career Development for Exceptional Individuals, 30*(2), 92–103. https://doi.org/10.1177/0885728807 0300020601

Turgut, G. (2013). International tests and the US educational reforms: Can success be replicated? *The Clearing House: A Journal of Educational Strategies, Issues and Ideas, 86*(2), 64–73. https://doi.org/10.1080/00098655.2012.748640

Vandercook, T., York, J., & Forest, M. (1989). The McGill Action Planning System (MAPS): A strategy for building the vision. *Journal of the Association for Persons With Severe Handicaps, 14*(3), 205–215. https://doi.org/10 .1177/154079698901400306

Waitoller, F. R., & King Thorius, K. A. (2016). Cross-pollinating culturally sustaining pedagogy and universal design for learning: Toward an inclusive pedagogy that accounts for dis/ability. *Harvard Educational Review, 86*(3), 366–389. https://doi.org/10.17763/1943-5045-86.3.366

Wenger, E., McDermott, R., & Snyder, W. M. (2002). *Cultivating communities of practice: A guide to managing knowledge.* Harvard Business School Press.

Yosso, T. J. (2005). Whose culture has capital? A critical race theory discussion of community cultural wealth. *Race ethnicity and education, 8*(1), 69–92. https://doi.org/10.1080/1361332052000341006

# LEADERSHIP, EQUITY, AND THE INDIVIDUALS WITH DISABILITIES EDUCATION ACT

**Catherine Kramarczuk Voulgarides**
*City University of New York, Hunter College*

Over 7 million students receive special education services under one of the most significant pieces of legislation affecting students with dis/abilities[1] in schools across the United States—the Individuals with Disabilities Education Act (IDEA 1997, 2004; National Center for Education Statistics [NCES], 2020). IDEA (2004) affects every aspect of the delivery of educational services to students with dis/abilities and it shapes educational practice in profound ways. IDEA is also a civil rights-based law that asserts that students with dis/abilities fundamentally deserve access to high quality educational services and opportunities despite a historical legacy of legally sanctioned exclusion from schools.

IDEA consists of several parts, each of which governs a different aspect of the special education process in schools across the United States. Part A

*Who Decides?*, pages 203–220
Copyright © 2022 by Information Age Publishing
www.infoagepub.com
All rights of reproduction in any form reserved.

provides the foundation for the legislation and its general provisions. Part B lays out how students with dis/abilities, ages 3–21, should be educated in schools. It is also associated with the six foundational principles of IDEA. Part C relates to infants and toddlers, birth to age 2, and the provision of early intervention services. Lastly, Part D is related to national activities and federal grants that support states in effectively administering IDEA and its foundational principles at the local level.

There are six central principles within Part B of IDEA (Yell, 2019). The principles are upheld via a plethora of individual protections that educators must comply with in practice. They include access to: a free appropriate public education (FAPE), the least restrictive environment (LRE), nondiscriminatory evaluations to determine dis/ability designation; educational services regardless of the severity of student's condition, procedural safeguards, and robust parental/caregiver participation. While the principles stand alone as separate concepts, they work together to protect the rights of students with dis/abilities in schools across the United States.

The IDEA principles, and compliance with them, should guide educators' actions when serving students with dis/abilities. However, many state education agencies (SEAs) and local education agencies (LEAs) are unable to achieve 100% compliance with IDEA (National Council on Disability, 2018; Stein, 2009; Wakelin, 2008; Wrightslaw, n.d.). Furthermore, the National Council on Disability (2018) asserts the Federal Government has not done "enough to force states to comply with federal law on special education" (p. 13). IDEA implementation is complicated though, and educators and leaders often do not have a strong legal understanding of the foundational principles of IDEA.

Zirkel (2015) asserts that teacher educators should increase their legal literacy around the foundational tenets of IDEA to assure proper compliance and correct implementation in practice. Similarly, educational leaders lack professional training and expertise to deal with special education law's technical complexities, such as properly complying with its foundational tenets. Administrators, both at the building and district level and special education or not, are unprepared to navigate the equity concerns that arise at the intersection of special education law and the administration of special education services in schools (e.g., Pazey & Cole, 2013; Pazey & Yates, 2018). Pazey and Yates (2018) argue special education leaders are required to "have an unusual breadth and depth of understanding across complementary disciplines" that is not explicitly taught in educational leadership programs and which is most likely acquired through trial and error in educational practice (p. 34). This is consistent with what Pazey and Cole (2013) had already argued, which was that special education and special education law courses should be added to educational leadership programs so that leaders are better prepared to effectively address special education concerns in practice.

Given the civil rights and social justice intent of IDEA, its complex legal structure, the importance of its foundational tenets, and the associated implementation challenges, it is important for educational leaders to not only thoroughly understand the purpose of IDEA, but also to understand how their everyday actions relate to broader inequities in special education. In this chapter, I briefly describe the foundational tenets of IDEA. I outline how the civil rights intent of IDEA morphs when it is applied to practice, as the IDEA procedural protections do not sufficiently uphold the civil rights intent of the legislation in practice. I argue that although the foundational principles of IDEA are legally robust and promising, consequential equity concerns remain in special education outcomes. I end with a brief discussion about how educational leaders can look beyond compliance with IDEA to more effectively achieve equity in special education outcomes.

## FOUNDATIONAL PRINCIPLES IN PART B OF IDEA

Students with dis/abilities have the right to FAPE via IDEA. FAPE requires that students with dis/abilities receive special education and related services that meet their unique educational and future needs [20 U.S.C. § 1401(d)(1)(a)]. FAPE is upheld and guaranteed through the creation of an individual education program (IEP) [20 U.S.C. § 1402(9)]. An IEP requires that for each student receiving services under IDEA: (a) present levels of performance are recorded; (b) annual social, emotional, behavioral, and academic goals are regularly monitored; (c) supplemental services and aids are provided to students with dis/abilities as deemed appropriate; and (d) accommodations are also provided to students as needed.

The principle of FAPE is deeply interconnected with LRE, Child Find, and the associated eligibility requirements for classification (Zirkel, 2015). The LRE provision and federal regulations for LRE outline a continuum of placement options (34. C.F.R. § 300.115), aids, and services to assure students with dis/abilities are educated, to the greatest extent that is beneficial, in a general education setting with their nondisabled peers. The LRE placement is indicated in the IEP. IDEA also requires state and local education agencies to identify, locate, and evaluate eligible students to receive special education services, known as Child Find [20 U.S.C. § 1412(a)(1)]. States must have policies and procedures in place to do this, and the provisions extend to children with dis/abilities who are homeless, wards of the state, and attending nonpublic schools, regardless of the severity of their dis/ability [20 U.S.C. § 1412(a)(3)]. Through the Child Find process, any resulting classifications are recorded in a child's IEP.

Children being considered for classification and placement in special education are also entitled to nondiscriminatory evaluations whereby each child is fairly and without bias evaluated to determine if they have a dis/ability or not. The results of nondiscriminatory evaluations are used to plan the types of services and aids a student receives in order to benefit from the schooling process. The results are eventually incorporated into an IEP and guide a student's learning plan. "Special factors" must be considered for each student who qualifies for special education services under IDEA. IDEA requires that an IEP accounts for how a student's behavior, limited English proficiency, blindness or visual impairment, communication needs and deafness, and use of assistive technology [§300.324(a)(2)] affect the services they are evaluated for, entitled to, and receive in schools via IDEA. The legislation mandates that students cannot be denied FAPE and the right to an IEP. The resulting Zero Reject principle [20 U.S.C. A§1401(1)] asserts that no child is denied an education, regardless of the severity of their dis/ability.

Additionally, IDEA Part B mandates caregiver/parent participation and due process when any education decision is made regarding a child's special education evaluation, referral, program planning, or assessment (20 U.S.C. § 1414 (e), 2004). Caregivers/parents must give informed consent for any special education evaluations, labels, and/or services that are suggested for their child and they can dispute a school's recommendation via IDEA's various procedural protections. Caregivers/parents have a considerable amount of power to advocate for their children via IDEA, and the IEP cannot be formalized or enacted upon without a caregiver/parent's consent. While the foundational principles of IDEA are robust and critical for securing the rights of students with dis/abilities, consequential inequities in special education outcomes have been recorded for decades (Dunn, 1968; Skiba et al., 2008). In addition, the social justice and civil rights impetus behind IDEA's foundational principles have become highly proceduralized, technical, and difficult to manage in practice.

## Equity and the Foundational Principles of IDEA

Globally, disproportionality in special education is a prominent issue. The significant disproportionate representation of Black Indigenous students of color (BISoC) in special education classifications, placements, and suspensions (U.S. Department of Education, 2020) is well-documented. For instance, 17.5% of American Indian/Alaskan Native students were identified as having a dis/ability under IDEA even though they only comprise 1% of students enrolled in public schools. On the other hand, White students represent 48% of public school students, but comprise only 14% of students served under IDEA (Hussar et al., 2020; NCES, 2018). BISoC with dis/abilities are also disproportionately subject to exclusionary disciplinary policies and practices (Losen, 2014; U.S. Department of Education, 2020). The U.S

Department of Education (2014) Office of Civil Rights report shows that students with dis/abilities are more than twice as likely to receive an out-of-school suspension (13%) as compared to nondisabled peers (6%), and the disparities are compounded by race and gender.

These racial disparities relate to the foundational principles of IDEA. There are inequities and implementation challenges associated with each principle. Ideally, these challenges should not occur *if* the principles were substantively applied to practice. The following parts of the chapter describe equity concerns associated with each foundational principle.

## Equity and Part B: Considerations and Concerns

FAPE, which is represented through a well-crafted IEP, remains an elusive reality in schools. The construction, implementation, and monitoring of an IEP in practice is not always accurate and IEPs are not always implemented appropriately (Hoover & Patton, 2017; Zirkel & Bauer, 2016). A well-crafted IEP includes such aspects as measurable individual goals aligned with a students' social, emotional, academic, and behavioral needs so that a student with a dis/ability has a carefully designed education program that can be tracked and documented (Gibb & Dyches, 2015). A poorly crafted IEP contains generic goals that are not as responsive to individual needs. Bray and Russell (2016, 2018) in their work examining IEP implementation, they found that poorly crafted IEP's were responsive to institutional pressures rather than to student needs, offering limited guidance on how to effectively provide special education services to students with dis/abilities. In addition, local interpretation of federal IDEA mandates do not specify how to create meaningful and culturally responsive IEPs that meet student needs (Tran et al., 2018).

FAPE, IEPs and parental/caregiver participation present unique equity concerns too. Wealthier, and often White, caregivers/parents are often better positioned to leverage IDEA and secure sound IEPs that benefit their children too (e.g., Ong-Dean, 2009). The U.S. Government Accountability report (U.S. Government Accountability Office [U.S. GAO], 2019a) examined patterns of caregiver/parent use of IDEA procedural protections, due process, and mediation requests. The report found racial and class differences in how IDEA legal mechanisms were used by caregivers/parents, citing difficulty in

> paying for attorneys and expert witnesses at a due process hearing[s], parents' reluctance to initiate disputes because they feel disadvantaged by the school district's knowledge and financial resources, and parents' lack of time off from work to attend due process hearings. (U.S. GAO, 2019a, p. 1)

The report also found that when caregivers/parents and school officials disagreed over special education services provided under IDEA and legal action was taken, there were lower levels of dispute in districts with more BI-SoC. The report indicated that language barriers, retaliation fears, and/or legal costs were possible factors affecting dispute activity. The trends mirror research which indicates that families from diverse and less economically advantaged backgrounds encounter unequal power relationships during the special education process (e.g., Harry, 2008; Harry & Ocasio-Stoutenburg, 2020), which also leads to lower quality IEPs that are not aligned with student needs.

Similarly, in another U.S. GAO report published in 2019, the U.S. GAO examined why the number of children receiving special education services at the state level varied across the United States. Specifically, the report focused on understanding how Child Find and the zero reject principle were applied to practice. It highlighted how the latitude afforded to states in determining special education eligibility and dis/ability definitions have become so muddled that "a child eligible for services in one state might be ineligible in another" (U.S. GAO, 2019b, p. 1). The findings were especially consequential for English learners (emergent bilingual) because, according to the leaders who were interviewed for the report and consistent with research on the subject, it is difficult to properly identify and evaluate emergent bilingual students for special education services (e.g., Hamayan et al., 2013; Shifrer et al., 2011). There is potential for conflation of language acquisition needs with special education needs. The report's findings put into question not only the way in which federal mandates are interpreted at the local level, but also how nondiscriminatory evaluations are, or are not, universally and equitably leveraged in practice to protect the rights of *all* students.

Similarly, the LRE provision has been inequitably applied to practice resulting in consequential racial disparities. LRE, in practice, is often interpreted as a space and place or as a ratio that considers the number of students with dis/abilities in a classroom to the number of qualified teachers in that classroom (Howe et al., 2018). The technical interpretation of LRE symbolically signals inclusive practices, but it does not ensure equity in inclusion. For example, in New York City over 1 million students are educated in the public school system. Rates of inclusion for students with dis/abilities rose from 53% in the 2009–2010 school year to 66% in the 2016–2017 school year. While the increase is impressive, these data also reveal that BISoC and students with labels such as autism, intellectual dis/ability, and emotional disturbance, as compared to White students with these dis/abilities, are still placed in more restrictive settings (Fancsali, 2019). The patterns illustrate how numeric inclusion may be achieved, but equitable inclusion can nonetheless be rare. Understanding why and how the described inequities manifest and how they relate to the work of educational leaders is of critical importance.

## Challenges Associated With IDEA Implementation and Procedural Compliance

IDEA is a highly proceduralized law. Zirkel (2015) states, "Special education is the most legalized segment of P–12 schooling" (p. 263), which affects how educators and educational leaders understand the original social justice and civil rights impetus of IDEA and how they comply with IDEA mandates in practice.

Through each reauthorization of IDEA (1997 and 2004), the U.S. Congress developed procedural standards of equal opportunity and access for students with dis/abilities (Zirkel, 2005). The dynamic was built into foundational legal cases that shaped the development of IDEA. For example, in the *Board of Education of the Hendrick Hudson Central School District v. Amy Rowley* (1982) case, which established a precedent for providing students with dis/abilities FAPE through an IEP, the *Rowley* court determined that the procedural requirements of IDEA reflect "a 'legislative conviction' that the *substance* of an appropriate education could be realized by simply meeting the law's *procedural* requirements" (Ong-Dean, 2009, p. 32). Two standards for FAPE were established by the *Rowley* Court, "(a) Did the school district comply with the various applicable procedures? and (b) Is the IEP 'reasonably calculated to enable the child to receive educational benefits?'" (Zirkel, 2015, pp. 206–207). A student's IEP need only be reasonably calculated to yield educational benefit, indicating "that any progress was better than no progress" (McKenna & Brigham 2019, p. 3) for students with dis/abilities. The procedural standards for FAPE create a low threshold for compliance with IDEA and at the same time, low expectations for students with dis/abilities.

The focus on procedural compliance over substantive compliance implies that a student's thoroughly completed IEP can signal sufficient compliance with the law. However, it does not assure that the IEP has been implemented in an equitable manner for that particular student. Therefore, if a correctly filled out IEP is taken to be evidence of compliance with the civil rights and social justice ideals of IDEA, irrespective of whether or not the IEP is equitably leveraged in practice, inequities are allowed to persist unabated under the guise of compliance.

This dynamic represents a form of symbolic compliance with civil rights-oriented mandates without actually needing to realize civil rights outcomes (Edelman, 2016). Compliance, therefore, is problematic when it becomes a means to an end—when the logic of compliance (Voulgarides, 2018, 2020), or the way that educators comply with and use IDEA, upholds norms and ways of being that perpetuate, rather than disrupt, inequities. In essence, seemingly benign acts of compliance with IDEA can (re)produce inequities in special education when compliance means complacency with discriminatory forces that do not promote equity, access, and educational opportunity for *all* students.

## ENACTING CHANGE AND CENTERING EQUITY DURING THE POLICY IMPLEMENTATION PROCESS

Given the enduring inequities in special education and the dynamics associated with IDEA compliance, leaders must push their staff and colleagues to reimagine the purpose of special education. It also requires that state departments of education, district leadership boards of education, and school leader training programs do the same. These educational stakeholders must examine how special education services are delivered to students in their schools and districts using an intentional equity lens.

In other words, educators must fundamentally shift how they view students at their intersections, how they organize their workflows, and how they see and imagine radical possibilities for change within their local contexts (e.g., Renee et al., 2010; Welner, 2001). Below, I describe what the zone of mediation is and provide some suggestions for challenging this zone.

## The Zone of Mediation

To reimagine the administration of special education services in schools, leaders must critically challenge problematic cultural norms, ways of being, and values that influence how policies are enacted and used within their local contexts. The process involves questioning how local power dynamics, related to deep-seated beliefs about race, dis/ability, language, and educability affect students. When leaders identify and challenge the practices and beliefs that contribute to inequities, they can work within their local zones of mediation and enact equity-focused change within their local context (Welner, 2001). The *zone of mediation* is the space where educators and leaders can act locally, given the resources at hand, and create equity-based changes. The zone of mediation is comprised of four locally determined components: the inertial, the technical, the normative, and the political dimensions of schooling (Welner, 2001).

### Inertial Forces

Inertial forces are taken-for-granted ways of being. They are the components of everyday educational practice that relate to what has always been, the way things always were, and so forth. Inertial forces allow for educators' professional capacities and beliefs, racial ideologies, ideologies about ability, and the social and contextual factors that negatively impact student outcomes and marginalize families to persist unquestioned. Leaders must identify the inertial forces that shape their practice and they have to actively work to disrupt the inertia. In doing so, they can identify levers for change that promote more equitable and fair practices.

Examples include, but are not limited to:

- ensuring that staff know that curricula should be critically interrogated for the accurate representation of all groups of students and that curricula sufficiently acknowledge structures of power and privilege in society;
- ensuring that there is community-wide knowledge of racial inequities and disproportionality occurring in the district via regular school and district communication channels; and
- ensuring that educational inequities are clearly described in district communications so that community and school coalitions can be formed to address the inequities.

These suggestions are loosely adapted from Bryk et al. (2010), Fergus (2016), and Klingner et al. (2005).

### Technical Forces

Technical forces are the concrete inputs that make schools work. They are the tangible, material, and temporal inputs that help a school and/or district function on a day-to-day basis. They give the organization its structure, the resources it needs to function, and the resource pathways that dictate how resources are allocated across and within schools in a district. Technical forces are also visible and they can be physically manipulated—like budgets, teacher schedules, and so forth. These inputs, and the ways in which educational leaders allocate both material and professional resources across districts and within schools, have to be critically examined for their equity impacts on diverse students. Leaders must ask questions about which groups of students get more resources, greater access to higher qualified teachers, and so forth. They must ask why decisions about how resources are distributed and to whom they are being distributed are being made and subsequently, unpack how technical inputs may sustain inequities through these decisions.

Examples include, but are not limited to:

- ensuring that funding, space, and time are regularly allocated for districtwide *collaborative* professional development related to issues of race, disability, ethnicity, equity, inclusion, diversity, sexuality, country of origin, and so forth;

- ensuring that within-school tracking is monitored for racial, ethnic, linguistic, and gender patterns;
- ensuring that a schoolwide equity plan and mission statement is established and abided by, that guides students' schedules and the allocation of experienced teachers to high-needs classrooms; and
- ensuring that the most qualified teachers are assigned to the highest-need classes and that there is diversity in the teaching force.

These suggestions are loosely adapted from Bryk et al. (2010), Fergus (2016), and Klingner et al. (2005).

### Normative Forces

Normative forces are the professional beliefs and values that shape educational practice. They are deeply entrenched within local communities and connected to racial and ability ideologies that define notions of achievement and shape teacher expectations about diverse students. Normative social forces are very difficult to challenge because they are connected to a person's core belief system about race, ability, and educability (Welner, 2001). It is important that leaders do extensive work around developing their own capacity to reflect on destructive normative beliefs and simultaneously push their teachers and staff to do so also.

Examples include, but are not limited to:

- ensuring that educators acknowledge that professional development is a lifelong learning process;
- ensuring that educators develop the capacity to have meaningful conversations with one another about how race, culture, diversity, equity, inclusion, sexuality, country of origin, and so forth relate to their educational practice and student outcomes;
- ensuring that staff are aware that culture is dynamic, complex, constantly evolving, and embedded in every aspect of the teaching and learning process; and
- ensuring that student perspectives are meaningfully included in the teaching and learning process and that deficit-based beliefs about students and families are not tolerated.

These suggestions are loosely adapted from Bryk et al. (2010), Fergus (2016), Klingner et al. (2005), and Voulgarides et al. (2017).

### Political Forces

Lastly, political forces are related to the power imbalances that exist within a community, school, and district. Political forces also extend beyond these locales. They are associated with local, state, and federal policy demands and expectations. Leaders must be aware of how local political dynamics affect school board decisions, how accountability policies and laws shape their managerial decisions around technical inputs, and so forth. Although it is difficult for leaders, at both the school and district level, to push back against political forces associated with local community dynamics and board of educations, leaders should create coalitions with colleagues, community members, and students to challenge the political forces that thwart equity in education at the local level.

Examples include, but are not limited to:

- ensuring that issues of equity are raised in personal and public forums between school and district officials and community and family members;
- ensuring that districts regularly communicate with local and state educational officials about issues of equity occurring in their local context and discuss how state officials can help them address these issues; and
- ensuring that coalitions are built between educators and community members that effectively allow for districts' and community members' needs to be communicated to local boards of education and state officials in the pursuit of educational equity.

## LOOKING FORWARD: PRACTICAL RECOMMENDATIONS FOR PURSUING EQUITY AT THE INTERSECTION OF LEADERSHIP AND SPECIAL EDUCATION SYSTEMS

Leaders should first disaggregate their data related to classifications, suspensions, and placements to identify patterns and inequities that manifest across race, dis/ability category, gender, language status, and so forth. Leaders, at both the district and school level, can begin by analyzing the special education referral process itself and discipline referrals in order to identify potential system gaps or instances where particular teachers may be referring students at a higher rate for special education services or exclusionary disciplinary outcomes. Leaders can critically analyze the data and engage in conversations with their staff about why certain patterns of achievement and/or disciplinary outcomes exist. The data-based conversations open up space for educators to examine how their biases and beliefs drive their practice (see Fergus, 2016 for a comprehensive example of these practices), which can facilitate efforts to disrupt normative and inertial forces. However, it is important to note that specific technical assistance and professional development must be targeted to help educators move from discussing racialized disparities to how their own belief systems relate to the identified inequities. Deficit models of thinking, places the responsibility of learning on individual bodies and does not sufficiently question how social structures, norms, and systems contribute to persistent inequalities in education. And it also—intentionally or not—locates the sources of academic failure and/or behavioral issues within students, their upbringing, or the families and communities that they come from (see Valencia, 2012; Valencia & Solórzano, 1997). If not directly addressed, deficit patterns of thinking can become reified in these conversations and they must be specifically deconstructed and addressed.

Second, leaders should not only require that IEP's are legally sound, but that they are also equitably leveraged in practice. Recommendations for practice include assuring that IEP meetings are not focused on efficiency over quality. Leaders can monitor the length of time that IEP meetings occur for different groups of students disaggregated by race, dis/ability category, gender, language status, and other salient identities. Technical inputs can be adjusted to assure that the identified inequities are addressed. Normative forces can also be challenged when leaders assure that IEP meetings are conducted in ways that promote nuanced engagement, involvement, and understandings of families, students, and their needs.

Third, the technical procedural protections of IDEA must be balanced with complex and inclusive notions of caregiver/parental engagement and involvement. It is important for teacher educators and leaders to advocate for and with caregivers/parents, rather than silence their needs and inadvertently deny access to high quality educational opportunities. Leaders, and the staff they oversee, should regularly reflect upon their assumptions, biases, and beliefs, about what constitutes a "good" caregiver/parent or "good" caregiver/parent engagement and involvement. Herrera et al. (2020) suggest that educators "engage, respect, and accept" the community and cultural wealth of all the caregivers/parents they work with on a daily basis (xvii). Leaders must assure that they, and their staff, see *all* parents and caregivers as partners who have a wealth of knowledge and expertise. The work requires that political forces are challenged at the local level because caregiver/parental influence on school practices are often influenced by wealth (Lareau, 2011) and deficit views of race (e.g., Yosso, 2005).

Fourth, leaders should engage in professional development that recognizes how intersectional identities, including a dis/ability label, affect how students are served under IDEA. For example, and in relationship to ELL students, it is important that educators and leaders have the skills to distinguish between language acquisition processes and a dis/ability designation. Although the language acquisition process often mirrors the observable characteristics of learning dis/abilities (Hamayan et al., 2013), educators must have the skills to determine if what they observe is part of the language acquisition process or is evidence of a dis/ability—the important distinction being that language acquisition processes are not, and should not, be treated as dis/abilities (Zacarian, 2011). Nondiscriminatory evaluations, authentic IEP meetings, and proper Child Find practices require this knowledge. It is important to note that this work requires departments that do not typically work together to share knowledge, interpret data, and make collective decisions about students at the intersection of language and dis/ability. This, alone, requires a restructuring of how schools and districts typically operate in the service of more equitably attending to student needs.

Fifth, the concept of LRE needs be understood in a way that moves beyond determining proper student to teacher ratios and placement patterns. Leaders have to reconceptualize the LRE provision as a call for creating more inclusive environments in schools. While there are many "checklists" that recommend best practices for creating inclusive schools (e.g., Villa & Thousand, 2005), a checklist does not rupture the assumption that the dual system of education, one that is "general" and one that is "special," is an appropriate way to organize and educate children. The distinction inherently reifies a medical model of dis/ability, which is deeply ingrained in the legal logics of IDEA. A medical model of dis/ability signals that an individual with a dis/ability has deviated from a prescribed "norm." They have limited "biological function resulting from a physical, cognitive, or sensory impairment" which subsequently "distinguishes between two states of being: normal and pathological" (Baglieri & Lalvani, 2019, p. 15). When the "normal" and the "pathological" are embedded into organizational practices through LRE and a continuum of placements, the medical model of dis/ability is taken for granted as truth. Thus, leaders must push themselves and their staff to associate the LRE provision, and compliance with it, with a more inclusive understanding of how to organize schools and serve students at their intersections.

Finally, educational stakeholders, including teachers and leaders, must understand how their complex work environments affect their daily decision-making processes. When educators are faced with multiple legal, procedural, and practice-based demands, they triage their workflow. The decisions they make are based upon personal and professional expertise and the knowledge they have about special education and the educative process. Educators adapt broad policy directives to the realities of their local contexts, while simultaneously meeting the requirements of IDEA and the managerial, organizational, and contextual needs of their local schools. They use personal and professional discretion to implement these policies with readily available, yet imperfect information—a form of bounded rationality (March & Simon, 1958). They also satisfice (March & Simon, 1958), picking and choosing from available information and resources to develop a solution that maximizes rewards and minimizes the costs of their work. Satisficing makes their workflow manageable, but when people satisfice they are not doing the "ideal job, but the doable job" (Bowker & Star, 2000, p. 24). They make decisions that align with their own understandings of the world, which may be fraught with unexamined biases and beliefs that can marginalize students and deny them educational opportunity and access. Leaders must push themselves and their staff to resist complying just to comply because it makes their workflow more manageable.

The steps outlined here are building blocks for identifying and challenging local zones of mediation. They collectively engage with and challenge inertial, technical, normative, and political forces. It is incumbent upon leaders to constantly find levers and mechanisms in practice that disrupt policies, practices, and procedures that sustain inequities.

## CONCLUSION

While the foundational tenets of IDEA are important and they secure the rights of students with dis/abilities in schools, the principles alone do not assure equitable outcomes. Due to this, leaders must focus on supporting students with dis/abilities and their caregivers/families in ways that go beyond compliance and technical understandings of IDEA. The work requires disruption of local zones of mediation in order to promote equity and lead to more expansive notions of leadership.

Ishimaru (2019) argues that leaders should operate with a *both/and* approach that centers collaborations between families, students, and educators. The approach recognizes "both the leadership of non-dominant youth, families, and communities *and*...the formal leaders and educators within educational systems" (Ishimaru, 2019, p. 140). It requires educational leaders overseeing special education programs that engage with both the substantive civil rights and social justice history of special education and assure that procedural compliance with IDEA is upheld so that the rights of students with dis/abilities are protected in schools. It also requires that both targeted efforts to address persistent racial inequities in special education and the pursuit of educational opportunity and access for all students coexist and drive the work of educators. The both/and approach recognizes that "our educational systems contain *both* historically rooted dynamics of oppression *and* possibilities for just futures and collective well-being" (Ishimaru, 2019, p. 140, emphasis in original). Thus, the both/and approach can lead towards more liberatory and inclusive educational spaces for *all* students so that equity in special education does not remain an elusive ideal.

## AUTHOR NOTE

Portions of this chapter were adapted from: Voulgarides, C. (2018). *Does Compliance Matter in Special Education?: IDEA and the Hidden Inequities of Practice*. Teachers College Press.

## ACKNOWLEDGMENTS

I would like to thank Dr. Alexandra Aylward and Natalie Zwerger, New York University for their invaluable feedback and contributions when preparing the chapter. Also Dr. Susan Etscheidt and Dr. David I. Hernández-Saca for their insights when conceptualizing the chapter.

## NOTE

1.  I use the term "dis/ability" with a slash to refer to the social construction and contextually determined nature of dis/ability. The choice rejects the idea that dis/ability is a fixed individual trait (e.g., Annamma et al., 2016; Davis, 1995).

## REFERENCES

Annamma, S. A., Connor, D. J., & Ferri, B. A. (2016). A truncated genealogy of Dis-Crit. In D. J. Connor, B. A. Ferri, & S. A. Annamma (Eds.), *DisCrit: Disability studies and critical race theory in education* (1st ed., pp. 1–8). Teachers College Press.

Baglieri, S., & Lalvani, P. (2019). *Undoing ableism: Teaching about disability in K–12 classrooms*. Routledge.

Board of Education of the Hendrick Hudson Central School District v. Rowley, 458 U.S. 176 (1982)

Bowker, G. C., & Star, S. L. (2000). *Sorting things out: Classification and its consequences*. MIT press.

Bray, L. E., & Russell, J. L. (2016). Going off script: Structure and agency in individualized education program meetings. *American Journal of Education, 122*(3), 367–398.

Bray, L. E., & Russell, J. L. (2018). The dynamic interaction between institutional pressures and activity: An examination of the implementation of IEPs in secondary inclusive settings. *Educational Evaluation and Policy Analysis, 40*(2), 243–266.

Bryk, A. S., Sebring, P. B., Allensworth, E., Luppescu, S., & Easton, J. Q. (2010). *Organizing schools for improvement: Lessons from Chicago*. University of Chicago Press.

Davis, L. J. (1995). *Enforcing normalcy: Disability, deafness and the body*. Verso.

DeMatthews, D. E., Edwards, D. B., & Nelson, T. E. (2014). Identification problems: US special education eligibility for English language learners. *International Journal of Educational Research, 68,* 27–34. https://doi.org/10.1016/j.ijer.2014.08.002

Dunn, L. M. (1968). Special education for the mildly retarded—Is much of it justifiable? *Exceptional children, 35*(1), 5–22.

Edelman, L. B. (2016). *Working law: Courts, corporations, and symbolic civil rights.* University of Chicago Press.

Fancsali, C. (2019). *Special Education in New York City: Understanding the Landscape* [Brief]. Research Alliance for New York City Schools.

Fergus, E. (2016). *Solving disproportionality and achieving equity: A leader's guide to using data to change hearts and minds.* Corwin Press.

Gibb, G. S., & Dyches, T. T. (2015). *IEPs: Writing quality individualized education programs.* Pearson.

Hamayan, E. V., Marler, B., Lopez, C. S., & Damico, J. (2013). *Special education considerations for English language learners: Delivering a continuum of services.* Caslon Publishing.

Harry, B. (2008). Collaboration with culturally and linguistically diverse families: Ideal versus reality. *Exceptional children, 74*(3), 372–388. https://doi.org/10.1177/001440290807400306

Harry, B., & Ocasio-Stoutenburg, L. (2020). *Meeting families where they are: Building equity through advocacy with diverse schools and communities.* Teachers College Press.

Herrera, S. G., Porter, L., & Barko-Alva, K. (2020). *Equity in school–parent partnerships: Cultivating community and family trust in culturally diverse classrooms.* Teachers College Press.

Hoover, J. J., & Patton, J. R. (2017). *IEPs for ELs: And other diverse learners.* Corwin Press.

Howe, K. R., Boelé, A. L., & Miramontes, O. B. (2018). *The ethics of special education.* Teachers College Press.

Hussar, B., Zhang, J., Hein, S., Wang, K., Roberts, A., Cui, J., Smith, M., Bullock Mann, F., Barmer, A., Dilig, R., Nachazel, T., Barnett, M., & Purcell, S. (2020). *The Condition of Education 2020* (NCES 2020-144). National Center for Education Statistics.

Individuals With Disabilities Education Act Amendments, 20 U.S.C. § 1400 et seq. (1997). https://www.govinfo.gov/content/pkg/PLAW-105publ17/pdf/PLAW-105publ17.pdf

Individuals With Disabilities Education Act, 20 U.S.C. §1400 et seq. (2004). https://sites.ed.gov/idea/statute-chapter-33/subchapter-i/1400

Ishimaru, A. M. (2019). *Just schools: Building equitable collaborations with families and communities.* Teachers College Press.

Klingner, J., Artiles, A. J., Kozleski, E., Harry, B., Zion, S., Tate, W., Zamora Durán, G., & Riley, D. (2005). Addressing the disproportionate representation of culturally and linguistically diverse students in special education through culturally responsive educational systems. *Education Policy Analysis Archives/Archivos Analíticos de Políticas Educativas, 13,* 1–40.

Lareau, A. (2011). *Unequal childhoods: Class, race, and family life.* University of California Press.

Losen, D. J. (Ed.). (2014). *Closing the school discipline gap: Equitable remedies for excessive exclusion.* Teachers College Press.

March, J. G., & Simon, H. A. (1958). *Organizations.* John Wiley & Sons.

McKenna, J. W., & Brigham, F. J. (2019). More than de minimis: FAPE in the Post Endrew F. Era. *Behavior Modification, 45*(1). https://doi.org/10.1177/0145445519880836

National Center for Education Statistics. (2018). *Digest of Education Statistics: Table 204.40. Children 3 to 21 years old served under Individuals with Disabilities Education Act (IDEA), Part B, by race/ethnicity and age group: 2000-01 through 2017–2018.* https://nces.ed.gov/programs/digest/d18/tables/dt18_204.40.asp?current=yes

National Center for Education Statistics. (2020). *Students with disabilities.* https://nces.ed.gov/programs/coe/indicator_cgg.asp

National Council on Disability. (2018, February 7). *Federal Monitoring and Enforcement of IDEA Compliance.* https://files.eric.ed.gov/fulltext/ED588516.pdf

Ong-Dean, C. (2009). *Distinguishing disability: Parents, privilege, and special education.* University of Chicago Press.

Pazey, B. L., & Cole, H. (2013). The role of special education training in the development of socially just leaders: Building an equity consciousness in educational leadership programs. *Educational Administration Quarterly, 49*(2), 243–271. https://doi.org/10.1177/0013161X12463934

Pazey, B. L., & Yates, J. R. (2018). Conceptual and historical foundations of special education administration. In J. Crockett, B. Billingsley, & M. L. Boscardin (Eds.), *Handbook of leadership in special education* (2nd ed., pp. 18–38). Routledge.

Renee, M., Welner, K., & Oakes, J. (2010). Social movement organizing and equity-focused educational change: Shifting the zone of mediation. In A. Hargreaves, A. Lieberman, M. Fullan, & D. Hopkins (Eds.), *Second international handbook of educational change* (pp. 153–168). Springer.

Shifrer, D., Muller, C., & Callahan, R. (2011). Disproportionality and learning disabilities: Parsing apart race, socioeconomic status, and language. *Journal of learning disabilities, 44*(3), 246–257. https://doi.org/10.1177/0022219410374236

Skiba, R. J., Simmons, A. B., Ritter, S., Gibb, A. C., Rausch, M. K., Cuadrado, J., & Chung, C. G. (2008). Achieving equity in special education: History, status, and current challenges. *Exceptional Children, 74*(3), 264–288.

Stein, E. B. (2009). The Individuals With Disabilities Education Act (IDEA): Judicial remedies for systemic noncompliance. *Wisconsin Law Review,* 801.

Tran, L. M., Patton, J. R., & Brohammer, M. (2018). Preparing educators for developing culturally and linguistically responsive IEPs. *Teacher Education and Special Education, 41*(3), 229–242.

U.S. Department of Education. (2014). *Civil rights data collection data snapshot: School discipline.* https://ocrdata.ed.gov/assets/downloads/CRDC-School-Discipline-Snapshot.pdf

U.S. Department of Education. (2020). *41st Annual Report to Congress on the Implementation of the Individuals with Disabilities Education Act, 2019.* https://sites.ed.gov/idea/2020-annual-report-congress-idea

U.S. Government Accountability Office. (2019a, November). *Special Education: IDEA Dispute Resolution Activity in Selected States Varied Based on School Districts' Characteristics* [Report to Congressional requesters]. https://www.gao.gov/assets/710/702514.pdf

U.S. Government Accountability Office. (2019b, April 11). *Special education: Varied state criteria may contribute to differences in percentages of children served* (GAO-19-348). https://www.gao.gov/products/GAO-19-348

Valencia, R. R. (Ed.). (2012). *The evolution of deficit thinking: Educational thought and practice.* Routledge.

Valencia, R. R., & Solórzano, D. G. (1997). Contemporary deficit thinking. In R. R. Valencia (Ed.), *The evolution of deficit thinking: Educational thought and practice* (pp. 160–210). RoutledgeFalmer.

Villa, R. A., & Thousand, J. S. (Eds.). (2005). *Creating an inclusive school.* ASCD.

Voulgarides, C. (2018). *Does compliance matter in special education? IDEA and the hidden inequities of practice.* Teachers College Press.

Voulgarides, C. K. (2020). Leadership and the Individuals With Disabilities Education Act (IDEA): Is compliance with IDEA a path toward educational equity? *Journal of Education Human Resources, 38*(2), 238–257.

Voulgarides, C., K. Fergus, E., & King Thorius, K. A. (2017). Pursuing equity: Disproportionality in special education and the reframing of technical solutions to address systemic inequities. *Review of Research in Education, 41*(1), 61–87.

Wakelin, M. M. (2008). Challenging disparities in special education: Moving parents from disempowered team members to ardent advocates. *Northwestern Journal of Law and Social Policy, 3*, 263.

Welner, K. G. (2001). *Legal rights, local wrongs: When community control collides with educational equity.* SUNY Press.

Yosso, T. J. (2005). Whose culture has capital? A critical race theory discussion of community cultural wealth. *Race Ethnicity and Education, 8*(1), 69–91. https://doi.org/10.1080/1361332052000341006

Zacarian, D. (2011). *Transforming schools for English learners: A comprehensive framework for school leaders.* Corwin Press.

Zirkel, P. A. (2005). Does *Brown v. Board of Education* play a prominent role in special education law? *Journal of Law and Education, 34*, 255.

Zirkel, P. A. (2015). Special education law: Illustrative basics and nuances of key IDEA components. *Teacher Education and Special Education, 38*(4), 263–275.

Zirkel, P. A., & Bauer, E. T. (2016). The third dimension of FAPE under the IDEA: IEP implementation. *Journal National Association Administration Law Judiciary, 36*, 409.

CHAPTER 10

# LATINX FAMILIES AND DISABILITY

## The Intersections of Identity, Experiences, and Siblinghood

**Denia G. Bradshaw**
*California State University, Los Angeles*

As a Latina, emergent bilingual, first-generation college student, and the eldest of my father's second family, I have had to learn to navigate different spaces throughout my education. In this respect, there are many students like myself that diverge from "the norm" in terms of cultural background, life experiences, and abilities. In this work, I add to the literature about how we can best support students like myself and my brother, who has been identified as "special needs" and whose cognitive diversity positions him as diverging from the norm.

Reflecting upon my own journey, I have been drawn to serve others like my youngest brother, who was born with a developmental disability. Having struggled with the *hegemonic institutionalization of the English language as a linguistically diverse child,* the rigor and creativity of my lifelong study of classical music paved the path to positive social-emotional experiences by fostering a sense of community and belonging. My musical training guided my own learning and actively minimized the barriers I otherwise faced. Strategic development, recognizing and detecting patterns, and creativity are skills I attribute to my study of classical music, along with my life experiences as a non-native English speaker and Latina. To note, my journey and experience with music was purposeful and empowering. It did not come about by itself and I recognize the support structures that have helped in my musical development. For me, it was the encouragement of my father, quality music lessons, and having a teacher that recognized my full potential in music that made a fundamental difference in my own growth. Through these experiences, I have identified essential support structures that have shaped my approach and dedication to empowering learners with diverse backgrounds and learning needs.

In the present chapter, I highlight my experiences as an older sibling to a younger sibling with a developmental disability, illuminating common themes between these experiences and the literature, and weave in theoretical and conceptual perspectives from the frameworks of disability critical race theory (DisCrit), intersectionality, funds of knowledge (FoK), and practices of inclusion and empowerment as they relate to these experiences.

I examine the observed experiences of my younger brother throughout his life in education. I explore his life as it relates to my own from his birth to present day, focusing on how well-intended educational experiences may have influenced his sense of self. Using narrative strategies, I delineate how practices, instruction, and school climate as a special education student may have contributed to shaping my brother's sense of self-efficacy. I also compared our experiences by examining the ways in which I witnessed and understood his lived experience as an older sibling, but also one that is considered to be typical-able bodied.

## DisCrit: Dismantling Notions of Disability

Annamma et al. (2013) merged tenets of critical race theory (CRT) and disability studies (DS) and have created a theoretical framework called DisCrit. Annamma et al. (2013) intentionally include the "/" in "Dis/ability" to disrupt distorted understandings of disability and bring forth awareness to how "disability" signals a misconception that there is an inability to execute "culturally expected tasks" that further define the individual as "unable to navigate society" (p. 24). DisCrit incorporates a dual analysis of race and ability with hopes to be applied when researching race and dis/ability within education and other areas (Annamma et al., 2013). The application of DisCrit when analyzing the educational experiences of students can powerfully inform and serve to cultivate best practices, enhance experiences and environments to empower students in their learning, and continue to humanize and include the visibility of dis/ability in key decision-making.

## Intersectionality: A Prism for Understanding Intersectional Identity Work

Many of the barriers students face are due to the lack of awareness and understanding of the multiple and intersecting identities that students possess in relation to teachers and systems in place (Crenshaw, 2013). A finding from a qualitative study I conducted about students with disabilities in community colleges, highlighted the notion of intersectionality when describing an older returning student that is hearing impaired and how proactive and inclusive practices can benefit them as a learner (Bradshaw, 2020). The participant in that study described the use of visuals and captioning as beneficial and can also benefit learners whose home language is other than English. These students may be more comfortable learning with their native language and in the process of learning an additional language, they could additionally benefit from closed captioning and visuals (Bradshaw, 2020). Unfortunately, when educators lack awareness of the intersectionality of identities among their students, they are limited in their practice; they also dishonor the lived experiences of students and as a result sustain these socially constructed stereotypes (Peña et al., 2016).

## Students' Gifts: Funds of Knowledge In and Out of the Classroom

Students who are economically, linguistically, and socially diverse, such as students with disabilities, are often consciously or unconsciously impacted in their education by deficit views. Moreover, university researchers in the late 1980s and early 1990s established the FoK framework and approach for purposes of identifying practices that could offset the negative effects of prevalent cultural deficit views and raise awareness on instructional best practices (Moll et al., 1992; Rodriguez, 2013). Among the rationale to improving teaching practices includes the intention to enrich learning experiences of diverse students through an inquiry process that enables educators to learn more about students' home lives and to then develop connections for learning between knowledge production at school and at home (Rodriguez, 2013).

## REMOVE, REVIEW, AND SALUTE:
### DISCRIT, INTERSECTIONALITY, FOK, AND HONORING THE BRILLIANCE WITHIN EVERY LEARNER

Further awareness of intersections of disability and additional identities can be improved and developed by adopting the frameworks of DisCrit, FoK, and/or intersectionality when engaging with diverse learners. DisCrit dismantles socially developed misconceptions around disability (Annamma et al., 2013), FoK encourages the educator to engage and connect with the lives of the learners' outside of the classroom, and intersectionality acknowledges that many of the oppressions that exist for students are outcomes from multiple circumstances unfolding at the same time due the intersectionality of multiple identities (Crenshaw, 2013). Students who have been historically marginalized and oppressed do not benefit from practices that continue notions of deficit and inability. Instead the better goal is to honor, empower, and invite learners to unleash their "natural brilliance" to radiate (Fritzgerald, 2020). Every student is brilliant in their own unique way and education should create conditions that nurture, invite, and celebrate the brilliance each learner possesses (Fritzgerald, 2020). Further, students have a higher sense of self-agency as a result of empowering inclusive practices. When students with disabilities are fostered to be self-determinant, educators attained relevant goals, improved self-determination, and students stated a sense of satisfaction from this method (Bandura, 1986; Wehmeyer et al., 2000). Self-determination in individuals enables them to become self-regulated problem-solvers, a skill necessary inside and outside of the classroom.

## NARRATIVE AND RESTORYING

This narrative inquiry is intended to provide my own reflections upon the experience of being an older sibling by focusing on the intersection of complex processes that have influenced and shaped the life of my younger brother with a developmental disability. This narrative provides a way of understanding the experiences of my youngest brother.

As the older sibling and the researcher, I analyze and reorganize our stories through the process of restorying (Creswell & Poth, 2018). With restorying, there is a gathering of stories and analysis of personal and social interactions; past, present, future, and situation (Clandinin & Connelly, 2000). Narratives and the power of narratives have power in their teachings by asking readers to listen.

A major goal of narrative inquiry is some form of authentic collaboration between research and participants that develops over time, in a place or collection of places, and in interactions of a person's social environment for purposes of understanding lived experiences (Clandinin & Connelly, 2000). Within these stories is an interlaced story of the researcher as an older sibling of a younger brother that has been identified by the school system as having a developmental disability. The story provides insight into how experiences in school have served as a turning point in my life to be an advocate and agent for change for underserved populations. While I am privy to sets of experiences that intersect with my brother's, and I occupy a position that may yield insights he may not have, in no way do I purport that my experiences are his. I recognize in working through my analysis the tensions in "speaking for" others, and hence why I am keen on writing from the first person throughout.

## INSIGHTS THROUGH MY OWN NARRATIVE

*The greatest gift our parents ever gave us was each other.*
—Unknown

As a way of analyzing my observations and experiences as an older sibling with a younger brother with a developmental disability, I am using narrative vignette as a strategy.

### A Baby Brother

Sibling relationships are unique in comparison to other relationships for several reasons. Sibling relationships are usually the longest relationships people have in their lifetime, are created automatically at birth (or in early childhood if adopted), and last until the passing of one of the siblings (Cicirelli, 1995). Despite differences in age, sibling relationships are usually egalitarian with both siblings having mutual feelings toward each other; siblings can have shared and nonshared experiences that can influence the development of each sibling and their relationship (Cicirelli, 1995). Growing up with a little brother that would later be diagnosed as having a disability was without prediction. These life experiences, however, have been nothing short of an opportunity to improve, become an agent for change, and be of service to those that would benefit from advocates.

When I was about 6 or 7 years old, my mother held me in her arms in our apartment porch and asked me if I wanted another little brother or sister. Excitedly nodding my head, she understood that as a yes. My youngest brother was born in May of 1996 when I was a little over eight and a half years old.

We were expecting him in August, however, due to severe complications, he was born by emergency cesarean section after a 29-week pregnancy. My baby brother was premature and weighed 1,116 grams, not even two and a half pounds. Having suffered from apnea at birth, he was intubated and placed in a neonatal intensive care unit (NICU). The doctor diagnosed him with premature birth and respiratory distress syndrome (RDS). RDS is a breathing disorder that is common among premature newborns because their lungs are not able to create enough of the substance, known as surfactant, that keeps the lungs fully expanded when they breathe in air when they are born (Soll & Blanco, 2001; Walther et al., 1992).

> When describing his tininess, my mother would always say that he could fit in a shoebox because he was so small.

She still says that to this day. I chose this vignette because my first memory of my little brother was looking at him from the outside in.

May of 1996 to July that year, my other brother and I would visit our youngest brother from afar. We were able to see him at the hospital from the outside through a tiny little window. His tiny little body would be kept safe and warm in the incubators at the NICU. About 2 months later, we would finally meet our baby brother in the NICU. When entering the NICU, we had to be extra careful and my memories of those visits included seeing other little lives being protected and cared for through incubators, warmers, multiple monitors, IV's (intravenous catheters), and feeding tubes.

> I remember seeing him for the first time. He opened his eyes and I wondered what hue his colored eyes would eventually become. Around that same time, we would finally be able to bring him home from the hospital.

In the earlier stages of neonatal care, preterm infants were commonly diagnosed with disabilities (Lawn et al., 2013). According to Ong et al. (2015), infants that are preterm are highly subject to developmental programming of adverse neurodevelopmental, body composition, and metabolic outcomes. Our family at that time did not know that he would later be diagnosed with a disability.

> After coming home, he had to wear these small stickers on his tiny chest with wires that connected to a monitor that would track his heart rate and number of breaths. If one of the electrodes came off, a loud siren would sound. As a child, this concerned me heavily and I was constantly checking on him in his crib. Being quite tiny and vulnerable, I worried a lot about him and feared that I would not be able to protect him. Being close to 9 years old at this point, I remember feeling those protective older sibling qualities developing. I wanted to keep my baby brother safe.

When he came home, my parents were given instructions and guidelines for taking care of my little brother. Among those, included guidelines for a successful home monitoring experience. Within this manual, were descriptions of terms such as: *Apnea* (not breathing); *bradycardia* (low heart rate); *CPR* (cardiopulmonary resuscitation to be used if the baby stops breathing or the heart stops); *cyanotic, cyanosis* (an "abnormal bluish skin color"); *electrodes* (small pads placed on the baby's skin to pick up heart and breathing impulses); *monitor* (a device that senses the baby's heart rate and respiratory rate); and pneumogram/pneumocardiogram (a recording of the baby's breathing and heart beats; Homedco, 1984, p. 3).

My little brother had to wear a belt with electrodes on it. The belt would be wrapped around his tiny chest between his armpits and lower ribcage. When the monitor alarm sounded, we would rush over to his crib. According to the manual, which we abided by, we were to respond to an alarm as quickly as possible (within 10 seconds; Homedco, 1984). The alarm did go off various times when he had to use the monitoring system, fortunately, it never sounded because he stopped breathing or his heart stopped. It almost always sounded because he was moving around in his crib which resulted in the electrodes moving and causing a "false alarm." The alarm jolted me and I was afraid he was going to die. I loved him very much and wanted to be sure that he was healthy and safe.

## "Normal"? Why Not "Mainstream" or "Status Quo"?

When he was 3 years 8 months old, it was determined that he was not developing "normally" and he was assessed through a psychological evaluation to determine if he would be eligible for regional center services. Being a preteen at the time and occupied with my middle school days, I have no recollection of these matters with my little brother. As I would grow, I would slowly learn more about his assessments, his needs, and his special education experiences.

### ¿Travesio o Curioso?

As an infant and toddler, he definitely possessed a curiousness and bravery beyond mine or my other brother's. At the time, what I am referring to as curiosity and bravery was often referred to by others as *travesuras* (engaging in mischievous acts). Our mother would often tell others that compared with my older brother and me at that early age, the youngest was very different. She would refer to us as easy and always being *bien calmaditos* (very calm), unlike the youngest who manifested high levels of energy. One can argue that the adventure in my other brother and myself, manifested in the youngest. However, from what I recall, this characteristic was not referred to from an assets-based lens because we were all expected to behave in a designated way and respect parental authority. However, safety was always top priority. With regard to safety there was no room to argue. An example I vividly remember of my little brother's sense of exploration and curiosity was when he was about 4 years old and we had made our first trip as a family to Las Vegas.

> After the long drive, we arrived at our hotel to relax. We weren't there long and we did not relax long until my parents realized the youngest had walked out of the room. Next thing we know we were all running around the hotel, taking different floors, calling out his name, searching and searching for my little brother. I remember worrying I would never see him again and I cannot remember at what other time in my life I have seen my mother in such a panic frenzy. I felt so much fear.

When my youngest brother took off that afternoon, we were afraid because he was at higher risk for injury or to get lost because he was so young and could barely communicate his needs. Kiely et al. (2016) found that elopement, the act of secret departure, was prevalent among children in the United States with developmental disabilities. In another study by Anderson et al. (2012), the findings concluded that 49% of the 1,218 sampled families with children with ASD had a history of wandering since the age of four. We would eventually find my little brother within the hour minding his own business drawing squiggles with a blue ballpoint pen on empty white paper behind a security officer desk. I will never forget the fear nor the sense of relief that existed within those moments.

Our family knew the youngest was curious and had a lot of energy. My parents would say things like, "He just never stops." When he was in first grade, my parents frequently met with his teacher and this teacher was very transparent about his hyperactivity. Our parents would leave these meetings laughing as they walked to the car because this one particular teacher would say things like "He's gonna kill me!" I appreciate that my parents never referred to him as *travieso* (being mischievous or naughty), but rather as highly active. I do remember being very defensive when people tried to define his behavior in ways that were highly negative.

## Sibling Dynamics, Bonding, and Influence Throughout the Years

Aside from our parents, my other brother and I spent a great deal of time looking after the youngest. During this time, and speaking for myself, I would experience a spectrum of emotions: affection, jubilance, and empathy, but also worry, irritability, and despair. Watching my little brother learn his firsts are among the most special regarded memories from my childhood. I remember we taught him "Twinkle Twinkle Little Star" and for the longest time he never sang all the words, just the words at the end of each stanza and we loved it. We would sing the beginning part of the lyrics and gradually slow down, a *ritardando*, in the music serving as a cue for his entrance.

Twinkle, twinkle, lit-tle...

*Pause*

Star!

How I won-der what... you...

*Pause*

Are!

These were joyous moments experienced as a sibling. States of being from the other end of the spectrum were, and are, about his current well-being, how society views him, and his future well-being. Kao et al. (2012) interviewed siblings of children with developmental disabilities and some participants reported sympathy and sadness for their sibling. The same study also reported an understanding of assuming caregiving responsibilities whenever their sibling needed help (Kao et al., 2012). Further, siblings play an influential and significant role in the lives of individuals with and without disabilities (Burbidge & Minnes, 2014). Moyson and Roeyers (2012) state that siblings are strongly concerned about the physical and mental well-being of siblings with developmental disabilities. Further stating that their sibling's well-being is so important to them, that they will do everything to improve it (Moyson & Roeyers, 2012).

When he was little and others would speak of his hyperactivity as being *travieso*, I would feel protective because I did not like hearing complaints about him. As he got older and would enter public school, the experiences to follow would provoke frustration with me because he would be treated differently from others. Having already observed such with people labeling him as "naughty," the frustration I would feel after he would come home upset because his class was "made fun of again" would upset me. Seeing him hurt and then hurting with him during those times is imprinted in my existence. There were times when he would tell me about situations like those described and I could somehow empathize. Other times, I would be powered by deep frustration and would verbalize to him that this is not okay and that this should not be happening to him nor to his classmates.

I remember the last time I heard of these experiences; I had said along the lines of "I am going to talk to the administrator. This needs to stop!" He urged me not to, almost in desperation. I did not want to worry him further. I agreed I would not take any action.

Ideally, I would like to imagine that these events of bullying and such ended because I no longer heard of them after my urgency to "stop this with the administration" comment. I know better and I know the truth. He feared retaliation and further bullying with action being taken. Zeedyk et al. (2014) note that there is reason to believe that youth with hidden disabilities experience more bullying than their "typically" developing peers. My brother chose to keep his experiences to himself and also away from me after that. I believe that he feared that his situation would get worse, and maybe it's a combination of things. Perhaps he knew it hurt me to know more. Watching loved ones be marginalized and oppressed is painful and I believe that a lot of the reasons we do social justice work is to actualize change because of what we have witnessed our loved ones endure.

Petalas et al. (2012) found that being the sibling of a brother with a developmental disability can have a positive impact, which includes increasing tolerance and the understanding of disability and diversity, along with sharing moments of joy. When I was in high school and early college I loved taking my little brother to the park. The second I would mention it, his face would light up and I can understand how special parenting can be because of moments that I was blessed to experience like this as an older sibling. When I took photography as a senior in high school, the majority of my shots included my little brother. He was my photography subject again and again. I would capture shots of him with geometric angles and corners from the jungle gym and tennis court (see Figure 10.1), the tenderness of him hugging and petting our golden retriever (see Figure 10.2), and the shadows of the fence gently covering his silly yet intensely goofy smile. Because of photography, we started a tradition to go on walks to the park for years after. The establishment of this tradition became one of every weekend when I would come visit.

Years later our family would get another dog, a pug mix named Buddy. Buddy was loveable and full of energy. My little brother took good care of

**Figure 10.1**  Little brother at the jungle gym.

**Figure 10.2**   Little brother petting our golden retriever.

Buddy and loved him very much. When I would visit my family, I would play with Buddy and my little brother would not be far away, ready to narrate on Buddy's behalf.

> As Buddy would look up at me, I would hear my little brother say in a lowered tone of voice: "Love me."

He and I bonded greatly over this dog as we took him to parks, walks, and car rides. Numerous times my little brother would put a sock on the pug's curly tail and we would giggle watching him chase that sock in circles and circles. Those memories that I shared with my little brother and Buddy are remembrances I hold dear.

My little brother deeply impacted my life. I added an additional career from my performing arts training and professional degrees, to serve those like him in postsecondary settings. It is interesting how those we love can influence the paths we take and the type of transformation we want to see for the future, not just in education, but in society. From my own experience, and as indicated by Camhi (2005), siblings who grow up with a sibling that has a disability have greater independence, a responsible attitude, greater empathy and compassion for others, and possess an enhanced awareness and sensitivity to the needs of others. Our youngest also influenced my other brother in his welfare and in the welfare of others like him. My other brother believes that good health and fitness are important attributes to the quality of life for all individuals, especially those with disabilities. My other brother is an adaptive physical education teacher in one of the largest school districts in the nation. Our youngest and his existence is a blessing because it inspired us to be an advocate, to serve, and to fight for change.

## I See and Admire Your Unique Brilliance

Disability is an identity marker, but not the only one: He is brilliant in his own unique ways. Firstly, my brother always exhibited a level of confidence that I did not possess. For instance, he has no problem dressing up as his favorite character even if it is not typical of societal expectations/norms for a young man. When I inquired about this, I asked if this level of confidence is due to being labeled and categorized as "*special* needs." My brother said, "Yeah it is." He mentioned how other classmates of his would probably not do this act, and later explained that he is more "ballsy" than the majority. He mentioned too that he felt our father had demonstrated a level of confidence that had influenced and resonated with him.

Throughout my life, I have noticed the unique brilliance of my youngest brother. An asset that he has is his ability to memorize facts. When he was much younger and we had cable television, his favorite channels were Discovery Channel and the History Channel. His teachers would tell my parents that my youngest brother would ask them the most challenging questions. Sometimes his teachers could provide an answer to his complex inquiries. Other times, as indicated by the teachers to my parents, they were perplexed and would have to sit down at a computer and Google it in order to answer his elaborate questions.

I remember a time when I had told him that I had taken astronomy for my general education requirements and he instantly lit up. He was beyond excited to participate in discourse about astronomy and immediately posed questions, presented interesting facts, and other concepts and vocabulary associated with astronomy that I had slowly forgotten over time:

> Did you know that stars that become planets are known as brown dwarfs? Interesting fact: Some scientists claim that brown dwarfs are not true stars because they do not have enough mass to ignite the nuclear fusion of ordinary hydrogen.

He had a clear and honest curiosity to learn more about stars and planets and a strong yearning to talk to someone about it:

> I enjoy asking him about random facts from a television series. If he is into it, he knows it like the back of his hand.

With English being my second language, learning to read in the beginning and reading independently was a struggle. The book series that made all of the difference when I was in elementary school were the Harry Potter book series by J. K. Rowling. I remember having the paperback to the first book of the series and hardcover of all the rest. I remember those hardcovers being expensive, however, my parents embraced my renewed conviction regarding reading. That said, my understanding of, and love for the world in which Harry Potter existed, was like no other. My brother has not read the novels however, he has done an immense amount of reading about them online and certainly knows the series far better than I do nowadays. I find myself approaching my brother often when I forget a name or an event in that series for answers. He will take a second, maybe frown a little, put his hand up to his chin, and inquisitively look up at the sky and reply with "I think it's..." and then he would respond. When unsure, my brother would utilize his resourcefulness and research the answer. According to Deci (1975), this intrinsic motivation to engage in a task genuinely out of curiosity (e.g., looking up facts), is evidence of possessing self-determination.

It fascinates me that my brother's developmental disability is classified as "disability," when he has such unique brilliance with his memory and enjoyment of learning:

> When he was about 2 years old, it was noted that he was not developing at the same rate as "typical" children, like my other brother and myself. His development was "delayed." He learned to walk at around one and half years old. Doctors told my parents he would not be able to talk, however, this was delayed also. He began to talk between 3 and 4 years old.

The term "delay" has a connotation of being late or behind. Arguably, it could be said that he was not delayed, rather he developed in his chosen time. Some of the language associated with disability is indicatively condescending. For instance, "hearing impaired" is far more detrimental than "hard of hearing." Why not "neural divergence" instead of saying "learning disability"? Individuals with disabilities, like my brother, have different abilities that should be recognized and honored. As stated earlier with DisCrit, disrupting the socially-developed constructs of what is able and what is not is a misconception that further remains to be dismantled.

Despite having a disability, my brother enjoyed going to school, did well in his classes, and continues to enjoy learning. At a very young age, my brother began various therapies in order to prepare him to be integrated into the general education classroom. However, this was not the result. My brother was in special education throughout the entirety of his preK–12 experience. He had individualized education plans (IEP) that were developed by a team that included my parents, his psychologist, and his teachers. IEPs are a provision outlined by the Individuals With Disabilities Education Act (IDEA, 2004). The Disabilities, Opportunities, Internetworking, and Technology (DO-IT) program describes the IEP as a plan developed to guarantee specialized instruction and related services for the academic success of students with disabilities in preK–12 (IDEA, 2004). With an IEP in place, my little brother would be supported throughout his educational experience. Interestingly, the majority of the IEPs did not request nor require my little brother's presence. According to my mother, the planning in these IEPs did not solicit or include the voice of my brother. McGahee et al. (2001) state that children with disabilities should be involved in their own IEP and be offered choices at a young age in order to begin the development of self-advocacy skills. Unfortunately, this was not the case for my youngest brother. Nonetheless, my parents advocated for him through the development of his IEPs:

> Our father was a strong advocate for my little brother and moved him from one school to another because he did not feel as though they were tapping into his potential. He knew the law and was sure to defend my little brother's rights.

An example of my mother advocating for my brother was when an acquaintance of the family who is not familiar with disability referred to him as being *enfermo* (ill, sick, or unwell). Our mother corrected them and informed him that is not the case because he is *muy inteligente* (very intelligent). We all did our best in advocating for him, including my other brother and myself:

> Once, he came home and said the little girl down the street called him "stupid." My other brother and I bolted to set things straight.

My other brother and I were in high school when this incident happened. We wanted to protect the youngest and were sure to let her know this was not ok and this was quite unkind. I remember her apologizing to us, and more importantly, apologizing to our little brother. Our brother may not have certain skills that society has deemed as preferred or regarded superior by being typical, or normal, or status quo, but he is undoubtedly intelligent and his brilliance should not be dimmed because of this existing deficit-based medical model of disability.

About 6 months into the COVID-19 pandemic, I was on a team playing trivia with colleagues, scholars, and doctoral students from the American Educational Research Association (AERA) on Zoom video conferencing. One of the questions that stumped myself and others on my team was: "What is the name of Zeus' father?" The members of my team, including myself, were in the breakout room clueless. At that moment it just happened that my brother was walking in and passed by. I took a chance and asked him that question, which I understand is "cheating." Like the physical inquisitive response described above, a curious look to the ceiling with his hand on his chin he responds, "Kronos" and walks away. I was quick to tell my team and since no one had any clue as to Zeus' father's name, we submitted that answer and we gained a point that round.

My brother may not have some of the skills determined by society to be normal or "typical," however, he does have brilliance. He has certain gifts and talents that I, a "typical" person that is not categorized as deficit in ability according society, does not.

Throughout my life, my friends who met my brother treasured him. They, like myself, know him to be quite intelligent with an exquisite sense of humor. I remember telling him this and he doubted me:

"Really?"

"Yes, really. They love you."

"Oh."

And shrugs it off, as if in disbelief. For years, I wondered why those mentions surprised him so. He is and was always memorable and exceptional to me and to many others in his unique ways of being.

## Reflecting on Educational Experiences and Their Impact: This Is Not OK

*Perceived self-efficacy refers to belief in one's agentive capabilities, that one can produce given levels of attainment.*
—Bandura, 1997

Now in his 20s, I decided to approach my brother and ask him about his experiences in school. Upon asking, he demonstrated a hesitance to share. I simply asked, "Would you be willing to share your positive and not so positive experiences when you were in school?" He frowned his face and shook a quick "No" in my direction. I advised him that he did not have to. I also told him that if he wanted to voice an experience, that this is an opportunity for that and an opportunity to inform others. I insisted that with new knowledge others may make different decisions that can benefit diverse learners, like himself, for the future. He accepted.

Probing, I asked, "How were your experiences with your teachers?" He said they were overall good and that they were kind. He further went on to explain that a lot of the issues he had with school were with the aides the teachers had in his classes. He mentioned an incident that had occurred with one of them that had really upset him. When I asked him if he was comfortable enough to explain it to me, he agreed. His lived experience with some of the assistants had been unprofessional, and in my opinion, dehumanizing behavior toward him. He also shared that these assistants could be unkind.

During our conversation, I probed about what he would have done differently to have improved his experience in school. He shared that he wished he were more motivated and "worked harder." He shared the same sentiment about his classmates lacking motivation. Additionally, he mentioned to me that he did what he was told, but realizes now, he feels he did not reach his potential when he was in school. I probed with more questions wanting to understand further as to why he felt that his experience would be better if *he* were more motivated and if he worked harder. Among those inquiries included questions around challenges in class, teacher empowering students, and classroom climate and culture. During this conversation, it dawned on me that he had included himself and his classmates as those to blame for this lack of motivation. What circumstances occurred throughout his schooling experience to provoke this thinking? According to Hammond (2015), the root of the problem is not that student's lack motivation, but rather their sense of self-doubt leads to a negative academic mindset which is what generates lack of motivation. Further, Hammond (2015) states that leading student's to motivation and engagement is reliant on what responsive educators "believe about belonging, effort, and the value of the task" (p. 129).

Overall, my little brother told me he enjoyed school. He also shared that one of his teachers had told him he is the smartest one in the class. Shortly after he mentioned this, I asked:

"Do you feel like you were challenged?"
"No."

"Were you challenged to do more because you possess the potential to?"
"No."

"Did anyone ever empower and let you know that you can do challenging things?"
"I don't think so."

To me, this is representative of several points, those being; problematic societal constructs, lack of teacher training, and lack of support for teachers in special education settings. I asked if anyone had ever told him that his future is bright and that he has a lot to offer to the world in his classes, he also said, "No." Within this conversation I found myself explaining to him that the motivation he and his classmates lacked was not their nor his fault. I explained to him that this is a lot to expect from a child seeking guidance at school.

Wiest et al. (2001) indicates that one of the most influential factors on students' academic intrinsic motivation is teacher competence. Teachers who are able to monitor progress, develop structured lessons with optimal challenge, and adapt instruction with purposes to increase engagement, are strategies that help students develop mastery at academic endeavors (Brophy, 2004). Further, when teachers provide opportunities for choice making, rather than control, students are granted the prospect of becoming independent learners (Deci et al., 1981). By allowing students to assume some element of control over the learning process "builds stronger intrinsic motivation and can make it more likely learners will want to go beyond requirements" (Posey, 2019, p. 137). As a learner myself, I emulated this when I first studied music as I excelled. My experience in music gave me access to humanizing the learning process, along with assuming control over this process. Further, this experience has shaped my approach when interacting with students. It is true that we shape each other as human beings.

Students with disabilities experience additional educational challenges than students without disabilities, however, they *can be* successful with certain strategic supports in place, and this includes high expectations (Cawthon et al., 2015). Teachers along with their aides can be empowering students like my brother, motivating and challenging them despite being in a special education class. If this were the case, would the feelings my brother has about himself not being motivated or working hard enough be different? Probably well-meaning, the cultural dynamic around special education and students with special needs unintentionally deprives students of their potential early on. My brother drew the fault within himself, rather than with the culture and the systems that are currently in place, the "status quo." These types of attitudes and beliefs are embedded and should be reconsidered, dismantled, and reconstructed, and educational systems should support their educators and leaders in doing that work. Vaz et al. (2015) recommend an acquisition of pedagogical knowledge related to students with disabilities in order to positively influence educator attitudes to be more inclusive. Furthermore, Vaz et al. (2015) found that low self-efficacy in teaching skills was associated with negative attitudes which further acknowledges the importance of supporting teachers and their teacher knowledge. The practice of fostering students with a positive sense of self and ability are compromised when students are not presented with any opportunities to develop those skills. Educators are presented with a gift, and that is to influence, facilitate, and foster these skills that are crucial to thrive in education. Truthfully, these skills apply to other life's circumstances and situations, including the resilience to rise from setbacks. According to Fast et al. (2010), people with higher self-efficacy have higher levels of desires and obligations, along with possessing the capacity to restore themselves after facing failure than those with lower dimensions of self-efficacy.

## DISCUSSION

When I was in middle school, I began to learn how to play the flute and joined band class. In sixth grade I struggled and in seventh I was advised if I wanted to continue in band, I had to purchase a better working instrument and I had to start taking private lessons. The majority of my classmates took lessons regularly and soon enough, I began to as well. I mention this because after I replaced my pawn shop flute with a music industry known brand and began taking private flute lessons, I began to thrive. From being last chair, with guidance (i.e., lessons) and proper equipment (i.e., nicer flutes), I moved up and began to place into district honor groups and would become principal flute for years to come in high school, community college, and during my master's degree at the university level. I also mention this because it was expensive for my family to support my musical endeavors. My father and my aunt would play a central role in helping me acquire nicer instruments so that I could thrive in my musical education. It was expensive and there were months where I could not take lessons because of funds lacking. Struggling to fit in when I was in school, learning English, succeeding academically—my involvement in music changed my life. That said, I always wondered if my little brother's sense of self would have changed if he received tutoring, or additional support outside of class, or if he participated in quality programs outside of public school, outside of "the system." Would he be more intrinsically motivated to go to college and get a professional degree?

The intersectionality of identities throughout a person's life can augment the interrelatedness and exchange of underlying barriers as it relates to a student's sense of self. Cortiella and Horowitz (2014) indicate that the number of students with disabilities of lower socioeconomic status are higher than in affluent homes. While there may be an overrepresentation of working class and racialized students, what I have found to make a fundamental difference are the quality of services and the support structures that need to be in place. Latina mothers, in research by Shapiro et al. (2004), reported feeling disappointment with the services within the educational system due to poor communication, lack of information, and the existing negative attitudes. Mortier and Arias (2020) further acknowledge that these conditions exist among other minorities as well. As it relates to intersectionality, students possess multiple identities and many of the obstacles they confront are a result of a lack of understanding of how intersectionality influences these experiences (Crenshaw, 2013). For me and my other sibling, being Latinx and learning Spanish was an important part of our home experience. As adults, we are now bilingual and see it as an asset in all we do. But I wonder: Could the rich Spanish that was spoken in our home have been embraced in my youngest brother's early schooling experiences? Could the special education services that my brother received have taken advantage of the rich Spanish language resources that were available to him at home, with support from his family? Just as my other brother and I learned Spanish at home, the youngest could have been given support in school to nurture the use of the Spanish language words and phrases. As I observe my little brother now, as an adult, learning Spanish phrases, it makes me happy; It would have made me and my family happy back then, if he would have been encouraged to learn Spanish language and phrases. For him, however, my mother was happy that he could learn one language and could talk at all. He did not start speaking until he was 3 or 4 years old, as a result there was less interest in learning any other language than English.

Education for students with disabilities is at a crossroads. It is recognized as such and needs to be recognized by those who are privileged and by those who are doubtful, perhaps lack awareness, of this current juncture. Further, there is a need to raise awareness among educators to the intersection of identities and experiences that students have and provide them with flexible and adaptable interactions within academic environments (Stack-Cutler et al., 2015). When learning, the barriers that emerge are within the environment, the interactions, and the curriculum, *not* within the student.

Whether it is general education or special education, when a student is not offered the opportunity to reach their potential and, therefore, are socialized with a sense of "I can't" or "I am unworthy," the educators and the system of education in their lives have failed them. This is not fair to students. All students deserve to have dreams and be inspired and empowered to find the pathways to reach them. The fault and the accountability for such failure to the future lies within educational systems, their leaders, and educators with outdated beliefs of the fault being that of the learner rather than the deficit-minded perspectives that have long existed and damaged the potential that their learners deserve from their education. Pernicious practices need to be replaced with affirming, humanizing practices that honor the spectrum of diversity that exists; is assets-based; provides opportunities for self-agency by providing flexibility and options in practice; creates community, safety, and trust; seeks ongoing professional learning; is growth-mindset oriented; and utilizes evidence-based best practices to reach all learners and the challenge is how to get there. Seeing people and their ability, like my brother, is an important step in this direction. While the research spells out what needs to take place as we develop holistic support structures for students like my brother, I recognize the challenges, often enduring, that prevent schools to better serve such children in humanizing ways.

It is noteworthy to acknowledge the lack of participation my youngest brother had with his own IEPs. As reported earlier by McGahee et al. (2001), self-advocacy skills should be started as early as possible and strategies for this can be by involving the child with a disability in their own IEP process. Regardless of a child's cognitive abilities, a child should be provided meaningful opportunities to be able to foster the development of voicing goals and learning preferences. By offering options to children with disabilities in their educational goals, whether through an IEP or not, they are granted choice, autonomy, and a chance of developing self-advocacy and self-determination. Students with disabilities may have self-awareness of their needs, however, as stated by Van-Belle et al. (2006), students with disabilities should be afforded opportunities to learn how to communicate what their needs are and to what rights and supports they are entitled to. Lastly, it has been proven again and again that education has not been responsive to the needs and dreams of students with disabilities. Sometimes individuals are the problem and in some cases it's individuals like administrators and teachers, in other cases, the system is not designed to deal with the challenges and issues that my brother's experiences raised. In my view... the research, empowerment, and advocacy for these learners must continue. In the words of Socrates: "Education is the kindling of a flame, not the filling of a vessel."

## CONCLUSION

By learning about my youngest brother's experiences and observing them as his older sister, I always found myself feeling uneasy. The culprit to this apprehension was "the system." The system, in which my parents, brothers, and I entrusted, failed my youngest brother. The youngest was the first child with a disability my parents had and they trusted that the system would take care of our family. The "system," as I refer to it in this context, is the hidden curriculum, the policy, the teachers, the counselors, the regional center, the schools, the doctors, the service coordinators, and so forth. If this system saw the potential my brother possessed along with his value to society, he would not be here today with this unmotivated attitude of: "I am not enough." My stance on this is that the system has been and continues to be influenced by outdated and pernicious practices and as a result issues emerge, such as people like him being excluded from opportunities to be empowered and grow in order to be able and ready to embark challenges. This is a flaw within beliefs and how those beliefs infiltrate the system and how they impair the bright futures they may have envisioned. Chavez and Longerbeam (2016) state that beliefs influence everyday behaviors and are often unconscious until they are encountered with a different underlying worldview. They further note the importance to be reflective of our own personal worldviews and understand where these beliefs and behaviors originated from (Chavez & Longerbeam, 2016). Reimagining so much can be uncomfortable, however, society and educational systems have a responsibility to reconstruct and rebuild such beliefs and practices to fulfill their purpose of serving students, which include diverse populations such as students with developmental disabilities.

A step toward changing beliefs and practices is by adopting a critical race lens. Visibility exists among inclusion and the removal of discrimination across identities such that of race and social class, yet disability continues to lack that visibility (Baynton, 2001; Liasidou, 2014). The lack of visibility can be attributed to a variety of circumstances in education, one reason being the type, or lack of preparation for educators and leaders in education. Annamma and Morrison (2018) assert that racism and intersections with other oppressions as contributing factors to dysfunctional education ecologies that can be addressed by drawing from a DisCrit approach to identify and disrupt ineffective systems. Notably, attitudes and responses that are deficit-based and negative toward students with disabilities creates anxiety and fear, inevitably impeding any kind of learning. Negative emotions, like feelings of "not enough" or "unworthy," "can taint perception, motivation, and subsequent learning" (Posey, 2019, p. 77). Under such circumstances, students will not learn effectively and connect with others if they are perceiving social or environmental environments, curriculum, and materials as "disabling" or "threatening" (Cohen et al., 2006; Hammond, 2015; Meyer et al., 2014). By being self-aware, drawing from the lens of DisCrit to examine current practices, and utilizing intentional and proactive pedagogical strategies to reach all learners, educational institutions can begin to remove the barriers that exist for students with disabilities.

Proactive and intentional strategies that can empower learners can be frameworks such as FoK, counternarratives, and universal design for learning (UDL). With FoK, rather than assume deficits, practitioners and leaders prioritize and leverage the presence of knowledge, skills, and strategies among students they developed in settings outside of school (Rodriguez, 2013). Further, educators have the opportunity to engage as co-creators of knowledge with their students when they increase awareness of the challenges students and families face outside of school and establish meaningful relationships where knowledge creation and exchange can be vitalized over time (González et al., 2011). Scholar hooks (1994) describes this further: "Any classroom that employs a holistic model of learning will also be a place where teachers grow, and are empowered by the process. That empowerment cannot happen if we refuse to be vulnerable while encouraging students to take risks" (p. 21). With counternarratives, a given reality that is inconsistent with what is considered the status quo or pervasive otherwise can be captured and utilized to inform research, theory, and practice (Ladson-Billings, 1998). Counternarratives provide rich opportunities to "reinterpret, disrupt, or interrupt pervasive discourses" that depict certain communities and identities as "deficit" (Milner & Howard, 2013, p. 542). Lastly, the UDL framework is evidence-based, informed by neurosciences, and upholds the notion that barriers exist within the environment and curriculum, not within the learner (Meyer et al., 2014). By utilizing UDL, practitioners are proactively and intentionally designing learning environments that anticipate learner variability with the goal of fostering expert learners that can guide their own learning (Nelson, 2014).

The narrative of being an older sibling to a younger brother with a developmental disability focused on our story and concludes with impacts of educational experiences on long term goals and sense of self. This is not meant to describe everyone's story, the restorying in this piece comes through my perspective. In our lives, none of us are afforded the choice to choose the circumstances we are born into. Whether students have disabilities, are in special education, have IEPs or 504 plans, all students deserve opportunities to be challenged, uplifted, empowered, and believed in. From our experiences it is clear that the impact of the negative and deficit-minded perspectives of people who have been historically oppressed, further disadvantages and disenfranchises its stakeholders due to negligence and dehumanizing attitudes and actions.

Education is a complex system and like other complex systems, natural and social, it's functions and obligations adapt to the needs of its dwellers, in this case it's learners. Forests need natural disturbance agents such as fires, pathogens, and insects to establish ecological balance, undoubtedly as do the rigid traditions of education and teacher preparation. Like natural disturbances, the current educational systems in place need reevaluation and reform to better serve the cognitive diversity that exists and the diversity that continues to evolve and grow among its educational ecosystem. Arguably, the intersectionality of identities that amplify diversity, which should be honored and valued, are the "disturbance agents" among education. They are prompting the educational system through their existence that it is time to change. Change is necessary and will always be necessary. As uncomfortable as change can be, it can also be transformational. Change can manifest by exercising flexibility; providing options; empowering learners, educators, and staff; all while, like nature, by trusting the process.

## REFERENCES

Anderson, C., Law, J. K., Daniels, A., Rice, C., Mandell, D. S., Hagopian, L., & Law, P. A. (2012). Occurrence and family impact of elopement in children with autism spectrum disorders. *Pediatrics, 130*(5), 870–877. https://doi.org/10.1542/peds.2012-0762

Annamma, S., Connor, D., & Ferri, B. (2013). Dis/ability critical race studies (Dis-Crit): Theorizing at the intersections of race and dis/ability. *Race Ethnicity and Education, 16*(1), 1–31. https://doi.org/10.1080/13613324.2012.730511

Annamma, S., & Morrison, D. (2018). DisCrit classroom ecology: Using praxis to dismantle dysfunctional education ecologies. *Teaching and Teacher Education, 73*, 70–80. https://doi.org/10.1016/j.tate.2018.03.008

Bandura, A. (1986). Social foundations of thought and action: A social cognitive theory. In D. F. Marks (Ed.), *The Health Psychology Reader* (pp. 94–106). SAGE Publications. http://dx.doi.org/10.4135/9781446221129.n6

Bandura, A. (1997). *Self-efficacy: The exercise of control*. W. H. Freeman and Company.

Baynton, D. (2001). Disability and the justification of inequality in American history. In P. K. Longmore & L. Umansky (Eds.), *The new disability history: American perspectives* (pp. 17–33). New York University Press.

Bradshaw, D. G. (2020). *Proactive design and inclusive practices: Universal design for learning in higher education* (Publication No. 13899) [Doctoral dissertation, California State University, Los Angeles]. ProQuest.

Brophy, J. (2004). *Motivating students to learn* (2nd ed.). Routledge. https://doi.org/10.4324/9781410610218

Burbidge, J., & Minnes, P. (2014). Relationship quality in adult siblings with and without developmental disabilities. *Family Relations, 63*(1), 148–162. https://doi.org/10.1111/fare.12047

Camhi, C. (2005). Siblings of premature babies: Thinking about their experience. *Infant Observation, 8*(3), 209–233. https://doi.org/10.1080/13698030500375776

Cawthon, S. W., Garberoglio, C. L., Caemmerer, J. M., Bond, M., & Wendel, E. (2015). Effect of parent involvement and parent expectations on postsecondary outcomes for individuals who are d/Deaf or hard of hearing. *Exceptionality, 23*(2), 73–99. https://doi.org/10.1080/09362835.2013.865537

Chavez, A., & Longerbeam, S. (2016). *Teaching across cultural strengths: A guide to balancing integrated and individuated cultural frameworks in college teaching*. Stylus Publishing.

Cicirelli, V. G. (1995). *Sibling relationships across the life span*. Plenum Press.

Clandinin, D. J., & Connelly, F. M. (2000). *Narrative inquiry: Experience and story in qualitative research*. Jossey-Bass.

Cohen, G., Garcia, J., Apfel, N., & Master, A. (2006). Reducing the racial achievement gap: A social-psychological intervention. *Science, 313*(5791), 1307–1310. https://doi.org/10.1126/science.1128317

Cortiella, C., & Horowitz, S. H. (2014). *The state of learning disabilities: Facts, trends, and emerging issues* (3rd ed.). National Center for Learning Disabilities. https://www.ncld.org/wp-content/uploads/2014/11/2014-State-of-LD.pdf

Crenshaw, K. (2013). *On intersectionality: Essential writings*. New Press.

Creswell, J. W., & Poth, C. (2018). *Qualitative inquiry & research design: Choosing among five approaches* (4th ed.). SAGE Publications.

Deci, E. L. (1975). *Intrinsic motivation*. Plenum Press.

Deci, E. L., Schwartz, A. J., Sheinman, L., & Ryan, R. M. (1981). An instrument to assess adults' orientations toward control versus autonomy with children: Reflections on intrinsic motivation and perceived competence. *Journal of Educational Psychology, 73*(5), 642–650. https://doi.org/10.1037/0022-0663.73.5.642

Fast, L. A., Lewis, J. L., Bryant, M. J., Bocian, K. A., Cardullo, R. A., Rettig, M., & Hammond, K. A. (2010). Does math self-efficacy mediate the effect of the perceived classroom environment on standardized math test performance? *Journal of Educational Psychology, 102*(3), 729–740. https://doi.org/10.1037/a0018863

Fritzgerald, A. (2020). *Antiracism and universal design for learning: Building express-ways to success.* CAST Professional Publishing.

González, N., Wyman, L., & O'Connor, B. (2011). The past, present, and future of "funds of knowledge." In B. Levinson & M. Pollock (Eds.), *A companion to the anthropology of education* (pp. 481–494). Wiley-Blackwell. https://doi.org/10.1002/9781444396713.ch28

Hammond, Z. (2015). *Culturally responsive teaching and the brain: Promoting authentic engagement and rigor among culturally and linguistically diverse students.* Corwin.

Homedco. (1984). *Home infant monitoring: Guidelines for a successful monitoring experience.*

hooks, b. (1994). Teaching to transgress: Education as the practice of freedom. *Journal of Leisure Research, 28*(4), 316. https://doi.org/10.4324/9780203700280

Individuals With Disabilities Education Act (IDEA), Pub. L. No. 101-476, 104 Stat. 1142. (2004). https://www.govinfo.gov/content/pkg/PPP-2004-book1/pdf/PPP-2004-book1-doc-pg869.pdf

Kao, B., Romero-Bosch, L., Plante, W., & Lobato, D. (2012). The experiences of Latino siblings of children with developmental disabilities. *Child-Care, Health and Development, 38*(4), 545–552. https://doi.org/10.1111/j.1365-2214.2011.01266.x

Kiely, B., Migdal, T. R., Vettam, S., & Adesman, A. (2016). Prevalence and correlates of elopement in a nationally representative sample of children with develop-mental disabilities in the United States. *PLoS ONE, 11*(2), e0148337. https://doi.org/10.1371/journal.pone.0148337

Ladson-Billings, G. (1998). Just what is critical race theory and what's it doing in a nice field like education? *International Journal of Qualitative Studies in Educa-tion, 11*(1), 7–24. https://doi.org/10.1080/095183998236863

Lawn, J. E., Davidge, R., Paul, V. K., Xylander, S., Johnson, J. G., Costello, A., Kin-ney, M. V., Segre, J., & Molyneux, L. (2013). Born too soon: Care for the preterm baby. *Reproductive Health, 10*(S1), S5–S5. https://doi.org/10.1186/1742-4755-10-s1-s5

Liasidou, A. (2014). Critical disability studies and socially just change in higher education. *British Journal of Special Education, 41*(2), 120–135. https://doi.org/10.1111/1467-8578.12063

McGahee, M., Mason, C., Wallace, T., & Jones, B. (2001). *Student-led IEPs: A guide for student involvement.* Council for Exceptional Children.

Meyer, A., Rose, D. H., & Gordon, D. (2014). *Universal design for learning: Theory and practice.* CAST Professional Publishing.

Milner, H. R., & Howard, T. C. (2013). Counter-narrative as method: Race, policy and research for teacher education. *Race, Ethnicity, and Education, 16*(4), 536–561. https://doi.org/10.1080/13613324.2013.817772

Moll, L. C., Amanti, C., Neff, D., & Gonzalez, N. (1992). Funds of knowledge for teaching: Using a qualitative approach to connect homes and classrooms. *Theory Into Practice, 31*(2), 132–141. https://doi.org/10.1080/00405849209543534

Mortier, K., & Arias, E. (2020). "The Latino community is not accustomed to arguing for the rights of their children": How Latina mothers navigate special education. *Journal of Latinos and Education.* https://doi.org/10.1080/15348431.2020.1804912

Moyson, T., & Roeyers, H. (2012). 'The overall quality of my life as a sibling is all right, but of course, it could always be better.' Quality of life of siblings of children with intellectual disability: The siblings' perspectives. *Journal of Intellectual Disability Research, 56*(1), 87–101. https://doi.org/10.1111/j.1365-2788.2011.01393.x

Nelson, L. L. (2014). *Design and deliver planning and teaching using universal design for learning.* Paul H. Brookes Publishing.

Ong, K. K., Kennedy, K., Castañeda-Gutiérrez, E., Forsyth, S., Godfrey, K. M., Koletzko, B., Latulippe, M. E., Ozanne, S. E., Rueda, R., Schoemaker, M. H., Beek, E. M., Buuren, S., & Fewtrell, M. (2015). Postnatal growth in preterm infants and later health outcomes: A systematic review. *Acta Pædiatrica, 104*(10), 974–986. https://doi.org/10.1111/apa.13128

Peña, E. V., Stapleton, L. D., & Schaffer, L. M. (2016). Critical perspectives on disability identity. *New Directions for Student Services, 2016*(154), 85–96. https://doi.org/10.1002/ss.20177

Petalas, M. A., Hastings, R. P., Nash, S., Reilly, D., & Dowey, A. (2012). The perceptions and experiences of adolescent siblings who have a brother with autism spectrum disorder. *Journal of Intellectual and Developmental Disability, 37*(4), 303–314. https://doi.org/10.3109/13668250.2012.734603

Posey, A. (2019). *Engage the brain: How to design for learning that taps into the power of emotion.* ASCD.

Rodriguez, G. M. (2013). Power and agency in education: Exploring the pedagogical dimensions of funds of knowledge. *Review of Research in Education, 37*(1), 87–120. https://doi.org/10.3102/0091732x12462686

Shapiro, J., Monzó, L., Rueda, R., Gomez, J., Blacher, J., & Taylor, S. J. (2004). Alienated advocacy: Perspectives of Latina mothers of young adults with developmental disabilities on service systems. *Mental Retardation, 42*(1), 37–54. https://doi.org/10.1352/0047-6765(2004)42<37:AAPOLM>2.0.CO;2

Soll, R., & Blanco, F. (2001). Natural surfactant extract versus synthetic surfactant for neonatal respiratory distress syndrome. *Cochrane Database of Systematic Reviews, 2.* https://doi.org/10.1002/14651858.cd000144

Stack-Cutler, H. L., Parrila, R. K., & Torppa, M. (2015). Using a multidimensional measure of resilience to explain life satisfaction and academic achievement of adults with reading difficulties. *Journal of Learning Disabilities, 48*, 646–657.

Van-Belle, J., Marks, S., Martin, R., & Chun, M. (2006). Voicing one's dreams: High school students with developmental disabilities learn about self-advocacy. *Teaching Exceptional Children, 38*(4), 40–46.

Vaz, S., Wilson, N., Falkmer, M., Sim, A., Scott, M., Cordier, R., & Falkmer, T. (2015). Factors associated with primary school teachers' attitudes towards the inclusion of students with disabilities. *PloS One, 10*(8). https://doi.org/10.1371/journal.pone.0137002

Walther, F. J., Benders, M. J., & Leighton, J. O. (1992). Persistent pulmonary hypertension in premature neonates with severe respiratory distress syndrome. *Pediatrics, 90*(6), 899-904.

Wehmeyer, M. L., Palmer, S. B., Agran, M., Mithaug, D. E., & Martin, J. E. (2000). Promoting Causal Agency: The Self-Determined Learning Model of Instruction. *Exceptional Children, 66*(4), 439–453. https://doi.org/10.1177/001440290006600401

Wiest, D. J., Wong, E. H., Cervantes, J. M., Craik, L., & Kreil, D. A. (2001). Intrinsic motivation among regular, special, and alternative education high school students. *Adolescence, 36*(4), 111–126.

Zeedyk, S. M, Rodriguez, G, Tipton, L. A, Baker, B. L, & Blacher, J. (2014). Bullying of youth with autism spectrum disorder, intellectual disability, or typical development: Victim and parent perspectives. *Research in Autism Spectrum Disorders, 8*(9), 1173–1183. https://doi.org/10.1016/j.rasd.2014.06.001

CHAPTER 11

# MULTITIERED PEDAGOGIES OF PATHOLOGIZATION

## Disability, Race, and Positive Behavioral Intervention and Supports in a Diverse Elementary School

**Irene H. Yoon**
*The University of Utah*

It is taken for granted that order and safety are basic conditions for schooling to proceed, though what constitutes "orderly" and "safe" may vary. Law and order have been interests of the neoliberal state for decades, and this agenda has expanded increasingly into schools (Annamma, 2017; Richie, 2012; Selman, 2017; Sussman, 2012). The Gun-Free Schools Act (1994) and the Safe and Drug-Free Schools and Communities Act (1994), passed as amendments to reauthorizations of the Elementary and Secondary Education Act, are widely discussed as launching an era of militarized policing in schools (Kalvesmaki, 2019; Sussman, 2012). This policy landscape and the close relationship between schools and prisons are often called the school-to-prison pipeline, or the "school–prison nexus" (Annamma, 2017;

*Who Decides?*, pages 247–281

Meiners, 2007).[1] School-based discipline has become a focal point in research on the school–prison nexus because exclusionary discipline is highly correlated with pushing youth of color out from schools and communities into state care and juvenile prisons (Irby, 2017; Lustick, 2017; M. W. Morris, 2016; Vaught, 2017).

Inseparable from the school–prison nexus and school-based discipline are their overwhelmingly disproportionate effects on youth of color and disabled youth. Disabled Black, Indigenous, and students of color (BISOC)[2] are overrepresented in punitive, exclusionary discipline decisions (Skiba, Horner, et al., 2011; Skiba, Michael, et al., 2002; Tobin et al., 2012), special education systems (Annamma, 2017; Annamma et al., 2013; Coutinho et al., 2002; Harris-Murri et al., 2006), substantially segregated special education placements (Coutinho & Oswald, 1996; Hart et al., 2010), juvenile justice systems (Adams & Meiners, 2014; Annamma, 2017; Meiners, 2007), and school pushout (M. W. Morris, 2016; Oswald & Coutinho, 1996). These disparities suggest that order and safety are not neutral but racialized and ableized, with narrow definitions of normal and safe behavior that are not intended to protect all students (Hart et al., 2010; E. W. Morris, 2005; M. W. Morris, 2016; Sussman, 2012).

In response, research has examined processes and policies that contribute to youth incarceration and the school–prison nexus because, though these policies and processes are race-neutral in language, they have clearly racist and ableist outcomes. Many studies have alluded to the importance of direct observations of behavior management and discipline practice in schools and classrooms because behavior management and discipline are cumulative and multidimensional processes that involve multiple levels of culture and power: schoolwide norms, interpersonal relationships, and community historical contexts, to name a few (Bal, 2015; Bal et al., 2012; Gillies, 2016; Harris-Murri et al., 2006). These cultural contexts are parts of interactions between people with differing relationships and access to resources, authority, and autonomy.

In this chapter, I utilize ethnographic observation to explore how behavior management in schools is a systemic and cultural set of practices that can pathologize and criminalize disabled BISOC. This suggests that the racist and ableist school–prison nexus begins before office disciplinary referrals (ODRs) and exclusionary discipline and originates in classroom behavior management. Specifically, I examine one school's behavior management through their implementation of positive behavior interventions and supports (PBIS). Across the United States and internationally, it is becoming difficult to find a school that does *not* use school-wide PBIS, which adapts the principles of response to intervention (RTI) from special education systems for behavior management and disciplinary procedures for all students. PBIS is a framework; schools utilize it as part of multitiered systems of support (MTSS) to identify and coordinate interventions, programs, and services for students across district, school, and community-based providers (Sugai & Horner, 2002). The expansion of schoolwide PBIS and MTSS into nearly every school (and into juvenile prisons; e.g., Gagnon et al., 2018; Jolivette et al., 2015) in the United States has been relatively rapid and written into the federal Individuals With Disabilities Education Act of 1997 (https://www.pbis.org).

This diffusion is worth critical attention because school systems—in response to the school–prison nexus—look to PBIS to shift behavior management from punitive control of behavior to equitable, consistent, educative processes (Sugai & Horner, 2002). So far, however, existing research has found that PBIS has not significantly reduced the race-disability disproportionality of exclusionary discipline and ODRs; both the frequency and the severity of disciplinary actions disproportionately target BISOC and students with disability labels (Lewis, 2018; Tobin et al., 2012; Vincent, Sprague et al., 2013; Vincent & Tobin, 2011). I argue in this chapter that carceral logics and pedagogies of pathologization (Annamma, 2017) are active processes in PBIS and stymie attempts at humanizing learning environments for all students (Waitoller & Thorius, 2015).

First, I share the conceptual framework and define carceral logics, pedagogies of pathologization, and their theoretical foundations. Next, I review literature on school behavior systems and PBIS, explaining critiques of the latter research base. Third, I share how I conducted this study and why before diving into ethnographic findings. Finally, I discuss how scholars and practitioners might center BISOC with emotional and behavioral disorder (EBD) labels through reframing fidelity, notions of positive, and love in school systems.

## CONCEPTUAL FRAMEWORK

This chapter is informed by theorization around carceral logics and pedagogies of pathologization. In the neoliberal "law and order" state, carceral logics of control and removal drive assumptions behind pedagogies of pathologization. In this section, I explain these phenomena, explicating their foundations in critiques of neoliberalism, intersectionality, and dis/ability critical race theory (DisCrit).

### Carceral Logics

*Carceral logics* are "the commonsense notion that the objective of society is to maintain safety and order through unquestioned social control"

(Annamma, 2017, p. 5). Hence, funding for mental illness, disability, poverty reduction, and violence reduction and prevention is funneled to prisons to contain individuals; laws and support services treat structural causes of these social problems as individual choices and pathologies, releasing the state from responsibility for them (Brent, 2019; Meiners, 2007; M. W. Morris, 2016; Richie, 2012; Selman, 2017). That is, criminalization and incarceration remove, rather than resolve, social problems related to oppression and injustice; they define who belongs in society and is deserving of the protections and dignities of membership (Richie, 2012).

Belonging matters because the neoliberal state emphasizes resource scarcity and competition by contracting state services out to the private sector and public–private partnerships (Selman, 2017; Waitoller & Thorius, 2015). Because of scarcity, economic growth is an unquestioned good through which elite wealth increases without labor, while young people's consumption is criminalized (Brent, 2019). From this perspective, schools and human services agencies monitor criminality and deviance to grow prison populations (Adams & Meiners, 2014; Annamma, 2017; Brent, 2019; Krueger, 2010; Ramey, 2015; Selman, 2017). Thus, carceral logics are essential for neoliberal state power partly because prisons are a growth industry under the guise of inevitable and natural responses to criminal and pathological deviance. People who break the law can easily be painted with broad strokes as deserving removal from society (Richie, 2012; Vaught, 2017).

## Carceral Logics in Schools

Neoliberal carceral logics also operate in schools, which are state-building projects that are ableist, racist, and misogynistic (Annamma, 2017; Meiners, 2007; Richie, 2012; Selman, 2017). Hence, behavioral management and discipline in schools—like in prisons and human services agencies—play a role in preparing disabled BISOC for surveillance, poverty, and dispossession through bodily controls such as lockdowns and searches; indignities of personal worth; attending school with behavior monitors and school resource (police) officers; and, ultimately, prison or institutionalization (Adams & Meiners, 2014; Hirschfield, 2008; Irby, 2017; Meiners, 2007; Selman, 2017; Sussman, 2012; Vaught, 2017).

These institutions and practices are about control and creating docile subjects (Bornstein, 2015; Sabnis et al., 2020; Selman, 2017). Neoliberal carcerality is written into school codes of conduct (Selman, 2017), the surveillance of student bodies (Annamma, 2017), and assumptions about motivation and behavior from economics (Franzén & Holmquist, 2014). Though individual schools and educators may defy carcerality, many are caught in the processes of the school–prison nexus despite their efforts (Adams & Meiners, 2014; Annamma, 2017; Annamma & Morrison, 2018).

## Intersectionality

Carceral logics operate differently for different people. Some people are protected by them from harm and responsibility for their actions, while others are hyperpoliced. In the United States, race, gender, disability, and socioeconomic status are primary organizers of who is affected by mass incarceration and carceral logics. *Intersectionality theory* explains how social location can affect how individuals and communities experience carcerality differently. Specifically, intersectionality articulates the ways that Black women are excluded from racial justice and feminist movements, being forced to choose between which aspects of their identities play bigger roles in their lives when their experiences of being Black are shaped by being women, and their experiences as women are shaped by being Black (Combahee River Collective, 1977; Crenshaw, 1991; Richie, 2012). Crenshaw (1991) described this exclusion as a legal problem of multiple marginalization that left Black women vulnerable to violence and exploitation (see also, M. W. Morris, 2016). For example, Richie (2012) and Vaught (2017) described the State's targeted punishment of poor Black mothers, who are publicly vilified as incompetent and neglectful parents whose children must be taken from them and institutionalized for their protection. Such state-sanctioned violence and removal blames individuals without acknowledgement of historical and structural conditions.

## DisCrit

Crenshaw's (1991) original intent to highlight the experiences and exclusion of whole groups of people from justice movements is relevant to understanding the disciplinary experiences of disabled BISOC in schools, who are both disabled and Black, Indigenous, or of color, and never solely one (Annamma, 2017). DisCrit builds on intersectionality theory's argument that experiencing both racism and sexism is unique from either racism or sexism to consider the interdependent co-construction of racism and ableism (Annamma et al., 2013). DisCrit asserts that students of color with dis/ability labels have qualitatively different educational experiences than their white peers with the same labels, and that dis/ability labels are used to rationalize removing students of color from general education settings. Furthermore, students of color with dis/ability labels experience racialization and ableism differently—such as the erasure of Indigenous students from nearly all special education and disability research, or the racial disparities in the assignment of different special education labels (Annamma et al., 2013).

DisCrit also builds on the prior work of conceptualizing how society values whiteness as representing goodness, intelligence, and a normative body; and that legal gains for dis/abled people of color occur through interest convergence with white dis/abled movements (Harris-Murri et al., 2006; Leonardo & Broderick, 2011; Smith, 2004). This is the fifth of seven DisCrit tenets (Annamma et al., 2013). The first tenet of DisCrit interrogates ideas of normal and the processes of normativizing versus pathologizing ability and race in educational settings. The remaining tenets are: (a) valuing multidimensional identities and troubling monolithic portrayals of any one dimension; (b) recognizing the social construction of race and ability, alongside their material and social realities; (c) privileging the knowledges of peoples traditionally unrecognized in or excluded from research; (d) exploring legal and historical contexts of dis/ability and race and how they have been used together to deny the rights of some citizens; and (e) requiring and supporting activism and resistance (Annamma et al., 2013). DisCrit and intersectionality articulate the nuanced ways that BISOC with EBD labels experience school behavior systems that are organized around neoliberal carceral logics.

## Pedagogies of Pathologization

Annamma (2017) calls school-based processes of the school–prison nexus *pedagogies of pathologization*. Pedagogies of pathologization refer to how educators interpret and treat disabled Black girls and girls of color as deviant, criminal, and disordered. These practices are pedagogical because they teach disabled girls of color they are pathological and abnormal, not to be trusted, expected to be violent or dishonest; these influence the girls' identity development and learning. Such criminalizing and pathologization occur through cycles of carceral surveillance, labeling, and punishment that go unquestioned (see also, Bornstein, 2015, 2017a; Brent, 2019; Ramey, 2015). These practices demand compliance and docility, assuming that disabled students of color are always "at risk" of losing control. They include separating and isolating students who are already in juvenile prisons; shaming students in front of their peers; neglecting students' questions and efforts to advocate for their learning; monitoring minute movements and dress; reducing students to labels and diagnoses; and scrutinizing behaviors, gender performance, and movements across spaces (hallways, bathroom, classroom, playground, etc.). Surveillance, labeling, and punishment often overlap and support each other. Importantly, these processes occur through interactions among individuals, organizations, and social structures (Annamma & Morrison, 2018). For incarcerated, disabled girls of color (the focal population in Annamma, 2017), the pedagogies reduce them to files of stereotypes, diagnoses, behavioral infractions, and disciplinary punishments.

Annamma (2017) is not the only study that explores the school–prison nexus and pedagogical processes of dehumanization and containment (see also, Gillies, 2016; Selman, 2017; Vaught, 2017). These studies have contributed to a growing research base that centers students' perspectives on being criminalized and pathologized in the school–prison nexus, though not all consider disability as a dynamic in their behavior or dispossession (Annamma, 2017; Gillies, 2016; Hart et al., 2010; Irby, 2017; M. W. Morris, 2016; Winn, 2010).

In this chapter, I apply frameworks developed in youth correctional settings to a traditional public school. I do this because the school–prison nexus is not unidirectional, from prisons to schools. Prison practices do not only inform school practices around behavior and compliance, in fact, school practices are often mimicked by prison schools (Vaught, 2017). In the school–prison nexus, BISOC, some with disability labels, make sense of carceral pedagogies of pathologization while they are trying to develop senses of self as worthy of privacy, learning, academic engagement, career fulfillment, health and well-being, trust, and aspirations (Annamma, 2017; Irby, 2017; M. W. Morris, 2016; Winn, 2010). While they may internalize some of the identities that educators construct for them, they also resist these lessons, insisting on their uniqueness and inherent value.

## REVIEW OF LITERATURE

In this review of literature, I connect my conceptual framework with educational research on school behavior challenges and PBIS. I pay particular attention to the intersections of race and disability in these phenomena, including critiques of behavior normalization in PBIS that demand more culturally responsive and justice-centered approaches.

### Pathologizing and Normalizing Behavior in School

In U.S. public schools, perceptions of student behavior—as challenging, inappropriate, prosocial, and so forth—tend to be influenced by the race, gender, class, and disability of students and educators, who are predominantly white (Hart et al., 2010; Lustick, 2017; Monroe, 2005). Thus, studies have found racialized, classed, and gendered patterns in excessive attention to controlling and monitoring behaviors of students of color—particularly disabled Black, Indigenous, and Latinx students (Hart et al., 2010; E. W. Morris, 2005; M. W. Morris, 2016). Relatedly, in special education research, EBD referrals and placements have been found to be notoriously malleable by educators' perceptions and can exemplify how racism, poverty, and gender work in collusion with ableist interpretations of behavior and emotion (Aho et al., 2017; Dolmage, 2018; Hart et al., 2010). Finally, behaviors considered to be appropriate and prosocial may be narrowly defined by educators in white, middle-class, cisheteronormative expectations of "boys" and "girls" (e.g., Apple, 2004; Hart et al., 2010; E. W. Morris, 2005; Reay, 2007).

For example, Black boys and Latinx boys are often interpreted as violent, intentionally misbehaving, disrespectful, and out of control, if they are acknowledged as children at all (Dumas & Nelson, 2016; Goff et al., 2014; Irby, 2017). In contrast, Black girls and Latinx girls are often constructed as unladylike—loud, attention-seeking, and prone to fighting (E. W. Morris, 2005; M. W. Morris, 2016). Underlying these harmful interpretations are white supremacist fantasies and ideologies that are built on anti-Black racism and fetishization that is focused on pathologizing BISOC and their families, as well as normativizing white middle-class bodies and lifestyles (Lensmire, 2012; Richie, 2012; Yoon, 2016).[3]

## Turning to Tiered Models of Intervention

With attention to reforming education systems for equity, Response to Intervention (RTI) was first used in education to improve identification of students for specific learning disability categories. It then began being used as an approach to identify and assess students who might benefit from behavioral interventions or special education resources for EBD categories (Harris-Murri et al., 2006; Sugai & Horner, 2009). RTI principles sought to provide opportunities through which all students could learn: proactive, supportive, and non-aversive intervention; data collection over time; respecting the dignity of persons and enhancing their quality of life; and improving instruction as a way to reduce removing and excluding disabled students from general education (Ferguson et al., 2001; Kincaid et al., 2016; National Center for Culturally Responsive Educational Systems [NCCRESt], 2005; Waitoller & Thorius, 2015).

Based on adapted RTI principles, PBIS has sought to improve reliability and consistency of behavior management and prevent behavioral disruptions through behavioral science, rigorous measurement of outcomes, and monitoring school implementation of interventions (https://www.pbis.org). To these ends, PBIS frameworks include three tiers of increasing intensity of intervention support. The first tier addresses teaching and reinforcing "appropriate" behaviors in general education classrooms. The second tier provides more intensive supports to students who do not adequately change behaviors after Tier I instructional practices (i.e., early intervention). These may be provided outside general education classrooms. Tier III interventions include intensive supports and data collection that assess students' behaviors with possibility of referral for special education labels and resources (https://www.pbis.org).

Many school systems across the country have adopted PBIS models—and, when implemented with high fidelity schoolwide, they can yield reductions in exclusionary discipline, reduce ODRs, and improve school climate (https://www.pbis.org). But there are mixed results when examining these outcomes for equity. Even with schoolwide improvements, exclusionary discipline and ODRs continue to disproportionately impact students of color and students with disabilities while improving for white students (Cramer & Bennett, 2015; McIntosh, Gion, et al., 2018; Tobin et al., 2012; Vincent, Sprague, et al., 2013). And while some schools have set equity as the focal point of PBIS models, they may have difficulty addressing racism and ableism head-on, leading to surface-level plans that are no more equitable or accessible than before (e.g., Bornstein, 2017b; McIntosh, Gion, et al., 2018; Vincent, Sprague, et al., 2013). These lingering inequities have been the primary focus of scholars who have shifted attention away from implementation and evaluation of PBIS models and interventions toward equitable and supportive learning experiences and environments for all students, particularly BISOC with disability labels.

## Addressing Limitations in PBIS

Inequities in implementation and outcomes may suggest limitations in PBIS and RTI principles and research paradigms (Finch, 2012; Wilson, 2015). Critiques of PBIS have ranged from those seeking to improve approaches for designing PBIS models to outright rejection of its underlying principles. For instance, some scholars have criticized an overemphasis on research over educational experiences for students. Methodological concerns such as consistency and fidelity distract PBIS research away from behavioral change or improvement from students' perspectives (Wilson, 2015). Furthermore, PBIS increases educators' use of data, but data to monitor behavior and PBIS implementation often comprises disciplinary decisions and ODRs, and does not document students' learning in terms of changes in behavior, social-emotional experiences, coping skills, or self-perceptions in relation to teachers and peers (Vincent, Tobin, et al., 2012; Wilson, 2015). However, calls for observation-based research on PBIS and RTI to understand behaviors in and across cultural contexts and practices for BISOC with EBD labels have been made for years (Harris-Murri et al., 2006; NCCRESt, 2005).

A second theme of critique is that, though PBIS and RTI implementation may reduce the overtly punitive nature of some behavioral management and discipline schoolwide, they are still based on deficit models of thinking about behavior as decontextualized, located in individual students with problems, and needing to be fixed (Sabnis et al., 2020; Waitoller & Thorius, 2015). Moreover, educator-driven expectations for "appropriate" or "prosocial" behaviors are likely to be culturally assimilationist, compliance-driven, and limited in effectiveness unless they are conceived with and by community members and students to be meaningful (Bal et al., 2012; Cramer & Bennett, 2015; Fallon et al., 2012; Harris-Murri et al., 2006; Hart et al., 2010; McIntosh, Moniz, et al., 2014; NCCRESt, 2005).

For 2 decades, scholars have argued that PBIS and RTI must beware of deficit approaches toward students, families, and communities and develop culturally adaptive and inclusive educational systems (Ferguson et al., 2001; Harris-Murri et al., 2006; NCCRESt, 2005; Sabnis et al., 2020). Several recommendations to respond to this problem include: culturally responsive PBIS (CRPBIS) designed for local relevance through participatory community-based processes (Bal, 2015; Bal et al., 2012; Fallon et al., 2012; Harris-Murri et al., 2006; NCCRESt, 2005), more discussion of race and racism in special education and discipline systems and decisions (Bornstein, 2017b; Carter et al., 2017; Lustick, 2017; Monroe, 2005), returns to transformative goals of RTI (Waitoller & Thorius, 2015), and changes in data collection and research to evaluate PBIS practices for justice-oriented outcomes (Bal et al., 2012; Finch, 2012; Wilson, 2015). Most also recommend ongoing professional development and community partnerships around these practices.

A third set of critiques of PBIS addresses underlying assumptions and logics behind the framework, primarily that PBIS still utilizes neoliberal medicalizing and carceral logics (Brent, 2019; Bornstein, 2017a; Ramey, 2015). Medicalizing logics assume that behavioral problems are static, innate, and individual deficits. Thus, in neoliberal scarcity, medical categorization and labeling are required for access to resources and supports (Harris-Murri et al., 2006; Ramey, 2015; Sabnis et al., 2020). Hence, PBIS does not fundamentally challenge educators' beliefs about students and behavior or the racist and ableist impetuses of neoliberal carcerality.

Despite critiques, there remains little discussion of how PBIS supports students with behavioral and social-emotional needs who are not outwardly disruptive in class. These "internalizing" behaviors can be related to structural conditions such as chronic stress and intergenerational trauma, but receive almost no attention in PBIS and RTI research (McIntosh, Ty, et al., 2014, is the only exception to my knowledge). This silence reflects how educators and researchers prioritize minimizing disruptions—that is, control—over educative processes that teach and support students through a spectrum of emotions, neurodiversity, and coping strategies (Wilson, 2015). In practice, neglecting internalizing behaviors also means that students learn that they belong in school as long as they hide their thoughts, feelings, and behaviors. This is a violence of a different nature, another side of carceral logics of belonging and exclusion.

## METHODOLOGY

This chapter draws from ethnographic research at Fields Elementary School, located in an inner-ring suburb of a major U.S. city.[4] Fields served about 650 students in Grades K–5 and, in the last decade, the school had shifted from serving a predominantly white and Protestant, English-speaking, working-class community to one that was highly diverse in language and culture, immigration status, race, and religion; most families were working-class or working poor (74% of students qualified for free or reduced-price lunch). About 40% of students were emergent multilingual. Fields Elementary also practiced special education inclusion with pull-out services, so all classrooms included students with disability labels, including EBD.

### Recruitment and Data Collection

Based on theoretical perspectives that pedagogical interactions will be, to some extent, informed by racism and ableism, and include cultural discontinuities between white women teachers and racially diverse students; I recruited white women teachers at Fields for this study. I explained my interest in if and how it mattered when predominantly white women taught in highly diverse schools, and that I was hoping to follow white women teachers because of their representation in the profession and at Fields Elementary. Three teachers volunteered, but one withdrew because she began family leave during the project period. The remaining two teachers were able to commit to the full study and became the two focal teachers, Theresa and Elizabeth. Both were white women.

Because of my focus on dynamics of race, gender, and disability in interactions and practice, I emphasized observation in data collection. I observed Theresa and Elizabeth in their classrooms and followed them into grade-level team meetings, planning periods, and professional development for 5 months, spending 20 hours per week, equally splitting time between them. (Team members consented to participate in the study when they were present, but I did not observe in their classrooms or interview them.) This approach afforded extended time in classrooms immersed in relationships, organizational practices and logics, and ideologies to contextualize pedagogical interactions.

I interviewed Theresa and Elizabeth formally at the beginning and end of the study, with informal interviews and conversations at every visit. These interviews supplemented observations with teachers' reflections, contextual information, interpretations of student behavior, and rationales for instruction that I could not have observed. I also interviewed the school principal for context about the school; she initiated an extended conversation about PBIS at Fields. I recorded observations with scripted field notes and audio recorded and transcribed individual interviews and small team settings.

## Participants

Theresa and Elizabeth were middle-class white women teachers at different points in their careers. Theresa was a white woman in her 40s who often mentioned her two children. Though she had 15 years of teaching experience, it was her first year teaching second grade and working closely with that team. The second focal teacher, Elizabeth, was a woman in her late 20s, the seventh year of her career. She had taught all 7 years at Fields. In the year of this study, Elizabeth taught a fourth/fifth split (with both fourth and fifth grade students in her class), so she was on both fourth- and fifth-grade teams.

Theresa had an affectionate style of teaching—she often called her class a family and engaged in playful banter with students. Theresa had three students on behavior plans out of 24 students, though she also struggled to give adequate academic and linguistic supports to other students. There was a wide range in academic achievement among her students.

Elizabeth was efficient, focused on academic talk and work, and was kind, but not overly affectionate with her students. I inferred that her students trusted her because they asked vulnerable questions in private and in front of the class, like after a lockdown drill for school shootings. Elizabeth had three students on behavior plans out of 26 students, all with different EBD labels. Elizabeth's class had a narrower spread of academic achievement than her colleagues' classes because she taught students from two grade levels who were at relatively close ranges of reading and mathematics achievement. This was intended to support her meeting two grade levels' standards.

For both Theresa and Elizabeth, all students with behavior plans were Black boys and boys of color, though both teachers closely watched behaviors of some girls of color.

## Analysis and Trustworthiness

I approached analysis iteratively and inductively, given the ethnographic approach of observation and the density of each interaction in my field notes (Emerson et al., 2011). During observations, I was primarily interested in teaching practices, but I also zoomed in and out on the scale of interactions from whole-class to student- and group-level (Annamma & Morrison, 2018; Emerson et al., 2011). Sometimes, such as during student group work, I picked one group of students to observe; other times, I followed the teacher around the room. I reflected on these observations with daily journaling (Emerson et al., 2011). I began to notice more and more of my observation and reflection related to behavior management and that teachers' talk about race and ability was often deracialized during these conversations (see Yoon 2016, 2018). My journals reflected my discomfort with implicit messages that students showed they were learning about themselves and each other, in ways that converged around disability, race, and gender.

After data collection ended, I continued to explore ideas about critiquing whiteness and white womanhood in behavior pedagogies. I approached analysis as cycles of reading and coding data with intermissions of reading theoretical and empirical literature (Charmaz, 2014). I created a log sheet that included major topics of each day's observations to check whether or not behavior talk was as extensive in practice as it seemed in my reflections (Miles et al., 2014). I hand-coded episodes in all field notes with broad topics such as "behavior," "silence," and "socialization," which I considered to be when teachers taught expected and desired behaviors as connected to school, learning, and individual student identities. These topics were embedded in nearly every teacher–student interaction, and behavior was the central topic or issue constantly, sometimes rapidly, throughout each day.

With confidence that behavior was indeed a major issue for participants and for me, I then reviewed data to examine the episodes where racialized, gendered, classed, and disability dynamics were involved in behavior management pedagogies and teacher discussion. I hand-coded these episodes for underlying dynamics of behavior management with inductive sub-codes for the broader topics described above (Miles et al., 2014). For example, I coded episodes that (a) used PBIS scripts, (b) reflected teachers' perceptions of ability and disability in behavior management, (c) adjusted scripts and protocols for students in different ways, and (d) used labels to comment on students' abilities and identities. Then I paused and (re)read research that could help contextualize these categories and sub-codes (Charmaz, 2014). Based on this check against literature, I developed codes including "PBIS scripts," "disciplining [student name]," and "passive aggressive." I also noted when teachers practiced behavior management in ways that were explicitly discouraged in the Fields PBIS framework ("not PBIS").

Next, I tested the connections between PBIS practices and compliance, criminalizing, pathologizing, and excluding. To do this, I grouped the prior inductive code categories into language and ideas from pedagogies of pathologization ("surveillance," "labeling," etc.; Miles et al., 2014). I found multiple access points to understand how PBIS scripts, PBIS framework, and PBIS framework principles accelerated pedagogies of pathologization at Fields Elementary in teacher teams and in focal classrooms. In this way, coding was iterative, with checks for trustworthiness and with increasing conceptual specificity (Miles et al., 2014).

After I completed analysis, I met with Theresa and Elizabeth individually to discuss analyses of their team conversations and classroom practices (see more in Yoon, 2016). They were open and reflective, not defensive. For additional analyses of Elizabeth's classroom interactions, I had more conversations with her about deracializing classroom talk (Yoon, 2018).

## Study Context: The PBIS Model at Fields Elementary

Schoolwide, the Fields PBIS system was based on the five expectations of "be safe, be respectful, be responsible, persevere, and do your best." Fields Elementary educators also developed a three-tier set of increasingly intensive behavioral and disciplinary interventions.

### Tier I

Following PBIS principles of providing consistency and explicit teaching, teachers and leaders at Fields agreed upon a shared set of language for monitoring behavior expectations. These "PBIS scripts" were frequently and consistently observed across classrooms. For example, teachers said, "I really appreciate how..." and then named students and the praiseworthy behavior (e.g., "I really appreciate how Shani and Mariana are showing me with their eyes that they're ready"). Both Theresa and Elizabeth primarily praised students who were being quiet, on task, and attending to the teacher. These behaviors were labeled "respectful" and "responsible," "successful," and "ready to learn."

Fields' PBIS scripts were reinforced by a recommended token system of rewards (OSEP PBIS Center, 2019). "Beary Treats" (slips of paper) were Fields' PBIS tokens, named for the school's bear mascot. Students received Beary Treats when teachers could "catch 'em being good" and spent them in a school "shop" with trinkets and candy. Monthly, Fields held an assembly where students with the most Beary Treats in each class were recognized as "Cool Cubs." Cool Cubs were called to the stage, had their pictures taken, and received certificates and buttons for their backpacks. At the end of the year, students who had been named Cool Cubs every month were celebrated in a "Best Bears" assembly with their families.

Finally, all teachers at Fields also agreed to a common step-by-step protocol of warnings and consequences for most student misbehavior. The final step was an Office Disciplinary Referral (ODR). ODR consequences could include suspension, expulsion, calling in parents for a conference, or other more serious actions.

### Tier II

Second-tier supports at Fields Elementary were not part of general instruction. For instance, Elizabeth had a student who participated in a pull-out "social skills group," which the interventionist explained as "how to be a friend." Some students had individualized behavior plans, with behavior goals and rewards connected to earning points for making their goals. This was a modified version of an additional Tier II intervention called the Bears' Den, in research called Check-In Check-Out (CICO; Vincent, Tobin, et al., 2012). The principal described the Bears' Den as

> a really euphemistic phrase for when you've been naughty. [chuckles]. Every morning these kids check-in with an adult, other than their classroom teacher, and every afternoon they check-out. They have points. They collect points through the day... They just love it. It's amazing—they think they're in some kind of really cool special club. And it actually, really works.

Behavior goals and rewards were personalized, so teachers maintained their own stashes of rewards separate from the school's Beary Treats "store." Some students also earned reward time; they could choose when to spend several minutes reading, playing an academic computer game, or some other pre-approved, nondisruptive activity.

### Tier III

The Fields principal explained: "Now, we still have a few kids that [Tier II] doesn't help and then we have to get out the big guns and start thinking, is this a kid that needs special education referral, is this a kid that maybe we need to completely change their program." Tier III included functional behavioral assessments (FBA; an intense surveillance and labeling process to document and gain insight into triggers and underlying needs of undesirable behavior), labeling with EBD diagnoses, and creating special education individualized educational plans (IEPs). PBIS Tiers II and III, therefore, created special education enrollment at Fields.

## FINDINGS

At Fields Elementary, I found that PBIS legitimized pedagogies of pathologization and exclusion around behavior. I present this idea in two parts: first, in *teacher talk*, which revealed perceptions of students and concerns about classroom dynamics; and second, in *patterns of practice* in classrooms. First, teacher talk revealed pathologized and criminalized students. Second, I describe three classroom patterns of practice that enacted PBIS as surveillance, labeling, and punishment in pedagogies of pathologization: (a) *catching 'em being good*, (b) *a responsibility rhetoric*, and (c) *trading goods and goodness*.

## Conceptualizing PBIS in Teacher Talk

Teachers at Fields Elementary had informal conversations about student behavior and discipline that provided insight into how they used PBIS to control behavior and to express frustrations about student behavior. The topic of student behavior came up in every team meeting in all three grade levels that I observed. One conversation on the fifth-grade team, and my debriefing about it with Elizabeth afterwards, exemplified carcerality in PBIS and the pathologization and criminalization in teachers' beliefs about students:

> It was a Friday morning; every Friday the school had a late start for students, giving teachers 90 minutes for team collaboration. Karen, a reading specialist, complained to the team about keeping her fifth-grade reading group on task. After explaining that four students distracted the others, she paused. "And, um—I don't know—I don't know what to do anymore."
>
> Fred responded first: "Welcome to Fields." He continued, describing that students at the school "lack thinking, lack effort, lack care—and part of it is the economy, their parents don't have jobs." He added that managing student behavior had been difficult "more this year than I've ever had in 11 years."
>
> Donna offered: "If you tell them about something, they won't get it. But if you let them move around..."
>
> Fred interrupted Donna in return: "But I sympathize, and Donna sympathizes." He added another suggestion: "I give them rewards. They're an immature group. Give them a skittle per detail, literally. Or give them a cookie. We're back to the drawing board with this group. Classroom management with this group—let me finish" (Karen had opened her mouth to respond). Fred concluded, "You've set the expectation, now you need to keep the line. You've got to find out what's the consequence that matters to them. It's bribery, are you with me?"

The group conversation continued for several more minutes, with two more teachers, Elizabeth and Bobby, adding examples of teaching around students' inability to focus and other deficits. Fred's first comment, "Welcome to Fields," did not challenge Karen's complaint, but indicated that behavioral challenges were representative of the grade ("this cohort") and school as a whole. Fred advocated responding to students with "bribery," utilizing candy or whatever currency (food) was meaningful to students. While Fred's mention of the economy might have seemed like consideration of structural contexts, he constructed students as manipulative adversaries and teachers as stuck in a power struggle they could not afford to lose.

In an interview, I asked Elizabeth about the conversation. She noted that she had wondered at the time how I perceived it. She explained that Fred and Donna had been frustrated with Karen's struggles because they had had similar conversations with her before—she was a "more traditional" teacher with limited active engagement strategies. Elizabeth added,

> Karen, like I said, a lot of her experience in teaching is with primary students and she has said she is afraid of fifth-graders; they scare her with their behavior and their size. They're big. They smell, they're big...

Elizabeth's first response was that Karen's struggles were individual and de-racialized her colleague's fear of BISOC (the majority of Fields students), only attributing Karen's fear to age, development (odor), and physical stature. But Karen's fear resonated with numerous studies that explicate white women's fear of Black men and boys, who are judged to be older than they are, considered to be animalistic and less innocent than their ages suggest (Goff et al., 2014; Irby, 2014; Lensmire, 2012; Vaught, 2017).

In this example, the fifth-grade team conflated individual situations or students with the entire school and talked about leading students along with candy and cookies, like motivating animals. They were not alone, however. I found similar talk about BISOC with EBD labels in the second-grade team, which several times discussed a Black girl student who "needed to be hog-tied" due to outbursts. Constructing students as out of control pathologized them and suggested that PBIS did not shift teachers' paradigms about BISOC and the taken-for-granted need for control over behavior. The ways that teachers conceptualized PBIS were reductive of students and of PBIS principles, and erased relationships between systemic oppression, chronic stress and historical trauma, and behavior and mental health.

## PBIS as Pedagogies of Pathologization in Classroom Patterns of Practice

Given the wealth of evidence in teacher teams that controlling behavior, race, and disability was a primary concern, similar patterns of control and exclusion arose across teaching styles and teams. Though the teachers used different tones and affect in delivery, both Theresa and Elizabeth used the school's PBIS scripts (e.g., "I really appreciate...") and protocols for warnings (e.g., "This is your warning"). These PBIS scripts were grounded in three functions: (a) interpreting positive support as "*catch 'em being good,*" (b) reproducing a *responsibility rhetoric*, and (c) establishing behavior as

264 • I. H. YOON

currency for *trading in goods and goodness*. Enacted *passive aggressively*, these patterns of practice emphasized silence and bodily discipline and made overlapping use of carceral surveillance, labeling, and punishment in pedagogies of pathologization, criminalizing and pathologizing students within the framework of PBIS.

### Catch 'Em Being Good

The Fields principal and Elizabeth both explained that one goal of PBIS was shifting teachers' mindsets about behavior from assuming that students were likely doing something "wrong." They stated the emphasis behind PBIS was to "catch 'em being good," which reframed but retained surveillance, and implicitly and by repetition came to mean quiet and still.

Both teachers repeatedly said, "I really appreciate how [student] is [some named behavior]" to label and articulate the behaviors they wanted to affirm. Theresa often used the phrases "[Student] is doing a good job," "I love it when students follow directions," or "I love those students who are working quietly." Given the direct recognition of compliant students as deserving Theresa's appreciation and love, the unspoken statement was that the unnamed students' behaviors would not be deserving. This was an implicit punishment of exclusion. To be clear, these scripts were not strictly in accordance with PBIS, which would ask for more specific feedback. Elizabeth, in her classroom, alternated "appreciating" with "I'm really impressed with...," as in, "I'm super impressed with the way Table 4 is waiting and not feeling the need to make noise... That's really responsible."

Though positive in content, this label emphasized compliance and silence as the primary ways to be "good" and "responsible." The "catching 'em" scripts were passive aggressive in delivery, implicit corrections that pointed out that some unnamed students were being "bad" or "not being responsible." (This also left students to discern if they were the ones being corrected.) The school-wide practice was directly taken from neoliberal logics of individual choice and responsibility as the arbiter of opportunity and reward. The running narration (surveillance) of what students were doing that was praiseworthy ("I appreciate how...") rationalized value in the token economy of Beary Treats. This token economy affirmed persons based on their productivity in behavioral compliance.

Furthermore, catching students "being good" did not stop teachers from catching students' not being good and subsequent punishments. It simply reformulated it. This practice maintained surveillance ("catching 'em") but made it somewhat nicer (cf. Sugai and Horner's [2002] "active supervision" concept). This principle and its accompanying PBIS scripts did not, therefore, change the perception of students who were labeled "behavior problems." It was built around the assumption that they would not be "caught being good."

## Responsibility Rhetoric

As noted above, the primary force behind PBIS scripts that affirmed "being good" was a neoliberal responsibility rhetoric about choice that positioned students as agents and their behaviors as representing intent. Responsibility rhetoric was a pillar in the school's expectations of being safe, respectful, responsible, persevering, and doing your best—all grounded in individualistic choice. Responsibility rhetoric justified the need for carceral control of irresponsible individuals through PBIS protocols of disciplinary consequences.

Elizabeth had developed efficient scripts for student discipline that framed choices—that is, actions—as having consequences. If students did not comply with her instructions—or if they chose to do something that was not her instructions—Elizabeth had students choose a "consequence" for their actions. By replacing the word "consequence" for "punishment," students had to be compliant with choosing something that would be experienced as a punishment while being told it was their choice and a result of their being out of compliance (a circular logic). Cascades of seeming choices, therefore, led back to the intended lesson that compliance was responsible, respectful, and doing their best. This logic released Elizabeth from responsibility for punishment and put the onus on students to change their behaviors without changing the contexts of those behaviors. It also positioned students to take responsibility for making choices that were decisions between multiple poor options that all resulted in punishment and exclusion from opportunities, functioning similarly to carceral logics of dispossession.

The trickiness of these responsibility rhetorics was evident in Elizabeth's disciplinary interactions with one of her students, Frank. One day, Frank was reading his own book instead of completing reading "centers" worksheets. The resulting interaction, below, lasted more than 20 minutes and was not a clear exchange of one action for a consequence. It followed a pattern of silent resistance that occurred with two of Elizabeth's students of color with EBD labels, Frank and Jason, nearly every time I was in the classroom:

Elizabeth was finishing a small group reading lesson when she called to Frank: "Frank, come sit by me, please." He complied, and she dismissed the reading group and began to talk with Frank quietly and without eye contact, looking at her notebook. I had been sitting a table away and walked over to join them as Elizabeth noted, "...and that includes centers work. Can you tell me why you're choosing not to do your centers work?" I scripted the rest of the conversation:

FRANK: I just want to read.
ELIZABETH: (dryly, impatient, but with moderated low tone) I know. I do too. I would love to just sit and read. But you know what, I

can't do that right now. I have other things I need to do first. What center work are you choosing to do?
(Frank is silent.)

**ELIZABETH:** Would you like some suggestions?
(Frank is silent.)

**ELIZABETH:** (the same low tone has a false brightness) OK, your silence is telling me that you don't need suggestions, you know what center you're going to do. So what center are you going to choose to do now?
(Frank is silent.)

**ELIZABETH:** (moves materials at the table) OK, now your silence tells me you are choosing not to go to recess. Recess and the classroom are places for people who choose to do their work. Recess is a privilege for those who have participated in the classroom. What center are you going to choose to work on?
(Frank is silent.)

**ELIZABETH:** (same low tone, less energy) OK, now your silence tells me you're choosing not to participate in the classroom. And that makes me sad. You'll stay in for recess today to work on your centers since you chose to take recess now.
(Frank silently goes back to his desk and continues reading his book.)

**ELIZABETH:** (calling out to the class) If you have a fluency packet and you haven't done your cold read yet, please bring it to the front table.
(Students come up to the table, pair up, and read to each other. They know the procedure. Elizabeth monitors them and then walks over to Frank, who is about 10 feet away.)

**ELIZABETH:** (to Frank) Do you have a center to work on or do you want me to bring you one?
(Frank is silent.)

**ELIZABETH:** Do you have a vocabulary worksheet, do you want to start with that? That is what you said you were going to work on ...

At the end of the interaction, Elizabeth's tone had softened a bit, as if she did not have the heart to continue policing. Her questions became looser: from forced choices, to genuine but closed choices between two options, to closed choices with open-ended options. Frank's stony silence resisted the control and punishment, and as Elizabeth's surveillance and forced choices eased, so did Frank's resistance. His cheeks were no longer red and his jaw was no longer tightly clenched. Elizabeth brought a vocabulary worksheet over to Frank, which he ignored but later completed during recess in about 3 minutes of messy, but accurate, work. It was difficult to say who had "won" the power struggle, though Elizabeth accomplished her goal that Frank would complete the reading centers. This détente illustrated how nobody wins in neoliberal carcerality, but some lose more than others.

In this episode, Elizabeth illustrated not only the countless planes of awareness that teachers operate on and switch between, but also how the structure of the class and of Frank's behaviors, responses, and coping were not well matched. Elizabeth did educative and patient interactions by the book: She explained everything explicitly. Her statements were not directed at Frank as a person, and Elizabeth gave him many opportunities to comply with instructions. She asked questions with two specific, closed-ended options, a strategy to effectively reduce choice and control behavior indirectly. She seemed to know he would avoid eye contact. She gave seconds and sometimes minutes of pause between attempts to engage Frank. Elizabeth did not call the behavior specialist or escalate to an ODR because Frank's behavior was nondisruptive. Also, Elizabeth did not give up on making sure Frank was accountable to his work. Finally, such exchanges occurred with Frank nearly every day; Elizabeth's patience and consistency were unassailable.[5]

However, considering affect, including Frank's stubbornness and resistance, Elizabeth laced passive aggressive moves into PBIS scripts based on responsibility rhetoric and turned the interaction into micro-punishments and power struggle. She utilized a neutral tone with a repetitive script that exaggerated reframing of Frank's silences into choices, feigned patience and empathy, and closed down choices and meaning. The tone and passive aggression silenced Frank and hardened his noncompliance, setting him up for punishment by removal from recess.

Following PBIS protocol and avoiding punishment did not shift the central conflict over compliance; the logic of choices, responsibility, and earned privileges was designed for students to demonstrate having learned compliance. As a result, classroom expectations fit the description of "total institutions" like asylums and prisons, as observed by Goffman (1961): little choice over time and schedule, activity, location, movement, and surveillance over persons whose primary identity labels in the institution were pathologies or crimes.

### Trading Goods for Goodness

Token economies are systems of material behavior rewards to encourage consumption and a myth of individual merit. Tokens (points, tickets, tallies) are distributed and tracked in exchange for positive behavior, recorded in ways that are noted to the whole class, and then rewarded in front of the whole school. In the Fields token system, the principal explained, "So the more Beary Treats [students] have, the more stuff they get to buy." Only some students earned enough tokens per month to afford anything in the school "store," so there was a class hierarchy in which students with more tokens bought more or more expensive prizes; and the ones with the most tokens also got celebrated in assemblies. That is, the rich got richer, and their tokens produced more accolades without having to produce more behavior. Tokens were the currency for goods and goodness, teaching students that behavior was tied to capitalism.[6]

Theresa frequently referred to Beary Treats to remind students that she was tracking students' behaviors. One day in April, Theresa announced her surveillance: "I have to give Beary Treats by [May] 1st, which is not too far away, and I'm looking for people who are not jumping over the couch, not rolling around... I don't want you to be surprised if you don't get a Beary Treat this month." The function of mentioning Beary Treats with the responsibility rhetoric of "I don't want you to be surprised if..." transformed rewards into punishment and shifted responsibility from Theresa onto the students. Punishment was not just given, but also practiced through withholding. In the token economy, reward and punishment both required surveillance, labeling, and passive aggressiveness.

Theresa encountered inequitable hierarchies of goods and goodness nearly every month. Because two students (boys of color on behavior plans) complained that some students always got Beary Treats and they never did, Theresa engaged the whole class in a lecture:

**THERESA:** I did want to talk to you about Cool Cubs. I had a lot—*I* didn't, this *class* had a lot of problems this month... So if we have 24 students in this class and I only put in 10 names, how many students [didn't get Beary Treats]? And how can those students get Beary Treats next time?
**STUDENT 1:** Work hard?
**STUDENT 2:** Be nicer?
**THERESA:** OK, these are all things that can help you get Beary Treats. Because it's hard on me. It's always hard on me. I want to nominate all of you... If your name isn't called, I want you to think—okay, in March, what could you have done?... Terry, Mohamed, I would love to see you called up on stage, I would be so proud, I would be like a proud mama down there, like a proud mama when all her chicks get called on stage. Does it mean I don't like you? [Students, chorally: "Nooo."] No. I love *all* my chicks. [They giggle.]

In addition to capitalistic hierarchy, token economies taught exclusion through responsibility rhetoric and labeling. When Theresa called to Terry (a Black, multiracial boy) and Mohamed (Black, Somali American boy) by name, she responded not only to their complaint of unfairness, but also implicitly labeled them to the class as never getting "called up on to stage." Also, Theresa leveraged her relationships with students in a way that centered herself to argue that withholding reward (i.e., punishment) was hard on her, the withholder. This positioned teachers' feelings and job conditions, rather than student learning, as the intended beneficiaries of positive school behavior. This is a move of whiteness-at-work in schools (Yoon, 2012). Also notable was Theresa's assertion that her behavior monitoring was not personal, but a reflection of affection or love; this affective move twisted exclusion and punishment into a sign of love.

Student learning, in the carceral logics of PBIS, benefited teachers, who were mostly white women, in the Fields behavior economy, because they were arbiters of who got currency. They were thereby able to buy compliance to be able to get through their day in the school–prison nexus. Students produced behavior for sale to adults who had power to give out Beary Treats (not all adults did). Students who did not produce enough good behavior were less valuable, earning fewer or no Beary Treats—what they had produced didn't count enough for a token—and thus they were working for no reward or compensation. Token economies formalized a hierarchical behavioral industrial complex. All students, regardless of race, disability, or gender, were involved in this system of exclusion and belonging.

The token economy also pathologized students who did not perform compliance and responsibility. It added racist and ableist cuts that two Black boys (one American, one an American immigrant) already under surveillance with behavior charts as a result of being labeled "in need of more intensive practice," to use the principal's words, were erased from the school's "good" student body by never being called up to stage for a Cool Cub photograph. Yet they were hypersurveilled in class when they were behaving poorly and went unnoticed most of the time that they were compliant.

## DISCUSSION

PBIS as it was practiced at Fields was intended to reduce behavioral disruptions and punitive responses. But, upon interrogation, I found that practices in the name of PBIS became teaching tools for racist and ableist labeling of children; they rationalized surveilling and punishing students by blaming them for behavioral "choices" while also considering them to be unmotivated, lazy, and corruptly open to "bribery." Punishment was stepwise and predictable, but still built up to removing students from classrooms, as opposed to preventing and ending removal. Here I discuss conceptual and practical issues that have implications for research and system design: intersectionality and carcerality, reframing "positive" and "fidelity," and decarcerating educational systems with love.

## Intersections of Carcerality

Race and disability, not to mention gender and sexuality, are intersectionally imbued with meanings that exclude disabled BISOC from school, and that preclude their belonging, self-determination, friendship, joy, and dignity in school (Annamma et al., 2013; Irby, 2014, 2017; M. W. Morris, 2016; Vaught, 2017; Winn, 2010). These are concerns that are related to, but run deeper than, the push to make PBIS more culturally responsive.

Like Annamma (2017) conceptualized, at Fields I found surveillance, labeling, and punishment to be hyperenacted with Black students and students of color with disabilities. In many instances, educators pathologized and criminalized students by drawing on multiple processes at once (e.g., both surveilling and labeling). But most situations did not feel affectively negative or intimidating. In fact, much of the labeling, surveillance, and punishment were technically faithful to the school's PBIS protocols and agreed-upon expectations.

There are several issues that might contribute to carceral logics in PBIS. One is a misunderstanding of "positive," which I discuss below. Another is that surveillance and internalizing discipline are part of the original intent of PBIS: "Teachers must engage in active supervision ... so that students learn that teachers are monitoring and evaluating their social behaviors" (Sugai & Horner, 2002, p. 34). A third dynamic is the impetus of whiteness-at-work (Yoon, 2012) and white supremacy to deracialize discussions of racial disciplinary disparities (Bornstein, 2017b; Carter et al., 2017; Lustick, 2017) and to cultivate fears of Black students in particular (Irby, 2014; Lensmire, 2012). The intersections of race, disability, and gender in oppression and governmentality are woven into how PBIS and multitiered systems are interpreted, practiced, and researched (Waitoller & Thorius, 2015). These critiques conceptualize how social and disciplinary exclusion dehumanizes, objectifies, and diminishes the dignity of students, particularly disabled BISOC (Annamma, 2017; Dumas & Nelson, 2016; Irby, 2017).

I do not cast judgment on the educators in this study. Though they bear responsibility for their actions, their words and practices were not uncommon and reflect structural contexts and ideologies that are much larger than any individuals. PBIS is but one element of the school–prison nexus that dehumanizes and pathologizes disabled BISOCs; participating in carceral logics to some extent is nearly inevitable as educators are surveilled and controlled while they contain and control students. These acknowledgements do not excuse their practices, but situate them in the mundane violence of white supremacy, ableism, and neoliberal carcerality.

## "Positive" Means "Educative," Not "Nice"

In PBIS, "positive" means educative approaches to changing behaviors rather than aversive practices and removing students from the classroom. However, it also can mean nice and non-confrontational, indirect, as was evident at Fields. This contradiction was evident in the Fields version of "positive," which was not any less punitive, shaming, or exclusionary than traditional behavior systems and disciplinary practices. They continued to close off opportunities to teach and practice communication, conflict, coping, and other skills (Wilson, 2015). This is a dangerous path to toxic positivity, where "normal" is happy and produces narrow versions of "nice" goodness. As with Frank and Elizabeth, Fields' (mis)interpretation of positive had the potential to be self-defeating, particularly when students resisted aspects of PBIS.

Positive support and reinforcement require a depth of relationships with students and families that is not about finding information that fuels pathologization. These kinds of support and reinforcement require multidimensional critical consciousness and engagement with complexity that current research about behavior support and PBIS does not adequately model. Future research must continue to address intersections of race and disability (and more), building on work such as humanizing pedagogies (Bartolomé, 1994; Camangian, 2015; Salazar, 2013), culturally sustaining pedagogies (Paris, 2012; Paris & Alim, 2014; Waitoller & Thorius, 2016), and identity confluence (Khalifa, 2018) to provide tools for practical and theoretical advances. More research with direct observations of behavioral and disciplinary scripts and routines, and of leaders' roles in influencing organizational logics for equity (Horn et al., 2015; Ishimaru & Galloway, 2020), is needed to shake up what gets taken for granted as disordered and disorderly, what is positive and educative, and what educators consider possible.

Such research does not necessarily mean abandoning PBIS and behavioral science, but positioning it in an array of responses to behavior and system design. At the same time, there are important ways for leaders and educators to shift carceral logics and what is considered successful implementation in PBIS. One way to start is to engage educators in self-study of their own practice: what behaviors they affirm, when, to whom, and why. I found three entry points to these self-studies. First, educators—and the PBIS scripts they created—located behavioral problems in individual students and ignored systemic issues or those that reflected poorly on themselves (Annamma & Morrison, 2018; Harris-Murri et al., 2006). Second, my data included countless missed opportunities to appreciate students' engagement, questions, collaboration, critical thinking, and helpful feedback to peers—behaviors that are certainly about learning and not focused on compliance. Third, I also found missed opportunities to intervene in students' learning to pathologize and criminalize each other. Recognizing and acting on such opportunities would help educators resist carceral logics and pedagogies of pathologization.

## Fidelity to Students

While there is a great deal of attention to fidelity of implementation in PBIS research; I suggest, instead, asking who maintains fidelity to the dignity of disabled BISOC and their families (Irby, 2014, 2017), to their complex personhood (Gordon, 2008), and to their dreams. PBIS research must shift attention to unlearning racist ableism in school policies, curricula, resource allocation, and underlying beliefs about themselves and each other. Current research and data collection on PBIS lacks this kind of richness at the level of what happens for students and communities, efforts to transform behavioral systems, or under what conditions and why.

Research-centered emphasis on fidelity and consistency also contributes to measurement and categorization that are part of carceral, racist, and ableist surveillance and labeling. For instance, partly as a result of Tier II behavior charts and Tier III functional behavioral assessments, disabled BISOC at Fields were hyperaware that they were under observation. Thus, the Fields PBIS model, though attempting fidelity to technical implementation, did not entail equitable learning about behavior and belonging in school.[7]

Through pedagogies of pathologization, students learn neoliberal carcerality and who deserves to belong in society. But the problems of exclusionary discipline and the dehumanization of BISOC with EBD labels or behavior plans did not occur solely because of classroom management, and cannot be fixed by just these practices, either. Perhaps conversations about behavior and discipline could be approached like truth and reconciliation commissions, with institutional actors and community members who are disabled BIPOC and who experienced behavioral and disciplinary exclusion in school (cf. Maine-Wabanaki State Child Welfare Truth & Reconciliation Commission, 2015). State agencies have done intense harm to families and communities by using behavior management, surveillance, and discipline; and these truths are dark, painful, and deeper than most educators allow themselves to admit.

## Love Decarcerates System Design

I was haunted by the carceral pathologizing and criminalizing of students, particularly BISOC with EBD labels, at Fields Elementary. The carceral demand for compliance stems from the racist assumption that students of color are prone to criminal violations. Compliance also excludes neurodivergence and students with intellectual, emotional, learning, or physical disabilities that make it impossible or painful to be orderly, quick, still, quiet, or visibly on task. As DisCrit argues, ableist notions about behavior and schooling almost always overlap with racist ones—such as stereotypes of loud Black students who are dangerous and too big to physically control. The co-construction of racism and ableism is not random (Annamma et al., 2013; Annamma & Morrison, 2018; Chapman et al., 2014; Richie, 2012).

I propose that love is the core of behavioral and disciplinary justice. Love is antithetical to the school–prison nexus. Love in system design assumes that belonging is unconditional and not to be revoked, even for those students who seem beyond "help."[8] PBIS frameworks may begin to hint at some of these questions, but do not follow them to their furthest potential (Waitoller & Thorius, 2015). As a result, PBIS cannot challenge the assumption that BISOC with EBD labels can and should be fixed, or else removed.

Love designs around the most excluded, disorderly, silenced students. This would require building in contingencies, flexibilities, and customizations for these students, with consideration of their disability labels, their particularities, their families, and their essential role in the school community. Contingencies, flexibilities, and customizations organized around love instead of normality would necessarily affect content, instruction, schedule, expectations and rules, as well as relationships and discipline. Along the way, these options could offer greater accessibility and choice for all students (cf. Ferguson et al., 2001; Harris-Murri et al., 2006).

## CONCLUSION

In this chapter, I analyzed how PBIS provided research-based legitimacy for surveillance, labeling, and a passive aggressive way of punishing students indirectly such that students were positioned as responsible for their own exclusion. This chapter built on previous critiques and argued that PBIS, despite intentions, calls upon carceral logics that pathologize and criminalize difference, particularly for BISOC with EBD labels. Behavior systems that do not interrogate common-sense control, normalization, and removal are unlikely to be transformative without critically grappling with the reality that state institutions like school systems will not love us, no matter how compliant we are (cf. Waitoller & Thorius, 2015, 2016).[9]

PBIS at Fields did not expand ideas of acceptable behavior or denaturalize the connection between race, disability, and behavior; PBIS was retrofitted to these paradigms. Three patterns in PBIS scripts included catching students being good, using a responsibility rhetoric, and trading goods for goodness. These patterns had overlapping dynamics of surveillance, labeling, and punishment—processes in pedagogies of pathologization.

Educators have long used behavior to pathologize and criminalize disabled BISOC and remove them from school. PBIS is the central model I questioned here, but the framework and implications could apply to other behavioral and disciplinary programs. PBIS scholars have taken up the challenge of addressing school behavior management and exclusion. However, carceral logics of compliance, orderliness, and deviance in PBIS do not—cannot—love disabled BISOC enmeshed in the school–prison nexus. Centering disabled BIPOC students, in response, probes the meanings of "positive" and "fidelity" and considers love in design.

## NOTES

1. I use the term "school–prison nexus" instead of the term "school-to-prison pipeline" because the metaphor of a "pipeline" is inaccurate, unidirectional, and over-deterministic. In using "school–prison nexus," I acknowledge the numerous ways that schools, child welfare agencies, juvenile justice systems, and criminal justice systems interact with each other and with other state-run institutions.

2. Though it is imperfect, I utilize the term BISOC for several reasons. First, it calls attention to the unique and interdependent roles that anti-Blackness and settler colonialism play in the United States. Second, it decenters whiteness while also acknowledging that all persons of color experience racism in different ways in a racial hierarchy that puts people of color in competition with each other. I also capitalize proper nouns, such as Black and Indigenous, because they are self-determined identities based on shared political, cultural, historical processes (Dumas, 2016). Asian American, Latinx, Native American, and Brown are other such self-determined identities. As Dumas incisively states, "*White* is not capitalized in my work because it is nothing but a social construct, and does not describe a group with a sense of common experiences or kinship outside of acts of colonization and terror. Thus, *white* is employed almost solely as a negation of others... Thus, although *European* or *French* are rightly capitalized, I see no reason to capitalize *white*" (p. 13). I follow this logic with reference to the adjective "white" that denotes the racial label.

3. There are significant differences in who gets services and for what disability labels, depending on race. Asian American students are underserved by special education resources, likely due to the model minority myth about high achievement, obedience, passivity, and respect for authority (Ng et al., 2007). Indigenous students are typically ignored in special education research, though they have the highest degrees of disproportionate representation of any racial group (Annamma et al., 2013). While Asian American students tend not to be pathologized, criminalized, and punished as Black, Latinx, and Indigenous students tend to be (and as no students should be), the model

minority myth obscures differences within the broad population of Asian, Pacific Islander, and Desi Americans (Harris-Murri et al., 2006).

4. More extensive description of the study site is in Yoon (2016, 2018).
5. Frank was one of Elizabeth's three students on a behavior plan. Frank was an Asian American (Vietnamese American) boy with attention deficit hyperactivity disorder (ADHD) as an EBD label, and his IEP included a behavior chart, but not the Bears' Den. Frank loved to read and draw and had a mind that was constantly moving from one plot to another. He was exuberant about potty humor. He had two common responses to disciplinary interactions with Elizabeth: Sometimes he talked in a high-pitched baby voice, and other times he turned sullen and red, refusing to speak or make eye contact with Elizabeth.
6. In many schools, these tokens are also called "bucks," making the connection to currency explicit.
7. I experienced this because my presence as a researcher (not to mention an adult) occasionally stoked students' anxiety about such surveillance. One Black boy with an EBD label in Elizabeth's class made comments about my note-taking and presence in the classroom as a "monitor" several times.
8. Here I am careful to discuss "belonging" rather than "inclusion," to avoid confusion with the definition of inclusion as location in space/classroom and amount of time in various spaces (i.e., the special education approach to the "least restrictive environment" clause of IDEA).
9. I use the first-person plural here because I am a disabled woman of color, though my "invisible" disabilities make it such that I am often taken to be nondisabled. I am aligned with, but different from, the students in this study. I also am Korean American and a cisgender woman, so I had privileges in that I was not targeted for punitive discipline in many of the ways I observe in schools. My behavior was not pathologized or criminalized, nor should it have been. However, I also was not served or aware of resources in schools as I could have been, because of the anti-Black, racist myth of the model minority (Ng et al., 2007).

# REFERENCES

Adams, D., & Meiners, E. (2014). Who wants to be special? Pathologization and the preparation of bodies for prison. *Counterpoints: From education to incarceration: Dismantling the school-to-prison pipeline, 453*, 145–164.

Aho, T., Ben-Moshe, L., & Hilton, L.J. (2017). Mad futures: Affect/theory/violence. *American Quarterly, 69*(2), 291–302.

Annamma, S. A. (2017). *The pedagogy of pathologization: Dis/abled girls of color in the school-prison nexus.* Routledge.

Annamma, S. A., Connor, D., & Ferri, B. (2013). Dis/ability critical race studies (DisCrit): Theorizing at the intersections of race and dis/ability. *Race Ethnicity and Education, 16*(1), 1–31.

Annamma, S., & Morrison, D. (2018). DisCrit classroom ecology: Using praxis to dismantle dysfunctional education ecologies. *Teaching and Teacher Education, 73*, 70–80.

Apple, M. W. (2004). *Ideology and curriculum* (3rd ed.). Routledge.

Bal, A. (2015). *Culturally responsive positive behavioral interventions and supports* (WCER Working Paper No. 2015-9). University of Wisconsin–Madison, Wisconsin Center for Education Research.

Bal, A., Thorius, K. A. K., & Kozleski, E. (2012). *Culturally responsive positive behavioral support matters.* The Equity Alliance at ASU.

Bartolomé, L. (1994). Beyond the methods fetish: Toward a humanizing pedagogy. *Harvard Educational Review, 64*(2), 173–195.

Bornstein, J. (2015). "If they're on Tier I, there are really no concerns that we can see:" PBIS medicalizes compliant behavior. *Journal of Ethnographic & Qualitative Research, 9,* 247–267.

Bornstein, J. (2017a). Can PBIS build justice rather than merely restore order? In *The school to prison pipeline: The role of culture and discipline in school* (Vol. 4, pp. 135–167). Emerald Publishing Limited.

Bornstein, J. (2017b). Entanglements of discipline, behavioral intervention, race, and disability. *Journal of Cases in Educational Leadership, 20*(2), 131–144.

Brent, J. J. (2019). Enduring dispositions: Examining punitive logics in the context of disciplinary reform. *Theoretical Criminology, 23*(1), 96–116.

Camangian, P. R. (2015). Teach like lives depend on it: Agitate, arouse, and inspire. *Urban Education, 50*(4), 424–453.

Carter, P. L., Skiba, R., Arredondo, M. I., & Pollock, M. (2017). You can't fix what you don't look at: Acknowledging race in addressing racial discipline disparities. *Urban Education, 52*(2), 207–235.

Chapman, C., Carey, A. C., & Ben-Moshe, L. (2014). Reconsidering confinement: Interlocking locations and logics of incarceration. In L. Ben-Moshe, C. Chapman, & A. C. Carey (Eds.), *Disability incarcerated: Imprisonment and disability in the United States and Canada* (pp. 3–24). Palgrave MacMillan.

Charmaz, K. (2014). *Constructing grounded theory* (2nd ed.). SAGE Publications.

Combahee River Collective. (1977). *The Combahee River Collective statement: Black feminist organizing in the seventies and eighties.* Kitchen Table/Women of Color Press.

Coutinho, M. J., & Oswald, D. P. (1996). Identification and placement of students with serious emotional disturbance, Part II: National and state trends in the implementation of LRE. *Journal of Emotional and Behavioral Disorders, 4,* 40–52.

Coutinho, M. J., Oswald, D. P., Best, A. M., & Forness, S. R. (2002). Gender and sociodemographic factors and the disproportionate identification of culturally and linguistically diverse students with emotional disturbance. *Behavioral Disorders, 27*(2), 109–125.

Cramer, E. D., & Bennett, K. D. (2015). Implementing culturally responsive positive behavior interventions and supports in middle school classrooms. *Middle School Journal, 46*(3), 18–24.

Crenshaw, K. (1991). Mapping the margins: Intersectionality, identity politics, and violence against women of color. *Stanford Law Review, 43*(6), 1241–1299.

Dolmage, J. T. (2018). *Disabled upon arrival: Eugenics, immigration, and the construction of race and disability.* The Ohio State University Press.

Dumas, M. J. (2016). Against the dark: Antiblackness in education policy and discourse. *Theory Into Practice, 55*(1), 11–19.

Dumas, M. J., & Nelson, J. D. (2016). (Re)imagining Black boyhood: Toward a critical framework for educational research. *Harvard Educational Review, 86*(1), 27–47.

Emerson, R. M., Fretz, R. I., & Shaw, L. L. (2011). *Writing ethnographic fieldnotes* (2nd ed.). University of Chicago Press.

Fallon, L. M., O'Keeffe, B. V., & Sugai, G. (2012). Consideration of culture and context in school-wide positive behavior support: A review of current literature. *Journal of Positive Behavior Interventions, 14*(4), 209–219.

Ferguson, D. L., Kozleski, E. B., & Smith, A. (2001). *On... transformed, inclusive schools: A framework to guide fundamental change in urban schools.* Education Development Center.

Finch, M. E. H. (2012). Special considerations with Response to Intervention and instruction for students with diverse backgrounds. *Psychology in the Schools, 49*(3), 285–296.

Franzén, A. G., & Holmqvist, R. (2014). From punishment to rewards? Treatment dilemmas at a youth detention home. *Punishment & Society, 16*(5), 542–559.

Gagnon, J. C., Barber, B. R., & Soyturk, I. (2018). Positive behavior interventions and supports implementation in secure care juvenile justice schools: Results of a national survey of school administrators. *Behavioral Disorders, 44*(1), 3–19.

Gillies, V. (2016). *Pushed to the edge: Inclusion and behaviour support in schools.* Policy Press.

Goff, P. A., Jackson, M. C., Di Leone, B. A. L., Culotta, C. M., & DiTomasso, N. A. (2014). The essence of innocence: Consequences of dehumanizing Black children. *Journal of Personality and Social Psychology, 106*(4), 526–545.

Goffman, E. (1961). *Asylums: Essays on the social situation of mental patients and other inmates.* Anchor Books.

Gordon, A. (2008). *Ghostly matters: Haunting and the sociological imagination* (2nd ed.). University of Minnesota Press.

Gun-Free Schools Act. 20 U.S.C. § 7961 (1994). https://www.govinfo.gov/app/details/USCODE-2015-title20/USCODE-2015-title20-chap70-subchapVIII-partF-subpart4-sec7961

Harris-Murri, N., King, K., & Rostenberg, D. (2006). Reducing disproportionate minority representation in special education programs for students with emotional disturbance: Toward a culturally responsive RTI model. *Education and Treatment of Children, 29*(4), 779–799.

Hart, J. E., Cramer, E. D., Harry, B., Klingner, J. K., & Sturges, K. M. (2010). The continuum of "troubling" to "troubled" behavior: Exploratory case studies of African American students in programs for emotional disturbance. *Remedial and Special Education, 31*(3), 148–162.

Hirschfield, P. J. (2008). Preparing for prison?: The criminalization of school discipline in the USA. *Theoretical Criminology, 12*(1), 79–101.

Horn, I. S., Kane, B. D., & Wilson, J. (2015). Making sense of student performance data: Data use logics and mathematics teachers' learning opportunities. *American Educational Research Journal, 52*(2), 208–242.

Irby, D. J. (2014). Revealing racial purity ideology: Fear of Black–White intimacy as a framework for understanding school discipline in post-Brown schools. *Educational Administration Quarterly, 50*(5), 783–795.

Irby, D. J. (2017). The indignities on which the school-to-prison pipeline is built: Life stories of two formerly incarcerated Black male school-leavers. In *The school to prison pipeline: The role of culture and discipline in school* (pp. 15–39). Emerald Publishing Limited.

Ishimaru, A. M., & Galloway, M. K. (2020). Hearts and minds first: Institutional logics in pursuit of educational equity. *Educational Administration Quarterly.* https://doi.org/10.1177/0013161X20947459

Jolivette, K., Boden, L. J., Sprague, J. R., Ennis, R. P., & Kimball, K. A. (2015). Youth voice matters: Perceptions of facility-wide PBIS implementation in secure residential juvenile facilities. *Residential Treatment for Children & Youth, 32*(4), 299–320.

Kalvesmaki, A. F. (2019). *Exploring policy connections of student discipline* [Unpublished doctoral dissertation]. University of Utah.

Khalifa, M. (2018). *Culturally responsive school leadership.* Harvard Education Press.

Kincaid, D., Dunlap, G., Kern, L., Lane, K. L., Bambara, L. M., Brown, F., Fox, L., & Knoster, T. P. (2016). Positive behavior support: A proposal for updating and refining the definition. *Journal of Positive Behavior Interventions, 18*(2), 69–73.

Krueger, P. (2010). It's not just a method! The epistemic and political work of young people's lifeworlds at the school–prison nexus. *Race Ethnicity and Education, 13*(3), 383–408.

Lensmire, A. (2012). *White urban teachers: Stories of fear, violence, and desire.* Rowman & Littlefield Education.

Leonardo, Z., & Broderick, A. A. (2011). Smartness as property: A critical exploration of intersections between whiteness and disability studies. *Teachers College Record, 113*(10), 2206–2232.

Lewis, M. M. (2018). Navigating the gray area: A school district's documentation of the relationship between disability and misconduct. *Teachers College Record, 120*(100307), 30.

Lustick, H. (2017). Making discipline relevant: Toward a theory of culturally responsive positive schoolwide discipline. *Race Ethnicity and Education, 20*(5), 681–695.

Maine-Wabanaki State Child Welfare Truth & Reconciliation Commission. (2015). *Beyond the Mandate: Continuing the conversation* [Report]. Maine-Wabanaki State Child Welfare Truth & Reconciliation Commission. http://www .mainewabanakitrc.org/wp-content/uploads/2015/07/TRC-Report-Expanded _July2015.pdf

McIntosh, K., Gion, C., & Bastable, E. (2018). *Do schools implementing SWPBIS have decreased racial and ethnic disproportionality in school discipline?* [Evaluation brief]. OSEP Technical Assistance Center on Positive Behavioral Interventions and Supports.

McIntosh, K., Moniz, C., Craft, C. B., Golby, R., & Steinwand-Deschambeault, T. (2014). Implementing school-wide positive behavioural interventions and supports to better meet the needs of Indigenous students. *Canadian Journal of School Psychology, 29*(3), 236–257.

McIntosh, K., Ty, S. V., & Miller, L. D. (2014). Effects of school-wide positive behavioral interventions and supports on internalizing problems: Current evidence and future directions. *Journal of Positive Behavior Interventions, 16*(4), 209–218.

Meiners, E. R. (2007). *Right to be hostile: Schools, prisons, and the making of public enemies.* Routledge.

Miles, M. B., Huberman, M., & Saldaña, J. (2014). *Qualitative data analysis: A methods sourcebook* (3rd ed.). SAGE Publications.

Monroe, C. R. (2005). Why are "bad boys" always Black?: Causes of disproportionality in school discipline and recommendations for change. *The Clearing House: A Journal of Educational Strategies, Issues and Ideas, 79*(1), 45–50.

Morris, E. W. (2005). "Tuck in that shirt!" Race, class, gender, and discipline in an urban school. *Sociological Perspectives, 48*(1), 25–48.

Morris, M. W. (2016). *Pushout: The criminalization of Black girls in schools.* The New Press.

National Center for Culturally Responsive Educational Systems. (2005). *Cultural considerations and challenges in response-to-intervention models: An NCCRESt position statement.* National Center for Culturally Responsive Educational Systems.

Ng, J. C., Lee, S. S., & Pak, Y. K. (2007). Contesting the model minority and perpetual foreigner stereotypes: A critical review of literature on Asian Americans in education. *Review of Research in Education, 31*, 95–130.

Oswald, D. P., & Coutinho, M. J. (1996). Leaving school: The impact of state economic and demographic factors for students with serious emotional disturbance. *Journal of Emotional and Behavioral Disorders, 4*(2), 114–125.

Paris, D. (2012). Culturally sustaining pedagogy: A needed change in stance, terminology, and practice. *Educational Researcher, 41*(3), 93–97.

Paris, D., & Alim, H. S. (2014). What are we seeking to sustain through culturally sustaining pedagogy? A loving critique forward. *Harvard Educational Review, 84*(1), 85–100.

Ramey, D. M. (2015). The social structure of criminalized and medicalized school discipline. *Sociology of Education, 88*(3), 181–201.

Reay, D. (2007). "Unruly places": Inner-city comprehensives, middle-class imaginaries and working-class children. *Urban Studies, 44*, 1191–1201.

Richie, B. E. (2012). *Arrested justice: Black women, violence, and America's prison nation.* NYU Press.

Sabnis, S., Castillo, J. M., & Wolgemuth, J. R. (2020). RTI, equity, and the return to the status quo: Implications for consultants. *Journal of Educational and Psychological Consultation, 30*(3), 285–313.

Safe and Drug-Free Schools and Communities Act. 20 U.S.C. § 7101 *et seq.* (1994). https://www.govinfo.gov/content/pkg/USCODE-2011-title20/html/USCODE-2011-title20-chap70-subchapIV.htm

Salazar, M. C. (2013). A humanizing pedagogy: Reinventing the principles and practice of education as a journey toward liberation. *Review of Research in Education, 37*(1), 121–148.

Selman, K. J. (2017). Imprisoning 'those' kids: Neoliberal logics and the disciplinary alternative school. *Youth Justice.* https://doi.org/10.1177/1473225417712607

Skiba, R. J., Horner, R. H., Chung, C. G., Rausch, M. K., May, S. L., & Tobin, T. (2011). Race is not neutral: A national investigation of African American and Latino disproportionality in school discipline. *School Psychology Review, 40*(1), 85–107.

Skiba, R. J., Michael, R. S., Nardo, A. C., & Peterson, R. L. (2002). The color of discipline: Sources of racial and gender disproportionality in school punishment. *The Urban Review, 34*(4), 317–342.

Smith, P. (2004). Whiteness, normal theory, and disability studies. *Disability Studies Quarterly, 24*(2). https://doi.org/10.18061/dsq.v24i2.491

Sugai, G., & Horner, R. (2002). The evolution of discipline practices: School-wide positive behavior supports. *Child & Family Behavior Therapy,* 24(1–2), 23–50.

Sugai, G., & Horner, R. H. (2009). Responsiveness-to-intervention and school-wide positive behavior supports: Integration of multi-tiered system approaches. *Exceptionality,* 17(4), 223–237.

Sussman, A. (2012). Learning in lockdown: School police, race, and the limits of law. *UCLA Law Review, 59*(3), 788–850.

Tobin, T., Horner, R., Vincent, C., & Swain-Bradway, J. (2012). *If discipline referral rates for the school as a whole are reduced, will rates for students with disabilities also be reduced?* [Evaluation brief]. OSEP Technical Assistance Center on Positive Behavioral Interventions and Supports.

Tyre, A. D., & Feuerborn, L. L. (2017). The minority report: The concerns of staff opposed to schoolwide positive behavior interventions and supports in their schools. *Journal of Educational and Psychological Consultation, 27*(2), 145–172.

Vaught, S. E. (2017). *Compulsory: Education and the dispossession of youth in a prison school.* University of Minnesota Press.

Vincent, C. G., Sprague, J. R., & Gau, J. M. (2013). *The effectiveness of school-wide positive behavior interventions and supports for reducing racially inequitable disciplinary exclusions in middle schools* [Report]. UCLA.

Vincent, C. G., & Tobin, T. J. (2011). The relationship between implementation of school-wide positive behavior support (SWPBS) and disciplinary exclusion of students from various ethnic backgrounds with and without disabilities. *Journal of Emotional and Behavioral Disorders, 19*(4), 217–232.

Vincent, C. G., Tobin, T. J., Hawken, L. S., & Frank, J. L. (2012). Discipline referrals and access to secondary level support in elementary and middle schools: Patterns across African-American, Hispanic-American, and white students. *Education and Treatment of Children, 35*(3), 431–458.

Waitoller, F. R., & Thorius, K. K. (2015). Playing hopscotch in inclusive education reform: Examining promises and limitations of policy and practice in the US. *Support for Learning, 30*(1), 23–41.

Waitoller, F. R., & Thorius, K. K. (2016). Cross-pollinating culturally sustaining pedagogy and universal design for learning: Toward an inclusive pedagogy that accounts for dis/ability. *Harvard Educational Review, 86*(3), 366–389.

Wilson, A. N. (2015). A critique of sociocultural values in PBIS. *Behavior Analysis in Practice, 8*(1), 92–94.

Winn, M. T. (2010). 'Our side of the story': Moving incarcerated youth voices from margins to center. *Race Ethnicity and Education, 13*(3), 313–325.

Yoon, I. H. (2012). The paradoxical nature of whiteness-at-work in the daily life of schools and teacher communities. *Race Ethnicity and Education, 15*(5), 587–613.

Yoon, I. H. (2016). Trading stories: Middle-class white women teachers and the creation of collective narratives about students and families in a diverse elementary school. *Teachers College Record, 118*(2), 1–54.

Yoon, I. H. (2018). Silencing racialized humor in elementary school: Consequences of colormuting and whiteness for students of color. *Berkeley Review of Education, 8*(1), 117–144.

# CHAPTER 12

# REIMAGINING EARLY EDUCATION LEADERSHIP

## Spiritual-Based Leadership Meets Democratic Experimentalism

**Angela Passero Jones**
*University of Wisconsin–Eau Claire*

**Roderick Jones**
*University of Wisconsin–Eau Claire*

In this chapter we consider how leadership in early education markets can be enacted through more humanistic and communal efforts based on spiritual orientations rather than capitalistic rationales. Initially, we present a case study of private preschool leaders' decision-making to offer examples of who and what decides enrollment and disenrollment in publicly funded (via vouchers) yet private prekindergarten programs. We then discuss spiritual-based leadership as an alternative to resist marginalizing practices that normalize ableist constructions in school choice programs. Finally, we rethink early education leadership by way of the *leadership within* framework (McDowall Clark

*Who Decides?*, pages 283–309

Copyright © 2022 by Information Age Publishing

www.infoagepub.com

& Murray, 2012) while challenging marketized models of early education in juxtaposition to democratic experimentalism (Moss, 2009).

## WHO DECIDES (DIS)ENROLLMENT? A CASE STUDY

The case study presented here revealed how notions of normality were implicated in decision-making processes that affected student disenrollment in one state's prekindergarten policy ecology. The state's prekindergarten ecological policy framework was predicated mostly on a privatized voucher system and included children who have or were perceived to have disabilities. Details about the study's policy context, methods, and findings follow.

### Policy Context

Preschools exist within policy ecology encompassing the convergence of multiple policies, each with its own history, discourses, and practices (Odom et al., 2004; Weaver-Hightower, 2008). Considering child care regulations, universal preschool initiatives and federal programs (e.g., Improving Head Start for School Readiness Act of 2007, Race to the Top Early Learning Challenge of 2011 [U.S. Department of Education, n.d.], and Preschool for All Initiative of 2013 [U.S. Department of Health & Human Service, n.d.]), and policies for children with disabilities (e.g., Section 619 of the Individuals With Disabilities Education Improvement Act of 2007, Section 504 of the Rehabilitation Act of 1973, and the Americans with Disabilities Act of 1990), the ecological system becomes increasingly complex for (pre)school children with disabilities.

In Florida, the state in which this study occurred, participation in prekindergarten programs was positioned as a constitutional right for all 4-year-olds. While penning a veto letter in response to state legislators' first attempt to implement the program, the governor identified three program goals: (a) provision of school choice, (b) establishment of high early learning standards with an emphasis on literacy, and (c) utilization of student assessments to ensure accountability (Bush, 2004). Policy interests negotiated in Florida's Voluntary Prekindergarten Program (VPK) embodied what Apple (2005) coined conservative modernism: "The complicated alliance behind...educational reforms that have centered around neo-liberal commitments to the market...neo-conservative emphases on stronger control over curricula...and new managerial proposals to install rigorous forms of accountability..." (p. 11).

#### Choice

VPK afforded parents choice over the type of program in which to enroll children. Choices included school-year programs delivered by private providers or public schools; summer programs delivered by private providers or public schools; or in the case of a child with an eligible disability, specialized instructional services programs in lieu of participation in VPK programs. According to state statute, "A parent may enroll his or her child with any private prekindergarten provider that is eligible to deliver the VPK program under this part; however, the provider may determine whether to admit any child" (§ 1002.53(6)(a-c), Fla. Stat); therefore, enrollment choice was at the discretion of parents and providers, and providers had choice in sustaining enrollment. Students who withdrew or were dismissed from a VPK provider for the following reasons were eligible to re-enroll with another provider (F.A.C. 6M-8.210(2)(c), 2010): failure to comply with VPK provider's attendance policy, illness of the student or family member, disagreement between parent/guardian and VPK provider, change in the student's residence, change in employment schedule of parent/guardian, or the provider's inability to meet the student's health or educational needs.

### Standards and Accountability

Governor Bush's (2004) veto letter promoted standardization and accountability via recommendations for "a system concerned with performance standards, outcome measures, and a curriculum that facilitates early literacy" (para. 3) and called for the Florida Department of Education to "establish performance measures and standards" (para. 5) and "refocus the statewide school readiness assessment on emerging literacy skills, develop literacy-focused curriculum standards, and lay the foundation for program integrity and accountability measurement" (para. 7).

The governor's push for prekindergarten program standards, outcome measures, and curricula focused exclusively on early literacy fomented debate in the early childhood community (Barnett, 2005; National Institute for Early Education Research [NIEER], 2005; Solochek, 2006). When he signed VPK into law, public outcry ensued in response to the statewide kindergarten readiness screening used as the accountability metric. According to state statute, evaluation of VPK programs is performed annually using the statewide kindergarten readiness screening (Fla. Stat. § 1002.67, 2014; Fla. Stat. § 1002.69, 2014). The National Institute for Early Education Research (NIEER) considered the screening policy "one of the most disturbing components of the newly elected Florida Legislation" (NIEER, 2005, p. 7). The director of NIEER, Steven Barnett, suggested that the screening policy "violates the cardinal rule of early educators that says, 'first do no harm'" (Barnett, 2005, p. 2) and policy makers' "simple approach" to accountability falsely assumed a single test upon entrance to kindergarten could assess the quality of a child's preschool experience. Screening results established the quality of providers' performance, need for corrective actions, and funding eligibility (Fla. Stat. § 1002.67(43)(c), 2014). Thus, funding for VPK providers was determined by how well students performed on the screening.

## METHODS

Case study design (Creswell, 2013) was employed to evidence how preschool leaders' decision-making processes appropriated prekindergarten policies. Three private prekindergarten programs were identified via purposeful sampling (Maxwell, 2008) to represent provider types in a local market whose demographics (i.e., socioeconomic status and race) simulated the state's. Two or three leaders at each preschool provided interview data (two interviews per participant transcribed by first author), observations (preschool tours), and policy documents (e.g., parent handbooks, curriculum materials, classroom behavior management systems, advertisements, etc.). Follow-up interviews were conducted to verify the interviewer's sensemaking of participants' stories; data from multiple sources was cross-referenced (interviews, observations, and document reviews), and thick description of the research preschools and participants was provided to ensure research quality. The data sources are discussed below.

### Interviews

Two interviews were conducted with each leader, tape recorded, and transcribed. The first interview was semi-structured and followed a protocol. Interviews were between 21 and 55 minutes and took place at a quiet location chosen by participants. First-round interviews provided background information pertaining to how leaders viewed their work in the VPK program. Questions addressed participants' perceptions of the program's purpose, significance, and benefits, and the challenges they faced delivering the program. Probing questions were asked to understand how leaders perceived children and families desired for enrollment in their respective programs.

Review of first-round interview data helped identify follow-up questions for the second interviews, sources for document review, and opportunities for observation. Second-round interviews lasted between 18 and 55 minutes and were used to gather missing information, address contradictions, and address ambiguously answered questions from the first interview.

### Observations

Center tour observations were conducted to learn about each center's enrollment process and to gain deeper awareness of how center leaders perceived their programs. The observations provided opportunity to understand language, routines and practices, and other rituals of sensemaking in each center. Field notes were taken during observations and included descriptions of the center's physical context as well as participants' actions and conversations (Hatch, 2002).

### Documents

Drawing from what Krippendorff (2013) referred to as "relevance sampling" that "aims at selecting all textual units that contribute to the given research question" (p. 120), a document review was conducted to develop a richer understanding of program phenomena. Center leaders provided relevant documents, which included center or school level policies for the VPK program. Additional documents spanning enrollment policies, behavior/discipline policies, dismissal/termination policies, program brochures and flyers, curriculum materials, parent communication forms, marketing materials, and the program's website or social media pages were examined. Included in the document review was enrollment information about student demographics, student assessment data, and the program's readiness rates obtained from the Florida Department of Education Kindergarten Readiness Rate Website (Florida Office of Early Learning, 2015).

## Analysis

Attention was given to participants' narratives, particularly how they understood and positioned ability as a social construct in their local policy-market ecology. Data was analyzed using a poststructural approach offered by Lather (1993). Lather provided "scandalous categories" (p. 685), a checklist of sorts for exploring validity in poststructural research. For the purpose of this study, we drew upon examples taken from Lather's "checklist," which suggest that validity from a poststructural vantage point can be appropriated in text that "searches for the oppositional in our daily practices...puts conventional discursive procedures under erasure...embodies a situated, partial, positioned, explicit tentativeness... [and] constructs authority via practices of engagement and self-reflexivity" (p. 686).

Central to this study was language and practices leaders invoked to aid their decision-making around student disenrollment. Of equal importance were oppositional discursive forces lodged in everyday language used by leaders and their attempts to understand and enact policy that functioned to reconstruct notions of normal, abnormal, able, and disable. Furthermore, this study questioned conventional discursive procedures of disenrollment through analysis of interview data and critically examined center policies and practices that functioned to reconstruct behavioral and academic expectations for young children. Data analysis identified findings which described ways leaders made decisions about student enrollment and disenrollment processes and how notions of disability were implicated in such processes.

## FINDINGS

Two cross-case themes, identity and reciprocity, emerged from data analysis. The sense of identity of the leaders influenced their interpretations of and reactions to program policies, local market pressures, and, subsequently, constructions of the "good consumer," a perceptual dyad of parent and child prepared for rigor with the exhibition of self-control (see Passero Jones & Jones, 2021). Additionally, findings suggested that good consumers reinforced leaders' desired identity. Undesirable or "bad consumers" were uncovered through discursive binaries as leaders referenced who or what constituted good consumers. Finally, the leaders justified disenrollment decisions amid a continuum of exchanges with consumers.

### Identity Maintenance and Development

The theme, identity maintenance and development, involved organizational and personal challenges leaders faced as they mediated their personal and business identities (i.e., their personal and business image, brand, ideal, etc.). While responding to market pressures and prekindergarten program requirements, leaders invoked (dis)ability through their identity lens based upon the activation of social roles (e.g., business owner, employer, teacher, parent, Christian, etc.) when engaged in disenrollment decisions. Disparate identity lenses influenced the leaders' perceptions of normal/abnormal, abled/disabled, and also affected their inclusion and exclusion of children as "others." As leaders made sense of policies, practices, and discourses through their identity lenses, they espoused leadership orientations that facilitated their preschool's willingness to be more or less inclusive of children with diverse needs.

Further, to understand how leaders developed and nurtured their personal and business identities, organizational portraits depicting each preschool's culture, core values (i.e., economic, educational) and identity themes (as an organization and as a leader) are illuminated in Table 12.1 and discussed below. Direct quotes from interviews are italicized to accentuate participants' accounts. Pseudonyms for participating preschools and leaders purposely reflect findings and help explicate participants' identity constructions. Only preschool owners or directors in charge of disenrollment decision-making are included in subsequent findings.

**TABLE 12.1 Center and Leadership Team Values**

| Center | Center Pseudonym | Center Type | Leadership Team | Values |
|--------|------------------|-------------|-----------------|--------|
| A | Affectionate Altruism Preschool | Family Owned | Maria | Affection and Altruism |
| B | Brainy Best Preschool | Franchise | Milton | Competition and Research |
| C | Careful Charity Preschool | Church | Esther | Charity and Care |

### *Affectionate Altruism Preschool*

When selecting a name for this preschool, the term affectionate was chosen to represent the owner's expressed desire to demonstrate care toward others. Altruism was evoked to describe the owner's repeated refrain to "look out for" others' welfare (i.e., her students and their parents, employees, and community). The owner touted her upbringing as a Christian and summoned the "golden rule" in her daily practices: "Do unto others as you would have them do to you." This perspective influenced her compassion and forgiveness toward parents when they missed payments. Also, at extra cost to her business, she occasionally hired one-on-one aides to help provide care for children with significant disabilities. According to the preschool's parent handbook, its mission focused on maintaining

> an inviting atmosphere for your child that promotes growth socially, emotionally, and intellectually. We will reach these goals with your child by having a soft, soothing, and comfortable environment that allows free choice of play throughout the day and planned learning activities. Our staff is well trained and displays love for children in their daily interactions.

**Maria.** The owner of Affectionate Altruism entered the childcare service field in 1987. She wanted to pursue a career she could balance with her young family. After working at a local church and in Montessori preschools for 22 years, she opened Affectionate Altruism in 2009 and fulfilled a variety of roles:

> from completing paperwork all the way to working in a classroom to taking out the trash and cleaning and mopping the floors...it's part of showing the staff that you're in there with them...willing to get your hands dirty just like they do.

Maria, as in Dr. Maria Montessori, was the pseudonym for this participant because she spoke often about how her school's curriculum, while not Montessorian, was influenced by her prior work experience in Montessori preschools.

**Decision-making practices: Adapting identity.** Responding to pressure from newly revised prekindergarten program policies enacted by the state office, Maria altered the curriculum approach traditionally used in the pre-kindergarten classroom at her preschool. While making the curriculum change, she struggled with the decision because she wanted her preschool program to maintain its Montessori roots. She lamented that the state ac-countability system had unfairly forced structured curriculum standards and teacher-directed instruction on students and teachers, causing her to acquiesce her Montessorian practices and beliefs. Despite relenting to the pressure, Maria eventually embraced the new "structured" prekindergarten program implemented at her preschool. This new curriculum approach (re)shaped Maria's disenrollment decision-making. While she made disen-rollment decisions based on "what I feel would be morally and ethically correct" based on her spiritual beliefs, she cited the program's structure as the reason some families were not a good fit: "We've had families that weren't happy with the way our structured [prekindergarten program] is where we've said, you know, maybe it's not for you."

In addition to confronting curriculum changes that influenced ways Ma-ria envisioned her preschool, Maria shared there were a few instances when she disenrolled children due to severe behavioral concerns—behaviors which included persistent biting, cussing, kicking, throwing and jumping off furniture. She recounted an incident when she told parents their child was "a danger to the other children," hoping her comments would encour-age the parents to get their child "some help." Yet, the parents decided to pull their child out of the program. The help Maria referred to was medi-calized, behavioral, or psychological in nature, a foretelling of the child's behavior as an abnormal manifestation or disabling condition.

The evolution of Maria's prekindergarten program from a Montessorian orientation to that which employed "structured" state-driven accountability measures required adaptation in how she saw her school and engaged chil-dren and parents. Notably, Maria's decision-making about disenrollment occurred when a child(ren) threatened to upend her program's stability and its concomitant identity as a place (from a business and personal per-spective) devoted to affectionate and altruistic care, despite considering a child(ren) with a disability as one who stands to potentially benefit most from human affection and altruism.

### Brainy Best Preschool

The pseudonym Brainy Best was chosen to illustrate themes of prestige/competition and research due to emphasis placed on the preschool's use of a "scientifically proven" curriculum. These themes surfaced from inter-views with the preschool's owner who lauded the importance of efficien-cy and punctuality in daily operational practices and routines. The term

"Brainy" signified the preschool's purported use of a "brain-based" curriculum vetted by corporate leadership. "Best" captured the preschool's vision to be the best in town, which was heralded in various marketed advertisements. According to its parent handbook, the preschool mission statement conveyed:

> [Brainy Best] provides a secure, nurturing, and educational environment for young children; a place for children to bloom into responsible, considerate, and contributing members of society.

> [Brainy Best] wants all children to have the opportunity to grow physically, emotionally, socially, and intellectually by playing, exploring, and learning with others in a fun, safe, and healthy environment.

> As a family owned and operated organization, [Brainy Best] welcomes positive family involvement and encourages a family-teacher approach where the needs of every child comes first to obtain a successful early childhood education.

**Milton.** In recognition of school privatization efforts promoted by economist Milton Friedman (Friedman, 1997), the pseudonym Milton connected Brainy Best's owner's prior career in the finance industry to his aggressive "best" in town preschool marketing campaign. While Milton expressed belief he was "putting back into something, in the lives of families, knowing they have somebody here that's committed for them than somebody...that has the mindset or a frame that revolves around dollars," he underscored his intentions to maintain the finest local preschool reputation.

**Decision-making practices: Protecting identity.** Brainy Best was the most expensive preschool that participated in this study, and given the high-quality service Milton believed his preschool provided, he was critical of parents who did not have good payment histories. This was an affront to his business interests and beliefs of personal responsibility. From his experience, parents typically pulled their child(ren) out of his preschool "because they haven't paid their bill," yet similar to Maria's account, Milton cited "serious [behavioral] disruption" as another leading reason for disenrolling a child. He further explained,

> I had a student that was literally tearing up the classroom and the student was doing it on a daily basis...really had no solution to the child and we had to disenroll the child.

Interestingly, while Milton recounted his decision to disenroll the student because he exhibited disruptive and destructive behavior, he allowed the student to return to the preschool whenever "it was fit and appropriate" for everyone's concern. When asked follow-up questions about disenrollment practices at Brainy Best, Milton appeared agitated and stated:

You have to be very careful disenrolling a student in that environment [pre-kindergarten program] because there are legal implications involved as well... [parents] can become argumentative, confrontational, you're treading on a fine line there. So there's a lot of ifs, whats, whens, questions and a lot of crossing the t's and dotting the i's I think. It's easier said than done. So, we disenroll very few students, but we have disenrolled several.

Milton's sense of caution or the need to protect his preschool's perceived identity as the foremost (best) childcare provider against parents' refusal to pay, uncontrollable children, legal missteps, and unhappy parents when making disenrollment decisions was a guiding concern. His use of the terms "fit" and "appropriate" not only situated the child's behavior within the purview of normality but also positioned classroom practices (e.g., curriculum, rules, routines, etc.) as the standard of normality.

### Careful Charity Preschool

At Careful Charity, preschool leaders considered the context of work as a ministry, first, and then a preschool. The term "careful" described how the director conscientiously sought to mediate conflict between her desire to minister to children/families and her personal and the preschool's capacity to serve students with special needs. Charity referred to the preschool's nonprofit status and the director's perception of her work as a sort of spiritual calling and gifting.

According to Careful Charity's parent handbook, its mission was "to teach and empower students through Christian education that they may uphold God's standard of truth, and make an impact on their world." Their vision statement reads:

> We believe in strong education for world change and it is our desire to be recognized and sought as a premiere Christian Preschool reaching, teaching, and unleashing our future world leaders. It is the desire of [Careful Charity] to work in cooperation with our families to discover the full potential God has for each student... The students will be surrounded with the love of God and Biblical principles on a daily basis. [Careful Charity] will be a safe environment where students will be encouraged to support each other with Godly integrity and accept each other unconditionally.

**Esther.** Given the preschool's position as a Christian ministry led by women, the director of Careful Charity was named after a female leader in the Bible. Esther worked in childcare for 25 years, a career she chose because of her love for children. "I love children," she said,

> I always have. I took childcare in high school. I have four children of my own and I wanted to do something where I could have my last child with

me ... that basically got me into it, but I always cared about children. I always loved them.

Esther worked at Careful Charity for 15 years although the preschool had provided the prekindergarten program for approximately 10 years. She described her career as "joyful." As she reflected on her experiences working with children, she explained:

> I enjoy watching them from the very beginning to the time they leave, what they learn, what impacts I have made on their lives. This isn't just a preschool. This is a ministry to me. So, I don't just do teaching and my teachers don't just teach. They minister to the children and the families.

**Decision-making practices: Conflicting identity.**  Interviews with the director unveiled internal tensions she obscured about decision-making processes resulting from her (in)ability to balance the preschool as a ministry, small business, and regulated childcare and prekindergarten provider. Additionally, though the preschool offered extensive written policies for document review, Esther's decision-making processes on student disenrollment relied more on personal leadership observations, experiences, and instincts. Further, she emphasized that decisions leading to the disenrollment of students who presented challenges induced her to engage in deep, spiritual reflection before acting upon her initial thoughts. Expressing a lack of absolution with respect to the disenrollment of a student in one particular case, she recounted,

> I'm not sure if I should've put my foot down and say "okay that's it. The child's leaving." But I've been kind of convinced that we should keep trying and see what we can do for the child.

According to Esther, prayerful reflection emboldened her ability to make decisions to disenroll students whom she questioned the preschool's aptness to serve. In the above case, when providing parents and their child a trial enrollment period because of the child's history (at other schools) of unmanageable behavior, Esther believed she and her peers "should keep trying" to help the family through interpersonal, job-embedded skills and, more importantly, prayer. She considered prayer a powerful way to seek God's wisdom and grace as she ministered to the child and attended to business and instructional demands (i.e., classroom interruptions, impact on other children's behavior, perception of other children's parents, etc.). Yet her spiritual convictions, when examined against her recollection of and experiences with the child, faltered and repositioned her decision to disenroll the child on the basis of his "angry" temperament:

He doesn't hurt anyone. I get concerned that he's gonna hurt himself, but he won't hurt anyone else. He just kinda wigs out on us and sometimes we can bring him back down but then there's other times it's so bad he just tears apart the room and we have to get all the children out of the classroom and just let him do his thing. Then when he's done, he actually goes and cleans it all up.

Esther's final comment—"Then when he's done [being angry and tearing the room apart], he actually goes and cleans it all up"—suggested when the child returns to a state of normalcy, he is capable of functioning like other (normal) students. From her statement, it can be inferred that if he refused to clean after himself, the tantrums would be abnormal or inexcusable. Taking this and additional comments into account, Esther affirmed the child's disenrollment was contingent upon several observable threats: (a) infliction of harm to another child or himself, (b) physical destruction of classroom environment, and (c) the child's refusal to clean up after dismantling the classroom environment. Despite prayerful reflection and a willingness to extend "grace" to the parents and the child's behavior, Esther finally acknowledged, "We're working on getting help for him. So we want to see how this turns out. Then if not, then we'll probably have to tell them that he'd have to leave the school."

Esther's ambivalence over whether to disenroll the student demonstrated how she struggled to maintain her sense of spiritual identity when dealing with complexities of operating a preschool. She interpolated discourses about her spiritual beliefs and practices and unknowingly qualified them in relation to the child's behavior, each time providing more perspective while simultaneously diminishing the threat, fear, or risk in moving from the problem toward possible solutions—or at best continued engagement and thus enrollment.

The aforementioned organizational portraits extend specific contextual frames through which discourses and perceptions held by preschool leaders worked to influence their personal and business leadership decision-making practices. Some participants' understandings of normality were framed through constructions and expressions of "service" as they emphasized the import of being service-oriented leaders. Additionally, leaders' perceived internal and external threats against their preschools and/or their individual identities influenced how they maintained and developed their identities in response to disparate demands. They made decisions that caused them to accept adaptations or changes to their identities (Affectionate Altruism), protect their identities (Brainy Best), and to negotiate conflict (Careful Charity) as they sought to do what they believed advantageous for their preschools and the children/families under their charge. These normalizing discourses surfaced as tensions between continuing enrollment for children whose behavior posed threats to the preschools' survival within the local market. Such tensions drove decision-making around disenrollment and functioned to shape perceptions of normality for pre-kindergarten students.

## Reciprocity (Good Versus Bad Consumers)

To the extent preschool leaders felt enabled to maintain their personal identity and business reputation, their narratives constructed children and parents as good or bad consumers. Children and parents as good consumers and the different ways in which their beliefs, motives, and actions aligned with leaders' identities and business interests conjoined to build relationships predicated on mutual benefit—or reciprocity. Consumers who positively reinforced leaders' identity and preschools' goals were considered "good." The extent to which leaders were able to depend on good consumers to sustain their personal identity and organizational goals informed their enrollment decision-making practices. However, discourses that depicted children as "unprepared," "unfit," or "angry," and parents as "rogues," "noncompliant," or "uninterested," functioned to blame children and parents, supporting leaders' decision-making around disenrollment.

For preschool leaders, the need to protect personal and business identities in the local market required positioning children and parents as consumer and commodity. As consumers, parents, and by consequence children, pursued services provided by the different preschools. Paradoxically, the preschools in this study were thought to be the quintessential good—the product or commodity marketed as propitious educational and childcare service. However, this study illuminated it was not merely what preschools were able to provide for parents and children, but reciprocally "the goods" children and parents were able to yield for preschool leaders.

## LEADING THROUGH IDENTITY CONSTRUCTIONS

While responding to local market pressures and prekindergarten program requirements, preschool leaders invoked (dis)ability through their identity lens. Participants' identities subsumed multiplicitous roles (i.e., as a business owner, employer, teacher, parent, Christian, etc.). These various identities influenced their perceptions of normal/abnormal and abled/disabled and affected their inclusion and exclusion of "others."

This study illustrated how prekindergarten policies, enrollment/curriculum practices, and market/spirituality discourses intersected to shape decision-making practices centered on disenrollment that constructed children in particular ways. Furthermore, leaders made sense of these policies, practices, and discourses via their own identity lenses. Whereas Maria and

Esther at the family-owned and church-run preschools enacted spiritual based leadership, Milton tended to embrace a transactional leadership approach. Participants' leadership efforts also oriented their preschools toward being more or less inclusive of children with diverse needs.

## (Pre)School Identity

School leaders make sense of policies based upon their perceived intended purpose of schooling and the role schools are expected to perform within that broader purpose (Jennings, 2010; Jessen, 2012). Research on leadership in choice schools has found that school leaders "manage[d] the school choice process to achieve the principal's desired ends—ends that have been established, in part, through the principal's sense-making about the local accountability environment" (Jennings, 2010, p. 230). In Jennings' (2010) study, participants' desired ends included the bottom-line, survival, or social justice. The signaling (recruiting through targeted advertising) and counseling out (encouraging parents to withdraw their children) practices engaged by these principals were means used to achieve the desired ends.

Additionally, Jennings' (2010) study of choice schools in New York City found exclusionary practices occurred most explicitly and frequently at a franchise school. This chapter's study identified a similar trend; however, leaders in the study presented herein were aware of various dynamics that affected students' and parents' choice. For instance, while Brainy Best's policies indicated they supported inclusive schooling environments, participants at this preschool made it clear that children with disabilities can be included as long as they fit into their classrooms. That is, no special accommodations, modifications, or changes were made to make the classrooms or curriculum accessible—children must fit in leaders' predetermined mold. This finding is consistent with Estes' (2004) study of charter schools in Texas, where her analysis of interview data revealed while the charter schools may not have explicitly denied the enrollment of students with disabilities, administrators admitted they "communicate to parents that their service provision is limited to what the parents see" (p. 263). Further, several administrators in Estes' (2004) study reported expelling "students who did not meet their behavior expectations, without providing services" (p. 263).

Jessen (2012) discovered in New York City that charter school leaders' perceptions of market and accountability pressures, excessive costs, and difficulty of teaching students with disabilities served to rationalize the exclusion of students perceived to have high levels of need. She also found school leaders "explicitly discussed their methods of screening out students with special needs, rationalizing that their academic requirements would not 'fit' with the school" (p. 449). Discussions of "fit" and practices related to what Jessen (2012) called signaling (how schools send signals to parents about the type of child desired for the school) was persistent across preschools participating in this current study. While signaling was most explicit at the franchise preschool (Brainy Best), particularly how they marketed themselves as using a "scientifically based" curriculum and were not inclined to change their curriculum or environments to accommodate diverse needs of students, evidence of signaling (and fit) were also apparent at the other preschools as they advertised as a specific faith-based community or touted a "structured" curriculum.

## Spirituality and Inclusion

Two leaders who participated in this study (Maria at Affectionate Altruism and Esther at Careful Charity) were influenced by a desire to be of service to others (servant leadership) as a manifestation of their spiritual and religious beliefs. Furthermore, enrollment practices employed by Affectionate Altruism and Careful Charity were more inclusive, as they were guided by the leaders' spiritual and religious convictions. Research on inclusion in schools (both preschools and K–12 systems) have found leaders who drew upon their spirituality in decision-making were more inclined to include students with disabilities in their schools than those who did not (i.e., Knoche et al., 2006; Keyes et al., 1999).

In another study, Jones (2020) similarly found former PreK–12 school principals based decision-making and inclusive practices on their spiritual beliefs, including how they resisted site-based and district-led initiatives as they worked to remove social barriers that traditionally marginalized students with disabilities in their schools. Retaliatory actions—by staff, parents, and district leaders—that resulted from the principals' decisions as they worked to socially transform their school's culture caused them to confront moral and spiritual tensions. Moreover, when leading on behalf of students with disabilities, the principals often questioned whether decisions they executed were ultimately for the betterment of and responsive to everyone's needs. A recurrent theme which allowed them to work through their role and values conflict was their spirituality.

Winston (2013) defined spirituality as "an expression of one's core values" (p. 24) and suggested a connection between spirituality in the workplace and enhanced creativity, honesty, trust, personal fulfillment, and an increased commitment to organizational goals. Likewise, Pruzan (2013) described spirituality as "an existential search for a deeper self-understanding and meaning in life—and living in accordance with what one finds" (p. 35). Similar to Maria's and Esther's experiences, Knoche et al. (2006) found childcare providers who were more likely to include children with disabilities perceived their work as a calling, rather than simply "a job with a paycheck" (p. 100). According to Molloy and Foust (2016), to view one's work a calling suggests that one's work is "fulfilling and positively influencing society" (p. 340) and often leads them to "invoke spirituality" (p. 341).

### Spiritual-Based Leadership

According to Pruzan (2013), fundamental to spiritual-based leadership (SBL) is "the leader's search for meaning, purpose and self-knowledge based on one's own spirituality" (p. 33). Considering an organization's leadership structure, rationality and spirituality interweave and influence decision-making processes. These influences affect decisions that work to maintain the sense of identity, purpose, vision, and success for organizations and leaders (Pruzan, 2013). Further, Pruzan (2013) suggested that SBL expands "concepts of success to include unselfish service and respect for all those who are affected by their action" (p. 39), thus providing a frame of reference and language for preschool leaders to lead with their heads and hearts.

Winston (2013) suggested that spiritual leadership entails decision-making on the basis of servitude and "the greater well being of the followers [in this case, teachers, children, and families] even at the potential expense of the organization" (p. 29). This was evidenced in the findings of altruism at Affectionate Altruism and charity at Careful Charity. Preschool leaders Maria and Esther drew upon a moral code, a divine directive of sorts, that went beyond the welfare of their business. Their decision-making was induced by a heightened concern for the welfare of children enrolled in their preschools, the well-being of their families, and the overall solvency of their business and local community. This was evident in risks they took to ensure that children and families were treated fairly, with compassion and grace. These risks included hiring one-on-one teachers to work with children with special needs, allowing parents to fall behind on payments (occasionally forgiving owed balances), and continuing enrollment for children who exhibited challenging behaviors. They viewed business success beyond monetary compensation—it was about serving others and God.

According to Keyes et al. (1999), spiritually guided leadership denotes three relational dimensions: the leader's relationship with self, a power greater than self, and others. These dimensions were apparent in Maria's and Esther's decision-making. They made decisions which (a) solidified an inner relationship within themselves as they pursued growth in their Christian faith, (b) strengthened their relationship with God as a power greater than themselves, and (c) fostered relationships with their employees, students, and parents as they attempted to demonstrate compassion and grace for others. For instance, Esther made decisions through prayerful reflection and felt compelled by a higher power to continue to include a child whose behavior she considered destructive. Maria reflected upon her upbringing as a Christian as she made decisions to sacrifice her business success (i.e., her profit margin) to meet the needs of children in her preschool.

When (pre)schools are managed by leaders who practice SBL, teachers may be more likely to view work as a calling and dedicate their efforts toward including children with diverse needs in classrooms (Knoche et al., 2006). Furthermore, this study suggests that as (pre)school leaders' decisions are guided by spiritual convictions, they may be more inclined to appreciate kinship among individuals, uphold an inclusive view of children with disabilities, and may be less likely to "other" children and their parents when challenges arise. However, when driven by a sense of prestige and monetary motives, preschool leaders may more readily embrace a perspective that upholds exclusionary practices based upon students' differences, business image, and robust profit-margins, resulting in a mechanistic, functionalist leadership orientation.

### SBL Versus Mechanistic Paradigm and Hypercapitalism

SBL merges dominant functionalist leadership paradigms that utilize rational decision-making imperatives along with one's core values and seeks harmony between one's thoughts, words, and deeds (Pruzan, 2013). Leaders who practice SBL constantly balance the spiritual and the rational as seen with Esther through her identity conflict as a minister and business leader as well as in how Maria drew upon various identities in her decision-making (mom, prekindergarten/child care provider, business owner, Christian, etc.). In contrast, leaders who do not draw upon spirituality tend to rely primarily on rationality as was illustrated with Milton at Brainy Best who enacted more of a mechanistic approach to leadership.

According to Winston (2013), Western management paradigms embrace mechanistic approaches to providing leadership of individuals in the workplace and ignore people's humanity and spirituality. In organizations that employ strict managerial paradigms, work is disconnected from the human soul and performed only to maximize output. Further, people are "elements of production and/or service only" (Winston, 2013, p. 24) and their basic needs are often trivialized. Considering Winston's (2013) assertions, although Milton stated he viewed his work as "putting back into something, in the lives of families, knowing they have somebody here that's committed for them than somebody... that has the mindset or a frame that revolves around dollars," he conveyed little remorse over terminating an employees or disenrolling children from his program.

Alternatively, in organizations managed by leaders who hold themselves accountable for embellishing others' lives as a manifestation of their spirituality, work itself becomes an expression of their calling. Work is perceived as a way to connect with others (i.e., employees, children, and parents) and to improve people's lives. Systems (policies, procedures, practices, etc.) in these organizations are in place to cultivate relationships as leaders and employees pursue shared (business, personal) core values. As evidenced by Esther's leadership orientation at Careful Charity, the need to increase or achieve a tangible, predetermined outcome/output was lessened by her motivation to lead her preschool as a ministry, first, and then as a (pre)school.

This study revealed a mechanistic leadership paradigm primarily at the franchise preschool. While Milton discussed emotional connections to his work (i.e., "it makes me a better person"), his daily decision-making and practices embraced a mechanistic orientation governed by timeliness, refusal to make modifications to the classroom structure or curriculum to meet the needs of children with disabilities, and the termination of an employee who threatened the preschool's prestigious reputation. Embracing an identity of prestige suggests a "better than" dynamic—an us versus them, the good and the other. Milton's leadership practices were guided by beliefs of economic advantage from operating a "multi-million dollar [preschool] facility" with advanced security technology and other resources. For Milton, this prestigious facility offered preschoolers the best learning curriculum, and, through vigorous advertising, informed families about a variety of the facility's pertinent child care benefits. Such beliefs are commensurate with what Cannella and Viruru (2004) referred to as hypercapitalism:

> a worldview grounded in the belief that money, markets, and power are synonymous and form the foundation for human functioning... [and] can be characterized by (1) interpretations of the world that are entirely based on capital, resources, and markets, (2) a fear of losing material commodities, and (3) a belief that capital (rather than Enlightenment/modernist science) [is] now the solution to human problems. (p. 117)

Canella and Viruru (2004) suggested that children, at a very early age, become agents of hypercapitalism and are reconstructed as political tools. This case study revealed how children functioned as both consumer and commodity for preschools: a consumer of the education provided by the prekindergarten program and one whose performance (as a commodity) solidified or threatened a preschool's survival in the market. Disenrollment decisions across centers were made around notions of "fit" (synonymous to normal), suggesting that preschools are more inclined to serve children who reinforce their leaders' desired identity and organizational goals. Without spiritually guided leadership or a greater moral purpose for the leaders' work, children can become marketplace pawns. As such, enrollment and disenrollment decisions become not only about what preschools can do for a child but also what the child can do for preschools, thus creating classrooms that exclude children on the precedent of difference—difference as disability and children as "good" or "bad" consumers based on what they and parents can do for and to preschools.

## TOWARD DEMOCRATIC EXPERIMENTALISM

*Because imagining other ways of being is the precursor of struggling to achieve them.*
—Peter Moss, 2004, p. 28

Ball and Vincent (2005) argued that preschools operate in and represent a peculiar market environment. They contended that although preschool markets are perceived to be rationally governed, they are laden with emotion. For instance, their research found parents were more concerned with finding and keeping their child enrolled in a preschool that provided caring, nurturing experiences than with curricular or facility considerations. That parents place paramount concern on selecting a preschool or childcare program based on its ability to ensure their child's safety and essential needs is not to suggest cost is of no or lesser significance. Conversely, it demonstrates emotional and financial antagonisms parents must alleviate in order to enroll their child in a preschool or childcare program when, given local market dynamics, choice is dictated by fewer options and affordability, making choice increasingly fictive. The situation is more restrictive and exasperating for parents of children with disabilities (Glenn-Applegate et al., 2010; Hanson et al., 2000; Knoche et al., 2006; Lovett & Haring, 2003). Yet, prekindergarten markets and policies in the United States continue to assume tenets of rational choice theory and hypercapitalistic orientations that play a decisive role in how leaders engage in organizational identity development and disenrollment practices. These assumptions continue to marginalize and exclude children and families that are not perceived to be "good" consumers. Given these realities, the question becomes: How can we reconceptualize preschool markets that embrace diverse social and learning experiences for every child?

To answer this beckoning call, we contend that preschool leaders are best-equipped to challenge marginalizing practices by stimulating discourses that empower themselves and other stakeholders to engage in stentorian projects of reimagination. Our research, predicated on how preschool leaders' decision-making practices affect the experiences and enrollment of children identified or perceived as dis/abled (Jones, 2020; Passero Jones & Jones, 2021), has encouraged us to question deeper the nature of education markets and how they can be otherwise constructed for all children and families. In doing so, it is incumbent upon us all to consider the kind of transformative education we desire for children. Cannella (2008) suggested that revolutionary reconstruction of childhood education should focus on concepts of human respect (value for all beings), multiple realities (diverse perspectives), agency (children as agents of their own lives), radical democracy (analysis of power), and revolutionary action (rooted in notions of social justice and care). Delving deeper into a proposed dramatic shift in education markets, we pivot initially toward rethinking preschool leadership as "leadership within" (McDowall Clark & Murray, 2012) and then propose, as Moss (2009, 2012, 2017) suggested, one alternative market framework: democratic experimentalism.

## Leadership Within

Our findings related to SBL and its influences on the experiences and enrollment of children with diverse needs have yielded an alternative way for us to conceptualize leadership within education markets. Leadership is socially constructed within circumstantial social, cultural, and policy ecologies. Considering the neoliberalism policy frame (standardization, competition, and accountability) undergirding the prekindergarten program in the above study, we considered complex influences that aided (pre)school leaders' decision-making processes. For example, while Maria and Esther—invoking their spiritual beliefs—expressed a desire to include children with diverse needs, they nonetheless resorted to normalizing practices influenced by their identities (business, personal) and interpretations of program policies. As a truth regime (Foucault, 1972 ), children are observed, measured, and judged by accountability tools (state and program policies) and amid teachers' and school leaders' beliefs or sense of identity, making them vulnerable as constructed objects (i.e., a line item on a schools' budget). According to Cannella (2008), such behavior is "an act of injustice" (p. 170). We suggest SBL provides a space to begin challenging normalizing and objectifying practices within education markets.

Considering SBL as a practice that is grounded in leaders' internalized beliefs and values systems, McDowall Clark and Murray (2102) argued for the importance of supporting dimensions of inner (understanding leaders' internal motivations such as spirituality) and diffused (understanding leaders' sense of mutual or shared responsibility across organizations) leadership in early childhood programs. Their research proposed a framework for reconceptualizing early childhood leadership called *leadership within*. This paradigm includes three interweaving features: (a) catalytic agency, (b) reflective integrity, and (c) relational interdependence. Each is unpacked below to help stimulate discussion on reimagining the role of (pre)school leaders.

## Catalytic Agency

Catalytic agency acknowledges the effects one's (a leader's) actions have on the betterment of society. Similar to SBL, catalytic leaders choose not to lead by meting out directives but by articulating shared purpose. The leader's agency, or proactive involvement, becomes catalytic when they harness the communal power of their role to induce broader change. Throughout this leadership process, leaders continually account for the beliefs and values of others in their organizations and consider their work "a shared journey" toward rebuffing the status quo (McDowall Clark & Murray, 2012, p. 35). When guided by spiritual beliefs that recognize and honor humanity and by providing space for teachers to question assumptions about childhood, preschool leaders can disrupt the marginalizing practice of the market.

## Reflective Integrity

Leadership within deems reflection an indispensable component of leadership at the individual and collective level. Leaders with catalytic agency prioritize space and time in schools for themselves and others to engage in reflective integrity, where they interrogate assumptions informing their beliefs, behaviors, and relationships. According to McDowall Clark and Murray (2012), "Leadership without reflection is not true leadership, as without reflection behaviours, actions, events and consequences go unexamined and the process becomes one of exertion of power...misguided leadership...unaware of what is really happening" (pp. 36–37). Similar to Freire's (2012) claim that action without reflection is mere activism or "action for action's sake" (p. 88), leading without reflection reifies marginalizing practices nested in the education market—even if this is not what leaders intend or believe. Reflective integrity permeates critical reflection and informs collective revolutionary action.

For example, when leaders are asked or required to engage in reflective activities that challenge perceived images, notions, and social constructions they hold about the children, such musings can become a source of catalytic agency and be used for instituting radical changes in a preschool. Leaders and other actors can critically consider ways in which children are dis/abled within their spaces (i.e., how curriculum and policies function to normalize ableist practices). Thus, the child (as a being) and her interests can then become reimagined through rights-based discourses, as promoted by the United Nations Convention on the Rights of the Child (United Nations Office of the High Commissioner for Human Rights, 1989), wherein the perspective of the child is acknowledged and valued (Polakow, 2007; Woodrow & Press, 2007). In such a reorientation of policy and pedagogy, practitioners can actively invoke discourses premised on the needs, vulnerabilities, and competencies of children. Reflective integrity, as a leadership within practice, affords opportunity for reimagining children as capable contributors and constructors of knowledge who are worthy of rights, dignity, and respect.

### Relational Interdependence

The final interwoven attribute of leadership within is relational interdependence. This attribute relies on relationships within and across the school to transform schools. In essence, when operating cognitively and emotionally through relational interdependence, leaders affirm "we need each other" (McDowall Clark & Murray, 2012, p. 39) to be effective in creating just, respectful, and dignifying preschooling experiences for all children. Relational interdependence transverses reflective integrity and catalytic agency. Leaders who facilitate a culture of relational interdependence support collaboration within and across their school, collaboration that values each person's input and impact. For example, in childcare and education markets, parents are not typically viewed as participants (Ball & Vincent, 2005; Vincent, 2000; Vincent & Ball, 2006). By acknowledging and valuing parents' perspectives, leaders who embrace relational interdependence will reject the common practice of blaming parents and instead create change by including them as critical partners in reimagining preschool for all children.

## Democratic Experimentalism

Moss (2009) argued that the traditional economic market model, *homo economicus*, is an expression of neoliberalism's deepest values and assumptions, one that particularly considers actors as autonomous and rational utility maximizers in the pursuit of self-interest. He suggested that neither parents nor practitioners in early childhood education programs willingly adopt roles ascribed to them in the market model. We contend, along with Moss (2009), that the problematic nature of the current market model superimposed on preschools can be reenvisioned to promote a new economy of care and democratic experimentalism capable of encouraging increased inclusion of children and families with manifold needs. According to Moss (2009), democratic experimentalism

> presumes a subject is capable and willing to adopt a public as well as a private role, with a sense of social justice and responsibility, and who is a citizen concerned with collective as well as individual well-being, bearing both rights and responsibilities. This subject can be child or adult, children being viewed as agents and rights-bearing citizens in the here and now, whose views and experiences need full expression in the process of democratic participation that are central to this model. Central values of this model are participation, dialogue, trust—and choice. (p. 32)

Furthermore, he proclaimed this model "is a moral ideal and way of life, both personal and collective, that needs constant attention and practice. It is about the inclusion and influence of everyone...it also requires faith in humanity" (p. 30).

We now turn to how democratic experimentalism interacts with tenets of SBL and the leadership within framework to disrupt normalizing and ableist practices. We offer discussion of how this alternative model may operate and be interpreted at various levels of the market (i.e., national/state, local, and school).

### National and State Levels

Democratic experimentalism necessitates collective dialogue for an unwavering national commitment to early education for all children. If done earnestly, this conversation would be geared toward establishing a clear national framework that provides autonomy for state and local levels of the market to make decisions based on their communities' diverse needs. Moss (2009) offered suggestions for how this work could be envisioned and enacted at the national level of the market:

- establishes access to and funding for early childhood programs as an entitlement for all children as citizens;
- positions early education as a public good and responsibility (not a private commodity);
- establishes a framework for curriculum including broad goals, allowing for local interpretation and augmentation; and
- commits to creating and maintaining a well-educated and well-paid workforce.

Finally, Moss (2009) explained that the national level can "articulate a vision for democratic experimentalism" (p. 38) and serve as a reference point for subsequent levels of the market.

### Local Level

Moss (2009) suggested at the local level of a democratic experimental market actors would collectively interpret and augment national and state frameworks. During this process actors would affirm the value of democracy within/across their respective communities and provide support for democratic practices at the preschool level. Furthermore, local officials would actively promote and nurture collaboration between actors within/across various social institutions to create networks and projects advancing democratic practices affecting children and families in local communities.

*School Level*

At the local, site-based level, the preschool, according to Moss (2009), would be responsible for providing four fundamental democratic elements: (a) collective decision-making process about the purposes and practices of the school by all those who are affected by them; (b) collaborative process of "meaning-making" of the work of early education; (c) contesting dominant discourses or regimes of truth to actively unpack assumptions and values; and (d) working toward change through critical reflection, reimagination, and action. Ultimately, it is at this critical level that we contend the leadership within the framework aligns with the elements outlined by Moss (2009) for local implementation of the democratic experimentalism market model.

This study illustrated how prekindergarten policies, enrollment and curriculum practices, and identity (spirituality/prestige) discourses intersected to form decision-making practices around enrollment. Leaders engaged in discursive practices that constructed children in particular ways—ways influenced by state education policies, local market pressures, and facets of their and their schools' desired identity. Moreover, they decided who could and could not participate in the prekindergarten market. We contend that a reimagining of education markets and leaders can challenge discourses and practices that exclude and dehumanize children and families. This reimagination extends from SBL and weaves into frameworks of leadership within and democratic experimentalism. Through these frameworks, we argue decision-making around schooling can become a collective process of inclusion that respects and honors the diverse perspectives and experiences of all children and families.

# REFERENCES

American's With Disabilities Act of 1990, Pub. L. No. 101-336, 104 Stat. 327.

Apple, M. W. (2005). Education, markets, and an audit culture. *Critical Quarterly*, 47(1–2), 11–29. https://doi.org/10.1111/j.0011-1562.2005.00611.x

Ball, S. J., & Vincent, C. (2005). The 'childcare champion'? New Labour, social justice and the childcare market. *British Educational Research Journal*, 31(5), 557–570.

Barnett, S. W. (2005, January/February). Florida screen falls short. *Preschool Matters: A Publication of the National Institute for Early Education Research*, 3(1), 2. https://nieer.org/wp-content/uploads/2016/08/31.pdf

Bush, J. (2004, July 9). [Letter to Glenda E. Hood, Secretary of State].

Cannella, G. S. (2008). *Deconstructing early childhood education: Social justice and revolution. Rethinking childhood* (Vol. 2). Peter Lang Publishing, Inc.

Cannella, G. S., & Viruru, R. (2004). *Childhood and postcolonization: Power, education, and contemporary practice.* Psychology Press.

Creswell, J. (2013). *Qualitative inquiry and research design: Choosing among five approaches* (3rd ed.). SAGE Publications.

Estes, M. B. (2004). Choice for all?: Charter schools and students with special needs. *The Journal of Special Education, 37*(4), 257–267. https://doi.org/10.1177/00 224669040370040501

Florida Administrative Code (F.A.C.) 6M2102c (2010). https://www.flrules.org/gateway/RuleNo.asp?title=Office%20of%20Early%20Learning%20-%20Voluntary%20Prekindergarten%20Education%20Program&ID=6M-8.210

Florida Office of Early Learning. (2015). *Readiness rate search* [Data file]. https://vpkrates.floridaearlylearning.com

Foucault, M. (1972). *The archaeology of knowledge and the discourse on language.* (A. M. Sheridan Smith, Trans.). Pantheon.

Freire, P. (2012). *The pedagogy of the oppressed.* Bloomsbury.

Friedman, M. (1997). Public schools: Make them private. *Education Economics, 5*(3), 341–344.

Glenn-Applegate, K. Pentimonti, J., & Justice, L. M. (2010). Parents' selection factors when choosing preschool programs for their children with disabilities. *Child & Youth Care Forum, 40*(3), 211–231. https://doi.org/10.1007/s10566-010-9134-2

Hanson, M. J., Beckman, P. J., Horn, E., Marquart, J., Sandall, S. R., Greig, D., & Brennan, E. (2000). Entering preschool: Family and professional experiences in this transition process. *Journal of Early Intervention, 23*(4), 279–293. https://doi.org/10.1177/10538151000230040701

Hatch, J. A. (2002). *Doing qualitative research in education settings.* SUNY Press.

Improving Head Start for School Readiness Act of 2007, Pub. L. No. 110-134, 121 Stat. 1363 (2007).

Jennings, J. (2010). School choice or schools' choice? Managing in an era of accountability. *Sociology of Education, 83*(3), 227–247. https://doi.org/10.1177/0038040710375688

Jessen, S. B. (2012). Special education and school choice: The complex effects of small schools, school choice and public high school policy in New York City. *Educational Policy, 27*(3), 427–466. https://doi.org/10.1177/0895904812453997

Jones, R. J. (2020). Variations in experience and meaning: Leadership involvement and identities with special education and disabilities. *International E-Journal of Advances in Education, 6*(17), 184–196.

Keyes, M. W., Hanley-Maxwell, C., & Capper, C. A. (1999). "Spirituality? It's the core of my leadership": Empowering leadership in an inclusive elementary school. *Educational Administration Quarterly, 35*(2), 203–237.

Knoche, L., Peterson, C. A., Edwards, C. P., & Joen, H. (2006). Child care for children with and without disabilities: The provider, observer, and parent perspectives. *Early Childhood Research Quarterly, 21*(1), 93–109. https://doi.org/10.1016/j.ecresq.2006.01.001

Krippendorff, K. (2013). *Content analysis: An introduction to its methodology* (3rd ed.). SAGE Publications.

Lather, P. (1993). Fertile obsession: Validity after poststructuralism. *The Sociological Quarterly, 34*(4), 673–693.

Lovett, D. L., & Haring, K. A. (2003). Family perceptions of transitions in early intervention. *Education and Training in Developmental Disabilities, 38*(4), 370–377.

Maxwell, J. A. (2008). Designing a qualitative study. In L. Bickman & D. J. Rog (Eds.), *The SAGE handbook of applied social research methods* (2nd ed., pp. 214–246). SAGE Publications.

McDowall Clark, R., & Murray, J. (2012). *Reconceptualizing leadership in the early years.* McGraw-Hill Education.

Molloy, K. A., & Foust, C. R. (2016). Work calling: Exploring the communicative intersections of meaningful work and organizational spirituality. *Communication Studies, 67*(3), 339–358.

Moss, P. (2004). Setting the scene: A vision of universal children's space. In Daycare Trust (Ed.), *A new era for universal childcare?* (pp. 19–28). Daycare Trust.

Moss, P. (2009). *There are alternatives! Markets and democratic experimentalism in early childhood education and care* (Working Papers in Early Childhood Development, Number 53). Bernard van Leer Foundation.

Moss, P. (2012). Governed markets and democratic experimentalism. In A. T. Kjørholt & J. Qvortrup (Eds.), *The modern child and the flexible labour market* (pp. 128–149). Palgrave Macmillan.

Moss, P. (2017). Power and resistance in early childhood education: From dominant discourse to democratic experimentalism. *Journal of Pedagogy, 8*(1), 11–32.

National Institute for Early Education Research. (2005, January/February). Florida's new public pre-k screening test raises alarm; It's a 'disturbing' provision, early educators say. *Preschool Matters: A publication of the National Institute for Early Education Research. 3*(1), 7. https://nieer.org/wp-content/uploads/2016/08/31.pdf

Odom, S. L., Vitztum, J., Wolery, R., Lieber, J., Sandall, S., Hanson, M. J., . . . Horn, E. (2004). Preschool inclusion in the United States: A review of research from an ecological perspective. *Journal of Research in Special Educational Needs. (4)*1, 17–49. https://doi.org/10.1111/J.1471-3802.2004.00016.x

Passero Jones, A. C., & Jones, R. J. (2021). Constructing (dis)ability through participations in early childhood markets: Preschool leaders' enrollment decision-making. *Journal of early childhood research, 10*(1), 60–82.

Polakow, V. (2007). *Who cares for our children?: The child care crisis in the other America.* Teachers College Press.

Pruzan, P. (2013). Integrating rationality and spirituality in leadership. *International Journal on Spirituality and Organization Leadership, 1*(1), 33–46.

Section 504 of the Rehabilitation Act of 1973, Pub. L. No. 93-112, § 504, 87 Stat. 394 (1973). https://www.ssa.gov/OP_Home/comp2/F093-112.html

Section 619 of IDEA, 20 U.S.C. § 1419 *et seq.* (2004). https://www.govinfo.gov/content/pkg/PLAW-108publ446/html/PLAW-108publ446.htm

Solocheck, J. S. (2006, July 26). State to test for success of pre-k: A two-part assessment will help show how much prekindergarten helped. But some say the test is flawed and out of context. *St. Pete Times.*

United Nations Office of the High Commissioner for Human Rights. (1989). *Convention on the Rights of The Child.* https://www.ohchr.org/EN/Professional Interest/Pages/CRC.aspx

U.S. Department of Education. (n.d.). *Early Learning.* https://www.ed.gov/early-learning/elc-draft-summary

U.S. Department of Health & Human Services. (n.d.). *Preschool for All.* https://www.acf.hhs.gov/ecd/preschool-all

Vincent, C. (2000). *Including parents? Education, citizenship and parental agency. Inclusive education.* Open University Press, Taylor & Francis Group.

Vincent, C., & Ball, S. J. (2006). *Childcare, choice and class practices: Middle class parents and their children.* Routledge.

Voluntary Prekindergarten Education Program, XLVIII Fla. Stat. §§ 1002-1002.51 -1002.79 (2015).

Weaver-Hightower, M. B. (2008). An ecology metaphor for educational policy analysis: A call for comlexity. *Educational Researcher, 37*(3), 153–167. https://doi.org/10.3102/0013189X08318050

Winston, B. E. (2013). Spirituality at Workplace: Changing Management Paradigm. *International Journal on Spirituality and Organization Leadership, 1*(1), 21–32.

Woodrow, C., & Press, F., 2007. (Re) positioning the child in the policy/politics of early childhood. *Educational Philosophy and Theory, 39*(3), 312–325.

# CHAPTER 13

# SEEING THE ABLE

## ~~Dis~~ability Through the Eyes
## of a Younger Sister

**Molly Greer**
*University of Central Florida*

I had the childhood that kids dream of. I experienced love deeply, had everything I needed and access to what I wanted. I was the youngest child and boasted in the glory of being the baby of the family. My bouncy golden curls, sassy attitude, and infectious smile lit up a room. I had my daddy wrapped around my finger, and I knew just how to play the baby card so that Micah, my brother, would get in trouble instead of me. Everything was exactly how I envisioned a family should be; I had a mom, a dad, and an older brother. Micah and I got along most days. You could find us splashing around in the pool or playing King of the Castle on our playset. Everything was perfect, until that day in 1996. That day is a blur in my mind, not because it was so long ago, but because I was only 4 years old. I couldn't comprehend the events that happened, but from my eyes this is how it looked.

I was enjoying watching the chameleon in the classroom. My preschool teacher had brought her to school that day. My friends and I watched the

*Who Decides?*, pages 311–331
Copyright © 2022 by Information Age Publishing
www.infoagepub.com
All rights of reproduction in any form reserved.

chameleon with great anticipation, but nothing was happening. Mom, who was working upstairs, came into my classroom. This was nothing uncommon; it was a perk of going to preschool in the same building as my momma. I saw Mom grab my backpack and jacket. She called me over to her. Confused and angry, I joined her. She quickly put my light jacket on me and threw my backpack over her shoulder. I had no idea what was going on.

I waved goodbye to my teacher and walked with Mom up the stairs and out the middle entryway. My 4-year-old brain quickly switched from confusion to a sense of adventure. I wondered where we were going, who we were driving to see, and what we were doing. As most young kids, my imagination soared as we drove our normal route home. That was, until we made the wrong turn. "Mommy, we don't go this way." I had ridden this route countless times; we missed the turn by the Biggs, and it was my favorite place to pass. It had a beautiful building.

Mom informed me that we were going to the doctor. I loved going to the doctor and typically mom had a smile on her face. Today that was different. I saw mom wiping something from her eye as she made the final turn into the parking lot. We rushed into the doctor's office and Dad was there. This was not normal. I looked at Dad, ran over to hug him and then saw Micah. He was lying on the big table and looked like he was asleep. I wanted to go see him, but I knew not to wake up Micah. I did not want him to wake up grumpy.

I sat in the room looking at the walls like I always do. The *101 Dalmatians* characters were prancing all over the tan walls. I imagined the movie scrolling in my mind, and waited to go home, wondering why we were there. I was praying I was not getting a shot; I hated shots. Micah woke up and grabbed his head, and the doctor walked in shortly. I was a kid, I didn't know the words spoken, but I saw the faces of Mom and Dad. There was concern in their eyes and Mom started to cry. Whatever they were talking about was not good.

We left the doctor's office and Mom brought both Micah and me home. We pulled in the driveway, I hopped out of the van and ran to the backyard yelling for Micah to join me. Mom stopped me, then said I needed to go inside. Sad, I walked up the stairs to the front door. Micah still wasn't feeling good. He said his eyes hurt to open them and that his head hurt. Mom had him lie on the couch to rest. I went to my room, pulled out some toys, and brought them to the living room. I offered Micah to play with me. He said nothing. Dad came in shortly after.

This was the day that my perfect world shattered and the new normal began. I climbed up on my Little Tikes table like I always had, but today, Micah didn't join me. This day was the start to many days where I played without my brother. Today changed my entire world and I was only four.

As a 4-year-old I couldn't have comprehended the events of that day. I just knew that my world had changed. It wasn't until much later in life that I was able to pinpoint this day in my memories and learned of the events of that day. Micah was in PE and was running around, when he collapsed with a seizure. The school called Mom immediately and that's where the story picked up with me. Mom rushed from work to meet Dad, who had picked up Micah, at the doctor's office. The doctors had told my parents the worst news that parents could hear, that he didn't know what caused the seizure. The sudden onset of seizures was worrisome to the doctors but they had no answers.

Pediatrics sent Micah to a neurologist. The events of this story continue to spiral downhill. The first neurologist sent Micah for a panel of blood tests and scans. Micah spent weeks in and out of doctor's offices, only for the neurologist to discover that Micah had a lesion on his brain. The lesion sat between the occipital lobe and parietal lobe. This neurologist prescribed medication and told my parents there was nothing more he could do. A lesion on a child this young was essentially untreatable and medicine had not experimented on children of Micah's age.

Devastated, my parents sought a second opinion. This is where the story turns from bad to worse. Almost a year after his initial diagnosis, Dr. Holmes took my brother in as his patient. Dr. Holmes assured us that medicine was progressing, but indeed neurosurgery to the extent Micah needed was only experimental at that time. Dr. Holmes walked our family through a challenging several months. The additional testing showed that Micah was having seizures more frequently than we were noticing. He was having multiple petit mal seizures throughout the day and tonic complex focal seizures were a result from a spike in Micah's blood pressure and heart rate due to physical activity or overstimulation. At this time, Micah was only presenting an average of one seizure a day, yet multiple seizures were happening without our knowing.

After about 6 months of working with Dr. Holmes and about a year into this journey, Dr. Holmes referred Micah to Dr. Trevethan and Dr. Warf, at the University of Kentucky, where they took over care. It was under their care that Micah endured weeks of testing in the hospital. As a child, I recalled walking in to visit my brother and seeing wires plugged into Micah's brain. These were in fact EEG leads showing the brain activity of my brother to gain a better understanding of Micah's condition. These images will forever remain in my mind, for seeing Micah in this way not only confused me, but it worried me. My parents were away from me for weeks at a time, and I only got to see my brother two times in the midst of this 2-week testing period. Life was hard, but was soon to get better. The new normal was going to shift one more time.

Micah's team at the University of Kentucky devised a plan. There was an experimental brain surgery that could assist Micah's lesion on his brain. Dr. Warf, his neurosurgeon, was confident that with the complicated surgery, Micah could live a more "normal" life. Dr. Warf and his team operated on my then 10-year-old brother in the summer of 1998, nearly 2 years after Micah's first seizure.

Micah's surgery was a success and about a year after his surgery my mom gave him the last dose of his seizure medication. Since then, 23 years later, Micah has not experienced a seizure. The normalcy in life that Dr. Warf and his team hoped for was a reality for Micah. Micah's life is one of triumph and pressing the limits of medicine. Micah was no longer restricted by seizures. At age 16, he got his driver's license, at 20, he became an emergency medical technician, 22 began driving a semitruck over the road, at 25 met the love of his life, 27 married her, 28 began working for one of the biggest shipping companies in the world, and at 29 welcomed a beautiful little boy into the world. Though Micah's life journey has led him to amazing places, life postsurgery brought new challenges.

At the onset of 1st grade, a year before Micah's diagnosis, my parents were called into school to discuss the possibility that Micah had ADHD. Testing for ADHD happened soon after and though he didn't meet the criteria, my family was now involved in the system of special education. Micah continued falling behind. Micah would frequently be found staring into space and inattentive which ultimately led him to miss a year of education prior to his diagnosis. Micah was given an IEP in first grade for learning disabilities in reading and mathematics. Throughout his diagnosis and treatment, the learning gaps expanded and it seemed as if he lost years of foundational education. We then navigated the life of a student with exceptional needs and I was in the middle.

## THE ROLE OF A YOUNGER SIBLING

### Not the Baby Anymore

I was the baby of the family and I was the only granddaughter on both sides of the family tree. As you can imagine, I was spoiled rotten. I hit the jackpot every Christmas, I wore all the pretty dresses (and hated them!), and I could get away with about anything. Until that day in 1996. On that day my whole world flipped upside down. I went from being the center of attention, in my eyes, to being the one toted along to all the doctor's appointments, or shipped off to a friend's or family member's place to spend a week or two while Micah was dealing with medical tests.

I was not the baby anymore; in a matter of minutes I grew up very fast and the multiple reassignments of my role in the family began. Each reassignment or additional role given to me shaped me into who I am today; they constructed the passions in my heart. My roles as a sibling shift from the younger sibling attributes to being the protector, advocate, and caregiver which are common roles that siblings acquire with a diagnosis such as my brother's (Rossetti et al., 2018). Throughout the next section of this chapter, I will share each change in role and the impacts these had on my education and direction in life. To conclude, I'll share how this journey led me to where I am today and how these experiences are shaping my future research.

## The Protector

The seizures Micah had, which my family saw, were dangerous. The onset typically happened when he was physically active or experienced repetitive bright lights. I wasn't even five yet when Mom and Dad sat me down at the kitchen table and gave me instructions for what to do when Micah experienced a seizure and how to help him when he came out of the seizure. At four years old I became my brother's protector. To this day, I can recall the steps I was supposed to take, how to count my way through his seizure, and the list of questions I had to ask him when he came out of the seizure. Unfortunately, I put this procedure into practice frequently. Micah would have a seizure on average two a week. As a kid I thought this was a lot, yet in reality, I responded to very few on my own. Nonetheless, I was a part of the response team, and each time, it took the whole team.

My most vivid memory of this role occurred right after my 5th birthday. Micah and I were playing with our best friend outside at church. We ran around the parking lot like always, but Micah ignored his warning signs and suddenly he was seizing. Our friend had not experienced Micah's seizures, and he started to panic. I ran to Micah as fast as I could, caught him as he was falling to the ground, I turned him to his side and made sure to put my knee under his head. I started singing my favorite song in my head, and yelled for our friend to go get my mom. This was the first time I did this solo.

I was singing the song when Mom came out, Micah was still seizing. I looked at her and I saw the smile of a proud momma. My song was the timing of the seizure, when I made it to a certain point in the song that's when we called 911. I hadn't made it there yet and Micah finally came out of his seizure. I proceeded to ask him the questions we always asked him, "Who are you?" and down the list to "How is your head?"

My mom grabbed his headache medicine and I walked my brother to the couch in the church where he laid down. I grabbed a blanket for him to cover his face then sat with Micah watching him fade into a shell of himself as he disconnected from the world. Mom and Dad finished their duties and we headed home. I was 5 years old. I was no longer just his sister, I was a trained protector.

Being the protector developed as life progressed. At daycare, I was the first responder, at church I always had an eye on him, and at school I was always checking with his teacher to be sure he was okay. I was scared. I watched my brother have seizures often and I had to be there to help him, to keep him safe.

## The Teacher

Micah's biggest challenges throughout his diagnosis and after surgery were at school. Micah had surgery which impacted portions of the brain that held short-term and long-term memories. Still to this day, he has not recovered some of his memories dating back to his very young childhood. Micah's surgery greatly impacted his ability to retain the information that he was learning and cleared countless banks of foundational education. Micah was given testing shortly after his return to school so that teachers had a better understanding of where he was academically. They confirmed he was at a first-grade level in reading and writing. They also confirmed a mathematics deficit comparable to a second-grade student.

Micah and I would sit together and do homework after school. This is where I received my first taste of teaching. I would work with Micah on various subjects, eager to share what I was learning with my big brother. I was an odd learner in accordance with the standards of teaching at the time. I too struggled with mathematics. My teachers were phenomenal in helping me understand mathematics and teaching me how to use various supports to succeed. I personally needed visual representation of concepts to complete problems, so I was building my toolbox to help my brother out.

Micah's learning gaps grew throughout his education. While I was still in high school and he in college, I would assist him in making sense of assignments, editing papers, providing him with strategies to organize his thinking, and share in the struggle with him. As a teacher to my brother, I found my love for modifying assignments, finding supports for assignments, and for breaking apart the learning process so that he had a chance to succeed.

## The Advocate

Being an advocate is the most influential role that I engaged in as a sibling. I started very young as an advocate for my brother. I attended my first ever IEP meeting during the fall of my first-grade year. I knew nothing about the meeting; I sat in the conference room coloring a picture. Though not engaged directly with the meeting, over the course of 3 years, I watched teachers come together to create a plan for Micah's education. I heard the conversations about how teachers would support Micah at school and then tips for my parents to support him at home. I learned what being an advocate was through this process. It wasn't much later that I got to apply these skills I had just learned.

In middle school his education took a turn for the worse. His case manager frequently canceled meetings, overlooked accommodations, and one year she forgot to hold an IEP meeting. This is where I learned about parent advocacy. I saw my mom, an educator herself, seek resources so that Micah could have access to the best education he could get. I watched Mom advocate for my brother in a way that empowered Micah. Her advocacy skills continued to teach me throughout Micah's high school career.

Through watching my mother, I found myself wanting to advocate for my brother. I started doing research on supports he could have in college, the steps he needed to take to ensure that he received these resources, and I worked with Mom to create a plan that benefitted Micah. My brother was about to be out of the public-school setting and he still needed resources. Through investigation of my own and conversations with the teacher I peer tutored for, along with Mom's conversations with her school's guidance counselor, we learned that Micah needed a 504 or IEP on file his senior year of high school so that he could receive services at the college he wanted to attend.

It was around this time that the school wanted to "graduate" him from special education. Mom and I couldn't understand why a school system would desire for a student that needed supports to leave that system. We couldn't let Micah go to college with no supports. He needed extended time on tests, a reader, technology, and more for him to be successful. Mom did all the advocating at the school level, but it was an honor to assist her in preparing each meeting. This is where I found my love for advocating and teaching. Through the shifts in roles, I was discovering who I was and where my passions were. There was a fire ignited in my heart as a young child and as I progressed through middle and high school my involvement with Micah added fuel to that fire.

Micah is not disabled, he is differently abled. No, he could not translate the thoughts in his head to the paper before him, but he had the most caring heart and would do anything for anyone to ensure that they received the care they needed. Micah's abilities only looked different from those of his peers. Throughout Micah's schooling teachers frequently missed his compassion for others, his ability to bring people together, his friendliness, his musical talent, his desire to care for others, and his loyalty to those he cared about. Instead, his reading, writing, and mathematics disability defined Micah. Teachers only saw the amount of extra work they had to do to support him or the extra required meetings to attend. Because of this, I had to do something to change the narrative. My brother and students with disabilities deserve to be celebrated for their amazing abilities and not be defined by the academics they cannot perform.

This next section will discuss how my journey, being parallel with Micah's, has shaped my teaching and now future research.

## MY STORY: SISTER TO RESEARCHER

My childhood was truly a great childhood, but like many siblings of children with disabilities, I had my challenging times. Reflecting on my childhood, I see my growth and development through the lens of a special education teacher. Though I learned to be a protector, teacher, and advocate, my childhood didn't always have a positive outlook. There were many nights I stayed in grandparents' or family friend's houses crying myself to sleep because I wanted my mom. I spent most of my high school life resenting my brother, and could even admit that I have resentment today.

My high school career was the only time during my education where the support I was providing my brother frustrated me. As a sibling of someone with a brain injury, the feeling of resentment and the feeling of grief is common, and typically felt at the time of diagnosis or injury (Tyerman et al., 2019), yet for me life didn't slow down enough for me to process my emotions until Micah left for college. It was in these 4 years that I grew weary of the life that I was thrust into and I wanted to focus on me. As a freshman, in high school Micah was a freshman in college. I assisted with editing his papers, sharing tips on note-taking, and helping him organize his thoughts for various assignments. It was at this time that I was trying to explore who I was and who I wanted to be.

I had challenges of my own in high school that revolved around boys, marching band, and other teenager problems. At this point in time in my life, I wanted to be me. I didn't want the responsibilities that I had once had. It was sophomore year that I had that moment of relief as Micah had ended his college career and pursued becoming an EMT. Even though Micah had transitioned into a job where I could no longer help, I was still angry at the reputations that I had to fight, the constant comparison that I had to overcome, and the childhood I was realizing that I had missed out on. It was in high school where I wanted to be the center of my parents' world again, I was the only one in school I deserved it (right?).

I was not always Micah's biggest supporter, yet these moments of resentment helped me define who I was and the passions that were ignited in my heart. Micah's medical journey impacted the family; for me, though, it changed my future.

I grew up like most 1990's children. I was one of the lucky girls who had a pretend beauty salon in my bedroom and I had this amazing veterinary kit.

When asked what I would be when I grew up, I would quickly blurt out, "I want to be a veterinarian." I loved animals and I wanted to care for the sick ones. That was until I saw the journey my brother had with his education. I was a protector, teacher, and advocate for my brother all throughout his primary and secondary education, yet my story doesn't end there.

Micah's junior year of high school was a year that impacted my future career decisions. Micah's IEP was due for an annual review and his case manager wanted to "graduate" him from special education by the following year. I heard mom and dad discussing this transition and I became very upset. Did these teachers not see what a struggle school is for him? Do they not understand the supports our family was providing him at home? Do they not know that if he is released from special education services he would have no supports at the university he wanted to attend?

I saw failure in the special education system, and my brother was the recipient of the consequences of this failure. To graduate my brother as a non-special education student, the school wanted to release him from the program. His supports would no longer be available to him and he would no longer have the tools available to him so that he could succeed. As his sister, I watched this unfold and it broke my heart. I saw Micah's journey in a different light. I had asked the special education teacher, I peer tutored for, to help me understand what was happening, where she replied that the school's decision could be due to upcoming funding changes. The potential that money came before the needs of my brother broke my heart.

It was around this time that I was beginning to think about college. I found myself changing my searches from schools of veterinary medicine, to schools of education. My brother's story had shaped who I was becoming and where my heart's passions were. It was during my eighth-grade year, Micah's senior year, that I decided I wanted to be a special education teacher. I wanted to show the love that he received in elementary school, fix the disorganization he experienced in middle school, and right the wrongs of his high school teachers. It was throughout Micah's journey that I saw the positives and the negatives of special education. Experiencing these changed my whole life. Special education had to be different, even if it just started with me, one teacher.

As I graduated with my undergraduate degree, a professor challenged me to think about why I chose special education. In that reflection I found four themes in the answer to why I chose to foster learning of students with exceptional needs.

## MY WHY

It's simple. Micah is my "Why," right? But it isn't that simple. Yes, my brother is a phenomenal man; he endured a life-altering surgery. Yet, my "why" is a true reflection of more than just my brother. My "why" involves his teachers, the school community, our community, bouts of failure, and our family. Teaching is a career that is heavily influenced on a person's lived experiences and the experiences of those close to them (Lortie, 2020). The choice to teach special education and now pursue my PhD isn't because of Micah's surgery and learning disability; it was because of every aspect of our lives from 1996–2006, when Micah graduated.

## The Power of a Teacher

Teachers were the lifeline for my family. Micah's first seizure happened at school and other seizures followed over the 2 years before surgery. Micah had phenomenal teachers in elementary school. These teachers came together to not only support my brother, but to support his family, including me. Many days I would go to after-school care and not see my brother anywhere, which panicked me. Then I would see Mrs. Watkins walk in, she would sit down next to me and let me know that Micah was sleeping in her tub, but he was okay.

Mrs. Watkins made the effort every time Micah had a seizure to let me know after school, because I would not see him in aftercare. As his sister, that already greatly worried about him, I appreciated this. What she did beyond this is what inspired me to be the best teacher I could be. Micah had migraine headaches after his seizures. Sound and light hurt his head even with the medication he was given. Mrs. Watkins would ensure that Micah was given his medication, then allow him to nest down in an old clawfoot bathtub she had as a cozy reading spot in her room. Micah would cover his head with the pillows, and she would turn the lights off in the classroom; then she continued instruction.

Mrs. Watkins's sainthood doesn't end with her physical care of Micah. After the first seizure Micah had in her class, she realized that he was missing hours of instruction to sleep off the headache, so she called my mom and asked if she could work with Micah during after-school care, so that he didn't fall behind. Mrs. Watkins had my brother in her classroom at least 3 days a week to help him catch up on instruction he had missed because he had a seizure. She selflessly put aside her planning and preparation time after school to help my brother. I have memories of Mom and I walking down to pick up Micah from Mrs. Watkins, and there she would be with the gentlest smile on her face, calmly working with Micah on math or reading 2 hours after school had ended.

Mrs. Watkins saw my brother's vulnerability and needs, and without hesitation modified her curriculum to meet those needs. It is through this flexibility and care that Mrs. Watkins changed my brother's life. Nel Noddings

(1995) refers to this level of care as a supporting structure, where the teacher meets the students where they are and builds instructional practices to support the student's learning. In a recent conversation with Micah, we discussed Mrs. Watkins and how she impacted his educational career, his one simple statement reflects Neddings' concept of care, "She did something for me that no teacher had to do. She cared for me and that is why she is my favorite teacher." Mrs. Watkins continued to care for my brother in a way that inspired me.

She is a saint, and Mrs. Watkins is a major reason that I chose education. She would hug Micah and encourage him, at the same time hug my mom and remind her that we would make it through this together, and finally she would hug me and remind me that we are taking care of my big brother. Micah was blessed with Mrs. Watkins, and I am fortunate that she left her fingerprint on my heart. Mrs. Watkins's care and love for my brother

Micah also had a phenomenal special education teacher in elementary school, Mrs. Kortum. She and Mrs. Watkins worked closely together to ensure that Micah's needs were being met, but also worked with Mom and Dad to ensure that she was providing them with supports for home. Mrs. Kortum had that same gentle smile. She would make sure to be up to date on transformers so that she could interact with Micah and his interests. She would smile at me in the hallway and when Micah had a seizure she would remind me that he was okay.

Mrs. Kortum managed Micah's IEP, and as a child I didn't understand what that meant, but in his IEP meetings I could hear her concern for my brother, and her advocacy for him. She was the driving force behind finding the appropriate accommodations and modification for Micah, as well as being his service provider. She and Mrs. Watkins co-taught before co-teaching was popular in the schools. Mrs. Kortum showed me the love and compassion a special educator needs to have for their students. To this day, when I run into her at the local grocery, she still inquires about my brother and my family.

These teachers were great examples of the love of a teacher as well as the heart of the teacher. I saw the flexibility and compassion paired with a genuine desire to impact students in these ladies, and through their teaching I saw my brother grow. I wanted to be that teacher, and because of their example, I was able to become as close to them as possible while adding my personal touch.

## The Power of a School Community

My elementary school holds many great memories on my educational journey. I walked into school daily and felt cared about and I knew that my teachers would do anything for me. The administration at the time was caring and invested in my family along with many other families. Camden Station, in Crestwood, Kentucky, ensured that every student felt like they belonged in the school community and that each student understood their worth.

I can't speak for my brother in regard to the school community, for I wasn't aware of this concept until much later in life. Upon reflection on the kind of community I wanted my dream school to have, I realized I was pulling inspiration from my elementary school community. When I walked into school, there were always adults smiling and excited to greet me; my teachers showed that they loved teaching, and I knew that if anything were to happen, I was safe. I only knew school with the looming of Micah's seizures and his disability, yet I never felt singled out because my brother was "that student."

It was quite the opposite. Camden Station rallied behind my family. My family formed close relationships with office staff, administration, special education teachers, and general education teachers. The Greer family and Camden Station Elementary became a team. It is this school and family community that created a vehicle for change (Epstein, 1995). This school/family collaboration empowered my family and allowed each of us, including me, an active part in my brother's education; a reason for my career and life choices. The ability of the school community to encourage and innovate gave my family the peace of mind that Micah's needs would be taken care of, as well as my needs. Elementary school provided me with a network of help if I were to need it. The school community allowed for personal growth and growth with my family. In the midst of the chaos happening at home, I was safe at school and I had a team of teachers supporting me, too.

The transition from elementary school to middle and high school was a bit more challenging. In elementary school I wasn't just "Micah's sister," I was Molly, which is very important when it comes to being a sibling of a student with a disability. I was not defined by the struggles my older brother had. As I transitioned to middle school, I was now "Micah's little sister." It isn't a title I was ashamed of, but it left an air around me that some teachers didn't want to associate themselves with. The reality is, Micah was a student with learning disabilities and I was a gifted and talented student, but because of the label, I had to work harder than most to show my skills.

This school community began to wear on me. I was a student that had perfect grades, no late work, and a spotless referral record. The constant comparison to my brother impacted that. I became the perfectionist. Some teachers didn't see me as an individual, but more as an extension to my brother. The celebration of my skills stopped in sixth grade, and never returned. This shift in school community continued through high school, and though my brother was never a "bad" student, he was a challenge.

I was Micah's little sister, and that now influenced the care that teachers had for me. The ethics of care that was once fueling my passion to learn had shifted. In elementary school teachers nurtured me as a mother would nurture their children (Noddings, 2013), yet in middle school that nurture quickly faded and the support I once thrived on was shifted to comparison. Ethics of care is a choice of active virtue; the natural sense of caring and then the ability to respond to that caring feeling (Noddings, 2013). I felt, as a student, that my sibling had impacted the support that was actively given to me. Was this a shift in the school culture? Or was it how I was seen as a middle school student? That answer I may never know, as a student I felt it was due to the relation to Micah and it caused turmoil in my heart.

I fought daily to prove my worth as a student, and to this day still don't know whether I ever won the battle. A school culture that was vibrant and life-giving for my family in elementary school shifted to dull and condescending in middle and high school. For some, this would have negatively impacted their academics. For me, it fueled me to make a change. School climates of my middle and high school influenced how I cultivated community within my classroom, with siblings of my students, and with parents.

## The Power of Failure

Failure. One word that I hate to hear. Failure is filled with negative connotations. Yet, in my story, failure had more positive power than negative. It wasn't the failure of Micah that was an issue, but it was the failure of teachers, the special education system, and the medical community. Micah struggled to write. Math didn't make sense to him and reading words on a page was too much for his brain to process, but that did not make him a failure. That made him a learner. Missed IEP meetings, lack of accommodations, teacher attitude, and lack of special education support were failures brought about by a culmination of a district learning Micah's needs and teachers learning on their own journey as a teacher.

We saw failures in many forms. The beauty of each of these failures is that each prompted more growth in our family and in the school system. In middle school, one of Micah's case managers missed an IEP meeting, nearly making the district out of compliance. Potentially an oversight or the stress of too many students on their caseload. Middle school was also a time where accommodations weren't effectively given or documented. In high school, data collection on Micah's IEP goals and his accommodation use did not happen. Again, this could be a direct result of overburdened or overworked teachers striving to meet the learning needs of all students.

These issues could be a result of under-prepared teachers, under-supported teachers, or the school culture. Impacts of new legislation, economic impact, teacher shortage, and teacher preparation can also contribute. As a member of the school and district community, I am thankful that the culture once experienced, seems to be a distant memory. Each aspect is important to be evaluated, and each aspect drives who I am today and my research agenda.

These failures drastically impacted my brother's education. This chapter title is Seeing the Able, because my brother was defined by his disability, not his ability, in middle and high school. Those 7 years wore heavily on the family. I was tired of seeing my family beaten down by teachers telling my mom that she didn't know what she was talking about, or the system not providing the supports that Micah needed. I was tired of seeing my brother struggle, and I was tired of feeling forgotten in the middle of it.

Failure in Micah's story ignited a fire in me. As I entered into my undergraduate studies, I knew that I wanted to change how teachers and administration saw students with disabilities. Through their failure I found my strength. I had seen the struggles my family endured throughout those years, so that when I entered a classroom I had a novel viewpoint.

Living through these moments of failure gave me a greater understanding of what my class's families were experiencing. I am thankful that Micah had the supports at home to help him overcome obstacles, but not every student has access to that. These understandings directed every conversation, every IEP meeting, every service provider meeting, and every interaction with families. I was not going to let these events happen to the families I served as a teacher.

## The Power of Family

Micah's journey was long. It took 2 years from his first noticeable seizure for him to have surgery, and after that, he navigated the remainder of his school years with a label, a disability. This was a challenge for my family. My parents were learning how to care for a son with a seizure disorder with no hope of finding a resolution for the issue. My parents were then teaching extended family, Micah's friends' parents, and church family how to react when Micah had a seizure.

Our perfect family was crumbling and all my parents could do was trust God for guidance and advocate for their son. From 1996–1998 our family grew from the four of us to an entire community of people composed of our extended family and our church family. Our church family rallied around us, offering to care for me while Micah was at appointments or had his hospital stays. Our extended family supported us coming in for appointments, transporting me back and forth from the hospital over an hour away so that I could see my family.

Our family continued to grow over the course of Micah's education, as many families do grow. People came into our lives teaching us something new, offering us support. Looking back on the many years of Micah's journey, I have experienced this beautiful chaotic and non-blood related family. Micah's journey was a challenge for my parents and for him, but as a sibling, I struggled on a different level.

I saw everything that was happening in the house. As many children experiencing trauma, I became the peacemaker of the family. At such a young age, I thought I had to fix things so that Mom and Dad didn't have so much stress. It wasn't until Ta and Randy came along that I realized the burden I was taking on as a kid. This couple invested their time and energy into me. My parents had gained two additional members of their community, ones they love and appreciate; I had gained bonus parents, ones I knew would be there for me through even the toughest times of my life.

I speak of Ta and Randy because they picked up on the stress of my role and the impact it was having on me long before my parents did. Meeting through church in 2000, Randy played bass guitar under the direction of my mother, the minister of music. Randy made a comment one day that he and his wife Tammy (We call her Aunt Ta) had no plans for spring break. My parents offered the couple an invitation to join us on vacation and a beautiful friendship grew. This is a unique relationship. Ta and Randy came into our lives after Micah's initial surgery, yet during some challenging times in his educational journey. Ta taught at a local high school as a resource teacher and Randy worked as a factory worker. Randy's journey is a story of its own, moving from building cars to social work, to an emotional and behavior disabilities classroom teacher, to an assistant principal. His schooling and mine happened around the same time, which provided a great support for both of us.

I was 8 years old when I first met this couple. We have many memories together. We have shared over 20 years of vacations, Sunday lunches, heartbreaks, celebrations, and more. These two people changed my world. Ta would see me trying to be perfect and remind me that my family loved me because of me, that I didn't have to fix things. I was able to be a kid around this couple. They invested in me and my brother equally, they supported my passions, came to my basketball games, my marching band competitions, encouraged my baking addiction (I am sure the sweets they received were a bonus!), and challenged me to be a kid and an individual. They saw me. Ta and Randy both poured into my life. Offering support and love as a child, yet that didn't cease as I have grown and began my journey as an educator.

As an adult, I still cherish the late-night chats around a campfire where they invest in me, challenge me, and encourage me. I am fortunate that our lives merged because of a random vacation invitation and cherish all of the love they have given me. Watching their interactions with me, even today, I try to implement what I have learned from them. Speaking life into the siblings and the parents is my main goal as someone who interacts with families.

Family is one of the biggest sources of my "Why." Without the support and guidance of our family, we would not have walked through the valley with as much grace as we did. Without family, I would not understand how systems outside the nuclear family influence students. Without family, my dreams that I am pursuing were at risk of being pushed aside.

Family is a concept that is unique to each person. For me family includes many that are not blood relatives. I have more people in my family that are not related, than those that are. Since the concept of family changes from person to person, it is important to understand that there isn't a wrong type of family or a right type of family. Family, in my terms, is the support you have around you, those that are there for you. This family could be small or large. Whoever they are, they are perfect for you.

As a teacher, I made sure to understand who was in the "family." I wanted to know the immediate family and those that were in close friend circles that students would interact with, for these people were the support groups. A strong family led to great outcomes for both myself and my brother, and my goal was to empower other families to include their tribe in the raising of their students.

## My Why in Action

My bachelor's degree is in moderate to severe special education and in elementary education and I held these themes close to my heart. I applied for eight jobs by the time I had walked across the stage at graduation, and after five of those jobs offered positions, I was gainfully employed only two days after I graduated. I went into each interview ready to share my story, and ready to share how I was going to change exceptional education. With each interview, I became more excited to be in the center of change.

When I received the call from my first-choice school, I knew this was where I needed to be. An empty classroom and seemingly unlimited resources were at my fingertips. This specific school nor the district had ever had a classroom like mine and they trusted this fresh graduate from Morehead State University to make a difference. I was so thankful for this 1 year. I made connections with paraprofessionals, administrators, and families in this year. I allowed my story (experience?) to drive every decision I made; how I interacted with families, siblings, service providers, and how I taught students. After 1 year, I chose to move back home and give back to the community who fostered the growth of my skills and dispositions.

I started my new job at Camden Station Elementary School, the place my journey with education and special education started. In my interview the principal asked me, "How do you plan to teach a group of students with significant special needs?" I took a deep breath and my heart spilled out before the interview committee:

I plan to teach the needs of the learner so that their passions and strengths have the opportunity to be seen. Each student has a unique ability and it is my job to figure out how to bring their ability to the forefront. A student's value does not come from what they cannot do, it comes from what they can do. So, each day I will ask myself, how can I foster growth in their abilities? I will also challenge you and families to take the same mindset.

One of the teachers in the interview wrote down my response word for word and gave it to me on my first day in the building. She informed me that this mindset was what swayed the interview committee to hire me instead of the inhouse hire.

This mindset is a direct consequence of Micah's journey and what I learned from those years. I shared this story with families at Camden and ensured that I would do everything so that their students saw success. I built great relationships with families and students, so much so that siblings would want to peer tutor and bring their friends. Provision to be innovative was granted to me and I was changing exceptional education instruction for the better. I saw my "Why" unfolding before my eyes.

I experienced life-changing medical issues during my fifth year of teaching. I ended up in the emergency room with life-threatening blood clots. Three weeks later and a transition to The Ohio State University, I underwent a rare lifesaving open heart surgery to remove clots that had rubberized in my lungs. Though the medical journeys of my brother and myself were not at all related, it was the influence of my cardiothoracic surgeon that challenged me to evaluate the impact I wanted to make and the steps I was taking to get there. Heading into surgery, before the anesthesia began making me drowsy, my surgeon looked at me and asked, "Have you made the impact on the world that you dreamed of making?" I couldn't say yes, I had much more to do, I shook my head no. It wasn't until Day 2 of recovery that he came into the room and said to me, "You made it through this, now go change the world." In the same conversation he told me that my current teaching position was no longer the best place for me due to the physicality of my job. It was then my world shattered before me. What was I going to do if I couldn't be in the classroom?

I am thankful for the 16 inches of blood clots. It put me in a position to leave the classroom so that I could pursue my PhD, a change I wasn't quite ready to consider prior to surgery. My "Why" shaped my story and it is still shaping it today.

## FUTURE RESEARCH AND TEACHER PREPARATION

Today, I am writing this as an exceptional education PhD student at the University of Central Florida, with a focus on math instruction. I would not be here without Micah. Micah's story wasn't just his own. He was the main character, but we were all impacted by his story. I would never wish for his story to be different, for his story revealed my identity. I have shared his story, my story, and some reasons why I chose special education. I want to further share with you how Micah's ability is shaping my future in research and future career aspirations.

### Shaping the Future of Research

I watched my brother struggle in the academic areas of mathematics, reading, and writing. I was very good at providing supports for him in the area of reading and writing, yet I was lost on how to support him in mathematics. Like Micah, I struggled with mathematics as well and the thought of having to go to math class made my stomach churn. It wasn't until I was in college that I had a professor who taught me how to do various mathematical processes where I could understand them. It was her patience and method of instruction that allowed me to develop the confidence to compute mathematical problems and also to teach them.

My future research direction involves mathematical instruction and students with mathematical learning disabilities. In education, mathematical disabilities are considered one category and all given similar treatment. It is my goal to help separate and categorize mathematical disabilities, and help develop specific strategies for teachers to use while teaching students with math disabilities.

My future research also includes gaining more understanding of mathematical anxiety in teachers and students. Through understanding the anxiety and providing supports for teachers and students with mathematical anxiety, a teacher's mathematical instruction strengthens and a student's ability to learn mathematics is not hindered by the fear of failure that is often associated with it.

The construction of IEP mathematical goals and supports is my final research direction and future dissertation topic. My goal is to understand the mathematical language used in the IEP for students with mathematical disabilities. I am looking to uncover if specific language indicates success of the student in mathematics.

### Preparing Teachers

Entering my PhD program, I wanted to influence teacher preparation, specifically how higher education is preparing exceptional education educators. Teachers, good and bad, heavily influenced my brother's educational journey. It is important for future educators to have a solid understanding of what exceptional education is, and also how to support students and families effectively. Throughout my undergraduate career, I received a strong foundational understanding of exceptional education and elementary education academic concepts. My training in college combined with my personal experience made me a strong candidate for any teaching position.

As I graduate from my program and begin teaching, I will focus on how teachers are prepared for the classroom, allowing them opportunities to enter their educational communities to be involved with teachers and students. Through bringing together a community and university, we have the opportunity to involve stakeholders in the teacher preparation process. Future teachers have the ability to be in the community teaching, serving, and learning while the community is benefiting from the bright minds of the teachers through various means. I hope to be involved in a university seeking to provide opportunities for future teachers such as tutoring programs, reading buddies, mentors, best buddies, and more. Bringing together a community and university has the potential to better both future teachers as well as community education efforts.

The only way to address the problems I saw in my brother's education was to become a teacher and start with me. I was innovative in the classroom, implementing technology, video modeling, and going above and beyond as many teachers do for the hope that I could connect to students. I spent hours in collaboration with my speech language pathologist, the district speech language pathologist, and our district moderate to severe disabilities coach designing, creating, and implementing a class-wide core vocabulary board. One where all students had the opportunity to respond and interact at whichever ability level of communication they were presently at. I welcomed co-teaching with a variety of service providers to ensure that students not only had the supports they needed but also saw collaboration and teamwork. I had the opportunity to implement the lessons taught to me and implement them to the best of my abilities. Finally, I wasn't afraid to try something new knowing that each attempt could either fail or succeed.

To continue the change, I want to prepare future educators to do more than I could do during my 5 years of teaching. Teachers have the power to change the world of all students and families; it is my hope to bring my experiences alongside the curriculum I'll be teaching to prepare future students to thrive in the classroom.

## CLOSING THOUGHTS

Who defines disability? This is the wrong question to ask. Education should ask, "Who defines ability?" Our world seems to fixate on what others can't do to the extent that some lose focus on what an individual can do. Knowing my brother's limitations (math, reading, and writing learning disabilities), what would you expect him to be now, 23 years later? I asked this of a couple of his teachers and some of their responses would shock you.

"Micah would be a wonderful nurse!"

"Micah is probably working somewhere he can do simple tasks."

"Oh Micah! I can see him being a first responder."

These are three responses from teachers he had throughout his educational career. Two of these teachers saw my brother's ability, and one of them defined him by the lack of his ability. What do you think? Where is he now? Micah is a highly desired over-the-road truck driver at one of the biggest shipping companies in the world. His ability, his heart, his drive, his compassion, and his desire to be the best he could be led him to this place. He was recently awarded a pin for being a 2020 Hero, because he went to work every day and delivered COVID-19 vaccines to some of the hardest hit areas. Some of his teachers were right, he has the heart to change the world, to care for and protect those around him, and to live the life he was called to live.

So, let me ask you again, who defines ability? If we had believed the teachers in middle and high school, Micah's life would not be as fruitful and impactful as it is. It isn't a teacher's job to see a disability. It is the teacher's job to see areas in which a student needs support and support them, as well as see the areas of strength and allow those to grow as well.

As educators, our calling is to ensure that every student succeeds and understand that every student's success does not look the same. It is not our place to define someone by a labeled disability. It is our role to see who the individual is and what their strengths are so that they see success every day.

As teachers, support staff, administration, and all those who foster the education and growth of students, I urge us to see our students as humans with unbounding ability. Each student has their own challenges to overcome, and we are here to provide the best accommodations and modifications to ensure that they have the greatest opportunity to shine. I learned from Micah's journey, that the teacher that saw his abilities provided the most access to education and they were the ones that left the biggest footprints on our hearts.

As we enter our classrooms, schools, or offices, I challenge us to look for the ability of our students, but also look for ways to connect to siblings, parents, and families. For these connections are vital for student success and for families to feel the value of their voice in the education of their students.

My final thought to leave with you today is to thrive in the midst of failure. Failure is inevitable, it's essential to the process of learning. Albert Einstein once said, "Failure is success in progress." We have a beautiful position as teachers, we can see our progress through victories and failures and we have students that learn from both. I strive to live in the lessons I have learned but bring my students into it, when appropriate. It is through our growth we become more effective and impactful teachers. Seek to see each student's amazing and beautiful abilities. You could be the only person they encounter that day that believes in their ability, and that can change the life of that student.

## REFERENCES

Epstein, J. L. (1995). School/family/community partnerships. *Phi delta kappa, 76*(9), 701.

Lortie, D. C. (2020). *Schoolteacher: A sociological study.* University of Chicago Press.

Noddings, N. (1995). Teaching themes of care. *Phi Delta Kappa, 76,* 675–675.

Noddings, N. (2013). *Caring: A relational approach to ethics and moral education.* University of California Press.

Rossetti, Z., Harbaugh, A. G., & Hall, S. A. (2018). Patterns of adult sibling role involvement with brothers and sisters with intellectual and developmental disabilities. *Journal of Developmental and Physical Disabilities, 30*(4), 527–543. https://doi.org/10.1007/s10882-018-9600-6

Tyerman, E., Eccles, F. J. R., Gray, V., & Murray, C. D. (2019). Siblings' experiences of their relationship with a brother or sister with a pediatric acquired brain injury. *Disability and Rehabilitation, 41*(24), 2940–2948. https://doi.org/10.1080/09638288.2018.1482506

# STUCK IN A POOR POST-SCHOOL OUTCOMES LOOP FOR STUDENTS WITH SIGNIFICANT DISABILITIES

## What We Can Learn From Arizona

**Erica S. McFadden**
*Independent Scholar*

**Julie Whitaker**
*Independent Scholar*

## ABSTRACT

Arizona's high schools have consistently measured student success based on ableist notions of academic success, while post-school outcomes for students with significant disabilities continue to deteriorate. In this chapter, we review findings from a 2015 Arizona study that surveyed 224 parents and guardians and 634 high school students with disabilities across 17 school districts. The goal of this study was to learn about students' experiences at school, and how

*Who Decides?*, pages 333–356
Copyright © 2022 by Information Age Publishing
www.infoagepub.com
All rights of reproduction in any form reserved.

these experiences were helping students and parents prepare for life beyond high school. The study also examined what variables education administrators could control that would lead to increased youth self-efficacy, and ultimately, improved post-school outcomes.

The overall finding was that Arizona's education system and other systems of student support suffered from overall lowered expectations for youth with disabilities due to generally ableist attitudes exhibited in the academic setting. These low expectations contributed to students' low levels of confidence and performance and eventually to poor post-school outcomes. In contrast, the study found there was a common theme among the districts, charter schools, private schools, providers, and businesses that were actively working to overcome barriers faced by students with significant disabilities—leadership's strong belief in students' "abilities" beyond the academic context. The collective goal and definition of success should be to build academic, vocational education, socialization, and employment skills and opportunities among *all* students; not just those who are deemed "able." This chapter seeks to reframe the conversation by focusing more on strengthening post-school outcomes as opposed to solely focusing on academic success promoted through an ableist lens.

Arizona faces an emerging trend that has gone largely unnoticed. In 2019, one of every two Arizona students with intellectual disabilities (ID) reported through the state's post-school outcomes (PSO) survey they were not engaged in any activity 1 year after exiting high school. They are effectively disconnected, continuing a trend of economic and community exclusion that tends to last throughout their lives. Over the last several years, there has been a federal movement to improve student outcomes like these, but where does Arizona stand? What are we currently doing to move the needle, and what do we still need to do? It is critical that high schools are prepared to educate and train youth with significant disabilities for life beyond high school.

This chapter begins by discussing key federal initiatives, which were designed to improve post-school outcomes—the federal Workforce Innovation and Opportunity Act (WIOA) of 2015 and the Individuals With Disabilities Education Act (IDEA) of 2004. Next, using data from the Arizona Department of Education (ADE) PSO from 2015 to 2019, we tracked the variations in engagement, employment, education, and other postsecondary opportunities for students enrolled in special education services. Based on a brief review of theoretical literature, we then argue that a school's construct of what "success" is and who is "able" limits the opportunities available to many students with disabilities and negatively impacts post-school outcomes. Making good grades and testing well on academic achievement tests are criteria that do not by themselves translate into vocational and life success for many students. And if some students are not able to meet these arbitrary definitions based on a school's perception of "ability," then schools, staff—and at times—families, lower expectations for these students.

To make the case on how the ableism construct presents itself in schools, this chapter then explores data from the 2015 Arizona *Graduation Cliff* study (McFadden et al., 2015) to better understand what and how certain variables may impact post-school outcomes in schools both statewide and nationally and how these variables are impacted by ableism. Finally, we close with a discussion of best practices—many of which are occurring nationally. These models have actively tackled the epistemology of what "ability" looks like for students with significant disabilities and what this has meant for their outcomes beyond high school.

## BACKGROUND: NATIONAL POLICY AND POST-SCHOOL OUTCOMES

There are a few key federal initiatives that were created to improve post-school outcomes—WIOA and IDEA. One of the goals of WIOA is to increase individuals with disabilities' access to high-quality workforce services to prepare them for integrated, competitive employment. Under WIOA, youth with disabilities are to receive extensive pre-employment transition services (Pre-ETS) before they are deemed "unemployable." Pre-ETS in Arizona is a state-sponsored career discovery and job readiness service that helps students with disabilities prepare for future employment. Pre-ETS workshops address such topics as job exploration counseling, work-based learning, counseling on postsecondary and training opportunities, work readiness training, and self-advocacy instruction.

In addition, IDEA mandates schools to prepare students with disabilities for adult employment, postsecondary education, independent living, and community participation. IDEA states that transition services "is designed to be within a results-oriented process, that is focused on improving the academic and functional achievement of the child with a disability to facilitate the child's movement from school to post-school activities" (IDEA 2004, Part B, 614, [d][1][A][VIII]; §300.43[a][1]). Yet, it has fallen short of meeting these goals.

In response to this void, the U.S. Department of Education spearheaded and funded many best practice programs that targeted predictors of post-school success. The National Technical Assistance Center on Transition (NTACT) identified more than 20 predictors of post-school employment, education, and independent living success for students with disabilities based on both promising and evidence-based practices. Some of these predictors include community experiences, inclusion in general education, interagency collaboration, paid employment/work experience, parental expectations and involvement, self-advocacy/self-determination, self-care/

independent living skills, social skills, and student support (NTACT, 2019a; Mazzotti et al., 2014).

Yet, even with all of these positive actions, Arizona's post-school outcomes remain stagnant with not much changing over the last 5 years. ADE began conducting a PSO survey in 2015, which tracks students' community engagement 1 year after graduating/exiting secondary education. Participants are asked to report on their level of community engagement. Survey options are "competitive employment," "postsecondary education," "other postsecondary education" (training/certificate program), "other employment," or "not engaged."

Overall results show that "not engaged" among all students with disabilities have remained fairly constant—from 27% in 2015 to 26.3% in 2019. Approximately 23% of students with disabilities enroll in higher education and that statistic has also remained stagnant over time. Competitive employment rates, however, have dropped from 36% in 2015 to 30.8% in 2019. The statistics become even more abysmal when analyzed by disability type. Among individuals with intellectual disabilities (ID), competitive employment rates have also dropped from 19% in 2015 to 15.4% in 2019; and higher education has only slightly increased from 4% to 5% over that same time span. The disconnection rate for this population, however, has remained at a staggering 50.3% (ADE, 2019).

These low outcomes are mirrored in employment statistics for the state. Data from the American Community Survey (ACS) indicate that working-age adults with disabilities are employed at a much lower rate than working-age adults without disabilities. Among those with disabilities, individuals with cognitive disabilities have the lowest rate of employment. ACS data show that in 2017, across the nation as a whole, 74.8% of persons with no disability were employed, while only 36.3% of individuals with a disability and 27.1% of individuals with a cognitive disability were employed. Similar disparities exist within Arizona, where in the same year, 72.7% of individuals without a disability, 36% of individuals with any kind of disability, and 26.3% of individuals with a cognitive disability were employed.

The disconnectedness of this population, especially among those with cognitive or ID, coupled by its growing number and sheer size should be a great cause for concern to the state. According to ADE enrollment numbers, more than 11% of Arizona's public high school students had disabilities in 2019. As more students are identified for services, enrollment of special education students in Arizona public schools has risen by 25.3% since 2003—significantly higher than the 18.6% total growth of the rest of the student population. In fact, in the 2019–2020 school year there were 130,909 6- to 21-year old students enrolled in special education, making up 12.5% of the student population. That is more than 1 in 10 students in special education. And with increased awareness of disability diagnoses, this number will only continue to grow. It is urgent that Arizona education leaders reexamine current evidence-based initiatives and how they are applied in our state. Systemic biases due to ableism may be hindering the success of students identified for special education services.

## LITERATURE REVIEW

For the last 30 years, the Americans With Disabilities Act of 1990 (ADA) brought about changes that have helped improve the lives of the growing number of individuals with disabilities across the United States. While the ADA was instrumental in advancing progress for individuals with disabilities, there is still a long way to go. Negative attitudes about the abilities, rights, and importance of inclusion of individuals with disability among community members can lead to fewer employment and postsecondary education prospects for individuals, particularly those with intellectual and developmental disabilities (Vornholt et al., 2017).

These negative attitudes can lead to the stigmatization of disability (Zheng et al., 2016) and are sometimes referred to as "ableism." Ableism is defined as the discrimination and oppression of disabled people; a societal belief that being able is "normal" and is preferred. It is also defined as a system of oppression that favors being able-bodied or able-minded at any cost, frequently at the expense of people with disabilities. Ableism describes a system that assigns value to individuals based on societally constructed ideas of intelligence, excellence, and normal behavior. This construct defines being able, both physically and mentally, as the normative and preferable way to be. Ableism is often used to justify discrimination and oppression of individuals with disabilities (University of Arizona, 2020).

Ableism is present not just on a relational level, but in the way structures and language are constructed in our society. For example, steps, but no ramps, make a building inaccessible to a person who uses a wheelchair. Similarly, buildings without automatic doors, or ones that require pressing a button to operate, ignore the fact that some individuals may have difficulty using their limbs, or may not have limbs at all. Ableism is also present in our language, which includes various slurs that have been seamlessly integrated into our everyday conversations, such as "retarded" and "spazz." Ableism is also highlighted by the lack of representation of individuals with disabilities in media, including having nondisabled actors playing roles of individuals with disabilities, a practice known as "cripping up" (Smith, 2017). It is so common that actors without disabilities have won Academy Awards for playing a character with a disability, including Tom Hanks in Forrest Gump.

But perhaps the most troubling setting in which ableism has taken hold is the education system. Despite the passage of the IDEA and the billions of dollars spent on education and services for students with disabilities each year, very little attention and emphasis has been given to helping students learn and practice the soft skills that will help them in their adult lives. Moreover, students with disabilities are often graded on ableist scales of success, such as academic achievements and the ability to learn the same content as their nondisabled peers. In addition, there is little representation of individuals with disabilities in K–12 curricula. Where it does exist, it is often presented as a negative construct (Bacon & Lalvani, 2019). For example, Captain Hook is the villain in Peter Pan or Tiny Tim is someone to be pitied in The Christmas Carol.

The call for ending ableist notions of success in the education sphere has been around for decades. In 2002, Harvard Professor Thomas Hehir explored how "ableist assumptions influence the education of children with disabilities and these assumptions undermine the educational attainment of these children" (p. 3). In his paper, he asserts that special education teacher preparation programs should "explicitly challenge the ableist assumption that the manner in which nondisabled children perform school-related tasks is always the preferred goal for disabled students" (p. 25).

Though Hehir's paper was published almost 20 years ago, his arguments still hold in schools across the nation. Taylor (2018) makes a similar argument stating that children with ID should not have separate educational aims from their nondisabled peers, but that instead, education should be approached from an inclusive standpoint, taking into account what works best for each child. And in 2019, Giangreco posits the reason why more students with severe disabilities are not included in the classroom is due to ableism. In effect, these students are excluded from the general education classroom, which is an indicator for successful post-school outcomes, because teachers have difficulty conceptualizing curricular inclusion of students with significant disabilities.

Ableism in education is also exemplified in the calculation of graduation rates. Only students who have graduated in 4 years with a regular high school diploma are calculated in most states' official graduation rates. Students with more significant disabilities, those who have limited English proficiency, and others who graduate in 5 or 6 year time frames (or with a GED) are not counted, unless their state obtains special permission from the United States Department of Education. For example, Arizona only publicly posts calculations of 4-year and 5-year graduation rates. In 2019 with a 4-year graduation rate expected of all students, ADE reports that only 68% of students with disabilities graduate. Among 5-year cohorts, however, that percentage increases to 76%. The gains aren't as great among students overall. Among 4-year cohorts, the graduation rate is 79% and increases only slightly to 82% with an addition of a year. This demonstrates that students with disabilities more greatly benefit when accommodations are made to standard measures of success; however, without graduation data publicly reported, it is hard to determine how Arizona is doing accommodating students in special education

In 2015, the reauthorization of the Every Student Succeeds Act (ESSA) allowed for states to develop a state-defined alternate diploma for their students with the most significant cognitive disabilities, which are able to be counted in their state's graduation rate. Though this is a step in the right direction, these alternate diplomas are still steeped in ableism since they must follow the same requirements as the state's regular diploma—they are standards-based—again measuring students with disabilities to see how they can be like their nondisabled peers. To date, only a handful of states have begun developing, or are implementing, a state-defined alternate diploma (NTACT, 2019b). For students with significant disabilities to be prepared to succeed in their lives after high school, attitudes, structures, and processes within the education field need to be changed to ensure that they have equitable access to equal opportunities.

## HOW ABLEISM IMPACTS SCHOOLS: REFLECTING ON THE 2015 GRADUATION CLIFF STUDY

There has been a dearth of research on students with more significant disabilities, how their school experiences shape their post-school outcome and how ableism may manifest itself in the school environment. However, in 2015, a report titled *The Graduation Cliff: Improving the Post School Outcomes of Students With Disabilities* described how Arizona was doing to prepare youth with disabilities for life beyond high school (McFadden et al., 2015). More specifically, the mixed methods study sought to gain an in-depth understanding of the transition process to postsecondary education and employment for Arizona youth with disabilities enrolled in special education; it also considered the hopes and dreams of middle and high school students and their parents, and what was being done to support these aspirations. Ten focus groups that included family members and middle and high school youth were conducted. The research team also interviewed 30 experts, youth, and families. All interviews were transcribed and imported into MAXQDA analytic software and open coded to identify key themes. As patterns and themes began to emerge across transcriptions, and relationships between categories became apparent, each one was revisited using axial coding, memoing, and other inductive analytical strategies.

The research team also surveyed 224 Arizona parents and guardians and 634 high school students with disabilities from 17 school districts across the state. The survey data collected through Qualtrics was analyzed using factor analysis and ordinary least squares (OLS) linear and logistic regression models using STATA12, a statistical software package. STATA12 was used to calculate frequency counts. It was also used to perform OLS linear multiple regressions to test causality and relationships between survey topics and questions. A comprehensive measure was also developed that identified the variables that contributed to positive school environments and higher aspirations among the students. Reliability of the combined values for the best practice was verified with Cronbach's alpha.

Arizona is a local control state, meaning the governing and management of public schools is conducted by elected representatives serving on school boards located in the communities served by the schools. To that end, responses varied by school and district. Some schools were doing great things in transition, while others were still developing. Overall, students were very hopeful about their futures and were preparing and participating in different activities. However, access to and the quality of preparation and activities varied according to the barriers that were present. While many more factors were discussed in the 2015 report, this chapter will highlight the importance of including social skills, student support, work experiences, and self-advocacy in all school curriculum to combat ableism and promote post-school engagement in vocational or academic life.

## Building Social Skills

Social skills, emotional intelligence, and personal habits are important for getting and retaining jobs and are highly predictive of student achievement and post-school employment. Employers agree that an absence of communication and social skills (i.e., soft skills) are the biggest barriers to individuals who desire to attend college or get a job after high school. Further, research has shown that those students who spend the most time with friends during school have a higher quality of life (Beelman et al., 1994; Denham & Almeida, 1987; Schneider, 1992; Forness & Kavale, 1996). And students with both informal and formal supports and social skills are more likely to land jobs post-high school than those without these supports and skills (Pierson et al., 2008). However, despite indicators pointing to their importance, they are often the last priorities considered in an academic setting.

### The Importance of Friends' Support

Students in this study reported that friendships offered such benefits as moral and emotional support, protection from bullying, help with homework, and information. For those transitioning from middle school, the number of friends they have in their new high school becomes extremely important, offering some stability amidst great change. However, some parents cited the difficulty in their children's ability to maintain relationships with friends without disabilities who lived across town or who did not understand their child's behaviors. As a result, some students became very depressed and lonely.

This study found that the frequency of having contact with friends with and without disabilities was correlated with students' hopefulness for their futures. Despite this finding, students with disabilities are overwhelmingly unable to hone their social skills inside or outside of school and are more isolated than others (Chung et al., 2012). Almost half of study participants, 47%, talked to friends outside school less than once a week; and 22% rarely or never talked to friends outside of school. There is a difference in these results by disability. A high percentage—about 1 in 3—of those with ID and autism stated that they "rarely" or "never" interact with friends outside school. Interaction in the study was defined as texting, talking on the phone, instant messaging, or visiting face-to-face, so transportation did not necessarily impact interaction.

### The Importance of Extracurricular Activities

The reason why these students were isolated can be found when looking at their involvement in activities. Only slightly more than half of this sample's students with disabilities were involved in school-related, extracurricular activities—an excellent avenue to making friends (Jorgensen et al., 2012). Parents expressed concerns and frustration with schools' procedural barriers their children faced in accessing programs. Many activities are offered only to general education students without disabilities, such as the ability to participate in high school level classes while in middle school or the ability to join some extracurricular activities. For example, in some schools, parents reported that general education students registered first, so popular courses and extracurricular activities filled up before the special education students were allowed to register; and for those enrolled in inclusive extracurricular activities, this study found that many students with disabilities were offered minor roles, if any. With so many other barriers facing families, involvement in extracurricular activities becomes the last priority. A parent of a student with multiple disabilities stated the issue:

> I don't know what club I could put him in that somebody understands his limitations or can see his strengths and be able to play off of those things. Do I have to go to club too, so that he can be in a club? I don't know. I work 8 to 5, how do I help him with a club?

Schools can rectify this in several ways. They can ensure that: IEPs include extracurricular activities that the student is interested in, class/activity enrollment times are equitable, fees are waived for students who cannot afford them, and that needed accommodations and supports are offered for the student to participate and engage to the same degree as their peers without disabilities. Yet, many schools still do not prioritize extra-curricular activities.

Thus, for the many students with disabilities uninvolved in clubs or outside activities, there are limited opportunities to socialize outside of school. If parents and students are unable to gain access to inclusive activities, parents often look to recreational organizations that are segregated, serving students with disabilities only to fill voids in their children's social and recreational lives. As a result, many students befriend other students with disabilities in these programs—a positive outcome—but because these programs are segregated, students continue to be excluded from mainstream social activities, and only have access to activities and friends based on biased perceptions of disability. They are missing out on inclusive opportunities to develop personal interests, practice social and functional skills, develop social relationships, feel like a valued member of the school community, and develop self-advocacy skills (Pence & Dymond, 2015).

### The Impact of Bullying

Parents expanded on the barriers to school activity involvement citing bullying by other students, a lack of support and understanding, and failure to make accommodations. Nearly 1 in 5 students reported being bullied or picked on by other students at least once a week. Parents gave a higher number—38%. Some disability groups were targeted more than others. Students with autism were 3 1/2 times more likely to be bullied than other students with disabilities; but for those with emotional disabilities, the difference was even more dramatic. Those with emotional disabilities were 7 times more likely to be bullied than others with disabilities and 4 times more likely to be physically attacked.

As a result, some students felt like they must hide their disability to fit in. A student with traumatic brain injury shared his experience: "I'm going into the special ed advisory. And the other kids are questioning, 'What's that? Are all the kids in there retarded? Are you retarded with them, too?'" However, others found ways to accommodate. They reported looking for others to befriend more like themselves. For example, parents of students with ID and autism report that most of their child's friends had similar disabilities. Some simply gave up on making friends with students without disabilities, because they felt they were never given opportunities to belong.

This research also found that bullying had a significant negative effect on students' future aspirations, self-efficacy, and school performance. These repeated, negative experiences of bullying made it difficult for them to fit comfortably into the world post-graduation. Those who were bullied believed they were less likely to graduate high school or support themselves financially after graduation than those who had not been bullied. Further, bullying led to fighting, or what student participants stated was "self-defense." A parent stated how this occurred with his son:

> He was getting picked on by other students...since we weren't getting any results from the teachers, I told him to defend himself. Then, that ended up getting him in trouble. When he tries to defend himself, he's labeled as the bad kid.

Being attacked or involved in fights at school were predictive of being suspended or expelled. This was a significant problem among students with disabilities in this sample, with 25% of students in the family sample having been suspended. Those with emotional disabilities were 10 times more likely to be suspended than others with disabilities. This negatively impacted their expectations to graduate high school or college and, for some, it was the beginning of the pipeline into the juvenile justice system (Mader & Butrymowicz, 2014). For some with disabilities, especially among students of color with disabilities, special education administered through an ableist system can increase the likelihood of students landing in jail.

## The Importance of Student Support

These findings underline the need for positive student support, so these students don't feel the need to hide or fight back. Access to both informal and formal support is essential to student success. Both parents and students noted a need for mentors—one for the student and one for the parent—in helping them throughout school and navigating post-high school options. Specific to transition to life beyond high school, students are seeking help from adult mentors with financial aid, college applications, scholarships, and other tasks to help them achieve their career goals. Three out of four Arizona youth with disabilities in this sample reported that their families were helping them get ready for life after high school.

Following parents/family, teachers play the second largest role in students' lives followed by friends. Help from teachers and school counselors serve as a positive influence and buoy students' hopes for their futures. Some of the ways in which students said teachers helped them were through tutoring, paying attention and listening to them, supporting them, helping them with problems, and providing them with information on how to reach their goals.

With different teachers come different personalities—some are more supportive than others. Half the students surveyed felt adults in their lives listen to them "only a little," if at all. For those with more significant disabilities, only 30% felt listened to "very well." The culture of the classroom and the students' perceptions of the teacher can inhibit or support students' access to help and perception of feeling listened to. In some classrooms, students are too embarrassed to ask for help. In other classrooms, teachers may forget or delay getting back to the students who do ask for help, impacting students' abilities to complete assignments correctly and on time. Both students and parents felt less likely to ask for or get help or support from teachers perceived as inflexible, strict, non-understanding, or uncaring. Due to the variability of teachers' personalities and approaches to students with disabilities, it is critically important that schools create a supportive environment with trusted adults who students and families can approach if they run into barriers in the classroom. In cases where that did not happen, students and their families felt excluded from the school.

While the majority of students in this study spent their time in integrated settings, those with more significant disabilities were not always offered that choice. Some parents felt a loss of control on where their students were educated. A parent of an entering high school freshman with multiple disabilities stated:

> These were decisions made without me. They have him on distance learning so he's on a computer in the classroom with this teacher...He's on the computer all day long. This is so different for him from what he was doing from second grade to eighth grade in an ED (emotional disability) classroom. There's no teacher interaction, student interaction going on for him.

Some parents believed students without disabilities were getting preferential treatment, more attention, and were being pipelined to better schools than students with disabilities. Parents of students with disabilities were often counseled on where their child would best fit based on their child's disability, which they didn't feel was always the most desirable option for their child—a direct consequence of ableism.

In the sample, parents of students with emotional disabilities and autism consistently ranked their schools lower than the overall average. One-half of parents of students with emotional disabilities didn't believe their school adequately met their child's individual needs, often trying to force them into a rigid system with few accommodations. This indicated there was a potential teacher training issue regarding these disabilities. Some parents felt they had to constantly advocate for their child's rights and often were unsure what the next step should be. Both parents and students had difficulty finding a balance between small enough classes that wouldn't cause anxiety and getting challenging coursework. Like many others, their child's school seemed to offer a "one size fits all" approach towards education.

As a result, some parents moved their children to specialized or individualized programming that catered to the student's disability but removed them from inclusive general education environments that are important to successful post-school outcomes. They felt they had no options through general education. The expectation and prescribed setting for the student were based on ableist assumptions of the child's abilities.

## The Importance of Career and Technical Education and Work Experience

Career and technical education (CTE) programs, which may be funded through local, state, and/or federal funds, target "hands-on learning" and expertise in a specific trade in high school. An abundance of research over the last several decades demonstrates significant positive outcomes for students with disabilities who take CTE courses. Involvement in these programs results in students being twice as likely to obtain full-time jobs after high school than students not involved. CTE program involvement also results in higher pay and a higher high school graduation rate (Theobald et al., 2019; Baer, Flexer, et al., 2003; Baker & Popowicz, 1983; Halpern et al., 1995; Harvey, 2002; Silverberg et al., 2004). But even with all of the evidence, it is an underused resource among students with disabilities with many never being given the option or made aware of CTE. For those special education students who are enrolled, CTE staff stated that they face attitudinal barriers from teachers in the CTE program. These teachers do not think students with significant disabilities can do the job or are able enough. Some teachers are unaware of the important role that accommodations can play in ensuring that students with disabilities are successful in a student's career path.

For example, if the student uses a wheelchair and wants to work on airplanes, they would not be able to do that particular job because of its inaccessibility; but the student could still work in the field of aviation mechanics. Most jobs can be adapted or jobs within the student's desired field can be located. Thus, educating others in the field, as well as teachers about accommodations is critical to removing barriers to access CTE and other training programs. However, additional training still needs to target the attitudinal barriers these groups may possess.

Despite the lack of access to CTE, on average, across all grades, 94% of youth study participants thought about their futures and, by senior year approximately 83% knew what they needed to do to achieve their personal goals and feel ready. Careful planning of transition activities during high school results in positive post-school outcomes. Work experiences and vocational training offer the opportunity to build soft and problem-solving skills, providing students with expertise in a trade to help them find and maintain a job. The positive effects of having a paid job among high school students with disabilities are impressive and well documented (Carter et al., 2012; Baer, Flexer, et al., 2003; Bullis et al., 1995; Doren & Benz, M, 1998;

Rabren et al., 2002.) and, there is no difference in this positive effect by the significance of the student's disability.

Students with paid work believe that after finishing high school they will very likely get a job and support themselves financially in the future. Holding a community-based job is also predictive of having greater problem-solving ability and self-efficacy. In effect, student aspirations are shaped by their work and volunteer experiences, their families, their friends, and what they enjoy doing.

Half of the youth study participants held some type of job. However, only 1 in 4 of these jobs were provided through the school, and they were targeted to those with primarily significant disabilities. School jobs tend to service the school population and are narrow in scope. School-based jobs mentioned in this study included working in the school store, helping in the school cafeteria, cleaning school bathrooms and other janitorial tasks, landscaping the school grounds, working in a copy/print shop, and delivering mail. While these school-based jobs help students acquire some needed skills, the temporary, training nature of these positions does not allow students to hold these jobs permanently. Further, some of the parents of those with more significant disabilities felt their students were being "pipelined" into menial positions based on what teachers thought they were capable of, which was either janitorial or food service, which did not reflect their students' interests. Other parents, however, felt this was all their child could do.

Alternatively, community-based jobs offer a wider path of career exploration, as well as more opportunities for permanent employment. In the study, students relied on family, friends, and themselves to find paid jobs in the community—only 11% of community jobs were provided through the schools. In many cases individuals were encouraged to start their own businesses, such as landscaping, home repair, or babysitting. In fact, over half of the jobs held in the community by individuals with disabilities were entrepreneurial.

Recognizing the importance of community-based employment for students' acquiring real job skills, networking with employers, and obtaining jobs, many schools are linking employers and students through transition programs, or creating their own school-based businesses, sometimes in partnership with the community. Increasingly, schools are moving away from setting sheltered employment and day treatment centers as the final goal for high school graduates with I/DD (intellectual and developmental disabilities). Businesses that join these partnerships often have a personal connection to disability. On getting a business to hire students with disabilities, Bob Enderle, the director of diversity, community relations, and organizational development from Medtronic states:

You have a tremendous talent that is available to you, (a) that we know is more productive, (b) has a higher retention rate, and (c) is more engaged in the organization. If you look at those characteristics, we know those are characteristics of higher performing organizations that have very significant business results. (McFadden et al., 2015, p. 35)

These businesses understand the barriers these students face as well as their potential, which directly confronts a paradigm based on ableism.

## Self-Determination/Self-Advocacy

Research finds that students with a sense of hope about their futures and self-determination/self-advocacy skills are more likely to achieve greater personal outcomes and achievement and be engaged in post-school employment and independent living (Carter et al., 2012; Hansford & Hattie, 1982; Holden et al., 1990; Valentine et al., 2004; Wehmeyer & Schwartz, 1997). Further, in the study, students who were motivated and had a specific plan said they were being "pushed" and encouraged by someone in their life who had confidence in them. The phrase "I know you can do it" from a parent or teacher serves as a tremendous motivator in the life of a student, regardless if he or she has disabilities, and is an indicator of the types of decision-making opportunities students are afforded.

But overall, the study found that students' voices were still lacking in school decision-making and were contributing to policies anchored in ableism. Some schools are trying to remedy this by implementing self-advocacy/self-determination training, which focuses on enhancing personal capacity by creating awareness of disability rights, developing meaningful opportunities for participation, and modifying the environment so barriers for participation are removed. In addition, the individualized education program (IEP) is the universal, school-based mechanism that can grow these skills. The IEP is a comprehensive assessment for each individual that connects their strengths and talents with the supports or training needed to achieve their desired goals. This is also a document that can ensure that NTACT predictors are incorporated in each individual's plan.

In Arizona, every student with an IEP must have a transition plan by the age of 16. The transition plan is based on a high school student's individual needs, strengths, skills, and interests. Transition planning is used to identify and develop goals which need to be accomplished during the current school year to assist the student in meeting his post-high school goals. The IEP with transition plan is the strategic framework that, when led by the student and followed by school personnel, families, and the student, can maximize the potential for each individual. The student can take ownership over their own goals and the plan to get there with supports in place.

Support given by the IEP can maximize the learning and leadership potential of every student when utilized correctly. With supports written into the IEP that mitigate learning barriers, students are able to better identify their own strengths and build their confidence. Further, students' involvement in their own IEP helps them identify their own abilities and weaknesses, which are essential in building self-advocacy skills.

The study found that a student's degree of control over the IEP shows significant positive effects in that youth's choice of meaningful activities linked to post-school success, including choice of classes, school activities, how they get to and from school, how they spend their free time at school, and feeling listened to by adults. However, not all students feel they have a lot of choice over their IEPs—only 48% of students with disabilities reported having a lot of choice over their IEP goals. If the student had an ID, only 21% reported a lot of choice.

Despite the benefits of student-led IEPs, many students do not take leadership in the process. Many don't speak up, don't know what's in their IEPs, rely on their parents, or just show up at the end of the meetings. Control over the IEP directly impacts how and in what capacity students are involved in their schools—either centrally or peripherally. In the study, many students felt limited on what courses they could take for example.

Unfortunately, student roles in the IEP and other decision-making opportunities are often overtaken by those in authority (including parents) for a myriad of reasons, including a lack of confidence in student abilities, inadequate time, student apathy, and/or over-protection by adults. One student reported, "Ever since I've been in school, I've never got to pick anything cuz I've always been stuck with things that they [teachers] said I could do." The lack of student leadership in these areas while in high school foreshadows their minimal involvement and limited success post-high school. Schools, families, and youth need to act now to counteract that trend.

In addition, there is a disconnection between adults and youth that may impede the latter's effort to set goals. For example, while 71% of Arizona youth with disabilities reported that their families were trying to help them get ready for life after high school, almost half of them felt that adults listen to them only a little, if at all. For those with more significant disabilities, that figure is 70%. In addition, when asked about their likelihood of graduating college, living away from home, and having a job to support themselves financially, students were positive. But parents' expectations, when controlled by the significance of the youth's disability, were slightly lower. In fact, 37% of parents believed that their student would go to a day program after high school. Parents of students with autism or ID were less likely to think that their child would get a job and support themselves than parents of children with other types of disabilities.

The study found, however, that there is a set of variables that education administrators control that show significant positive effects on youth self-efficacy, regardless of the students' disability significance, race/ethnicity, or school location. That set of variables included "students feeling listen to," "not being bullied," "having choice of activities," "control over their IEP," and "paid work experiences." However, the presence of these conditions in schools varies widely.

Study data revealed that districts with youth reporting higher aspirations and greater self-efficacy did have one thing in common: A strong belief among district leadership—including school board members, superintendents, and special education directors—in their transition programs and their students' abilities to succeed. This commitment by leadership to a model that challenges ableism leads to sustainable best practices in transition, such as self-determination/self-advocacy training and IEPs linked to meeting postsecondary goals that are established by the student. In effect, transition programs should not be limited in their view of what special education is. Rather, they are part of a school-wide effort and partnership with general education teachers and staff. The collective goal is to build academic, vocational education, and employment opportunities among *all* students, so that ableism can finally be successfully confronted.

## DISCUSSION

The refrain is a familiar one: "The disability doesn't define the person." Yet, we see that overall schools expect less from populations with significant disabilities because of the presumed weaknesses associated with their labels. The overall school system itself suffers from overall lowered expectations for youth with disabilities. Historically, not enough resources have been allocated to employment, training, recreation—even education—for youth with disabilities, yet there has been an uneven emphasis on day programs and family support to help families care for youth with disabilities who are not expected to participate fully in the community.

The *Graduation Cliff* (McFadden et al., 2015) findings showed that almost all the students surveyed thought about what they would like to do after high school, but students had more optimism about their prospects than the parents did. The students expressed the desire to have a job, but worried that they would not be able to support themselves or live on their own. It was common for these students to be excluded from social and leadership opportunities in school and feel like they had limited influence over their own IEPs. The study also found that those who found jobs in high school did do so primarily through family, friends, and neighbors—the individuals in their lives who have a different, more positive construct of that individual's "ability." Finally, the study found that students with disabilities simply were not offered the same choices as their peers without disabilities. CTE options continued to weed out students not seen as "able" enough. In this context it is no surprise that Arizona PSO outcomes have remained relatively stagnant over the last 5 years, and ACS employment outcomes have lagged.

Currently, Arizona schools approach their students with disabilities through a largely deficits-based model, where the focus continues to be on what the person cannot do. In this view, students with ID who are capable of learning and reading may instead be redirected to work preparation activities instead of improving their reading skills or may not be expected to take leadership over their IEP or hold a paid job in the community. These prescribed beliefs challenge the notion of person-centered planning and self-determination, which are critical to successful post-school outcomes. The disability field is moving to a supports-based model of disability where an examination of the person's skills and the environment facilitates an understanding of what supports need to be in place so the person can be successful. This is facilitated through person-centered planning and provides more opportunities for socialization and self-determination.

## Person-Centered Planning—An Important Tool to Building Social Capital

A person-centered plan targets the individual's vision for his or her future and determines ways to get there. It directly combats ableism by helping those involved with the student with a disability see the total person, recognize their strengths, desires, and interests, and discover completely new ways of thinking about the future. The informal person-centered team meets to identify opportunities for the individual to also develop personal relationships, participate in their community, increase control over their own lives, and develop the skills and abilities needed to achieve their goals.

These plans help inform IEPs and the transition plan by providing background about the person and his or her goals. Research on outcomes of person-centered planning has shown an improvement in social networks, closer contact with family and friends, and greater involvement and engagement in group activities. In essence, it leads to greater inclusion, quality of life, and builds the individual's social supports needed to help reach their in-school and post-school goals.

Providing parents and adolescents with inclusive social interaction opportunities with peers and families without disabilities—such as extracurricular activities, school-wide initiative communities, and incentives for businesses to connect with the disability community—can create new connections. These connections can provide unique information, which is a form of social capital. These connections by members of the student's person-centered planning team typically involve a heterogeneous group of people encountered at work, in the community, and through other friends. Since the information provided by these members is not disability-focused, it often leads to greater access and more diversity to options in education, social activities, and employment, and can spur greater physical and mental health outcomes and well-being, breaking the student with a disability out of an ableist lens.

Without social capital, the resources and information to which students and parents have access are bounded by the limited options provided through a formal system of programs and services dictated by the disability, for example, state disability programs. But, the aforementioned person-centered plan offers a way out of this bounded system. Students and their support teams can use these plans to begin to map out the connections one has to support their aspirations, identify where holes in his/her connections are and where new connections need to be identified.

Moreover, the use of informal supports—friends, family, neighbors—leads to positive education and employment outcomes among youth with all types of disabilities. Teachers, parents, and students should not be afraid to ask friends, neighbors, co-workers, the businesses they frequent, and others for mentoring advice, for an internship, or even for a job. Most community members want to help. They just have never been asked, or don't know how. Consequently, those businesses personally invested in participating in school community-based work programs tend to personally know someone with a disability. All of these informal supports outside of a school-based system are less likely to look at the individual through an ableist lens and more likely to approach them understanding their strengths, which can also combat ableist practices that hinder post-school outcomes.

## Incorporating Best Practices

Additionally, district-wide and school-wide policies can promote student self-efficacy in the face of ableism. For example, instituting school-wide positive behavioral interventions and supports (PBIS) policies promotes positive behavior, reduces bullying, and emphasizes inclusive environments among all students. In instances where bullying does occur, PBIS schools and districts can institute policies that promote conflict resolution rather than punishment so that problems can be solved in an open and constructive way. Stronger collaboration among schools, agencies, ADE, and Arizona's institutions of higher education can improve outcomes for transition-aged youth. Such activities may include increasing accessibility of college opportunities for youth with disabilities and increasing capacity and technical support for all stakeholders via certifications, programs, and technical assistance. Project SEARCH and the Youth Leadership Forum (YLF) are also initiatives that schools can access to challenge assumptions of what youth with disabilities can do.

Project SEARCH is offered in many states, including Arizona. It prepares transition-aged youth with ID for competitive employment. The program provides real-life work experience combined with training in employability and independent living skills to help youth with significant disabilities make successful transitions from school to adult life. The Project SEARCH model involves an extensive period of training and career exploration, innovative adaptations, long-term job coaching, and continuous feedback from teachers, job coaches, and employers. As a result, at the completion of the training program, the goal is for students with disabilities to be employed in nontraditional, complex, and rewarding jobs. The presence of a Project SEARCH high school transition program can bring about long-term changes in business culture that have far-reaching positive effects on attitudes about hiring people with disabilities and the range of jobs in which they can be successful.

DiverseAbility in Arizona operates the YLF, which is also offered in many states. YLF is an innovative, intensive 5-day training program for high school sophomores, juniors, and seniors who have significant disabilities. The focus of the forum is to strengthen self-advocacy and self-efficacy. The program includes structured small and large group activities, field trips, a dance, a formal banquet, and a tour of the state capitol. It provides educational programs on topics such as: positive self-concept, options after high school, the history of disability as a culture, and leadership responsibilities. Staff and presenters who engage with the student delegates include disability community leaders, legislators, and numerous role models who have disabilities. Student delegates are assisted in developing a personal leadership plan which includes specific action items that they complete when they return to their communities. Following completion of YLF, student delegates serve as a youth voice to inform the Arizona State Plan for Independent Living (SPIL), and are assigned a mentor for on-going support for 1 year. For many participants, YLF is the first time they ever spent a night away from home by themselves.

Pre- and post-tests reveal that most who began YLF were not previously aware of services or how they could access postsecondary education. But after involvement with the program, participants knew about assistive technology and independent living, laws that affect them, and their IEPs and how they work. All of the participants felt more confident and informed after completing the program and were able to more strongly advocate for themselves both at home and at school, including through their IEPs.

Both Project SEARCH and YLF change the paradigm regarding students with disabilities from deficit- to strengths-focused. Project SEARCH aims to change for businesses their approach to overall hiring. The business recognizes the individual gifts and needs of the student as it customizes jobs based on the strengths of that student. YLF seeks to re-enforce for students with disabilities their value, their rights, and how to advocate for themselves to help them be successful. In essence, both initiatives are paradigm changing in that they do not put the student in a box. Both allow the student to take risks, fail, learn grit, and hone their strengths, which is what is needed in our schools to help them be successful. In the *Graduation Cliff* study, a student stated best how important it was to take risks as they approached their future, "I'm worried about getting my own apartment, and paying bills, and being on my own. To work on it is to work on your fears and just keep on going" (McFadden et al., 2015, p. 39).

## CONCLUSION

Though post-school outcomes have shown modest improvement overall nationwide, disconnection rates of students with ID have remained consistently high. More needs to be done to confront the ableism that exists in societal expectations, work opportunities, and inclusion in school life. To minimize the effects of ableism, we must raise our expectations of students' potential, enhance their opportunities for genuine inclusion in school and societal activities, and structure a system that provides them with the skills they need to get the jobs they seek.

Properly preparing our youth for life beyond high school should not just be a goal for those who are considered able enough. Thus, a commitment by leadership to expand the definition of "ability" and commit to combatting ableist attitudes toward achievement leads to sustainable best practices that combat staff turnover, low pay, and a shortfall in funding for the state's education and employment programs. A culture is then created that fosters higher expectations for youth with disabilities. These higher expectations motivate more opportunities for student self-determination at home and at school, genuine inclusion in school and community activities, and planning that provides students with the skills they need for the careers they seek. This paradigm change guides post-school placements towards meaningful employment and inclusion in the community.

With the support of their families, communities, and a shift in attitudes away from ableism, students with significant disabilities can lead engaged, fulfilling lives after high school. Personal relationships that both emotionally bond families facing similar challenges and bridge resources outside of the limited formal support system can help youth, families, and the overall community recognize that all students with disabilities have gifts and that everyone has a place to contribute to society. Having a school leadership, parental involvement, and an informal system that supports these efforts can change the paradigm, so that having low, if any, expectations for students with significant disabilities is no longer the expectation and ableism can be effectively mitigated in school settings once and for all.

## REFERENCES

Arizona Department of Education. (2019). *State of Arizona 2019 post school outcome survey results for school year 2017–2018 exiters.* https://www.azed.gov/special education/transition/post-school-outcomes

Bacon, J. K., & Lalvani, P. (2019). Dominant narratives, subjugated knowledges, and the righting of the story of disability in K–12 curricula. *Curriculum Inquiry, 49,* 4, 387–404.

Baer, R. M., Flexer, R. W., Beck S., Amstutz, N., Hoffman, L., Brothers, J., Stelzer, D., & Zechman, C. (2003). A collaborative followup study on transition service utilization and post-school outcomes. *Career Development for Exceptional Individuals, 26,* 7–25.

Baker, S. B., & Popowicz, C. L. (1983). Meta-analysis as a strategy for evaluating effects of career education interventions. *Vocational Guidance Quarterly, 31,* 178–186.

Beelman, A., Pfington, U., & Losel, F. (1994). Effects of training social competence in children: A meta-analysis of recent evaluation studies. *Journal of Clinical Child Psychology, 23,* 3, 260–271.

Bullis, M., Davis, C., Bull, B., & Johnson, B. (1995). Transition achievement among young adults with deafness: What variables relate to success? *Rehabilitation Counseling Bulletin, 39,* 130–150.

Carter, E. W., Austin, D., & Trainor, A. A. (2012). Predictors of postschool employment outcomes for young adults with severe disabilities. *Journal of Disability Policy Studies, 23*(1), 50–63. https://doi.org/10.1177/1044207311414680

Chung, Y., Carter, E. W., & Sisco, L. G. (2012). Social interactions of students with disabilities who use augmentative and alternative communication in inclusive Classrooms. *American Journal on Intellectual and Developmental Disabilities, 117*(5), 349–367. https://doi.org/10.1352/1944-7558-117.5.349

Denham, S. A., & Almeida, M. C. (1987). Children's social problem-solving skills, behavioral adjustment, and interventions: A meta-analysis evaluating theory and practice. *Journal of Applied Developmental Psychology, 8*(4), 391–409.

Doren, B., & Benz, M. R. (1998). Employment inequality revisited: Predictors of better employment outcomes for young women with disabilities in transition. *The Journal of Special Education, 31,* 425–442.

Forness, S. R., & Kavale, K. A. (1996). Treating social skill deficits in children with learning disabilities: A meta-analysis of the research. *Learning Disability Quarterly, 19,* 1, 2–13.

Giangreco, M. F. (2019). "How can a student with severe disabilities be in a fifth-grade class when he can't do fifth-grade level work?" Misapplying the least restrictive environment. *Research and Practice for Persons With Severe Disabilities, 45*(1), 23–27.

Halpern, A. S., Yovanoff, P., Doren, B., & Benz, M. R. (1995) Predicting participation in postsecondary education for school leavers with disabilities. *Exceptional Children, 62*, 151–164.

Hansford, B. C., & Hattie, J. A. C. (1982). The relationship between self and achievement/performance measures. *Review of Educational Research, 52*(1), 123–142.

Harvey, M. W. (2002). Comparison and postsecondary transitional outcomes between students with and without disabilities by secondary vocational education participation: Findings from the National Education Longitudinal Study. *Career Development for Exceptional Individuals, 25*, 99–122.

Hehir, T. (2002). Eliminating ableism in education. *Harvard Educational Review, 72*(1), 1–32.

Holden, G. W., Moncher, M. S., Schinke, S. P., & Barker, K. M. (1990). Self-efficacy of children and adolescents: A meta-analysis. *Psychological Reports, 66*(3), 1044–1046.

Jorgensen, C. M., McSheehan, M., Schuh, M., & Sonnenmeier, R. M. (2012). *Essential best practices in inclusive schools.* https://scholars.unh.edu/cgi/viewcontent.cgi?article=1069&context=iod

Mader, J., & Butrymowicz, S. (2014, October 29). *For many with disabilities, special education leads to jail.* The Hechinger Report. http://hechingerreport.org/content/pipeline-prison-special-education-often-leads-jail-thousands-american-children_17796/

Mazzotti, V. L., Test, D. W., & Mustian, A. L. (2014). Secondary transition evidence-based practices and predictors: Implications for policymakers. *Journal of Disability Policy Studies, 25*(1), 5–18. https://doi.org/10.1177%2F1044207312460888

McFadden, E., Daugherty, D., Lee, S. E., Fisher K. W., Hack, A., & Spyra, E. (2015, May 1). *The Graduation Cliff: Improving school outcomes of students with disabilities* [Summary report]. Arizona State University Morrison Institute. https://addpc.az.gov/sites/default/files/media/Graduation%20Cliff%20Summary%20Report_1.pdf

National Technical Assistance Center on Transition. (2019a). *Effective practices matrix.* https://transitionta.org/wp-content/uploads/docs/Predictors-by-Outcome-Area_New_08-02-2021.pdf

National Technical Assistance Center on Transition. (2019b). *2019 Part B FFY 2017 SPP/APR indicator analysis.* https://ectacenter.org/~pdfs/grads360/18278.pdf

Pence, A. R., & Dymond, S. K. (2015). Extracurricular school clubs: A time for fun and learning. *TEACHING Exceptional Children, 47*(5), 281–288. https://doi.org/10.1177/0040059915580029

Pierson, M. R., Carter, E. W., Lane, K. L., & Glaeser, B. C. (2008). Factors influencing the self-determination of transition-age youth with high-incidence disabilities. *Career Development for Exceptional Individuals, 31*, 115–125.

Rabren, K., Dunn, C., & Chambers, D. (2002). Predictors of post-high school employment among young adults with disabilities. *Career Development for Exceptional Individuals, 25*, 25–40.

Schneider, B. H. (1992). Didactic methods of enhancing children's peer relations: A quantitative review. *Clinical Psychology Review, 12*(3), 363–382.

Silverberg, M., Warner, E., Fong, M., & Goodwin, D. (2004). *National assessment of vocational education: Final report to Congress.* U.S. Department of Education, Office of the Under Secretary, Policy, and Program Studies Service.

Smith, L. (2017). *#Ableism.* Center for Disability Rights. http://cdrnys.org/blog/uncategorized/ableism/

Taylor, A. (2018). The logic of deferral: Educational aims and intellectual disability. *Studies in Philosophy and Education, 37*(3), 265–285.

Theobald, R. J., Goldhaber, D. D., Gratz, T. M., & Holden, K. L. (2019). Career and technical education, inclusion, and postsecondary outcomes for students with learning disabilities. *Journal of Learning Disabilities, 52*(2), 109–119. https://doi.org/10.1177/0022219418775121

University of Arizona. (2019). *Ableism 101: What is ableism? What is disability?* [PowerPoint slides] https://drc.arizona.edu/cultural-center/ableism-101-part-one-what-ableism-what-disability

U.S. Census Bureau. (2017). American community survey 1-year estimates, Table B18120: Employment status by disability status and type.

Valentine, J. C., Du Bois, D. L., & Cooper, H. M. (2004). The relation between self-beliefs and academic achievement: A meta-analytic review. *Educational Psychologist, 39*(2), 111–133.

Vornholt, K., Villotti, P., Muschalla, B., Bauer, J., Colella, A., Zijlstra, F., Van Ruitenbeek, G., Uitdewilligen, S., & Corbiere, M. (2018). Disability and employment—Overview and highlights. *European Journal of Work and Organizational Psychology, 27*(1), 40–55.

Wehmeyer, M., & Schwartz, M. (1997). Self-determination and positive adult outcomes: A follow-up study of youth with mental retardation or learning disabilities. *Exceptional Children, 63*, 245–255.

Zheng, Q., Tian, Q., Hao, C., Gu, J., Tao, J., Liang, Z., Chen, X., Fang, J., Ruan, J., Ai, Q., & Hao, Y. (2016). Comparison of attitudes toward disability and people with disability among caregivers, the public, and people with disability: Findings from a cross-sectional survey. *BMC public health, 16*(1), 1024. https://doi.org/10.1186/s12889-016-3670-0

# SECTION IV

## EXPERIENCE AND POWER IN SCHOOLS

The five chapters in this section include critical narratives and counternarratives that weave together disability studies, social justice literature, decolonizing frameworks, critical disability, and critical race theory. The chapter authors illuminate various perspectives and conceptual frameworks related to studying in and leading K–24 educational institutions. Taken together, the chapters examine power in ways that reveal marginalizing practices and provide for new possibilities for practice.

In the opening chapter, "In Our Own Words: Special Education Teachers of Color With Dis/abilities," Kulkarni, Bland, and Gaeta provide three parallel narratives of how disability is experienced from the perspectives of graduate students and a professor. The authors employ DisCrit analysis to frame discourses in special education and on the paucity of work focusing on special education teachers of color (SETOCs) who also identify as having dis/abilities. Utilizing their collective experiences as both students and educators, they seek to provide counternarratives to racism and ableism in schools by focusing on the intersection of racism and ableism, and asserting that racism and ableism too often "operate as interdependent identities." Their narrative concludes with a window into the experiences of SETOC teachers from a public institution attempting to navigate the creation of appropriate virtual spaces for themselves and for their students.

In the following chapter, "Who Decides? Teachers With Disabilities and the Role of School Administrators," Damiani asks the reader to consider: "Who decides who can teach, how teachers can teach, and what constitutes 'good' teaching?" She argues that schools are organized around ability constructs that shape the experiences of disabled students, staff, teachers, and administrators. Damiani draws on data from interviews and letter writing to highlight the experiences of teachers with disabilities. Damiani's analysis of narratives of teachers with disabilities underscores the value of professors possessing an inclusive educational vision as well as values and dispositions that respect and fully recognize students with disparate learning needs. Situated in a joint framework of transformative leadership and disability studies in education, Damiani suggests ways to move forward in a shared leadership model with teachers with disabilities as teacher-leaders. The chapter additionally highlights several leadership strategies that can be employed in fostering an educational environment in universities where all bodies (and voices) are recognized and valued.

In "Experiences of Disability in One Canadian Faculty of Education: Recognition and Resourcing as a Social Justice Response to Supporting Students Living With Disabilities," Brideau and Bishop draw on a social justice model to frame two first-person narratives from the authors who, between them, have more than 60 years of work and formal learning in numerous Canadian and Australian education settings: one from the perspective of a physically disabled student with particular focus on her experiences as a master's and PhD student; and the other from the standpoint of a university professor who was formerly a K–12 teacher and principal. The authors also highlight significant gaps in the literature related to recognizing and honoring the lived experiences of students with disabilities in university settings. Learning from the lived experiences of students with disabilities may ultimately inform the quality of solutions developed for a multitude of systemic, attitudinal, and environmental barriers, which continue to impact the educational experiences of this student population. Pertinent areas discussed in the chapter include: (a) engaging in class activities that reflect an inclusive educational vision; (b) developing attitudes, values, and dispositions that respect and fully recognize students with disparate learning needs; (c) providing professional learning and critical understandings specific to those living with disabilities; and lastly (d) identifying leadership strategies which can be employed in fostering an educational environment where all bodies (and voices) are recognized and valued.

Recognizing the value of all, unfortunately, has not always been commonplace in education. Delgado, Greene-Woods, Lawyer, and Alofi engage a decolonizing-intersectionality framework in "Climbing the Mountain: Power, Privilege, and Equity" to describe the experiences of Deaf and Hard of Hearing (D/HH) as a minoritized group in educational administration. Seeking to fill a gap in the research surrounding D/HH administrators working in D/HH programs, the authors document the various challenges D/HH leaders face in both preparation and practice. The decolonizing-intersectionality framework is founded partially on the idea that schools can be sites of perpetuating stratified social positions for both students and educators. Using this framework, the authors employ a multiple-case instrumental case study method to detail how D/HH educational administrators attained positions of authority and how they center themselves as Deaf individuals and educational leaders.

The ways in which leaders who advocate for inclusion and socially just education implement practice and policy have direct effects on the lived experiences of students. In "Rolling My Way in Leadership: Perspectives From an Educator With Cerebral Palsy," Vergara presents a personal narrative involving her life as an individual with cerebral palsy (CP), and as a wheelchair user. Vergara first explores how her educational experiences were impacted by her disability, moving from K–12 through higher education. She then analyzes how her disability motivated her in the struggle for professional growth and leadership in education. The experiences are narrated through DisCrit frames as Vergara explores how dis/ability and race, as systems of oppression, have intersected throughout her life. In constructing the narrative, Vergara aims to conscientize readers about implicit or explicit societal challenges that individuals with disabilities encounter in their quest for equity, and to set the conditions for empowerment of individuals with disabilities to continue demanding justice while working within institutional contexts.

Cooper and Otis finish the section by introducing readers to a framework on college going culture. In their chapter, "Dis/Abled Students in College-Going Cultures: Examining How Dis/Ability Is Understood in a "College for All" Culture," Cooper and Otis ask readers to work through and grapple with the meaning behind "college for all." They ask what it means to be college ready? Who is college ready? And conversely, are colleges "ready" for students labeled with learning disabilities, emotional disturbance, Autism, and other labels. Motivated by issues of racial inequity, tracking, and unequal access and opportunity and drawing from a large study of college going culture in schools in California, the authors present a conceptual framework that seeks to help practitioners and researchers alike to understand the many ways that schools, as institutions, might function to serve every student. The chapter is organized around two fundamental questions: "How can school leaders utilize a framework of equity and inclusive college going on their campus?" and "How might we adapt existing frameworks for college-going cultures to be more equitable and assuming of students with disabilities?"

# CHAPTER 15

# IN OUR OWN WORDS

## Special Education Teachers of Color With Dis/Abilities

**Saili S. Kulkarni**
*San José State University*

**Samuel Bland**
*San José State University*

**Joanna Marinia Gaeta**
*San José State University*

The education system is filled with examples of how students of color with dis/abilities[1] are positioned as unintelligent, at risk, or behaviorally deviant (Broderick & Leonardo, 2015). Because schools draw upon Eurocentric cultural knowledge and behavior (Yosso, 2005), students of color with dis/abilities are among the most marginalized groups in educational spaces. This parallels some of the inequities we see in teaching. While research on racism has predominantly identified the ways in which students of color experience it in schools, less is known about the experiences of

*Who Decides?*, pages 361–381
Copyright © 2022 by Information Age Publishing
www.infoagepub.com
All rights of reproduction in any form reserved.

teachers of color (Pizarro & Kohli, 2020). Among teachers of color is a subgroup of teachers, special education teachers of color (SETOCs), who have been overlooked and underserved in both research and critical spaces (Kulkarni et al., 2021). Additionally, there is limited research on teachers of color who identify with visible and invisible dis/abilities as defined through learning, mental health, trauma, and health. Often, teachers of color are aware of racial injustices through personal experiences in schools yet are framed as underprepared (Irizarry & Donaldson, 2012; Kohli et al., 2017). Additionally, teachers with dis/abilities have experienced further marginalization and segregation in schools. There is a critical need to learn from voices and stories of SETOCs with dis/abilities who are committed to providing transformative educational opportunities for their students who experience similar marginalization.

What little research that exists on SETOCs tends to focus on a few key areas including the recruitment of SETOCs (Brown, 2014). Progress in this area, however, has been made in California, where Cooc and Yang (2016) note that there has been a substantial increase in the number of SETOCs. Still, Bettini and colleagues (2020) note that nationally, SETOCs are underrepresented in the literature and field. As Boveda and Aronson (2019) contend, to date there are few studies that specifically include the voices of SETOCs. These authors used a mixed-methods study of preservice SETOCs and found that teachers noted complexities of understanding the sociocultural differences of their students and interpretation of their own experiences with discrimination.

## CRITICAL AFFINITY SPACES

Leonardo and Porter (2010) argue that White people and people of color enter spaces of racial dialogues from very different positions and experiential knowledge. It is imperative, therefore, that there can be spaces which help people of color collectively access support. Even the most critical teachers of color face enormous constraints structurally as well as personally in educational spaces (Achinstein et al., 2010). Moving from a trauma-informed approach toward a healing-centered framework (Ginwright, 2015) emphasizes the need for teachers of color to collectively heal and reimagine pedagogies of activism and resistance in their classrooms (Pour-Khorshid, 2018). Martinez et al. (2016) explain that as educators work to resist White supremacist ideologies in the classroom, they may experience isolation, further necessitating spaces to build with others collectively.

Teachers working at the intersections of racism and ableism in schools have the added challenges both from critical, collective spaces, which rarely include disability as an identity (Baglieri & Lalvani, 2020) and from special education which employs a deficit framing of students of color, students' disabilities and abilities. Working at this critical nexus requires careful attention to the interdependence of racism and ableism (see Annamma et al., 2013). It also requires an affinity space that specifically acknowledges the specific needs of special education teachers.

The current chapter utilizes DisCrit (Annamma et al., 2013) to shift dominant narratives of special education teachers, leaders, and teacher education and to highlight SETOCs with dis/abilities. We offer narratives sharing our own journeys as SETOCs with dis/abilities and counter existing narratives about dis/ability which employ race and ability-neutral policies. We draw from experiences of racism and ableism as students and educators in the school system. Specifically, we lean on DisCrit Tenet 2, which highlights how racism and ableism operate as interdependent identities. We describe implications of our experiences for teachers as leaders and for leadership at large to understand how the intersections of dis/ability and race influence the experiences of SETOCs. We also draw directly from our work to build a critical affinity group of SETOCs at a public 4-year institution in the Bay Area and how the experiences of creating this space virtually during the global pandemic reified some of our own complex understandings of our identities as people of color, as people with health and dis/ability considerations, and as educators.

## DR. K: TEACHING AS A TEACHER EDUCATOR OF COLOR WITH DIS/ABILITIES

My story negotiates my identity as a South Asian female with invisible dis/abilities. I draw from my experiences as a student, teacher, and teacher educator in majority-White educational spaces and how these different positionings impact my framing of ability, dis/ability, and leadership. I begin by describing my teaching experiences in the Bay Area and then draw from how these experiences were complicated by the opportunity to attend graduate school and learn specifically about dis/ability studies and critical race theory from leading scholars in the field.

I spent the first 2 years of my undergraduate degree in Boston figuring out what I wanted to major in and what my career options would be after graduating. I went from the self-imposed rigidity of thinking that I had to become a doctor to grappling with complex poetry in the English department and finally landing on psychology. My last few semesters were spent assisting a developmental psychology professor with some of her research on language, child development, and dis/ability. It was there that I began to see education as a viable career option.

Like most undergraduates at private and elite institutions, I was an easy target for alternatively-certified programs such as Teach for America (TFA) and the New Teacher Project (TTNP). These programs were an easy way for me and my colleagues who were drawn to volunteering and service in college to see teaching as a mission to help students in underserved, urban schools. I look back on this perspective and my complicity in this problematic system with reservation and some regret, though I know it also helped to shape my current belief system and eventual (un)learning of these values and ideologies.

During my first few years as a special education teacher, my beliefs began to shift through practices and opportunities to work directly with students in the classroom. These daily interactions in schools were a pivotal part of shaping who I later became. It is important to note, however, that if they weren't also structured by strong mentorship by credential program instructors and a critical program through the Teacher Education for Advancement of Multicultural Society (TEAMS) program sponsored by AmeriCorps at the University of San Francisco, I would have continued to hold the same deficit views of communities of color and students with dis/abilities that the New Teacher Project refused to challenge.

My assigned teaching fellows program was in Oakland, California. I moved to Oakland from Boston, never having lived in the Bay Area and not having a community there. Immediately, one of the things I draw upon now, as a teacher educator, is how important these things are for new teachers. Not having that immediate support network while navigating a new environment presented challenges during my first year. My assigned classroom was a middle school portable in the back of the school buildings, over 100 yards away from the main school building (see Figure 15.1). That main school building

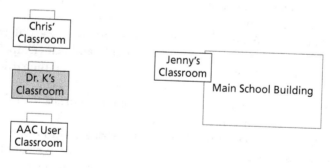

**Figure 15.1** Layout of Dr. K's middle school as a special education teacher. *Image Description:* Representation rectangles labeling main school building, Jenny's classroom attached to main school building, distance from the left and three classroom portables represented by rectangles. Dr. K's classroom is left center and colored in gray and Chris' classroom and AAC user classrooms are on either side of Dr. K's classroom.

was where "general education" students were allowed to attend classes. My colleague Jenny, who taught students with "mild dis/abilities" was allowed to be in the main building, but her segregated classroom was at the very edge of the building, like the tip of the island (see Figure 15.1).

Attitudes toward dis/ability, even in the mid 2000s when I began to teach, were incredibly racist and ableist. The simple task of trying to get some of the students with whom I worked to engage in extracurricular courses such as physical education (PE) or art was met with incredible discomfort or outright refusal. Students with the complex support needs I taught in my first year were often rendered invisible, infantilized, or dehumanized. Unsurprisingly, yet still as painful, these students were all students of color. My participation in Saturday seminars for teachers committed to multicultural education never addressed significant dis/ability; it is important to note this erasure is often the case in critical spaces (Kulkarni et al., 2021). Nevertheless, I was grateful for the space in developing frameworks with which to draw on my own experiences as a person of color and those of my students as students of color. Learning from scholars such as Dr. Jeff Duncan Andrade and Dr. Geneva Gay was an invaluable opportunity.

My work as a special education teacher was around the time I had to come to terms with my own struggles with mental health and a physical pelvic floor dis/ability (see Kulkarni et al., 2021). I attended bi-weekly physical therapy sessions for a pelvic floor dis/ability at a time when this was not quite as common as it is today. Physical therapy for pelvic floor disorders is a combination of biofeedback to reduce muscle tightness in hips, groin, and hamstrings, as well as lower back pain. Muscle tightness for me was both physical and psychological (directly linked to some anxiety). Coming to terms with my own dis/abilities is something that will continue to be a lifelong process for me, but as I have gotten older, I have also become a little less nervous and learned to deal with the internalized ableism I once harbored.

My time in graduate school allowed me the privilege of time to continue to wrestle with these tensions of dis/ability identity, positionality, relationality and intersectionality. I was fortunate enough to learn about dis/ability studies in education through a graduate school professor with whom I was assigned to work as a teaching assistant, Dr. Eunjung Kim. For most of graduate school, I recognized a discomfort with the way that special education portrayed and researched people with dis/abilities. I didn't see my students and their lived realities as something special education research seemed to value. Dis/ability studies opened up a world of possibilities around understanding ableism, how it intersected with racism and how to undo our conceptions of normality in schools. It changed the way I began to view my work as a doctoral student and eventually as a teacher educator. My dissertation, for example, utilized a critical dis/ability studies framework married with culturally relevant pedagogy. This was work being done at the intersections of dis/ability and race around the time when Drs. Connor, Ferri, and Annamma developed the first book for DisCrit. Dr. Kim encouraged me to read across the field of dis/ability studies and to develop my own definition of dis/ability studies as it related to my own work and the research I planned to conduct for my dissertation. I wrote that dis/ability studies encompassed a lens as well as a field. Drawing from the social model of dis/ability, it highlighted the importance of dis/ability as identity and lived experience rather than deficit. Additionally, dis/ability studies encouraged the valuing of the lives of disabled people(s) in their own care, education, and research; rather than having these aspects decided for them. In developing this definition, I have since expanded my understanding to include activism and resistance and nuance around the fact that dis/ability studies still have to reckon with its own whiteness.

I was delighted to find that dis/ability studies field had a group of powerful South Asian scholars and activists from whose work I could draw meaning for my own work in teacher education. I learned from the important work of Dr. Nirmala Erevelles, Dr. Priya Lalvani, Dr. Srikala Naraian, Dr. Subini Annamma, and other important South Asian educators broadly. Being able to fully draw from these identities, as women of color and as disabled, have shaped the ways in which I prepare teachers in my current role as a faculty member.

In particular, I note that it is important that teachers understand the complexities of identity and representation. My role, therefore, is to help them negotiate their multiple identities and the identity they bring in as teachers. This harkens back to DisCrit Tenet 1, which describes how racism and ableism operate interdependently. In my role as a teacher educator, I want to make this interdependence and intersectionality very apparent for students. We do this through a series of critical readings representative of the lives of disabled people of color. It is also to expose them to the lived realities of intersectional lives of other people of color with dis/abilities. We draw heavily on readings from Dr. David Connor and Dr. Subini Annamma, and their earlier work on DisCrit, for this reason; as both have shared the narratives and accounts of students that have helped expand these understandings.

In moving forward, the next steps for me as a teacher educator are to be able to share a bit more about my own lived experiences with the teachers with whom I work. I also have plans to connect with educational leaders and administrators for this work, especially in my roles as part of our educational leadership doctoral program and the emancipatory leadership master's programs at San José State University. It is through both of these programs that I hope to also provide opportunities to delve into the intersections of racism and ableism, dis/ability studies critical race theory (DisCrit; Annamma et al., 2013) and the lived experiences of disabled people of color that can inform how leaders include and understand dis/ability as an identity rather than a deficit.

## SAMUEL: NEGOTIATING DIS/ABILITY IDENTITY

When I started school on the eastside of San Jose, at Evergreen Community College, I had challenges related to having speech problems and related to having a speech delay. I was born prematurely and this is part of the explanation for some of these delays with my speech. I did not start speaking until close to 4 years of age. When I started elementary school, it was really difficult for me to pay attention in large groups because I did not understand what the material meant. I remember being in the first grade. We would, as a class, take a timed test that would make me feel stressed because of my lack of understanding of the concept of addition and subtraction. Still, the test meant I was timed and compared with other students. I tended to be disappointed by the results I would receive when I got my worksheet back. I also felt disappointment at not being mentioned on the wall, where the teacher put the work of students who were excelling. When some kids are seeing other students succeeding, it can make them feel like they do not belong in the classroom or are not capable of doing the same work.

Teachers in school noticed I was struggling and recommended me to a special education resource room. During this time, I was pulled out of my larger classroom and placed into small groups throughout the school day to develop my writing and reading skills. When working in small groups, I felt better because I was not being constantly compared to my whole class in terms of my test scores and grades. As I entered third grade, my family moved to South San José. I was able to get into a special education classroom traveling on a small, yellow school bus from Curtner to Los Alamitos in Almaden every day. The bus ride was 1 hour every morning. The students at my new school were majority White and the neighborhood consisted of students from a higher socioeconomic status than my former school. I quickly learned that I was the fifth Black student at the school and was placed in an inclusive special education classroom because parent involvement and a high amount of staff was available. My classroom was located in front of the school, but everyone knew it was the special education classroom because they placed the moderate and severe classroom right behind our portable (see Figure 15.2).

I was treated differently because I was in special education and as one of the few Black students in the school. Students would always refer to my class as "the small class." Being able to be in an inclusive classroom gave me the opportunity to grow academically, improved my reading and my ability to construct sentences on my own. Teachers in my class provided consistent

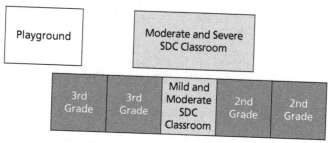

**Figure 15.2** Samuel's elementary school layout. *Image Description:* Representation rectangles labeling Samuel's elementary school. On the top center is the name of the moderate/severe special day class (SDC) classroom in light grey. Top left is the playground in white. Bottom across the center are dark grey squares indicating third grade classrooms and at the center bottom is the mild/moderate special day classroom in blue, where Samuel was "placed." Note that the moderate severe classroom was actually that large, equivalent to 2–3 classrooms in the main building.

scaffolding and helped me to fill in the blanks. The different area was also life changing because I was able to see some schools provide art and music compared to my old school which did not have these resources. I started to get into the habit of drawing things and I started to pursue art, for which my mother bought me a huge art kit during Christmas. Again, it was interesting to see how different this new school was from my previous one, especially in terms of racial makeup and resources.

As a student who attended a special education program, I often faced embarrassment, internalized ableism and shame about dis/ability. As I went to middle school, news came out I was placed in special education from other students who would gossip before school. The majority of the teachers at this school, including my special education teachers, were White. The first time I was able to experience having someone I could relate to was when I met Coach Drake. Coach Drake was a Black male and shared my background. He also enjoyed the same music and sports that I did. It was very compelling to have someone who I could see myself in and who held a professional position. I also had another Black teacher who taught history. She was very supportive of my learning because I had anxiety when we needed to read in front of the class and because I had difficulties pronouncing certain words. Many of my friends in the special education classroom wanted to be in general education classes, because these classes were thought of as ideal. I was in general education courses for math and history. When being pushed into a general education classroom, I struggled with learning the concepts because I did not have the foundational skills related to literacy and math. I knew academic success meant better jobs and opportunities, so by the end of middle school I was only in special education to receive some advising and I persisted in my general education courses to try and carve out this desired success.

By the time I started high school, I was able to adapt socially but I continued to struggle with math. My grades started to be affected because I was not performing well on exams. Half way through my first year of high school my family moved to Fremont where I went to a high school, again with a majority of White students. When I began school, there wasn't transportation and my sister and I had to walk two miles every morning to school. School started early and I struggled to be on time. My English teacher would give me a hard time and would not listen to me. During science, I was often called Urkel from the 90s television show *Family Matters* because of having glasses and being Black. A few times, other White students at the school also called me "monkey" without any students receiving any consequences. I started to skip school at the end of my freshman year and my grades began to worsen.

I transferred schools again, this time to a high school where the demographics and educators were more mixed. At this school, my progress improved because teachers were willing to understand and be compassionate toward what I was not getting at the time. I also had teachers who were really honest and direct, relating to how my current situation would align with my future situation. One of my areas of need during high school was my writing skills. This was because I did not receive reinforcement related to foundational skills such as grammar, sentence structure, and organization which were taught in elementary and middle school. As I completed high school, I still felt that I was not on the same level with my peers. I was not going to attend a 4-year college right after high school because I did not meet the college admission requirements. This feeling of not being on the same level and this sense of insecurity followed me even when I went to college because I was unaware of how to "play the game." I struggled to obtain financial aid and navigate the process of higher education.

In college, I had a newly found freedom and autonomy of not attending classes if I chose not to. I was placed in remedial math and English courses. When I was in these classes, I did not take them seriously and I typically attended them to get to the next level. I believe that high school should provide additional supports related to reading and writing so that students would not need to be placed in remedial classes. When I started my second quarter of college, I missed many of my assignments and put in very little effort. I received all Fs during my second quarter right before the summer. During the summer, I was able to refocus and receive the academic support for students with dis/abilities related to tutoring, extended time on exams, and counseling through the education opportunity program (EOP) for first generation college students.

These services helped me to excel in my classes, but at times I felt a high amount of stress related to succeeding. In the middle of my sophomore year, I struggled with writing and I did not pass the required writing class. My teacher thought I needed to repeat the class, therefore, she told me I needed to meet with her at 7 o'clock if I wanted to improve my grade. Unfortunately, I was not able to meet with her at that time due to the lack of transportation and also juggling an unstable job. The professor was not flexible or understanding and had not provided me with explicit instruction, which caused me confusion related to writing prompts. The teacher did not present any examples of the writing assignment and probably thought all of the students understood her directions. As a result, I was really confused and when I tried to ask questions she did not have the time to support me during instruction time or after class. After not receiving support from my teacher, I kind of felt like giving up.

When I transferred to San Jose State University, I believed my writing skills were improving. When I was admitted in the Child Development Department, my professors would tell me my writing was poor and I was at fault for my progress. It was like two different worlds coming from De Anza and entering San Jose State University including different rules related to academic achievement and excellence. During my first year at San Jose State University, I dealt with a high amount of stress, lack of being organized, and did not have support in place to help me with my academics. After my first year, I sought help in writing and I was supported by a writing counselor who helped me with my papers. My grades started to improve, but I dealt with anxiety during this time and imposter syndrome. Did I really belong in college? After college I knew that I wanted to work with kids, but I did not want to pursue this right away with the high amount of stress and burnout I experienced on campus.

After completing my bachelor's degree, I worked for Santa Clara Unified School District in various positions. My first job was really hard because it was a split shift and my schedule was not consistent. I dealt with depression because I gave 6 years of my life to receive little pay and did not have a stable life. Things started to change when I pursued a role as a paraprofessional educator. Suddenly, my outlook was different and I enjoyed my time working with kids. Even as a person with a dis/ability, I still was unsure about working with kids with dis/abilities. My first 2 years as a paraeducator, the teacher I supported had a difficult time with organization and behavior management. She spent so much time controlling student behavior and I started to recognize that this was problematic. I also experienced a high amount of stress and started to rethink the job. The teacher went to a different school because she was burnt out. The next teacher was a game changer. She focused on building collaborative relationships with her staff. I was really impressed with her management skills when dealing with the students and of having compassion and being flexible because several students came with different learning styles. She attempted to present different ways to solve problems academically and socially because several students dealt with anger issues. Lastly, she was also understanding of how the students felt in the classroom in which she treated them with respect and dignity with a listening ear.

Leadership was also a critical piece of my experience working as a paraprofessional educator. The administrator at my job was very supportive of me and helped me to become a teacher. He saw the potential in me. He was well liked but everyone did not like the fact that he was a bit less strict in his approach to discipline. It's interesting how that authoritarian way of acting in schools is so engrained somehow! When I was growing up and began working as a paraprofessional in several of the mainstream classrooms, and in my own classroom as aide, several teachers demanded that the students were quiet for the majority of the school day and sit in their seats. Teachers demanded that students listen to them "or else." When teachers would speak to students this way, they generated a one-way dialogue in which the teacher was the only individual to partake in the conversation. As a result, several students were placed in punishment for having to be placed on the wall or sent to the office during recess or lunch. Largely hearing conversations in the lunchroom, several teachers blamed the students but did not account for the student background or family history. It was really difficult because around this time, I saw lots of reports of high amounts of students of color being suspended included in special education. Primarily, the teachers at my school were White and when working in their classroom they didn't understand what it meant to be culturally sustaining. Somehow, seeing what not to do helped me realize what I was committed to.

As DisCrit (Annamma et al., 2013) affords us, racism and ableism were present in my story of interactions with teachers as a student of color with disabilities. We do not have enough teachers who are flexible, understanding, and compassionate in their academic instruction or related to their students' social emotional learning. Relating to my own experience, having a teacher in your corner to be able to understand your own learning and behavior style and being able to adapt the curriculum to your strengths instead of your weaknesses can help elevate the understanding related to the curriculum being taught. School leaders should look for teachers who are flexible in presenting content to students that are engaging, present cultural backgrounds, and provide relatable experiences from students' lives to stay engaged and focused in the classroom.

The school system presents several barriers for teachers, administrators, and students to become successful. The school system is designed as a maze for students of color who are at a disadvantage related to the resource gap that is presented in schools to be lost and forgotten. Several schools in disproportionate zoning districts are not receiving the same quality of instruction and school buildings in comparison to their counterparts living in suburban neighborhoods. The school system has been historically designed to hold students of color back from opportunities, generating an opportunity gap, which prevents students from building their own network and long-term success.

## JOANNA'S STORY: SCHOOL AND TRAUMA-INFORMED INSTRUCTION

My family and I just recently moved from the East Side of San Jose to the South side. With the move, came the obvious repercussion of changing schools: being on the waitlist and doing school from home. At the time, I thought it was normal to be at home for as long as I was, but as a kid you don't understand the concept of being on "a waitlist" to get into school. Finally, after about 3 weeks of instruction, I was enrolled as a first grader in an elementary school in the Morgan Hill School District.

As a second grader, I felt I knew what to expect. I had my first-grade teacher, my friends, the librarian, and the playground; I looked forward to returning to safety and the familiar. As a teacher, I feel we sometimes forget that school is a safe place for students. Even for students like me.

This is the year that I was abused by my father multiple times. My mom had been a stay at home mom for the longest time and decided to return to the workforce. She eventually found out about the abuse which caused my parents to get into a big argument that revealed my dad had a drug relapse and started his habit, again. After the explosive argument, my mom kicked my dad out of the house.

My mom had a restraining order placed against my father, and that was that. I never spoke to my mom about the trauma I experienced, and neither did she. There were about 3 years I didn't know what was going on in the classroom. How can you begin to think about school when something traumatic happens to you? As a child, I didn't know how to even express myself verbally as I was barely learning how to read high-frequency vocabulary words and construct sentences. How was I expected to function at school? Yet at the same time, school became my safe haven and place of hope over my own home.

When I entered my third-grade year, I started to have chronic kidney and bladder infections. This meant that I was out of school due to being sick and often hospitalized. One memory is burned in my mind that I can still clearly see today. We all came back from morning recess. It was math time and we were all in our whole group seats. My teacher went to the front of the class and asked everyone a question: "How many of you know your multiplication facts?" When I looked around, I only saw two of my classmates raising their hands. She seemed pleased and replied, "The two of you come in the back with me. The rest of you, stay in your seats and color."

At first, it was a dream come true. Coloring after recess wasn't a norm, so we all welcomed the change! As I looked back, I wanted to go to the back so I could learn this new word called "multiplication" and what it meant. I felt discouraged because I wasn't part of the group who was learning multiplication. I remember feeling something was wrong with me, with all of us, who remained in our whole group seats, coloring. I thought, maybe if my hair was blonde, if my skin was light, and my eyes were colored rather than brown like the two students, I could learn multiplication too.

Oftentimes teachers are found doing this very same thing to their students: focusing on what students don't know rather than focusing on what they have the potential to learn. As teachers and administrators, we need to continue to communicate and foster learning and growth for the learning differences our students bring to the classroom. I am not against skill-level groupings, but when this is used as a comfort rather than a support, it can have detrimental effects on the students as a whole. In this case, the idea of gift sharing could have been utilized by using the student "mentors" who knew about multiplication to assist in small group activities. Another idea that teachers can implement is rotating groups. While this allows students of various levels to engage with each other, it also gives students the experience of individuals with different abilities and how to work together to foster understanding.

Our home in the Southside of San Jose had been sold. We lived on the property where they were going to build a power plant in this part of San Jose. With our 30 day notice almost up, my mom applied to a couple of homeless shelters. After living out of our car for almost a year and a half, there was an opening at a homeless shelter in San Martin. From the homeless shelter in San Martin, I would take the 68 bus early in the morning to my old elementary school. From there, I would take the school bus to the fourth through sixth grade campus on Monterey Road.

As a teacher, I've had 3 homeless students come through my classroom, all middle school boys. Every single one of them came to school tired due to transportation difficulties (either due to using public transportation, sometimes being late due to bus delays, car troubles, etc.). Oftentimes teachers would share how these students would fall asleep in class or were tardy. I was able to advocate for my students' experiences with the staff and how transportation can be a difficult barrier that affects multiple areas such as attendance and healthy sleep (and lack of). Check-ins with our students can help to shed light on what they need so we are able to support them over the barriers that they face.

When we hear these stories as teachers, we think from the perspective of an educated adult. As a teacher now, I have some students who are facing similar situations of trauma, and some of the rhetoric from teachers sounds like this: "Why don't the parents get them therapy?" or "Why don't their parents care?" or "The student just doesn't care." These are destructive statements that teachers need to reflect on and transform. Rather, constructive measures like referring outside agencies for therapy and help, empathy, and compassionate communication can go a long way when we are connecting with our students and their families.

Growing up in a conservative Mexican-Christian household, I was raised believing that mental health wasn't real. You had to be strong mentally and pray for strength. It wasn't until I started learning more about mental health in college that I talked with my doctor and was diagnosed with anxiety and depression. After my initial diagnosis, I was conflicted because I felt there was something more going on beneath the surface that I couldn't figure out myself. After my doctor did a little digging at this point, I was diagnosed with PTSD (post traumatic stress disorder) due to multiple, ongoing traumas I experienced from second grade until early college.

Mental health is a crucial part of our student's well-being that all educational staff need to take into consideration. Our approach to classroom situations can set off triggers within our students, initiating walls that separate us from them. When students experience trauma or have dis/abilities, their reaction is always going to be one that protects. It's important that school isn't just a physical safe place for our students but a mentally/emotionally safe space. As teachers, we can create a supportive environment where students can finally be at ease. Feeling at ease is one of the important ways to connect with our students and then initiate learning. Safety is primary and learning is secondary.

Lastly, all behavior is an indication of what is taking place internally within our students. Students who have experienced trauma/s, have dis/abilities, are homeless, and so forth, have reactions that manifest in different ways. As an educator I have seen the hardcore student who isn't in touch with their emotions, the student who doesn't "care" about anything, and the student who is resilient, just to name a few. What's common between all of these students is that these students have teachers, aides, counselors, and so forth, who are able to help guide their choices and make a connection. All these students, our students, require understanding that their reactions, behaviors, and words are not meant to disrespect or torment a classroom community, rather, to bring it together. Inclusivity, connection, and empathy are paths that assist our students who are on these journeys. The question is, "How do you connect with a student if your experience is worlds different than theirs?" The answer is to get to know who your students are. Cumulative files have more knowledge to offer us than we expect but can't be our only source for student information. For example, this paired with day to day classroom observations can illuminate behavioral patterns and triggers for students. As a result, one can discover more effective ways of meeting the students' individual behavior needs. I go into this in much more detail later. On a deeper level, asking questions about what your students are into is a great way to break the ice. If they recommend *Between Shades of Grey* by Ruta Sepetys (2012), read it. If they share their culture and what they did with their family the night before, listen. Students share what they like and what is important to them. The job for us as educators and administrators is to seek out knowledge of who they are.

I was hired as an instructional assistant (IA) for a middle school mild/moderate dis/ability classroom. The 2 years of experience I had as an IA allowed me to exercise skills in connecting with my students, working 1:1 with students with various needs and students with diverse educational and behavioral needs. As an IA providing behavior support, I had information about my student's experiences, learned their triggers, and how to meet them where they were at in order to provide them with the support they needed. Upon completing my CSET test, I was hired as a teacher, under a special education emergency certificate, teaching in the middle school mild/moderate dis/ability setting. This placement occurred during my second year of teaching at the school site where I was working and in the third semester enrolled in a teaching credential program.

At the beginning of my second year of teaching, I had a student who was mocking me as I reviewed the school expectations. I ignored it and, as a second-year teacher, I had the feeling I wanted to write a referral on this student for being disrespectful, one who repeats everything the teacher says with a mocking tone and looks at the class for encouragement or laughs. Once the 2:30 p.m. bell rang, I ended up going to the students cumulative file. It turned out that this student exhibited similar behaviors in his elementary classes. It was a cycle in the form of a stack of referral copies. He would mock the teacher, the teacher would write a referral, the student would escalate and act out (usually by swearing, throwing things in the classroom, and leaving the classroom), and then parents would get involved. As I read referral after referral, it was evident that writing a referral on this child would do more harm than good. There was some disconnect that the teachers weren't aware of or understanding, and this stared me in the face.

After getting the class started on their assignment, I asked the student to come outside with me so I could speak with him. I asked him if he remembered mocking me in class yesterday. He nodded. I told him,

I looked in your file and noticed that this was something you did back in elementary and you know what? I know writing referrals doesn't work for you. So instead, I will be talking with your parents about what's going on in class.

This student's parents and I worked as a team to support our student and eventually got him to attend the meetings as well. Being his case manager for 2 years, I learned everything about him. He had fetal alcohol syndrome, which affected his learning, hearing, and different developmental areas. Even after our talk and him crying, I became one of his favorite teachers. Having this level of understanding resulted in reaching out to the parents and communicating with them about behaviors that were manifesting in the classroom. As this student's case manager and teacher, I would've never known that his family would've been so supportive if I didn't take the first step and reach out. This is a practice I have taken with me since. No matter how challenging the situation, you never know how your student and their families will respond. As educators and administrators, it is better to build a community connection and work together as a team with one goal in mind: the student. Our students need a community of support from teachers, paraeducators, counselors, administrators, and family.

Oftentimes as teachers, there are "minor" behaviors that start out as either a cry for help or attention. With this particular student, he wanted to be liked and included by his peers. He sought this by engaging in disruptive behaviors. We ended up making a hand signal, so I knew when he needed to take a break and have a reset. This was very successful in my classroom due to our communication and consistency about our signal use. Unfortunately, even though this signal was part of his behavior intervention plan (BIP), not all of his teachers adhered to it. He ended up having the hardest time in a few of his classes due to inconsistencies. There was an incident that escalated in class, and the teacher didn't use the signal and the situation got out of hand. The student was wandering around the school campus, yelling and swearing at the top of his lungs, and eventually went back into the classroom and was swearing at the teacher who triggered the escalation. He was yelling in his face. Finally, after asking him to come with me to my classroom, he came. My classroom was empty so there was a place he could unload the frustration. He cussed, yelled, and cried in my classroom, with me sitting at a desk and him pacing around the classroom. I allowed him to express his frustration and not once did he cuss at me, just about the situation. I had him stay in my classroom the entire period so he could have a safe place to process the situation.

He was still escalating and yelling when I was asking him questions like, "Do you want a tissue to wipe your nose?" I knew the swearing wasn't toward me. He just went through a familiar cycle that triggered many emotional responses dating back to elementary. Again, I made sure to reach out to his parents to let them know what happened at school. This situation, and many like this one, are testaments to how we as teacher's can transform the discipline process for our students if we educate ourselves about our students' needs. As teachers, we need to educate ourselves on our students, their experiences, and use this information to support our students. This is a critical piece for teacher preparation and dispositions.

These stories emphasize the need for trauma-informed teaching and pedagogies that allow us, as teachers and leaders, to move past assumptions and allow students, families, and communities to process pain. My own experiences with trauma shaped who I was and who I am as a teacher. I learned later about mental health, trauma, and behavior and how these things impact my own journey with education as well as my students' journeys. Understanding mental health dis/ability and learning to support students in holistic ways has deeply informed the ways in which I approach teaching. It also helps me to implore and advocate with leadership for restorative approaches to discipline at my middle school.

## DISCUSSION AND CONCLUSION

As evidenced from our stories above, we negotiated the identities of dis/ability with our statuses as teachers and leaders. We note the instances of how racism and ableism were interdependent in all of our school experiences as teachers and learners. Specifically aligning our work with DisCrit's first tenet and noting that racism and ableism uphold notions of normalcy, our stories noted how special education spaces continued to be segregated, racist spaces in schools. We note the specific feelings of imposter syndrome that dis/ability and race generate for the identities of teachers of color with dis/abilities (as evidenced by Samuel's story) as well as the challenges of the work of SETOCs in critical, social justice spaces (as noted in Dr. K's story), from which we are often denied entry. We also note the importance of trauma-informed pedagogies to help students process their experiences (Joanna's story). To begin to build together, combat imposter syndrome, trauma, and feelings of inadequacy entrenched in internalized ableism, we provide here the importance of building affinity groups for SETOCs and some implications for anti-racist, anti-ableist leadership practices.

### SETOC Affinity Groups

As noted in the introduction, SETOCs are an overlooked and underserved group in education. Given the isolation and feelings of inadequacy that come from internalized racism and ableism, it is critical that SETOCs be provided spaces to process their identities as teachers, students, and leaders. Our journey toward sharing our stories stems from a virtual critical affinity space of which we were a part during the global pandemic. Our affinity space dealt with the intersections of racism and ableism using Zoom focus groups bi-weekly and created a space in which we could process racism, ableism, and the challenges of teaching. We note that this space is just the beginning, but that teacher education programs should incorporate such spaces for students of color. Kulkarni et al. (2022) highlighted the importance of SETOC support in their work on minoritized special education teachers working toward equity. We similarly felt that creating a collective space for us to vent, process, and be heard was important to sustaining our on-going work in special education and as teachers of color. As noted in our literature review, critical affinity spaces, especially for teachers of color, provide a much-needed space for healing (Pour-Khorshid, 2018).

Miller (2020) notes that in order to be anti-racist, leaders need to be aware of the fact that culture shapes leadership and leadership shapes culture. Because school leaders have the capacity to shift the culture of schools toward anti-racist and anti-ableist understandings of dis/ability and difference, they are critical to enacting meaningful changes. Sustainable leadership that engages anti-racism and anti-ableism is needed by engaging school stakeholders. This is critical to move beyond deficit frameworks of special education and meaningfully engaging dis/ability in classroom spaces, both as it relates to teachers' identities and P–12 students. It is our hope that by sharing our stories of SETOCs with identified dis/abilities, that we can begin to shape a much-needed conversation and note an erasure of such representation both in the field of special education and in its implications for educational leadership.

## Suggestions for Leaders

Based on our stories and our own experiences, we have several suggestions for school leaders who are working alongside SETOCs with disabilities and in support of students of color with disabilities. Primarily, we believe that school leaders need experiences unpacking disability as an identity construct. These experiences should start in leadership and administration credential and educational programs, where future leaders are supported in understanding disability as a marker of difference and identity rather than a deficit.

Second, we highlight the importance of connections between special education teachers, leaders, and other educational stakeholders such as families and instructional assistants. All of these key stakeholders are critical in the educational development of students with disabilities and their future success in postsecondary settings (Harry & Kalyanpur, 2014). Generating opportunities and spaces where families, teachers, and leaders can come together outside of traditionally structured meetings such as individualized education plan annual meetings, provides the opportunity to build positive relationships and provide ongoing support for students with disabilities.

Importantly, leaders need to expand their definitions of diversity and inclusion. Diversity and inclusion in higher education are common catch phrases that code the importance of racial equity initiatives. Moving beyond this framework, leaders need an expansive understanding of race as its intersections across social identity, including disability which is often removed from such conversations. In special education, inclusion refers to the opportunities for students with disabilities to learn alongside same-aged peers in general school settings. It is important for leaders to expand both definitions and understand how racism and ableism operate interdependently to uphold notions of normalcy in schools (Annamma et al., 2013).

Finally, it is important that leaders become attuned to move beyond the quantitative data often presented in professional development school spaces and listen to the narratives of multiply marginalized youth and educators. We hope that such narratives humanize the experiences of disability and race in schools and allow leaders to understand the complexities that these identities embody. We hope that "our own words" have an impact on the ways in which educational professionals and leaders educate students of color with disabilities.

## AUTHORS' NOTE

We have no known conflict of interest to disclose.

## NOTES

1. We use the slash in dis/ability to indicate a fracture between abled and disabled identities and the tensions these identities create in schools and educational spaces.

## REFERENCES

Achinstein, B., Ogawa, R. T., Sexton, D., & Freitas, C. (2010). Retaining teachers of color: A pressing problem and a potential strategy for "hard-to-staff" schools. *Review of educational research, 80*(1), 71–107. https://doi.org/10.3102/0034 654309355994

Annamma, S. A., Connor, D. J., & Ferri, B. A. (2013). Dis/ability critical race studies (DisCrit): Theorizing at the intersections of race and dis/ability. *Race, Ethnicity and Education, 16*(1), 1–31. https://doi.org/10.1080/13613324.2012.730511

Baglieri, S., & Lalvani, P. (2019). *Undoing Ableism: Teaching about disability in K–12 classrooms.* Routledge. https://doi.org/10.4324/9781351002868

Bettini, E., Gilmour, A. F., Williams, T. O., & Billingsley, B. (2020). Predicting special and general educators' intent to continue teaching using conservation of resources theory. *Exceptional Children, 86*(3), 310–329. https://doi.org/10.1177/0014402919870464

Boveda, M., & Aronson, B. A. (2019). Special education preservice teachers, intersectional diversity, and the privileging of emerging professional identities. *Remedial and Special Education, 40*(4), 248–260. https://doi.org/10.1177/0741932519838621

Broderick, A. A., & Leonardo, Z. (2015). What a good boy. In D. J. Connor, B. A. Ferri, & S. A. Annamma (Eds.), *Dis/ability studies and critical race theory in education* (pp. 55–67). Teachers College Press. https://doi.org/10.1080/13613324.2012.730511

Brown, K. D. (2014). Teaching in color: A critical race theory in education analysis of the literature on preservice teachers of color and teacher education in the US. *Race Ethnicity and Education, 17*(3), 326–345. https://doi.org/10.1080/13613324.2013.832921

Cooc, N., & Yang, M. (2016). Diversity and equity in the distribution of teachers with special education credentials: Trends from California. *AERA Open, 2*(4), 1–15. https://doi.org/10.1177/2332858416679374

Ginwright, S. A. (2015). Radically healing Black lives: A love note to justice. *New directions for student leadership, 2015*(148), 33–44. https://doi.org/10.1002/yd.20151

Harry, B., & Klingner, J. (2014). *Why are so many minority students in special education?* Teachers College Press.

Irizarry, J., & Donaldson, M. L. (2012). Teach for America: The Latinization of US schools and the critical shortage of Latina/o teachers. *American Educational Research Journal, 49*(1), 155–194. https://doi.org/10.3102/0002831211434764

Kohli, R., Pizarro, M., & Nevárez, A. (2017). The "new racism" of K–12 schools: Centering critical research on racism. *Review of research in education, 41*(1), 182–202.

Kulkarni, S. (2021a). Journey as a special education teacher of color with dis/abilities. In D. Connor & B. Ferri (Eds.), *How teaching shapes our thinking about dis/abilities: Stories from the field* (pp. 277–290). Peter Lang.

Kulkarni, S. (2021b). Shifting special education teacher beliefs about dis/ability and race: Counter stories of goodness and smartness. *Curriculum Inquiry, 51*(5), 496–521. https://doi.org/10.1080/03626784.2021.1938973

Kulkarni, S. S., Bland, S., & Gaeta, J. M. (2022). From support to action: A critical affinity group of special education teachers of color. *Teacher Education and Special Education, 45*(1), 43–60. https://doi.org/10.1177/08884064211061189

Kulkarni, S., Nusbaum, E., & Boda, P. (2021). DisCrit in conversation with teacher education at the margins. *Race, Ethnicity and Education.*

Leonardo, Z., & Porter, R. K. (2010). Pedagogy of fear: Toward a Fanonian theory of 'safety' in race dialogue. *Race Ethnicity and Education, 13*(2), 139–157. https://doi.org/10.1080/13613324.2010.482898

Martinez, A. N., Valdez, C., & Cariaga, S. (2016). Solidarity with the people: Organizing to disrupt teacher alienation. *Equity & Excellence in Education, 49*(3), 300–313. https://doi.org/10.1080/10665684.2016.1194104

Miller, P. (2020). Anti-racist school leadership: Making 'race' count in leadership preparation and development. *Professional Development in Education, 47*(1), 7–21. https://doi.org/10.1080/19415257.2020.1787207

Pizarro, M., & Kohli, R. (2020). "I stopped sleeping": Teachers of color and the impact of racial battle fatigue. *Urban Education, 55*(7), 967–991. https://doi.org/10.1177/0042085918805788

Pour-Khorshid, F. (2018). Cultivating sacred spaces: A racial affinity group approach to support critical educators of color. *Teaching Education, 29*(4), 318–329. https://doi.org/10.1080/10476210.2018.1512092

Sepetys, R. (2012). *Between shades of gray.* Penguin.

Yosso, T. J. (2005). Whose culture has capital? A critical race theory discussion of community cultural wealth. *Race ethnicity and education, 8*(1), 69–91. https://doi.org/10.1080/1361332052000341006

CHAPTER 16

# WHO DECIDES?

## Teachers With Disabilities and the Role of School Administrators

**Michelle L. Damiani**
*Rowan University*

## ABSTRACT

Who decides who can teach, how teachers can teach, and what constitutes "good" teaching? Schools are organized around ability constructs that shape the experiences of disabled students, staff, teachers, and administrators. Achieving equity in education requires that all stakeholders interrogate the implications of their policies and practices. Equity-oriented leadership implores school leaders and administrators to examine the effects of ableism and to use their power to eliminate inequities for diverse teachers. This chapter draws on data from teacher interviews and letter writing that inform recommendations for school administrators who share responsibility for creating supportive school cultures, ensuring equitable access, and building capacity in education. Situated in a joint framework of transformative leadership and disability studies in education, this chapter concludes with ways to move forward in a shared leadership model with teachers with disabilities as teacher leaders.

*Who Decides?*, pages 383–412
Copyright © 2022 by Information Age Publishing
www.infoagepub.com
All rights of reproduction in any form reserved.

Who decides who can teach, how teachers can teach, and what constitutes "good" teaching? As the United States recently celebrated the 30th anniversary of the Americans With Disabilities Act (ADA), a critical examination into ableism in schools and the experiences of disabled teachers/teachers with disabilities is both timely and necessary. Schools are organized around ability constructs that shape the experiences of disabled students, staff, teachers, and administrators. The guiding principles of equity-oriented leadership implore school leaders and administrators to examine the effects of ableism in their schools/districts, and to use their power to eliminate inequities for diverse teachers.

The findings presented in this chapter draw on a larger empirical study that was designed to understand the lived experiences of teachers with disabilities in P–12 settings. This inquiry included consideration about the ways that teachers' experiences with disability figured into their professional identities, into their classroom practices, and into their experiences in school contexts. This chapter is informed by data from interviews and letter writing that highlight the experiences of teachers with disabilities and inform recommendations for school administrators who share responsibility for creating supportive school cultures, ensuring equitable access, and building capacity in education.

Readers will notice the use of both person-first language (teacher with a disability) and identity-first language (disabled teacher) in this chapter. Using both language frames allowed me to honor the explicitly stated preferences of teachers who contributed to this research while also using the language of the disability studies discipline which recognizes that environmental, attitudinal, and systemic barriers create the conditions whereby various ways of being and doing are constructed as disability in comparison to able-bodied norms or expectations. Use of the terms "disabled" and "nondisabled" in this chapter are intended to highlight the ways that teachers are disabled by inaccessible and oppressive social structures in the educational system. These language distinctions are important in efforts to question power, decision-making, and conceptualizations of ability and disability.

More to this point, the history of using disability labels to mark disability as inferior and students with disabilities negatively in comparison to "general education students" created the need to reframe language. Some teachers in this research had firm expectations that all educators including administrators should understand the importance of person-first language. Take for example when Rachel expressed anger with teachers who called her by her disability, rather than by her name. They referred to her as "the deaf girl" to which she emphatically questioned, "Person-first language, don't you know anything?" Because education conceptualizes disability as a deficit, many students, and teachers, have not had opportunities to develop or express positive disability identities in the context of school. Thus, while person-first language has encouraged a move toward recognizing person-hood ahead of disability, it has also fallen short in terms of valuing disability as an inseparable aspect of identity and culture, and in terms of under-standing disability as a social construction and a result of societal barriers.

Three of the teachers in this study identified as deaf with a stated prefer-ence for person-first language. For these teachers, their use of lower-case deaf was consistent with Padden's (2000) explanation of deaf which refers to the audiological condition of deafness and other noncultural aspects of disability. Alternately, identity-first language and capitalized Deaf is pre-ferred by the Deaf community in recognition of their identity as a cultural and linguistic minority. I come back to this discussion and importance of language later in this chapter in the implications. I hope that this explana-tion is useful to readers, and particularly for administrators, as they engage in the important tasks of developing school cultures that are welcoming of disability and that serve as sites of disruption to ableism.

## DISABILITY STUDIES AND EDUCATIONAL LEADERSHIP

### Teachers With Disabilities

To situate the discussion of teachers with disabilities in the literature that follows, this section provides an overview of the research pertaining to the experiences of educators with disabilities. There is a slowly growing body of research that specifically addresses the experiences of elementary and secondary teachers with disabilities (e.g., Clayton 2009; Duquette, 2000; Ferri, Connor, et al., 2005; Ferri, Keefe, et al., 2001; Gerber, 1992; Gerber, 1998; Jackson, 2012; Nam & Oxford, 1998; Neca et al., 2020; Stenger, 2013; Valle et al., 2004; Vogel & Sharoni, 2010). In addition to research, there are many first-person narratives that further underscore the critical influ-ence of administrative decisions and decision makers in K–12 education (e.g., Cohen & Wysocky, 2005; Corcoran & Carlson, 1994; Jeffress, 2018; Smith, 2013; Solis, 2006). Documented throughout these writings is the critical role that school leaders have in creating inclusive school cultures around disability and supporting diverse educators. Also important is the fact that the numbers of teachers with disabilities and administrators with disabilities in the United States is known to be disproportionately low, but there is no reliable statistic about their prevalence (Anderson, 2006; Jack-son, 2012; Williams et al., 2013), and there are no systematic procedures in place to document this underrepresentation.

## Disability Studies in Education

The majority of literature around disabled educators and their experiences is grounded in disability studies (DS). Disability studies recognizes disability as a social phenomenon and challenges traditional medical and clinical conceptualizations of disability (Taylor, 2006). In schools, disability is often positioned as a "problem," and as an issue of special education (Ferri, 2006; Gabel & Connor, 2009; Linton, 1998; Marks, 1997; Taylor, 2006). The negative positioning of disability in education has supported a system of approaches that intentionally and unintentionally exclude disabled students, faculty, and administrators from opportunities, access, and equitable participation. Accurate representation of disability and disability history are also largely absent in the curriculum. This messaging reinforces negative attitudes toward disability in schools and throughout society. In fact, just recently two states, California in 2011 (S.B. 48, Section 51204.5) and New Jersey in 2019 (P.L.2019, c006), passed the first educational laws or measures requiring schools to "adopt instruction that accurately portrays the political, economic, and social contributions of persons with disabilities and lesbian, gay, bisexual, and transgender people, where appropriate" (n.p). Such measures have important implications for improving our use of culturally responsive and culturally sustaining practices, as well as for addressing the critical need to diversify the teacher workforce. Disabled teachers and disability culture need to be part of that conversation and administrators are integral to ensuring that happens in their schools or districts.

## Ableism in Education

Hehir (2005) argues that "progress toward equity is dependent first and foremost on the acknowledgment that ableism exists in schools" (p. 17). Ableism, as Hehir (2002) defines it, is "the devaluation of disability" where nondisabled ways of being and doing are preferable to disabled ones (p. 1). Critical disability theory "is a framework for the analysis of disability which centers disability and challenges the ableist assumptions which shape society" (Hosking, 2008, p. 16). Studies in ableism (SiA) is a theoretical framework that interrogates ability, rather than disability, and the systemic structures that allow ableist norms, policies, and practices to go unquestioned (Campbell, 2009). In this research aimed at understanding the experiences of teachers with disabilities, I centered the voices of teachers guided by critical disability theory and SiA through a disability studies in education (DSE) lens.

Various forms of ableism contribute to low levels of educational attainment and employment (Hehir, 2002). Professional norms that are rooted in ability expectations have excluded teachers with disabilities from employment in the education field, or in some cases have relegated them exclusively to positions related to special education (Rousmaniere, 2013). Case law demonstrates that faculty are largely unsuccessful in challenging disability discrimination through the courts. In addition to these legal outcomes, there are many more incidences of disability discrimination among disabled teachers than are reported or that rise to the level of litigation (Abram, 2003; Euben, 2004). So while laws exist, and while laws may progress over time, discriminatory practices persist and/or entities find ways to persist with existing practices that uphold ableism in education. We see the same pattern with educational policies and initiatives; policy changes or changes in the conditions under which schools and school leaders operate does not mean that there are substantive shifts in how leadership is practiced (Elmore, 2005).

For teachers, ability standards, inaccessible environments, and an oppressive culture of equating disability with a lack of being qualified or competent have guided who can become a teacher and how teaching can be accomplished. By comparison, DS scholar Rosemarie Garland-Thomson (2012) argues that experiences of disability are valuable, generative to meaning-making in the world, and that valuing disability diversity as an asset would require that we honor "because of" rather than "in-spite of" interpretations of disability. Brad Cohen, an elementary school teacher and later principal, offered an example of the interpretation that Garland-Thomson advocates for when as a professional he insists that he is not successful as a teacher despite Tourette syndrome, but rather is a good teacher because of it. In Cohen's experiences of education, Tourette syndrome led him to become "The teacher I never had" (Cohen & Wysocky, 2005, p. 137).

Positive disability identities and professional disability identities are not easily accepted within the teaching profession. Disabled teachers continue to be discredited for the successful and labor-intensive work that they do to advocate for themselves, for their students, and as change agents within an oppressive system. However, as Anderson (2006) contends, disabled bodies, and specifically, teachers with disabilities, are "bodies of possibility" that can transform educational spaces and ways of teaching (p. 369). At present, the field of education aims to be inclusive, but seems largely unaware and unwilling to consider teaching with a disability as an asset to the profession.

## Educational Leadership

Educational leadership represents a long-standing and well-developed field with an extensive body of literature around a range of school issues and practices. However, even as educational leadership has expanded its scope to address issues of social justice, equity, and diversity, bringing DSE and leadership for social justice together remains undertheorized (Manaseri & Bornstein, 2018). DisCrit, dis/ability critical race studies, brings together theory and praxis considerations of DS and critical race theory (Connor et al., 2016). Recently, DeMatthews (2020) specifically connected disability to educational leadership. He argued for a DisCrit leadership framework for principals whereby it is recognized that

> racism and ableism are built into educator and principal practices, which contribute to the reproduction of inequitable systems and outcomes. Yet, principals are in a key position to challenge dominant narratives about race and ability and facilitate equity-oriented change. (p. 27)

These critical theorizations are necessary to help us understand the shifting landscape of educational leadership, and to address inequities in practice for students and other critical contributors, such as teacher leaders. Empirical research about the impact of school administrators on the school experiences of educators with disabilities is also scant. A search for the terms "disabled teachers," "disabled educators," "disabled administrators," "teachers with disabilities," "educators with disabilities," and "administrators with disabilities" produced no results in prominent educational leadership journals.

Much of the writing about disability in educational leadership has been around preparing leaders to serve students with disabilities and their roles in the administration of special education programming. Thus, the growing body of research around socially just leadership and inclusive school reform is also critically important to preparing leaders beyond the deficit-driven and marginalizing organization of special education (Capper et al., 2006; Capper & Young, 2014; Pazey & Cole, 2013; Theoharis, 2009). Early in the inclusive education movement, educational leadership literature reflected discussions about the socially constructed nature of disability and the medical and social models of disability (Bishop et al., 1993; Goor et al., 1997). Goor et al. (1997) took up the impact of attitudinal barriers around disability including how feelings of lack of preparedness, being unaware of the extent of their responsibilities, and having negative beliefs about disability impacted leaders' approaches to students and led to resentment toward providing resources and programming for students with disabilities in their schools.

In the 1980s, the field of educational leadership began focusing on instructional leadership as necessary to improve teaching (Hallinger, 2010; Neumerski, 2012). The move to instructional leadership suggested that school administration was not only about management, and it called for a distributed leadership approach across various leaders, including teacher leaders and instructional coaches (Neumerski, 2012). This development in the conceptualization of school leadership grew into a body of literature around teacher leaders that is an important precursor to my work. Recent writing in educational leadership has focused on ideas such as responsible leadership (Starratt, 2005), accountable leadership (Elmore, 2005), teachers as leaders (Lieberman & Miller, 2005; Portner & Collins, 2014), and teachers and administrators leading together (Berg, 2018; Eckert, 2018; Portner & Collins, 2014). These interests of scholarship represent important opportunities for pursuing transformative practices in education including those that engage more nuanced conceptualizations of power within the role of educational leadership. A thread across this literature is the value placed on what Elmore (2005) describes as "distributed leadership" where school teachers and administrators are leading together toward a common goal and collective efficacy. Elmore indicates that collective efficacy requires a shift from individual accountability to collective norms that work within formal mechanisms. However, Neumerski (2012) noted bodies of knowledge around principals and teacher leaders remain separate, and that discussions of teacher leaders remain largely principal focused. I add that it is not clear that educational leadership has considered how individual accountability on the part of administrators, collective expectations within schools, and formal mechanisms for navigation and assessment are bound up in problematic ways with ability norms that conflate difference with specific skills and ways to demonstrate them.

Thus, it is impossible to ignore the aspects of power that school principals and administrators have. As Elmore (2005) points out, the heavy focus on managerial duties has not shifted even as the social, economic, and cultural context of public schools have changed dramatically. How accountability is operationalized at any given time "deeply affects how teachers and school leaders think about their work, how they determine their authority, how that authority is defined and circumscribed, and for what they are accountable" (Elmore, 2005, p. 135). Unsurprisingly, the focus on external accountability based on standardized achievement in educational leadership transfers to evaluating teacher abilities and teacher effectiveness (Elmore, 2005; Lieberman & Miller, 2005). So, while the field of educational leadership has been conceptualizing the work of leadership in much more inclusive and equity-oriented frameworks over the last 15 years, the practice of educational leadership related to disability, and especially the approaches to disabled educators, has remained primarily transactional.

Disability history and policy have demonstrated that individuals with disabilities need to be involved in all decisions about disabled people. This expectation for representative involvement of people with disabilities, and for teachers in consideration of reasonable accommodations at work, is codified in the ADA. Here it is worth pointing out that representative involvement has been a priority of the disability rights movement captured through the call for "Nothing about us without us" (Charlton, 1998). Acknowledging the need and expectation for teachers with disabilities to be involved in school-based decisions that affect them is inextricably aligned with the shared leadership approach to shaping school culture presented by Portner and Collins (2014).

The move to examine transformative leadership has grown alongside a rapidly growing body of literature in equity-focused, justice-focused, and culturally responsive leadership. Shields (2010) takes transforming leadership a step further by distinguishing *transformative* leadership in education from both *transactional* and *transformational* leadership. According to Shields, transformative leadership is focused on dismantling issues of inequity as a necessary means of achieving leadership for inclusive and socially just learning environments. Some of the critical elements of transformative leadership that she writes about include

> a combination of both critique and promise; attempts to effect both deep and equitable changes; deconstruction and reconstruction of the knowledge frameworks that generate inequity; acknowledgment of power and privilege; emphasis on both individual achievement and the public good; a focus on liberation, democracy, equity, and justice; and finally, evidence of moral courage and activism. (Shields, 2010, p. 562)

Together, transformative leadership and critical disability theory offer new trajectories for inclusive school cultures that value all members of the school community, including disabled teachers.

Here I have intentionally put the frameworks for DS and educational leadership in conversation with one another, particularly as they relate to leading together for social justice and the role of administrators among teachers with disabilities. In a combined framework, "We must also be willing to examine how disability is defined, whose knowledge we value, whose voices we privilege, and how the experiences of teachers with disabilities can contribute to broader goals for social justice in education" (Damiani, 2019, p. 62). Achieving equity-oriented leadership implores school leaders and administrators to value teachers with disabilities and to use their power to simultaneously disrupt systems of oppression to provide equitable and asset-oriented opportunities for diverse teachers as an intentional element in social justice leadership.

## METHODS

The data discussed in this chapter are drawn from a larger study that involved a series of 21 in-depth semi-structured interviews and eight written letters. Eleven teachers participated in this study, all of whom self-identified as teachers with a disability(ies). This study did not focus on any one category of disability, but instead reflected a range of disability experiences. Participants were representative of both general education and special education teachers who were employed in P–12 (preschool to Grade 12) teaching positions in various U.S. locations. Teachers in this study participated from seven different states that were representative of U.S. regions, including the Northeast, the Southeast, the West, and the Midwest. More specific locations and the information about the school settings are not reported as a consideration of anonymity for participants.

This study was reflective of teacher experiences at varying stages of their teaching career, including beginning, developing, experienced, and veteran teachers. Based on the number of years of teaching experience, this sample included one beginning teacher (1–2 years of experience), two developing teachers (3–4 years of experience), three experienced teachers (5–9 years of experience), and five veteran teachers (10 or more years of experience). This group of teachers with disabilities reported considerable mobility within the field. Teachers at every experience marker described above reported changing teaching positions. In fact, only three of the teachers, all veteran teachers, indicated that they had never changed teaching positions. Comparatively, most of the teachers, 8 out of the 11, had been in their current teaching position for 5 years or fewer and some teachers were still interested in pursuing new teaching positions.

Each interview lasted between 60 and 90 minutes and addressed teachers' lived experiences with disability broadly and their specific experiences with disability in education. Written letters were also requested from each of the participating teachers. The prompt for letter writing was intentionally open-ended, asking what a current teacher with disabilities would like to say to future teachers with disabilities and/or allies. All interviews were transcribed verbatim and pseudonyms were assigned for all participants, individuals' names, schools, school districts, and specific locations. I used NVivo qualitative analysis software to systematically code all de-identified and member checked data involved in this study. I also used NVivo's (2016) visual analysis tools to understand themes in the data as a whole, as well as focused data within the letters. I conducted data analysis in a constant comparative grounded theory approach (Creswell, 2013) supplemented with narrative analysis methods (Riessman, 2008). In this chapter, I focus my discussion and examples on how teachers' experiences may inform school administrators in their role as educational leaders.

# FINDINGS

Here I have demonstrated my research findings through a selection of teacher experiences involving their P–12 administrators. The section begins with an introduction of teachers' contrasting experiences with their school administrators. These experiences serve as a starting point for understanding the subsequent research themes and recommendations presented in this chapter. I organized relevant themes topically as three dilemmas that teachers with disabilities faced involving administrators in their professional practice. The three dilemmas are: (a) decisions about disclosing disability to administrators, (b) accessibility for teachers and in teaching, (c) the school culture around disability. Each dilemma is supported with examples from data and relevant literature, and a discussion. Following that is a section on implications for practice that addresses recommendations for each dilemma as it relates to principals, school leaders, and/or district administrators who are making decisions about teachers and disability in their schools. Informed by these considerations, the chapter segues into a discussion about ways to move forward in a shared leadership model with teachers with disabilities as teacher leaders.

## Teachers' Experiences With Administrators

As reported in Damiani (2019), each of the 11 participating teachers discussed that the role of administrators was critical to whether they had positive or negative experiences as a teacher with a disability. Overall, this group of teachers had 1 of 3 impressions of their administrators. Teachers described their school principals, and sometimes their vice principals or district-level administrators as (a) informed and supportive school leaders who created space for teachers with disabilities by increasing access and challenging the assumptions of others; (b) responsive to teachers' needs, but still guided by ignorance, fear, uncertainty, or unintentional ableism; or (c) authoritative, close-minded, and sometimes knowingly creating additional barriers for teachers with disabilities.

While 8 of the 11 teachers discussed times where an administrator was supportive, only 3 of the 11 teachers (27%) had consistently positive impressions of their school principals or felt that their administrators consistently and adequately supported them as teachers. In situations where teachers reported adequate support, they provided examples of attention to accessibility, the ability to request accommodations and suggest changes, and confidence in their administrator's support of them as qualified teachers (p. 143). Detailed examples of what support or lack of support involved are highlighted in the dilemmas that follow. It is important to note that several of the same teachers who talked about positive leadership from one administrator, simultaneously described neutral or even hostile experiences with other administrators in the same school building (e.g., with the principal and vice principal) or in the district (e.g., with two different building principals or with the principal and district special education administration).

Consistently, however, it was *individual administrators* who engaged in transformational leadership as it related to teachers with disabilities. Therefore, teachers' positive, inclusive, or specifically anti-ableist experiences with administrators were the result of individuals who were expressly committed to supporting teachers with disabilities. For teachers in this study, administrators' attitudes and expectations around disability, whether positive or negative, became standards of practice in each of their schools. As Zachary said, we need more administrators that "go to bat" for teachers with disabilities like his principal did, rather than those who Rachel explained, only "accommodate disabilities from a managerial perspective." The difference in the ways that these two participants summarize what they and other teachers with disabilities need from administrators points to some of the key differences between transactional leadership and transformative leadership, and how these approaches impact teachers with disabilities.

In their research about cross-cultural dimensions of transformational leadership, Santamaria and Jean-Marie (2014) identified the need for "a paradigm shift to the way in which educational leadership is practiced nationwide," particularly as the preK–12 student body becomes increasingly diverse (p. 333). Supporting the need for a large-scale shift in practice, Elmore (2005) noted that educational leadership approaches continue to reflect individual decision-making and a lack of responsiveness to the ever-evolving and more diverse context of education. Simply put, students need to see people like themselves represented and successful in positions of power in education. And, all students (disabled and nondisabled) need to experience individuals with disabilities in schools as expected and normal, whether those individuals be their peers, their teachers, or their principals. As an increasing number of students with disabilities are pursuing teacher education (Clayton, 2009; Valle et al., 2004) and as the needs of those aging in the teacher workforce continue to shift (Milchus, 2008), the number of teacher candidates and teachers with disabilities in the teacher workforce will rise.

Not surprisingly, teachers' positive and negative experiences with administrators influenced their decision(s) about whether or not to disclose disability to their administrators and whether or not they felt comfortable exercising their rights to access and reasonable accommodations. Teachers' experiences also highlighted many specific examples of workplace discrimination in action and showed how the pressure to hide or pass as nondisabled at school is coded into the school climate around disability and the teaching profession. Each of these thematic findings is discussed below as a dilemma. Understanding these experiences creates an onus for school leaders to respond in their individual and collective practices.

### Dilemma 1: Decisions About Disclosing Disability to Administrators

Detailed patterns emerged in the interview and letter data that indicated how teachers made intentional decisions about if, and when, they disclosed their disability to students, colleagues, administrators, and parents (Damiani, 2019). The results of those findings showed that these 11 teachers disclosed most often and most openly with their students, and least often or most restrictively with administrators and parents. This finding indicated an inverse relationship related to power whereby as authority increases, teachers' willingness to disclose decreases.

Teachers explained in detail how they prepared for disclosure at different points in their careers, especially when administrators are involved. Teachers shared their experiences "obtaining employment, maintaining employment, securing tenure, and defending their professional reputation" (Damiani, 2019, p. 144). At each career stage, many of the teachers' examples pointed to evidence of workplace discrimination and stigma.

Zachary described how challenging it was for him to secure a full-time teaching position as a certified teacher with a visible physical disability that affects his verbal communication. After substitute teaching, Zachary had interviewed for several permanent positions and "every time I would get denied and I don't know why I did." Following unsuccessful interviews, the principal at one of the schools approached him:

> I want you here. I want you to work here. Fill out an application...If you go for an interview, they are going to have a hard time understanding you. So I am going to write a letter saying that I know you; you've taught with us and I know your work.

Zachary and Heather both expressed that the time required to adequately explain teaching with a disability to others further influenced their disclosure decisions.

> If you know the administrator or the people on the interview committees, then you can talk about it more and explain why having disabilities would be advantageous in teaching. Then it can be helpful. In a screening interview essay where you have 3–6 minutes to explain why disability is not a bad thing, then it wouldn't be helpful...And I think that it's important the way I present myself. I don't walk into the room and say, "Hi, I'm someone with a disability who can't do anything." I walk into a room and say, "Hi, I'm a teacher, how can I help?" And, I think that affects how other people think.

Diane, Heather, and Zachary's experiences were representative of both visible and invisible disabilities. Choosing not to disclose became problematic to some teachers' professional interactions with their administrators, though many teachers with invisible disabilities chose to pass whenever possible or when presented with an option. For many, hiding or passing was not a personal preference, but rather a realistic understanding of how disability is viewed negatively in schools and employment, and the associated implications for disclosing under such conditions. As with identity research related to race, gender, and sexual orientation,

> disability identity development is both a question of social categorization and meaning-making, as well as fundamentally physical and biological. People with disability must negotiate their own (visible and invisible) impairments in addition to the social meaning assigned to those impairments as they form an identity around disability. (Forber-Pratt et al., 2017, p. 204)

By comparison, teachers cited disclosing to students as a way to be transparent with students in an effort to normalize disability in their classroom and as potentially valuable for students with disabilities in an effort to help them understand their disability experiences. Several teachers discussed that the action of disclosing to students produced opportunities for sharing insider knowledge between students with disabilities and teachers with disabilities, as well as increased respect and trust between them. As Rachel wrote,

> Be open about your unique learning needs; students will respect so, SO, much more. When I recently began wearing hearing aids again, I explained it and talked to my students (who all have visual impairments). They asked questions and touched/explored the hearing aids and have since been more willing to open up with me about their disabilities and their needs (what is challenging for them, etc.).

**Discussion.**    Consistent with Evans' (2019) writing about three primary forms of disability disclosure, participating teachers indicated that their purposes for disclosing to administrators were mostly related to advocating for their needs as a teacher or protecting themselves from unfair judgment.

Diane had been a strong proponent of disclosure with workplace leaders including with school administrators; she had even chosen to provide her colleagues with additional information about her disability and how they could most successfully work together. She gave them a business card that she said was intended to be "a quick and easy reminder to just stop and think" about ensuring that faculty materials and meetings were accessible; it offered quick tips as it related to working together as classroom teachers or school professionals, and requested that colleagues "respect me enough to ask." Despite her proactive approach and efforts to educate others through a frame of successful collaboration, Diane's negative experiences led her to shift her position and disclose more selectively with colleagues and administrators, but she did still always disclose with students. Many more participants indicated that they would not disclose disability to their administrator at any stage due to blatant experiences of discrimination, fear of retaliation, or having had experiences where disclosure backfired. Patterns in teachers' experiences made it clear that hiding disability or passing as nondisabled was personally and professionally safer (less professionally risky) for teachers, especially where administrators were involved. Ultimately, disclosure was a complex and individualized process layered by teachers' lived experiences, their efforts to navigate systemic ableism in education, and for some by internalized ableism.

The interview process often requires sustained and fast-paced verbal interactions. These able-bodied expectations could easily put a teacher applicant at a distinct disadvantage in the interview process. In Zachary's case, he "agreed that his principal acted as an advocate, and as a facilitator to the interview process that allowed him to have equal consideration by the hiring committee" (Damiani, 2019, p. 144). Here Zachary's principal appears to have moved beyond the role of an ally to what Bettina Love describes as a "co-conspirator." According to Love (2019), a co-conspirator is someone who takes a risk for somebody else by putting something on the line and using their power and privilege to benefit someone else who does not have that same form of privilege. Though she should not have had to write a letter to her administrative colleagues, Zachary's principal recognized the need for this upfront and intentional method of providing a professional reference when the teacher was denied the opportunity to speak for himself. Diane described this denial of representing yourself to people in positions of power as a right that is taken away and "trumped by someone else's opinion."

Attitudes and conditions of the workplace environment strongly influenced whether or not teachers with disabilities chose to disclose in school settings (Valle et al., 2004). Disabled people, including teachers, frequently express that attitudinal barriers are often the most challenging barriers to navigate. Aligned with the social model of disability, teachers make assessments about how the school and professional culture around disability might lead to responses where disability is created, intensified, reduced, or eliminated. Thus, teachers evaluate the risks and benefits of "coming out" in relation to how disability is positioned at their school, by their degree of self-acceptance as a person with a disability (Valle et al., 2004), and by the expectation for teachers to have a socially legitimatized professional identity (Coldron & Smith, 1999).

The importance of relationship building is well established in education, but there is little or no attention to the impact of relationships between disabled and nondisabled school professionals, or about the transformative possibilities of leading together with teachers with disabilities in distributed leadership approaches. This chapter addresses that gap. Ultimately, teachers cannot do this alone. "Administrative attitudes set the tone for both teachers and students; teachers seemed to associate a culture of inclusion for students with an administrative willingness to also go to bat for inclusion and success of teachers with disabilities" (Damiani, 2019, p. 144).

### Dilemma 2: Accessibility for Teachers and in Teaching

The Americans With Disabilities Act (ADA, 1990) mandated that school environments be accessible, with the right to reasonable accommodations, and the right to nondiscrimination on the basis of disability. As Milchus (2008) noted, "The process for determining accommodations should be interactive, and involve both the employee and the employer" (p. 147). Knowledge of workplace protections and processes are critical understandings for principals and school leaders who are all responsible for ensuring equity in their schools and working together with teachers with disabilities to determine how to meet their professional needs.

Table 16.1 shows examples of the kinds of accommodations that participating teachers requested from their administrators to support their teaching (Damiani, 2019, p. 156). In addition to these physical space and material needs, teachers also discussed how access considerations extend beyond their individual classrooms. Attention to accessibility is needed in all work of the profession including faculty meetings, school events, and professional development activities. Expanding the scope of accommodations and reframing access as a school-wide priority rather than an individual issue

**TABLE 16.1  Participants' Examples of Accommodations Used for Teaching**

| Accommodations Category | Participants' Examples |
| --- | --- |
| Classroom Equipment | • Classroom projectors (ELMOs and Smartboards)<br>• Podium stand<br>• Large screen computers<br>• Magnification tools |
| Specialized Software and Related Materials | • Large print materials<br>• Screen reader software<br>• Screen reader accessible PDFs<br>• Audio texts<br>• Office management software (Occasions)<br>• Assistive educational technology and literacy software (Kurzweil and Solo Suite) |
| Environmental Modifications | • Classroom location<br>• Scheduling adjustments<br>• Lighting adjustments<br>• Establishing classroom routines<br>• Establishing reminders with colleagues |
| Communication Access | • Interpreters |

requires attention to all aspects of inaccessible environments and attitudinal barriers that adversely impact individuals with disabilities in schools.

In an interview, Nora shared the following scenario as she discussed the need for accessible transportation in order to participate in a leadership opportunity that she was selected for based on her expertise.

> I was asked by my director of our school to be a mentor at another school . . . and I'm very qualified for it. I feel at this point in my teaching career I'm confident in mentoring others . . . And it's something that I am interested in . . . I recently wanted to become more of a mentor whether it's for colleagues at my school or whether it's people elsewhere . . . the only issue is getting to the school. I can't drive there. A bus or rideshare program would take 1½–2½ hours compared to 30 minutes by car. Therefore, I would require support with transportation.

The administrators involved interpreted this to mean that another teacher would need to be off-campus, would need to have a substitute teacher in their classroom, and there would be an additional cost associated with providing access for this teacher as opposed to another qualified teacher. In the end, Nora was not afforded this opportunity based on her need for accommodations and another nondisabled teacher at her school took the opportunity, an outcome that Nora described as "a disappointment" and "a huge barrier."

As a qualified teacher with a visual impairment, Nora and I discussed this as a problem of access, as well as, a significant limiting of her professional opportunities on the basis of her disability. Though these were unintentional consequences, Nora was denied this opportunity to be a teacher leader, to grow her involvement in teacher mentorship, and it limited her wage-earning power as this was a paid consultant position. Furthermore, Nora's lack of presence in this role contributes to the invisibility of teachers with disabilities in schools and in leadership positions.

Access and equity struggles occurred in schools individually and publicly. In interviews, Cara, Rachel, and Diane talked about experiences where their principals stepped in to address faculty complaints about teachers with disabilities receiving reasonable accommodations. In each of these situations, a colleague complained about a perceived issue of fairness, often stemming from teachers with seniority. In Cara's case, the complaint came from a senior teacher who was angry about Cara having an assigned classroom, rather than her needing to rotate classrooms as other teachers did. This colleague raised the issue publicly in a faculty meeting where Cara was in attendance. All three teachers indicated that their administrators addressed these incidents immediately and directly with the individuals involved. Teachers were grateful for this administrative support; however, we also discussed how none of the administrators addressed the issues of equity versus equality that were inherent in these situations, nor how these incidents relate to the overall school culture. These responses underscore how opportunities to discuss disability as a school community may be missed; perhaps because administrators are unsure of how to do this within the confines of confidentiality mandates or because administrators lack situational awareness about the impact of various disability responses. Consequently, members of the school community could have been left with questions or discomfort about these situations, and/or interpreted administrators' private approach as unintentional modeling of the idea that disability is a taboo topic that should not be discussed publically or professionally. This may also further reinforce the notion that access is an individual issue rather than a shared or collective responsibility of all members of a school community.

**Discussion.** As a matter of policy, P–12 schools are generally not prepared to meet the needs of teachers with disabilities beyond a minimum compliance approach with the law. "Schools have unique opportunities to become models for universally designing how they provide reasonable accommodations" for employees. "As findings from this study revealed, education is an underutilized, but fertile ground for universally designing school spaces, curricular approaches, and instruction that make the most effective use of shared resources and educational technologies" (Damiani, 2019, p. 278).

The oppressive systems of both special education and workplace accommodations have produced consequences of marginalization, limited access, and reduced opportunities for many disabled teachers. The fact that teachers in this study experienced getting accommodations as a hidden or mysterious process added to the perception that disability should remain invisible and to the stigma around needing accommodations. From a critical studies perspective, the use of and process for acquiring professional accommodations needs to be de-medicalized. Normalizing the use of accommodations in a proactive, transparent, and accessible approach could move schools beyond minimum compliance with the law while still protecting individuals' privacy and confidentiality. Essential to this kind of transformative shift is the recognition that ableism is a problem in schools and needs to be deconstructed. From there, school leaders can make decisions about needs for and how to remove environmental barriers as an issue of disability justice within a commitment to social justice.

### Dilemma 3: The School Culture Around Disability

School administrators' perceptions of disability and competence determine whether teachers with disabilities are welcome and valued in their schools (Clayton, 2009; Cohen & Wysocky, 2005; Corcoran & Carlson, 1994; Stenger, 2013). Participating teachers confirmed that attitudinal barriers (myths, fears, stereotypes, etc., that cause prejudice and discrimination) make having a disability in a school setting most difficult (Shapiro, 1993). As a result, teachers with disabilities had developed sophisticated strategies for anticipating and responding to ableism in their teaching and with their students.

Nora and Zachary explained how their principals established inclusion as a priority at their schools, including teachers with disabilities. In these scenarios, administrative actions represented exemplars for the field. However, many more teachers shared negative experiences. In one situation, Zachary arrived at a substitute teaching assignment where

> people would just give me fast looks. I would go in as a teacher and they would call an extra aide in the room and tell the aide to act as the teacher. So, the aide would basically take over. That's a school where I definitely did not feel included or accepted.

The clear message at this school was that teachers with disabilities would not be allowed to act in the capacity of teachers. "In the interview, we discussed that in addition to that school losing him as a teacher, the administrative action of assigning a teaching assistant to take over for a teacher whom they believe is incapable sent a visible and powerful message to all in the school" (Damiani, 2019, p. 144) about the culture around disability at school.

**Discussion.** Ultimately, both DSE and educational leadership acknowledge that administrators have a critical role in establishing the school culture, including attitudes and responses towards disability (Clayton, 2009; Cohen & Wysocky, 2005; Corcoran & Carlson, 1994; Gerber, 1992; Goor et al., 1997; Portner & Collins, 2014; Williams et al., 2013). In writing about a comprehensive model for training effective school principals, Goor et al. (1997), argued that "the principal established the overall climate and influences instructional practices—in fact the key predictor of a program's success is the principal's attitude toward it" (p. 133). Secondly, they argued that comprehensive leadership training must address essential beliefs, knowledge, skills, and reflective behavior for preparing school principals. Preparation that focused on knowledge and skills alone was not enough—administrative leaders needed to be critically reflective practitioners who *can* and *do* examine their assumptions.

Again, the first step for school leaders towards countering problematic practices or trends around ability and disability is acknowledging that ableism is a problem in schools and bringing a commitment to reflective practice and change. Writing about ableism, Campbell (2019) draws on Butnor and McWeeny's (2014) point that the purpose of engaging in critical frameworks is not to fit into existing frames of reference, "but to shift our frames altogether so that we see things differently from another perspective, a unique angle, and the standpoint of a new location" (Butnor & McWeeny, 2014, p. 11, as cited in Campbell, 2019, p. 3). Only through critical study and engaging in critical conversations will the field of educational leadership be able to push forward toward leadership training and practices that intentionally work to dismantle ability constructs, attitudinal barriers, and the adverse effects of both for all in schools.

Thus, addressing the dilemma of school cultures around disability means expanding our understanding of what it means to be inclusive. Specifically, creating cultures of inclusion require attention to all aspects of diversity and equity in education, including disability-related inequities. Instead, disability has been bound up in meanings of difference as undesirable and/or challenging. The separate systems of "general education" and "special education" further undermine efforts toward achieving school cultures of inclusion.

## Implications for Practice

I begin this discussion about implications for practice by first coming back to Portner and Collins' (2014) critical call for educational leaders to become more comfortable and more accepting of what they do not know. Dismantling ableism in education through equity-oriented leadership necessitates a willingness for administrative leaders to learn about inequities in their systems, and particularly for educational leaders to learn from those who have experienced school as sites of struggle, marginalization, and oppression. To understand the barriers and the inequities at work for disabled educational professionals, it is necessary to authentically engage them as critical knowers and partners in the process. This kind of relationship necessitates trust as the mediating variable between teachers and school administrators (Tschannen-Moran & Gareis, 2015). Trust is a critical foundation if you "don't know what you don't know." Such a position allows for critical discussion (learning and unlearning) beginning with a navigation of difference, rather than sameness that values the authority of lived experiences.

I write about the need for trust with caution and attention to who and how we are asking for trust. It would be unreasonable and irresponsible to ask disabled educational professionals to implicitly trust or be willing to trust either individual school leaders or the oppressive and multiply marginalizing educational systems in place. Disabled people are continually asked to disclose personal information and experiences that nondisabled people are not. For educational professionals, there is also a clearly defined power structure in schools. Evidence from disabled teachers' experiences in this and other studies show how complicated teacher–administrator relationships can be and how that translates to professionally supportive or professionally detrimental leadership depending on the administrator's understanding and beliefs about disability. Thus, in an equity-oriented leadership approach it is the responsibility of school leaders and administrators to earn the trust of disabled teachers through their interactions, policies, and practices with attention to who is privileged and how, and what needs to be done to intentionally disrupt the status quo and provide equitable opportunities in education.

As the key determinant of school culture, school leaders set the tone and expectation for whether difference and diversity will be valued in their schools or not. School leaders have an opportunity, and I argue a responsibility, to model their willingness to learn and intentionally expand their perspectives as practice of transformative leadership. This approach to leadership may serve as a model for all in schools and may address the common phenomena of administrators having different perspectives that produce different outcomes for students and teachers. Seeing intentional acts of school leaders being co-conspirators (Love, 2019) and "going to bat" for teachers and students are perhaps the kinds of shifts that are needed among leaders who are intentionally working to disrupt the various intersectional injustices that continue to occur in schools. Inclusive schools need inclusive and equity-focused leaders. Teachers, and especially marginalized and minoritized teachers, cannot do this work in isolation, nor should they be expected to. Inclusive leadership is a necessary part of enacting systemic change.

Here I revisit each of the specific dilemmas identified in this chapter and discuss specific actionable recommendations. The chapter closes with a discussion about moving forward to enact change with teacher leaders.

## Dilemma 1: Decisions About Disclosing Disability to Administrators

In recognizing disability as necessary diversity in schools and as an asset to the instructional outcomes expected in schools, administrators must learn more about disability identity and disability identity development as an essential consideration to professional identity development and teacher identity development. An initial resource for administrators could be the Council for Exceptional Children's Policy on Educators With Disabilities (CEC, 2016). As a leading professional organization in special education, the CEC sets forth clear written expectations for all educational entities to support teachers with disabilities at all levels in terms of identity and disclosure, securing reasonable accommodations, and backing educators' rights and educational institution's legal responsibilities (full text available at https://journals.sagepub.com/doi/full/10.1177/0014402916651880).

In connection to supporting teachers in cultivating teacher identities that could include disability, I come back to the discussion of person-first and identity-first language from the introduction. As educational leaders consider how to value difference and understand difference as generative to school communities and teaching, it is important to understand the language used to discuss disability. Language is powerful. As educational leaders are the most influential factor in how school cultures develop, school

administrators need to be knowledgeable of the history and use of different language frames. Without this critical context, school leaders risk using
language that undermines the important work of transformational leadership. Understanding various language preferences would allow leaders to
consciously use, model, and discuss the impact of language around disability and facilitate the kinds of open discussions that are needed in schools related to social justice. As Diane said, "Respect me enough to ask." This form
of respect may also serve to build trust in leadership and support opportunities for disclosure among teachers with disabilities who choose to do so.
School leaders could use respecting and honoring disability language preferences as an actionable example of transformative and DS aligned leadership as opposed to accommodating disability in a transactional, and too
often minimum compliance approach, for disabled teachers and students.

### Dilemma 2: Accessibility for Teachers and in Teaching

Achieving a culture of inclusion requires that administrators create a
culture of access in their schools and an expectation for shared responsibility for ensuring access within school communities. Achieving a culture of
access requires that school leaders systemically review and revise school procedures to remove barriers and opportunities for implicit bias, disability discrimination, and professional marginalization. One way that school leaders
might do this is by reenvisioning and reorganizing the mechanisms for requesting and obtaining professional accommodations through a universal
design approach. For example, schools should expect that employees could
need to make use of accommodations and make information readily available such that prospective and current employees should know where and
how to access this information at any time it might be needed. District leaders might also consider whether a centralized or decentralized approach
to accessing additional resources and materials would most effectively and
efficiently serve the needs of students, staff, faculty, and administrators. In
this research, several teachers with disabilities thought that having a single
point of contact might streamline the process and allow for a more comprehensive understanding of all the resources available in the district and
where they are located.

### Dilemma 3: The School Culture Around Disability

In order to ensure that the field is comprised of educational leaders who
are critically reflective, equity-oriented, and who *can* and *do* examine their
assumptions, requires changes to administrative leadership and educational leadership training. Educational leadership training should engage critically with disability and DS in education perspectives as essential content for
school leadership. Note that this recommendation is *not* referring to special
education training and is not isolated to special education, but instead to

understanding conceptualizations of disability and ableism in education as inequity that requires intentionally addressing attitudinal, environmental, and systemic barriers at school. However, the impact of practices associated with these conceptualizations do also have important implications for inclusive special education training and inclusive school reform that should intentionally challenge deficit-based practices and traditional models of special education.

Like teachers, all educational leadership candidates for certification or licensure need to be held to professional expectations for culturally responsive and equity-oriented approaches to leadership that are supported with opportunities to critically examine current practices, plan for change making, and practice enacting these leadership skills while training. Additionally, those already established in the field as administrative leaders and educational leaders need similar opportunities, including access to ongoing training, and mandatory accountability measures that demonstrate how school leaders are analyzing what is occurring in their schools and action planning for results, sharing successful and transformational experiences and practices, and continuing to ask questions.

## A WAY FORWARD: PRACTICING SHARED LEADERSHIP WITH TEACHERS WITH DISABILITIES

If we are to achieve inclusive school cultures that welcome and support all members of school communities, then we need to practice inclusivity within the profession and model inclusive professional communities of support in schools. Building on early discussions about collaboration, it continues to be important to share authority with teachers and involve teachers in school decisions (Cook & Friend, 1993). To move the field forward, teachers' involvement in decision-making processes must be meaningful, substantive, and valued even if those recommendations challenge our beliefs and existing practices in ways that are critical and perhaps even uncomfortable.

Disability studies literature has consistently recognized the generative knowledge and contributions of disabled educators and teaching with disability (Garland-Thomson, 2012; Anderson, 2006), but these contributions and the intersecting implications with disability have received considerably less attention in other fields. Thus, in this chapter, I have purposefully highlighted some of the important points of connection and the departures between DS in education and educational leadership. Writing about supporting emerging teacher leaders within powerful leadership, Portner and Collins (2014) affirm that teacher leaders may have creative approaches to solving difficult issues that require changes in their schools, but that creative thinking and change imply risk, and risk-taking requires a safe environment where teacher leaders are confident that they will not be criticized or penalized for offering up ideas (p. 4). This is not to suggest that there should not be constructive discussion or debate about any given idea or recommendation, but it is written more to the point of power and direction of authority between individuals in schools—administrators to teachers, and nondisabled to disabled. Teachers cannot engage in broad-based participation if they are denied opportunities, and they cannot build trusting team relationships if they are fearful of professional repercussions.

My research (Damiani, 2019) demonstrated that teachers with disabilities comprise a skilled community of educators. Disabled teachers have much insight and experience to offer the profession in areas including, but not limited to, teaching methods, student programming and supports, individual and shared accommodations, faculty development, and evaluating school approaches. In her letter, Daniella wrote the following advice for future teachers with disabilities: "Just because you might do something differently than they do does not make your way wrong, and it is beneficial for your students to see there is more than one way to solve a problem." Daniella also advised, however, that in using different teaching methods, teachers with disabilities should anticipate questions and value judgments from others (teachers, administrators, parents). This was representative of just one of the many ways that teachers with disabilities in this research discussed anticipating and responding to ableism, where navigating those value judgments can lead to others learning from the contributions of teachers with disabilities and accepting more diverse approaches. Thus, disabled teachers serve as leaders and problem-solvers in multiple ways within the profession.

The current reality is that, in the existing power structure, speaking out is more likely to be detrimental for disabled teachers than it is to be viewed as a progressive critical contribution. In fact, research by Keller et al. (1998) found that disabled teachers' knowledge, experience, and recommendations have even been viewed by some educators and administrators as posing a threat to institutional maintenance of power and control. Specifically, they found that

> educators with disabilities apparently threatened those educators, especially special educators, who have held power and have been paternalistic in their approach with students who have disabilities. Instead of perceiving educators with disabilities as a resource, Ron observed that often teacher-educators and administrators saw them as obstacles and a source of extra work. (p. 4)

Expounding on the issue of administrators feeling threatened by teacher leaders, Portner and Collins (2014) offer that some administrators might possibly feel threatened when teachers emerge as leaders. They may fear that ambitious teacher leaders will somehow determine their own authority. Yet there is nothing in the concept of teacher leadership that conflicts with the essential role of administrative leadership. (p. 12)

What will it take for educational leadership to demand a move away from transactional approaches to disability toward an expectation for inclusive transformative leadership, noting that this also means shifting the conceptualization of disability in schools? How do we ensure that disabled teacher leaders are expected in the profession and afforded the same opportunities as nondisabled teacher leaders? The recommendations included in this chapter offer a starting point toward achieving that goal. Additionally, the position that the field of educational leadership takes on these questions will determine what leadership training and models will look like for current and future educational administrators and should specifically address how to engage in shared leadership with teachers with disabilities. These decisions will also influence the conditions that shape school culture. Recognizing that culture cannot be imposed on a school, it is up to school leaders to create school environments where inclusive school cultures develop through the course of social interactions and inclusive community expectations and shared accountability (Portner & Collins, 2014).

In writing about becoming a more powerful leader through shared leadership, Portner and Collins (2014) offer well-developed guidance for achieving high leadership-capacity schools, empowering teacher leaders, and building a leader of leaders culture in schools. According to the authors, "Teacher-leadership is more about empowering teachers by increasing their access to resources, information, and expertise in order to positively affect school change" (p. 34). In a shared leadership approach, "responsibility and accountability becomes a shared belief that can be utilized as a catalyst for change in the school community" (Ankrum, 2016, p. 151).

Though there is growing support for the idea that "teacher leaders are an untapped resource in schools" (Ankrum, 2016, p. 158), there continues to be both an absence of positive representation and an invalidation of "good teaching" in connection with disability. Toward the aims of DSE and equity-oriented leadership, "We must be willing to examine how disability is defined, whose knowledge we value, whose voices we privilege, and how the experiences of teachers with disabilities can contribute to broader goals for social justice in education" (Damiani, 2019, p. 62). Achieving this goal requires progressive educational leaders who identify themselves as change agents (Williams et al., 2013). As a basis for serving in this capacity, administrators must become more accepting of the foundational idea that leading together begins with acknowledging that we (administrators) "don't know what we don't know" (Portner & Collins, 2014). This framing creates space for valuing disabled teachers' expertise and recognizes them as the authorities of their lived experiences. Drawing on their knowledge of lived experience, teachers with disabilities not only seek to make a difference for their students, but also bring particular skills and attributes to their work. By their very presence, teachers with disabilities challenge deficit-based models of disability or the norms around how to be a professional. Naming disability as valuable and an asset pushes the physical and imaginary boundaries of deficit-driven interpretations of disability in education.

Just as teachers with disabilities offer unique knowledge and skills to the work of teaching, so do administrators with disabilities offer much to the work of school leadership. Further research is needed around the experiences of disabled administrators/administrators with disabilities. The absence of disabled voices in educational leadership limits the administrators themselves, as well as their school communities and the broader field who also miss out on these critical professional contributions. As Santamaria and Jean-Marie (2014) aptly argued, the identity of educational leaders from historically underserved and underrepresented backgrounds impacts leadership practice. Thus, I argue that disabled educational professionals must be part of any practice of inclusive education and equity-oriented leadership.

## CONCLUSION

In closing, inclusive and equitable leadership is the responsibility of all. Hosking (2008) states that critical theory must "explain what is wrong with current social reality, identify the actors to change it, and provide both clear norms for criticism and achievable practical goals for social transformation" (p. 3). Currently, in terms of valuing and supporting teachers with disabilities, individual administrators are working in isolation as individual actors at individual schools. This is simply insufficient to create large-scale change and achieve equity within the discipline. Expanding what it means to be inclusive, to practice inclusive education, and to practice inclusive school leadership requires a shift from administrators who see their role as being effective leaders of special education programming, to those who support disability as a valuable aspect of diversity and who locate themselves as change agents within the system. This presents a call to action and an opportunity for all educational leaders to live inclusion through shared leadership.

Administrators and school leaders often navigate differences in criteria of match between those in charge of determining abilities and ethical commitments towards a more inclusive and/or just set of practices. This chapter begins the conversation about ethical leadership practices related to teachers with disabilities; however, this is a topic that requires deeper investigation. Just as DS has challenged the field of traditional special education, so too should equity-oriented leadership challenge the restrictive thresholds around disability that have been the basis for practice in traditional spaces in educational leadership. Working together in an interdisciplinary approach creates the best possibilities for praxis aligned to social justice.

The recommendations outlined in this chapter are intended to encourage ongoing critical conversations about policies and practices related to teachers with disabilities that have long gone unquestioned. In *School Trouble: Identity, Power, and Politics in Education,* Youdell (2011) described a goal of bringing together "tools and tactics for intervening into contemporary education in ways that have the potential to destabilize the endurance of inequalities and loosen the constraints of its normative knowledges, meanings, practices, and subjects" (p. 1). For teachers with disabilities, mobilizing such practices necessitates reframing what it means to be a "good teacher" and how we believe that "good teaching" is accomplished. It requires recognizing value in disability and disabled teachers' knowledge as it relates to identity, pedagogy, and best practices in education. Further, it implores us to create school cultures that demand access, celebrate diverse teachers' professional contributions, and empower teacher leaders.

# REFERENCES

Abram, S. (2003). The Americans With Disabilities Act in higher education: The plight of disabled faculty. *Journal of Law and Education, 3*(1), 1–20.

Americans With Disabilities Act of 1990, Pub. L. No. 101-336, § 1, 104 Stat. 328 (1990). https://www.eeoc.gov/eeoc/history/35th/thelaw/ada.html

Anderson, R. C. (2006). Teaching (with) disability: Pedagogies of lived experience. *The Review of Education, Pedagogy, and Cultural Studies, 28,* 367–379. https://doi.org/10.1080/10714410600873258

Ankrum, R. J. (2016). Utilizing teacher leadership as a catalyst for change in schools. *Journal of Educational Issues, 2*(1), 151–165. http://dx.doi.org/10.5296/jei.v2i1.9154

Berg, J. H. (2018). *Leading in sync: Teachers and principals working together for student learning.* ASCD.

Bishop, K., Foster, W., & Jubala, K. (1993). The social construction of disability in education: Organizational considerations. In C. Capper (Ed.), *Educational administration in a pluralistic society* (pp. 173–202). SUNY Press.

Butnor, A., & McWeeny, J. (2014). Feminist comparative methodology performing philosophy differently. In Butnor & McWeeny (Eds), *Asian and feminist philosophies in dialogue: Liberating traditions.* Columbia University Press.

Campbell, F. K. (2009). *Contours of ableism: The production of disability and abledness.* Palgrave Macmillan.

Campbell, F. K. (2019). Precision ableism: A studies in ableism approach to developing histories of disability and abledment. *Rethinking History, 23*(2), 138–156. https://doi.org/10.1080/13642529.2019.1607475

Capper, C., Theoharis, G., & Sebastian, J. (2006). Toward a framework for preparing educational leaders of social justice. *International Journal of Educational Administration*, 44, 209–224. https://doi.org/10.1108/09578230610664814

Capper, C., & Young, M. (2014). Ironies and limitations of educational leadership for social justice: A call to social justice educators. *Theory Into Practice*, 53, 158–164. https://doi.org/10.1080/00405841.2014.885814

Charlton, J. I. (1998). *Nothing about us without us: Disability oppression and empowerment*. University of California Press.

Clayton, J. (2009). Teacher with a learning disability: Legal issues and district approach. *Journal of Cases in Educational Leadership*, 12, 1–7. https://doi.org/10.1177/1555458909336842

Cohen, B., & Wysocky, L. (2005). *Front of the class: How Tourette syndrome made me the teacher I never had*. St. Martin's Griffin.

Coldron, J., & Smith, R. (1999). Active location in teachers' construction of their professional identities. *Journal of curriculum studies*, 31(6), 711–726. https://doi.org/10.1080/002202799182954

Connor, D. J., Ferri, B. A., & Annamma, S. A. (Eds). (2016). *DisCrit: Disability studies and critical race theory in education*. Teachers College Press.

Cook, L., & Friend, M. (1993). Educational leadership for teacher collaboration. In B. Billingsley, *Program leadership for serving students with disabilities*. ERIC Clearinghouse.

Corcoran, J., & Carlson, C. (1994). *The teacher who couldn't read: The true story of a high school instructor who overcame his illiteracy*. Focus on the Family Publishing.

Council for Exceptional Children. (2016). *Policy on educators with disabilities*. https://journals.sagepub.com/doi/full/10.1177/0014402916651880

Creswell, J. (2013). *Qualitative inquiry and research design: Choosing among five approaches*. (3rd ed.). SAGE Publications.

Damiani, M. L. (2019). Transforming understandings about who can teach: Experiences and approaches of teachers with disabilities (Publication No. 22616492) [Doctoral Dissertation, Syracuse University]. ProQuest Dissertations Publishing.

DeMatthews, D. (2020). Addressing racism and ableism in schools: A DisCrit leadership framework for principals. *The Clearing House: A Journal of Educational Strategies, Issues, and Ideas*, 93(1), 27–34. https://doi.org/10.1080/00098655.2019.1690419

Duquette, C. (2000). Examining autobiographical influences on student teachers with disabilities. *Teachers and Teaching*, 6(2), 215–228. https://doi.org/10.1080/713698718

Eckert, J. (2018). *Leading together: Teachers and administrators improving student outcomes*. Corwin.

Elmore, R. (2005). Accountable leadership. *The Educational Forum*, 69(2), 134–142. https://doi.org/10.1080/00131720508984677

Euben, D. (2004). Disabilities and the academic workplace. *Academe*, 90(5), 1–1.

Evans, H. D. (2019). Trial by fire: Forms of impairment disclosure and implication for disability identity. *Disability & Society*, 34(5), 726–746. https://doi.org/10.1080/09687599.2019.1580187

Ferri, B. (2006). Teaching to trouble. In S. Danforth & S. Gabel (Eds.), *Vital questions facing disability studies in education* (Vol. 2, pp. 289–306). Peter Lang.

Ferri, B., Connor, D., Solis, S., Valle, J., & Volpitta, D. (2005). Teachers with LD: Ongoing negotiations with discourses of disability. *Journal of Learning Disabilities, 38*(1), 62–78. https://doi.org/10.1177/00222194050380010501

Ferri, B., Keefe, C., & Gregg, N. (2001). Teachers with learning disabilities: A view from both sides of the desk. *Journal of Learning Disabilities, 34*(1), 22–32. https://doi.org/10.1177/002221940103400103

Forber-Pratt, A. J., Lyew, D. A., Mueller, C., & Samples, L. B. (2017). Disability identity development: A systematic review of the literature. *Rehabilitation Psychology, 62*(2), 198–207. https://doi.org/10.1037/rep0000134

Gabel, S., & Connor, D. (2009). Theorizing disability: Implications and applications for social justice in education. In W. Ayers, T. Quinn, & D. Stovall (Eds.), *Handbook of social justice in education* (pp. 377–399). Taylor & Francis.

Garland-Thomson, R. (2012). The case for conserving disability. *Bioethical Inquiry, 9,* 339–355. https://doi.org/10.1007/s11673-012-9380-0

Gerber, P. (1992). Reflections on "being learning disabled and a beginning teacher and teaching a class of students with learning disabilities." *Exceptionality, 3,* 259–263. https://doi.org/10.1080/09362839209524819

Gerber, P. (1998). Trials and tribulations of a teacher with learning disabilities through his first two years of employment. In R. Anderson, C. Keller, & J. Karp (Eds.), *Enhancing diversity: Educators with disabilities* (pp. 41–59). Gallaudet University Press.

Goor, M., Schwenn, J., & Boyer, L. (1997). Preparing principals for leadership in special education. *Intervention in School & Clinic, 32*(3), 133–141.

Hallinger, P. (2010). Developing instructional leadership. In B. Davies & M. Brundrett (Eds.), *Developing successful leadership* (pp. 61–76). Springer. https://doi.org/10.1007/978-90-481-9106-2

Hehir, T. (2002). Eliminating ableism in education. *Harvard Educational Review, 72*(1), 1–33.

Hehir, T. (2005). *New directions in special education: Eliminating ableism in policy and practice.* Harvard Education Press.

Hosking, D. L. (2008, September 2). *Critical disability theory* [Paper presentation]. Lancaster University, United Kingdom. https://www.lancaster.ac.uk/fass/events/disabilityconference_archive/2008/abstracts/hosking.htm

Jeffress, M. S. (Ed.). (2018). *International perspectives on teaching with disability: Overcoming obstacles and enriching lives.* Routledge.

Jackson, E. M. (2012). *Virginia educators with disabilities survey results: Report to the board.* Virginia Board for People With Disabilities, 1–11.

Keller, C., Anderson, R., & Karp, J. (1998). Introduction. In R. Anderson, C. Keller, & J. Karp (Eds.), *Enhancing diversity: Educators with disabilities* (pp. 3–13). Gallaudet University Press.

Lieberman, A., & Miller, L. (2005). Teachers as leaders. *The Educational Forum, 69*(2), 151–162. https://doi.org/10.1080/00131720508984679

Linton, S. (1998). *Claiming disability.* New York University Press.

Love, B. (2019). *We want to do more than survive: Abolitionist teaching and the pursuit of educational freedom.* Beacon Press.

Manaseri, H., & Bornstein, J. (Eds.). (2018). Forum introduction: Dismantling ableism: The moral imperative for school leaders [Special issue]. *Review of Disability Studies: An International Journal, 14*(3). https://rdsjournal.org/index.php/journal/article/view/772

Marks, D. (1997). Models of disability. *Disability and Rehabilitation, 19*(3), 85–91. https://doi.org/10.3109/09638289709166831

Milchus, K. (2008). Aging educators with disabilities: Experiences with accommodations. *Aging, Disability and Independence,* 141–150. https://doi.org/10.3233/978-1-58603-902-8-141

Nam, C., & Oxford, R. (1998). Portrait of a future teacher: Case study of learning styles, strategies, and language disabilities. *System, 26,* 51–63. https://doi.org/10.1016/S0346-251X(97)00070-5

Neca, P., Borges, M. L., & Pinto, P. C. (2020). Teachers with disabilities: A literature review. *International Journal of Inclusive Education,* 1–20. https://doi.org/10.1080/13603116.2020.1776779

Neumerski, C. M. (2012). Rethinking instructional leadership, a review: What do we know about principal, teacher, and coach instructional leadership, and where should we go from here? *Educational Administration Quarterly, 49*(2), 310–347. https://doi.org/10.1177/0013161X12456700

NVivo. (2016). Qualitative data analysis software: Version 11 Pro: QSR International Pty Ltd.

P.L.2019, c006, S1569 2R, 2019 Reg. Sess. (New Jersey. 2019). https://www.njleg.state.nj.us/2018/Bills/PL19/6_.HTM

Padden, C. (2000). The deaf community and the culture of deaf people. In M. Adams, W. Blumenfeld, R. Castaneda, H. Hackman, M. Peters, & X. Zuniga (Eds.), *Readings for diversity and social justice: An anthology on racism, antisemitism, sexism, heterosexism, ableism, and classism* (pp. 343–351). Routledge.

Pazey, B., & Cole, H. (2013). The role of special education training in the development of socially just leaders: Building an equity consciousness in educational leadership programs. *Educational Administration Quarterly, 49,* 243–271. https://doi.org/10.1177/0013161X12463934

Portner, H., & Collins, W. E. (2014). *Leader of leaders: The handbook for principals on the cultivation, support, and impact of teacher-leaders.* Pearson.

Riessman, C. K. (2008). *Narrative methods for the human sciences.* Sage Publications.

Rousmaniere, K. (2013). Those who can't teach: The disabling history of American educators. *History of Education Quarterly, 53*(1), 90–103.

S.B. 48, Education Code 51204.5, (California. 2011). https://www.cde.ca.gov/ci/cr/cf/senatebill48faq.asp

Santamaria, L. J., & Jean-Marie, G. (2014). Cross-cultural dimensions of applied, critical, and transformational leadership: Women principals advancing social justice and educational equity. *Cambridge Journal of Education, 44*(3), 333–360. http://dx.doi.org/10.1080/0305764X.2014.904276

Shapiro, J. (1993). *No pity: People with disabilities forging a new civil rights movement.* Three Rivers Press.

Shields, C. (2010). Transformative leadership: Working for equity in diverse contexts. *Educational Administration Quarterly, 46*(4), 558–589. https://doi.org/10.1177/0013161X10375609

Smith, P. (Ed.). (2013). *Both sides of the* table*: Autoethnographies of educators learning and teaching with/in [dis]ability*. Peter Lang.

Solis, S. (2006). I'm "coming out" as disabled but I'm "staying in" to rest: Reflecting on elected and imposed segregation. *Equity and Excellence in Education, 39*(2), 146–153. https://doi.org/10.1080/10665680500534007

Starratt, R. (2005). Responsible leadership. *The Educational Forum, 69*(2), 124–133. https://doi.org/10.1080/00131720508984676

Stenger, J. K. (2013). *The life that chose us: Educators with tourette syndrome*. JKS Press.

Taylor, S. J. (2006). Before it had a name: Exploring the historical roots of disability studies in education. In S. Danforth & S. Gabel (Eds.), *Vital questions facing disability studies in education* (pp. xii–xxiii). Peter Lang Publishing.

Theoharis, G. (2009). *The school leaders our children deserve: Seven keys to equity, social justice, and school reform*. Teachers College Press.

Tschannen-Moran, M., & Gareis, C. (2015). Principals, trust, and cultivating vibrant schools. *Societies, 5*, 256–276. https://doi.org/10.3390/soc5020256

Valle, J., Solis, S., Volpitta, D., & Connor, D. (2004). The disability closet: Teachers with learning disabilities evaluate the risks and benefits of coming out. *Equity & Excellence in Education, 37*, 4–17. https://doi.org/10.1080/10665680490422070

Vogel, G., & Sharoni, V. (2010). "My success as a teacher amazes me each and every day"—Perspectives of teachers with learning disabilities. *International Journal of Inclusive Education, 15*(5), 479–495. https://doi.org/10.1080/13603110903131721

Williams, J., Pazey, B., Shelby, L., & Yates, J. (2013). The enemy among us: Do school administrators perceive students with disabilities as a threat? *NAASP Bulletin, 97*(2), 139–165. https://doi.org/10.1177/0192636512473507

Youdell, D. (2011). *School trouble: Identity, power and politics in education*. Routledge.

CHAPTER 17

# EXPERIENCES OF DISABILITY IN ONE CANADIAN FACULTY OF EDUCATION

## Recognition and Resourcing as a Social Justice Response to Supporting Students Living With Disabilities

**Melissa Brideau**
*Western University*

**Pam Bishop**
*Western University*

At a time when some leaders want to stereotype, blame, or dismiss someone who looks, thinks, speaks, or lives differently from them, school and university leaders can offer a more expansive and inclusive way of "walking the talk." Educational leaders have the privilege of leading a core part of democracy, namely schools, universities, and their respective communities. Despite multiple attempts by various politicians, governments, and agencies

*Who Decides?*, pages 413–438
Copyright © 2022 by Information Age Publishing
www.infoagepub.com
All rights of reproduction in any form reserved.

**413**

to curb the efforts of progressive school and university leadership, communities across the globe are showing an increasing desire to have welcoming, open, and inclusive schools in their neighborhoods (Ainscow, 2020; Campbell, 2020; Oakes, 2017; Riehl, 2000). Most parents realize schools play a crucial role in helping their children and their neighbors' children prosper. Many parents understand that for the 21st century, their children's learning has to be in settings that reflect the diversity of their community, state, or nation (Ainscow, 2020; Hartley, 2015; Oakes, 2017). In addition, many parents want schools and universities with teachers and professors who know how to skillfully and genuinely nurture classrooms that are comprised of a diverse range of students (Campbell, 2020; Hoppey et al., 2018; Jacklin et al., 2007; Ryan & Struhs, 2004).

Our chapter is intended to be both hopeful and strategic because we realize how effective it can be to work with, learn from, and place faith in university students who are on their way to becoming the next generation of educators, social workers, psychologists, and so on, in the course of making faculties more inclusive places of learning. If we are to change disabling attitudes or behaviors, providing professional learning for university personnel is a wise way forward. We offer several suggestions to support learning about becoming a more inclusive faculty member or university leader than one might otherwise be. Along the way, we note the increasing trend toward legitimizing the learning needs of students living with disabilities (DeMatthews et al., 2020; Jacklin et al., 2007). We draw on literature and our lived experiences to contextualize what it can feel like as a student living with disabilities to not be fully recognized, respected, or included (as a student who, like other class members, needs to learn).

We also note the challenges wrought by a neoliberal backdrop to the education sector that often creates a chronic lack of resourcing and extreme work intensification for educators (Blackmore, 2019; Connell et al., 2009; Rezai-Rashti & Segeren, 2020). Despite the challenges of a neoliberal backdrop, educators "of all stripes" need to be a part of a systemic effort to better support students living with disabilities. By employing a social justice model (Evans et al., 2017) we progress an underlying argument that disability is less about a deficit view or a student's inability and more about universities adapting to remove institutional barriers (including cultures, structures, and policies) that, at their core, are exclusionary and ableist in nature. A social justice model actively seeks to support students living with disabilities; increase understandings of the oppressive and highly problematic nature of many historic and contemporary views assigned to those deemed "disabled" and create genuinely inclusive campus environments where differences are potential strengths and valued (MacKinnon et al., 2004). More specifically, the social justice model is intended to eliminate ableism, refine understandings about what counts as normal and equitable, and view disability identities in a positive way (Evans et al., 2017). The chapter is ordered in the following way: context, social justice model, Melissa's story, discussion, professor's story, reflection, and conclusions.

## CONTEXT

Michael Apple (2012) suggests "telling the truth about relations of inequality" is important for critically oriented researchers (p. 230). Apple also argues that capturing "where possible actions can be and are going on that challenge these inequalities... and the actual daily lives of the actors who work so hard to alter current realities" (p. 230) matters. Historically, too often students with disabilities in schools and universities have not been a common feature in the work of researchers in the field of education (Borland & James, 1999). Yet almost regardless of age, students with disabilities understand about relations of inequality—even if they are too young to have read about or spoken of them. For example, many students with disabilities in elementary and high schools "may be segregated into separate classrooms or programs, or they may be teased or bullied for looking or acting differently than other students" (Ostiguy et al., 2016, p. 302). School students with disabilities may also be tracked and tested, or even withdrawn from annual standardized testing regimes that education systems across much of the world impose in the name of accountability. These are, as Oakes (2017) asserted, additional by-products of neoliberalism which have diminished the aspirations for common good because of an over-emphasis on "the economy and individual interests" (p. 101). Schools have been positioned in competition with one another.

Governments regularly underscore the need to privilege academic success of students in literacy, numeracy, and science. Those student performances are in turn marketed by the publication of annual school testing results both locally and between countries (Gunter, 2018). Rather than addressing and supporting the social and academic learning needs of all students, one consequence of neoliberalism is an overly narrow focus on a school's academic performance metrics to the virtual exclusion of student achievements that contribute to being a good team player; sharing; winning and losing well; being affirming of others; and being supportive of differences in individuals, communities, and societies. Neoliberalism is a term assigned to "free market economic thinking where . . . the individual is seen as more important than the collective and economics is separable to politics because it does not allow any particular self-interest to dominate" (Thomson, 2020, p. 28). However, as Thomson (2020) notes, far from there being equal competing self-interests in the market, factors of power and status are involved and result in an "outcome that is inevitably unequal—there will be winners and losers" (p. 28).

A recent study by Rezai-Rashti and Segeren (2020) points to an increasing pressure on public school principals in Ontario and British Columbia, Canada to be conscious of and implement neoliberal reforms such as marketization and high-stakes testing. According to Rezai-Rashti and Segeren, such reforms are problematic for many marginalized students. Rezai-Rashti and Segeren (2020) note that "these shifts also have ramifications for the practice of school leadership, especially practices aimed at addressing equity and social justice" (p. 15). Indeed, the complexities, tensions, and contradictions reported by principals in this study led Rezai-Rashti and Segeren to observe: "With increasing amounts of time devoted to measuring, marketing and managing, school leaders have far fewer resources—time or financial—to devote to equity and social justice work" (p. 15). In the end, neoliberalism not only has shaped the work of schools but it "has changed the relationship between the state and the individual, imposing greater responsibility on the individual regardless of circumstance" (Blackmore, 2019, p. 178). Neoliberalism has also reinforced a longstanding view that those who do not prosper in education are themselves responsible for such outcomes through insufficient individual effort or capacity. Entrenching an explanation about access, retention, or achievement that omits earlier "multiple indirect social and cultural benefits of education" (Blackmore, p. 178) underestimates the complexities faced by students living with disabilities and ignores the pernicious nature of ableism.

The intended or unintended consequences of ableism and neoliberalism that are manifest in testing regimes and placements in many schools are also evident in the higher education sector. Dolmage (2017) claims "ableism makes able-bodiedness and able-mindedness compulsory" (p. 17). In other words, those with disabilities in universities are negatively constructed against a set of practices, assumptions, norms, and values associated with so-called able-bodied and able-minded individuals. Dolmage argues, "Academia powerfully mandates able-bodiedness and able-mindedness, as well as other forms of social and communicative hyperability" (p. 7). Part of the explanation for this cultural norm in the academy can be traced to the early history of European universities in the 11th century that were "closely tied to the hierarchy of the Christian church and monasteries and empires of the day" (Toswell, 2017, p. 5). Those students were destined to take up leading roles in business and society. Although in the past century universities have admitted women, for Indigenous and people of color there has been a longstanding assumption that universities function to serve academically strong and able-bodied individuals from privileged economic and social backgrounds.

From Dolmage's (2017) assessment of census data in the United States, Canada, and the United Kingdom, a markedly smaller percentage of citizens

25 years and older with a disability have a bachelor's degree compared to citizens without a disability. Dolmage's claim is supported by Mitchell (2016) who notes that "people with disabilities remain noticeably absent in higher education" (p. 18). Certainly across the United States, Canada, Australia, and the United Kingdom, parity is a long way off. Mitchell posits that universities are continuing to reproduce "practitioners of normalization" (p. 19) especially as lawyers, doctors, psychologists, and special education teachers. In many communities and universities, the notion of disability has been viewed as abnormal and deficient (Evans et al., 2017). Somewhat ironically, while universities have constantly been at the forefront of creating new and highly advanced knowledge on the one hand, they have uncritically reproduced many existing social norms. A greater recognition of students with disabilities being accepted into universities and graduate studies in particular is a vital part of contributing to broader diversity in many professions (Hartley, 2015; Smith, 2010). To achieve greater representation of students with disabilities in universities there are numerous actions needed to make them inclusive learning institutions: admissions criteria that include elements in addition to academic achievement; access to housing and transport; curricula that are genuinely accessible and based on universal design principles (Saltes, 2020); and extending scholarship funding to effectively respond to the needs of particular students with disabilities (who may start their education less financially secure than many students), providing employment transition support for students who have completed their degrees, and many others. Without explicit, evidence-informed actions on the part of universities, and especially their senior leaders, many prospective or existing students living with disabilities will continue to experience longer time in some programs than students deemed to be without disabilities because the learning framework in universities is often based on a normative view of students being without disabilities. More attention needs to be given to the impact "that attending universities has on the lives of students with disabilities" (Borland & James, 1999, p. 85), including possible scheduling implications for personal care workers, booking and availability of specific transport, and proximity to supermarkets. Without a more holistic approach to supporting students with disabilities prior to and once in universities, they will continue to experience underemployment over a lifetime, risk greater exposure to poverty (Dolmage, 2017; Saunders, 2006), limited career opportunities (Dolmage, 2017), and restricted opportunities to live independently compared to others in the community (Barnes, 2005).

Expecting students with disabilities to disproportionately carry the costs of making educational institutions more inclusive is unjustifiable if viewed through a social justice lens. For educational leaders who are values-led and possess a social justice outlook, it is past time that schools (or school systems) and universities shoulder more of the costs associated with formally educating students with disabilities. As Black and Simon (2014) suggest, organizational policies and inclusive leadership can be advanced to enact educational reform that strongly supports inclusive practices across the organization.

# A SOCIAL JUSTICE MODEL

In this chapter, we adopt a lens that relies on a social justice model rather than framework because "most disability models are closer to paradigms than they are to theories in that they present a certain way of viewing disability based on people's perceptions, beliefs, and experiences rather than research data" (Evans et al., 2017, p. 54). A social justice model of disability draws from civil rights, women's and other movements that were evident in the United States in the 1960s and 1970s. "Social justice is both a goal and a process" (Bell, 2016, p. 1). Principles or concepts of social justice such as access to resources and recognition are used in the course of critically analyzing individual, social, and institutional structures and cultures (Adams, 2016). In so doing, the social justice model enables an unveiling of privilege of dominant groups or interests and oppression of nondominant groups or interests (Evans et al., 2017). Further, a social justice model addresses diversity and "the intersectionality of experiences, roles, and identities" (Evans et al., 2017, p. 73). One potential advantage of including intersectionality factors is that it allows a consideration of multiple aspects of an individual or group and hence may counter one-size-fits-all understandings of people with disabilities or contexts in which they work, study, or live.

A further advantage of nesting this chapter in a social justice model is that it is particularly well suited to the education sector due to its advocacy potential. Drawing on this influential research of MacKinnon et al. (2004), Evans et al. (2017) suggested that social justice involves

> providing support to students with disabilities; educating both students with disabilities and those who are not disabled about the existence of disability oppression, working with them to create an environment that values differences and teaching them to advocate for their own and others' liberation; and working to change institutional structures and policies that support oppression of those with disabilities. (p. 74)

These features broadly help us ask "why is $x$ the case and not $y$?" (Apple, 2012, p. 230). In this chapter disability is defined as "the loss or limitation of opportunities to take part in the normal life of the community on an equal level with others due to physical and social barriers" (Barnes, 1991,

p. 2). In a complementary way, it is clear that "disability is a political and cultural identity, not simply a medical condition" (Dolmage, 2017, p. 5).

## MELISSA'S STORY

In this section, Melissa shares her story of the various challenges she has faced throughout her postsecondary career and how the collective assistance of numerous key figures within her network of support has been crucial in her ability to attain educational goals.

### Managing a Circle of Care

Growing up with a disability that limited my physical level of functioning has meant that I must depend on the help of personal support workers (PSW's) to complete many activities of daily living. The PSWs assist me with a variety of tasks related to dressing, toileting/showering, grooming, meal preparation, as well as transferring to and from my wheelchair. While I am indeed very grateful to be in receipt of such care, the system is not without its challenges—which, to my mother's credit, I was always made to take care of as independently as possible. However, prior to moving away from home to attend university, my mother was always there should I have required immediate assistance or her support/guidance as I worked to resolve an issue, but once I moved out, I could no longer rely on my mother in the same manner (as she resides an hour away from where I attend school). Thus, I had to learn fairly quickly how to balance academic duties with navigating the trials and tribulations that are, unfortunately, far too common in the home health industry.

One of the first challenges for me was making sure that my care schedule did not conflict with my classes. This was a huge stressor for me, as I knew that if I were not able to meet basic needs, it would be virtually impossible for me to participate in any aspect of the higher education community. In other words, having appropriate care set up would be integral to my success within the academy. Thus, in order to alleviate some of the anxiety associated with what I felt was a monumental task, I had a care conference (prior to the start of classes) where I met with representatives from the various healthcare agencies that would be providing me with assistance, as well as staff from the school's disability service office. The goal of this conference was for all parties to gain some clarity around the extent of my needs and how my care could be arranged to ensure that I could adequately fulfill my duties as a postsecondary student. However, this proved to be an incredibly arduous task as it became increasingly evident that the availability of PSWs was quite limited and meant that I had very little say in not only who would be providing my care, but also when it would occur. In order to properly illustrate the extraordinary nature of the circumstances, it is important to note that at one point in my postsecondary career, there were six agencies that provided my personal care (each responsible for different days/times throughout the week) and I often had to go to bed between eight and nine at night to accommodate the PSW's schedules.

In addition, working with so many different people, and managing such a chaotic schedule led to many other complications which impacted not only my physical health, but also caused me to struggle emotionally as I frequently felt isolated and alone. This was a consequence of the fact that while I was indeed living independently, I had very limited freedom or autonomy in my own life as I was constantly forced to adapt to the needs of the agencies/staff, often at the expense of my overall health and well-being. For instance, due to the lack of flexibility on the part of these healthcare agencies, I did not always have the chance to participate in academic and social events that occurred on campus, as there were only certain times when PSWs could assist me. Another troubling aspect of having to rely so heavily on attendants is that some individuals sent by the agencies were very inconsistent/unprofessional. One occurrence that stands out as particularly traumatic is the time that my PSW neglected to show up to assist me with a morning routine leaving me stuck in bed unable to get to the bathroom, much less attend classes. By the time my PSW finally arrived 5 hours later, I had not only missed a class in which I was supposed to give a presentation, but I was in excruciating pain that left me physically/emotionally drained, and therefore, unable to tend to any school-related tasks I had planned for the day.

Today however, my life has become a bit easier in this regard as I now have all of my care provided through one agency. While this is indeed great news, I must also tell you that I continue to deal with a multitude of frustrating situations on a daily basis. This includes not knowing which PSW is coming to assist me and having the agency schedulers change my booking times without notifying me. Although this experience is not nearly as bad as those mentioned previously, I still have moments where I feel as though my time and my being are neither valued nor respected. Even in the face of this adversity, I have found pockets of brightness that have helped me to evolve both personally and professionally. First, I have had the pleasure of meeting some amazing PSWs who exude warmth, kindness, and compassion in all aspects of their work. Second, as a result of interacting with such a diverse group of people/agencies, I have not only been able to strengthen important skills such as time management, organization, and conflict resolution, but I have also developed increased knowledge about the home healthcare system. Last but not least, gaining these valuable insights has inspired me to use my voice to advocate for others in similar circumstances who may not be able/have the opportunity to speak up for themselves, and most importantly, to let them know that they are not alone.

## Invisible Barriers

Perhaps the most difficult of all the barriers I have faced in my higher education journey has been the invisible challenges I must contend with on a daily basis. First, the negative attitudes of other students and staff have most certainly impacted my collegiate experience. One realm where these attitudes have become readily apparent to me is when having to interact with or ask for support from faculty in order to meet my unique needs. For instance, due to the nature of my disability, I must frequently ask for accommodations such as flexibility with assignment deadlines. While most faculty have been tremendously supportive and helpful when I have communicated my needs to them, there have been others who have indicated that providing me with such flexibility is not a possibility as it would be unfair to grant me an extension of time without offering the same leniency to the rest of my classmates. Responses of this sort inhibit my ability to physically function; if I'm not able to properly pace myself, I can experience extreme fatigue and flare-ups in my chronic pain, which in turn can cause debilitating muscle spasms. Further, neglecting to consider my diverse learning needs only serves to impede the development of a more inclusive learning environment and essentially invalidates my very existence as a physically disabled student in the academy. While situations like this are thankfully few and far between (as most professors have been incredibly supportive and understanding), I am grateful to have the support of fabulous disability service staff as they have assisted me in gaining the confidence to have critical conversations with my educators around the accommodations needed and how we can work as a team to ensure a rich learning experience for both parties.

Along with a lack of understanding/awareness from faculty, I've also had numerous occasions in which other students felt entitled to ask questions related to my disability that were largely inappropriate such as wondering if I'm able to speak or asking for specific information related to my medical history. As you can imagine, dealing with these situations is extremely frustrating/exhausting and requires a considerable amount of my emotional energy in not only managing how I react to others, but most especially, how I confront my own problematic inner dialogue that comes as a direct consequence of trying to fit into a world that, ultimately, was not made for people like me. As a result of experiencing events such as those mentioned above, I have been forced to tend to another workload on top of my various academic responsibilities: combating the ever-present effects of internalized ableism. For me, this includes the intense feelings of shame and frustration I feel when I am not able to complete tasks in the same manner, or at the same pace, as my peers. In addition, I must grapple with the fear and anxiety that occur every time I need to ask for accommodations as I often worry that my colleagues/ superiors will think that I am lazy, lack motivation, or that I am simply taking advantage of their generosity. This concern over how I am perceived then leads to other negative emotions such as feelings of unworthiness—that I do not deserve the opportunities being a graduate student has afforded me (despite knowing that I have worked extremely hard/overcome numerous obstacles to get myself where I am today). Although I make every effort to remind myself of these facts, engaging in this type of extra labor as well as that which is required to navigate inherently ableist structures, policies, practices, and attitudes within the higher education community comes at a high cost to my emotional and psychological well-being.

On a brighter note, even in the face of these challenges, it is also equally important to me that I share with you how lucky I feel as I have been blessed with numerous sources of support that have helped me immensely and carried me through some of my darkest moments. First and foremost, the informal support I have received from my family and friends has assisted me in shaping/maintaining my positive outlook, sense of humor, and resilient spirit. Second, the formal support I have received from members of the academy including supervisors, faculty, administrative staff and those in disability services has been incredible and enabled me to increase my confidence both personally and professionally (as many of these individuals saw the light in me when I did not see it in myself). Finally, I would be remiss if I did not mention one being that has made my quality of life infinitely better: my service dog, Freya. Freya not only allows me to be as independent as possible by providing physical assistance such as picking up items that I have dropped; pulling off clothing; opening doors, cupboards, and drawers; but she also gives me unwavering emotional support in the form of unconditional love and understanding. Moreover, in working and learning from Freya, she has taught me many valuable lessons. For example, she has shown me what it means to be unapologetically authentic; that it is okay to rest when I need to rest; and that by continuing to learn and challenge myself, I will lead a happier, more meaningful, and fulfilled life. Last, but not least, she is the best co-author I could ask for (she is lying under my feet as I write this)! For her (and so many others in my life), I am forever grateful.

## Barriers to Community Participation

When thinking about going away to school, I was not only tasked with figuring out how to manage academic life, but also how to manage moving from a small rural town to a larger city in Ontario, Canada. Along with the opportunity to pursue my educational goals, I was filled with a flurry of excitement when thinking about how the move (from an area with very few supports designed to assist disabled people in their quest for independence, to a city where resources are more readily available) would allow me to increase my participation in the surrounding community. From the start of the planning process, I knew that a key element to this successful transition would be my ability to obtain adequate and accessible housing. Despite being aware of how challenging finding housing to meet my unique needs could be (as differing ideas around the notion of accessibility can make this particularly difficult), I did not let this daunting reality dissuade me from my goal of partaking in an experience common to many first-year university students: living in residence.

Preparing for such an endeavor required me to set up a meeting with the residence manager to discuss ways in which they could improve the built environment so that I could effectively and efficiently access and move freely around my living environment. Now, at this juncture, it is important to share that prior to this meeting, staff from the schools' disability service office met with staff in the residence office to provide education and advocacy focused on the nature of my needs, and to prepare them for the fact that renovations would need to be completed before the start of the semester. Upon meeting with the residence manager, I was quite nervous because my previous experiences of asking for any type of accommodations/retrofitting of spaces had often been met with resistance due to the time, energy, and cost it takes to carry out these renovations. However, I'm happy to say that thanks to the phenomenal advocacy work of the school's disability service professionals, and the residence manager's willingness to listen and take action, this was not the case. Instead, I was met with kindness, compassion, and understanding which served to put me at ease when discussing the types of renovations that would be required. The accessibility features discussed in this meeting included: remote controlled doors, a roll-in/wheelchair accessible shower, and the installation of grab bars set at just the right height to allow me to self-transfer. Along with improving the physical accessibility of the space, we also discussed other practical issues such as: setting up a lock box outside the main door to my residence that would allow my attendants access to the building so that they could assist me with my personal care; and bringing in an accessibility consultant that would provide expertise on what to do in case of an emergency situation (i.e., a fire in the middle of the night when I'm in bed and cannot get to my chair). At the end of the meeting, I was assured that everything I needed to be done would be put in place before my arrival on campus. Thus, this meeting served to alleviate some of my worries in the sense that I knew my living space would be set up in a way that would enable me to meet my daily needs.

As a result of these positive experiences early on, I was able to make the most of my time on campus. Living in residence not only made it easier for me to access crucial academic support necessary to achieve success in my studies, but it also made it easier to develop relationships with peers. Being surrounded by peers allowed me to meet and interact with many wonderful people who have each touched my life in their own unique way. While it is indeed true that my first year in residence was a memorable one filled with some of the best and most fruitful times of my life, it is also true that the end of that first year was considerably more challenging for me. This is because I had to make the difficult decision to stay in residence in order to ensure I had the energy required to remain successful in my studies. I knew this was the right choice for me as I was well aware of the numerous hurdles that came with trying to find housing that is both accessible and affordable to those on a fixed income. Further, I did not feel that I would be able to handle the stress of navigating the waitlists for social housing or the renovations that would inevitably be required as well as balancing my academic duties. That being said, it was still incredibly painful coping with the reality that while those around me would be moving out, and on to another exciting phase of life, I would be staying put.

After 4 years of living in residence, I made the decision to take a leap of faith and move off campus with some friends. In our search for accommodations, we learned some very valuable lessons such as: We would need to be very specific around what we meant by accessibility as we were often told that places were accessible only to realize once inside that I could not make it beyond the front door; and that the spaces that would meet my needs were too expensive for us to afford on our limited student budgets. Eventually, we came upon a space where the landlords gave us permission to retrofit the apartment to suit my needs. It was decided that I would take the master bedroom as it had enough space for me to move around in my wheelchair. In addition, it was equipped with an en suite bathroom that with the toilet removed, and a ramp (built by my stepdad), would allow me to take a shower. However, if I wanted to use the bathroom I had to transfer into my shower chair, as it was not possible for me to fit through the door of the main bathroom with my wheelchair. Thus, I spent a large amount of time and energy working to meet basic needs. To put it in perspective, I had to transfer four times just to use the bathroom: from my wheelchair to shower chair; shower chair to toilet; the toilet back to shower chair; and finally, the shower chair back to my wheelchair. This move also came with other costs as well. For instance, living off campus meant that I no longer had access to the school's accessible transportation service and so I often had to go in my wheelchair to school or use the city's accessible transportation system which requires you to book your ride 3 days in advance. Both of these options were difficult at times as driving myself to school became more challenging in harsher weather conditions and using the city's services was frustrating as I was unable to go to campus on the spur of the moment for study purposes, or to participate in other events on campus. Moreover, even if I had booked a ride on time, the service was very unreliable, often picking me up late from home (making me late for class) or picking me up late from school (making me late to meet one of my personal care attendants at home).

Despite the various obstacles mentioned above, these experiences only made me physically and emotionally stronger. I was able to have the opportunity to live on my own and it gave me increased insight and awareness of the challenges other students may be facing as they attempt to secure appropriate housing. Finally, this journey allowed me to meet other individuals who (through their support and dedication to ensuring that I had adequate housing) made a tremendous impact on my life. In what follows, we discuss Melissa's story in light of social justice considerations of recognition and resourcing.

## DISCUSSION

In this section, I, as Melissa's supervisor (and co-author of this chapter), conceptually reflect on her lived experiences and provide some links with relevant literature. To me, Melissa's story shines a light on some of her lived experience in relation to her postsecondary education and how she accessed resources—or did not. Her story also reveals several instances linked to matters of recognition both in terms of how she understands being recognized and the variations in how others recognized her. Issues of recognition for students who live with disabilities are matters of social justice (Bell, 2016; Evans et al., 2017). How "nondisabled" individuals view students with disabilities may be informed by oppressive assumptions and stereotypes (Ostiguy et al., 2016). There are numerous elements raised that I believe explain Melissa's significant challenges and achievements. Having a mother whose values, beliefs, and actions encouraged Melissa to be independent has been important for her—and a contrast to the dependence enforced by a necessary reliance on personal care workers. Melissa's flexibility in juggling her time requirements with those of the personal care workers' availability with whom she had limited control (because up to six agencies were involved in that service provision) evidences a substantial capacity for dealing with tensions between the needs of herself and others—and adapting. Having to do "workarounds" and accommodate the needs of others is a common experience for students living with disabilities (Dolmage, 2017; Ostiguy et al., 2016).

In my view, it was Melissa's recognition of power held by agencies that was both complicated and stressful to manage and beyond her capacity to govern. She also recognized the improvement in ultimately having to deal with only one agency, although she still had to adapt to fit in with the agency's scheduling parameters. Melissa astutely recognized that the agency's valuing of her time was much more limited than their concern for their personal care workers' time. Melissa's clear explanation of how problematic situations can become for her if a scheduled personal care worker does not arrive underscore the dependence at play—and a practical limit to independence. Many agencies that support students living with disabilities face chronic underfunding from the government and hence often experience personnel shortages and service requests that cannot be entirely met (Hartley, 2015).

It was clear to me that by understanding her own needs better than those students or professors who stereotype and ask ignorant, entitled, and invasive questions, Melissa actively sought to recognize the "pockets of brightness" in her life such as the richness of friendships, familial relations, and others who saw her in a strengths-based way. Regularly facing negative attitudes and behaviors is common to those on the margins, but that frequency does not diminish the disappointment, affront, energy loss, and anger that can come from constantly justifying one's worth, ability, and potential (Dolmage, 2017; Evans et al., 2017). I was struck by Melissa's enduring generosity towards others. The advocacy that Melissa engaged in for others, and especially those less able to advocate, underscores her compassion and commitment to principles of equity and social justice.

Like me, most professors were responsive to Melissa's self-advocacy regarding her class or academic needs suggesting that they recognized the legitimacy of those arguments. By having to grapple with some professors' responses for Melissa's requests for "reasonable consideration," such as extra time, placed a burden on her that should have been shouldered by the faculty via communication about relevant policies and practices. The extra time in those situations is a resource—and it can be provided or withheld by professors. Positioning Melissa's requests as potentially contributing to inequities for other class members highlights an ignorant attitude toward a student who lives with a disability and a shallow grasp of multiple advantages enjoyed by many students in the class. Indeed, the advantages are so embedded that those professors did not see nor recognize them. Put another way, when ableist views prevail, students who live with disabilities are, according to Bell (2016), "subordinated and disadvantaged" (p. 9).

I believe the failure of some professors to understand that Melissa required additional time to complete assignments and denial of her requests for that consideration was problematic. Not only did those decisions place Melissa under additional (and unhealthy) pressure to complete assignments in unnecessarily compressed time frames, but it also contributed to a sense of her requests—and herself—being unreasonable. However, the matter of a student with a disability needing more time to complete assignments should not necessarily only involve a student and their instructor or supervisor. The institutional policies should enable provision to be made for assignments to be handed in, for example, at the end of a term. Such a provision may work well for many students who are living with disabilities. That said, it may be problematic if an accurate gauge of a student's academic progress is only evident toward the end of term (after the first assignment is marked) and there is insufficient time to provide additional support or the student appeals a grade on the grounds that, following feedback on their first assignment there was insufficient time for them to take into account the feedback and make appropriate changes to the remaining assignments. In addition, for some students who are living with disabilities it may be realistic to expect them to take longer to complete a thesis. On equity, retention, achievement, and completion grounds additional funding should be available to support students in those situations. Put another way, treating members of different population groups the same based on norms of progress or markers of success that were designed for a dominant group may end up thwarting the larger purposes of inclusion and diversity in higher education at this stage in the 21st century.

Importantly, in my view, Melissa has created numerous informal and formal networks and those personal resources have provided critical support for her in multiple ways including for her studies. Melissa's service dog, Freya, has provided unconditional love and established herself as a crucial part of the support needed both for household tasks, study, and companionship purposes. Suitable rental accommodation in the private market sector proved to be difficult to find—and required Melissa to arrange for various modifications to be made to the houses. By contrast, Melissa experienced a much more responsive reaction from the university where she ended up staying for the duration of her studies. Although human rights legislation and related government regulations in Canada may apply to all providers of rental properties, in this instance, the university proved to be more willing to recognize and respond to Melissa's accommodation needs and access to physical resources than the private rental sector. As is the case for many of us, Melissa's housing requirements were fundamental to her being able to function effectively in her studies. That housing tenancy, in effect, made her visible to the university. Time spent by Melissa ensuring she could access functional living arrangements was greater for her than many students due to most rental housing not being designed for universal accessibility. The time use was invisible to almost everyone but was necessary in her efforts to access university education.

In all, for Melissa's university studies to progress well—or indeed at all—it meant she needed to plan well, be effective with time management/scheduling of appointments, handle conflict when it arose and adopt a highly flexible approach in the course of achieving her housing/rental and care needs. It was clear to me the inclusive leadership, values, and disposition of the student-housing manager ensured that the university provided what Melissa identified as necessary for her living arrangements. That contribution by way of recognition and resourcing was highly supportive and stands in sharp contrast to the professors who interpreted Melissa's request for the needed resource of extra time to complete assignments in a deficit way. Along the way, that lack of recognition delegitimized both the request and Melissa. Those professors either did not know of Melissa's legal rights to reasonable adjustments, did not care, or had little understanding of ableism and their part in contributing to or reducing that in the university setting. Ableism is concerned with and almost invariably assumes able-bodiedness and able mindedness (Dolmage, 2017). In higher education, professors' situating of students as able-bodied or able-minded can limit understandings of students who may not identify or be identified in that way. Professors who do not recognize students living with disabilities can unknowingly or deliberately render them invisible. I am heartened that a majority of professors did not take such a deficit-based approach and supported such requests from Melissa. Most professors did not make Melissa's task of gaining time extensions overly complicated or difficult. Some professors used universal design principles in their courses and course outlines. Others recognized Melissa as being fully human and identified their need to adapt their teaching and assignments to her learning needs.

Next, we turn to consider the influence of two graduate students' experiences on me as a professor and administrator who then worked with Melissa and other faculty, staff, and administrators to develop an explicit plan to provide scholarships to attract students living with disabilities and Indigenous students into MA and PhD programs.

## PAM'S STORY

Several years ago, I was in an exam and the chair provided an opportunity for all those present to take a 5-minute break, halfway through proceedings. The PhD student, a talented researcher, elected to go to the bathroom nearby. Because the bathroom really wasn't fully accessible, it turned out that he was unable to use the bathroom stall: John's (pseudonym) wheelchair was wider than the stall door. His access to a resource that most students take for granted was denied because it was built to only accommodate particular users. The faculty's only "accessible" bathroom was in another part of the building—and it would have taken about 4 minutes to get there. John decided against going—and went back to the room where his exam was being held. Even though the exam chair, who was from another faculty, had no idea of the barrier the student faced in attempting to access a restroom, John elected to put up with the consequences of that exclusion and successfully completed the exam. Once the exam had concluded, John shared with examiners details of attempting to use the bathroom during the 5-minute break in proceedings. At the time, John and another individual were the only graduate students living with "known visible" physical disabilities. The graduation of John almost coincided with the admission of Melissa into the PhD program. She was then 1 of 2 students living with a physical disability amongst a graduate student population of 1,000.

The numbers alone pointed to barriers being present that at least in part explained why there were only two students indicating they had physical disabilities. Those numbers plus the quiet advocacy of Melissa also provided an impetus to reconsider how the faculty could attract—and support—a more diverse student population. As Melissa's supervisor, I learned much in our weekly supervision meetings—including the pragmatic and not-so-pragmatic realities experienced by many students living with physical disabilities. Through discussions about the nature of the doctoral research Melissa wanted to pursue, my understandings about ableism (including my own) in higher education grew significantly. Together and on our own we read about social justice and critical disability research and theories. If I had known what I learned from Melissa and countless articles, books, and other literature earlier, I would have acted more quickly to address some of the inequities that students with disabilities of one sort or another experience. Although I had been involved with social justice initiatives for decades, they did not really address students living with disabilities. Melissa worked at staying positive in the face of many challenges that would have elicited complaints from many "able-bodied" graduate students (and professors) were they to have faced those same circumstances. In the course of getting to know her as an individual as well as graduate student, I learned about how small changes made to the physical layout and setup of accessible student accommodations can be profound in their impact on quality of life. For example, once apprised of the need, the university put in a transfer bar for Melissa to use in her bathroom. Without the specific facility Melissa sometimes fell as she endeavored to transfer out of her wheelchair—and then an ambulance would be called to assist to help pick her up. Melissa's deep understanding of the cumulative effects of intersectionality and disadvantage experienced by disparate marginalized communities was also shared with me to build on readings and discussions of theories and research.

In all, these weekly face-to-face meetings (prior to the pandemic) between Melissa and me as her supervisor, contributed to a suggestion by me to increase the number of graduate students in thesis-based programs. In particular, during the course of a subsequent graduate programs review, it was advocated to the external reviewers that more students who were living with disabilities and more Indigenous students should be evident in the faculty's MA and PhD programs. As an outcome of the external reviewers agreeing with and endorsing that claim, an ad hoc committee was set up to develop a plan to attract more students living with disabilities. Melissa was a member of that committee and, ultimately, it agreed to advocate for targeted scholarships. In brief, the committee proposed that the faculty fund three PhD and two MA scholarships annually for 4 consecutive years for students living with disabilities and the same allocation for Indigenous students. In all, the scholarship investment amounted to approximately $2.3 million—all of it sponsored by faculty funds. Because of the size of the potential outlay, the provost and other senior university personnel needed to agree with and support the plan—which they did. The first of the scholarships will be awarded early in 2020 so that recipients may begin their graduate studies in Fall 2021. Critically, the PhD and MA scholarships are important resources offered to recipients in addition to other awarded scholarships. For students living with disabilities and Indigenous students, that feature may have significant benefits. For example, it may enable recipients to obtain better suited and higher standard rental housing. At a minimum, all PhD recipients will each receive the $80,000 over 5 years plus the university's guaranteed graduate scholarship that pays tuition plus $12,000 annually as part of an assistantship arrangement. MA recipients will receive $10,000 for 2 years in addition to the possibility of a scholarship of $12,500 over that timeframe.

These scholarships recognize the complicated and embedded challenges that many students living with disabilities and Indigenous students experience in their efforts to access university education. The scholarships should result in up to 12 students living with disabilities achieving their PhDs and up to eight MA students with disabilities completing their degrees. Along the way, it is hoped that the faculty's student population will become, and appear, more diverse. It is also hoped that these scholarships are not the only initiatives undertaken by the faculty in the coming years as it attempts to become a truly accessible site for all graduate students. While Melissa's insights and lived experiences were an impetus for these scholarships, she will not be a recipient of them as they are available only to incoming students. Melissa is extremely pleased that the initiative stands to benefit many students and ultimately lead to employment opportunities that were previously not available. This significant investment drew on values and purposes connected to equity, diversity, and inclusion. These scholarships recognize the need for additional resource support being available that complements other more widely available scholarships. The investment could be made because the faculty had sufficient funds to sponsor this "values-led" initiative. There was a critical mass of key central and faculty administrators, equity scholars, graduate office staff, and Melissa who recognized that for historical reasons and ableist assumptions, more access to resources would be vital for some prospective students. Together, those university members worked in support of what has finally emerged: an opportunity to better recognize and resource graduate students living with disabilities and Indigenous students in one Canadian faculty of education. Below, we turn to some of the literature, which provides further insights into supporting the access and success of students with disabilities and the higher education sector.

## LITERATURE REVIEW

From her standpoint of having worked as a disability practitioner as well as an equity manager in the higher education sector for more than 25 years, Hartley (2015) suggests that encouraging progress has been made in regard to increasing the number of students with disabilities participating in Australian higher education. However, Hartley also accepts that a major challenge remains; namely, creating "a system that is representative of the wider community and values that knowledge, skill, and experiences that people with disabilities bring to their learning, ultimately becoming places where people with disabilities can flourish" (p. 413). Like Hartley (2015), the National Centre for Student Equity in Higher Education (NCSEHE, 2017) reported the number of students with disabilities in universities increased markedly in Australia, claiming "between 2008 and 2015 the number of undergraduate students with disability increased by 88.6 per cent, more than double the rate of growth of total undergraduate students nationally, representing 6.2 per cent of the overall undergraduate student body" (p. 3). The NCSEHE report also observed that many higher education institutions were struggling to adequately meet the needs of the increased numbers of students with disabilities. In that respect, the NCSEHE echoed Hartley's claim concerning the current state-of-pay not valuing or enabling students with disabilities to flourish. NCSEHE identified three priority areas that required institutional attention: retention, success, and outcomes; teaching and institutional cultures; and support policies and strategies. In addition, NCSEHE identified several policy recommendations that need to be implemented in higher education. For example, improved data collection on students with disabilities, more inclusive teaching practices and technology, comprehensive disability training for university personnel and students, and more flexible study options. Definitions of types of disability currently recognized by the federal Department of Education and Training include "hearing, learning, mobility, vision, medical and 'other'" (NCSEHE, 2017, p. 8). However, there are many subclassifications of disability not covered under these six areas. Going forward, the need to disaggregate data in order to better recognize disability subgroups was identified by NCSEHE as necessary to being more responsive to highly specific needs of students with disabilities. DeMatthews et al. (2020), in the United States, identified the importance of creating and conveying a vision, facilitating high-quality learning for students, building capacity, and a supportive culture when making an organization more inclusive for students with disabilities.

Self-disclosure of a disability is another aspect that can impact the university experiences of students who live with disabilities. Whether at the application or enrollment stages or during studies, self-disclosure is the "primary mechanism for accessing disability support, adjustments and accommodations at university" (NCSEHE, 2020, p. 11). A self-disclosure approach relies on an individual to indicate that they have a disability in order to access needed support from the university. Self-disclosure may be viable for many students but not all. For example, some students may not trust that their disclosure will be respected or viewed without negative judgements such as shaming or doubting being formed by university personnel. By and large, in a study by Jacklin et al. (2007), students with disabilities indicated that they elected to self-disclose to their university to ensure support or avoid a problem during their studies. In response to self-disclosure and supporting students with disabilities, most universities draw from a medical model of disability, which largely positions impairment as the locus of the problem. Perhaps not surprisingly, in a similar vein, the Americans With Disabilities Act, 2008 defines disability as an impairment, whether mental, physical, episodic, or in remission. Notably, the legal definition of disability is concerned with whether an individual's impairment "substantially limits one or more major life activities" (Ostiguy et al., 2016, p. 301). Definitions of disability that have impairment at their center have often been an impetus to an individual, rights-based discourse that, for example, recognizes the inherent value and dignity of each person. Over the last 4 decades, universities in North America, the United Kingdom, Australia, and other democracies have generally accepted those principles. In more recent years, the enactment of those rights-based principles has, in broad terms, improved.

By contrast with the medical model, a social model of disability takes a broader view and considers structural, social, economic, political, and environmental factors that represent inequities or barriers to those living with disabilities. Both the social model and the rights-based model of disability have gained traction over the last 15 years (Bonati, 2019). Indeed, Bonati suggests the shift to a broader understanding of how disability engages with attitudes and the environment shaped some of the preamble to the United Nations Convention on the Rights of Persons With Disability (2006). Countries such as Australia, Canada, and the United States are signatories to the UN Convention on the Rights of Persons With Disability and in turn, compliance requirements of universities by the government often reflect the spirit and principles of that UN Convention. Policy in universities then becomes a key mechanism for administrative, legislative, and pedagogic interventions needed to lessen disadvantages experienced by students with disabilities.

Students living with disabilities continue to experience some professors and staff not adhering to university policies that apply to them, especially concerning making reasonable adjustments in the classroom (Evans et al., 2017; NCSEHE, 2017). Hartley (2015) argues that progress made by universities toward people with disabilities can be checked against equity and quality of student experience data and learning experiences of students with disabilities. According to Hartley, "Findings from the 2013 University Experience Survey developed by Graduate Careers Australia and the Social Research Centre, provide … evidence that the learning experience of students with disabilities is qualitatively different from that of students not reporting a disability" (p. 415). Students with disabilities were less satisfied in 4 of the 5 main areas surveyed: teacher quality, learner engagement, learning resources, and skills development. The one area where students with disabilities were more satisfied than other students was in the area of student support. Hartley's analysis implies that a deficit view of students with disabilities is still prevalent in the culture at many Australian universities. "A deficit view is also strongly reflected in much of the literature about students with disabilities who are viewed as intrinsically problematic, 'deviant' from the 'norm,' and in need of 'remediation'" (Ryan & Struhs, 2004, p. 76).

Universities need to collaborate on and coordinate their data collection and exchange so that knowledge sharing can heighten the efficacy of policy implementation and better benefit students with disabilities across the sector. Vickerman and Blundell's (2010) study of disabled students' lived experiences in one higher education setting in England found that a "gap between rhetorical policy and practice is evident, with most students struggling to receive support" (p. 30). A study by Shevlin et al. (2004) investigated the quality of access and participation by students living with disabilities in Irish institutions of higher education, and they also noted a fragmented approach with only some universities actively grasping the need to change admission, curricula, assessment policies, and procedures. Several years later, the NCSEHE (2017) report also acknowledged that retention and success has remained an ongoing issue in universities so far as degree completions and employment outcomes are concerned for students with disabilities. Perhaps not surprisingly then, students with disabilities encounter notable disadvantages when attempting to find employment or careers once they graduate. The NCSEHE report also found that students with disabilities who actively seek support in their universities have typically experienced higher rates of retention and academic success. Institutional cultures in many universities are part of the explanation for not "applying reasonable adjustments" (NCSEHE, 2017, p. 8) where students with disabilities are concerned, hence the need for more professional learning and awareness training for all university employees.

Black and Simon (2014) argue that learning should be a core element in organizational life when any inclusive change effort is directed toward supporting students with disabilities. Addressing the learning needs of students with disabilities is critical but must be accompanied by learning from all members of the university (Evans et al., 2017; Saltes, 2020). In turn, such investments require substantial funds at a time when public education budgets are strained. However difficult it may be to locate funding from the government, it is critical to have adequate financial support because every member of society is entitled to a solid start in their education. This fundamental right is not yet truly available for all and indeed Barnes (2005) suggests societies must change and become more inclusive if people living with disabilities are to realistically have a chance to live independently. For that chance to materialize, there must be better and more inclusive alternatives to what is currently on offer in education and other realms of institutional and social life. Barnes (2005) is hopeful but clear about what this will take:

> For disabled people this alternative must be a society in which all human beings regardless of impairment, age, gender, sexual orientation, social class, minority ethnic status can coexist as equal members of the community, secure in the knowledge that their needs will be accommodated in full and that their views will be recognized, respected, and valued. It will be a very different society from the one in which we now live. It will be a society that is truly democratic, characterized by genuine and meaningful equal opportunities and outcomes with far greater equity in terms of income and wealth, with enhanced choice and freedom, and with a proper regard for environmental and social interdependence and continuity. (p. 255)

In her 2016 American Educational Research Association Presidential Address, Jennie Oakes (2017) urged members to "engage in public scholarship—joining with educators, political leaders, storytellers, and activists—to produce and use knowledge in concert to shift cultural norms and political power toward equity and inclusion" (p. 91). Also, Oakes believes that "despite all of their failings, public schools and universities remain society's most democratic institutions" (p. 101). As Oakes indicated, stories are one means by which norms that enhance the quests for equity and inclusion can be effective. Stories also help educators and students to connect "explicit, formal, symbolic presentations of knowledge and the practical knowledge found in individuals' effective actions" (Danzig & Harris, 1996, p. 197). Some stories offer a view from the personal side of an individual that may not be as easily divulged in the course of university life. Stories can serve multiple purposes such as sharing ethical ways of understanding one's own or others' experiences, principles, or what Danzig and Harris (1996) describe as "practical theories." Those practical theories may serve as an impetus for action—as happened with the two stories shared in this chapter. More than $2 million was allocated in scholarships to support MA and PhD students living with disabilities and Indigenous students in one Canadian faculty of education. Stories are also an important way for members of marginalized communities to reveal experiences that were previously hidden, ignored, or passed over.

## CONCLUSIONS

One of our intentions in this chapter was to give voice to and provide insight into the lived experiences of one PhD student in a Canadian faculty of education, given the paucity of attention assigned to the voices of students with disabilities. Another intention was to show how, through Melissa's story, as (told here but) shared in several faculty conversations, practical knowledge and effective actions (Danzig & Harris, 1996) followed. Learning about Melissa's lived experiences as she has navigated her university education showed that the journey required many different challenges to be worked around, and much more pre-planning and management than most students are required to give as a matter of course. Consistent with the literature, her story points to a level of ableism that is manifest in universities across the globe. Taken-for-granted assumptions, exclusive attitudes, and values, and a deficit approach to her equity-linked requests for extra time to complete assignments for some professors were evident throughout her journey. Amidst the disabling ways of a few professors was an institutional and collegial response to invest in scholarships that were targeted at supporting students living with disabilities and Indigenous students. There was a reliance on Melissa's views to inform the way in which scholarship criteria were worded and the marketing framed so as to gain strong interest in those opportunities. Involving students with disabilities in such resource allocations is not only helpful but consistent with the literature and values regarding inclusive leadership and university settings.

Directing resources to better support students with disabilities is critical in terms of universities becoming more inclusive in their outlook as well as in admission, teaching, and learning actions. The quest to become more inclusive invariably involves tensions—the neoliberal backdrop prizes the market, generation of money, and "timely" program completions by students. While this backdrop casts a troubling shadow over the challenges faced by universities, it nonetheless provides a context in which leaders, faculty, staff, and students can work together to identify which leadership actions, organizational visions, values, and dispositions will lead to a more inclusive place for all—rather than mostly for those who have historically been well served by the university sector. As our social justice model indi-cated, recognition and resourcing remain crucial matters to address when considering the access and success of students with disabilities in univer-sities. At this stage in the 21st century, we have not heard enough about these issues directly from university students living with disabilities. Univer-sities' efforts to make their institutions more inclusive and accessible will be advanced by better understanding the complexities, challenges, and op-portunities faced—and told—by students with disabilities. To help universi-ties further advance their efforts to become, as Hartley (2015) and Oakes (2017) suggest, more representative of the wider community, leaders, pro-fessors, and staff must engage in professional learning that enables them to understand the embedded nature of ableism and its inequitable social, cul-tural, material, and educational effects on students living with disabilities.

# REFERENCES

Adams, M. (2016). Pedagogical foundations for social justice education. In M. Ad-ams & L. A. Bell (with D. Goodman & K. Joshi). (Eds.), *Teaching for diversity and social justice* (3rd ed., pp. 27–53). Routledge.

Ainscow, M. (2020). Promoting inclusion and equity in education: Lessons from international experiences. *Nordic Journal of Studies in Educational Policy, 6*(1), 7–16. https://doi.org/10.1080/20020317.2020.1729587

Americans With Disabilities Act of 2008. 42 U.S.C.12102 et seq. 2008. https://www .eeoc.gov/statutes/ada-amendments-act-2008

Apple, M. W. (2012). Some lessons in educational equality [Review of the book *Les-sons in educational equality: Successful approaches to intrac*table *problems around the world*, by J. Heymann & Adèle Cassola, Eds.]. *Educational Researcher, 41*(6), 230–232. https://doi.org/10.3102/0013189x12449379

Barnes, C. (1991). *Disabled people in Britain and discrimination.* Hurst.

Barnes, C. (2005). Independent living, politics and policy in the United Kingdom: A social model account. *Journal of Learning Disabilities, 36*(3), 248–258.

Bell, L. (2016). Theoretical foundations for social justice education. In M. Adams & L.A. Bell (with D. Goodman & K. Joshi). (Eds.), *Teaching for diversity and social justice* (3rd ed., pp. 3–26). Routledge.

Black, W., & Simon, M. (2014). Leadership for all students: Planning for more inclusive school practices. *NCPEA International Journal of Educational Lead-ership Preparation, 9*(2), 153–172. ERIC. https://files.eric.ed.gov/fulltext/ EJ1048067.pdf

Blackmore, J. (2019). Feminism and neo/liberalism: Contesting education's pos-sibilities. *Discourse: Studies in the Cultural Politics of Education, 40*(2), 176–190. https://doi.org/10180/01596306.2019.1569877

Bonati, L. (2019). Social justice and students with intellectual disability: Inclusive higher education practices. In K. Freebody, S. Goodwin, & H. Proctor (Eds.), *Higher education, pedagogy and social justice* (pp. 207–224). Palgrave Macmillan.

Borland, J., & James, S. (1999). The learning experience of students with disabilities in higher education: A case study of a UK university. *Disability & Society, 14*(1), 85–101.

Campbell, C. (2020). Educational equity in Canada: The case of Ontario's strategies and actions to advance excellence and equity for students. *School Leadership & Management, 41*(4–5), 409–428. https://doi.org/10.1080/13632434.2019.1709165

Connell, R., Fawcett, B., & Meagher, G. (2009). Neoliberalism, new public management and the human service professions [Introduction to the special issue]. *Journal of Sociology, 45*(4), 331–338. https://doi.org/10.1177/1440783309346472

Danzig, A., & Harris, K. (1996). Building competence by writing and reflecting on stories of practice. *Journal of Educational and Psychological Consultation, 7*(2), 193–204.

DeMatthews, D., Billingsley, B., McLeskey, J., & Umesh, S. (2020). Principal leadership for students with disabilities in effective inclusive schools. *Journal of Educational Administration, 58*(5), 539–554. https://doi.org/10.1108/JEA-10-2019-0177

Dolmage, J. T. (2017). *Academic ableism: Disability in higher education.* University of Michigan Press.

Evans, N. J., Broido, E. M., Brown, K. R., & Wilke, A. K. (2017). *Disability in higher education: A social justice approach.* Jossey-Bass.

Gunter, H. (2018). *The politics of public education: Reform and ideas.* Policy Press.

Hartley, J. (2015). Australian higher education policy and inclusion of people with disabilities: A review. *Journal of Postsecondary Education and Disability, 28*(4), 413–419.

Hoppey, D., Black, W., & Mickelson, A. (2018). The evolution of inclusive practice in two elementary schools: Reforming teacher purpose, instructional capacity, and data-informed practice. *International Journal of Educational Reform, 27*(1), 22–45. https://doi.org/10.1177/105678791802700102

Jacklin, A., Robinson, C. O'Meara, L., & Harris, A. (2007, February). *Improving the experiences of disabled students in higher education.* The Higher Education Academy [Project period August 2005–November 2006]. University of Sussex.

MacKinnon, F. J., Broido, E. M., & Wilson, M. E. (2004). Issues in student affairs. In F. MacKinnon (Ed.), *Rent'z student affairs practice in higher education* (3rd ed., pp. 387–402). Charles C. Thomas.

Mitchell, D. T. (2016). Disability, diversity, and diversion: Normalization and avoidance in higher education. In D. Bolt & C. Penketh (Eds.), *Disability, avoidance and the academy: Challenging resistance* (pp. 9–20). Routledge Advances in Disability Studies.

National Centre for Student Equity in Higher Education. (2017). *NCSEHE focus: Successful outcomes for students with disability in Australian higher education* (pp. 1–15). Curtin University, Perth, Western Australia.

National Centre for Student Equity in Higher Education. (2020). *Discussion paper on the 2020 review of the disability standards for education 2005 September.* Curtin University, Perth, Western Australia.

Oakes, J. (2017). Public scholarship: Education research for a diverse democracy [2016 AERA Presidential address]. *Educational Researcher, 47*(2), 91–104. https://doi.org/10.3102/0013189X17746402

Ostiguy, B. J., Peters, M. L., & Shlasko, D. (2016). Ableism. In M. Adams, L. Bell, with D. Goodman & K. Joshi (Eds.), *Teaching for diversity and social justice* (3rd ed., pp. 299–337). Routledge.

Rezai-Rashti, G. M., & Segeren, A. (2020). The game of accountability: Perspectives of urban school leaders on standardized testing in Ontario and British Columbia Canada. *International Journal of Leadership in Education, 23*(6). https://doi.org/10.1080/13603124.2020.1808711

Riehl, C. (2000). The principal's role in creating inclusive schools for diverse students: A review of normative, empirical, and critical literature on the practice of educational administration. *Review of Educational Research, 70*(1), 55–81.

Ryan, J., & Struhs, J. (2004). University education for all? Barriers to full inclusion of students with disabilities in Australian universities. *International Journal of Inclusive Education, 8*(1), 73–90. https://doi.org/10.1080/1360311032000139421

Saltes, N. (2020). It's all about student accessibility. No one ever talks about teacher accessibility: Examining ableist expectations in academia. *International Journal of Inclusive Education.* https://doi.org/10.1080/13603116.2020.1712483

Saunders, P. (2006). *The costs of disability and the incidence of poverty* [Discussion Paper No. 147]. Social Policy Research Centre, University of New South Wales, Sydney, Australia.

Shevlin, M., Kenny, M., & McNeela, E. (2004). Participation in higher education for students with disabilities: An Irish perspective. *Disability & Society, 19*(1), 15–30. https://doi.org/10.1080/0968759032000155604

Smith, M. (2010). Lecturer's attitudes to inclusive teaching practice at a UK university: Will staff "resistance" hinder implementation? *Tertiary Education and Management, 16*(3), 211–227. https://www.tandfonline.com/doi/full/10.1080/13583883.2010.497378

Thomson, P. (2020). *School scandals: Blowing the whistle on the corruption of our education system.* Policy Press.

Toswell, M. J. (2017). *Today's medieval university.* Arc Humanities Press.

United Nations. (2006). *Convention on the rights of persons with disabilities.* UN General Assembly.

Vickerman, P., & Blundell, M. (2010). Hearing the voices of disabled students in higher education. *Disability & Society, 25*(1), 21–32. https://doi.org/10/1080/09687590903363290

# CLIMBING THE MOUNTAIN

## Power, Privilege, and Equity

**Natalie Delgado**
*Lamar University*

**Ashley Greene**
*Lamar University*

**Gloshanda Lawyer**
*Utah Valley University*

**Abdullah Alofi**
*Saudi Arabia Ministry of Education*

Educational leadership requires an intentional, deliberate approach and continually evolving practice; it includes responsibility, collaboration, fairness, self-control, and emotional, as well as social intelligence (DiPaola & Hoy, 2015; Moffett, 2008; Taylor, 2013). Leadership, defined as "a process whereby an individual influences a group of individuals to achieve a common goal," has long been considered a significant position in political

*Who Decides?*, pages 439–470
Copyright © 2022 by Information Age Publishing
www.infoagepub.com

life and in the organizational structure of society (Northouse, 2004, p. 3; Üstün, 2017).

When considering the experiences of leaders in the field of education, research is available on educational leadership in general education and administrative perception in special education schools (see Bays & Crockett, 2007; Cooner et al., 2005; Lashley, 2007). However, when the focus shifts to the experiences and challenges that are directly connected to administration in deaf and hard-of-hearing (D/HH) programs, the availability of such research is limited and sporadic (Balk, 1977; Keller, 2015; Knudson, 2003), despite the fact that deaf education is considered the oldest field in special education (Moores, 2001). When narrowing the scope to administrators in D/HH programs who also identify as D/HH themselves, research is significantly more limited. The shortage of literature on leadership practices in deaf education has resulted in a lack of knowledge about how D/HH educators obtain and remain in the positions of superintendents, directors, and principals in residential schools for the deaf and in mainstream programs in the United States (Balk, 1997; Kamm-Larew & Lamkin, 2008; Kamm-Larew et al., 2008). Deaf education therefore represents a unique part of the administration umbrella. The purpose of this chapter is to describe D/HH administrators in education; the disabling of D/HH individuals; and the issues of equity, power, and privilege within educational leadership. In addition, we demonstrate the challenges that D/HH professionals face when taking on administrative roles in schools such as training, hiring, and preparing for administrative roles. Finally, determining the current state of D/HH professionals within the field of educational leadership is essential to this research.

This study utilized the decolonizing-intersectionality framework (Lawyer, 2018), which was developed to analyze how colonization manifests in the schooling of Deaf, DeafBlind, DeafDisabled, and Hard-of-Hearing individuals within the United States. Specifically, the decolonizing-intersectionality framework provides a lens to examine how schools can be sites for perpetuating systems that condition students and school personnel alike into their inferior or superior social positions. We applied the decolonizing-intersectionality framework to a multiple-case instrumental case study (Baxter & Jack, 2008; Stake, 2006) to examine how school leaders were able to assume their administrative positions, their perspectives of the journey, and their roles, particularly as Deaf individuals. Decolonization in the field of deaf education is a powerful concept that could align with the goals of empowerment to embrace a nonhierarchical view and equal opportunities in the field (Anglin-Jaffe, 2015). Additionally, we discuss the implications of the study on educational policy, especially in higher education, which includes teacher and administrator preparation, and the K–12 level which includes school administrators, teachers, and other school personnel (Lawyer, 2018).

## LITERATURE REVIEW

### Forgotten: Tracing the History of D/HH Administrators

In educational leadership, research demonstrates that administrators are placed in the spotlight, on the front lines in the eyes of their superiors, and these administrators must effectively lead their instructional staff and ensure a quality education for their students (Hilliard & Jackson, 2011). School leaders are responsible for curricula, instructional practices, test scores, safety, and support for all staff and students. They are no longer seen as "managers" of a group of people; instead the narrative has shifted to highlight them as educational leaders and models (Barnett, 2004). School administrators are expected to be "moral stewards, educators, and community builders," in which they clarify the purposes of their programs, maintain their positions as educational experts, and foster community within their faculty and staff, students' learning community, and stakeholders of the public (Murphy, 2002, p. 176).

Though some could argue that literature in educational leadership could be broadly applied to or encompass deaf education, there is little explicit focus on D/HH administrators within the field. Instead, what little literature can be found that involves D/HH administrators, deals with details of educational leadership perceptions of deaf education teachers (Lartz & Litchfield, 2005; Teller & Harney, 2005) or how to prepare deaf education leaders for jobs in the field (LaSasso & Achtzehn, 1996). One example from Knudson (2003) indicates that the manner in which a superintendent of a deaf school interacts with the Deaf community is a reflection on their identity. It was also found that the superintendent's quality of relationship with the school board also appeared to be dependent on how the superintendent identified themselves (e.g., hearing or Deaf; Knudson, 2003). What little we know regarding D/HH administrators has only just begun to uncover the significant under-representation of this population (O'Brien et al., 2014).

There are several layers to unpack in the discussion of the under-representation of D/HH administrators both in the literature and the field of educational leadership. For example, Simms et al. (2008) found that less than 40% of the deaf education field is made up of D/HH professionals; only 22% of teachers and 14.5% of administrators are D/HH. When race is considered in addition to Deaf identity, a mere 2.5% of teachers in the field of deaf education identify as both D/HH and as persons of color (POC; Simms et al., 2008). Even more concerning is that only three D/HH administrators of color were found throughout the United States (Simms et al., 2008). It is not surprising that administrators of deaf education programs and schools are mostly comprised of White, heterosexual, able-bodied, Christian men

(Knudson, 2003; LaSasso & Achtzehn, 1996). While the exact number of D/HH administrators in the entire United States remains unknown, along with the number of hearing administrators in deaf education, research shows the limited number of D/HH administrators in schools for the deaf. As of 2017, there were 40 hearing top-level administrators and 24 D/HH top-level administrators in schools for the deaf across the United States. Top-level administrators in this report were superintendents or directors (Wheeler, 2017). These demographic data alone suggest that the roots and impact of systemic oppression are pervasive in the field of educating D/HH students. Furthermore, a decolonizing-intersectionality framework requires that we address systemic barriers that prevent D/HH and D/HH administrators of color from obtaining administrative positions at the rate of hearing and White administrators.

As the focus of public education has evolved, there has been a push for administrators to receive more formal training and education for educational leadership development (Murphy, 2002). This type of programming is expected to prepare potential administrators for leadership roles through field studies, real-life applications, engaging in professional development, and even enrolling in mentorship programs. Programs are also increasingly focused on establishing socially just educational spaces (Pazey & Cole, 2012). Some programs have expanded their mentorship offerings, focusing on mentorship candidates from a variety of racial and ethnic backgrounds, women instead of exclusively men, curricula that focus on interpersonal relations, reflective writing, and other such programming (Jackson & Kelley, 2002). Mentorship programs have been steadily on the rise, with an experienced administrator lending support to the newer administrator (Jackson & Hilliard, 2013). However, such mentorship programs often do not consider ability within their socially just framework and tend to be designed for abled, hearing prospective administrators, and do not include the mentorship needed for prospective D/HH administrators. One exception to this rule is the Conference of Educational Administrators of Schools and Programs for the Deaf (CEASD, https://www.ceasd.org), which offers mentorship programs and a leadership academy for aspiring principals, directors, and superintendents. There is a great need for D/HH administrators to have access to quality mentoring programming from administrators who understand their educational contexts and linguistic preferences just as their hearing counterparts do.

The need for appropriate programming and mentorship for D/HH administrators is crucial, as deaf education is different from other special education contexts due to the development of different pedagogical settings. Due to the different educational philosophies and approaches to deaf education that exist today (Garberoglio et al., 2012), administrators must be prepared to work in various settings, such as schools for the deaf, oral schools, or mainstream schools. The campus communication philosophies for each setting may also differ, and a D/HH administrator must also be knowledgeable in listening-and-spoken language, total communication, and bilingual-bicultural philosophies, among others. In addition to ASL, children in the aforementioned educational settings may be instructed using manually coded English, simultaneous communication, and total communication. Manually coded English is a signed system based on written English, incorporating English grammatical structure and syntax. Manually coded English differs from American Sign Language (ASL), which has its own grammatical structure and syntax that does not echo that of written English (Gustason et al., 1974). Settings that use manually coded English may use simultaneous communication, meaning use both spoken language and a signed system at the same time (Gustason et al., 1974). Others may use total communication, which originally referred to using any given method that worked for a specific student in that particular moment (Holcomb, 1967, as cited in Scouten, 1984). In other words, it was intended to provide flexibility to switch between languages and communication methods as needed. Though its original intent was to accommodate for individual language and communication needs, "total communication" is now used synonymously with simultaneous communication, and refers to talking and signing concurrently. In the last 2 decades, bilingual/bicultural approaches have been gaining more traction as methods that expose D/HH students to ASL and written English in tandem with Deaf culture and the hearing community culture (Ashton, 2012; Cokely, 2005). As bilingual/bicultural methods are making their way through the deaf education system, deaf education administrators and the schools they serve must remain vigilant to the ever-changing recommendations from the field.

Continued development in the field of deaf education requires administrators to be conversant with emerging trends in curriculum and communication approaches (Hilligoss, 2014). Also, administrators in schools that serve D/HH students should be in positions to manage the provision of education to students by undergoing proper training in language and communication skills while appreciating the accommodation of D/HH students, given that they vary widely depending on their needs. Thus, administrators should be well-versed in the educational needs of D/HH students as well as approaches to meeting those needs to support their instructional staff (Andrews & Covell, 2006; Musyoka et al., 2015).

It is essential to understand the social factors that impact D/HH individuals in the United States and the education of these individuals—namely colonization, the construction of disability, and intersectionality—in order to clearly understand how D/HH administrators continue to be overlooked in the literature and hampered from assuming and/or excelling in leadership roles in deaf education. Part of understanding such omission is seeing how educational leadership training and preparation programming nationwide contributes to the dearth of D/HH administrators in education settings.

## Colonization and the Construction of Disability

Lawyer (2018) traced how the social construct of disability and the U.S. schooling system function as mechanisms of colonization in the United States with uniquely negative impacts for Deaf, DeafBlind, DeafDisabled, and Hard-of-Hearing individuals with multiply marginalized identities (e.g., immigrant, person of color, raised in a non-English speaking home, LGBTQIA+, low socioeconomic background, etc.). Colonization includes the various ways that groups of people are indoctrinated into subordinated and superordinated positions. Both the subordinated and superordinated groups become conditioned to follow a system of inequity that uses "formal and informal methods (behaviors, ideologies, institutions, policies, and economies) that maintain the subjugation or exploitation of... peoples, lands, and resources" (Waziyatawin & Yellow Bird, 2005, p. 2). In this chapter, we are referring to a system that uplifts White hearing people into educational leadership positions and places barriers for D/HH people—in particular, D/HH POC—to assume the same leadership positions. Such colonization takes place within the kyriarchical structures of society, referring to the complex interweaving of superiority and inferiority on the basis of one's race, class, gender, sexual orientation, ability, and so on (Fiorenza, 2001).

The social construct of disability results in an "Othering" of those whom society deems inferior or unworthy due to their deviation from the norm or revered normative standard. This concept of othering allows for the dominant identity groups to create a hierarchy in which they are superordinated and others rejected from the normative standard are subordinated. In the case of the United States' D/HH population, hearing people have been superordinated and D/HH people have been minoritized or subordinated, forced to strive for and conform to the hearing normative standard; schools are primary sites for indoctrination of these superordinated and subordinated positions (Lawyer, 2018). Such systems are designed to perpetuate the indoctrination of these superordinated and subordinated positions; for example, how an educational program serving students who are D/HH is designed has real-life consequences for the paths that these students will travel in life and how they will negotiate for true participation in society (E. Garrett, personal communication, November 29, 2020). For instance, D/HH people are frequently pushed to learn to speak and use amplification devices such as hearing aids and cochlear implants to acquiesce to the hearing way (Valente, 2011). Improving hearing status and conforming to hearing society (e.g., speaking, listening, not using sign language) has been a major focus of the field of deaf education in the last 200 years in the United States, often coming at the expense of a solid education (Baker, 2011). The dominant (hearing) population's perception of D/HH people as inferior, and using disability as a frame to communicate this inferiority as well as the need to be "cured" is just one way that kyriarchy is upheld and abled (hearing) people remain in positions of power particularly in educational settings, including special education and deaf education contexts.

It is through this kyriarchy of multiple systems of super- and subordination that D/HH people may experience barriers in upward mobility within the deaf education system. While the hierarchy may not be clear to students and those around them, it may become clear to students that the teachers and educators surrounding them are representative of the majority population (i.e., White, hearing, abled; Knaus, 2016). The impacts of the demographic imperative (Banks, 2004, 2008, 2010) or demographic urgency (Sleeter & Milner, 2011)—the mismatch of student identities with those of their teachers and school administration—has been shown to be correlated with the opportunity gap, that is the continued denial of students of color to have the opportunity to receive appropriate and equitable classroom instruction (Goldenberg, 2013). Even though it has been named the oldest field in special education (Moores, 2001), deaf education remains predominantly hearing orientated with the large majority of teachers reporting to be White, hearing women. To better understand the colonization of D/HH individuals and the current state of deaf education, the history of deaf education must first be explained.

Historically, D/HH individuals have faced years of oppression due to the dominant pathological and medical perspective (Ladd, 2003; Lane, 1992; Padden & Humphries, 1988) often held by hearing parents, administrators, and educators. After the Milan Congress in 1880, there was a shift to the oral method of educating D/HH children that stressed the significance of speech and lipreading skills rather than the use of sign language to communicate; thus, oralism in schools for children spread like wildfire, taking hold as the only method used in D/HH schools across the world (Ladd, 2003). Consequently, D/HH educators were not able to work as teachers during the oralism period and very few D/HH professionals were able to serve in administrative or leadership positions that were already occupied by hearing educators (Gannon, 1981). However, it should be noted that during this time, schools for the D/HH were primarily segregated and the oralism movement spread primarily in White deaf schools. In contrast, Black deaf schools in the United States largely still used sign language in the early 1900s, which led to the development of Black ASL, which was largely dismissed by White individuals at the time as an inferior language (McCaskill et al., 2011). The detrimental segregation in language remained until sign language was permitted once again in White deaf education in the late

1960s with the combination of speech as a form of communication known as *total communication.*

The year 1988 saw a radical shift, beginning with the Deaf President Now (DPN) movement at Gallaudet University in which students led a week-long protest that drew national and global attention. From the Milan conference until this movement, there had been virtually no D/HH administrators at any type of educational institution. Movements such as the DPN movement allowed the focus to shift from oralism back to manualism; this opened the door for D/HH educators to return to work in the residential schools for the deaf from where they had been shunned during the oralism period (Gannon, 1981; Moores, 2001). This time period also saw the emergence of school leadership by more D/HH professionals (Balk, 1997). Throughout all these historical changes, it is clear that D/HH educators had been firmly placed on the back burner, only to resurface after an extensive battle regarding the most appropriate language of use for D/HH individuals with the hegemonic group.

## Intersectionality

Further complicating the layers underlying colonization and oppression is intersectionality, which seeks to understand interconnected identities working together (such as race, class, or dis/ability) and how our social and legal systems compound discrimination and oppression for each of these identities when taken together (Shaw et al., 2012). For D/HH people who have intersecting identities (e.g., D/HH people of color, D/HH LGBTQ+, D/HH women, or even all of the above), there are even smaller numbers represented in educational leadership, as demonstrated by examining the number of D/HH professionals in leadership positions in the field and by examining scholarly literature within the United States. As mentioned earlier, as Simms et al. (2008) discovered, the lack of representation of D/HH individuals with other marginalized identities within educational leadership (a mere 2.5%) is further evidence of the effectiveness of these systems of oppression and the need to address them.

In order to build on the scarcity of literature that exists on D/HH administrators, we aim to shed light on the current experiences of deaf educational leadership as a whole. The present study will reinforce Knudson's (2003) discussion on the lack of marginalized groups represented in administrative roles within deaf education, particularly by focusing on D/HH individuals. We hope this study highlights how the landscape of deaf education has long been made up of the majority and demonstrates the need to prepare the landscape to fit the diverse population of students we are shaping.

## METHODS

We used the decolonizing-intersectionality framework to guide this study (Lawyer, 2018). This framework is an analytical tool that helps analyze dis/ability, race, class, language use, and other identity aspects that are considered different from the normative White, abled, English-speaking, heterosexual standard in the United States, with emphasis on how students embody many of these identities (Lawyer, 2022). The purpose of the framework is for those in positions of power, including researchers, school leaders, teacher preparation programs, and teachers, to recognize how their actions may continue to sustain schooling practices that are oppressive to students with multiply marginalized identities and to move into critical self-assessment (Bhattacharya, 2018). It also explores alternative methods and pedagogies that challenge those practices. It was developed to describe the ways in which one of the authors navigated interrogating the curriculum of colonization and to be a recommendation for application at the policy, higher education, and K–12 teaching and research levels (Lawyer, 2018). This study applied the decolonizing-intersectionality framework at the K–12 school administration and higher education administrator preparation levels. Specifically, we wanted to understand what practices were in place that either permitted or impeded entry of Deaf administrators into administration, and once in administrative positions, what allowed or motivated these administrators to remain in their positions.

We conducted a multiple case study in which six participants, or cases, volunteered. The purpose of this case study was to better understand the similarities and differences between administrators (Ivankova & Stick, 2007; Kaur et al., 2015; Stake, 2006) and to gain a more updated picture of the school administrator demographic for D/HH programs and/or deaf schools in the United States. We divided the United States into four regions: West, Midwest, South, and East Coast/New England. We searched individual states within each region for administrators who worked at schools for the deaf and/or mainstream programs that served D/HH students. A distribution list was developed with the names and email addresses of all identified school administrators. We did not include administrators who worked in or served sites that were not K–12 (e.g., standalone early childhood programs, standalone transition programs).

### Survey

An electronic survey consisting of 38 questions was distributed to 253 school administrators across the United States; it was also used to identify administrators who would be willing to be contacted for an interview.

The questions were presented as closed-ended and open-ended items. The closed-ended items included demographic questions, information about school settings and their respective communication philosophies, as well as several questions in regard to administrator qualifications (i.e., type of degree, type of certifications or licensure, etc.). The open-ended items allowed for more in-depth understanding of the respondents' experiences and included questions regarding the type of barriers experienced as well as situational anecdotes. Based on survey results, we had six respondents who volunteered to provide us further insight, each with different perspectives, into the experiences of D/HH administrators.

### Participants

The participants who completed the electronic survey ($n = 47$) were asked to self-identify their ethnicity. The question was left in an open-ended format so as to not limit participants; the majority self-identified as Caucasian, White, European American, or WASP ($n = 32$). The remaining participants reported their ethnicity as African American ($n = 3$), American ($n = 1$), European Hispanic ($n = 1$), Latinx ($n = 1$), and some participants ($n = 9$) chose not to identify their ethnicity. Geographic region of the participants varied, with most participants being from the South ($n = 13$), followed by the East ($n = 10$), Midwest ($n = 10$), and West ($n = 2$); the remaining participants chose not to specify a geographic region ($n = 12$). To help identify possible participants for follow-up interviews, the participants' hearing status was asked, and participants self-identified as Deaf ($n = 12$), hearing impaired ($n = 1$), and hearing ($n = 34$). The data from this survey reflected the findings of Simms et al. (2008), Knudson (2003), and LaSasso and Achtzehn (1996) in that the majority of our participants were White and hearing.

## RESULTS

### Initial Survey Findings

Survey participants who shared their experiences and barriers in the journey to becoming administrators cited examples of their experiences involving components of their identity such as race, age, sex, and hearing status. Only one participant out of all 47 reported that they did not experience any type of barriers in the journey to become an administrator. When asked to identify whether they still experience such barriers as a current administrator, 35 respondents reported *yes*. The different types of barriers that were reported are listed below.

## Race

A participant was a Black woman who felt she experienced barriers from higher-level administration and from colleagues who were White men. She stated that "working in a deaf school the positions at higher levels are very limited... once the opportunity presented itself to be promoted, people who were less qualified than me, and of the majority race got the position over me."

## Age

Some of the respondents felt that their age led to limitations in their career, reporting that "some of the teachers I lead are younger than 40 years old. They are more technology savvy than I am. I am open to their ideas, but it may take me longer to embrace their ideas." Another survey respondent shared similar concerns, stating "younger teachers (millennials) require a different approach than older generations. They respond more to a sales approach while older generations do the job when told."

## Sex

Several respondents from the survey cited experiencing issues pertaining to sexism. One participant reported resistance from the campus she worked for, stating "some people questioned my ability to lead a residential school for the deaf as a hearing woman." Another woman found a barrier in being "a female in a male-dominated administration." To compound being in a male-dominated environment, another felt that her administrators were looking for colleagues that "fit the student profile more closely," and felt her identity as a "White hearing female in a deaf school that was predominantly male and minority" proved to be a barrier.

## Hearing Status

Survey respondents experienced a range of barriers pertaining to their hearing status. One survey participant lamented that "Deaf [people] cannot do the job on the same level as hearing peers." Other survey participants believed they were experiencing audism, with one stating, "It is difficult not having immediate access to conversations among staff and parents. They question my ability to lead because I'm deaf, and because of my age, it requires more 'work' on my part to get things done." These administrators believed that expectations were lower for them, or that others did not perceive them to be competent or capable of being effective leaders. Another participant shared that other staff members feel it is an inconvenience to have to call the participant using a videophone or find and pay for interpreters for meetings. On the opposite side of the coin, a hearing participant reported feeling isolated in a Deaf-centric environment.

## Interviews

Of the 13 individuals in the survey who identified as "Deaf" or "hearing impaired," six volunteered to be interviewed to provide more insight into their experiences as Deaf administrators. The interviews resulted in six participants who: (a) identified as Deaf, male, and White; (b) got their start in the field as teachers with over 80 years of experience combined; and (c) are currently working as administrators in the field of deaf education. The identified participants will be referred to by their pseudonyms, which were chosen at random: Tom, Bob, Carl, Jeremy, Eric, and James. The administrators worked in a variety of settings, with one working in a mainstream program, and five working in deaf residential schools or special separate schools for the deaf. We did not anticipate having all interview participants that identified as White males. However, the limited representation in our participants might be viewed as an example of who has the most access to administrative roles in deaf education. Therefore, our exploration of their experiences focused primarily on how educational experiences and language backgrounds could have impacted their ascension to school administrator positions. Due to the participants' identities, we were unable to explore how race and other social inequities may have impacted their journeys to becoming school administrators. We are certain that these additional identity factors will provide a qualitatively different experience for D/HH administrators who are also women, people of color, queer, from different socioeconomic backgrounds, and so forth, as theorized in intersectionality.

### Setting

Semi-structured interviews were conducted remotely, using either video conference or videophone per the participants' communication and technology preferences. All participants requested that the interview be conducted in ASL. Each participant was informed that the interview would be recorded for later data analysis and gave verbal consent to the recording. The interviews were approximately 40 minutes long.

### Analysis

Members of the research team transcribed and translated the interviews from ASL into written English. We used a three-step data analysis process, called constant comparative analysis, that included utilizing open and axial coding to reach a core category. Close reading of the text allowed for the emergence of open codes by identifying frequent concepts from the data (Fram, 2013). Once open codes were identified, constant re-coding across team members was done to reduce data and develop axial codes, which were *barriers, support, administrative experience and qualities, understanding the school culture,* and *being Deaf in the workplace.* The third step included further comparing the axial codes to each other and other incidents of data, then reducing the codes to identify a core category (Charmaz, 2001). Through the process of analyzing axial codes, the researchers were able to identify the overarching message from participants that led to a core category entitled *Climbing the Mountain: Power, Privilege, and Equity.* Below we introduce our case participants and discuss the aforementioned categorical codes.

## MEET THE ADMINISTRATORS

### Tom

Tom is a White Deaf man born to a Deaf family. He has a bachelor's degree and a master's degree, and has worked his way up from teaching in the classroom to now working as a superintendent of a Deaf and Blind school. Tom oversees the work of 204 full-time employees and 30 substitutes. Tom envisions himself staying as an administrator for another 15 years, before considering working for a teacher training program. He is fortunate to have the support of a strong board and is proud of the teachers he supervises. Tom advises prospective D/HH administrators to begin preparing now for their dreams, attending workshops, working toward administrative certification, and finding a mentor.

### Bob

Bob is a White Deaf man born to a hearing family. He has a bachelor's and master's degree, in addition to completing hours for his administrative certificate. He also served as a teacher for 14 years prior to his current position, where he has remained for 10 years. Bob currently oversees 80 employees in deaf education and visually impaired programming throughout 14 districts. He states that he feels "content right now" with his position, but wants to eventually get superintendent certification or work behind the scenes educating the school board in another position. Working in a mainstream program, Bob also feels that it can be lonely to work in a hearing-dominant environment. Bob emphasizes that prospective administrators must build relationships with their staff and students, and to keep high expectations for everyone.

### Carl

Carl is a White Deaf man with a doctoral degree in Deaf studies and Deaf education. Carl served as a teacher for 8 years and principal for 6 years prior to his current title of superintendent at a private deaf school. He oversees 102 teachers and staff that service 143 students, in addition to 13 early intervention staff. While this number appears to be almost a 1:1 ratio for staff to students, it should be noted that these staff members also include school counselors, speech language pathologists, school psychologists, and others who provide required services as mandated by the students' individualized education plans. Carl is content with his position as superintendent. When considering the future, he is interested in using himself as a driving force to change deaf education throughout the country, perhaps through working with the Department of Education. His advice to future administrators is, "Don't try to overanalyze yourself to the point where you get down on yourself"; going on to encourage that they stay true to themselves, be genuine, keep reflecting on their actions, and maintain a growth mindset.

## Jeremy

Jeremy is a White Deaf man with a master's in deaf education and an administrative certificate. He served as a teacher for 14 years prior to becoming an administrator 3 years ago. Jeremy currently works as the director of transition services and also oversees elective offerings at his deaf school. He is responsible for 15 teachers and aides that service 94 high school students. To explain the difficulties that D/HH candidates experience in their quest to move up in administration, Jeremy uses the phrase "a glass ceiling" to show that D/HH candidates often hit a roadblock and cannot advance as easily as their hearing counterparts. He believes that having supportive higher-up administration is "key." However, he encourages potential administrators to be flexible and maintain open communication with staff.

## Eric

Eric is a White Deaf man with principal certification. He served as a teacher and educational program specialist working in a cooperative program, state deaf school, and a charter school. Eric now works as the secondary principal of a deaf charter school and oversees 25 teachers and aides. He endured many barriers and struggles to obtain his position, and now commutes from a lengthy distance to work, going home only on weekends. Eric's goal is to improve his professional development capacity for his faculty and staff, citing the diverse range of students they serve and the need to prepare his teachers for those students. He believes prospective administrators need to "start now, however long it takes," and begin preparing for their future as soon as possible. All the while, prospective administrators should bear in mind the importance of having a clear vision, and recognize that tough decisions are made frequently. Eric cites that "being able to help [staff] be effective and successful" is essential for a quality administrator.

## James

James is a White Deaf man who has a PhD in educational studies. Prior to serving as an assistant principal for the state deaf school where he is currently employed, James worked as a teacher and a literacy coach. From the time he entered the field as a middle school teacher, it took James approximately 14 years to become an administrator. James oversees 21 employees this year in his setting. He feels satisfied with his current position and does not seek to move up unless a better opportunity presents itself. James does not feel heavily impacted by any barriers in his workplace, which is a predominately D/HH workplace in a city with a large D/HH population. He suggests that potential future administrators stay patient and try different experiences and opportunities for work.

## CLIMBING THE MOUNTAIN: POWER, PRIVILEGE, AND EQUITY

For persons who do not reside at the top of the socially constructed hierarchy of who "belongs," the act of breaking into a field that is dominated by White, hearing, and abled presences often feels like they are climbing a mountain without the necessary equipment to help them succeed, while wearing a weighted vest. At the peak of the mountain is the height of their careers as educational administrators, conquering obstacles in their way and being given the respect and freedom they need to accomplish the tasks at hand. Despite having experience in the field, being educated, and obtaining the necessary certification or licensure in order to work in an administrative position, our D/HH participants required the assistance of hearing individuals in power to guide them through the process of breaking through multiple systems of super- and subordination in their quest to climb the mountain and resolve issues of power, privilege, and equity. Their first task while tackling the great heights of the mountain of moving into administration, was to manage, or even move, the barriers that were set in their path.

# BARRIERS

*I felt a disconnect [working at] state schools, the state . . . they had too much authority.*
*To be honest with you, they don't know any better [about deaf education].*

—Carl

Due to the limited locations at which D/HH individuals can work as administrators with full access to communication, D/HH individuals often find that there are scarce pickings throughout the United States. Instead, their circumstances often require that they relocate to other states to pursue employment in their chosen field, regardless of their level of education or the number of certifications they possess. The tremendous sacrifices required that might deter many from becoming administrators can be seen in the stories of Tom, Carl, and Jeremy who chose to rise in the face of adversity and make the decision to uproot to several different states in search of opportunities to become K–12 administrators. In Eric's case, his journey meant he had to choose between pursuing his dream career or supporting his wife's already established career. Rather than making that choice, Eric currently resides in a state separate from his family for career reasons. Despite job shortages and relocations, Carl reported that the "only thing that carried me over was patience, persistence, and focus. If anyone told me no, I refused to accept that. I did what I believed was right." Such sacrifice is a stark contrast from that of other educational administrators who do not identify as marginalized populations and do not have to filter their job search by the prospects of having full access to communication. These administrators, unlike their D/HH counterparts, do not have to concern themselves as heavily with settings that are less aware of, and less sensitive to D/HH-specific needs.

Not only are D/HH administrators faced with limited opportunities in the field, they are faced with what may be described as a mountain climber's nightmare: a lifeline that is just barely out of their reach. Despite their educational, personal, and professional backgrounds, our administrators' abilities to gain footing in their field was dependent upon who they knew and who was willing to become a gatekeeper for their entrance to an administrative position. For instance, we can examine Bob's journey, which was fraught with roadblocks from the beginning. As a young adult, Bob often reflected on his experiences as a mainstreamed D/HH child and he knew he wanted to be able to work in the mainstream setting at a public school to give back, so to speak. However, he almost did not get the opportunity to watch his goals materialize. As he neared the end of his education, he had one thing standing between him and his dream as an administrator at a public school: internship. "The process of finding an internship in a public school was so frustrating" compared to his hearing classmates, who quickly and effortlessly secured internship opportunities. After some time searching and ultimately missing the deadline to secure and complete his internship, Bob's graduation was postponed.

> I ended up being lucky because I knew a hearing person who was an administrator at the school where I [currently] work. That person encouraged me to apply and was a part of the interview committee; [that person] had the power to sway the interview in my favor. I ended up getting the internship.

If it had not been for that hearing gatekeeper, would Bob have been able to secure an internship before having to defer graduation once again? Would that experience have deterred him from continuing up the mountain?

Similarly, the other administrators in this study reported that a hearing people who happened to be administrators of higher authority acted as gatekeepers to assist them in securing employment as administrators. Though James and Carl began their journey in a deaf-centric environment, both of these men were unable to break into the field without a gatekeeper. In Carl's case, it was that gatekeeper who planted the idea of running a school in Carl's head—and then invited him to run the school where the gatekeeper worked. James's ability to quickly climb the mountain was boosted by his connections with other administrators in the field. It was these connections that allowed James the opportunity to have a less tedious journey than the other administrators in this chapter. On the opposite side of the mountain, Jeremy found himself on a more treacherous trail, where he was unable to become an administrator out of the gate. Rather than turn around and give up, Jeremy accepted positions for which he was overqualified and slowly worked his way up. It was not until he had a supervisor who was deaf-centric and willing to extend a rope that Jeremy was able to climb up to the top and become an administrator. Receiving a certain level of support from individuals in higher positions appeared to be crucial in the ability of these administrators to move up in the workplace.

Once the participants were able to break into a field that is typically dominated by hearing, abled individuals, they faced another barrier in regard to the need to be conscious of their communication options by ensuring they have the best team and options possible. For some of our participants, the environment in which they work provides very little access to direct communication and requires the participants to rely on the use of technology or interpreters. Take James's story for instance; he felt that his job options were limited due to his status as a Deaf person. While he felt he was open to the idea of working at different schools, James believed that mainstream programs dominated by hearing people would reject him because he does not speak or hear at all. He felt like he had fewer systemic barriers (specifically, audism) working at a Deaf school, and that is where he chose to make his home as an administrator. Eric is another administrator who shared the same feelings of restrictions based on the environment. Eric has worked in three different settings and reported that working in a hearing-centric environment that did not support a bilingual philosophy quickly wore him down as an individual. The ability to lead while not being supported proved to be akin to an avalanche on the side of a mountain, one that Eric quickly figured his way out of. He currently works in a deaf-centric environment where he feels his expertise as a Deaf man is more valued.

Adding to the already stressful daily responsibilities of an administra-tor, our administrators also have to prepare ahead for any encounters with other individuals who do not possess the ability to use sign language. Such preparation is essential for clear communication and transparency as an administrator. In order to do so, Bob and Tom emphasized the need of securing a team of interpreters with whom they are comfortable and who are familiar with their typical vocabulary choices. The use of specific inter-preters is a conscious choice as frequently hearing individuals will attach any misunderstanding on the interpreters' part to the D/HH individual. Having specific interpreters also allows the administrators the ability to communicate freely without any additional burden of monitoring the inter-preter's veracity. When arranging last-minute meetings, Bob is often forced to devise solutions that are appropriate for the other participants but not always the best choice for him, such as reading lips or using a video relay interpreting (VRI) service. Likewise, Tom reported concerns about using VRI, or videophone to communicate because frequently one is unable to control which interpreter is online, which may have a detrimental impact on the quality of the conversation or the perception of the caller regarding the administrator. Jeremy appeared to have a more positive experience, re-porting that his school has staff interpreters who are always there. Jeremy's school also had a different hierarchy, in which Jeremy typically only inter-acted with other signers and did not often have to figure out alternative communication strategies.

Based on his experiences as a D/HH individual working in a hearing en-vironment with frequent misunderstandings between D/HH and hearing staff due to language differences, Tom settled on the belief that "language creates conflict." Eric echoed the same sentiments, reporting that many of his frustrations stemmed from coworkers assuming language preferences of D/HH employees. Despite working in a system that caters to the educa-tion of D/HH children, many of those hearing individuals required that Eric interact with them using their preferred language or communication method, rather than the language Eric uses. In managing these many bar-riers, the administrators had varying levels of support helping them push through, which we describe below.

## SUPPORT OF A COMMUNITY AND NETWORK

*This job can be lonely. You are the only Deaf individual,*
*fully immersed in the hearing world.*

—Bob

The act of climbing a mountain requires a carefully chosen team, preparedness, and support from those around you. The carefully chosen team can
be reflected in the current teams with whom our administrators work. The
preparedness can be reflected in the education and certification programs
our administrators went through prior to ascending the mountain. The support, however, proved to be different for each administrator, but all agreed
that their ability to reach the top of the mountain was directly correlated to
the type of support they received from others in their journey. For instance,
James and Tom found themselves in the middle of the Deaf community at
a young age, which afforded them the opportunity to create connections
with individuals who would eventually become their mentors. Such connections were forged through participation in several youth leadership organizations, sports, previous jobs, or Deaf community events which created a
large circle of support for James and Tom. This network proved to be a critical part of James's ability to obtain employment as an administrator. While
Carl did not grow up in the same type of environment, his connections as
an adult led to the same level of support from others in the field. Interestingly, Carl began his career in a field that had no relevance to education.
An individual came to speak at the university where he was enrolled; this
individual saw administrative qualities in Carl and gently encouraged him
to consider a career as an administrator. Carl admitted that if it had not
been for that individual and the words of encouragement, he would have
never considered a career shift. Rather than clambering up the mountain
of administration aimlessly, these individuals received a guiding light in the
form of support from others in their personal and professional lives. That
guiding light became the driving force that has motivated and shaped their
leadership potential as school administrators.

Interestingly, all participants reported a desire to provide a high level
of support for their employees. In regard to advice for future administrators, each participant echoed the same sentiment: "Get ready now. Do not
wait for an opportunity to arise. Get your education, get the experience
you need and be ready." While Tom fears the possibility of not being able
to continue to support others, his focus is on his current employees, with
the desire to create a collaborative and conducive workplace in which all
employees feel adequately supported and have the resources needed to
perform their jobs to their best potential. Like Tom, Bob always seeks to
provide support to others. When asked what he recommends his employees

do if they want to become administrators, Bob emphasized, "Get an education and then apply for jobs. Set yourself up for success." The importance of a strong educational background will help pave the way in obtaining employment in the field of administration and in being an effective leader.

As an individual who has experienced firsthand how the presence of someone in power has a significant impact on oppressed groups, Tom seeks to pass on the baton and become a gatekeeper, while expressing that he is concerned. "Those who want to become administrators do not have a job here. We are a small school, and we just don't have any open positions. They all will have to leave and grab whatever is open." Despite the possibility of losing some of his best employees, Tom recognizes and supports the need for more D/HH individuals to ascend in the field of deaf education in order to create a more representative environment for the younger generation of D/HH students. Such recognition has become a driving force for Tom, whose purpose as a leader is to give advice to the future generation of D/HH K–12 administrators. He said, "Get ready now, administrators are beginning to retire, and we do not have D/HH people ready to take over. We need more D/HH individuals to get their degrees in the administrative field and be ready."

The ultimate goal as an administrator and effective leader, Jeremy reported, is to empower teachers and trust that they are doing their jobs effectively. Additionally, Jeremy believes that making himself accessible and visible on campus helps create an environment in which students and teachers feel supported, respected, and valued. Many of the participants reported that while they had received sufficient support from others prior to becoming an administrator, after they became an administrator, that level of support from others quickly dwindled. One such example is Bob, who is the sole D/HH administrator in the entire district. He frequently is not provided with full access to communication in last-minute meetings, which further increases his isolation during his climb on the mountain. He describes his position as being on an island alone, surrounded by hearing individuals. Joining Bob in feeling isolated, James cites that he would ideally like more support from other administrators, believing that existing support structures favor higher-level administrators such as superintendents. Eric, however, is fortunate to have more extensive support, in which his administrator colleagues share ideas and offer advice. Overall, while the administrators sought to support others, they were all in need of support for themselves too.

As part of their duty to support others beyond their staff, many participants reported their desire to adequately support the students. To create connections with students and let them know he cares about them, Jeremy believes that being approachable on campus rather than being holed up in his office goes a long way. Likewise, Bob expresses the desire to have a positive life-long impact on D/HH students. In order to give students that level of support, Bob goes beyond the call of duty by arranging one-on-one meetings with principals on several campuses that have D/HH students in their building. The purpose of these meetings is to establish rapport with the principals and to become a model upon which their perspective of D/HH individuals can build, and establish clear, valid expectations of the students. Bob's leadership approach is reflective of his experiences of isolation as a hard-of-hearing child educated in a mainstream setting. Bob reported that due to this isolation, he did not become secure in his own identity as a D/HH person until he became an adult. It is that experience that led Bob to want to pursue a career as an administrator where he could personally ensure that other D/HH students in mainstream settings had access to role models. Bob does not wish to see the same isolation in his programs, and especially not for the children they serve. Some ways Bob has attempted to build in positive identity and support include creating inclusive community-based experiences, such as setting up open-captioned movie nights and establishing a direct mentoring program between hearing families with D/HH children enrolled in his programs and D/HH adults.

Carl also shared Bob's sentiments of supporting students, albeit in a different manner. Carl mentioned that in the education system there is a large push for students to fit into society's expectations of attending a 4-year university after graduation. To combat this push, he makes an effort to introduce his students to other occupations that do not require a degree, stating that not every student is college-bound and that is perfectly acceptable. What is not acceptable to him, however, is diminishing or dismissing those students in favor of supporting the college-bound students. These two administrators recognize the importance of providing support for others within the community and the life-long impact this support will have on D/HH students.

## ADMINISTRATIVE EXPERIENCE AND QUALITIES

Administrators have a difficult job that requires personal and professional sacrifice. The act of being a leader in education requires that the leader stay abreast of the latest practices and remain intentional and reflective practitioners (DiPaola & Hoy, 2015; Moffett, 2008; Taylor, 2013). To understand if there are similar qualities and traits that each administrator shares, we analyzed each administrator's perception of the critical qualities administrators should exhibit, and what their individual experiences looked like up until they became administrators. One common quality that was observed in the participants was their desire to be "people first," as Tom put it. As a relatively new administrator, Tom constantly feels the pressure to effortlessly balance several responsibilities with his desire to support his employees. He stated,

> At work, my desk is always covered in paperwork. It never ends, but that's okay. I can work on the paperwork later at night or on the weekends. While I'm here, my focus is on the people. I'm very people-centered.

Eric also aims to embody people-centered leadership, allowing his staff to work without peering over their shoulders. He says to "trust the people you work with, and know how to make them be effective and successful—don't nitpick, let them do their jobs." Carl shares the same sentiment, expressing that he feels he is simply a "tool to drive things forward."

To continue to drive his work forward, Tom refuses to settle or become stagnant in his field. He strives to continuously grow as an administrator by attending workshops, remaining up to date on research, and looking for ways to improve the programs he serves. James also cites that he tries to remain open-minded, flexible, and willing to adapt to ever-changing needs and trends. Tom declares that he is "never satisfied; [he] always want[s] to see growth, change, and improvement." Tom continuously takes initiative in identifying areas of need within his programs, providing solutions, and hoping to encourage others to do the same. However, being able to identify these needs, develop one's vision, and clearly communicate that vision is difficult, lamented Eric. In climbing the mountain, it is essential that administrators are able to self-reflect on their vision and on their abilities to execute that vision.

Part of being an administrator in a school setting is understanding one's own leadership style and leadership qualities. The administrators all mentioned the leadership qualities they embodied or sought to embody, as well as those they deemed important in others. Jeremy felt that his leadership style stemmed from his experience as a teacher prior to becoming an administrator. As a result, he believes that he understands where teachers are coming from and knows what they need to be effective teachers. This understanding led to Jeremy being a leader who strives to create a positive, teacher-centric environment at his school.

All of the administrators in this study sought to grow their leadership qualities, whether through professional development, conferences, or mentorship. This was a point of frustration for Bob who has difficulties proving to his district that D/HH administrator-oriented workshops and/ or conferences are worth the investment, and his loneliness on the mountain is further compounded each time his district denies his requests. Many conferences focus on K–12 administrators of public schools with typically developing, monolingual, abled children. There is only one conference currently in the United States for administrators in deaf education which is the Conference of Educational Administrators of Schools and Programs for the Deaf (CEASD), and its location around the country changes yearly. James echoes the sentiment of needing more collaboration between D/HH administrators, believing that more outlets than just a yearly CEASD meeting are needed to stay abreast of the latest practices in deaf education and school leadership.

Like their counterparts, Bob and Eric believe that it is vital to keep current on changing trends and that it is equally important to remain unbiased and transparent as an administrator. James believes that exchanging information about what is happening at each school will lead to new ideas and more opportunities for students in their respective school settings. Additionally, James' maintaining transparency with his employees leads them to trust in him as an administrator. The other participants shared this belief that communication, transparency, and trust are essential for a positive work environment. These qualities are not only important for fostering positivity in the workplace, but also set the stage for the school culture.

## UNDERSTANDING THE SCHOOL CULTURE

*For example, my first year here, did I suddenly make changes? No, you can't do that.*
*You wait for the first year, see what needs to be improved or changed. Really,*
*some changes take a few years of slow [incremental changes].*

—Bob

Our participants shared that based on their experiences, it is imperative that new administrators take the pulse of the workplace and begin to study the school culture. Ideally, administrators slowly ease their way into their new environment prior to making any major changes. Our participants had a learned understanding of how to assess and learn their setting and staff's way of interacting with each other, with students, with expectations, and with other critical components of a school's culture. While our participants came from different backgrounds and work in different settings, they all understood their respective school cultures. For instance, Eric has worked in three different types of educational settings and reported that each environment had a direct impact on his ability to do his job. He found that understanding the "system," whether that be the state department of education, the school board, or other body of power, was most helpful in making administrative decisions. Other administrators also found that understanding the "system" was advantageous to their ability to navigate their day-to-day work with others, especially those outside of deaf education. Jeremy's approach to working in his school closely mirrored Eric's, in which he already understood the system that was in place before he arrived.

Additionally, Jeremy emphasized the importance of knowing your place as an administrator and what you are "allowed" to do to change the school culture. For example, Jeremy's school strictly follows a chain of command in which he does not have many interactions with those higher than his direct supervisor. Given that D/HH individuals have historically been oppressed, it typically is more difficult for their leadership to be recognized in a system that favors the dominant pathological and medical perspective uplifting abled, hearing people (and their way of being) over deaf ones (Ladd, 2003; Lane, 1992; Padden & Humphries, 1988). In that regard, James emphasized the importance of knowing your position in the educational system. He believes that the ability to adapt to different cultures and expectations is a crucial part of being a successful administrator. Jeremy echoes the same sentiments, expressing that it is important to take initiative to learn the school culture rather than expecting others to adapt to you. For Tom, the two campuses where he works have very different cultures and he had to learn how to adapt to the culture at each campus; such experiences were not uncommon for these administrators trying to build bridges between cultures or groups of people. Tom tried to bring the cultures together, attempting to grow the schools' relationships and provide opportunities to share resources. In these ways, each administrator learned how to manage their work within the systems and settings that employed them.

Understanding the system in which one works is beneficial because it allows administrators to more effectively navigate any potential barriers they may face, as well as know how to make effective use of their connections. For instance, in a hearing-dominated setting, Eric felt as if he spent most of his time advocating for his own needs. The constant advocating for himself led Eric to feel as if he was not able to contribute his efforts fully to the students he was responsible for; instead, he was occupied battling his own fight for access. Now in a Deaf-centric setting, Eric reports that his experience as an administrator is in stark contrast to his previous experience. While he is still new to the school, he feels as if the other administrators support him equally and allow him the opportunity to be a full, contributing member of the team. Like Eric, Carl also expressed feeling limited by the ways the school culture at a previous school restricted his abilities to lead the school in a manner he felt was most appropriate for the student population. Carl cited difficulties challenging the long-ingrained school culture in his current setting, and he dreams of making changes to craft a more Deaf-centric school setting. Overall, these administrators had to learn to "play the game," and learn their individual school cultures in order to more effectively lead their schools and the staff and students in their classrooms. All the while, even while "playing the game," they still advocated for change within their respective systems. Such skills and know-how become necessary gear in the administrator "backpack," so to speak, and the climb uphill without such tools would be fraught with resistance.

## DISCUSSION

Though the administrators who were interviewed were at the top of the D/HH hierarchy as educated White men, they still all experienced barriers in a variety of ways on their journey to the peak of the mountain. As a novice climber would not tackle Mount Everest alone, our administrators each had a gatekeeper and network of individuals who lent them a hand along their journey. Some climbs may prove treacherous, but our administrators forged ahead, finding barely noticeable pathways in order to continue on their journey. It should be noted that other administrators who fell down the mountain likely did not make our sample, nor did they have the opportunity to share their stories.

One pathway that remains heavily trodden and seemingly cemented is the face of deaf education in general. Every day, D/HH children all over the United States walk into their school buildings, greeted by their teachers and administrators, the team of people working together to serve them. Who are the faces of these teachers and administrators? As we discussed, the majority of them are White, hearing, abled people, and this information was reflected in our findings from the survey and interviews. The D/HH administrators who volunteered to be interviewed were all educated White men, who had no other identified disabilities, who are the faces that stand out the most in deaf education, and whose messages reverberated the loudest from the mountaintop.

The authors pondered why the only D/HH people who volunteered to be interviewed were White men—where were the women? Where were the POC administrators? Why did they not volunteer to be included in follow-up interviews? Was the lack of diversity in interviews simply a reflection of the low number of female administrators or D/HH POC administrators? Did the research process itself prove to be a barrier in successfully recruiting POC participants? Did the reason lie farther off the pathway to the top of the mountain, a pathway laden with danger and tightropes, leading that group to feel unsafe sharing their experiences? Further investigation into the experiences of female D/HH administrators or D/HH POC administrators is necessary to gain a full understanding of D/HH administrators. More research is needed with an explicit focus on D/HH administrators using a larger sample, as well as further research on D/HH administrators with additional marginalized identities. Such research would benefit from partnership with advocacy organizations, such as National Black Deaf Advocates (NBDA), to identify research participants. The addition of such research will allow for a deeper understanding of the systemic oppression of

D/HH professionals in the United States and assist in ensuring that more D/HH administrators garner opportunities to take leadership roles in the field of deaf education.

While more work is necessary to understand the D/HH administrator's journey to the top of the mountain, one thing is clear. In the stories of these six administrators, the act of a D/HH individual obtaining employment in the field of educational leadership required the presence of a hearing person in power to act as a gatekeeper. The key strategies in finding an administrative position are to master foundational administrative skills and find gatekeepers. The gatekeepers should value the knowledge, skills, and competencies the prospective administrator possesses while remaining unbiased in recognizing which applicant has the competencies best suited for their institution. As one of the most common sayings heard when conducting a job search goes, it is not only "what you know, but who you know." Such barriers for advancing into an administrative role means that D/HH individuals seeking to become administrators in the field of K–12 deaf education will likely face the same challenges our participants faced. While administrators of schools and programs for the D/HH often reflect that their population is misunderstood and that ideally, an administrator should be D/HH, current trends do not reflect such beliefs (E. Garrett, personal communication, November 29, 2020). One organization that is an instrument of change for elevating D/HH administrators is CEASD, which serves to provide a larger social network with respect to school leadership. Perhaps the competition to justify D/HH programs or schools with an orientation that is seemingly counter to integration results in the perpetuation of a closed network for D/HH individuals to advance, as such a closed network means limited access to opportunities (E. Garrett, personal communication, November 29, 2020).

Hearing gatekeepers can either break down the systemic barriers (as in the case of the hearing administrators who paved access for these D/HH colleagues) or they can uphold systemic barriers, such as audism. When considering reasons that D/HH individuals are often not considered for these leadership positions, spoken language ability/communication access is often brought up as an area of concern. However, as evident in Bob's case, he is able to comfortably communicate through spoken English and still he considers communication to be a barrier. Currently, the system does not allow for marginalized individuals to effortlessly move up on their own, especially in positions that are largely held by the dominant hearing group. With respect to POC administrators, even in 2020 there are so very few; this lack of representation in leadership is often assumed to be by design (E. Garrett, personal communication, November 29, 2020). The current prominence of the Black Lives Matter (BLM) movement, especially this year, may have an impact on the presence and prevalence in D/HH educational leaders of color in the days ahead (E. Garrett, personal communication, November 29, 2020). An understanding of the system and the various pathways to reach the top of the mountain is crucial to a successful journey. Despite barriers in upward mobility within the deaf education system, these administrators show incredible resilience; they refuse to give up in the face of adversity.

## Implications and Future Recommendations

It is not simply enough to understand what is happening in deaf education today; we must look ahead and identify strategies that will help us strengthen the practice of educational administration. As we discovered in the cases of the administrators in this study, hearing gatekeepers and mentors were key to their professional journeys, seemingly more important than education or credentials. Such experiences raise the question about qualified individuals who could not get in the door due to a lack of a hearing gatekeeper or mentor—where are they? What type of impact would they have had on their schools? Are we directly and indirectly harming D/HH children by continuing to maintain a system that values the expertise of hearing individuals higher than D/HH individuals? With that understanding, educational administration training programs that focus on leadership in deaf education should provide mentorship from within the program, or establish partnerships with schools in which students can intern. In an attempt to alleviate Tom's concerns regarding not having enough people to take over once the current generation of administrators retires, schools for the deaf would be wise to establish administrative internships in which the intern can shadow an experienced administrator, much like a student-teaching experience for classroom teachers-in-training. Such efforts could be expanded to include mainstream settings with deaf education programs with established partnerships with a given university program. Developing such relationships would help build a larger network, but the systemic issues mentioned by our participants still remain.

Another lesson from the administrators was the need to combat systemic issues that specifically impact D/HH administrators, such as audism. In return for partnerships and internship opportunities for their students, university programs with educational leaders in training can offer professional development for school and district leadership regarding D/HH sensitivity, hiring practices, accommodations in the workplace, and other pertinent topics that may affect D/HH administrators in their given settings. Providing such training can reduce concerns from higher-level administrators regarding how to work with D/HH administrators and their needs, and how to maximize communication with them. Furthermore, such partnership will bring the educational leadership community together and provide internal structures to help combat systemic issues.

Within educational administration training programs, care should be taken to ensure that the coursework is reflective of the diverse needs of students and staff. For instance, coursework should include information on equitable and socially just practices, both at a leadership level and at the classroom level. Such coursework should also be essential to teacher preparatory programs throughout the country, so that all levels within a school setting are engaging in social justice work and are culturally aware and sensitive. A true pipeline is what is needed so that Deaf people, especially Deaf POC, can be exposed to the opportunities and experiences needed to qualify for leadership positions (E. Garrett, personal communication, November 29, 2020).

## CONCLUSION

The goal of climbing the mountain is to reach that proverbial flag at the top: the ability to support the future generation of D/HH individuals. This goal seemed to be a large driving force in these six administrators, even at the cost of making tremendous personal sacrifices. For instance, some of our administrators currently reside in a state apart from their spouses and/or children in order to maintain employment, a sacrifice that is typically not seen with hearing administrators. While sitting at the top of the mountain may feel lonely, as in Bob's case, the journey to arrive at the destination was an experience that helped shape and mold the participants into the successful leaders they are today. Each role model and mentor they encountered on their way served as an important influence on the future of not only the participants but of all the students they serve. The support from role models and other individuals has been shown to be a critical key in helping D/HH individuals navigate various barriers (Cawthon et al., 2016). Understanding the landscape of the administration mountain, so to speak, will allow individuals within the system to recognize their power, privilege, and equity as well as how each individual has the ability to influence others' upward mobility.

## REFERENCES

Andrews, J. F., & Covell, J. A. (2006). Preparing future teachers and doctoral level leaders in deaf education: Meeting the challenge. *American Annals of the Deaf, 151*(5), 464–475. https://doi.org/10.1353/aad.2007.0000

Anglin-Jaffe, H. (2015). De-colonizing deaf education: An analysis of the claims and implications of the application of post-colonial theory to deaf education. In

K. Lesnik-Oberstein (Ed.), *Rethinking disability theory and practice* (pp. 76–97). Palgrave Macmillan.

Ashton, G. R. (2012). *Deaf leaders: The intersections of deaf culture, leadership, and professional associations* (UMI No. 3530360) [Doctoral dissertation, Union Institute and University]. ProQuest Dissertations and Theses Global database. https://search.proquest.com/openview/06940e1a771d9b2ac64329c3f4fc44d7/1?pq-origsite=gscholar&cbl=18750&diss=y

Baker, C. (2011) *Foundations of bilingual education and bilingualism* (Vol. 79). Multilingual Matters Ltd.

Balk, J. W. (1997). *Leadership practices of superintendents at residential schools for the deaf.* [Unpublished doctoral dissertation]. University of Nebraska.

Banks, J. A. (2004). *Diversity and citizenship education: Global perspectives. Global perspectives.* Jossey-Bass.

Banks, J. A. (2008). Diversity, group identity, and citizenship education in a global age. *Educational Researcher, 37*(3), 129–139. https://doi.org/10.3102/0013189x08317501

Banks, J. A. (2010). Multicultural education: Characteristics and goals. In J. A. Banks & C. A. Banks (Eds.), *Multicultural education: Issues and perspectives* (7th ed., pp. 3–30). Wiley & Sons Inc.

Barnett, D. (2004). School leadership preparation programs: Are they preparing tomorrow's leaders? *Education, 125*(1), 121–129.

Bays, D. A., & Crockett, J. B. (2007). Investigating instructional leadership for special education. *Exceptionality, 15*(3), 143–161. https://doi.org/10.1080/09362830701503495

Baxter, P., & Jack, S. (2008). Qualitative case study methodology: Study design and implementation for novice researchers. *The Qualitative Report, 13*(4), 544–556. https://nsuworks.nova.edu/tqr/vol13/iss4/2

Bhattacharya, K. (2018, April 25). *Learning to do "woke" qualitative research: How to break the master's rules and tools* [Video webinar]. https://wokeresearch.weebly.com/dr-kakali-bhattacharya.html

Cawthon, S. W., Johnson, P. M., Garberoglio, C. L., & Schoffstall, S. J. (2016). Role models as facilitators of social capital for deaf individuals: A research synthesis. *American Annals of the Deaf, 161*(2), 115–127. https://doi.org/10.1353/aad.2016.0021

Charmaz, K. (2001). Qualitative interviewing and grounded theory analysis. In J. Gubrium & J. Holstein (Eds.), *Handbook of interview research: Context and method* (pp. 675–694). SAGE Publications.

Cokely, D. (2005). Shifting positionality: A critical examination of the turning point in the relationship of interpreters and the deaf community. In M. Marschark, R. Peterson, & E. A. Winston (Eds.), *Perspectives on deafness. Sign language interpreting and interpreter education: Directions for research and practice* (pp. 3–28). Oxford University Press. https://doi.org/10.1093/acprof/9780195176940.003.0001

Cooner, D., Tochterman, S., & Garrison-Wade, D. (2005). Preparing principals for leadership in special education: Applying ISLLC standards. *Connections: Journal of Principal Preparation and Development, 6*, 19–24.

DiPaola, M., & Hoy, W. K. (2015). *Leadership and school quality.* Information Age Publishing.

Fiorenza, E. S. (2001). *Wisdom ways: Introducing Feminist biblical interpretation.* Orbis Books.

Fram, S. M. (2013). The constant comparative analysis method outside of grounded theory. *The Qualitative Report, 18*(1), 1–25. https://doi.org/10.46743/2160-3715/2013.1569

Gannon, J. R. (1981). *Deaf heritage: A narrative history.* National Association of the Deaf.

Garberoglio, C. L., Gobble, M. E., & Cawthon, S. W. (2012). A national perspective on teachers' efficacy beliefs in deaf education. *Journal of Deaf Studies and Deaf Education, 17*(3), 367–383. https://doi.org/10.1093/deafed/ens014

Goldenberg, B. (2013). White teachers in urban classrooms: Embracing non-White students' cultural capital for better teaching and learning. *Urban Education, 49*(1), 111–144. https://doi.org/10.1177/0042085912472510

Gustason, G., Pfetzing, D., & Zawolkow, D. (1974). *Signing exact English.* Modern Signs Press.

Hilliard, A., & Jackson, B. T. (2011). Current trends in educational leadership for student success plus facilities planning and designing. *Contemporary Issues in Education Research, 4*(1), 1–8. https://doi.org/10.19030/cier.v4i1.976

Hilligoss, T. (2014). *Principals who supervise teachers of the deaf: A mixed methods study* [Doctoral dissertation, University of Nebraska]. https://digitalcommons.unl.edu/cgi/viewcontent.cgi?article=1204&context=cehsedaddiss

Ivankova, N. V., & Stick, S. L. (2007). Students' persistence in a distributed doctoral program in educational leadership in higher education: A mixed methods study. *Research in Higher Education, 48*(1), 93–135. https://doi.org/10.1007/s11162-006-9025-4

Jackson, B. T., & Hilliard, A. (2013). Too many boys are failing in American schools: What can we do about it? *Contemporary Issues in Education Research, 6*(3), 311–316. https://doi.org/10.19030/cier.v6i3.7901

Jackson, B. L., & Kelley, C. (2002). Exceptional and innovative programs in educational leadership. *Educational administration quarterly, 38*(2), 192–212. https://doi.org/10.1177/0013161X02382005

Kamm-Larew, D., & Lamkin, M. (2008). Survey of leadership programs: Valued characteristics of leadership within the Deaf community. *Journal of the American Deafness and Rehabilitation Association, 42*(1), 48–69. https://repository.wcsu.edu/jadara/vol42/iss1/4

Kamm-Larew, D., Stanford, J., Greene, R., & Heacox, C. (2008). Leadership style in the Deaf community: An exploratory case study of a university president. *American Annals of the Deaf, 153*(4), 357–367. https://doi.org/10.1353/aad.0.0057

Kaur, A., Noman, M., & Awang-Hashim, R. (2015). Exploring strategies of teaching and classroom practices in response to challenges of inclusion in a Thai school: A case study. *International Journal of Inclusive Education, 20*(5), 474–485. https://doi.org/10.1080/13603116.2015.1090489

Keller Jr., M. P. (2015). *Investigating workplace ecology for superintendents at schools for the deaf in the United States* [Unpublished doctoral dissertation]. Lamar University.

Knaus, C. B. (2016). 'We talk but we don't say shit': Education and the silencing of voice. In N. N. Croom, J. S. Brooks, D. E. Armstrong, I. Bogotch, W. H. Sherman, & G. Theoharis (Eds.), *Envisioning a critical race praxis in K–12 leadership through counter-storytelling* (pp. 3–23). Information Age Publishing.

Knudson, B. G. (2003). Superintendents of American residential school for the deaf: A profile. *American Annals of the Deaf, 148*(1), 49–55. https://doi.org/10.1353/aad.2003.005

Ladd, P. (2003). *Understanding deaf culture: In search of deafhood.* Multilingual Matters Ltd.

Lane, H. L. (1992). *The mask of benevolence: Disabling the deaf community.* Knopf.

Lartz, M. N., & Litchfield, S. K. (2005). Administrators' ratings of competencies needed to prepare preservice teachers for oral deaf education programs. *American Annals of the Deaf, 150*(5), 433–442. https://doi.org/10.1353/aad.2006.0007

Lashley, C. (2007). Principal leadership for special education: An ethical framework. *Exceptionality, 15*(3), 177–187. https://doi.org/10.1080/09362830701503511

LaSasso, C. J., & Achtzehn, J. C. (1996). Leadership personnel needs in the education of deaf and hard of hearing children: Results of two national surveys. *American Annals of the Deaf, 141*(4), 229–302. https://doi.org/10.1353/aad.2012.0389

Lawyer. G. (2022). Theorizing the curriculum of colonization in the U.S. Deaf context: Situating DisCrit within a framework of decolonization. In S. A. Annamma, B. Ferri, & D. Connor (Eds.), *DisCrit expanded: Inquiries, reverberations & ruptures* (pp. 179–198). Teachers College Press.

Lawyer, G. (2018). *Removing the colonizer's coat in Deaf Education: Exploring the curriculum of colonization and the field of Deaf Education* [Unpublished doctoral dissertation]. University of Tennessee-Knoxville.

McCaskill, C., Lucas, C., Bayley, R., & Hill, J. (2011). *The hidden treasure of Black ASL: Its history and structure.* Gallaudet University Press.

Moffett, A. W. (2008). *Power base perceptions of school administrators at residential schools for the culturally deaf* [Doctoral dissertation, University of Southern Mississippi]. https://aquila.usm.edu/dissertations/1172

Moores, D. F. (2001). *Educating the deaf: Psychology, principles, and practices.* Houghton Mifflin Company.

Murphy, J. (2002). Reculturing the profession of educational leadership: New blueprints. *Educational Administration Quarterly, 38*(2), 176–191. https://doi.org/10.1177/0013161x02382004

Musyoka, M. M., Gentry, M. A., & Bartlett, J. J. (2015). Voices from the classroom: Experiences of teachers of deaf students with additional disabilities. *Journal of Education and Training Studies, 4*(2), 85–96. https://doi.org/10.11114/jets.v4i2.1131

Northouse, P. G. (2004). *Leadership: Theory and practice.* SAGE Publications.

O'Brien, C., Kuntze, M., Appanah, T., Lindsey, R., Robins, K., & Terrell, R. (2014). Culturally relevant leadership: A deaf education cultural approach. *American Annals of the Deaf, 159*(3), 296–301. http://www.jstor.org/stable/26234963

Padden, C. A., & Humphries, T. L. (1988). *Deaf in America: Voices from a culture.* Harvard University Press.

Pazey, B. L., & Cole, H. A. (2012). The role of special education training in the development of socially just leaders: Building an equity consciousness in educational leadership programs. *Educational Administration Quarterly, 49*(2), 243–271. https://doi.org/10.1177/0013161X12463934

Scouten, E. L. (1984). *Turning points in the education of deaf people.* Interstate Printers & Publishers.

Shaw, L. R., Chan, F., & McMahon, B. T. (2012). Intersectionality and disability harassment: The interactive effects of disability, race, age, and gender. *Rehabilitation Counseling Bulletin, 55*(2), 82–91. https://doi.org/10.1177/0034 355211431167

Simms, L., Rusher, M., Andrews, J. F., & Coryell, J. (2008). Apartheid in deaf education: Examining workforce diversity. *American Annals of the Deaf, 153*(4), 384–395. https://doi.org/10.1353/aad.0.0060

Sleeter, C., & Milner IV, H. R. (2011). Researching successful efforts in teacher education to diversify teachers. In A. F. Ball & C. A. Tyson (Eds.), *Studying diversity in teacher education* (pp. 81–103). Rowman & Littlefield.

Stake, R. E. (2006). *Multiple case study analysis.* The Guilford Press.

Taylor, M. M. (2013). Leadership: Perspectives from Deaf leaders and interpreter leaders. *International Journal of Interpreter Education, 5*(2), 43–53.

Teller, H., & Harney, J. (2005). Views from the field: Program directors' perceptions of teacher education and the education of students who are deaf and hard of hearing. *American Annals of the Deaf, 150*(5), 470–479. https://doi.org/ 10.1353/aad.2006.0011

Üstün, A. (2017). Effects of the leadership roles of administrators who work at special education schools upon organizational climate. *Universal Journal of Educational Research, 5*(3), 504–509. https://doi.org/10.13189/ujer.2017.050323

Valente, J. M. (2011). Cyborgization: Deaf education for young children in the cochlear implantation era. *Qualitative Inquiry, 17*(7), 639–652. https://doi .org/10.1177/1077800411414006

Waziyatawin, A. W., & Yellow Bird, M. (Eds.). (2005). *For indigenous eyes only: A decolonization handbook.* School of American Research Press.

Wheeler, J. (2017, September 12). *Updated list of deaf superintendents in America–24 deaf and 40 hearing* [Video]. Facebook. https://www.facebook.com/groups/ ASLTHAT/permalink/2038261169738713

# CHAPTER 19

# ROLLING MY WAY INTO LEADERSHIP

## Perspectives From an Educator With Cerebral Palsy

**Sofia Vergara**
*Educator/Co-founder Bridges to Inclusion*

In this personal narrative, I will present excerpts of my lived experience as an individual with the disability of cerebral palsy (CP), and a wheelchair user. To put things in context, I must clarify that although CP impacts individuals in a myriad of different development aspects, my limitations manifested themselves physically making me a quadriplegic. In conversations with my parents, I learned that despite my diagnosis, they were convinced of my intellectual prowess. Consequently, they had no mercy in demanding diligence and academic excellence of me as they did for my three able-bodied siblings.

I will focus here on two general themes: First, I will explore how my schooling experience, from K–12 through higher education, was impacted by my disability; I will then analyze how my disability has become a

*Who Decides?*, pages 471–489
Copyright © 2022 by Information Age Publishing
www.infoagepub.com
All rights of reproduction in any form reserved.

motivational force in my struggle for professional growth and leadership in education. Throughout this narrative, I will use part of the material included in my autoethnographic doctoral dissertation (Vergara, 2017) while highlighting the most influential moments of my educational experiences. Further, I will contextualize and expand on this material taking advantage of the perspective that I have gained during my postdoctoral years as a high school teacher and college professor. The ensuing story aims to conscientize (Freire, 2008) the general readership about implicit or explicit societal challenges that individuals with disabilities encounter in their quest for equity, and to set the conditions for empowerment of individuals with disabilities to continuing demanding justice from within. Furthermore, my experiences will be told within the framework of DisCrit (Annamma et al., 2016) by exploring how dis/ability and race, as systems of oppression, have intersected throughout my life.

## NAVIGATING MY K–12 SCHOOL YEARS

I spent my primary and first 2 years of secondary education during the years 1986 to 1998 in the public-school setting, and before getting into the narrative, I will offer some legislative context that impacted my lived experience.

In the educational realm, landmark court decisions, such as *Pennsylvania Association for Retarded Children v. Commonwealth of Pennsylvania* (1971) and *Mills v. Board of Education of District of Columbia* (1972), established that every child with a disability should be educated based on the equal protection clause of the 14th Amendment to the United States Constitution. These and other legislative victories pushed the agenda in favor of comprehensive legislation to increase educational opportunities for children with disabilities (U.S. Department of Education, 2010) and culminated with the passage of the 1975 Education for all Handicapped Children Act (Education for All Handicapped Children Act, 1975), which provided federal money to fund states and local agencies in order to ensure that "handicapped children" and adults ages 3 to 21 be educated in the "least restrictive environment" to the maximum extent appropriate, that is, they are educated with children who are not "handicapped" and that special classes, separate schools, or other approaches that remove children from their regular educational environment are only enacted when the severity of the "handicap" prevents the possibility of education in regular classes (U.S. Department of Education, 2010).

The above-mentioned legal framework was reaffirmed and expanded with the passage of two historic amendments to existing law: the Americans With Disabilities Act of 1990 regulations (ADA, 1990) and the Individuals With Disabilities Education Act Amendments of 1997 (IDEA, 1997). This latter legislation (IDEA) included provisions to facilitate the transition of students with disabilities from high school to adult living, meaning that each student's individualized education program (IEP) should include transition plans for identifying adequate employment opportunities and/ or other appropriate options for her/his adulthood. Consequently, IDEA highlights the importance of a well-executed IEP as the central component for the overall success of students with disabilities.

My public-school years were tremendously difficult for me: At an age when fitting in was, or at least seemed to be, a matter of life or death, I stuck out like a sore thumb. I did not belong anywhere; I was receiving the services of a one-on-one aide from the special education department, and at the same time, I attended all general education honors classes. This categorized me as a "mainstreamed" student. However, though my only "special education" class was adapted PE, because of my disability, no one would speak to me, not even my teachers.

Teachers, in general, would rather not deal with me and just placed me in the back of the room where I was out of the way. Despite being mainstreamed, I felt as if I were always asked to prove my intellect to them only because I could not write on my own and needed others to scribe for me. This attitude of distrust was specifically noticeable from my eighth-grade science teacher, who would question me verbally after completion of every homework assignment (typically scribed by my mother) just to be sure that I knew the content; oddly, I never saw him do this with other students.

Looking for a social niche, I spent time in the special education classroom. I would hang out there during lunch and I was eventually allowed to become a teaching assistant (TA) for the class. At first, I was thrilled: a place where I belonged! However, as time passed by, I felt stuck between two worlds: I craved the intellectual and social acceptance of my nondisabled peers, but I struggled to connect with my peers with disabilities. They, too, pushed me away because they perceived me as part of the "other" group. Obviously, there was a great division between my peers and me, this reinforcing my feeling of not belonging!

To cope with the situation, I distinctly remember making up (and telling) stories about how many parties I had gone to, how many friends I had, how many boys were interested in me, and so forth. This illusion made it seem as if I was much happier than I really was, but it also created a deep sense of frustration and sadness in me.

If I thought elementary and middle school were a bad dream, high school was an awful nightmare. From the very beginning I was tormented for being the mainstreamed "disabled" girl in the honor classes. I was almost daily called "cripple," laughed at, and students would disconnect the power to my motorized wheelchair so that I couldn't move; all I was trying to do was to "fit in." It would have been bad enough if I felt antagonized only by fellow students outside the class, but what made it torturous for me was that the teachers and administrators were nonchalant in their judgment and usually sided with the bullies. The situation became so volatile that I started questioning my safety, something that neither I (nor my parents) had previously imagined while in elementary and middle school.

First and foremost, I felt as if I was a burden on both administrators and teachers who were unprepared to adequately handle my socioemotional and physical needs, let alone educate a mainstreamed student with a disability. But my feelings were justified. For example, when I entered my classes I did not have desks that I could pull up to my wheelchair. Below is an excerpt of a letter written by my parents to the principal approximately a month after the school year began, and my repeated requests had been ignored, in which they expressed concern over the situation.

Dear Mr. K:

Our daughter Sofia is without a desk in three of her classes. The teachers in those classes have been requested by Sofia to correct this problem. Mrs. O., her counselor, has also been informed. Nothing has been done yet.

Needless to say, a desk is indispensable for Sofia. Already, in one test she answered a question incorrectly because she did not have the written questionnaire in front of her.

Notably, after this letter, it took at least another 2 weeks for the issue to finally be resolved.

The sheer fact that I had to demand desks in my classes, an accessible bathroom in the school, and adequate one-on-one assistance, demonstrate both an inadequate implementation of the ADA, and an extremely limited understanding of the concept of "least restrictive environment," which is the cornerstone of the IDEA. Furthermore, IDEA mandate that each student's IEP should ensure not only that the educational setting provides the least restrictive environment for the growth and development of students with disabilities, but also facilitates their transition from high school to adult living. The problem is that, as I clearly remember, my participation in the IEP process was only nominal. For instance, the "present level of performance (PLOP)" and "goal-setting" sections of my IEP, which are critical components of the process, were typically contentious discussions in which my parents and I vied for my academic progress and physical access to facilities within the school, while the administrators and teachers were mostly focused on adapted PE goals. Sadly, although there was a clear disconnect between our desires and what the school administrative team would actually commit to, we ultimately signed every IEP document with a sense of fate rather than with satisfaction in the process.

A blatant consequence of the unpreparedness of school administrators and teachers to deal with my concerns regarding my future goals and/or safety issues was that I fell through the cracks and was in danger of becoming one of the public-school statistics for students with disabilities who drop out of high school (Snyder & Dillow, 2015). To avoid this situation, my parents and I were forced to enter mediation and eventually took legal action against the school system for not providing adequate accessibility and accommodations; the school's inaction in these areas finally led to my emotional distress and physical injury. I distinctly remember that after I started crying about contentious arguments raised during my last public-school IEP, seeing my distress, our lawyer took me out of the room, calmed me down, and asked me bluntly, "What do you want to happen?" I replied, "The only thing I want is to get out of this school." Unbelievably, less than a week later, I was injured (hairline fracture of my right femur), while being transferred to an inaccessible bathroom. That was the last straw, and I never set foot in that school again.

After a month of recovery and the hectic process of finding an adequate (this time) private school, I finally found my way to Olympia High School. At the time, Olympia was a new school founded only 3 years prior to my arrival that emphasized diversity, social equality, and a personalized learning environment. Here, I felt socially accepted almost immediately by everyone at the school. The students had few preconceived notions of what a girl with a disability can, or cannot, do. I was just another member of the motley crew that made up the student population of Olympia High School. I was famous for acting as the taxicab that would drive multiple people to and from classes. Academically, there was no need for a one-to-one aide because all the teachers were more than willing to make all the necessary accommodations for me to succeed, including making photocopies of students' notes, extending time on exams when necessary, and being my scribe when I was unable to type an assignment. This openness made it easy for me to reach my full academic potential and allowed me to follow the same path as my able-bodied peers. In retrospect, many factors may have contributed to the comparatively positive experience that I had at Olympia with respect to those in the public-school setting. First and foremost, Olympia was a newly funded school with a small student body of 43 students. In addition, the school culture, at the time, successfully embraced diversity and inclusion amongst its community. Finally, its size also allowed for a student-centered approach to education and curriculum.

My transition from the public-school setting to this independent school seemed almost utopic at the time. However, in retrospect, I am not entirely certain if it was the goodness of Olympia School or the contrast with the traumatic experience that I endured in public school that influenced my state of mind. There were still times of awareness of my "difference," and even frequent episodes of isolation with respect to my peers, but I rationalized my feelings as typical teenage angst, largely because I was no longer being tormented by the flagrant bullying.

Overall, my K–12 experiences validate the contention that, unless concerted efforts are made to increase the participatory voice of students with disabilities in IEPs and other educational activities, many students with disabilities will potentially remain unprepared for an equitable adult life. Fortunately, in recent years there has been a push to encourage students with disabilities to take a proactive role in decision-making, not only at the level of IEPs, but into their postsecondary lives (National Center on Secondary Education and Transition, 2011). My lived experience shows that although IEPs are necessary transitional planning tools for students with disabilities, they are not sufficient. It is also necessary that school administrators and teachers embrace inclusive practices with the true commitment of setting conditions to empower the students towards self-determination.

## INDEPENDENT LIVING: MY AWAKENING

When the time came that I had to face postsecondary planning, I knew that I wanted to attend college, but multiple questions surfaced: Could I move away from home? If so, how would that work? Could I ever have the typical college experience as is often shown in movies? I knew that unless I moved away from home, the answer would be "No." In the middle of this struggle, I was ecstatic to learn that there was a program at UC Berkeley which would make this dream come true. From that day forward it was my mission in life to be accepted into the, now sadly nonexistent, UC Berkeley Disabled Students' Residence Program (DSRP).[1]

That dream came true in 2000. Being a part of DSRP, and a UC Berkeley student, changed me forever. It made me realize that others had come before me and built a community around their disability while at the same time being included in everyday college life. This instilled in me an instant sense of empowerment! I was not ashamed to tell my story anymore; instead, I embraced the negative experiences of my early high school years and contrasted them with my future.

Soon after I received my letter of acceptance, my parents and I drove the nerve-wracking 5½ hours from Los Angeles to Berkeley to tour the UC Berkeley campus with the director and the co-director of the DSRP. During our time together, the director, a wheelchair user, would often take me aside and tell me just how great it will feel for me to live an independent life. This did not fully sink in until, as we were strolling along the campus, we encountered a DSRP resident who was also a wheelchair user. We talked for about 15 minutes, he shared his experiences, and invited me to join the Disabled Students Union (DSU) as soon as I arrived in August. This brief conversation affirmed my gut instinct that I was going to find myself on that campus. The anxiety I felt when presented with information about having to hire my own personal staff, deal with timesheets, schedule every aspect of my daily needs, on top of the everyday course work of a UC Berkeley undergrad was somehow mitigated by the exhilaration of becoming independent! I felt that I was ready for this new experience in my life.

I moved to Berkeley by mid-August 2000. The whole concept of scheduling every aspect of my life was very foreign to me, and even more so, was the idea of having multiple people (of all genders) assist me with intimate needs. I remember the first day in which my parents were not present for my morning routine, a man walked into my dorm room. His name was Robert. During the routine, we chatted about trivial things and when it came time to do my hair, I thought that I was going to be in trouble; but I was very wrong: Robert made my hair look better than anyone before in my life. At that moment, I realized that everything would be okay for me there!

During my years at Berkeley, I still had to confront a social scene laden with "norms." My able-bodied peers dressed a certain way, attended parties, went on road trips, had relationship flings, and so forth. The societal expectation that I could not, nor would I want to, engage in these behaviors was saddening and segregating, especially when this rationale was used by my boyfriends as an explanation for failing romance and intimacy. My lived experience confirms the contention by Hanna and Rogovsky (1991) that the stigma that one carries as a person with a disability is used as a justification for avoidance between the abled-bodied individuals and people with disabilities. In my case, the burden of this struggle was made lighter because I was part of the disability community (and its allies) in Berkeley.

Like clockwork, on Wednesday evenings I would pull up to the automatic door of one of the largest buildings on the UC Berkeley campus and take the elevator to the second floor to find my people. There, our discussions would range from planning disability awareness weeks to coping with bad encounters with graduate student instructors (GSIs). We would also discuss how we could strategically participate in national campaigns to promote disability rights. These meetings almost always ended with impromptu dinner-and-drink sessions at a local bar.

One of the most memorable experiences I had as a first-year member of DSU was my trip to Sacramento along with my friends and fellow advocates Rebecca and Luisa. We were invited by the World Institute on Disability to testify in front of the State Assembly committee on behalf of Assembly Bill 925. The bill was introduced by Assemblywoman Dion Aroner (D-Berkeley) and proposed to let adults with severe disabilities retain Medi-Cal benefits until their yearly income reached $75,000 and remove the so-called marriage penalty so that assets of a spouse did not limit eligibility. Assembly Bill 925 passed the Assembly, but it was rejected by the California Senate based on "no-necessity" arguments.[2] This advocacy experience propelled me to become more involved in activism through the DSU to the extent that I became co-president in 2002. As leaders, my co-president and I made it our goal to increase the awareness of the disability experience among the general university population. To this end, we participated in and organized a multitude of diversity panels for students and faculty and wrote several editorials for the college newspaper.[3] Through our advocacy, the collective disability voice grew stronger on the UC Berkeley campus and, simultaneously, the power of my voice and activism grew in me with each passing moment.

My active participation in activities within a group with the common sociopolitical goal of visibility reinforced my understanding of the importance of not falling prey to self-pity and shame, which are implicit attitudes of oppressed members of society (Barnes et al., 1999; Charlton, 1998; Mitchell, 2007). Most importantly, it empowered me to fight against these feelings by adopting the lens of critical disability studies and the social model of disability (Devlin & Pothier, 2006; Linton, 1998; Ware, 2009; Wendell, 1996). The social model of disability offers individuals with disabilities a place from which we can fight back against societal misconceptions about disability, impairment, and handicap, and put forward the concept that disability is, in and of itself, a social, cultural, and political construct (Barnes et al., 1999; Charlton, 1998; Linton, 1998; Mitchell, 2007; Shapiro, 1994; Wendell, 1996). I responded to my internal call for activism by pursuing a major in political science, a minor in both Spanish and disability studies, and further becoming a leader within the campus community as co-facilitator of "Inclusion Initiative," a student-led course on the disability rights movement.

The ever-present life story of Ed Roberts and his colleagues, who pioneered first the independent living movement and later the disability rights movement (Shapiro, 1994), gave me the fortitude to never give up finding my place in the world, and to consider myself a "person first," notwithstanding my disability. Living with a disability offers an individual the opportunity to explore a unique dimension of what Charlton (1998) calls "raised consciousness," which he defines as:

> An experientially evolved awareness of self. Most often, raised consciousness involves a change in consciousness whereby the (false) notion of disability as a pitiful, medical condition has been replaced by the (true) awareness of disability as a social condition. This consciousness is profoundly liberating. (p. 118)

My years as an activist within and on behalf of the disability community, which included a 2½ week State Department-sponsored trip to Russia and a semester abroad in Chile, were some of the most fulfilling in my life. Having the opportunity to meet, and at times work with prominent disability activist leaders provided me with role models to emulate and to use as guides for leadership; this propels me to this day. Interestingly, throughout my academic pursuits, I have had the opportunity to read the stories of many activists with disabilities who speak of struggles and awakenings similar to mine in the realm of acceptance and political activism during their college years (see Ritvo, 2017).

## IT'S A HARD KNOCK LIFE: BECOMING A PROFESSIONAL

After years of activism and my graduation from UC Berkeley, I was hopeful (yet realistic) about my employment prospects as a college graduate with a disability. I knew that this would be difficult in my case because society, by sustaining an exclusionary stance towards people with disabilities (Barnes et al., 1999; Gleeson, 1999) would be stacking the cards against me in terms of job market options (U.S. Bureau of Labor Statistics, 2021). The root of this problem undoubtedly stems from marginalizing practices, institutional and societal, which results in the underrepresentation of people with disability in the workforce[4] and, by extension, in leadership positions. The magnitude of the problem was predicted by Barnes et al. (1999) when they state, "The historical experience of so many disabled people is of exclusion from, or marginalization and powerlessness at, the workplace" (p. 110).

This reality came to a head for me when, having made the decision that I wanted to become a teacher, I began applying for jobs. In early 2005, as a college senior, I entered an information session conducted by a well-known teacher placement agency. I was overly excited at the prospect of being part of this particular "family," about which many of my friends had positive things to say. After the initial overview of the organization by one of the team members, I engaged in a brief conversation with a woman who was in charge of placement in the region. It went something like this:

**Sofia:** Hi, thank you so much for coming to talk to us today.
**Woman:** Hello, how can I help you?
**Sofia:** My name is Sofia Vergara, and I will be graduating in May. I would be interested in joining your organization after I graduate. However, I was wondering if you have had applicants with disabilities in the past, and how their placement was handled.
**Woman:** [Looking me up and down before speaking again.] Well, I am not aware of anybody in a wheelchair being placed by our organization in the past. During training, our teachers live together in houses that are not accessible, and that could be a difficulty.
[End of conversation]

I had had this kind of interaction with people on many occasions before and also after this incident. However, what impacted me the most about this one instance was the abruptness with which the possibility of inclusion was disregarded, particularly from a person vested in the educational field. Furthermore, this person's attitude was in stark contrast to my experience in college since, at that particular moment, I remained in charge of the Inclusion Initiative course.

After this encounter, when filling out applications, I purposefully debated whether to explicitly disclose my disability or to leave it undisclosed until meeting in person. I tried this experiment both ways. When I first applied for a job at a tutoring company, I disclosed the fact that I was a wheelchair user during a phone interview at the start. That resulted in them not asking me for a second (in-person) interview. The second time, when I applied for a similar job, I did not disclose my disability until the in-person interview. They took one look at me and they did not make an offer. After many frustrating cycles with the same outcome, I reached out to the head of school at Olympia who had expressed to me previously his desire for me to come back to work there after graduation from college. I began my work there in October 2005. My first day on the job, I met with my former Spanish teacher and we discussed my being his assistant, while at the same time stepping in as a substitute for other teachers when needed.

Fortunately for me, it almost immediately became necessary that I take over a Spanish I class which had become too big for one teacher and needed to be split into two sections. Even though there were some students and their families that openly questioned my ability to teach because of my disability and young age, I persisted. To this day, I enjoy observing the students' willingness to adapt to "my difference," which often comes out in the way I teach. I cannot write on the board; thus, I use slide presentations. I cannot easily pass out papers; thus, I ask a student for that assistance. The students are always willing to help me to tidy up the classroom, and so forth. The bond that I typically create with my students is due in large part to the mutual flexibility in the relationship, and trust that I show them and that they show me. I am by no means an easy teacher; yet it feels good that each year many students tell me that they learn a lot more than just Spanish in my class.

After my first full year at Olympia, I applied, and was admitted (in 2007), to a local university's secondary education master's program and bilingual, cross-cultural, language and academic development (BCLAD) credential. At that time, I was still employed at Olympia School as an intern, although I had a full-time teaching load. Perhaps because of my history with the school, but surely in relation to my disability, I never felt acknowledged by the administration as a valuable part of the teaching faculty. In fact, I was explicitly told that there were questions from other people in the administration about how well I could handle more teaching responsibility.

During the 2 years of coursework while enrolled in a master's in education and credential program, I remember thinking that I would finally be valued as a qualified member of the faculty at Olympia High School. I was wrong. Even when I proved my dedication to the school, my career goals as an educator, and completed the necessary teaching credential and master's degree, some administrators felt entitled to question my competence and effectiveness without due cause, and only because of their preconceived notions that I may not be able to handle the classroom or the workload.

The obvious contradiction was that I already had a full-time load, and by all accounts (from most students, many parents, and other faculty), I was handling my responsibility very competently. Being loyal to the school and afraid of facing the need to find another job elsewhere given my disability, I accepted the inequity. But I was very aware of the discriminatory situation I was being boxed into; other less-qualified teachers with equivalent loads were more respected by the administration and contracted as full-time teachers. After many months of internal debate and advocacy, I was reclassified (though not retroactively) as a full-time teacher; nevertheless, this only happened after I demonstrated the completion of my master's program coursework (in 2009) and provided the school with the master's diploma from the university.

## My Relentless Struggle for Leadership at Olympia

During the ensuing years as a bona fide Spanish teacher with a master's and teaching credential, I enjoyed the collaborative learning environment that I created with my students and I strived to always give them my best. However, I am not sure that my workplace appreciated me as a potential transformative teacher leader, no matter how many innovative ideas and didactic tools I contributed to the school community. For example, 4 years ago, the position for modern language department head, previously occupied by a colleague with whom I worked very closely throughout my years at Olympia, became available. I made it clear to the newly hired school director that I was interested in the position, and I had the full support of a senior Spanish colleague. Making a long story short, I was sidelined: in a department composed of four Spanish teachers, one American Sign Language (ASL) teacher, and one part-time Mandarin teacher, the ASL teacher was chosen for the job. The decision allegedly was made because another Spanish teacher who also applied for the position apparently had too much "history" with me. The perplexing reality is that the "history" between me and this colleague stemmed from this teacher's false and discriminatory stance that the school cut me too much slack and that, consequently, he had to purportedly carry the burden of my disability. Despite the facts, the newly recruited school director took this male teacher's allegations seriously while squashing my aspirations and I was asked to continue with my teaching job. After much turmoil in the subsequent years—including an ugly incident where the person verbally accosted me and planted himself in front of my chair—he left the school that year. This ultimately opened the door for the creation of a new position as curriculum coordinator of the Spanish division. In September of 2016, I was offered and accepted this position.

At this point, you may wonder why I have accepted the obvious inequity that I have encountered in my current job at Olympia school. In answering this question, I must further examine the harsh reality that I have faced as a Latina with a disability when navigating through the multiple barriers encountered in finding, maintaining, and advancing in the ranks of employment in multiple realms.

## Reality Check

My disability has created in me a dialectical tension between accepting a certain level of dependence on family and friends in order to achieve a good quality of life and struggling to prove in the eyes of society that I am an independent person fully capable of achieving professional and leadership goals. Perhaps the most delicate aspect of this struggle is the awareness that because I am a woman with a physical disability, it has been challenging to achieve the typical social outlets that many women my age find. Admittedly, I have a very tight-knit group of friends and an amazing family, but at the same time, I do not have a partner, my own family, and so forth. Consequently, I tend to mask this loneliness by throwing myself wholeheartedly into my job and career as an educator and could not fathom the prospect of that not being a huge part of my identity. This is the main reason why, like it or not, I have kept myself in the educational realm and employed at Olympia school.

## Tolerant Utilization and Marginalizing Practices

My situation at Olympia falls squarely within the terms of "tolerant utilization" and "marginalization" that Linton (1998) uses to categorize people with disabilities in the eyes of society. It is obvious to me that, while I am necessary, adequate, and suitable for the school, the administration embraces the societal view and perceives me as little more than a good worker and a diversity check they can tick off. Furthermore, my struggle for recognition as an educational leader is tainted by marginalizing and biased perceptions of some colleagues and administrators who believe that, due to my physical limitations, I am unable to reach their standards of effective school leadership. Being treated this way makes me ponder why the school at times highlights my virtues as a "poster child" for disability (Longmore, 2016), while at the same time does not afford me the respect and equity that I merit, so that I might advance into a leadership post.

Regardless of now having a doctorate in educational leadership for social justice (since 2017) and being a curriculum coordinator in my school, I wake up every day feeling emotionally drained by my perceived irrelevance. My attempts to bring up issues regarding curriculum matters in departmental meetings do not always receive equivalent consideration by the department head as those from other colleagues. This person's infantilizing approach, echoed by some of my colleagues, interferes with the flow of the discussions, and ultimately weakens or undermines my opinions.

It seems paradoxical that whenever it is convenient for the school to show the diversity of teaching faculty in front of potential parents, review teams, or donors, and so forth, I am typically chosen for a classroom visit and my disability is talked about and/or exalted as "special."

Despite their awareness of my preparedness for educational leadership, certain members of the school administration, and many of my colleague teachers, are still not ready to accept that my opinion matters at least as much as theirs. This creates a sense of frustration that consumes my interest in being heard, and the only reason that I persevere in this endeavor is my passion for social justice education for the benefit of my students.

## Doors Open and Close: Doctoral and Postdoctoral Opportunities

Frustration and anger can be great motivational forces, and I channeled this energy into furthering my quest for growth in the realm of educational leadership. Indeed, my years in the doctoral program were transformative; we (as a cohort) were asked to grapple with what being a leader for social justice meant and had to forge our own path toward that goal. Establishing relationships with professors who not only embodied social justice leadership but were also capable of seeing beyond my disability and understood me as a person first, was an invigorating experience that ultimately guided me to the road of self-discovery and culminated in a doctoral dissertation of which I am incredibly proud (Vergara, 2017). There were moments of difficulty and not all the professors in the program equally embodied a critical awareness of social justice or of disabilities. Overall, however, and given my past experiences in other settings, the good far outweighed the bad.

In the weeks leading to graduation, I received a phone call from the university's communications office telling me that I was nominated to be pictured on the official graduation posters for the School of Education and invited me to schedule a photo shoot. After much struggling and reflection with the idea of becoming, once again, the "poster child" that I have always dreaded becoming, I wrote him an email and accepted the invitation. In this instance, the honor extended felt meaningful and outweighed my discomfort or fears about why I had been chosen. My life has truly been a paradox!

After receiving my doctorate, I had the (perhaps) naïve impression that it would be "easier" to find leadership positions in K–12 administration or professorships in higher education institutions. On the positive side, I was hired as a part-time lecturer at the same university from which I received my EdD degree. This gave me the opportunity to maintain my teaching position at Olympia while teaching evening classes to future educators in the areas of special education and disability. The topics covered in the five courses I taught ranged from multicultural awareness, behavioral support, IEP development at the undergraduate level, to the development of multitiered systems of support and response to intervention, at the graduate level. I put my heart and soul into developing the curriculum and delivering the content in an engaging way, and I thoroughly enjoyed my collaboration with graduate and undergraduate students alike, established great rapport with them, and received the highest marks in student evaluations. Nonetheless, although I remained ready when this university has more openings, a full-time faculty position has never been offered regardless of my multiple applications for such positions when they have been posted. In the absence of a concrete offer for full-time employment at my alma mater, I have often applied for similar positions at other universities and/or administrative leadership positions at K–12 institutions, but I have never passed the interview stage.

I recognize that it is not easy to separate, at any given moment, which of my identities (i.e., cultural, gender, or disability) is the dominant source for discriminatory treatments to which I have been subjected. The fact that I am a Latina woman with a disability places me at a greater disadvantage in obtaining leadership positions than even individuals with a disability from the dominant culture. McDonald et al. (2007) and Mitchel (2007) note that marginalization becomes exacerbated when a person belongs to multiple oppressed groups compared to what they might experience if there was only one contributing factor for oppression by society. What is safe to say is that the intersectionality of all three of these subjugated positionalities have contributed to the struggles I have faced in my efforts to contribute as an educational leader.

## OTHER CAREER PATHS

### Board of Directors

As it may be clear so far, I have devoted an important part of my adult life fighting for equity for individuals with disabilities. An interesting opportunity came my way in 2018 when my mother was asked to apply to participate on the board of directors of an organization dedicated to serving individuals with developmental disabilities. My mother immediately suggested that I would be a much more adequate person for such a job and that spring, I began serving on this board. The advocacy aspect of this board appointment reactivated, at a higher level, the passion for activism that had been dormant in me since my college years. Consequently, I dedicated myself to the work on the board's activities with great energy and dedication. This dedication was recognized when the position of board chair opened, and I was approached by its executive committee asking to serve as an interim chair. Interestingly, I became the first person served by this organization to be elected in 2019 as board chair.

My time in this role, which ended in July 2020, was full of ups and downs. On one hand, I learned a great deal about organizational management, governance, and communication, and had the opportunity to work intensely with fellow disability advocates with the goal of pushing the organization to set conditions of empowerment for the people served. I also made great friends among very accomplished colleagues. However, it is unfortunate that my election as board chair segregated the board members into two factions: (a) those who believed that I was a capable leader who provided a fresh perspective and was not afraid of asking the hard questions about the institution, and (b) those who saw me as a little more than a "token." Members of the latter group were happy to have me as the board chair as a figurehead of inclusion, but they had serious difficulties accepting my value as a leader. In fact, in meetings my opinions and action plans were only fully considered after these initiatives were first endorsed by able-bodied members who agreed with me. Interestingly, in their literature review, Beckwith et al. (2016) note as a major systemic flaw the fact that individuals with developmental disabilities are often invited to participate on boards of policy-making organizations with roles often being symbolic gestures that result in presence without genuine inclusion. It is very unfortunate that this might have been true in my case.

All things considered, while I was the chair, the board had the job of hiring a new executive director for the institution. I was able to lead the search committee towards the accomplishment of this major task effectively in a timely manner. Unfortunately, the divisions amongst board members for the reasons described above started to impair my effectiveness as chair and I did not want to participate in dysfunctions that could ultimately impact the individuals served by the organization in a negative way. For this reason, I resigned as chair, but I remain on the board (as requested by members of the community), and as an ex-officio member of its executive committee.

An important reason for this continuation is my strong conviction that individuals with disabilities must individually and collectively break the current paradigm of marginalization that society attempts to impose on us in order to attain the leadership positions for which we are qualified and deserve. Today, this means that we must make our voices heard either in social media, or as active participants in protests, to constantly fight for our rights for independence and inclusive education. My experiences on the board of directors have taught me that organizations which are committed to serving people with disabilities and promoting their empowerment should vigorously reject tokenism and develop an atmosphere of inclusivity and awareness among all personnel, most importantly in the upper leadership tiers. This awareness must be geared towards the dismantling of structural and attitudinal barriers, and the typically engrained notion that people with disabilities cannot perform at the level of an able-bodied person. Unfortunately, organizations that effectively embrace these principles are rare. Some organizations that clearly embrace these principles are nonprofit institutions such as the Centers for Independent Living, World Institute on Disability, and Disability Rights and Education Defense Fund. I propose that an effective path for organizations attempting to equalize the opportunities for leadership for employees with disabilities, would be to approach these well-known institutions and inquire about their hiring practices, training of human resources (HR) personnel, professional development activities, and employment turnover rate.

## Bridges to Inclusion

After much iteration of successes, failures, frustrations, and nonstarters, I have come to believe in the words of Michael Jordan: "Some people want it to happen, some wish it would happen, others make it happen" (Jordan, n.d.). In my case, "it" is a leadership role in which I am valued for all that I bring to the table.

For many years, a colleague from Olympia and I had been entertaining the idea of establishing a company entirely devoted to the promotion of inclusive education, professional development for educators, and disability awareness in general, as well as the direct support of individuals with disabilities (and their families) who need educational advocacy. With these goals in mind, we recently founded Bridges to Inclusion (http://www.bridgestoinclusion.org). We are excited that the company has obtained great traction, and already has had the opportunity to deliver professional development workshops to a local arts university, as well as to develop webinars offering direct support for faculty members and students as they embark on remote learning. As co-founders of Bridges to Inclusion, we believe administrators, teachers, school personnel, and in general all inclusion-driven organizations, should be given the opportunity to engage in professional development that specifically focuses on the integration of disability awareness into their curriculum and/or business models. I believe that this commitment will help correct implicit and explicit biases that marginalize, isolate, exclude, and oppress individuals with disabilities. Conversely, we hope it will encourage all participants to empower their constituents with disabilities to assume leadership roles within organizations and their community at large.

## BEING AT PEACE WITH MY DISABILITY

I hope that my brief exploration of the challenges and experiences in my journey as an educator highlights and exposes issues that may be determinant of the limited representation of people with disabilities in educational leadership—on one hand, and on the other, helps to guide future practices to ensure equitable opportunities for those who wish to pursue this path. I have shared epiphanies and included episodic data in order to give voice to the dialectic of empowerment and oppression of people with disabilities (Charlton, 1998) and to also create the space for critical transformative leadership within the disability community, as well as to call for inclusive spaces for transformative leaders with disabilities outside the context of the disability community.

## NOTES

1. The DSRP program at UC Berkeley was closed in 2014 when the California Department of Rehabilitation changed its funding model and decided not to fund residential programs outside of independent living centers run by the state.
2. *The Los Angeles Times* published on July 26, 2001, an editorial entitled "Staying Poor to Stay Alive" in reference to my testimony and arguing in favor of AB 925.
3. For example, disabled students' services, Daily Californian letter to the Editor, April 19, 2002, http://archive.dailycal.org/article.php?id=8398
4. The above referenced report by the U.S. Bureau of Labor Statistics states, "In 2019, the employment-population ratio for persons with a disability between ages 16 to 64 edged up to 30.9 percent, while the ratio for persons without a disability in the same age group increased to 74.6 percent." (p. 1)

## REFERENCES

Americans With Disabilities Act of 1990, Pub. L. No. 101-336, § 2, 104 Stat. 328 (1991) C.F.R (1990).

Annamma, S. A., Connor, D. J., & Ferri, B. A. (2016). Dis/ability critical race studies (DisCrit): Theorizing at the intersections of race and dis/ability. In *DisCrit: Disability studies and critical race theory in education* (pp. 9–32). Teachers College Press.

Barnes, C., Mercer, G., & Shakespeare, T. (1999). *Exploring disability: A sociological introduction.* Cambridge University Press.

Beckwith, R.-M., Friedman, M. G., & Conroy, J. W. (2016). Beyond tokenism: People with complex needs in leadership roles: A review of the literature. *Inclusion, 4*(3), 137–155. https://doi.org/10.1352/2326-6988-4.3.137

Charlton, J. (1998). *Nothing about us without us: Disability oppression and empowerment.* University of California Press.

Devlin, R., & Pothier, D. (Eds.). (2006). *Critical disability theory: Essays in philosophy, politics, policy, and law.* UBC Press.

Education for all Handicapped Children Act, no. Pub. L. No. 94-142, 89 Stat. 773 (1975).

Freire, P. (2008). *Education for critical consciousness.* Continuum.

Gleeson, B. (1999). *Geographies of disability.* Routledge.

Hanna, W. J., & Rogovsky, B. (1991). Women with disabilities: Two handicaps plus. *Disability, Handicap & Society, 6*(1), 49–63.

Individuals With Disabilities Education Act Amendments of 1997, Pub. L. No.105-17, 111 Stat. 37 (1997).

Jordan, M. (n.d.). *Michael Jordan quotes.* BrainyQuote. https://www.brainyquote.com/quotes/michael_jordan_167382?src=t_make_it_happen

Linton, S. (1998). *Claiming disability: Knowledge and identity.* NYU Press.

Longmore, P. K. (2016). "Heaven special child": The making of poster children. In L. J. Davis (Ed.), *The disability studies reader* (pp. 35–42). Routledge.

McDonald, K. E., Keys, C. B., & Balcazar, F. E. (2007). Disability, race/ethnicity and gender: Themes of cultural oppression, acts of individual resistance. *American Journal of Community Psychology, 39*(1–2), 145–161. https://doi.org/10.1007/s10464-007-9094-3

Mitchell, D. D. (2007). *Crises of identifying: Negotiating and mediating race, gender, and disability.* The University of Alabama.

National Center on Secondary Education and Transition. (2011). *Self-determination for middle and high school students.* http://www.ncset.org/topics/sdmhs/default.asp?topic=30

Ritvo, A. (2017). From poison ivy to live oak: How transferring colleges changed my perception of disability. In M. Jarman, L. Monahan, & A. Quaggin Harkin (Eds.), *Barriers and belonging: Personal narratives of disability* (pp. 25–31). Temple University Press.

Shapiro, J. P. (1994). *No pity: People with disabilities forging a new civil rights movement.* Three Rivers Press.

Snyder, T. D., & Dillow, S. A. (2015). Digest of education statistics 2013 (NCES 2015-011). National Center for Education Statistics, Institute of Education Sciences, U.S. Department of Education.

U.S. Bureau of Labor Statistics. (2021). *Economic news release: Persons with a disability: Labor force characteristics summary.* [Economic news release]. https://www.bls.gov/news.release/disabl.nr0.htm#:~:text=Employment%20In%202019%2C%20the%20employment,percentage%20point%20over%20the%20year.

U.S. Department of Education. (2010). *Thirty-five years of progress in educating children with disabilities through IDEA.*

Vergara, S. (2017). *Lived history of a transformative leader with disability: An evocative autoethnography for social justice* [Loyola Marymount University]. http://search.proquest.com/openview/1caed4efd4209c467ce5be7f5fd89d90/1?pq-origsite=gscholar&cbl=18750&diss=y

Ware, L. (2009). Writing, identity, and the other: Dare we do disability studies? In A. Darder, M. Baltodano, & R. D. Torres (Eds.), *The critical pedagogy reader* (pp. 347–416). Routledge.

Wendell, S. (1996). *The rejected body: Feminist philosophical reflections on disability.* Routledge.

CHAPTER 20

# DISABLED STUDENTS IN COLLEGE-GOING CULTURES

## Positing Frameworks for a "College-for-All" Culture

**Robert Cooper**
*University of California, Los Angeles*

**Brande M. Otis**
*University of California, Los Angeles*

Improving access to college for marginalized students and students of color has been a focus of educational research and practice in the K–16 pipeline, and many practitioners and scholars would agree that all young people should have the opportunity to attend college. Previous research reports that students of color often aspire to college, but many students are often encouraged into community colleges with no promise or plan to transfer (Pérez & McDonough, 2008) or attend schools where relevant college preparatory materials and coursework are provided to students tracked into higher academic hierarchies (Oakes et al., 2006). Despite efforts to

*Who Decides?*, pages 491–514
Copyright © 2022 by Information Age Publishing
www.infoagepub.com
All rights of reproduction in any form reserved.

improve college matriculation and readiness for all students, students of color with disabilities are still enrolling in college at lower rates than their nondisabled peers (Newman et al., 2011; Smith et al., 2012). And while the Individuals With Disabilities in Education Act (2004) mandates that schools help plan for postsecondary opportunities for special education students, little is known about the impact this policy has for students of color receiving special education services.

Data that details the increased enrollment of Black and Latinx students and disabled students, while positive, often do not employ an intersectional lens of the ways that race and disability work together. Furthermore, it is less clear the rates at which students of color with disabilities are enrolling in (and completing) college, and subsequently, how secondary schools are supporting transitions into college. Drawing from literature around college-going cultures and critical theories of disability and race, this chapter builds upon an original conceptual framework for building college-going cultures, to accommodate for and address the needs of disabled students of color.

This chapter's purpose is to think with and extend existing literature around college-going culture, as well as push the authors' conceptual frameworks of college-going cultures. For the purposes of this chapter, college-going cultures are defined as school cultures that include caring environments to support all students and families in obtaining the information, tools, and resources necessary to ensure access to and success in postsecondary education (Cooper et al., 2016). Not included within this definition, however, is the inherent complexity of the processes and factors that contribute to college-going for marginalized students. The phenomena of college going and college access are complex and are mediated and impacted by a myriad of factors, including the social, cultural, political, structural, and procedural elements of communities and schools. However, for the purposes of this chapter, the focus is on the practices, behaviors, and systems enacted by school staff that support or inhibit college going for disabled students of color.

The processes that inhibit or support disabled students of color in college going are complex, and should be considered as such. This chapter explores how an original conceptual framework might support high schools and school administrators in developing college-going cultures that truly support all students. This means acknowledging how special education and disabled students are often structurally and practically siloed in ways that inadvertently leave such communities out of conversations about college going. This also means reckoning with the power that special education has to label and prescribe education for disabled students, in addition to considering how high schools also prepare disabled students of color for the social and political aspects of college life.

## Purpose, Context, and Position: The Reason to Expand

The authors served as a research and documentation team for the efforts of 10 California public secondary schools in their attempts to build and sustain college-going cultures. Named the "College-Going Culture Grant" (CGCG), the research and documentation included school-level survey data and hundreds of interviews with school administrators, teachers, students, and families geared towards understanding what it means and what it looks like to develop a college-going culture. Led by the first author, the team developed a college-going culture conceptual framework that consisted of (a) clear expectations, (b) faculty involvement, (c) student identity, (d) continuous learning and improvement, (e) school-wide equity, and (f) a culture of care to understand and implement what it meant to develop a school climate and culture that was centered on college going for all students. Motivated by educational issues of racial inequity, tracking, and unequal access and opportunity to college-preparatory coursework, the original college-going culture framework was to help schools, practitioners, and researchers understand the many ways that schools, as institutions, might function to serve every student.

Throughout the time of the project, the framework was used in schools by administrators to help develop the systems, procedures, and policies necessary to support college-going cultures and subsequently, college going for traditionally underrepresented students. And, as this project continued, researchers with different kinds of expertise came and went, one of whom (the second author) helped the team think more capaciously about how to include the particular needs of students with disabilities. This project continues to be a rigorous and reflective space in which researchers, practitioners, and communities engage in a continuous process of learning and growth.

In this chapter, the authors pursue a conceptual project that explores the ways that leaders and educators might build and sustain college-going cultures in secondary schools, challenging and critiquing the existing framework to move towards a true "college for all" culture. Here, the authors ask that readers work through and grapple with the meaning of "college for all," as they think with such questions as, "What does it mean to be college ready?"; "Who is college ready?"; and conversely, "Are colleges 'ready' for students labeled with disabilities?" The following questions are used as guides for the conceptual goals of this chapter:

1. How might we adapt existing frameworks for college-going cultures to be more equitable and accepting of students with disabilities?
2. How can school leaders utilize a framework of equity and inclusive college going on their campus?

In pursuing the above questions, the authors provide a brief description of college-going cultures and their relevancy in supporting equity and access for traditionally marginalized students. Next, the authors ground the guiding questions by historicizing intersectional marginalization for racially/ethnically minoritized and disabled secondary school students. Next, the authors' originally posed framework is presented and critiqued for where it falls short in serving and supporting disabled students, drawing upon professional experience and academic scholarship to generate suggestions for how the framework can be improved. This chapter concludes with guiding thoughts for high-school leaders and administrators, who are working towards building and sustaining college-for-all cultures, and implications for how to build beyond K–12 and challenge higher education institutions to equally support college going for disabled students of color.

## Race, Disability, and Access to Higher Education

Inequitable schooling cannot be divorced from this country's longstanding history of oppression for marginalized groups, particularly for those with disabilities (Artiles, 2019). Disability labels in public education have a longstanding history of unaddressed ableism, racism, and classism in schools. As such, the intersectional relationships between disability and race are complex, and Annamma et al. (2013) write that we must interrogate "why so many students labeled with a dis/ability, particularly students of color, are either experiencing failure or being perceived as failing and on what grounds" (p. 6).

Historically, associations between race and disability were used to justify unfair and unequal treatment, in addition to violence (Erevelles & Minear, 2010), and it is necessary to wrestle with disability labeling as having been historically used to segregate and overtly discriminate against disabled students of color (Ferri & Connor, 2005; Graves & Mitchell, 2011; Menchaca, 1997; Valencia, 1997). However, the practices of ableism are not confined to schools. During the eugenics movement, understandings of disability shifted from the *symbolic* to the *medical* (Connor & Valle, 2015), leading to the understanding that disability was a pathology meant to be "cured, corrected, or rehabilitated" (Couser, 2011, p. 22). Those who could not be "cured" were declared unfit for society and were thought to be the cause of some of society's problems, and in the 1920s many people of color deemed "feebleminded" were sterilized and/or subjected to mistreatment (Connor & Valle, 2015).

Similar ideas carried over into schools, as students of color were disproportionately declared intellectually or emotionally unfit for education and pushed into segregated classrooms with less rigorous and/or enriching curriculum (Sleeter, 2010). Such practices stratified disabled students of color and justified pre-existing educational inequities (Sullivan & Artiles, 2011). In cases like *Larry P. v. Riles* (1972) and *Diana v. State Board of Education* (1970), students of color with disabilities were placed into what were termed "dead-end" classes that provided little room for academic enrichment or engaging curriculum (Cruz & Rodl, 2018). This history is not isolated, nor singular, and in fact reflects larger ideological projects that systematically sustained the ideas that Black, Latinx, and Indigenous students were intellectually, behaviorally, and emotionally unfit for education. Similar ideas persist today and are among the several factors contributing to the disproportionate representation of Black, Latinx, and Indigenous students in the special education categories of intellectual disability, specific learning disability, and emotional or behavioral disorders (Harry & Klingner, 2014; Losen & Orfield, 2002). These categories, also known as high-incidence disabilities, are often interpreted as more subjective as they rely primarily upon professional judgment and are bound less to physical markers (Annamma et al., 2013). Students of color with high-incidence disabilities will be the focus of this chapter due to the complicated relationship between such disability labels, race/ethnicity, and educational opportunity.

Students of color in special education do not often receive the benefits of special education, and instead, may face increasing marginalization at the intersection of disability status and race/ethnicity (Artiles et al., 2016). When we consider issues of college access and opportunity, the intersections of both race and disability nuance conversations around who goes to college, who does not, and why. While high-incidence disabilities like learning disabilities make up a significant population of disabled students who go to college, this conversation is highly racialized, and students with learning disabilities who go to college are more likely to come from White and middle to upper class backgrounds (Newman et al., 2009). This is in spite of the fact that many students with high-incidence disabilities aspire towards college (Lipscomb et al., 2017). Although we see that disabled students (particularly those of color) are enrolling in college at increasing rates,[1] they are still underrepresented on college campuses (Gregg, 2007; Newman et al., 2009; Pena et al., 2015; Snyder et al., 2019).

## Disabled Access and Preparation for College: What Does it Mean to Be College Ready?

Federal legislation and pushes for college readiness in secondary schools has been a topic of concern for over a decade (Monahan et al., 2020). College readiness is understood to be a "level of preparation a student needs in order to enroll and succeed, without remediation, in a credit-bearing

general education course" (Conley, 2008, p. 4). Updates to the Individuals
With Disabilities in Education Act (IDEA, 2004) mandate that students receiving special education services have a coordinated and individualized set
of goals, services, and activities designed to prepare them for postsecondary
opportunities. Specifically, the Individualized Transition Plan (ITP) supports college planning, vocational/career planning, and assisted living if
appropriate (Monahan et al., 2020). Some scholars argue that the addition
of mandatory transition planning has led to the increased representation
of students with disabilities on college campuses (Madaus & Shaw, 2006).
However, this connection is not as apparent for disabled students of color
(Baer et al., 2011), as they are still underrepresented on college campuses.

For disabled and nondisabled students alike, their success in college
is often, in part, predicated on the level of support and preparation they
received in high school and the level of institutional and social support
offered at their college of choice (Cooper & Davis, 2015). Many disabled
students of color, including those with high-incidence disabilities, do attend community colleges and 4-year universities and can successfully attend
to the intellectual demands of college curriculum, provided there is support (Trainin & Swanson, 2005; Troiano et al., 2010). However, without adequate academic and social preparation from their secondary institutions,
their efforts may be less successful. Hence, the authors find that there is a
need for a college-going culture aimed at supporting these transitions—focusing on institutional, structural, and systematic changes that support all
students in their matriculation to college.

## College Going and the Need for College-Going Cultures

Normalized processes in schools inevitably shape who is consistently afforded access to college through (a) opportunities to take and succeed in
rigorous coursework, (b) learning and hearing about college applications
and their processes, and (c) receiving clear and uplifting messages about
college as a viable option. These affordances, however, are repeatedly and
normatively provided to those students tracked into Honors/AP courses,
students declared as "gifted," and students who have learned to navigate
traditional schooling structures. This system of opportunity serves to maintain existing ideas about who is "right" for college, by continuing to provide
access and privileges to those who have traditionally benefited from and
enrolled in college. Those who fall outside of the norm are left out of many
systematic opportunities for college preparation, and their lack of enrollment in college is seen as a personal failure and deficit rather than a reflection of the privileges afforded by their institution.

The growing understanding of the ways that college access and college
preparation are stratified has led to a shift in academic scholarship. More

and more, educators and researchers are arguing for college-going cultures, a system of support set up to provide all students with equitable access to information, guidance, and support so that any student has the option to go to college (McKillip et al., 2013; McClafferty et al., 2002). College-going cultures are schools that provide access to rigorous coursework for all students (Corwin & Tierney, 2007), build positive school identities aligned with college going and develop college-going knowledge (Conley, 2007), and maintain high expectations for all students (McKillip et al., 2013). Such a culture attempts to ensure that all students have access to information about college, are prepared for college, and have access to comprehensive counseling through organized institutionalized supports. Additionally, such cultures consist of school-wide practices like consistent and ongoing communication with families, clear college expectations in all classrooms, and strong college partnerships.

Research shows that high school cultures are powerful influences on students' aspirations to attend college (Cooper & Davis, 2015). Aspects of high school cultures that influence student preparation and aspiration include, but are not limited to, coursework, teacher and staff expectations, college exposure, and college preparatory resources (e.g., PSAT/SAT tutoring; McClafferty-Jarsky et al., 2009). Movements towards equitable access to college means accounting for these factors and transforming schools at the political, technical, social, and cultural levels (Cooper et al., 2020); education leaders have a crucial role to play in these kinds of transformations.

Building a college-going culture means constructing and maintaining a strong mission and vision for the school, strengthening partnerships among school staff, and supporting school staff in their respective roles (McKillip et al., 2012). In a study of college-going culture development in an urban high school, counselors were given the flexibility and autonomy to work across classrooms and grade levels to connect staff members and students and view the systemic challenges and barriers to access schoolwide (McKillip et al., 2012). School principals can develop a school-wide mission and vision aligned with college-going culture, and support school counselors in developing the relationships and partnerships needed to address the needs of every student.

Previous research has noted the importance of positive school leadership in supporting students of color in their college-going ideations and realizations (Yavuz, 2016). For many students without access to college-going knowledge and preparation at home, schools are often the only exposure to college knowledge that some students have. While designated school staff like academic counselors are helpful for students in preparing for college and receiving college-going information, in large public schools, one or two designated professionals are often not enough to reach all students—particularly disabled students of color. Instead, we argue that a focus on supporting students at the school-wide level is crucial to encouraging all students to go to college, making school-wide leadership and vision vastly important.

Building such a college-going culture is predicated upon consistent and clear expectations for the school. School leadership, both "informal" or charismatic leaders and administrators who possess decision-making and positional power, are important for sustaining and carrying out a vision for the school.

## AN ITERATIVE CONCEPTUAL FRAMEWORK FOR BUILDING COLLEGE-GOING CULTURES

Theory helps us identify, interpret, and refine our ideas of and practices geared towards college-going cultures in schools. It is important to ground theory in the experiences, needs, and wants of the communities they are meant to support and serve (Annamma et al., 2019). As stated previously, this conceptual framework was initially aligned with and for visions of racial equity, with the primary goal of supporting schools in dismantling barriers to college for students of color. Upon reviewing the conceptual framework (see Figure 20.1), the authors concluded that it did not include a consideration of the unique barriers to college that disabled students of color face, and how schools and school leaders might dismantle them.

**Figure 20.1**   Original conceptual framework from CAPP college-going culture project.

The following are the domains of the college-going culture conceptual framework. Each domain exists as it did in the initial framework, however here, the authors spend time discussing what these domains mean and look like for disabled students of color. Drawing from collective experience in the field of education and special education, critical scholarship in race and disability and college-going cultures, the authors take this opportunity to explore how these domains can be used to advance the dreams and aspirations of disabled students of color.

## First Domain: Clear College Expectations

In experience working with college-going culture schools, the authors found that many schools struggled to communicate clear college expectations. The idea of clear college expectations encompasses a school's (and its stakeholders) belief that all young people are capable of attending and succeeding in college. The definition of clear college expectations builds upon the work of McClafferty and colleagues (2009) who argued:

> If all students are to be prepared for a full range of postsecondary options when they graduate from high school, then the explicit goals of this preparation must be clearly defined. These goals must be communicated in ways that make them part of the culture of the school, such that students, family members such as parents, teachers, administrators, and staff recognize the role that each plays in preparing students for college. (p. 4)

Consistent with previous literature around expectations, high expectations are often correlated with more favorable outcomes (Reveles & Brown, 2008). For a school and its staff to have clear college expectations for disabled students would mean that educators are operating from the assumption that disabled students should be and can be prepared for college success.

The original conceptual framework for student-centered college going did not consider the pervasive language and ideology of ableism within special education and school systems—particularly, the ways that the exclusion of disabled students from college going are "justified." Special education in schools employs a positivist, legalized, and medicalized framing and understanding of disability, which often dictates that disabilities are deficits that are located in young people, rather than in a complex interplay of sociopolitical and physical barriers and inaccessibility (Ong-Dean, 2005; Runswick-Cole & Hodge, 2009). Special education's discourse around disability makes it easy to dismiss disabled students and disabled students of color as *unfit* for college, due to the "deficits" of their disability. For example, in schools, school staff use state law to define and determine eligibility. Such definitions are often (but not always) aligned with medical language. The California Education Code (Eligibility

Criteria, Cal Code of Regulations, 3030) defines an emotional disturbance as a condition that "cannot be explained by intellectual, sensory or health factors," and an "inability to build or maintain satisfactory interpersonal relationships," as well as "inappropriate types of behavior or feelings under normal circumstances" (5 CCR 3030). While there is little research that examines the language around students labeled with emotional disturbances, author experience shares that often, students of color labeled with emotional disturbances (often boys) are associated with criminalization rather than college going. Schools must develop clear college expectations and preparation for disabled students of color—operating from an equity and justice framework, as well as a critical, sociocultural understanding of disability.

The clear college expectations domain reflects the practices that teachers employ to communicate their high expectations that all students be prepared for college. This includes regular conversations about college, "Where would you like to go to college, and why?" in addition to engaging students with rigorous curriculum and materials, designed for diverse and disabled learners. Here, in the expansion of this framework, the authors suggest that schools utilize the ITP space as a way to document and structure rigorous postsecondary planning for students with disabilities. Additionally, part of this domain means that disabled students must also be provided with multiple opportunities to succeed in coursework that will support college preparation.

The implementation and sustaining of this particular domain are often easier said than done. Although most educators are committed to the well-being and success of their students, the concept of clear college expectations is still predicated upon a student's perceived aptitude for college, leaving many young people with disabilities entirely out of school-wide conversations concerning college access. It is therefore important for school leaders and administrators to enact a vision for the school that breaks down assumptions and ideas about who should go to college. This could include engaging in professional development that shifts discourse around disability from medical/legal to a more sociocultural and critical framing. This might also include working with educators to analyze school data that illuminates academic achievement and discipline referrals for students of color with disabilities. Analyzing this kind of data can reveal inequitable trends and practices that result from staff expectations.

## Second Domain: Faculty Involvement in the College-Going Process

The faculty involvement in the college-going process domain refers to the ways that school professionals must intentionally and tangibly be involved in the college preparation, planning, and application processes of their students. This includes developing and sustaining meaningful relationships with young people and their families as predicates to supporting college ideation and matriculation. For school staff to be involved and active planners for disabled students of color, they must be understanding and supportive of the many ways in which a young person's disability "shows up." Too often disabled young people are not met with the level and consistency of support and space and care that they are owed. And while there are inevitable struggles of schooling and education within our current systems, educators can (and wish to) provide targeted care to young people.

Educators should be actively involved within the ITP and advocating for its start well before a child turns 16. While the ITP is a useful space, and should be used as a way to communicate and enact college expectations, much of the college-going literature states that postsecondary planning for students should start as early as eighth grade (Cooper & Liou, 2007). School staff can utilize this space to structure the support that disabled students of color receive. Educators should be discussing and positing a variety of opportunities and options for young disabled people in collaboration with parents and families. This means being flexible with course assignments (what they are "meant" to look like) and providing a variety of opportunities and methods for students with disabilities to receive proper feedback on college application materials.

Institutionally, school leaders can support nonacademic relationships between school staff and students by incorporating an advisory period into the regular school day (McKillip et al., 2012). During advisory, school staff can meet with students and go over concrete steps for navigating the college preparation, required coursework, the college application process, financial aid, and more. Such relationships allow all students to meet with an educator around what college-going and college-choice looks like for them.

## Third Domain: Healthy Student Academic Identity

In the third domain, a healthy student academic identity is a construct that is student-centered and determined. As such, the authors draw heavily upon student affirmations and understandings of academic identities. Here, the authors question the term "healthy," and welcome critiques, suggestions, and recommendations for how to envision academic identities that do not necessarily communicate visions of "wellness."

In short, this domain refers to the opinions and beliefs that young people have of and for themselves in academic spaces. The authors spent time with school staff building college-going cultures in schools, and during that time wondered about how student academic identity impacted college-going ideation and enrollment. However, here, the purpose is to think more about how disabled students, particularly those of color are positioned, understood, and felt in classrooms. How do disabled students of color perceive and understand themselves within academic spaces? Are such young people encouraged, affirmed in their complexity as humans, to be their full, brilliant, curious selves? An interpretation of "healthy student academic identity" should be aligned with a drive to free young people from the constraints of identifying with an institution that may not necessarily serve them, and instead encourage the development of an alignment with a purpose, value, or belief that might guide them in their futures.

Part of doing this includes giving space for disabled students of color to develop self-determining practices and beliefs and support their agency. School leaders have opportunities to lead schools in developing student-led IEP meetings and encouraging the systems and supports that help young people develop more agency within special education processes. While less practiced in schools, student-led IEP meetings are meaningful opportunities for young people to engage with the political and legal components of their education planning; increase their own advocacy and agency within school structures; and develop further ownership over the ways their accommodations, modifications, and services are structured (Mitchell et al., 2019).

In a study of students who were Deaf and Hard-of-Hearing, a student-led IEP and self-determination program helped students develop further understandings of their legal rights within the special education process. It also supported the college-choice process by having programming and conversations about the competence and philosophy of the disability services centers at colleges of interest and made connections with current college students who were Deaf or Hard-of-Hearing (Mitchell et al., 2019).

Additionally, healthy academic identities are supported when students see young people, like themselves, who are successful in college. This might mean creating an alumni program of volunteers who can provide advice, mentoring, or support for like-disabled students of color, being careful to align folks with similar disabilities (e.g., a student with dyslexia might benefit from support from another student with dyslexia).

## Fourth Domain: Continuous Improvement in Teaching and Learning

The fourth domain, continuous improvement in teaching and learning is interested in detailing the ways that educators might exercise and practice a mindset of growth and learning towards teaching. This domain was posited to frame the ways that educators might continue to refine their craft, and use professional development, experiences within the classroom, and tips from other educators to shape the way they support their students' college going. Educational leaders must engage their school teams in regular, data-based conversations about disproportionality in special education and discipline. To further this domain, the authors encourage special educators and general educators to build upon one another's practices, working collaboratively so that more and broader opportunities are available to disabled students of color. In light of some districts' and states' pushes toward inclusion, general educators should become increasingly adept at supporting, accommodating, and uplifting disabled students in their classrooms.

## Fifth Domain: School-Wide Focus on Academic Equity

The school-wide focus on academic equity domain refers to a general need for schools to think about issues of equity broadly, and not as sole features of classrooms or individuals. Key features of this domain are interested in equitable and restorative discipline practices, abolishing tracking, providing equitable and widespread access to "A–G" requirements (a sequence of high school courses that students must pass with a grade of "C" or higher to be eligible for CSU/UC admittance), Honors/AP coursework, and developing systems in which all students are provided with resources and services that fit their needs.

In the authors' own experiences within college-going culture schools there were still several conversations where educators communicated a lowered expectation—and thereby limited opportunity—for disabled students of color. Some educators spoke of capacity and what seemed "reasonable" for certain disabled students of color. Yet, such narratives and belief systems again place responsibility on disabled students of color for not successfully navigating a system that was not built with them in mind. Similarly, school administrators can work to shift conversations, narratives, and belief systems about whose responsibility it is to ensure that all young people thrive. This domain is pushed forward to encourage school leaders and schools to challenge the school-wide power structures that shape who is provided with diverse opportunities (enrollment in Honors/AP courses, college application support, access to college trips, planning towards a variety of postsecondary options) and who is not.

Furthermore, school-level policies around discipline also play a role in equitable access to educational opportunities, and education administrators and school leaders have a role to play in defining the approach their school takes in discipline. Despite legal protections from IDEA (2004), disabled students of color (particularly Black boys) are still suspended/expelled at higher rates than their nondisabled and disabled peers (Losen et al., 2014). In the same study, Losen et al. (2014) found that disabled students of color were more likely to be in classrooms with novice educators, which the authors hypothesized was a contributing factor to their overrepresentation in suspensions. Furthermore, school administrators can commit to a school-wide focus on academic (and discipline) equity by providing support for novice teachers and ensuring that school policies do not predominantly filter disabled students of color into classrooms with inexperienced educators.

## Sixth Domain: Institutional Culture of Care

The last domain is centered around an institutional culture of care and serves as foundation and sustenance for college-going culture work in schools. An institutional culture of care refers to a set of procedures, systems, and processes that ensure that every young person is cared for. An assumption is that school staff are invested in the futures of young people and *feel* care for their students. However, care is a *demonstration*—not a feeling—that is an embodiment of a genuine concern and hope for students. Womanist understandings of care position care as a communal responsibility, as political, and as risky (Beauboeuf-Lafontant, 2002). In short, care should be critically informed and aimed at supporting the social, political, and emotional rights of all students (Antrop-González & DeJesús, 2006), including those at the intersections of race and disability.

Care looks different for educators and students. While some educators believe that care means rigid expectations, firm discipline, or even failing, most students interpret care as regular check-ins, one-on-one conversations, and meaningful connections with families (Cooper et al., 2020). In a study of college-going cultures at an urban school, researchers found that students appreciated relationships with school leadership, such as the principal. Some students reported feeling a sense of care and connection to their school when their principal knew them on a first-name basis and recognized them on their campus, describing the principal's office as a "safe space" (McKillip et al., 2013).

Care is understood to be an overt demonstration. Pulling students aside, asking questions, and providing support are elements that help young people feel cared for. Within disabled communities, care can take on different meanings. While we will not fully explore this here, we do wonder about the implications of "care" in a culture that understands many disabled people to be in specific need of care. We all need and require care; none of us are "independent," or truly divorced from a need of community or support. And while we conceptualize care at a school-wide level, we also caution educators and researchers alike to consider the ways that messages of care have been used to patronize, paternalize, and limit the lives of disabled people.

However, care work for disabled students of color is political in unique ways—as the care provided to disabled students is aimed at dismantling multiple barriers to accessibility. The emphasis within this domain is centered at the institution. Because of this, a culture of care should be built into the institution—through accessible buildings and classrooms, environmental supports and considerations, and restorative and healing spaces. The institutional culture of care domain stresses the importance of ensuring that all students are cared for in meaningful ways—and part of this means ensuring that every student has an adult on campus with whom they can have a reliable and positive relationship.

## CONTINUING TO EXPAND A FRAMEWORK FOR "COLLEGE-FOR-ALL" CULTURE

### Collaboration and Partnership With Families in Pursuit of a "College-For-All" Culture

Families and parents of students with disabilities are considered, legally, to be an indispensable voice on the matters of student services and supports within special education. The Individuals With Disabilities in Education Act (IDEA, 2004) mandates the rights of families within the special education process, as well as their engagement. Yet for years, education researchers have documented how racial/ethnic minoritized families have been delegitimized, excluded, discriminated against, and/or disadvantaged within and by special education systems and processes (Artiles, 2019; Artiles & Trent, 1994; Ferri & Connor, 2005; Losen & Orfield, 2002; Sullivan, 2011).

In short, the IDEA mandates do not guarantee genuine and collaborative engagement for parents, nor do they account for the varying degrees of access to social, cultural, and foundational capital (Bourdieu, 1986) that many marginalized communities experience. Trainor (2010) argues that access to various forms of capital means that many privileged families can "engage" in the IEP process in ways that support the accommodations and services of their child, contrasting with the experiences of many families of color who often do not have the same access. For example, knowledge about special education processes such as referral, assessment, and eligibility, is important capital as parents and families participate in meetings about the appropriateness of various assessments, the reasons for referral, and appropriate eligibility. Parents with this kind of knowledge can further advocate for their child in meaningful ways and take concrete steps towards ensuring the needs of their child are met (Trainor, 2010).

The college-going process also involves families, and schools should be communicating regularly with families about what the process entails and how to navigate it. In the original college-going culture framework, community and family engagement was understood to be crucial—however, for parents of students with disabilities, this engagement might look different. In addition to regular parent conferencing and college-going workshops and information seminars, schools can distribute targeted and specific kinds of information to parents of students with disabilities. School counselors might host a parent night specifically for students with disabilities about how to secure disability accommodations at the college level; how to connect with disability cultural centers or services centers within the community; and provide a space for parents to share resources, tips, and experiences navigating the college-going process with their child.

School leaders and school staff should be committed to dismantling the barriers that prevent many families of color from wanting to or feeling like they can engage with schools. This might include a collaborative group model where educators, administrators, families, and students alike meet outside of the IEP space to discuss the specific needs of disabled students of color.

## The Role of Leadership in Building and Sustaining Partnerships

Partnerships formed between middle schools and high schools are incredibly important for disabled students as they transition into the ninth grade (Cooper & Liou, 2007). As disabled students transition into high school, so does their IEP and its accompanying services and accommodations. However, the cultural and personal knowledge about students built at the middle school do not transition. To further this domain, we suggest that eighth grade IEP teams and coordinators should arrange a meeting with the student's ninth grade IEP team to discuss goals and services in order to support the student's transition into high school. This would mean that middle schools and high schools have strong partnerships with one another. Such a partnership could ease a student's anxiety about navigating a new school, as this meeting could give them the opportunity to meet with their future teachers, explore their new campus, and become familiar with the culture of the school before transitioning. School administrators have an important role in making the connections between their high school staff and neighboring middle schools, and can work with middle school administrators in setting up a summer program that helps with this transition.

Successful components of college-going cultures also include establishing and sustaining partnerships with colleges and universities. Due to poor accessibility, inclusivity, and accommodations, disabled students of color often do not feel supported in postsecondary institutions. While documents like the ITP can support students in planning their futures and thinking about what they can do now and in the next years to support arriving at their postsecondary futures, ITPs are not always helpful in addressing the structural and institutional blockades that many disabled persons will face in postsecondary institutions.

Education leaders in secondary schools must work to develop partnerships with community colleges and 4-year universities. These partnerships need to be ongoing and meaningful and should inform the ways that students with disabilities are supported both in secondary schools and in universities. Secondary schools can work to inform colleges/universities of what kinds of supports and accommodations may be needed for students with disabilities when they reach the campus.

A key support system is to include visits to disability centers on college campuses during campus visits and support students in obtaining resources and information about how they will be supported on a specific campus. In addition to visits to disability centers, school leadership and/or administrators might also co-organize with college campuses to pay disabled students at the campus to speak on their experiences at a specific university and any tips they would give to disabled students. Such a panel should center the experiences of disabled students of color and their particular, intersectional experiences at the university.

## Beyond K–12: Higher Education Institutions and Their Role

To remark upon the impact of college-going cultures, it is also important to discuss the relationships between higher education institutions and their admissions requirements, and the academic structuring and tracking of secondary schools. California (the state in which the CGCG took place) has unique requirements as it relates to "college-readiness." With two prestigious 4-year public university systems (University of California or UC, and Cal State University or CSU), California places demands on secondary schools to prepare students in specific ways. Students must meet A–G requirements to be eligible for a school in the UC or CSU system. A–G refers to a list of approved subjects by the CSU/UC system. These A–G subjects include history, science, English, language other than English, college prep, visual/performing arts, and mathematics. These requirements are a series of specific courses that theoretically prepare students for college. In addition to meeting A–G requirements, students must hold a certain grade point average, and in some cases, score well on standardized assessments. However, this is the minimum, and educators and school professionals know that for students to be competitive, students must take and succeed in rigorous coursework (Honors and AP), do very well on their SAT, and participate in extracurricular activities.

California State University recently attempted to update its A–G quantitative reasoning high school requirements to 4 years instead of 3. This change would lead to dramatic shifts in the ways that K–12 mathematics education functions and could exacerbate the inequitable access to rigorous mathematics that many students of color, poor communities, and disabled communities face. Not only would such a change restructure mathematics education in secondary schools, it would make access to the affordable, public universities within the CSU system that much more difficult for disabled students of color. While CSU's suggested 4-year quantitative reasoning was quickly rebutted through proposition AB 1930, this suggestion is representative of the ways that public university systems influence the ways that secondary schools are structured.

Not all secondary schools are created equal. While some schools offer several Honors and AP courses, available to any and all students, other schools offer a handful—cherry picking who can take such courses and be competitive in college applications. The schools with more resources, serving higher income, White and Asian families, are more likely to have such courses. In the 2017–2018 school year, just 10% of students with disabilities within the state of California were prepared for college, as measured by the college-going indicator on the California Dashboard (State of California, 2019), indicating a need to examine the ways that disabled students are being prepared for college, as well as the need to question the eligibility guidelines put in place by higher education institutions.

Lastly, it is not enough to simply help disabled students of color enroll in college, but to help them graduate and be and feel successful. Higher education institutions are historically (and currently) ableist institutions that perpetuate the ideologies of individualized labor and decentralize the care work that is integral to many disabled people and communities, and many higher education professionals are not adept at supporting students with disabilities (Pena et al., 2015). There are many barriers for disabled students on college campuses, including: securing helpful and functional accommodations, and faculty refusal or failure to implement agreed upon accommodations (Toutain, 2019). Additionally, higher education settings are often not inclusive, and many instructors do not incorporate practices to support the needs of diverse learners.

Additionally, many students with "invisible disabilities" (high-incidence disabilities like learning disabilities, emotional disorders, intellectual disabilities that are more difficult to discern), feel the pressure to hide their disability for fear of stigma, and/or being considered "lazy" (Olney & Brockelman, 2003; Osborne, 2019). Particularly for students of color, who may already have internalized racist confrontations and concerns about their intellectual or professional capacity, disclosing one's disability may present additional concerns. And yet, students must not only disclose, but also prove their disability to their college institution to receive accommodations. This combination of structural, physical, ideological, and social barriers and oppressions can make college campuses emotionally and intellectually stressful spaces for disabled students of color.

There is a need for higher education institutions to create space for undisclosed and disclosed disabled students alike to create community. One study found that queer and disabled students found aspects of disclosure as a form of activism—empowering them to discuss their disability outside of the parameters of medicalized and institutional language (Miller et al., 2019). Additionally, disclosure can also be a way for disabled students to find community with other disabled students. Universities might encourage disability cultural centers to serve as this space, where disabled students can disclose to a social community if they choose, without fear of stigma from the larger institution.

Disability services centers are typically designed to meet legal mandates for accessible education and ensure that disabled college students have access to appropriate services. However, Chiang (2020) draws attention to disability cultural centers—which are separate from disability services centers—which provide safe havens and a cultural space for disabled college students to connect, be, and express disabled cultures in (ideally) safe ways. Chiang (2020) proposes that ideally the cultural center could exist in a central location on campus and would engage in programming and resources like inviting disability activists to speak on campus, creating a communal library, scheduling social events, and working with students to design inclusive programming. Chiang (2020) writes that a disability cultural center can serve students by "normalizing disability as well as communicating value for disability," and can help bring disabled students together to organize for social change (p. 1184).

## Concluding Thoughts

It is important that practices shift towards challenging institutions themselves and the ableist systems and structures that keep disabled students of color from enrolling in, and succeeding in college. Expanding existing conceptual frameworks similarly help in enacting more expansive and inclusive school cultures. And while the purpose of this chapter was to think through a conceptual framework that supports college-going at secondary schools, it is equally important for higher education institutions to interrogate and address the practices and systems that exclude and harm disabled students.

Lastly, this chapter also encourages a critique of the proposed framework: Is it appropriate to adapt a framework to consider the needs of students with disabilities, or is it necessary to build a new framework with students with disabilities at the center, to inform a truer "college-for-all" framework? Disability is not a monolithic category of identity. People who identify as disabled have different disability labels that mean different things for the ways that they experience and navigate the world. It is equally important, when supporting disabled students of color, to recognize and attend to the diversity amongst and within disability labels, and to further complicate this understanding with students' gender, race/ethnicity, language, sexuality, and class. How does a college-for-all framework consider and account for these complications? How does such a framework account for disabled students with intellectual disabilities? What definitions of college readiness need to be (re)considered in the push to be more inclusive of students with disabilities? And lastly, how might educators and school staff within the K–16 pipeline create and build education structures that fully support the needs, wants, and dreams of disabled students?

## NOTE

1. In 2015–2016 school year, 18% of Latinx undergraduates identified as disabled, and 17% of Black undergraduates identified as disabled (Snyder et al., 2019).

## REFERENCES

Annamma, S. A., Anyon, Y., Joseph, N. M., Farrar, J., Greer, E., Downing, B., & Simmons, J. (2019). Black girls and school discipline: The complexities of being overrepresented and understudied. *Urban Education, 54*(2), 211–242.

Annamma, S. A., Connor, D., & Ferri, B. (2013). Dis/ability critical race studies (DisCrit): Theorizing at the intersections of race and dis/ability. *Race Ethnicity and Education, 16*(1), 1–31.

Antrop-González, R., & De Jesús, A. (2006). Toward a theory of critical care in urban small school reform: Examining structures and pedagogies of caring in two Latino community-based schools. *International Journal of Qualitative Studies in Education, 19*(4), 409–433.

Artiles, A. J. (2019). Fourteenth annual Brown lecture in education research: Re-envisioning equity research: Disability identification disparities as a case in point. *Educational Researcher, 48*(6), 325–335.

Artiles, A. J., Dorn, S., & Bal, A. (2016). Objects of protection, enduring nodes of difference: Disability intersections with "other" differences, 1916 to 2016. *Review of Research in Education, 40*(1), 777–820.

Artiles, A. J., & Trent, S. C. (1994). Overrepresentation of minority students in special education: A continuing debate. *The Journal of Special Education, 27*(4), 410–437.

Baer, R., Daviso, A., Queen, R., & Flexer, R. (2011). Disproportionality in transition Services: A descriptive study. *Education and Training in Autism and Developmental Disabilities, 46*(2), 172–185.

Beauboeuf-Lafontant, T. (2002). A womanist experience of caring: Understanding the pedagogy of exemplary Black women teachers. *The Urban Review, 34*(1), 71–86.

Bourdieu, P. (1986). The forms of capital. In J. Richardson (Ed.), *Handbook of theory and research for the sociology of education* (pp. 241–258). Greenwood.

Chiang, E. S. (2020) Disability cultural centers: How colleges can move beyond access to Inclusion. *Disability & Society, 35*(7), 1183–1188. https://doi.org/10.1 080/09687599.2019.1679536

Conley, D. T. (2007). *Redefining college readiness.* Educational Policy Improvement Center. https://www.ct.edu/files/pdfs/p20/RedefiningCollegeReadiness.pdf

Conley, D. T. (2008). Rethinking college readiness. *New Directions for Higher Education, 2008*(144), 3–13. https://doi.org/10.1002/he.321

Connor, D. J., & Valle, J. W. (2015). A socio-cultural reframing of science and dis/ ability in education: Past problems, current concerns, and future possibilities. *Cultural Studies of Science Education, 10*(4), 1103–1122.

Cooper, R., & Davis, J. C. (2015). Problematizing the discourse: A quantitative analysis of African American high school students' academic aspirations and motivation to excel. *The Journal of Negro Education, 84*(3), 311–332.

Cooper, R., Davis, J., Munzer, A., Salazar, M., & Sanchez, S. (2016). *CAPP college-going culture grant schools: Clear college expectations.* https://static1.squarespace .com/static/5cd335742727be5f36f9b677/t/5eb0acaf2d668b7c8250dc24/ 1588636857741/CAPPReport_SP16_CGCGSchools_FINAL.pdf

Cooper, R., & Liou, D. D. (2007). The structure and culture of information pathways: Rethinking opportunity to learn in urban high schools during the ninth grade transition. *The High School Journal, 91*(1), 43–56.

Cooper, R., Otis, B., & Green, G. (2020). *Institutional culture of care and college-going cultures* [Unpublished manuscript]. The EASE Project, University of California Los Angeles.

Corwin, Z. B., & Tierney, W. G. (2007). *Getting there—And beyond: Building a culture of college-going in high schools.* Center for Higher Education Policy Analysis, University of Southern California.

Couser, G. T. (2011). What disability studies has to offer medical education. *Journal of Medical Humanities, 32,* 21–30.

Cruz, R. A., & Rodl, J. E. (2018). An integrative synthesis of literature on disproportionality in special education. *The Journal of Special Education, 52*(1), 50–63.

Diana v. State Board of Education, Civil Action No. C-70-38 (N.D. Cal., 1970, further order, 1973).

Erevelles, N., & Minear, A. (2010). Unspeakable offenses: Untangling race and disability in discourses of intersectionality. *Journal of Literary & Cultural Disability Studies, 4*(2), 127–146.

Ferri, B. A., & Connor, D. J. (2005). Tools of exclusion: Race, disability, and (re) segregated education. *Teachers College Record, 107*(3), 453–474.

Graves, S., & Mitchell, A. (2011). Is the moratorium over? African American psychology professionals' views on intelligence testing in response to changes to federal policy. *Journal of Black Psychology, 37*(4), 407–425.

Gregg, N. (2007). Underserved and underprepared: Postsecondary learning dis/abilities. *Learning Dis/abilities Research and Practice, 22,* 219–228.

Harry, B., & Klingner, J. (2014). *Why are so many minority students in special education?* Teachers College Press.

Individuals With Disabilities in Education Act, 20 U.S.C. § 1400 et seq. (2004).

Larry P. v. Riles, 343 F. Supp. 1306 (N.D. Cal. 1972), aff'd, 502 F.2d 963 (9th Cir. 1974); 495 F. Supp. 926 (N.D. Cal. 1979), aff'd, 793 F.2d 969 (9th Cir. 1984).

Lipscomb, S., Haimson, J., Liu, A. Y., Burghardt, J., Johnson, D. R., & Thurlow, M. L. (2017). *Preparing for life after high school: The characteristics and experiences of youth in special education. Findings from the National Longitudinal Transition Study 2012. Volume 1: Comparisons with other youth: Full report* (NCEE 2017-4016). National Center for Education Evaluation and Regional Assistance, Institute of Education Sciences, U.S. Department of Education.

Losen, D. J., & Orfield, G. (2002). *Racial inequality in special education.* Harvard Education Press.

Losen, D., Hodson, C., Ee, J., & Martinez, T. (2014). Disturbing inequities: Exploring the relationship between racial disparities in special education identification and discipline. *Journal of Applied Research on Children, 5*(2), 15.

Madaus, J. W., & Shaw, S. F. (2006). Disability services in postsecondary education: Impact of IDEA 2004. *Journal of Developmental Education, 30*(1), 12.

McClafferty, K. A., McDonough, P. M., & Nunez, A. M. (2002). *What is a college culture?* Facilitating college preparation through organizational change.

McClafferty-Jarsky, K., McDonough, P. M., & Nunez, A.-M. (2009). Establishing a college culture in secondary schools through P-20 collaboration: A case study. *Journal of Hispanic Higher Education, 8*(4), 357–373. https://doi.org/10.1177/1538192709347846

McKillip, M. E., Rawls, A., & Barry, C. (2012). Improving college access: A review of research on the role of high school counselors. *Professional School Counseling, 16*(1), 2156759X1201600106.

McKillip, M. E., Godfrey, K. E., & Rawls, A. (2013). Rules of engagement: Building a college-going culture in an urban school. *Urban Education, 48*(4), 529–556.

Menchaca, M. (1997). Early racist discourses: The roots of deficit thinking. In R. R. Valencia (Ed.), *The evolution of deficit thinking: Educational thought and practice* (pp. 13–40). Taylor & Francis.

Miller, R. A., Wynn, R. D., & Webb, K. W. (2019). "This really interesting juggling act": How university students manage disability/queer identity disclosure and visibility. *Journal of Diversity in Higher Education, 12*(4), 307.

Mitchell, V. J., Moening, J. H., & Panter, B. R. (2019). Student-led IEP meetings: Developing student leaders. *JADARA, 42*(4), 8.

Monahan, J. L., Lombardi, A., Madaus, J., Carlson, S. R., Freeman, J., & Gelbar, N. (2020). A systematic literature review of college and career readiness frameworks for students with disabilities. *Journal of Disability Policy Studies.* https://doi.org/10.1177/1044207320906816

Newman, L., Wagner, M., Cameto, R., & Knokey, A.-M. (2009). *The post-high school outcomes of youth with disabilities up to 4 years after high school. A report of findings from the National Longitudinal Transition Study-2 (NLTS2)* (NCSER 2009-3017). SRI International.

Newman, L., Wagner, M., Knokey, A. M., Marder, C., Nagle, K., Shaver, D., Wei, X., with Cameto, R., Contreras, E., Ferguson, K., Greene, S., & Schwarting, M. (2011). *The post-high school outcomes of young adults with disabilities up to 8 years after high school: A report from the National Longitudinal Transition Study-2 (NLTS2)* (NCSER 2011-3005). SRI International.

Oakes, J., Rogers, J., Silver, D., Valladares, S., Terriquez, V., McDonough, P., Renée, M., & Lipton, M. (2006). *Removing the roadblocks: Fair college opportunities for all California students.* UC All Campus Consortium for Research on Diversity and UCLA IDEA.

Olney, M. F., & Brockelman, K. F. (2003). Out of the disability closet: Strategic use of perception management by select university students with disabilities. *Disability & Society, 18*(1), 35–50.

Ong-Dean, C. (2005). Reconsidering the social location of the medical model: An examination of disability in parenting literature. *Journal of Medical Humanities, 26*(2–3), 141–158.

Osborne, T. (2019). Not lazy, not faking: Teaching and learning experiences of university students with disabilities. *Disability & Society, 34*(2), 228–252. https://doi.org/10.1080/09687599.2018.1515724

Pena, E. V., Stapleton, L. D., & Schaffer, L. M. (2015). Critical perspectives on dis/ability identity. *New Directions for Student Services, 154,* 85–96

Pérez, P. A., & McDonough, P. M. (2008). Understanding Latina and Latino college choice: A social capital and chain migration analysis. *Journal of Hispanic Higher Education, 7,* 249–265.

Reveles, J. M., & Brown, B. A. (2008). Contextual shifting: Teachers emphasizing students' academic identity to promote scientific literacy. *Science Education, 92*(6), 1015–1041.

Runswick-Cole, K., & Hodge, N. (2009). Needs or rights? A challenge to the discourse of special education. *British Journal of Special Education, 36*(4), 198–203.

Sleeter, C. (2010). Why is there learning disabilities? A critical analysis of the birth of the field in its social context. *Disabilities Studies Quarterly, 30,* 210–235.

Smith, F. A., Grigal, M., & Sulewski, J. (2012). *The impact of post-secondary education on employment outcomes for transition-age youth with and without disabilities: A secondary analysis of American community survey data* (Think College Insight Brief, Issue No. 15). University of Massachusetts Boston, Institute for Community Inclusion.

Snyder, T. D., De Brey, C., & Dillow, S. A. (2019). *Digest of Education Statistics 2017* (NCES 2018-070). National Center for Education Statistics.

State of California. (2019). *Academic performance* [College/Career]. California Dashboard. https://www.caschooldashboard.org/reports/ca/2019/academic-performance#college-career

Sullivan, A. L. (2011). Disproportionality in special education identification and placement of English language learners. *Exceptional Children, 77*(3), 317–334.

Sullivan, A. L., & Artiles, A. J. (2011). Theorizing racial inequity in special education: Applying structural inequity theory to disproportionality. *Urban Education, 46*, 1526–1552. https://doi.org/10.1177/0042085911416014

Toutain, C. (2019). Barriers to accommodations for students with disabilities in higher education: A literature review. *Journal of Postsecondary Education and Disability, 32*(3), 297–310.

Trainin, G., & Swanson, H. L. (2005). Cognition, metacognition, and achievement of college students with learning disabilities. *Learning Disability Quarterly, 28*(4), 261–272.

Trainor, A. A. (2010). Diverse approaches to parent advocacy during special education home—school interactions: Identification and use of cultural and social capital. *Remedial and Special education, 31*(1), 34–47.

Troiano, P. F., Liefeld, J. A., & Trachtenberg, J. V. (2010). Academic support and college success for postsecondary students with learning disabilities. *Journal of College Reading and Learning, 40*(2), 35–44.

Valencia, R. R. (1997). Conceptualizing the notion of deficit thinking. *The evolution of deficit thinking: Educational thought and practice, 19*(1), 1–12.

Yavuz, O. (2016). Educational leadership and comprehensive reform for improving equity and access for all. *International Journal of Education Policy & Leadership, 11*(10). https://doi.org/10.22230/ijepl.2016v11n10a684

# SECTION V

## ADVOCACY, LEVERAGE, AND THE PREPARATION OF SCHOOL LEADERS

This last section of chapters turns readers attention to questions around navigating institutional inertia while leveraging institutional resources. As this book is a volume in the IAP series Research and Theory in Educational Administration, we also feature chapters that have significant implications for the preparation of school leaders.

Hancock opens Section V with a conceptual piece aimed at understanding and changing "family–educator" relationships. "Power and Partnerships: Families, Educators, and Implications for School Leaders" addresses multiple power dynamics often present in the decision-making interactions that take place between families and educators. Informed by tenets of DisCrit, Hancock analyzes ways in which socially constructed norms shape power relations between marginalized communities and public schools, especially through interpersonal discourse. The norms of discourse are both implicit and manifest in the structure of typical school interactions, which include parent–teacher conferences and the utilization of various standardized documents. Hancock suggests that school leaders are uniquely positioned and by virtue of their positional authority, educational leaders should strive to increase transparent communication and inclusive participation, as well as provide opportunities for shared decision-making among parents and school educators.

Inclusive practices and effective communication inform the work of Semon, who provides a narrative that focuses on her struggles as a teacher navigating efforts to support full inclusion for an English language learner in a large Florida public high school. In "Engaging Sebastian: Advocating for the Inclusion of a High School English Language Learner Labeled With

**515**

an Intellectual Disability," Semon reflects on the structural and institutional norms and processes that she and Sebastian faced, particularly as these processes are connected to the "low expectations" of her coworkers. Semon narrates how Sebastian's relationship with his teachers inspired her to grow professionally, especially regarding her efforts to counter the "illegal decisions" made by school authorities in Sebastian's name. She presents this chapter, in part, to demonstrate some of the ways programs and philosophies designed to assist students like Sebastian fail to reach their potential without fierce advocacy on the part of teachers and families.

The question of who has decision-making power is central to many chapters in the book. In the chapter, "They Decide: Empowering Transition-Age Youth With Disabilities by Promoting Self-Determination," Scheef, Mahfouz, and Hagiwara examine how too often individuals with disabilities find themselves in situations where decisions are made for them by others. The chapter argues for the importance of putting decision-making power in the hands of individuals with disabilities themselves. In order to accomplish this, Scheef and colleagues argue for direct instruction and training in self-determination skills. Doing so provides greater opportunities for youth with disabilities to better understand and anticipate the future. In the authors' view, many of these efforts will come from the special education teachers who work with students directly, as well as indirectly through administrators who develop a school culture that facilitates the development of individual student self-determination skills. The chapter provides a pragmatic overview of self-determination skills for youth with disabilities and gives specific recommendations for school administrators looking to augment existing self-determination training in their schools.

Scholastic experiences are, of course, only one part of a student's journey. Green posits that diagnosis is not the starting point of a person's journey as a person with a disability. Often a person faces many obstacles before receiving any diagnosis, which then impacts their capacity to advocate for their needs. Her chapter, "Journey of Self-Determination for a Woman With Epilepsy" uses a self-determination framework to explore her journey as a woman with epilepsy. Through different important stages, she explains how her disability has impacted her ability to advocate for her needs, wants, and goals. She also provides recommendations for education-related personnel to ensure students with disabilities receive individual opportunities to explore and identify their needs.

Students with disabilities, as discussed in the previous chapters, have a variety of needs and assets that are too often unrecognized. Paes de Carvalho, Pedrosa de Camargo, and Magalhães Kassar provide a study of their efforts to understand and report on both policy and leadership practice related to students with disabilities in Brazil. Their chapter, "Contribution of Disability Studies to the Training of School Leaders in Brazil" features a historical policy analysis along with surveys and interviews of school leaders in Corumbá, a municipality located in the Mato Grosso do Sul State on the border between Brazil, Bolivia, and Paraguay. Despite the passage of progressive legislation and policy guidance that aimed to create more inclusive schools, the school leaders in their study struggled both locally and systemically in their effort to include and advocate for students with disabilities in substantive ways. Theory and practice, while mutually influential, often have significant discrepancies and the authors argue for greater examination of ableism and use of disability studies in professional development and support of school leaders in Brazil.

With a similar end in mind, Wilson and Umpstead propose a framework to support leaders in building the mindset and practices to create equitable learning environments for all students, especially those identified with disabilities. The approach utilized in their chapter, "Remembering What Matters Most: A Framework for Transforming Schools Into Inclusive Spaces for Students With Disabilities," uses servant leadership, social justice leadership, and transformative leadership frameworks, and the literature related to disability studies and intersectionality, to create a new framework with three pillars: care, connection, and collaboration. As with other chapters in this section, Wilson and Umpstead provide a pragmatic framework to guide more inclusive leadership practice.

We conclude the section with an eye towards leadership preparation. Almager and Valle's chapter, "Preparing Socially Just and Equitable Leaders: Centering Special Education Leadership and Advocacy in Aspiring Leaders Curriculum" presents the findings of three aspiring leaders in a 15-month principal preparation residency and their experiences observing, leading, and implementing special education best practices in rural, suburban, and urban school and district settings. The aspiring leaders engaged with district leaders and campus principal mentors in their daily practices, policy and law implementation, and progress monitoring services provided to students in special education. Interview and study findings revealed inconsistencies between district special education expectations and campus implementation. Almaguer and Valle discuss specific ways school districts, schools, and principal preparation programs can provide training for the support of both aspiring and current leaders to effectively lead more inclusive schools.

# CHAPTER 21

# POWER AND PARTNERSHIPS

## Families, Educators, and Implications for School Leaders

**Christine L. Hancock**
*Wayne State University*

### ABSTRACT

Meaningful participation in educational decision-making by families from multiply marginalized backgrounds is recognized as a key element of social justice which school leaders must address to promote equitable outcomes for students and families. The purpose of this conceptual paper is to present a framework to analyze ways in which power is reflected and constructed at ideological, institutional, and interactional levels during family–educator decisions. By attending to power, school leaders can deepen understandings of decision-making, and ultimately transform school systems for shared decisions. First, issues of power and asymmetry in family–educator relationships will be briefly outlined. Next, theoretical foundations of the framework will be addressed. Empirical support for the framework will then be provided, and a case example will be presented. Finally, implications for school leaders and recommendations to redistribute decision-making power will be provided.

*Who Decides?*, pages 519–546

**519**

The importance of family participation in educational decision-making is made clear through empirical, legal, and ethical rationales. Researchers have found improvements in academic and equitable outcomes when families engage in school decision-making (Ishimaru, 2013; Welton & Freelon, 2018). Parent participation in educational decision-making regarding their child with a disability is a foundational principle of the Individuals With Disabilities Education Act (IDEA, 2004), which mandates that families are afforded opportunities to participate on individualized education program (IEP) teams. School leaders (i.e., principals, administrators) enacting ethical commitments to just education affirm the importance of meaningful participation in decision-making by individuals from marginalized groups, such as families of color, families who are linguistically diverse, and families experiencing poverty (e.g., DeMatthews et al., 2016; Furman, 2012). This need is further magnified for families from multiply marginalized backgrounds, such as children and families of color with disabilities.

While schools and educators often intend to form meaningful partnerships with families, family engagement policies often socialize parents from multiply marginalized backgrounds into dominant cultural norms, offer narrow participation opportunities for families, and privilege professional expertise over that of families (Ishimaru et al., 2016). As a result, educators hold decision-making power over families, as demonstrated through a growing body of research documenting interactions wherein educators make decisions *for* rather than *with* families (e.g., Bacon & Causton-Theoharis, 2013; Canary & Cantú, 2012; Cheatham & Ostrosky, 2013; McCloskey, 2016). Further, parents report unsatisfactory experiences and exclusion during special education decision-making (Elbaum et al., 2016; Fish, 2006; Love et al., 2017).

How families and educators collaborate and make decisions about children's education plays an essential role in maintaining school organization (Ishimaru, 2020). When decisions regarding placement, planning, and discipline are carried out through practices that exclude and marginalize children, such as disciplinary practices that surveil and pathologize actions of Black children, inequitable legacies are maintained (Migliarini & Annamma, 2019). As families and educators make decisions, they evaluate strengths and support needs of children and youth (e.g., Alasuutari, 2014; Hjörne, 2005). In doing so, decision-making reflects and constructs notions of ability and disability, further maintaining school organization around these concepts.

Efforts for equitable education necessitate that school leaders develop nuanced understandings of power relationships between families and schools, including how policies and practices may uphold White supremacy by comparing families from multiply marginalized backgrounds to expected norms of whiteness, ability, and middle class values (DeMatthews, 2020; Ishimaru, 2020). School leaders have unique positions to set school policies, yet also are likely to face exclusionary and deficit-based district policies that label families and learners based on race and ability, such as highly segregated special education programs, enrollment boundaries that maintain racial segregation, and high-stakes accountability measures that identify certain schools as failing (Annamma & Morrison 2018; DeMatthews, 2020).

## Decision-Making Discourse and Ideological, Institutional, and Interactional Contexts

Researchers have defined decision-making as an incremental process that takes place through language in interaction (i.e., discourse) and results in commitment to future action (Dall & Sarangi, 2018). To illustrate, during IEP meetings, educators and families make decisions such as choosing goals to promote child learning and development. These decisions take place through discourse as educators and family members discuss goals and implementation strategies.

Decision-making processes are shaped by a number of factors which reflect and construct broader power relationships. As a result, many aspects of decision-making can constrain meaningful participation of families from multiply marginalized communities. Social norms regarding families and schools (i.e., ideologies) shape decisions through assumptions about normalcy that typically position families from these communities as deficient. For example, educational policies that depict parents of color, parents experiencing poverty, and parents who are immigrants as learners lacking resources or knowledge have been criticized for disregarding parent and community knowledge and framing parents as "needy" (Bertrand et al., 2018). Further, decision-making by families and educators takes place in an institutional context, and program philosophy, requirements, and resources contribute to how decisions are made (e.g., Alasuutari & Markström, 2011). Institutional processes necessarily serve the needs of the institution, which can further limit family participation. In addition, because decision-making takes place through discourse, it requires interactional skills such as questioning and listening, which involve culturally bound expectations for language use (e.g., Cazden, 2001; Gee, 2007), which can especially affect families who are bilingual (e.g., Howard & Lipinoga, 2010).

Inclusive education for all children and youth perceived as different (e.g., students with disability labels, students of color) calls for redistribution of decision-making opportunities to ensure families can meaningfully participate in decisions about their child's education (Waitoller & Kozleski, 2013). Such redistribution can take into account varied contributions to decisions to more fully transform hierarchies that maintain school organization around ability and disability and impede meaningful family participation in decisions. Examining power relationships between families and schools and deconstructing discourse that maintains inequitable power re-lationships can ultimately facilitate renegotiation of roles and create new opportunities for more shared decisions (Ho et al., 2020) in alignment with more democratic models of professionalism (e.g., Skrtic, 2013; Valle & Aponte, 2002).

The purpose of this conceptual paper is to present a framework to ana-lyze ways in which power is reflected and constructed at ideological, in-stitutional, and interactional levels during family-educator decisions. By attending to power, school leaders can deepen understandings of decision-making and ultimately transform school systems for shared decisions. First, issues of power and asymmetry in family–educator relationships will be briefly outlined. Next, theoretical foundations of the framework will be ad-dressed. Empirical support for the framework will then be provided, and a case example will be presented. Finally, implications for school leaders and recommendations to redistribute decision-making power will be provided.

## POWER AND ASYMMETRY IN FAMILY–EDUCATOR RELATIONSHIPS

Decision-making by families and educators necessarily involves participants from different social groups (i.e., parent, educator). In this context, power can be defined as an "asymmetric relationship among social actors who have different social positions or who belong to different social groups" (Reisigl & Wodak, 2016, p. 26). Asymmetry is inherent in two aspects of family–educator relationships: (a) institutional interactions (Heritage, 2013) and (b) professional knowledge (Bledstein, 1976; Skrtic, 1995).

First, according to Heritage (2013), asymmetry is a primary characteris-tic of institutional interactions, which require specific roles for profession-als (i.e., educators) and laypeople (i.e., family members) related to institu-tional goals (e.g., selecting goals for student learning). The need to carry out institutional goals also constrains how speakers contribute to discus-sion, as these goals shape what topics are and are not considered important to the conversation (Heritage, 2013). As a result of these roles, goals, and constraints, knowledge of conversational topics and routines are differen-tially distributed such that professionals have more access to conversational resources that shape how interactions unfold, such as information about what student learning goals are most easily addressed through planning because they are aligned with curricula. In turn, educators are likely to initi-ate discussion topics that maintain institutional roles, goals, and constraints (e.g., asking about student progress only in areas relevant to school). As a result, professionals have more opportunities than parents to shape deci-sions (e.g., Mehan et al., 1986).

Additionally, educators' professional roles require specialized knowledge and expertise (Bledstein, 1976; Skrtic, 1995), which can further contribute to asymmetrical relationships with families (Valle & Aponte, 2002). Objective knowledge regarding child ability and progress is highly prized in traditional views of special education (Skrtic, 1995), creating a context that necessitates and privileges educators' specialized knowledge and expertise. The assumption that scientific knowledge is more indicative of children's abilities than anecdotal, everyday knowledge can create a hierarchy where professional expertise is more valued than family expertise. Such hierarchies have been reported by many researchers investigating family-educator decision-making (e.g., Canary & Cantú, 2012; Harry et al., 1995; Kalyanpur & Rao, 1991; Klingner & Harry, 2006; Lea, 2006; Rao, 2000). Ultimately, beliefs regarding the value of scientific, objective knowledge and expertise can create a context where professionals are viewed as the most qualified to make decisions regarding a child's education (Bacon & Causton-Theoharis, 2013; Cheatham & Ostrosky, 2013; Harry et al., 1995; Hwa-Froelich & Westby, 2003; Klingner & Harry, 2006; Lea, 2006; Lo, 2008; Sheehey, 2006). Further, these beliefs maintain medicalized notions of need and intervention that pathologize family and child experiences, which further impedes partnerships (Lalvani, 2015; Vaughan & Super, 2019). At the same time, the most recent IDEA reauthorization imposed more responsibilities on parents, placing them in a position of monitoring educators' work and decisions (Haines et al., 2017; Turnbull et al., 2007). In other words, IDEA places the onus for advocacy on families, and presumes that parents know and can effectively advocate for their children (Goss, 2019). This role is in conflict with expectations that educators should act as authorities and experts. Thus, families are placed in a double bind wherein they are expected to be involved, but only in particular ways and to a limited extent (Lai & Vadeboncoeur, 2013; Valle & Aponte, 2002).

## THEORETICAL FOUNDATIONS

This section will draw on disability critical race theory (DisCrit; Annamma et al., 2013) and discourse theory (e.g., Gee, 2014; Reisigl & Wodak, 2016) to discuss power in the context of family-educator decisions about children from multiply marginalized backgrounds.

### DisCrit

DisCrit (Annamma et al., 2013) provides a framework to understand and analyze the interconnected nature of racism and ableism in educational decision-making. DisCrit builds from traditions of disability studies and critical race theory, offering an intersectional lens to uncover how racism and ableism simultaneously construct whiteness and ability as normal and marginalize those who are not perceived as normal, through processes that predominantly appear neutral (Annamma et al., 2013). In doing so, DisCrit reveals how the co-construction of race and ability can produce exclusionary social structures in educational systems (Annamma et al., 2013; Annamma & Morrison, 2018). Annamma et al. (2013) presented seven tenets through which DisCrit problematizes notions of normalcy and uncovers how social constructions of race and ability operate interdependently and influence one another, with real consequences for the lives of individuals who are labeled as raced and/or disabled (Annamma et al., 2013). DisCrit also recognizes ways in which people from multiply marginalized backgrounds have been denied equal rights and legal protections, while individuals perceived most in alignment with norms of whiteness and ability receive benefits (Annamma et al., 2013). To disrupt these normative practices, DisCrit advocates for centering experiences and perspectives of those who have been marginalized because of their identities in research, policy, and practice, and ongoing resistance against marginalization (Annamma et al., 2013; Annamma & Morrison, 2018).

DisCrit affords insights for school leaders to examine power relationships and foster equitable change by countering problematic notions of race and ability that uphold whiteness and ability as norms (DeMatthews, 2020; Kozleski et al., 2020). Thus, DisCrit can expand and deepen understandings of how schools are organized around notions of race and ability, and how decision-making interactions between families and educators enact such organization.

## Discourse Theory

Discourse theory (Gee, 2014; Reisigl & Wodak, 2016) supports identification of specific ways in which families and educators carry out educational decision-making, offering further insight into how families and educators construct race and ability during interactions. Through language use, individuals reconstruct ideologies (Gee, 2007, 2014), including racism and ableism. For example, speakers engage in actions that can provide or withhold social goods such as desired identities (e.g., engaged parent) or decision-making outcomes (e.g., preferred IEP goals, needed special education services). Discourse both reflects and constructs socially situated identities and actions (Wodak & Meyer, 2016). For example, when a special educator says, "We're here to provide the best services to meet your child's needs" during a meeting, this reflects the educator's assumption about shared knowledge (i.e., a purpose of special education is to provide individualized child services). At the same time, discussion of services in these terms reinforces this assumption, creating a context where actions maintain the educator's perspective (i.e., selected strategies provide individualized services rather than alter the environment). Further, discourse constructs power within interactions (Reisigl & Wodak, 2016). For example, when an educator begins a conference by reporting a child's school performance, this reflects ideological, institutional, and individual beliefs about the educator's specialized knowledge while constructing power through control over conversational topics.

Combining DisCrit and discourse theory supports detailed consideration of ways in which power is enacted during educational decision-making. DisCrit offers essential understanding of ways in which racism and ableism are embedded together in educational contexts, while discourse theory offers a means to uncover specific aspects of language use through which notions of race and ability are enacted.

## FRAMEWORK

Power infuses decisions made by families and educators. The following sections will outline how power is reflected and constructed through discourse at ideological, institutional, and interactional levels. Examples within each section highlight seemingly neutral and invisible ways race and ability are co-constructed (Annamma et al., 2013) during decision-making, as well as ways in decision-making typically operates to benefit children and families perceived closest to norms of whiteness and ability (Annamma et al., 2013). The reviewed research investigated interactions between educators and families, such as parent-teacher conferences and IEP meetings. Figure 21.1 presents a summary of the framework.

### Power and Ideological Aspects of Decision-Making

Families and educators make decisions in a sociocultural context (Ruppar & Gaffney, 2011; Wallerstein & Duran, 2010), and history, culture, and politics contribute to choices through taken-for-granted assumptions regarding normalcy and appropriate thoughts, behaviors, and actions, including who should and should not receive social goods such as status, worth, and material goods (Gee, 2007). DisCrit reveals how these social goods benefit those perceived closest to norms of Whiteness and ability, and predominantly withheld from those perceived to be outside of those norms, such as children and families from multiply marginalized backgrounds (Annamma

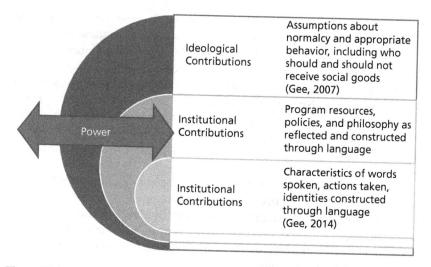

**Figure 21.1** Power in ideological, institutional, and interactional aspects of decision-making.

et al., 2013). Historical family-educator practices, cultural values embedded within educational policy, and educator interpretations of family resistance will be outlined.

### Historical Family-Educator Practices

Historical practices of education and special education contribute to family-educator decisions. In the 19th century, parents of color, parents experiencing poverty, and parents with disabilities were typically blamed for perceived child deficiencies and positioned as morally unfit to care for their child (Baquedano-López et al., 2013; Ferguson, 2002). In this context, children with disabilities (Ferguson, 2002; Turnbull et al., 2015) and indigenous children (Baquedano-López et al., 2013) were forcibly removed from the purported negative influence of their parents. Parents were pressured to cede decision-making to professionals, who were seen as more fit surrogate parents in alignment with norms of whiteness and ability. Practices that position families as passive have endured, shaping educators' and parents' expectations for and experiences of decision-making. For example, Vaughn et al. (1988) found few changes in parent participation during elementary IEP meetings 10 years after the implementation of P.L. 94-142, concluding that educators continued to dominate decision-making. Similarly, Harry (2008) asserted that despite significant changes over time in professional views regarding collaboration with families from diverse backgrounds, many barriers continued to limit the extent to which equitable partnerships were realized. As such, historical practices can continue to legitimize professional decision-making power over families from multiply marginalized backgrounds.

## Cultural Values

Dominant cultural values embedded in educational policies represent another ideological contribution to decision-making, and tend to use a White, Eurocentric perspective to make determinations about abilities (e.g., Souto-Manning et al., 2018). In particular, IDEA (2004) is based on a premise of highly valuing equity, individual rights, and freedom of choice (Kalyanpur et al., 2000). Families from ethnically diverse backgrounds may not share, and indeed may oppose these beliefs (Kalyanpur & Harry, 2012). For example, families may not value equity, and instead value differential familial or professional roles based on status or hierarchy (Kalyanpur et al., 2000). European American values embedded in IDEA (2004) create a context wherein educators can assume that the values represented are neutral and universal, and thus do not merit explanation or negotiation, although that is not the case (Kalyanpur et al., 2000). Moreover, the deeply embedded nature of these assumptions can contribute to obscuring the fact that these values lead to domination over families from multiply marginalized backgrounds and continued experiences of racism and ableism.

Differences in cultural values may also lead to disconnects between families' and educators' perceptions of disability, and when disconnects arise, teams and decision-making processes typically favor European American priorities, as these are embedded within the law (Kalyanpur & Harry, 2012). For example, researchers investigating educational decision-making have reported that families of color often perceive a wider range of normalcy than educators, and as a result may question the label of disability for their child (e.g., Harry et al., 2005; Hart et al., 2010; Hwa-Froelich & Westby, 2003; Kalyanpur & Rao, 1991; Lea, 2006; Rao, 2000; Sheehey, 2006). However, IDEA (2004) necessitates more rigid definitions of ability (Skrtic, 1995), creating a context wherein families' more nuanced views are rendered less relevant to educational decision-making, further marginalizing families (Kalyanpur & Harry, 2012).

## Educator Interpretations of Family Resistance

Although interactions with schools and educators may construct parents as passive, this does not mean that families do not have power and do not engage in a variety of strategies both within and outside of these interactions to resist domination (Graff & Vazquez, 2014). For example, Ho et al. (2020) found that Chinese parents of children with attention deficit hyperactivity disorder labels engaged in multiple forms of resistance. Through cognitive resistance, parents rejected schools' rules, routines, and determinations as inappropriate for their child. Through behavioral resistance, parents acted to secure their child's safety and emotional well-being, such as negotiating practices with educators, rejecting medicalizing their child's support needs, and in some cases changing school systems. Through transformative resistance, parents reimagined the purpose of education and challenged taken-for-granted assumptions about the mission and orientation of schooling (Ho et al., 2020).

Traditional avenues for family engagement such as attending parent-teacher conferences, participating in school committees, and volunteering in classrooms are largely dictated by school systems to parents, with little opportunities for parents to reshape these opportunities (Carreón et al., 2005). Further, parents who participate in ways aligned with these expectations are constructed as "good," whereas families who do not participate in "right ways" (e.g., agreeing, carrying out educators' recommendations) are seen by educators as in denial, apathetic, or disengaged (e.g., Goss, 2019; Kalyanpur & Harry, 2006; Lea, 2006; Rao, 2000). Professionals may use perceived lack of parental engagement as justification for limiting a family's role in decision-making (e.g., Klingner & Harry, 2006). These perceptions of family participation in their child's education further construct deficit-based perceptions of families from multiply marginalized backgrounds, and can result in rationalizing educators' domination over parents by enacting racialized assumptions that these parents lack skills and knowledge to independently support their child's learning (Carreón et al., 2005; Ishimaru, 2020).

## Power and Institutional Aspects of Family-Educator Decision-Making

In addition to being part of a sociocultural context that favors educators over families, decision-making takes place in an institutional context. As such, program philosophies, requirements, and resources contribute to how decisions are made (Ruppar & Gaffney, 2011; Wallerstein & Duran, 2010). Although there are many institutional contributions to decision-making, this section focuses on meeting procedures, program paperwork, and IDEA regulations. DisCrit uncovers ways in which these seemingly neutral processes serve to co-construct race and ability in ways that uphold whiteness and ability as norms (Annamma et al., 2013).

### Meeting Procedures

Meeting procedures such as step-by-step decision-making protocols adopted by institutions shape how teams evaluate options and make decisions. Such protocols tend to highlight professional expertise and prioritize objective knowledge through data analysis. Pressure to adhere to protocol and efficiently make decisions may prevent teams from considering alternate solutions or discourage educators from taking time to explain the process of decision-making, define terms, or check for understanding, limiting the extent to which family members can actively participate. Opportunities for parent participation in venues such as prereferral intervention teams appear limited, and may include being informed of educators' decisions, or providing information to educators (e.g., Chen & Gregory, 2011), reinforcing educator expertise as most important.

Availability and quality of institutional resources regarding language interpretation can afford or constrain opportunities to participate in decision-making for families from linguistically diverse backgrounds (Canary & Cantú, 2012; Schoorman et al., 2011). In particular, training and availability of language interpreters can shape the extent to which families understand and participate in decisions (Klingner & Harry, 2006; Lo, 2008; Schoorman et al., 2011), as well as differing expectations for family-educator interactions. To illustrate, Howard and Lipinoga (2010) found that parents who were Mexican immigrants indicated that they had questions for teachers prior to kindergarten conferences, but when topics and formats were different than what they expected, parents declined to raise concerns during the conferences.

### Program Paperwork

Because paperwork is likely to reflect the interests and needs of the institution that created it, it further reflects and constructs institutional authority. For example, completion of paperwork often emphasizes legal requirements (e.g., Hwa-Froelich & Westby, 2003), which serve the interest of the institution by documenting compliance or legitimizing institutional authority to make decisions. Focusing first on the needs of the institution creates structures that force needs of children and families to be constrained to align with institutional needs. Bray and Russell (2016) noted that the institutional influence of meetings resulted in meetings that looked and sounded the same despite the fact that the students had unique needs and were at different high schools using different models of inclusion. Further, as professionals are responsible for completing paperwork, when paperwork dominates decision-making interactions, professionals also dominate interactions as they facilitate reading and discussing the paperwork, relegating families to more passive roles (Bray & Russell, 2016).

Paperwork and other documentation such as meeting agendas create a "text-talk" link wherein the sequence and topics represented in written documents regulate the structure for discussion throughout an interaction (Markström, 2009). Control over discussion agendas constructs power by shaping what topics are introduced and prioritized (Cheatham & Ostrosky,

2011, 2013; Howard & Lipinoga, 2010; Hwa-Froelich & Westby, 2003; Klingner & Harry, 2006; Lo, 2008). Text-talk links have been shown to play a significant role in educational decisions with families, because completion of required paperwork and documentation structures interactions (Bray & Russell, 2016; Canary & Cantú, 2012; Harry et al., 1995; Lo, 2008; Rao, 2000; Ruppar & Gaffney, 2011; Sheehey, 2006).

### Legality and IDEA Regulations

In the 2004 reauthorization, IDEA coupled parent rights with responsibilities, thus placing the onus on parents to seek out information and training regarding IDEA or risk losing the benefits and rights it confers (Turnbull et al., 2007). According to Turnbull et al.'s (2007) policy analysis, these actions result in decision-making power that privileges local educational agencies (i.e., institutional authority). Such power can be viewed in instances wherein administrators and/or educators overrule family requests and attempts to advocate during decision-making (Bray & Russell, 2016; Hjörne, 2005). For example, Rogers (2002) demonstrated how a Black mother's attempts to advocate against her daughter's placement in special education were unsuccessful, and she ultimately acquiesced to the educators' recommendations, stating "If she have to go in, she can go into special ed" (Rogers, 2002, p. 213). Further, Rogers revealed how institutional authority over the style and type of evidence presented allowed for a child's continued placement in a separate special education classroom, despite contradictions in what counted as evidence across different meetings. In particular, the "deficits" that initially led to labeling the child as "multiply disabled" were presented as strengths in a review meeting and depicted as evidence of the placement's effectiveness. As such, institutional authority can complicate families' opportunities to participate in decisions.

Researchers have also reported emphasis on legality during partnership efforts, including labeling and categorizing disability (Bacon & Causton-Theoharis, 2013; Rao, 2000). Bray and Russell (2016) found that reading aloud documents mandated by IDEA (2004) such as educator reports of student progress, behavior, and evaluation reports constituted 29–54% of words spoken during IEP meetings. Additionally, the role of family participation in decision-making was linked to bureaucratic policies and definitions of participation, both in IDEA (Sheehey, 2006) and in individual program policies (Hwa-Froelich & Westby, 2003). These institutional definitions of parent participation shaped how educators approached families. While educational policy often confused and disempowered families, differing interpretations of policy mandates also led professionals to view their actions as controlled by the policies, requiring them to be inflexible and unable to exert professional judgment (Goss, 2019; Klingner & Harry, 2006).

# Power and Interactional Aspects of Family-Educator Decision-Making

While ideological and institutional factors contribute to how families and educators participate in decision-making, it is through interactions that specific decisions are made (Dall & Sarangi, 2018). Interactions between families and educators not only reflect power present in the social world, but also construct power through words spoken, actions taken, and identities constructed through language (i.e., discourse; Gee, 2014). As such, manifestations of power are present in interactional aspects of family-educator decision-making. Accordingly, features of discourse such as word choice, topic control, turn-taking, overlapping talk, and pauses play a role in how decisions are made (Dall & Sarangi, 2018). While there are many possible interactional contributions to decision-making, this section focuses on participation structures, control of discussion topics, and speech acts, as these are foundational practices that may impede participation of families from multiply marginalized backgrounds from decision-making.

## *Participation Structures*

Participation structures, patterns for how family-educator interactions are expected to proceed in particular contexts, such as setting child learning goals or evaluating child needs, reveal minimal parent participation (e.g., Howard & Lipinoga, 2010). In particular, educators have been found to talk more than parents during decision-making interactions (Alasuutari, 2014; Bray & Russell, 2016; Cheatham & Ostrosky, 2013; Lo, 2008; Rogers, 2002; Vaughn et al., 1988). When parents do contribute, their responses were likely to be more minimal, such as "mm-hm" or "okay" (Alasuutari, 2014). For example, Bray and Russell (2016) found that during high school IEP meetings, special educator talk ranged from 43–73% of words spoken, while parent talk ranged from 2–23% of words spoken, and student talk > 1–16% of words spoken. In addition, broader patterns of communication (e.g., questioning styles) and decision-making indicated that educators predominantly controlled interactions (e.g., Alasuutari, 2014; Cheatham & Ostrosky, 2013; Hjörne, 2005), and conversation outcomes (Alasuutari, 2014; Alasuutari & Markström, 2011; Cheatham & Ostrosky, 2011, 2013; Hjörne, 2005; Markström, 2009; McCloskey, 2016; Mehan et al., 1986; Rogers, 2002).

## *Control of Discussion Topics*

Educators construct power during decision-making through control of conversational topics. For example, Cheatham and Jimenez-Silva (2012) discussed how control of conversational topics allowed educators to move discussion away from a Mexican American parent's attempts at advocacy during a preschool parent-teacher conference, ultimately maintaining professional control of the decision regarding a child's transition to kindergarten, although the parent tried to leverage family cultural values to demonstrate the importance of her daughter's transition to attend school with her siblings. Howard and Lipinoga (2010) also reported that through control of discussion topics, kindergarten teachers signaled what was (and was not) considered important to them to discuss during parent-teacher conferences. Similarly, professional control over when and how discussion topics were introduced allowed educators to dismiss family efforts at negotiating a more inclusive environment for their child (McCloskey, 2016) and attempts to discuss instruction and child learning (Bray & Russell, 2016). In addition, the use of wait time can reinforce institutional authority and maintain topics or introduce new topics. While educators leaving little or no wait time before moving on can prevent family members from sharing their perspectives, extended wait time can also be used to imply that a response is expected, or that a parent's reply is not acceptable to the teacher (Cheatham & Ostrosky, 2009), thereby constructing and enacting social power and influence inherent in professional models of collaboration (Spino et al., 2013).

### Speech Acts

Educators use speech acts that highlight their expertise at the expense of parents' contributions, such as advice-giving (Cheatham & Ostrosky, 2011), evaluating children's skills (Hjörne, 2005), and constructing agreement (Lea, 2006). Agreement is typically a preferred response within discussion for its ability to be indicated without altering conversational flow (Pomerantz, 1984). In contrast, disagreement requires more conversational work to shift discussion, and speakers may need to use strategies such as pausing or mitigation to present disagreement (Pomerantz, 1984). Investigations of family-educator conversations suggest that decision-making interactions are often structured to promote agreement. For example, educators create a context for agreement by focusing on consent rather than more meaningful family participation in discussing a range of options (Canary & Cantú, 2012). Some researchers reported that educators presumed agreement by not asking for parent participation (Hwa-Froelich & Westby, 2003; Lo, 2008; Schoorman et al., 2011), thereby minimizing parents' opportunities to disagree or raise alternate views.

Educators can also construct power in interactions through complimenting. For example, educators are often encouraged to soften negative accounts of a child by creating a "compliment sandwich" wherein positive statements are introduced before and after the account (e.g., Power & Clark, 2000). However, this pattern of talk also serves to maintain conversational control (Bacon & Causton-Theoharis, 2013; Gathman et al., 2008). By placing the account between the compliments, educators create a sequence in which it is less likely for other speakers (i.e., parents) to take up the topic of the account (Gathman et al., 2008). This is an important strategy to maintain control of conversational topics, because accounts are more "vulnerable" to questions and other talk, whereas compliments are more likely to be simply acknowledged (Gathman et al., 2008). Such speech acts reflect professional power to construct educators as knowledgeable experts essential to the decision-making process. In contrast, parents can be constructed as passive recipients of professional expertise.

## EXPLORING HOW POWER IS ENACTED
## THROUGH A CASE EXAMPLE

The following transcript excerpt presented by Canary and Cantú (2012) illustrates how power is simultaneously enacted through ideological, institutional, and interactional aspects of decision-making by families and educators. During this IEP meeting, a Black mother (M) advocated for her son's continued participation in an extended school year program held over the summer. The exchange occurred with her son's teacher (T), one of six professionals in attendance at the meeting.

> **M:** How is it he can't remember after school vacation? He forgets the stuff he just learned two weeks before.
> **T:** It happens to all kids. Mostly it's because they have been home and not doing anything regarding school work.
> **M:** No, I work with him.
> **T:** I did put him in [extended school year] last year. Did he go?
> **M:** He went two weeks. And I had to stop taking him because we had a death in the family and then I just couldn't get him there.
> **T:** Oh, if you can take the responsibility to get him there—
> **M:** There was a transportation problem.
> **T:** They have to provide transportation.
> **M:** No, there was no transportation for him last year.
> **T:** I filled out the paper.
> **M:** A lady called me and said no transportation.
> **T:** I didn't know.
> (Canary & Cantú, 2012, pp. 286–287)

## Ideological Aspects of Decision-Making

During this exchange, power was embedded in ideological aspects of decision-making, highlighted in the teacher's responses that minimize the value of home-based learning for families from multiply marginalized backgrounds (e.g., Baquedano-López et al., 2013). Although the mother opens with a specific question about her son's ability to retain information (Lines 1–2), the teacher responds that this typically happens "because they have been home and not doing anything regarding school work" (Lines 3–4). This comment reflects long-standing ideological assumptions that school-designated learning opportunities are most meaningful for children's growth and development (i.e., historical practices). Importantly, these school-designated activities are predominantly aligned with experiences of White, European American families (Ishimaru, 2020). Certain families may be given the benefit of the doubt that their daily routines and activities support their child's learning, and that their home environment provides appropriate academic stimulation. However, the benefit of the doubt was not extended to this Black family, necessitating that the mother explain her efforts with her son (Line 5).

The exchange also demonstrated how educators may interpret family resistance as disengagement (e.g., Goss, 2019). As the conversation progressed to discuss the child's participation in the extended school year program, the mother shared that due to extenuating circumstances her son only attended the program for 2 weeks (Lines 7–8). The educator's response highlights the mother's responsibility, suggesting that the issue was one of apathy or disengagement (Line 9), reflecting racialized assumptions that this Black mother may be less involved in her child's education (e.g., Kalyanpur & Rao, 1991; Rao, 2000). As a result of these embedded ideological assumptions that uphold whiteness and ability as norms, the mother was positioned as deficient from the outset of decision-making, rather than positioned as a partner.

## Institutional Aspects of Decision-Making

Power was also infused through institutional aspects of decision-making in this exchange, as demonstrated in the discussion of paperwork and specific aspects of transportation and attendance policies (i.e., legality). These institutional constraints kept discussion of the child's participation in the program narrow and focused on adherence to policies and paperwork rather than details of the child's experiences or engagement. For example, the teacher opened this part of exchange by referencing enrollment processes, and then asking about attendance ("Did he go?"; Line 6). After the mother explained why her son stopped attending (Lines 7–8, 10), the teacher pointed to policy to counter the mother's statement, asserting "They have to provide transportation" (Line 11). When the mother restated that transportation was not available (Line 12), the teacher described how she completed the required paperwork (Line 13). This emphasis on processes and requirements reflect and construct power that maintains traditional organization of schools around the notions of race and ability. Institutional authority helps legitimate claims during decision-making, which can allow educators to maintain decision-making power over families, as demonstrated in this exchange.

## Interactional Aspects of Decision-Making

Interactional contributions to decision-making enacted power throughout this exchange, particularly through control of discussion topics and speech acts that allowed the educator to draw on her expertise as a professional and maintain authority over the mother. Although the mother opened with a specific question about her son's ability to retain information (Lines 1–2), the teacher did not take up this discussion topic about the child's particular skills in context. Instead, the educator drew on her general knowledge of children, noting that this "happens to all kids" (Line 3). In shifting to respond in this broadly applicable way, the educator utilized strategies associated with indirect advice-giving (Cheatham & Ostrosky, 2011) and implied that a potential solution would be for the parent to ensure that the child engages in schoolwork at home (Line 4). Although the mother stated that she did work with her child at home (Line 5), the teacher did not respond to this statement and instead introduced a new discussion topic, prior program attendance (Line 6). By initiating a new topic of discussion, the teacher indicated that the details of how the parent worked with her son were not important to this conversation, and maintained control of the conversational agenda.

Similarly, the educator minimized opportunities for the parent to share by using closed-ended questioning (Line 6) and presenting the educator's understandings as statements of fact, such as "They have to provide transportation" (Line 11) and "I filled out the paper" (Line 13). As a result, the mother had to counter incorrect assumptions and assert her own experiences multiple times (Lines 5, 10, 12, 14). Engaging in direct disagreement may impede decision-making opportunities for families in a variety of ways. First, researchers recognize disagreement as more difficult discursive work than agreement, because agreement maintains the sequence and flow of conversations (Pomerantz, 1984). Because the educator did not use speech acts such as questioning, checking for understanding, or summarizing that would naturally allow the parent to clarify her child's experience within the flow of the conversation, the onus was placed on the parent to assert herself. In doing so, another facet of collaborative decision-making may be impeded and the parent may be positioned as "difficult" for these attempts at advocacy (Valle & Aponte, 2002). Further, as a Black woman, her advocacy attempts may be minimized or dismissed based on racialized attitudes and social stereotypes about "angry" Black women (e.g., Ishimaru, 2020). These interactional contributions to decisions are heavily influenced by both family and educator perceptions of educator expertise, which allows educators to position themselves as more knowledgeable than parents, and therefore most suited to make decisions.

## IMPLICATIONS FOR SCHOOL LEADERS

These manifestations of power work together to position educators as active educational decision-makers and families as informants or recipients of expertise. Because consideration of power is needed to fully understand and support shared decision-making by educators and families from diverse backgrounds, this paper presented a framework that accounts for ways in which power is reflected and constructed in ideological, institutional, and interactional aspects of decision-making. The many ways in which power is reflected and constructed in family-educator decision-making often contribute to constructions of parents as passive recipients of professional expertise. As a result, educators can more easily maintain power and minimize or dismiss family concerns (Cheatham & Ostrosky, 2011; Hwa-Froelich & Westby, 2003), ultimately limiting family participation in decision-making. By attending to decision-making power, school leaders can deepen understandings of family-educator decision-making. Further, school leaders can apply these understandings to transform school systems for shared decision-making. Accordingly, here are three recommendations for school leaders: (a) interrogate ideological contributions to decision-making, (b) reimagine institutional contributions to decision-making, and (c) acknowledge interactional contributions to decision-making. Each recommendation will be discussed below.

## Interrogate Ideological Contributions to Decision-Making

To address ways in which power is embedded in assumptions about families, school leaders can interrogate ideological contributions to decision-making by engaging in critical reflection to identify assumptions and how they are enacted in school policies and family-educator interactions. Addressing these assumptions is essential to recognizing and redistributing decision-making power: How principals perceive parents contributes to the extent to which principals welcome and cultivate family participation in decisions (Bertrand et al., 2018; Ishimaru, 2013). Deficit-based assumptions rooted in racism and ableism allow schools and leaders to presume that families from multiply marginalized backgrounds require assistance and remediation and are therefore less capable of supporting school agendas (Bertrand et al., 2018). Simultaneously, such assumptions minimize the value of families' agendas, which often envision broader aims for education than schools (Ishimaru, 2020). To counter these notions, principals can draw on DisCrit (Annamma et al., 2013) to cultivate critical understanding of ways in which racism and ableism operate interdependently within schools and reject problematic notions of normalcy that further marginalize children and families by reinforcing dominant norms of whiteness and ability through practices such as labeling (DeMatthews, 2020). DeMatthews (2020) also recommends school leaders apply DisCrit to take up an intersectional and interdisciplinary lens and engage in activism and resistance to counter marginalization of children and families. For example, school leaders can resist deficit-based perspectives of families and actively take up alternate ways of thinking that highlight the strengths and expertise of families and communities of color, such as funds of knowledge (González et al., 2005) and community cultural wealth (Yosso, 2005). School leaders can draw on these perspectives to purposefully identify family expertise and position families as knowledgeable leaders in decision-making (e.g., Ishimaru, 2020).

In alignment with research that a primary practice of successful principals is to build vision and set direction (Leithwood et al., 2008). Billingsley et al. (2018) found that leadership for inclusive schools required that principals articulate a specific vision for inclusion and take steps to help the school community understand the importance of that vision. Following DeMatthews (2020), principals can model critical reflection through review of school policies for ways in which racism and ableism may be marginalizing children and families. Such review can consider not only assessment, evaluation, and intervention procedures for children with disabilities, but also broader policies related to curriculum, instruction, and discipline. Further, principals can pay particular attention to how they construct race and ability through their communications about school vision and mission, analysis of school achievement and outcomes, plans for improvement, and family engagement opportunities (Bertrand et al., 2018; DeMatthews, 2020). For example, principals can reject the construction of family engagement opportunities as workshops that "train" families and provide knowledge parents do not have. Instead, school leaders can support efforts to frame the opportunities as spaces for co-constructing knowledge as a school community where families, educators, and school leaders learn together, or as spaces where school staff are learners and families teach about their own practices (Bertrand et al., 2018). Such efforts can legitimize families' visions for their children.

## Reimagine Institutional Contributions to Decision-Making

To address ways in which power is embedded in program resources, policies, and procedures, school leaders can reimagine institutional contributions to decision-making by acting on family and community priorities and recommendations. Many current institutional policies and procedures contribute to a context for decision-making that reinforce the authority of programs and educators to make decisions *for* rather than *with* families, most often serving the needs of the institution over those of families and children. Such decisions are likely to reinforce problematic school arrangements and organization. In contrast, envisioning new institutional approaches to decision-making based on family and community perspectives helps to redistribute decision-making power and recognize multiple ways of knowing and being, enriching the process of school governance (Bertrand et al., 2018). Such efforts might be supported through new approaches to meeting procedures. For example, school leaders can counter bureaucratic approaches to planning by promoting ad hoc collaborations (Skrtic, 2013; Ware, 1994). In addition to examinations of school-based data, protocols might be adopted that center family expertise, such as McGill Action Planning, which follows a sequence of describing a child, exploring the child's history, discussing the team's dreams for the child, addressing fears, identifying how to meet child needs, and then developing an action plan (see Haines et al., 2018).

By opening decision-making more fully to families and community stakeholders, school leaders can become part of community-based change and better align school practices with community resources and priorities (Bertrand et al., 2018; Warren, 2005). To begin this process, school leaders might seek training from community-based organizations regarding grassroots leadership (Welton & Freelon, 2018), and professional development and coaching that can reframe their visions of themselves as community organizers (Ishimaru, 2013). Leithwood et al. (2008) found that successful principals redesign school organization through collaborative practices. Extending this framework to analysis of successful school leadership for inclusive education, Billingsley et al. (2018) found that leadership for inclusive schools involved collaborative redesign of exclusionary policies and practices that previously reinforced segregation of children perceived as different.

Principals can create space for families to share not only their experiences regarding how racism and ableism operate interdependently in schools, but also families' solutions, recommendations, and visions for more just and equitable education (Bertrand et al., 2018; DeMatthews, 2020). Families from multiply marginalized backgrounds have frequently demonstrated their abilities to lead change efforts for more equitable education, particularly regarding racist and ableist policies regarding school discipline, school closures, and anti-immigrant policies (Welton & Freelon, 2018). However, these advocacy efforts have often had to occur in opposition to school leadership. Instead, principals can do more to welcome and develop recommendations for more equitable policies and practices in collaboration with families, educators, and children and youth (Bertrand et al., 2018). Successfully redesigned inclusive practices included refining grading policies, eliminating segregated special education classes, adjusting school schedules, and identifying additional resources (Billingsley et al., 2018; DeMatthews 2015). In addition, Billingsley et al. (2018) found that successful principals of inclusive schools provided ongoing professional development that fostered inclusive practices, such as differentiating instruction and collaborative teaching models. Bertrand et al. (2018) also identified that institutional practices supporting family engagement in school-based meetings included the availability of language interpretation and childcare.

## Transform Interactional Contributions to Decision-Making

To address ways in which power is embedded in characteristics of words spoken, actions taken, and identities constructed through language, school leaders can transform interactional contributions to decision-making through steps that reprioritize meaningful family contributions. Decisions are ultimately made through interactions, and any efforts to redistribute opportunities for participation in decisions must attend to specific ways in which ideologies and institutional practices are enacted through language by families and educators.

The text-talk link shapes interactional features of decision-making by dictating conversational agendas and topics via required paperwork (Markström, 2009). School leaders are well-positioned to alter how decision-making is carried out by altering paperwork. For example, paperwork designed to highlight options can refocus conversations on parents' role in making choices about their child's education. In addition, school leaders can enact school-level policies that set the stage for more meaningful conversations, particularly by ensuring that parents and educators have adequate time and resources for shared decision-making. For example, principals can create coverage and flexibility so that all members of a team can participate in a full conversation, rather than dropping in to share a report and then leaving to return to a classroom or attend other meetings. Similarly, De-Matthews (2015) detailed how an elementary school principal's review of children's IEPs revealed that many children had identical goals; as a result, additional IEP meetings were held, and IEPs were rewritten to ensure that children's goals were appropriately individualized.

## CONCLUSIONS

By exploring how decisions about race and ability are constructed through discourse by families and educators and shaped by ideological, institutional, and interactional aspects of power, this paper contributes to efforts for educators and school leaders to better understand how students and families are likely to be further marginalized through decision-making interactions, resulting in inequitable education and outcomes (e.g., Harry et al., 2005; Hart et al., 2010; Howard & Liponoga, 2010; Klingner & Harry, 2006; McCloskey, 2016). Addressing how power is embedded and enacted in decision-making is essential to understand and support active and equitable participation by all families. By interrogating ideological contributions to decision-making, reimagining institutional contributions to decision-making, and acknowledging interactional contributions to decision-making, school leaders can set the stage to redistribute power and opportunities for decision-making, ultimately facilitating more shared decision-making with families.

## REFERENCES

Alasuutari, M. (2014). Voicing the child? A case study in Finnish early childhood education. *Childhood, 21*(2), 242–259. https://doi.org/10.1177/0907568213490205

Alasuutari, M., & Markström, A. M. (2011). The making of the ordinary child in preschool. *Scandinavian Journal of Educational Research, 55*(5), 517–535. https://doi.org/10.1080/00313831.2011.555919

Annamma, S. A., Connor, D., & Ferri, B. (2013). Dis/ability critical race studies (DisCrit): Theorizing at the intersections of race and dis/ability. *Race Ethnicity and Education, 16*(1), 1–31. https://doi.org/10.1080/13613324.2012.730511

Annamma, S. A., & Morrison, D. (2018). DisCrit classroom ecology: Using praxis to dismantle dysfunctional education ecologies. *Teaching and Teacher Education, 73*, 70–80. https://doi.org/10.1016/j.tate.2018.03.008

Bacon, J. K., & Causton-Theoharis, J. (2013). "It should be teamwork": A critical investigation of school practices and parent advocacy in special education. *International Journal of Inclusive Education, 17*(7), 682–699. https://doi.org/10.1080/13603116.2012.708060

Baquedano-López, P., Alexander, R. A., & Hernandez, S. J. (2013). Equity issues in parental and community involvement in schools: What teacher educators need to know. *Review of Research in Education, 37*(1), 149–182. https://doi.org/10.3102/0091732X12459718

Bertrand, M., Freelon, R., & Rogers, J. (2018). Elementary principals' social construction of parents of color and working class parents: Disrupting or reproducing conflicting and deficit orientations of education policy? *Education Policy Analysis Archives, 26,* 102. https://doi.org/10.14507/epaa.26.3546

Billingsley, B., DeMatthews, D., Connally, K., & McLeskey, J. (2018). Leadership for effective inclusive schools: Considerations for preparation and reform. *Australasian Journal of Special and Inclusive Education, 42*(1), 65–81. https://doi.org/10.1017/jsi.2018.6

Bledstein, B. J. (1976). *The culture of professionalism: The middle class and the development of higher education in America.* W. W. Norton.

Bray, L. E., & Russell, J. L. (2016). Going off script: Structure and agency in individualized education program meetings. *American Journal of Education, 122*(3), 367–398. https://doi.org/10.1086/685845

Canary, H. E., & Cantú, E. (2012). Making decisions about children's disabilities: Mediation and structuration in cross-system meetings. *Western Journal of Communication, 76*(3), 270–297. https://doi.org/10.1080/10570314.2011.651252

Carreón, G. P., Drake, C., & Barton, A. C. (2005). The importance of presence: Immigrant parents' school engagement experiences. *American Educational Research Journal, 42*(3), 465–498. https://doi.org/10.3102/00028312042003465

Cazden, C. B. (2001). Variations in lesson structure. In *Classroom discourse: The language of teaching and learning* (pp. 53–79). Heinemann.

Cheatham, G. A., & Jimenez-Silva, M. (2012). Partnering with Latino families during kindergarten transition: Lessons learned from a parent–teacher conference. *Childhood Education, 88*(3), 177–184. https://doi.org/10.1080/00094056.2012.682551

Cheatham, G. A., & Ostrosky, M. M. (2009). Listening for details of talk: Early childhood parent–teacher conference communication facilitators. *Young Exceptional Children, 13*(1), 36–49. https://doi.org/10.1177/1096250609347283

Cheatham, G. A., & Ostrosky, M. M. (2011). Whose expertise? An analysis of advice giving in early childhood parent–teacher conferences. *Journal of Research in Childhood Education, 25*(1), 24–44. https://doi.org/10.1080/02568543.2011.533116

Cheatham, G. A., & Ostrosky, M. M. (2013). Goal setting during early childhood parent–teacher conferences: A comparison of three groups of parents. *Journal of Research in Childhood Education, 27*(2), 166–189. https://doi.org/10.1080/02568543.2013.767291

Chen, W. B., & Gregory, A. (2011). Parental involvement in the prereferral process: Implications for schools. *Remedial and Special Education, 32*(6), 447–457. https://doi.org/10.1177/0741932510362490

Dall, T., & Sarangi, S. (2018). Ways of 'appealing to the institution' in interprofessional rehabilitation team decision-making. *Journal of Pragmatics, 129,* 102–119. https://doi.org/10.1016/j.pragma.2018.03.012

DeMatthews, D. E. (2015). Making sense of social justice leadership: A case study of a principal's experiences to create a more inclusive school. *Leadership and Policy in Schools, 14*(2), 139–166. https://doi.org/10.1080/15700763.2014.99 7939

DeMatthews, D. E. (2020). Addressing racism and ableism in schools: A DisCrit leadership framework for principals. *The Clearing House: A Journal of Educational Strategies, Issues and Ideas, 93*(1), 27–34. https://doi.org/10.1080/00098655 .2019.1690419

DeMatthews, D. E., Edwards, D. B., & Rincones, R. (2016). Social justice leadership and community engagement: A successful case from Ciudad Juárez, Mexico. *Educational Administration Quarterly, 52*(5), 754–792. https://doi .org/10.1177/0013161X16664006

Elbaum, B., Blatz, E. T., & Rodriguez, R. J. (2016). Parents' experiences as predictors of state accountability measures of schools' facilitation of parent involvement. *Remedial and Special Education, 37*(1), 15–27. https://doi.org/ 10.1177/0741932515581494

Ferguson, P. M. (2002). A place in the family: An historical interpretation of research on parental reactions to having a child with a disability. *The Journal of Special Education, 36*(3), 124–131. https://doi.org/10.1177/0022466902036 0030201

Fish, W. W. (2006). Perceptions of parents of students with autism towards the IEP meeting: A case study of one family support group chapter. *Education, 127,* 56–68.

Furman, G. (2012). Social justice leadership as praxis: Developing capacities through preparation programs. *Educational Administration Quarterly, 48*(2), 191–229. https://doi.org/10.1177/0013161X11427394

Gathman, E. C. H., Maynard, D. W., & Schaeffer, N. C. (2008). The respondents are all above average: Compliment sequences in a survey interview. *Research on language and social interaction, 41*(3), 271–301. https://doi.org/10.1080/ 08351810802237867

Gee, J. P. (2007). *Social linguistics and literacies: Ideology in discourses* (3rd ed.). Routledge.

Gee, J. P. (2014). *An introduction to discourse analysis: Theory and method* (4th ed.). Routledge.

González, N., Moll, L. C., & Amanti, C. (Eds.). (2005). *Funds of knowledge.* Routledge.

Goss, A. C. (2019). Power to engage, power to resist: A structuration analysis of barriers to parental involvement. *Education and Urban Society, 51*(5), 595–612. https://doi.org/10.1177/0013124517747363

Graff, C. S., & Vazquez, S. L. (2013). Family resistance as a tool in urban school reform. In E. B. Kozleski & K. K. Thorius (Eds.), *Ability, equity, and culture: Sustaining inclusive urban education reform* (pp. 80–106). Teachers College Press.

Haines, S. J., Francis, G. L., Mueller, T. G., Chun-Yu, C., Burke, M. M., Kyzar, K., Shepherd, K. G., Holdren, N., Aldersey, H. M., & Turnbull, A. P. (2017). Reconceptualizing family–professional partnership for inclusive schools: A call to action. *Inclusion, 5*(4), 234–247. https://doi.org/10.1352/2326-6988-5.4.234

Haines, S. J., Francis, G. L., Shepherd, K. G., Ziegler, M., & Mabika, G. (2018). Partnership bound: Using MAPS with transitioning students and families from all backgrounds. *Career Development and Transition for Exceptional Individuals, 41*(2), 122–126.

Harry, B. (2008). Collaboration with culturally and linguistically diverse families: Ideal versus reality. *Exceptional Children, 74*(3), 372–388. https://doi.org/10.1177/001440290807400306

Harry, B., Allen, N., & McLaughlin, M. (1995). Communication versus compliance: African American parents' involvement in special education. *Exceptional Children, 61*(4), 364–377. https://doi.org/10.1177/001440299506100405

Harry, B., Klingner, J. K., & Hart, J. (2005). African American families under fire: Ethnographic views of family strengths. *Remedial and Special Education, 26*(2), 101–112. https://doi.org/10.1177/07419325050260020501

Hart, J. E., Cramer, E. D., Harry, B., Klingner, J. K., & Sturges, K. M. (2010). The continuum of "troubling" to "troubled" behavior: Exploratory case studies of African American students in programs for emotional disturbance. *Remedial and Special Education, 31*(3), 148–162. https://doi.org/10.1177/0741932508327468

Heritage, J. (2013). Language and social institutions: The conversation analytic view. *Journal of Foreign Languages, 36*(4), 2–27.

Hjörne, E. (2005) Negotiating the 'problem-child' in school. *Qualitative Social Work, 4*(4), 489–507. https://doi.org/10.1177/1473325005058648

Ho, H. W. M., Ma, J. L. C., & Lai, K. Y. C. (2020). Power relations in a school context: Resistance of Chinese caregivers of school-aged children with attention-deficit hyperactivity disorder. *International Social Work*. Advance online publication. https://doi.org/10.1177/0020872819896825

Howard, K. M., & Lipinoga, S. (2010). Closing down openings: Pretextuality and misunderstanding in parent–teacher conferences with Mexican immigrant families. *Language and Communication, 30*(1), 33–47. https://doi.org/10.1016/j.langcom.2009.10.004

Hwa-Froelich, D. A., & Westby, C. E. (2003). Frameworks of education: Perspectives of Southeast Asian parents and Head Start staff. *Language, Speech, and Hearing Services in Schools, 34*(4), 299–319. https://doi.org/10.1044/0161-1461(2003/025)

Individuals With Disabilities Education Improvement Act of 2004 (IDEA), P.L. 108-446, 20 C.F.R. § 1400 et. seq. (2004).

Ishimaru, A. M. (2013). From heroes to organizers: Principals and education organizing in urban school reform. *Educational Administration Quarterly, 49*(1), 3–51. https://doi.org/10.1177/0013161X12448250

Ishimaru, A. M. (2020). *Just schools: Building equitable collaborations with families and communities.* Teachers College Press.

Ishimaru, A. M., Torres, K. E., Salvador, J. E., Lott, I., Joe, Cameron Williams, D. M., & Tran, C. (2016). Reinforcing deficit, journeying toward equity. *American Educational Research Journal, 53*(4), 850–882. https://doi.org/10.3102/0002831216657178

Kalyanpur, M., & Harry, B. (2012). *Cultural reciprocity in special education: Building family–professional relationships.* Paul H. Brookes.

Kalyanpur, M., Harry, B., & Skrtic, T. (2000). Equity and advocacy expectations of culturally diverse families' participation in special education. *International*

*Journal of Disability, Development & Education, 47*(2), 119–136. https://doi .org/10.1080/713671106

Kalyanpur, M., & Rao, S. S. (1991). Empowering low-income Black families of handicapped children. *American Journal of Orthopsychiatry, 61*(4), 523–532. https:// doi.org/10.1037/h0079292

Klingner, J. K., & Harry, B. (2006). The special education referral and decision-making process for English language learners: Child study team meetings and placement conferences. *Teachers College Record, 108*, 2247–2281.

Kozleski, E. B., Stepaniuk, I., & Proffitt, W. (2020). Leading through a critical lens: The application of DisCrit in framing, implementing and improving equity driven, educational systems for all students. *Journal of Educational Administration, 58*(5), 489–505. https://doi.org/10.1108/JEA-12-2019-0220

Lai, Y., & Vadeboncoeur, J. A. (2013). The discourse of parent involvement in special education: A critical analysis linking policy documents to the experiences of mothers. *Educational Policy, 27*(6), 867–897. https://doi.org/10 .1177/0895904812440501

Lalvani, P. (2015). Disability, stigma and otherness: Perspectives of parents and teachers. *International Journal of Disability, Development and Education 62*(4), 379–393. https://doi.org/10.1080/1034912X.2015.1029877

Lea, D. (2006). "You don't know me like that": Patterns of disconnect between adolescent mothers of children with disabilities and their early interventionists. *Journal of Early Intervention, 28*(4), 264–282.

Leithwood, K., Harris, A., & Hopkins, D. (2008). Seven strong claims about successful school leadership. *School Leadership & Management, 28*(1), 27–42. https:// doi.org/10.1080/13632434.2019.1596077

Lo, L. (2008). Chinese families' level of participation and experiences in IEP meetings. *Preventing School Failure, 53*(1), 21–27. https://doi.org/10.3200/ PSFL.53.1.21-27

Love, H. R., Zagona, A. L., Kurth, J. A., & Miller, A. L. (2017). Parents' experiences in educational decision making for children and youth with disabilities. *Inclusion, 5*(3), 158–172. https://doi.org/10.1352/2326-6988-5.3.158

Markström, A. M. (2009). The parent–teacher conference in the Swedish preschool: A study of an ongoing process as a 'pocket of local order.' *Contemporary Issues in Early Childhood, 10*(2), 122–132. https://doi.org/10.2304/ciec.2009.10.2.122

McCloskey, E. (2016). To the maximum extent appropriate: Determining success and least restrictive environment for a student with autism spectrum disorder. *International Journal of Inclusive Education, 20*(11), 1204–1222. https://doi.org/ 10.1080/13603116.2016.1155667

Mehan, H., Hertweck, A., & Meihls, J. L. (1986). *Handicapping the handicapped: Decision making in students' careers.* Stanford University Press.

Migliarini, V., & Annamma, S. A. (2019). Classroom and behavior management: (Re)conceptualization through disability critical race theory. In R. Papa (Ed.), *Handbook on promoting social justice in education* (pp. 1511–1532). Springer. https://doi.org/10.1007/978-3-030-14625-2_95

Pomerantz, A. (1984). Agreeing and disagreeing with assessments: Some features of preferred/dispreferred turn shapes. In J. M. Atkinson & J. Heritage (Eds.),

*Structures of social action: Studies in conversation analysis* (pp. 57–101). Cambridge University Press.

Power, S., & Clark, A. (2000). The right to know: Parents, school reports and parents' evenings. *Research Papers in Education, 15*(1), 25–48. https://doi.org/10.1080/026715200362934

Rao, S. S. (2000). Perspectives of an African American mother on parent-professional relationships in special education. *Mental Retardation, 38*(6), 475–488. https://doi.org/10.1352/0047-6765(2000)038<0475:POAAAM>2.0.CO;2

Reisigl, M., & Wodak, R. (2016). The discourse-historical approach (DHA). In R. Wodak & M. Meyer (Eds.), *Methods of critical discourse studies* (3rd ed., pp. 23–61). SAGE Publications.

Rogers, R. (2002). Through the eyes of the institution: A critical discourse analysis of decision making in two special education meetings. *Anthropology & Education Quarterly, 33*(2), 213–237. https://doi.org/10.1525/aeq.2002.33.2.213

Ruppar, A. L., & Gaffney, J. S. (2011). Individualized education program team decisions: A preliminary study of conversations, negotiations, and power. *Research & Practice for Persons with Severe Disabilities, 36*(1–2), 11–22. https://doi.org/10.2511/rpsd.36.1-2.11

Schoorman, D., Zainuddin, H., & Sena, S. R. (2011). The politics of a child study team: Advocating for immigrant families. *Multicultural Education, 18*(4), 31–38.

Sheehey, P. H. (2006). Parent involvement in educational decision making: A Hawaiian perspective. *Rural Special Education Quarterly, 25*(4), 3–15. https://doi.org/10.1177/875687050602500402

Skrtic, T. M. (1995). Special education and student disability as organizational pathologies: Toward a metatheory of school organization and change. In T. M. Skrtic (Ed.), *Disability and democracy: Reconstructing (special) education for postmodernity* (pp. 190–232). Teachers College Press.

Skrtic, T. M. (2013). The civic professional in Deweyan democracy. *Borderlands, 2*, 1–16.

Souto-Manning, M., & Rabadi-Raol, A. (2018). (Re)Centering quality in early childhood education: Toward intersectional justice for minoritized children. *Review of Research in Education, 42*(1), 203–225. https://doi.org/10.3102/0091732X18759550

Spino, M. A., Dinnebeil, L. A., & McInerney, W. F. (2013). Social power and influence: Understanding its relevance in early childhood consultation. *Young Exceptional Children, 16*(4), 17–30. https://doi.org/10.1177/1096250613493191

Turnbull, H. R., Stowe, M. J., & Huerta, N. E. (2007). *Free appropriate public education: The law and children with disabilities* (7th ed.). Love.

Turnbull, A., Turnbull, R., Erwin, E. J., Soodak, L. C., & Shogren, K. A. (2015). *Families, professionals, and exceptionality: Positive outcomes through partnerships and trust* (6th ed.). Pearson.

Valle, J. W., & Aponte, E. (2002). IDEA and collaboration: A Bakhtinian perspective on parent and professional discourse. *Journal of Learning Disabilities, 35*(5), 471–481. https://doi.org/10.1177/00222194020350050701

Vaughan, K. P., & Super, G. (2019). Theory, practice, and perspectives: Disability studies and parenting children with disabilities. *Disability & Society, 34*(7–8), 1102–1124. https://doi.org/10.1080/09687599.2019.1621741

Vaughn, S., Bos, C. S., Harrell, J. E., & Lasky, B. A. (1988). Parent participation in the initial placement/IEP conference ten years after mandated involvement. *Journal of Learning Disabilities, 21*(2), 82–89. https://doi.org/10.1177/002221948802100204

Waitoller, F. R., & Kozleski, E. B. (2013). Working in boundary practices: Identity development and learning in partnerships for inclusive education. *Teaching and Teacher Education, 31*, 35–45. https://doi.org/10.1016/j.tate.2012.11.006

Wallerstein, N., & Duran, B. (2010). Community-based participatory research contributions to intervention research: The intersection of science and practice to improve equity. *American Journal of Public Health, 100*(S1), S40–S46. https://doi.org/10.2105/AJPH.2009.184036

Ware, L. P. (1994). Contextual barriers to collaboration. *Journal of Educational & Psychological Consultation, 5*(4), 339–357. https://doi.org/10.1207/s1532768xjepc0504_4

Warren, M. R. (2005). Communities and schools: A new vision of urban school reform. *Harvard Educational Review, 2*(75), 133–173. https://doi.org/10.17763/haer.75.2.m718151032167438

Welton, A., & Freelon, R. (2018). Community organizing as educational leadership: Lessons from Chicago. *Journal of Research on Leadership Education, 13*(1), 79–104. https://doi.org/10.1177/1942775117744193

Wodak, R., & Meyer, M. (2016). Critical discourse studies: History, agenda, theory, and methodology. In R. Wodak & M. Meyer (Eds.), *Methods of critical discourse studies* (3rd ed., pp. 1–22). SAGE Publications.

Yosso, T. (2005). Whose culture has capital? A critical race theory discussion of community cultural wealth. *Race Ethnicity and Education, 8*(1), 69–91. https://doi.org/10.1080/1361332052000341006

CHAPTER 22

# ENGAGING SEBASTIAN

## Advocating for the Inclusion of a High School English Language Learner Labeled With an Intellectual Disability

**Sarah R. Semon**
*University of South Florida*

## ABSTRACT

This narrative focuses on my struggle, as a special educator, to negotiate the inclusion of an English language learner identified as having an intellectual disability in the context of a large high school in Florida. My narrative begins when I left high school teaching and began my current role as a visiting faculty member in the special education teacher preparation program in a nearby university. This narrative consists of my reflections on the realities of teaching in a self-contained classroom and the low expectations held by my colleagues as a way to explain the need for inclusion. I share my efforts to reach Sebastian, a seemingly noncompliant ninth grader, famous for sleeping in class. As the story unfolds, I relate how Sebastian's words and my perceptions of his lack of faith in teachers prompted me to do more than I might have otherwise done, given my personal need for employment and propensity to avoid conflict. I also share the barriers presented by the special education

*Who Decides?*, pages 547–568
Copyright © 2022 by Information Age Publishing
www.infoagepub.com

**547**

administrators who opposed my efforts to change Sebastian's disability label and special education placement. Moreover, I describe the unexpected support from general educators and other allies. The narrative also reveals how uncovering the illegal decisions made for this child in middle school served to swing the tide in his favor.

Thus, success for Sebastian was thus contingent and hard won. And while I recognize that any success should be celebrated, I remain haunted by all of the other students who remain excluded and underserved. My story concludes with how this case continues to echo and shape all of my efforts as a teacher educator in special education. By sharing this story, I hope to illuminate why inclusion for students with intellectual disabilities—particularly those who also have cultural or linguistic differences—are so difficult to achieve.

> *Once the "individual" is assigned to a category (or aggregate), he or she does not belong to other categories, most specifically the category understood to be "normal." He or she must therefore be dealt with accordingly, which almost inevitably involves segregation and exclusion.*
>
> —Gallagher, 2010, p. 36

## WHERE IT ALL BEGAN

It was my first day back in the classroom. I soon learned that my nine self-contained special education students would just call me "Miss," not Dr. Semon, not Mrs. Semon, just "Miss" or "Hey, Miss" when they needed my attention. As they filed in and enthusiastically greeted each other like old friends, one student entered the room silently. He looked different from the rest of my group. He looked like a kid from a Nike or Target ad—clean-cut and stylish with hip name-brand clothing and side-slung courier bag—giving the impression that he took time every morning to thoughtfully put together an outfit. He wore an insulin pump on his hip, reminiscent of a beeper. He looked cool. This was Sebastian. He acknowledged the other students with a head nod and had no choice but to tolerate their goofiness and hugs. As soon as he could, he found a seat and put his head down. Sebastian, the other students informed me, was from Puerto Rico, spoke only Spanish, and never did any work. The teachers in middle school, they said, gave up and allowed him to put his head down every day. Well, I thought to myself, I have experience teaching in self-contained special classrooms and was a professor in special education. So, I was confident that I could figure out what he was interested in and get him engaged. Not speaking Spanish myself, I wasn't sure how to communicate and provide instruction most effectively for him, but I knew it was my responsibility to figure it out. Looking back, I can still hear my students teasing me, "Hey Miss, you so wrong!" Sebastian would prove to be more of a challenge than I thought.

## MY RETURN TO THE CLASSROOM

I returned to teaching special education in my town's largest high school (serving a majority low-income African-American and Hispanic student population). When I applied for the position, as an introverted middle-class White woman in her 30s, I wonder now if I came across as either oblivious to the challenges of this type of school or someone with a savior complex. The reality was (and is) that I have a strong passion for social justice, ethics, and equity.

I grew up in the 1980s with activist parents in a low-income neighborhood near one of the housing projects in the Tampa Bay area. Environmentalism and helping others were central issues provoking my family's activism. We were part of a grass-roots effort to reopen the Sulphur Springs pool (which failed) and we produced a show called "Save Our Earth" on the local public access television station where my mom worked. My parents regularly helped drive children from the housing development to school and community events (like free-skating night on Wednesdays) in our 1971 Volkswagen van. After high school, I went away to a nearby state college and then moved a little closer to home to complete the final 2 years of my undergraduate program in teacher preparation at a small, private liberal arts college, which I paid for with scholarships, federal grants, Florida's critical teacher shortage tuition-reimbursements, and the income from my various jobs.

While in college, after a string of retail and coffee shop jobs, I began running the respite care program for Camp Fire (formerly Camp Fire Boys & Girls). In this position, I trained volunteers in procedures for providing in-home respite for families and served as a liaison between families and the volunteers. I also served as a counselor and nature specialist at a respite care camp for children and adults with developmental disabilities in California. In this work, I found my passion for working with kids with disabilities and earned a dual degree and teaching certification in specific learning disabilities and elementary education in 1999.

From there, I entered my first year as a teacher, confident that I held the specialized knowledge required to help and alleviate whatever disorders my students might present. In short, my conceptual understanding of my students as having disabilities, as being deficient, and as being in need of "fixing" was steeped in the traditional medical model of disability and unquestioned assumptions regarding culture, language, socioeconomics, and race. As their teacher, I viewed my role within a technical framework that views the act of teaching as the practical implementation of specialized procedures aimed at remediation (see Apple, 2004; Iano, 1990).

## BEGINNING TO TEACH

In my first year of teaching, I was given the freedom to decide how to structure the curriculum for the self-contained program at my school. This was around 1998, a time when the standards-based focus was just gaining ground there were no substantive expectations for teachers to adhere to academic standards for students who earned special diplomas (Morningstar et al., 1999). I registered for training to implement a life skills-focused curriculum and worked with my team to provide a variety of hands-on experiences and student-run enterprises, including car detailing, running a café, volunteering at local events, and engaging in local holiday art displays.

In that same year, I was involved in special education staffing for a sixth-grade girl who had recently immigrated from Haiti (even though she was not a student in my class or on my caseload). The staffing specialist decided to classify her as "other health impaired" since she didn't fit any other categories. The team, including myself, agreed because we all wanted to get her some help. Her individualized education plan (IEP) was created to provide 30 minutes of resource room support per day. I didn't fully understand the implications of her special education eligibility decision until I saw her again as she entered ninth grade. During the three intervening years, her placement had become progressively more restrictive until she was placed in a fully self-contained classroom setting. Thus, she eventually walked into my classroom, where I soon realized how capable she was and how wrong that eligibility decision had been for her. I was informed that she was too far behind to be put back into general education classes and that she didn't need the stress of having to pass the Florida Comprehensive Achievement Test. I didn't argue, the parents never complained, and the girl was content to be my special assistant that year. Although I left the classroom for my doctoral studies at the end of that year, this event resurfaced as I learned about the social model of disability and racial discrimination in graduate school. From this experience, I learned how special education had disabled this child.

Looking back, I see that my distinctly vocational approach was squarely situated in a deficit view of my students that was informed by the medical model of disability. I viewed my work as fixing and caring for students who needed my help. I have come to see special education as doing harm to many students. While many view special education as beneficial (smaller classes, more attention, teachers with specialized training), my experience has shown me that children in special education often suffer from stigmatization, labeling, and lowered expectations. All of which impact their postsecondary outcomes.

This hit home one day, a few years later, when I ran into a former student. Luis shared that he was in college. He said, "See, you guys thought I couldn't do it." This caught me completely off-guard. I never thought a student would internalize that message while in *my* classroom. I began to see that the tacit assumption I brought to my decision-making was that my students lacked the capacity for grade level appropriate academic work. I did not question my pedagogical decisions at the time because I lacked the conceptual background to do so. And why, after all, should such questions be necessary given the interlocking symmetry of the medicalized framework assumed in my undergraduate program? After 3 years as a special education teacher, I began graduate school, where the façade of that interlocking symmetry fell apart. This was a time when the scholarly discourse in special education was beginning to focus more on improving access to general education curriculum as compared to functional and vocational curriculum (Morningstar et al., 1999).

## DOCTORAL YEARS: UNLEARNING AND RELEARNING TO TEACH

I consider myself fortunate to have had an extraordinary doctoral student experience filled with intellectually invigorating philosophical explorations as well as exposure to professionally transformative ideas. I did not enter graduate school to become a special education teacher educator; I merely had a vague idea of wanting to improve the field of special education. However, through my doctoral coursework, I learned about the longstanding and seemingly intractable problem of disproportionate representation of minority students in special education classes (Artiles et al., 2010; Townsend-Walker, 2014). I discovered that Black and Brown children are also subject to more frequent and severe disciplinary measures (e.g., suspension and expulsion) at disproportionately higher rates than their "normal" peers for the same or lesser offenses (Klingner & Artiles, 2003; U.S. Government Accountability Office, 2018). However, what stood out most to me were the abysmal post-school outcomes for students with disabilities due to low expectations and their lack of access to the general education curriculum. Most crucially, I came to understand that these inequities in special education emerge from traditional medical model assumptions regarding the nature of disabilities and that finding a solution first requires a shift to the social model of disability. Furthermore, I began to recognize systemic inequities for children of color, and how—as a privileged White woman—my teaching practice was implicated in what I was learning. I realized I should have spoken up to prevent the girl from Haiti from being labeled at all. I should have advocated for a different approach to serving students who challenged the norms of general education classrooms. At the time, I did not have the knowledge or courage to engage.

Upon completion of my doctoral program, I moved to the Midwest to work as an assistant professor. While at this university, I began to explore ways of connecting the social model of disability and understandings about multicultural education to my pedagogy as a teacher educator. I discerned that implicit bias about race and the social model of disability shifts the responsibility from the deficits within students to the instructional decisions made by teachers and the policies, procedures, and decisions made by educational institutions, such as the work being done by Dan Losen and colleagues at the Civil Rights Project at UCLA. I began my scholarship exploring questions of how the existing special education system fails students in terms of their post-school outcomes (Morningstar et al., 2013).

As a teacher educator, I now share how the social model of disability empowers teachers with the knowledge that the system is set up to sort, select, promote, and fail certain learners, and that this construction must be questioned, dismantled, and replaced with a more humane approach to education. Teachers may have the ability—given a little ingenuity—to include some students, however we must take on our implicit biases toward students with learning differences. In my view, teachers must begin with high expectations and presumptions of the competence of their students. We must redesign schooling to be universally accessible to learners regardless of race, class, and disability. However, without this vital perspective, educators continue to view students as "failed normals" who are best served by a vocationalized curriculum delivered through a technified/reductionist approach to teaching (Iano, 1990). Unfortunately, the protection-oriented stance grounded in the medical model often serves to reinforce stigma and further marginalize students.

## RETURNING TO THE CLASSROOM AFTER DOCTORAL STUDY

For family health reasons, I later returned to my home state and to teaching high school special education. Coming full circle back to the classroom, I was able to witness firsthand the very tangible ways that the medical model of disability and institutional racism continue to create educational inequality for special education students. Almost a decade after I began my career, my new special education colleagues in the self-contained classrooms at this majority-minority high school reminded me of my former self. They filled the school day with games and toys, taught students to cook and clean, or gave them "jobs" such as laundering uniforms for the baseball team. For them, the vocational approach was still legitimate and necessary.

During the time when this case took place, special education in this high school, and others throughout Florida, were set up with self-contained classes for students with intellectual disabilities and units for students with emotional and behavioral disabilities (EBD). Teachers in these classes were responsible for providing daily instruction and managing the IEPs of students in their classes (typically 10–15). Students with disabilities who were included in most high school classes were supported by special education support teachers or support facilitators. These support teachers may teach a class of learning strategies daily or the school may have one such teacher teach the learning strategies classes all day—this typically served as a study hall. While the support teachers had less instructional responsibility, they often had higher caseloads (20–30) depending on the school size and staffing. In the current day, most of Florida's EBD self-contained units have been disbanded, however, self-contained units for students with intellectual disabilities remain (or have been centralized in a few schools throughout a district). Most large high schools in Florida have a team leader who serves as the local education administrator who is able to represent and authorize services in the school during IEP meetings. The school I was at had two local education administrators—the team leader and the special education teacher who had an office near my classroom. The structure of special education may provide helpful context for the rest of the case.

With a sense of urgency to improve post-school outcomes, I now worked to develop and provide an academically focused curriculum in my self-contained classroom. I advocated for inclusion for all of my students despite push back from administrators who insisted—some actively and others passively—that my students were not viable candidates for the general education classrooms based on their disability designations, low achievement, and difficult behavior. For example, when I asked for a set of grade level textbooks (for my small class of 9 students) I was told that it was more appropriate to use whatever I could find in the Exceptional Student Educators book closet. In this closet, I found piles of 10-year-old vocational skills textbooks and even older academic skills books. When I asked if other students in my class could be included and supported in other academic classes, I was told that they could not keep up and that the ESE support teachers were already overwhelmed. While these arguments are legitimate—resources are scarce and everyone is overworked—looking back, I feel I should have tried even harder to get the resources and inclusion that all of my students needed and deserved.

Instead, as Sebastian's case illustrates, the administrators and I talked past each other, never directly stating our underlying concerns, arguments, or perspectives. Ultimately, his inclusion was accepted due to a mistake that his middle school IEP team had made rather than an engaged conversation with the administration and teachers about how we as a school construct maintain an education system that benefits some students while excluding and marginalizing others.

The student I focus on in this case study was a non-English speaker labeled as having an intellectual disability. His name was Sebastian. During his IEP meeting, we discovered that he had essentially been denied legally mandated support for English speakers of other languages since the sixth grade. The team ultimately changed his placement and found that, indeed, he flourished with English language instruction and academic support. Notably, the resistance I faced regarding the inclusion of this student was not from the general education teachers. In fact, they were most receptive, while my special education colleagues and administrators were obstructive and unpersuaded. I recall feeling so frustrated with them at the time.

To be fair, they were well-meaning people upholding a system they believed served students well. I did not engage them in discussions about how the system fails students, especially those caught in the intersection of disability and race. I did, however, try to show them how to build a more inclusive pedagogy. I provided a workshop on universal design for learning, but the teachers in the room were either already on board or expressed resistance due to how much more work this would create for them. My energy might have been better spent first directly addressing the implicit assumptions about race, class, and disability and the very real, but unspoken questions about holding students with disabilities to the same "high standards" that are applied to all other students in the school. For me, engaging in difficult conversations and providing a moral education and connecting this to post-school outcomes data is needed to begin exploring pedagogical alternatives (Gallagher et al., 2019). I now encourage my preservice teacher to consider these things as a way to think about each of their students and work with others to provide an appropriately ambitious education for them.

## UNDERSTANDING SEBASTIAN

Sebastian was short for a ninth grader and one of two Hispanic students in my self-contained special education class. In the hallways with the general education population, Sebastian behaved like all the other kids—walking, talking, laughing, and joking around with age-appropriate ease. However, he hung his head as if to make himself disappear before he was seen entering my self-contained classroom. It was one of three classes in the school for students with intellectual disabilities. Inside the classroom, I interpreted his demeanor as saying that he didn't want to be in this class and felt a deep sense of stigma. While I did not journal or take observation notes, I recall that he refused to talk in class. The other kids said he could not speak English and that all he ever did was sleep in class. They reported that the teachers in middle school just let him sleep all the time.

During my year teaching Sebastian, he continued refusing to participate in lessons or activities and put his head down, despite my best efforts to build rapport with him and incorporate his interests into my lessons. During the first 2 months of the school year, I had only sporadic paraprofessional support due to the chronic shortage and high turnover of support staff. Fortunately, one temporary paraprofessional spoke Spanish. She attempted to get Sebastian engaged in class and was able to begin the process of helping me understand him and why he didn't want to be in a self-contained classroom.

## A CULTURE OF LOW EXPECTATIONS

I came into this teaching role critical of the lack of rigor in self-contained classrooms. I would have preferred to not work in a self-contained setting and made my inclusive philosophy clear during my interview. Unfortunately, this was the only type of position open due to a hiring freeze in the district at the time. As such, the self-contained classroom I designed was significantly different from the other two self-contained classrooms for students with intellectual disabilities at the school. One was equipped with a full kitchen and laundry room, while the other classroom was full of board games, puzzles, and toys. The classroom with a living skills focus was reserved for the most severe of the students in 10th–12th grade, while the game-oriented room was for those with "less severe" disabilities (i.e., mild intellectual disabilities, physical disabilities, and emotional/behavioral disabilities).

The teachers in these classrooms strictly enforced the segregation of their students. They did not allow them to walk in the halls when the general education students were switching classes. These teachers encouraged their students to go pick up their lunches and eat in the classroom while watching movies every day. In contrast, I encouraged my students to interact with their non-labeled peers during times for changing classes and lunch as much as possible. My students enjoyed this time and got to see their friends. Midway through the year, the school administration required me to restrict my students to the classroom during class switching time due to an incident where one of my students was implicated in drug use under the influence of general education peers in the bathroom. They also requested that my students eat lunch in the classroom. Despite my administration's request for my students to eat in the classroom, I advocated for them to be allowed to maintain one of the few times they could socialize with their "typically developing" peers. Therefore, it was decided by the administration that my students were required to sit together in one area of the cafeteria (nearest the staff lunchroom) where my paraprofessional was required to sit to monitor them as needed.

I provided an academic focus in my classroom, mirroring the general education structures of bell work, whole- and small-group instruction, and time for independent practice. I engaged the students in science projects and engineering design challenges that I found in Florida's lesson plan website. I also allowed the students to lead word study lessons. My class also ran the weekend backpack food bank (at the end of the week, after their academic work was complete). We also participated in multiple community-based field trips. During these trips, I required my students to complete budgeting activities and engage in real-life activities (while the other teachers just let their students window shop and socialize). As an example, when visiting a shopping plaza with an attached movie theater, my students completed job applications on-site and the manager conducted mock interviews and shared employability tips. These and other activities were ways in which I sought to reduce the monotony of being in the same classroom with the same students year after year. I often wished to be able to change the structures that segregated and isolated my students from their general education peers. I dreaded the fact that my students who loved challenges and hard work would be relegated to the life skills classroom or the game room for the rest of their high school careers.

## THE WORDS THAT MOVED ME

Sebastian seemed all too aware of the differences between his classroom and the classes of his general education peers. He had two older twin brothers, one grade ahead of him, who undoubtedly had different homework expectations. I soon learned that he was not served in a separate special education class in Puerto Rico. He hated being in special education and refused to participate because he wanted to be with the other kids in general education classes. He knew a little bit of conversational English, but was not proficient enough to be successful academically which would require intervention on the part of the school staff. When I had the Spanish-speaking paraprofessional, Miss Valle, work with him, it became clear that he was more than capable of doing the work. Realizing that his placement might not be correct, I told him I would see what could be done to get his classes changed for him. I spoke with the Special Education Department chair about the process. I was told to speak with a general education teacher to see if he could observe the class and assess whether or not he thought he could manage it. He could observe and participate, but had to be able to perform as well as the other students in order to be placed in the class.

Later that month, Miss Valle was reassigned to work as a one-to-one aide for a different student in general education classes, and Sebastian's head went down again. However, during that time I learned that he was very interested in cars and becoming a mechanic. Therefore, I spoke with Mr.

Darr, the auto shop teacher who agreed to let Sebastian observe one of his classes. Sebastian was excited and happy to do this. When I walked him down the hall to introduce him to the shop teacher, who asked Sebastian about his academic skills, Sebastian answered that his reading and math were "bad," but that he would work hard and do his best. On the walk back from the meeting, he spoke his first full sentence to me, asking about changing all of his classes. I said I was working on it, but that it might take time. Clearly skeptical, he said, "You will never do it, Miss. You will never change my classes." I was stunned at his conviction and became even more determined to help him.

In preparation for Sebastian's upcoming IEP meeting, I invited the school's Title I Family Liaison, Mr. Anthony, to conduct the required transition assessments with Sebastian in Spanish. I also asked him to explain how important it was for him to perform well in the auto shop class if he wanted to prove that he could move into other classes. During the assessment and interview, Mr. Anthony learned that Sebastian was not happy with the special education class and that he wanted to be in all general education classes, or even in a class for English language learners. He stated that he wanted a general education diploma, not "a stupid fake diploma," and that he wanted to learn things, do science, and be with his friends. Sebastian did not believe that adults would help him make these changes happen and he felt that he would be stuck in special education forever. Mr. Anthony and I were amazed that he had so much to say. Additionally, the in-depth transition interview revealed that he had specific plans to attend Northern Ohio's Auto Technology Program one day. Until then, Sebastian shared that he would live at home while he completed automotive courses offered at the local technical school. Additionally, he wanted to get married and start a family when he turned 22. He had more coherent plans than most of the ninth graders in general education.

After hearing Sebastian's plans, I was even more convinced that he was in the wrong setting to be able to achieve his goals. I asked Mr. Anthony (the school's Spanish speaking family liaison) to call Sebastian's mother and ask her opinion about changing his classes. I asked him to explain that parent advocacy for changes of this nature would be important. He found that Sebastian's mother was supportive of changing his classes and that she just wanted him to be happy; however, she did not want to upset the school staff.

## EARNING ENTRY

Sebastian started attending the auto shop class in the middle of the semester, which made the content very challenging because he lacked the background and context his classmates received earlier in the year. Further, the teacher had a very fast-paced and traditional lecture and book-work approach to instruction. The shop teacher complained that Sebastian was "acting like a bump on a log" in the classroom and was starting to put his head down because he was unable to do the work. I sent my newly hired paraprofessional, Mrs. Kelly, to see if she could help. Sebastian was very angry and embarrassed to have her sit next to him, but he got a bit more work done each day. Mrs. Kelly reported that the teacher's pace of speaking was lightning fast and the assignments were even difficult for her to understand. I wondered how Sebastian could keep up? How could he ever meet the auto shop teacher's expectations without some alteration to how instruction was provided? Would he be able to make it? Retrospectively, it is clear that locating the problem within the child was the problem, when providing resources such as translated texts or other alternative ways of learning for English language learners that could help so many students succeed in such classes.

## QUESTIONING PLACEMENT

At this point, I was questioning the accuracy of Sebastian's special education placement, which was based on his intellectual disability diagnosis. I wondered if changing his placement required changing how he was categorized by the system. Would a specific learning disability category be required to move him into general education classes? Would dismissing him altogether be the solution? Could he be moved out of the self-contained classroom for part or all of the day regardless of the diagnosis?

I, again, sought out the support of the leadership at my school and at the district level. This was unhelpful, as many stated that Sebastian would first have to prove that he could be successful in the general education classes before we could even start talking about changing placements. Three administrators also indicated that, regardless of his performance, it was already too far into the school year for Sebastian to catch up and be successful. These responses were to be expected as I assume they felt obligated to uphold the status quo and they were protecting the school staff from the extra work of making a change that had not been earned by Sebastian. My frustration with this is that the system and this way of thinking reflects educators' illogical beliefs about the normal curve. A system where students are sorted and selected into tracks and classes. A system where some students are able to be successful and have access to the classes they want to take and those who struggle are relegated to remediation or special education.

In their critique of Herrnstein and Murray's 1994 text, *The Bell Curve*, Dudley-Marling and Gurn (2010) thoroughly debunk the idea that human behavior is accurately reflected in statistically normal distributions. Dudley-Marling and Gurn (2010) highlight the research of numerous statisticians and influential figures in the history of psychological assessment. They point out that while the normal curve can be reflective of random events, such as gambling or petals on flowers, it does not translate well with human traits and behavior which are significantly influenced by social, cultural, and economic factors. For example, height, weight, strength, taste, response to signals, academic achievement, task completion time, and social conformity do not distribute normally. However, the idea of the normal distribution has proven to be sticky among educators. Dudley-Marling and Gurn (2010) illustrate how this concept remains at the heart of special education. They explain how attempts to dismantle this misguided way of thinking have not been received well in the field.

Still under the impression that I had to first change his diagnosis before considering a different placement, I spoke with the school psychologist about re-evaluating Sebastian. He said the team would need to determine if a re-evaluation was necessary and that typically by the time students get to high school, they have already been re-evaluated three times, so there is usually no need to do it again. "Especially, since things like intelligence quotient (IQ) scores are fairly reliable and do not change over time or with more testing." I knew that IQ test scores are only one of three aspects that determine intellectual disability, but I knew that the IQ often mattered most in special education decisions, which was clearly the case with Sebastian. I shared my concern that Sebastian was likely to drop out if something was not changed. The psychologist agreed that the team would need to look at all the data and decide if a re-evaluation was necessary. I realized that the case against making a permanent and significant change for Sebastian based on disability eligibility was not strong. He was far below grade level, refused to participate when he was not interested, and could not communicate effectively in English. It was already halfway into the semester and Sebastian was losing hope.

## THE INDIVIDUALIZED EDUCATION PLAN MEETING

With the IEP meeting coming in a few days, I spoke with the special education teacher next door regarding my concern that testing and re-evaluation would not provide adequate data to support the move. Mrs. Hines said,

You know what? We really don't need a re-evaluation or to change his label . . . so why don't we just go ahead and put him out there. He could give it a shot and we could always back him out of full-time general education classes—he would probably have to go into remedial classes anyway. And if the team decided he needs a new English language learner evaluation, maybe he could be put into the class for English language learners. All we really need is for the team to agree to the plan.

She volunteered to be the school representative at the IEP meeting—this would mean that I did not need to invite one of the other administrators in the school. This would be helpful as it would ensure that only people who knew Sebastian well would be a part of the IEP meeting.

At the start of the meeting, I presented the details of his case. While reviewing Sebastian's file, the psychologist noticed that when Sebastian arrived from Puerto Rico, he was not tested to determine if he needed services as an English language learner. The middle school team based their decision on his IQ score and intellectual disability label, and then proceeded to place him in a self-contained class. The document said that this special education setting would be able to address his English language learners' needs. We were stunned, as this was an unethical approach given that Florida is under a consent decree to provide appropriate English language services and teachers with appropriate certification.

Sitting around the table, the team unanimously decided that Sebastian deserved and required a full evaluation for English language learners and that he deserved the opportunity to be in general education classes. The auto shop teacher agreed to keep him in the program and to set him on the 4-year course of study toward an automotive certification. We put him on the standard diploma track, indicated that he no longer needed self-contained service, documented the need for in-class support services, and recommended a learning strategies class. We hoped that he would be placed into a class English language learners after the evaluation. Furthermore, we agreed to ask his teachers to complete a daily progress form and for him to check in and out daily with Mr. Anthony or myself. Mr. Anthony made it clear that the ball was in Sebastian's court, that he *might* fail ninth grade and be required to repeat classes, but that there would be ample support available. If he kept his head up, did all of his work, and tried hard, he *might* pass. Sebastian and his mother agreed that they understood the stakes. Free tutoring options were discussed, and everyone signed forms to get the process initiated. Mr. Anthony asked Sebastian what he thought of the outcome. With a pleased smile, Sebastian said, "Esto es un milagro" (It is a miracle). At this point, I was relieved that I had been able to fulfill my promise to make a change for him. I think this was the point when I began to understand the need for a true critique of the policies and procedures that perpetuate inequities in special education.

## AWAITING THE SCHEDULE CHANGE

After the meeting, Mrs. Hines notified the guidance counselors of the need to change the schedule, but nothing happened for nearly 3 weeks. Sebastian waited in the self-contained classroom and asked about the new schedule every day. He did what he wanted to do in class and started to put his head down—losing hope once again. I began sending him to the guidance office to ask for himself so that he would know I was not lying about the delay. We learned that Sebastian's IEP meeting took place during a busy time and the guidance department had decided to wait an additional 3 weeks until the end of the quarter so that he would have a fresh start.

The special education team leader called me to his office. He was upset that I had not followed protocol and said that I should have had Sebastian observe classes until he could prove he could handle the workload. For my part, I explained the team's decisions and the plan put in place to support Sebastian. I explained that they would be meeting again in a month, if necessary, to see what might need to be changed.

The schedule was ultimately changed at the start of the next term. Unfortunately, Sebastian was unable to remain in the physical education and auto shop classes. The guidance counselors did not discuss the schedule with the team, and his schedule was set up similarly to most students in the school with identified learning disabilities. Schedules for these students were presumably set up in this manner to facilitate support from the school's four special education teachers, who provided push-in services in those classes. Whoever made this decision might have also believed that Sebastian needed to be "remediated" since he had been in self-contained classes for so long. Sebastian's schedule included algebra and remedial math as well as English and remedial reading—both subjects taught as a block of two classes together—followed by the class for English language learners (which would consist of learning English via Rosetta Stone computer software), and a learning strategies course with Mr. Morris (the teacher next door to me) at the end of the day.

I remember being outraged at the schedule. Taking him out of the course he was most interested in was contrary to what I knew about keeping students from dropping out of school. The team had stipulated that he stay in the auto shop class, but I also knew he struggled with its content. I wondered if the extra remedial classes would be helpful or at least a way to keep him afloat while he made the transition into general education classes and auto shop the following year; therefore, I did not fight it. Perhaps on some level, I was relieved that the schedule had been created at all.

I asked Sebastian to discuss his schedule with Mr. Anthony, who emphasized that although he would get out of self-contained classes, the schedule was designed to bring him up to speed and help him improve his English so that he could succeed. Notably, he was told that he would begin the automotive program in the following year. While Sebastian was upset about having to be in remedial classes and not taking auto shop, he did not argue because he knew this class schedule would get him out of the dreaded self-contained classroom.

To cheer him up about the process, I bought him a black binder the next day with easy-open rings, tabs for each class, plenty of paper for notes, and a box of pencils. I was nervous for him to do well, but he was just as anxious to get out of my class. From then on, he came and checked in with me in the mornings and then went to his classes. His learning strategies class was at the end of the day and situated next door to my room, so he often came in to show me his teachers' comments and ask for help with work or tests when needed.

## WHOSE RESPONSIBILITY?

As soon as I could after his new schedule was in effect, I met with the algebra/remedial math teacher and explained Sebastian's story. The teacher was very welcoming and accustomed to working with English language learners. However, I noted that he might benefit from the in-class assistance provided by the special education teachers. Therefore, I emailed Mr. Dupree, the special education team leader, to find out who would be assigned as Sebastian's in-class support teacher. His reply was a forwarded email message from the regional staffing specialist stating that I should be the one to do the in-class support and have my paraprofessional cover the self-contained class since I "knew Sebastian so well."

Due to how uncooperative he had been earlier in the year, I was not surprised that Mr. Dupree was unwilling to assign an in-class support teacher to help Sebastian. However, for the staffing specialist to indicate that I should provide support in the general education classroom in addition to teaching my self-contained classroom was beyond surprising. I felt that Sebastian, or my recommendations for him, were being set up to fail so that he would have to be placed back into the self-contained classroom.

This response highlights the extremely low priority placed on teaching the students in the self-contained classroom. It also potentially indicates an unwillingness on the part of the other special education teachers to assist students with intellectual disability. Understandably, they have large caseloads and struggle to find the time to meet student needs. Nevertheless, it remains part of their job description to support *all* students regardless of their disability classification.

I did not respond to his email about in-class support and was unsure about how to proceed. The assistant principal requested a meeting with me, so I decided I would wait and discuss it with him. In the meantime, I found an opportunity to meet with the district intellectual disability supervisor once again to explain the situation. This supervisor was appalled and told me to inform the assistant principal that it would not be possible to provide support given my required teaching duties. Predictably, the meeting with the assistant principal was delayed due to administrative scheduling issues.

In the interim, while knowing that Sebastian required support, I sent my paraprofessional to help him. He hated this attention and once again put his head down the instant she came into the room to help him. From day one, Sebastian was vigilant about having his teachers sign his progress report papers daily; he got perfect reports, was participating, behaving, and on-task with his classwork without fail. The teachers often paired him with a student who could translate the assignments. However, he continued to complain about the paraprofessional coming to help him. I explained that the paraprofessional was required to attend his class, but that he did not have to talk to her unless he needed help. I told the paraprofessional to stay away from him and help the teacher or other kids as much as possible to reduce his embarrassment. When the district special education administrator finally visited, I explained that Sebastian appeared to be doing well, and noted his refusal to work when the paraprofessional came in. The district special education administrator recommended reducing paraprofessional support and even moving him to a monthly or weekly consultative status if he did better without assistance.

## ADMINISTRATIVE RESPONSE

Three weeks after the IEP meeting, I finally met with the assistant principal. He told me that he believed I had done nothing wrong and that he was aware that the team had acted together. However, he asked to be informed of the process in greater detail so that it would not be a surprise. He agreed that it was not my role to support Sebastian and suggested that I communicate with the English language learners teachers about providing more support for him. This was very telling, as the assistant principal did not indicate that another special education teacher would be assigned to assist Sebastian. By this time, I realized that having any special education personnel entering the classroom to assist Sebastian would only increase his stigma, so I did not push the matter. While I was relieved to not be reprimanded or required to leave my classroom, I left with the distinct impression that Mr. Dupree had gotten his way.

Interim reports came out in December: Sebastian received a C in algebra, B in remedial math, D in English and remedial English, F in the class for English language learners, and C in learning strategies. I asked the English language learner classroom teacher if it would be possible to provide more support for Sebastian, and I also spoke with the bilingual paraprofessional, who agreed to start attending his English/reading classes. Furthermore, I began building a relationship with the special education teacher who taught the self-contained behavior class. This teacher agreed to take Sebastian on at the next session where caseloads were assigned and support him as needed.

By the middle of the third quarter, Sebastian was struggling to do the work in his classes. However, he worked from bell to bell and the teachers rewarded his efforts. One day, I saw his class in the library. While many of his classmates were chatting and playing on their phones, Sebastian was steadily taking notes from the projector screen and ignoring his peers. He continued to obtain perfect comments on daily progress reports from each teacher.

## SEBASTIAN'S SUCCESS

Now, Sebastian strutted around campus with a pair of white wireless headphones around his neck, big diamond earring studs in both ears, and a new orange Ecko hoodie over his T-shirt (and, of course, his spotless white Adidas sneakers). When he began the year, he seemed withdrawn, small, and utterly sad. Now, he smiled and looked around himself confidently when walking down the halls. He seemed to be filling out physically, becoming taller and fuller in the face. He was coming out of his shell in other ways as well. He had a chat with Mr. Anthony and said that he did not want his teachers to "just give me grades or answers." He said he wanted to learn it all. He began to ask me for help more regularly. With Mr. Morris' permission, he went straight to my room at the end of the day (instead of the learning strategies class), where his old classmates hugged him and told him they missed him. He smiled, hugged them back, and would then get started on his work. It was a definite change for the better.

## SEBASTIAN—ONE YEAR LATER

I did not stay in this school after that year, there were a few other breaches of professional conduct—not chronicled in this chapter as they did not relate to the case, but which resulted in my loss of confidence in the leadership there. I was sad and scared to leave my students—particularly Sebastian, however, one of the special education teachers I worked with there agreed to add Sebastian to her caseload. She sent me text message updates about Sebastian every so often. He was passing all of his general education classes, including algebra. He struggled with the remedial class and the class for English language learners, but only because he did not want to be in them at all. He was on track to graduate and realize his future.

I took a fourth-grade general education position in a school where an inclusive stance was welcomed. I needed a space where I could work closely with like-minded professionals—reading and math coaches, the guidance counselor, and special education teachers (which were all titled "inclusion teachers" in this new school). I also wanted to test myself, to step into the shoes of the general education teacher and see how I would fare at including students in my classroom. The staff at this school held implicit beliefs about the social model of disability, they presumed that all children were competent and just needed different levels of support (the MTSS process helped with this—but that is another chapter) and we were able to consistently include many students who would otherwise be segregated in a self-contained classroom. The fact that this school received many students from the nearby orphanage may have contributed to helping the staff realize that *normal* is relative and that *all* students need the opportunity to succeed in the most inclusive setting possible.

## 2020: AN UNEXPECTED UPDATE

While writing this, Mr. Anthony's wife—who is now a doctoral student in our department—called me one Saturday with surprising news. Mr. Anthony had just run into Sebastian and his mother at Walmart. Sebastian remembered him and me as well! They were still glad we made this change for him. He is not yet in an automotive technical school as he had hoped, but he is doing well, looking good, driving, and still wanting to achieve his dream.

## FINAL THOUGHTS

After I left that high school, I also began volunteering for my local Guardian Ad Litem program. In this role, I research and advocate for the best interests of children in the foster care system who have been abused, neglected, or abandoned. I find in this role that I am able to be a more active third party involved in providing information that will help judges make decisions to support children and families. It has opened my eyes to the realities of poverty, drug abuse, and the ways that systems can disenfranchise or empower youth.

These experiences helped me understand the reasons why special educators and general educators desperately need to collaborate. They have also helped me see why they often struggle to do so. The amount of knowledge I have gained over the 2 decades of my career really only scratches the surface of my own understanding. Specifically, I feel I need to know more about how systems and policies work and can be challenged and changed by teachers. I want to understand more about the perspectives and priorities of stakeholders particularly those whose philosophies and approaches are different from mine. And I am intensely interested in how to enact an anti-racist and anti-ableist philosophy within the context of where I work and live.

This case has also taught me that early intervention is crucial if students are to be included and stay included in general education classrooms. Unfortunately, it seems early intervention is often undone once students with more intensive academic and behavioral needs reach middle school. Where they are often moved into self-contained settings and stay in these settings throughout high school. Middle and high schools in Florida require students to navigate larger campuses, multiple classes and teachers, and complex schedules. There are few to no supports in place to assist students with disabilities in making this transition. This is a time when children mature a great deal and with the right supports could be included in regular classes, but are never given the chance. In my opinion, the self-contained placement decisions made in middle school often are a dead end street. I feel there needs training and support for this transition period and procedures to review placement decisions made in middle and high school to ensure the opportunity to be included is maximized. In this scenario, the burden of proof of success should no longer be on the child to "prove" they are capable—they should just be afforded the opportunity to begin high school supported in inclusive settings.

I have now returned to teach in special education teacher education program at the large urban university where I earned my doctorate. I remain painfully aware that many of my special education colleagues teaching in the K–12 setting have not had the opportunity to test their own assumptions as I did. It is all too clear when I visit local high schools and see youth in "transition programs" sitting around tables making buttons to support the football teams or performing "work-study" that consists of cleaning the lunchroom after the other students return to class. I read about in the research literature, which has documented no significant changes in placements and service provision for students labeled as having intellectual disabilities in the last decade (Kurth et al., 2019). In fact, Agran et al. (2020) assess the root of the issue in this way:

> Placement decisions for students with severe disabilities have often been based less on the students' unique learning needs but more on beliefs and presumptions about student learning, entrenched school district policies that restrict program delivery options, and other variables unrelated to student needs. (Agran et. al., 2020, p. 1)

While I recognize that administrators must juggle complex logistics, budgets, policies, and personalities, I can only concur with the statement from Argan and his colleagues, which makes my current work all the more important. I also find it true when working with children in the foster care system, group home workers I meet may know that a child was placed in foster care through no fault of their own. As these children grow up in these difficult and often institutional settings, they are often labeled and treated as delinquent or worse in their group home or school settings.

When working with preservice teachers in such schools, I find myself grappling with how to share my experiences and teach them about the social model of disability while also allowing them to draw their own conclusions. However, I have found several ways to integrate my learning into coursework and field experiences. I pose questions, play devil's advocate, have them read counterpoint narratives about special education published in non-special education journals, and try to create opportunities that allow them to challenge their own assumptions. I speak with them about my first years of teaching and the guilt I carry for not being a better advocate, for not questioning decisions, and for not knowing enough about the implications of my actions. I share that the social relationships they develop with other professionals and their level of knowledge about history and societal issues will play a factor in their ability to advocate for their students. I encourage them to continue their education, to earn a PhD one day. Or at the very least participate in as much professional development and reading as they can to ensure they have the confidence to speak up and engage in critical conversations. Moreover, I explain what I would have done differently. I often wonder if this will have been sufficient when I look back in 8 to 10 years?

In one of our recent behavior management classes, I presented a case about a boy who threw his books on the floor whenever he entered the hall with other students to switch classes. In this scenario, the paraprofessional always picked up the books and the boy was always late to his next class. I asked my students to come up with ideas for intervention. The first and most common suggestion was to have the boy not switch classes with everyone else—to stay in his classroom and wait. I reminded them of the principle of normalization and pressed them for alternative solutions. They ended up with a solution involving peer support, positive reinforcement from teachers at each doorway down the hall and fading of the paraprofessional. I then shared my experience working with Sebastian and applauded their solution. My preservice teachers seemed to enjoy the process of generating alternative solutions. I only hope the administrators and leaders in their schools' value this as much as I do. Until then, I will continue to advocate for all of the Sebastians struggling to have their voices heard within the special education system.

## REFERENCES

Agran, M., Jackson, L., Kurth, J. A., Ryndak, D., Burnette, K., Jameson, M., Zagona, A., Fitzpatrick, H., & Wehmeyer, M. (2020). Why aren't students with severe disabilities being placed in general education classrooms: Examining the relations among classroom placement, learner outcomes, and other factors. *Research and Practice for Persons With Severe Disabilities, 45*(1), 4–13. https://doi.org/10.1177/1540796919878134

Apple, M. W. (2004). *Ideology and curriculum* (3rd ed.). Routledge Falmer.

Artiles, A. J., Kozleski, E. B., Trent, S. C., Osher, D., & Ortiz, A. (2010). Justifying and explaining disproportionality, 1968–2008: A critique of underlying views of culture. *Exceptional Children, 76*(3), 279–299.

Dudley-Marling, C., & Gurn, A. (2010). *The myth of the normal curve* (Vol. 11). Peter Lang.

Gallagher, D. (2010). Educational researchers and the making of normal people. In C. Dudley-Marling & A. Gurn (Eds.), *The myth of the normal curve* (Vol. 11, pp. 25–38). Peter Lang.

Gallagher, D. J., Petersen, A. J., Cowley, D. M., & Iqtadar, S. (2019). A sentimental education: Insights for inclusive reform from a university/school district partnership. *The SAGE Handbook of Inclusion and Diversity in Education* (pp. 146–158). SAGE Publications.

Iano, R. P. (1990). Special education teachers: Technicians or educators? *Journal of Learning Disabilities, 23*(8), 462–465.

Klingner, J. K., & Artiles, A. J. (2003). When should bilingual students be in special education? *Educational Leadership, 61*(2), 66–71.

Kurth, J. A., Ruppar, A. L., Toews, S. G., McCabe, K. M., McQueston, J. A., & Johnston, R. (2019). Considerations in placement decisions for students with extensive support needs: An analysis of LRE statements. *Research & practice for persons with severe disabilities, 44*(1), 3–19. https://doi.org/10.1177/1540796918825479

Morningstar, M. E., Kleinhammer-Tramill, P. J., & Lattin, D. L., (1999). Using successful models of student-centered transition planning and services for adolescents. *Focus on Exceptional Children, 31*(9), 1. https://doi.org/10.17161/foec.v31i9.6770

Morningstar, M., Knollman, G., Semon, S., & Kleinhammer-Tramill, J. (2013). Accountability for what matters: Using postschool outcomes to build school and community renewal. In L. C. Burrello, J. Kleinhammer-Tramill, & W. Sailor (Eds.), *Unifying educational systems: Leadership and policy perspectives* (pp. 156–169). Routledge.

Townsend-Walker, B. L. (2014). Sixty years after "Brown v. Board of Education": Legal and policy fictions in school desegregation, the Individuals With Disabilities Education Act, and No Child Left Behind. *Multiple Voices for Ethnically Diverse Exceptional Learners, 14*(2), 41–51.

U.S. Government Accountability Office. (2018). *K–12 education: Discipline disparities for Black students, boys, and students with disabilities*. (GAO-18-258). https://www.gao.gov/products/GAO-18-258

CHAPTER 23

# THEY DECIDE

## Empowering Transition-Age Youth With Disabilities by Promoting Self-Determination

**Andrew R. Scheef**
*University of Idaho*

**Julia Mahfouz**
*University of Colorado, Denver*

**Mayumi Hagiwara**
*San Francisco State University*

## ABSTRACT

Individuals with disabilities often find themselves in situations where decisions are made for them by others on their behalf. To put decision-making power in the hands of individuals with disabilities themselves, school-based special education services should feature instruction and training in self-determination skills. Doing so provides greater opportunities for youth with disabilities to better understand what they want for their future and implement

*Who Decides?*, pages 569–591

a plan to achieve future goals. Although much of these efforts will come from the special education teachers who work with students directly, school administrators can play a significant role in developing a school culture that facilitates the development of individual student self-determination skills. This chapter provides a general overview of self-determination skills for youth with disabilities and then gives specific recommendations for school administrators looking to augment existing self-determination training in their schools.

Individuals with disabilities often defer to others to make decisions on their behalf. Recognizing this, international efforts have supported the rights of individuals with disabilities to retain power to make personal decisions (e.g., Article 12 of the Convention on the Rights of People With Disabilities; United Nations, 2006). Efforts to increase student self-determination has become the foundation for policies, goals, and social systems involving individuals with disabilities (Loman et al., 2010). Self-determination generally involves the notion that individuals are empowered to take control of their lives; self-determined individuals know what they want and understand how to get it while recognizing their strengths and limitations (Field et al., 1998). Individuals with disabilities who have developed a greater sense of self-determination may experience improved employment outcomes and greater community access (Shogren, Wehmeyer, Palmer, Forber-Pratt, et al., 2015). Strong self-determination skills allow all people, including those with disabilities, to become genuine decision makers.

Individuals with disabilities are faced with the challenge of thriving in a world that has been established and molded by ableist mindsets. In broad terms, ableism represents societal preference for individuals with typical abilities, resulting in discrimination against those with disabilities (Wolbring, 2008). Ableism has shaped all aspects of society, and in doing so has become "one of the most socially entrenched and accepted isms" (Wolbring, 2008, p. 253). Brittain et al., (2020) make the argument that ableism "is, in itself, an exercise in power and control" (p. 218). As such, promoting self-determination for individuals with disabilities is a push against the promotion of ableist views, policies, and mindsets. Self-determined individuals with disabilities challenge traditional power structures reinforced by ableism by taking command of their personal life path.

## Contextual Factors Influencing Self-Determination Skills

The extent to which an individual is self-determined cannot be recognized by identifying specific choices or actions; these are individual in nature and vary based on the uniqueness of each person. However, it is the nature, function, or context of individualized decisions where self-determination can be found. When understanding student self-determination and delivering self-determination instruction, it is imperative to consider contexts as influential factors. Shogren et al. (2014) defined a context as "integrative concept that provides a framework for describing personal and environmental factors, supports planning, and policy development" (p. 111). Personal factors include age, gender, race/ethnicity, family backgrounds, and life experiences. On the other hand, environmental factors include community, organization, system, and policy and practices. Shogren et al. (2020) introduced the multidimensional model of contexts and highlighted the intersectionality of different contextual factors influencing human functioning and personal outcomes in complex ways. For example, culture, family backgrounds, gender, age, and support needs are some of the most often discussed contextual factors impacting self-determination for students with disabilities (Wehmeyer et al., 2011).

Although the definition of self-determination is universally applicable, how people engage in self-determined actions and what self-determination opportunities are available might be significantly varied by these contextual factors. Specifically, families from individualistic cultural backgrounds may value decision-making and goal setting around individual future aspirations, while families valuing community or collectivism might encourage family decision-making and family preferences over individual goals (Achola & Greene, 2016). Moreover, depending on the intensity of support needs that individual students require, how they demonstrate self-determined action may look different, but with appropriate supports, they can be self-determined even with extensive support needs (Shogren et al., 2020).

## Self-Determination Instruction in Schools

The development of self-determination skills is an essential component of special education services for students with disabilities, which may be especially true for high school students who are preparing for post-school transition (Burke et al., 2020; Shogren et al., 2020; Shogren, 2013). Secondary education is an exciting and challenging time for young adults; it heralds the transition between childhood and adulthood. During this time, youth are refining professional goals and aspirations while preparing to enter the complex world of adulthood. As such, the extent to which an individual is self-determined may be a key factor in their ability to achieve post-school goals (Test et al., 2009).

Secondary special education teachers are tasked with providing supports and services to help youth with disabilities achieve their individualized post-school goals. Promoting opportunities to develop student self-determination should be a key component of instructional plans. For students with disabilities (low- or high-incidence) targeted instruction can improve the extent to which individuals are self-determined (Burke et al., 2020; Wehmeyer et al., 2013). Research suggests that instruction in skills related to self-determination can have a positive impact on student outcomes, including those related to academics, employment, and community access and engagement (Dean et al., 2017; Shogren et al., 2012; Shogren, Wehmeyer, Palmer, Rifenbark et al., 2015). Mazzotti et al. (2021) updated the literature review conducted by Test et al. (2009) which identified predictors of positive post-school outcomes for youth with disabilities. They also found self-determination/self-advocacy instruction to be a key component of school-based services. Other studies have found similar results (e.g., Mazzotti et al., 2016; McConnell et al., 2012; Southward & Kyzar, 2017). The importance of self-determination skill development is further exemplified by its inclusion as one of the five areas of vocational rehabilitation pre-employment transition services offered to secondary students with disabilities (Workforce Innovation and Opportunity Act, 2014).

## The Roles of School Administrators

School administrators also play a role in cultivating these self-determination skills and ensuring that programs in their buildings meet the education needs of all students to promote college and career readiness. Carter, Lane, et al. (2015) surveyed elementary and secondary school administrators about their perspectives of self-determination and found that administrators recognized the importance of delivering instruction on self-determination skills. However, the study also identified the need for practitioner professional development (e.g., in-district, in-school workshop, mentorship) to develop proficiency in delivering self-determination instruction. Furthermore, Karvonen et al. (2004) studied how exemplar schools were implementing self-determination instruction across a building and found that students identified not only teachers but also other school professionals, including administrators, as important sources of support in developing self-determination. Notably, it took one person who had a belief in self-determination and motivation to spread out self-determination instruction throughout the school. This one person could be any school professional, including school administrators (Karvonen et al., 2004).

Substantial research and policy works have been established to guide the roles and responsibilities of school administration in special education (e.g., Council of Administrators of Special Education). For example, responsive leadership interventions and system progress monitoring, problem-solving, and developing collaborative leadership practices are considered crucial competencies that school administrators need to practice (Boscardin, 2007). Additionally, research has shown the importance of leadership in creating inclusive schools that meet the needs of all students (e.g., DeMatthews et al., 2020). Research has also shown a positive relationship between school administrators' understanding of special education and their attitude toward inclusion (Angelle & Bilton, 2009; Wakeman et al., 2006). A national study of 362 secondary school administrators found that principals who reported better understanding of special education were more proactive in being engaged and supporting special education teachers and the programs (Wakeman et al., 2006). The National Council of Accreditation of Teacher Education (NCATE), the Council for Exceptional Children, and the Council of Administrators of Special Education (CASE) have established professional standards to identify the knowledge and skills that characterize competent school administrators of special education. While these standards articulate the priorities for ethics and practice for school leaders in the field of special education administration, they are not specific to school principals. How school administrators could support opportunities for students to develop these essential self-determination skills is still not fully explored.

In this chapter, we will describe the characteristics of self-determination and then propose recommendations that school leaders may utilize to promote self-determination based on existing literature and our own experiences.

## SKILLS ASSOCIATED WITH SELF-DETERMINATION

Self-determination is not one single skill, but rather a collection of associated skills and competencies. Causal agency theory defines self-determination as a dispositional characteristic as people act as causal agents in their life "in service to freely chosen goals" (Shogren, Wehmeyer, Palmer, Forber-Pratt et al., 2015, p. 258). These authors explained that self-determined actions include (a) volitional action, making a conscious choice based on one's preferences and strengths; (b) agentic action, identifying pathways that lead to a specific goal or outcome; and (c) action-control beliefs, believing that one has the ability to take action and reach the goal.

Wehmeyer et al. (2000) identified seven essential components, which have become the foundation for much of the literature focused on self-determination and individuals with disabilities, including (a) decision-making, (b) choice making, (c) problem-solving, (d) setting and attaining goals, (e) self-advocacy and leadership, (f) self-knowledge and self-awareness, and (g) self-management and self-regulation. Table 23.1 provides a case study showing how each of these skills may relate to a student with a disability considering attending postsecondary education. In addition, each of these seven skills are described below.

**TABLE 23.1  A Case Study Displaying How the Characteristics of Self-Determination May Impact a Student Considering Postsecondary Education Attendance**

| Self-Determination Characteristic | Example of Potential Impact on Post-School Success |
|---|---|
| Decision-Making | The student researches and evaluates if attending postsecondary education is the right choice for them. |
| Choice Making | The student has decided to attend postsecondary education and must make a choice between possible college or university options. |
| Problem Solving | Funding postsecondary education is a barrier to enrollment. As such, the self-determined student seeks to explore ways to address this barrier. |
| Setting and Attaining Goals | The student develops a plan to increase their grade point average in order to receive a specific scholarship to attend the college of their choice. |
| Self-Advocacy and Leadership Skills | The student leads their own IEP meeting, allowing them to become more comfortable talking about their disability and accommodations. |
| Self-Knowledge and Self-Awareness | The student recognizes that the academic stresses of attending college will be substantial, which could be compounded by difficult relationships with a roommate. They seek to have a single-resident dorm room. |
| Self-Management and Self-Regulation | Recognizing that supports in postsecondary education are more limited, the student works to develop greater independence in tracking their academic responsibilities. |

## Decision-Making

The ability to make decisions is an essential component of self-determination (Wehmeyer & Shogren, 2017; Wehmeyer et al., 2000) and is also a predictor of positive post-school outcomes for youth with disabilities (Mazzotti et al., 2016). In order to effectively make a decision, an individual must (a) identify possible action alternatives, (b) understand potential consequences of each of these actions, (c) recognize the likelihood of each consequence occurring (if that particular action were to be taken), (d) identify the value or importance of each consequence, and (e) synthesize this information to realize the most desirable course of action (Beyth-Marom et al., 1991). Recently, the supported decision-making movement has emerged to promote self-determination for individuals with disabilities (especially intellectual disability) who may struggle in this process. Supported decision-making offers individuals with disabilities opportunities to control major life decisions, including the need for a legal guardian (Kohn et al., 2012).

## Choice Making

The decision-making process allows an individual to evaluate a scenario and develop options, which results in choice making. Ensuring that individuals with disabilities have opportunities to make their own choices is the foundation of self-determination. Choice making opportunities contribute to moving forward from a history of forced decisions made by others to giving individuals with disabilities more control over their life. Especially for individuals with intellectual or developmental disabilities, choice making may need to be taught (Agran et al., 2010). In addition, those facilitating the choice making must ensure that mechanisms and systems are in place to support the realization of choices made by the individual.

## Problem-Solving

Wehmeyer (2007) identified close connections between decision-making and problem-solving, noting that decisions one makes are often an essential piece of the problem-solving process. Problem-solving entails recognizing long- and short-term obstacles and the development of plans to overcome these obstacles. These skills are useful when students encounter various situations that require independence and competence at school and in the community, especially when students are expected to engage in tasks independently. Problem-solving can also be useful in relationships; students should have the capacity to navigate social difficulties with others. However, many individuals (including those with disabilities) may struggle with finding a potential solution to a problem. As such, developing these skills may be part of a comprehensive self-determination learning plan.

## Setting and Attaining Goals

Self-determined individuals are able to identify goals and develop a course of action to achieve these goals. As a result, youth with disabilities who successfully set goals may be more likely to achieve positive post-school outcomes (Mazzotti et al., 2016). School-based self-determination training may focus on goals involving different skill areas (e.g., academic, social, personal, career), durations (e.g., short-term, long-term), and environments (e.g., classroom, job site, community).

## Self-Advocacy and Leadership Skills

There is a close connection between self-determination and self-advocacy, so much so that Test et al. (2009) included them together in their study of predictors of positive post-school outcomes for youth with disabilities. Without the ability to advocate for one's self, it is difficult to have personal choices realized. Test et al. (2009) identified four components to self-advocacy, the first of which is *self-awareness*. Before one is able to express their needs and wants to others, they must have a strong understanding of themselves. Next, in order to feel confident that requests are appropriate, individuals must have *knowledge of rights*. With an understanding of legal rights and protections, individuals with disabilities gain power and confidence to advocate for their needs. However, without proper means to express these needs, requests may be ignored. As such, individuals with disabilities must have the *communication* skills to express preferences and advocate for their rights. Finally, *leadership* represents the transition from being a self-advocate to being someone who can advocate for others. These opportunities strengthen one's ability to advocate for themselves.

## Self-Knowledge and Self-Awareness

Self-determined individuals have knowledge about themselves, allowing them to better understand the extent to which goals are appropriate and reasonable. Instances of self-knowledge and self-awareness occur at a variety of levels. Recognition of personal strengths and needs to set goals or make decisions may be at the foundation of self-awareness for any individual. For individuals with disabilities, this may include recognition and self-acknowledgement of their disability and how it impacts daily living. Acknowledgement of one's disability can result in higher self-esteem, thus increasing the extent to which the individual is self-determined (Nario-Redmond et al., 2013). When faced with difficult situations, students with disabilities may access these skills to focus on their strengths, have better understanding of their own preferences, and thus achieve success.

## Self-Management and Self-Regulation

Self-management strategies allow individuals to "monitor, evaluate, and reinforce their own behavior and set their own goals" (Wehmeyer, 2007, p. 88). In order to experience success regarding other components of self-determination, individuals must be able to self-manage and self-regulate to realize the options they have decided to pursue. For students with disabilities, increased levels of self-management skills may lead to improved academic pursuits and an increased understanding of skills related to post-school transition (Berkeley & Larsen, 2018; Wehmeyer et al., 2007).

## WHAT CAN SCHOOL LEADERS DO
## TO PROMOTE SELF-DETERMINATION?

Secondary special education teachers are on the frontline of providing appropriate transition services to students with disabilities; they design and deliver instruction to meet IEP and post-school goals. However, school administrators can have a significant impact on the extent to which student self-determination is taught and fostered in schools. Increased sense of student self-determination for students with disabilities pushes back against traditional ableist mindsets by giving individuals with disabilities the power to be genuine decision makers. The following recommendations for school administrators interested in promoting the development of self-determination for students with disabilities have been grouped into three broader categories, including: influencing school culture, supporting special education teachers with curricular decisions, and staffing and external supports. A roadmap of strategies is included in Figure 23.1.

### Influencing School Culture

*Foster Meaningful Family Supports, Family Involvement,*
*and Community Partnerships*
  Decades of research have linked parental involvement in schooling to improvements in academic, social, and emotional performance in their children

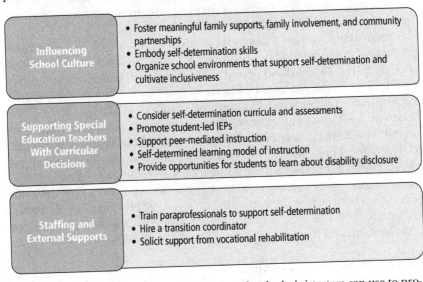

**Influencing School Culture**
- Foster meaningful family supports, family involvement, and community partnerships
- Embody self-determination skills
- Organize school environments that support self-determination and cultivate inclusiveness

**Supporting Special Education Teachers With Curricular Decisions**
- Consider self-determination curricula and assessments
- Promote student-led IEPs
- Support peer-mediated instruction
- Self-determined learning model of instruction
- Provide opportunities for students to learn about disability disclosure

**Staffing and External Supports**
- Train paraprofessionals to support self-determination
- Hire a transition coordinator
- Solicit support from vocational rehabilitation

**Figure 23.1**  A roadmap outlining strategies school administrators can use to promote the development of self-determination for students with disabilities.

(Brown et al., 2011; Castro et al., 2015). Research has consistently shown that collaboration between home and school increases both the number and duration of positive school outcomes (Mazzotti et al., 2021; Wilt & Morningstar, 2018). Additionally, parent engagement is not only important for academic success (Domina, 2005), but also crucial for increasing students' social capital, social control, motivation, and competence (Hill & Taylor, 2004; Marchant et al., 2001; Trainor, 2008). As schools rapidly become culturally diverse across the nation, the need for culturally responsive school culture has been urgent. School administrators play a major role in developing school culture where families of students with disabilities from diverse cultural backgrounds feel welcomed, respected, and supported. This culturally responsive partnership enhances engagement efforts and activities between school teachers and families. Such efforts will provide contextual information about families for schools to design, plan, and implement self-determination instruction in culturally responsive ways. This will ultimately support students to develop their self-determination skills.

At the same time, school administrators should provide professional development opportunities for teachers to become proficient in delivering self-determination instruction in culturally responsive ways (Carter, Lane, et al., 2015; Raley et al., 2020). Also, school administrators need to provide the resources needed for families to facilitate self-determination and enhance the skills of their children at home. This could involve sessions where families can expand their network with others sharing similar cultural backgrounds, better understand practices to develop self-determination, and gain access to community resources that will support the growth of student self-determination at home and in community.

School administrators should establish connections with the local community as a way to provide opportunities for their students (Gooden, 2005; Ni et al., 2018). Establishing strong connections with businesses and other organizations in the community fosters support for the vision of the school and stronger collaborative relationships (Sanders & Harvey, 2002). The increased "civic capacity" that results from building community alliances can cultivate healthy "mental models of schooling" (Goldring & Hausman, 2001, p. 199). Thus, through effective family and community partnerships, school administrators help their schools gain access to local organizations' networks, resources, and power to create growth opportunities for their students who are known by the community (Green, 2018; Warren et al., 2009). Students will be able to make informed decisions as they also get a chance to understand and have the support of their communities.

### Embody Self-Determination Skills

Principals who embody self-determination skills in their leadership and practices are able to empower transition-age youth and promote self-determination throughout school operations. School leaders are key players in a school's or district's commitment to implement programs, policies, and practices that support student self-determination (Karvonen et al., 2004). School administrators who exemplify self-determination skills can effectively build and maintain positive and trusting relationships among their administrative and teaching staff, and these relationships are essential to encouraging students to emulate such behaviors. Therefore, it is not surprising that school administrators play such a vital role in the success of self-determination program implementation, as school leadership may be one of the top factors affecting student learning and instruction. Thus, it is important that the school administrator shows genuine investment in special education by learning about all their students in the building and being ready to talk with them, and advocate for them. School administrators need to reevaluate their own beliefs and values and strategize how self-determination and inclusiveness are part of their leadership. Additionally, accomplishing the types of changes needed to integrate self-determination skills throughout the school requires culturally responsive transformative leadership from principals and administrators who are willing to realign structures and relationships to achieve genuine, sustainable, and equitable change.

### Organize School Environments That Support Self-Determination and Cultivate Inclusiveness

Since principals set the tone of the school community, they can be the chief advocates for special education. Traditional ableist views may be prominent in school culture, however the actions of school administrators can help promote truly inclusive mindsets. Effective special education practices and an environment that support the learning of all students and encourage agency in the learning process may take several years to evolve. However, in order to thrive in such environments requires the support, the deep work, of the school administrator to facilitate the changes in the system to establish practices and processes that breed self-determination and inclusive education throughout the school operations. This could be enacted by ensuring that students with disabilities have equal access to and are part of all activities that happen at the school (e.g., extracurricular activities, sports, field trips, social activities, clubs). Principals should ensure that students have opportunities to apply self-determination knowledge and skills. Thus, principals should emphasize self-determination and advocacy, integrate self-determination skills in the mission of the school, offer special courses related to self-advocacy and leadership, and develop opportunities for students to self-advocate and be part of all aspects of school life.

## Supporting Special Education Teachers With Curricular Decisions

### Consider Self-Determination Curricula and Assessments

In order to support the development of student self-determination, school administrators should support the delivery of related curricula for students with disabilities. These can be delivered by special education teachers, or any support personnel (i.e., peers, paraprofessionals, transition coordinators). Although commercially available curricula exist, students may find success with resources that are available at no cost. In addition to curricula, school administrators should recommend assessment tools to measure student self-determination. These could be appropriate for monitoring IEP goals or making data-based decisions regarding curricular activities for students. Table 23.2 includes descriptions of no-cost self-determination curricula and assessments, all of which are available from the Zarrow Center at the University of Oklahoma (https://www.ou.edu/education/centers-and-partnerships/zarrow).

### Promote Student-Led IEPs

Students are not required participants in individualized education program (IEP) meetings; however, the Individuals With Disabilities Education Act (IDEA, 2004) states that students should be invited when the team feels this is appropriate. As parents may have varying beliefs and perspectives on disability and schools are given vague guidelines by IDEA, student participation in IEP meetings is inconsistent. Wagner et al. (2012) found that approximately 50% of students ages 11–14 attended their IEP meetings, whereas about 70% of high school students attended their meetings. Of students who attended their meetings, approximately half felt they were able to provide *some input*. Students may be excluded from the process because school personnel may be unaware of how involvement in the IEP development can support student self-determination (Konrad, 2008). Additionally, students with lower social and cognitive skills are less likely to lead their IEP meeting (Wagner et al., 2012); a barrier that should be recognized and understood by school personnel interested in promoting student-led IEPs.

In order to increase student attendance and involvement in the IEP process, school administrators should encourage special education teachers to train their students to lead their own IEP meeting (as appropriate). Student involvement in their IEP has been identified as an evidence-based practice for instruction of students with disabilities (National Technical Assistance Center on Transition, 2017). Facilitating student-led IEPs can support development in each of the seven previously described characteristics of self-determination. Additionally, it may be especially valuable in providing opportunities for students with disabilities to increase skills related to

**TABLE 23.2  Examples of No-Cost Self-Determination Curricula and Assessments**

| Tool | Description | Access Link |
|---|---|---|
| Whose Future Is It Anyway (Curriculum) | This workbook is focused on developing self-determination by preparing students to lead their own IEP meetings. Schools interested in implementing student-led IEPs should consider this resource to guide the process. | https://www.ou.edu/content/education/centers-and-partnerships/zarrow/transition-education-materials/whos-future-is-it-anyway.html |
| Me! (Curriculum) | The 10-unit curriculum is designed to improve student self-awareness and self-advocacy. Each lesson includes PowerPoint presentations to guide instruction, worksheet activities for students, a summative unit quiz, and information describing how each lesson aligns to the Common Core Standards. Materials in Spanish are also provided. | http://www.ou.edu/education/centers-and-partnerships/zarrow/transition-education-materials/me-lessons-for-teaching-self-awareness-and-self-advocacy |
| Choice Maker (Curriculum) | The curriculum aims to support development of student self-determination by including lessons in three primary domains, including; choosing goals, expressing goals, and taking action. Each lesson includes a PowerPoint and student activities. There is an emphasis on student-led IEPs as a means to increase student self-determination. | https://www.ou.edu/education/centers-and-partnerships/zarrow/choicemaker-curriculum |
| Self-Determined Learning Model of Instruction (SDLMI; instructional model of promoting self-determination) | The SDLMI is a teaching model designed to enable teachers to promote self-determination by teaching and providing students with opportunities to engage in self-determination skills. Teachers can use the SDLMI with any type of goal and overlay it within any content area. | https://selfdetermination.ku.edu/homepage/intervention/ |
| ARC Self-Determination Scale (Assessment) | This assessment involves student self-evaluation that yields a total self-determination score, as well as scores in four subdomains (autonomy, self-regulation, psychological empowerment, and self-realization). | https://www.ou.edu/education/centers-and-partnerships/zarrow/self-determination-assessment-tools/arc-self-determination-scale |
| AIR Self-Determination Scale (Assessment) | In addition to providing a student self-determination self-assessment, the AIR includes forms for family members and school personnel to complete. Two larger domains (capacity and opportunity) are comprised of multiple sub-categories that relate to self-determination. Spanish and French versions of the assessment are also available. | https://www.ou.edu/education/centers-and-partnerships/zarrow/self-determination-assessment-tools/air-self-determination-assessment |
| Self-Determination Inventory: Student Report (SDI: SR; Assessment) | This online assessment is based on causal agency theory. Students with and without disabilities ages 13 and 22 respond to 21 items in regards to their ability to be self-determined. | https://selfdetermination.ku.edu/homepage/assessments/ |

setting goals, self-advocacy, leadership, and self-awareness. In order to lead a meeting, students need to be keenly aware of their rights, goals, and personal strengths and needs. In addition to student-led IEP training materials included in self-determination curricula described in Table 23.2, school administrators can arm special education teachers with materials compiled by the National Technical Assistance Center on Transition (NTACT, n.d.).

### Support Peer-Mediated Instruction

In order to promote inclusive educational opportunities for students with disabilities, schools may offer opportunities for peers without disabilities to provide targeted instruction and supports for students with disabilities (often those with intellectual and developmental disabilities). These peer-mediated instructional opportunities result in many benefits to students with disabilities, including increased social opportunities with peers, larger social network inside and outside of school, and additional access to academic tasks assigned to the general class (Brock & Huber, 2017; Carter et al., 2016). When considering the potential of developing a system of offering peer-mediated instruction, school administrators should recognize that these opportunities may support the development of self-determination in students with disabilities.

Peers may be well-suited to lead conversations related to the seven components of self-determination. They are learning these skills themselves and may be able to share strategies that have been effective for them. In addition, learning more about the abilities of peers with disabilities may help them better understand ableism and ways they can be advocates for inclusion and equality. In order to facilitate these conversations, it may be possible for a peer to deliver components from a self-determination curriculum. School administrators interested in developing peer-mediated instructional programs may consult Carter, Moss, et al. (2015) for guidance.

### Implement Self-Determined Learning Model of Instruction

In order to increase opportunities for students, including those with disabilities, and to develop self-determination skills, school administrators may consider providing teacher training on the self-determined learning model of instruction (SDLMI). This instructional model of teaching involves supporting student learning through three phases. The learning activity begins as students are provided with an opportunity to develop goal setting skills by answering the question "What is my goal?" Next, students practice self-management and self-regulation skills by answering the question "What is my plan?" After the learning activity is finished, students self-evaluate to answer the question "What have I learned?"—a step that impacts future goal setting and action planning (Wehmeyer & Shogren, 2017).

SDLMI has been identified as an evidenced-based practice to teach transition skills to youth with disabilities and may also be effective in increasing student on-task behavior (Rowe et al., 2021). School-wide implementation of SDLMI may lead to improvements in how students set goals that are aligned with in-school post-school successes (Graber & Raley, 2019). One principal emphasized, "We need to teach students how to navigate in a changing world before they graduate and promoting self-determination is the missing piece to engaging students in the learning process" (Graber & Raley, 2019, p. 23). Due to the individualized nature of SDLMI, the process can be taught to entire classes through a series of mini lessons featuring large group discussion and individual work time. Preparing and training students to have ownership over the process can lead to increased interest in goal attainment and enhanced self-determination.

### Provide Opportunities for Students to Learn About Disability Disclosure

Individuals with disabilities, especially invisible or nonapparent disabilities, are often faced with the decision whether to disclose their disability. These situations may present themselves in the workplace, community, postsecondary education, and in social situations.

Societal ableism has created potential barriers to disclosure, which may include discrimination, stigma, limited knowledge of supports and how one might access them, type of disability, avoidance of discomfort of others, and personal coping styles (Lindsay et al., 2018). When looking at obtaining employment, there are mixed views about when and how to disclose a disability (Jans et al., 2012). Whereas individuals with visible disabilities (e.g., people who use wheelchairs) may decide to be more open about discussing their disability in a job interview due to the visual existence of a disability, individuals with hidden disabilities may have a more difficult decision. School administrators should encourage secondary special educators to have conversations about disability disclosure with their students. Teachers may consider using *The 411 on Disability Disclosure* (National Collaborative on Workforce and Disability for Youth, 2005), a no-cost workbook that provides guidance for conversations about accommodations and disclosure in postsecondary, job, community, and social settings.

## Staffing and External Supports

### Train Paraprofessionals to Support Self-Determination

Paraprofessionals (paraeducators) are an essential piece of comprehensive school-based services to support instruction and inclusive educational opportunities for students with disabilities in the United States. Being that many paraprofessionals may be hired with limited previous training in education, training opportunities are essential to promote professional growth and their ability to effectively support students in the classroom (Carter et al., 2009). In addition, societal ableist mindsets may have caused paraprofessionals to believe that individuals with disabilities are helpless and need extensive supports. Although many paraprofessionals have a general understanding of self-determination, they may not be properly trained to support student development in these skills (Carter et al., 2011; Lane et al., 2012).

As school administrators work to identify, evaluate, and develop training packages for paraprofessionals, they should consider options that involve promoting self-determination for students with disabilities. These trainings should go beyond surface-level self-determination skills, such as simple choice making. Although these fall under the self-determination umbrella, trainings focused on the seven aforementioned self-determination domains should be delivered. Some recommendations for developing student self-determination that can be delivered by trained paraprofessionals, include: (a) supporting student self-monitoring of self-determination skills, (b) delivering a self-determination curriculum, (c) providing students with opportunities for leadership roles, (d) modeling choice making by sharing their own thought process when weighing decisions (e.g., choices about snack or lunch option), (e) talking through potential solutions when a student is faced with a problem, (f) facilitating role play sessions in a variety of environments where students practice self-advocating, and (g) working with students to self-direct academic choice making and goal setting based on their unique strengths and needs (Cabeza et al., 2013; Rowe et al., 2015).

### Hire a Transition Coordinator

Special education teachers in secondary schools may be tasked with providing instruction and supports relating to both academics and post-school transition. As such, school administrators may advocate for the hiring of a transition coordinator, a certificated special education teacher whose primary purpose is to address the post-school transition (nonacademic) needs of secondary students with disabilities (Asselin et al., 1998; Scheef & Mahfouz, 2020). The roles of transition coordinators vary, but these practitioners are able to provide instruction and support student development in a wide range of areas, including self-determination. Although some of the aforementioned strategies can be connected to academic instruction (e.g., SDLMI), others would be more likely to be realized with the support of a transition coordinator (e.g., student-led IEPs). School administrators may consider shifting job responsibilities of existing special education positions in order to create a new position that focuses specifically on supporting post-school transition.

## *Solicit Support From Vocational Rehabilitation*

For secondary students with disabilities, schools may consider reaching out to vocational rehabilitation (VR) to support the development of student self-determination. VR is a federal- and state-sponsored service designed to assist people with disabilities to find and maintain employment. As IDEA (2004) guides school-based services for eligible students with disabilities, the Workforce Innovation and Opportunity Act (WIOA, 2014) outlines VR services provided to individuals with disabilities. The 2014 reauthorization of WIOA included a mandate that states VR agencies allocate at least 15% of their program spending on supporting vocational goals on eligible school-aged youth with disabilities (students receiving special education services and also students who have Section 504 accommodation plans). These pre-employment transition services (Pre-ETS) include services in five areas, one of which is instruction in self-advocacy (WIOA, 2014).

This mandate to direct funding to supporting school-aged youth means that schools may have access to services from VR personnel. Although interagency collaboration is a hallmark of post-school transition services for students with disabilities (Kohler et al., 2016), secondary special education teachers may be unaware or confused about WIOA policy changes and the delivery of Pre-ETS services (Pacheco, 2019). Because many secondary special education teachers are focused on providing academic support to students, they may be unable to deliver transition-related activities and may have limited knowledge related to interagency collaboration (Benitez et al., 2009; Sprunger et al., 2018). School administrators should be aware that VR may be able to provide direct services to students within the school-based settings, including instruction in self-advocacy and self-determination.

## CONCLUSION

The development of student self-determination is critical to all youth. This may be particularly true for individuals with disabilities, who may be marginalized by traditional ableist mindsets and have personal choices made by others on their behalf. While the competencies of self-determination are interrelated and multifaceted, school administrators can develop their school environment in which self-determination becomes embedded in all facets of schooling on a student, teacher, leadership, and systems level to create a culture where all students can thrive in and outside school.

# REFERENCES

Achola, E. O., & Greene, G. (2016). Person-family centered transition planning: Improving post-school outcomes to culturally diverse youth and families. *Journal of Vocational Rehabilitation, 45*(2), 173–183. https://doi.org/10.3233/JVR-160821

Agran, M., Storey, K., & Krupp, M. (2010). Choosing and choice making are not the same: Asking "what do you want for lunch?" is not self-determination. *Journal of Vocational Rehabilitation, 33*(2), 77–88.

Angelle, P., & Bilton, L. M. (2009). Confronting the unknown: Principal preparation training in issues related to special education. *AASA Journal of Scholarship and Practice, 5*(4), 5–8.

Asselin, S. B., Todd-Allen, M., & DeFur, S. (1998). Transition coordinators define yourselves. *Teaching Exceptional Children, 30*(3), 11–15.

Benitez, D. T., Morningstar, M. E., & Frey, B. B. (2009). A multistate survey of special education teachers' perceptions of their transition competencies. *Career Development for Exceptional Individuals, 32*(1), 6–16.

Berkeley, S., & Larsen, A. (2018). Fostering self-regulation of students with learning disabilities: Insights from 30 years of reading comprehension intervention research. *Learning Disabilities Research & Practice, 33*(2), 75–86.

Beyth-Marom, R., Fischhoff, B., Quadrel, M. J., & Furby, L. (1991). Teaching decision making to adolescents: A critical review. In J. Brown & R. V. Brown (Eds.), *Teaching decision making to adolescents* (pp. 19–59). Routledge.

Boscardin, M. L. (2007). What is special about special education administration? Considerations for school leadership. *Exceptionality: A Special Education Journal, 15*, 189–200.

Brittain, I., Biscaia, R., & Gérard, S. (2020). Ableism as a regulator of social practice and disabled peoples' self-determination to participate in sport and physical activity. *Leisure Studies, 39*(2), 209–224.

Brock, M. E., & Huber, H. B. (2017). Are peer support arrangements an evidence-based practice? A systematic review. *The Journal of Special Education, 51*(3), 150–163.

Brown, G. L., McBride, B. A., Bost, K. K., & Shin, N. (2011). Parental involvement, child temperament, and parents' work hours: Differential relations for mothers and fathers. *Journal of Applied Developmental Psychology, 32*(6), 313–322

Burke, K. M., Raley, S. K., Shogren, K. A., Hagiwara, M., Mumbardó-Adam, C., Uyanik, H., & Behrens, S. (2020). A meta-analysis of interventions to promote self-determination for students with disabilities. *Remedial and Special Education, 41*(3), 176–188. https://doi.org/10.1177/0741932518802274

Cabeza, B., Magill, L., Jenkins, A., Carter, E. W., Greiner, S., Bell, L., & Lane, K. L. (2013). *Promoting self-determination among students with disabilities: A guide for Tennessee educators.* Vanderbilt University. https://vkc.vumc.org/assets/files/resources/psiSelfdetermination.pdf

Carter, E. W., Asmus, J., Moss, C. K., Biggs, E. E., Bolt, D. M., Born, T. L., Brock, M. E., Cattey, G. N., Chen, R., Cooney, M., Fesperman, E. Hochman, J. M., Huber, H. B., Lequia, J. L., Lyons, G., Moyseenko, K. A., Riesch, L. M., Shalev, R. A., Vincent, L. B., & Weir, K. (2016). Randomized evaluation of peer support arrangements to support the inclusion of high school students with severe disabilities. *Exceptional Children, 82*(2), 209–233.

Carter, E. W., Lane, K. L., Jenkins, A. B., Magill, L., Germer, K., & Greiner, S. M. (2015). Administrator views on providing self-determination instruction in elementary and secondary schools. *The Journal of Special Education, 49*(1), 52–64. https://doi.org/10.1177/0022466913502865

Carter, E. W., Moss, C. K., Asmus, J., Fesperman, E., Cooney, M., Brock, M. E., Lyons, G., Huber, H. B., & Vincent, L. B. (2015). Promoting inclusion, social connections, and learning through peer support. *TEACHING Exceptional Children, 50*, 9–18. https://doi.org/10.1177/0040059915594784

Carter, E., O'Rourke, L., Sisco, L. G., & Pelsue, D. (2009). Knowledge, responsibilities, and training needs of paraprofessionals in elementary and secondary schools. *Remedial and Special Education, 30*(6), 344–359.

Carter, E. W., Sisco, L. G., & Lane, K. L. (2011). Paraprofessional perspectives on promoting self-determination among elementary and secondary students with severe disabilities. *Research and Practice for Persons with Severe Disabilities, 36*(1–2), 1–10.

Castro, M., Expósito-Casas, E., López-Martín, E., Lizasoain, L., Navarro-Asencio, E., & Gaviria, J. L. (2015). Parental involvement on student academic achievement: A meta-analysis. *Educational Research Review, 14*, 33–46.

Dean, E. E., Burke, K. M., Shogren, K. A., & Wehmeyer, M. L. (2017). Promoting self-determination and integrated employment through the self-determined career development model. *Advances in Neurodevelopmental Disorders, 1*(2), 55–62.

DeMatthews, D. E., Kotok, S., & Serafini, A. (2020). Leadership preparation for special education and inclusive schools: Beliefs and recommendations from successful principals. *Journal of Research on Leadership Education, 15*(4), 303–329. https://doi.org/10.1177/1942775119838308

Domina, T. (2005). Leveling the home advantage: Assessing the effectiveness of parental involvement in elementary school. *Sociology of Education, 78*(3), 233–249.

Field, S., Martin, J., Miller, R., Ward, M., & Wehmeyer, M. (1998). *A practical guide to teaching self-determination.* Council for Exceptional Children. https://eric.ed.gov/?id=ED442207

Goldring, E. B., & Hausman, C. (2001). Civic capacity and school principals: The missing links for community development. *Community Development and School Reform, 5*, 193–210.

Gooden, M. A. (2005). The role of an African American principal in an urban information technology high school. *Educational Administration Quarterly, 41*(4), 630–650.

Graber, M., & Raley, S. K. (2019). Self-determination and student engagement: A Kansas high school finds the missing piece in learning. *Impact, 32*(1), 22–23.

Green, T. L. (2018). School as community, community as school: Examining principal leadership for urban school reform and community development. *Education and Urban Society, 50*(2), 111–135.

Hill, N. E., & Taylor, L. C. (2004). Parental school involvement and children's academic achievement: Pragmatics and issues. *Current Directions in Psychological Science, 13*(4), 161–164.

Individuals With Disabilities Education Improvement Act of 2004. Pub.L.No.108-446, 118 Stat. 2647 (2004) [Amending 20 U.S.C. §§ 1400 et seq.]. https://www .govinfo.gov/content/pkg/PLAW-108publ446/html/PLAW-108publ446.htm

Jans, L. H., Kaye, H. S., & Jones, E. C. (2012). Getting hired: Successfully employed people with disabilities offer advice on disclosure, interviewing, and job search. *Journal of Occupational Rehabilitation, 22*(2), 155–165.

Karvonen, M., Test, D. W., Wood, W. M., Browder, D., & Algozzine, B. (2004). Putting self-determination into practice. *Exceptional Children, 71*(1), 23–41.

Kohler, P. D., Gothberg, J. E., Fowler, C., & Coyle, J. (2016). *Taxonomy for transition programming 2.0: A model for planning, organizing, and evaluating transition education, services, and programs.* Western Michigan University. https://www.cde .state.co.us/cdesped/transitnprogtxnmy

Kohn, N. A., Blumenthal, J. A., & Campbell, A. T. (2012). Supported decision-making: A viable alternative to guardianship. *Penn State Law Review, 117,* 1111–1158.

Konrad, M. (2008). Involve students in the IEP process. *Intervention in School and Clinic, 43*(4), 236–239.

Lane, K. L., Carter, E. W., & Sisco, L. (2012). Paraprofessional involvement in self-determination instruction for students with high-incidence disabilities. *Exceptional Children, 78*(2), 237–251.

Lindsay, S., Cagliostro, E., & Carafa, G. (2018). A systematic review of barriers and facilitators of disability disclosure and accommodations for youth in post-secondary education. *International Journal of Disability, Development and Education, 65*(5), 526–556.

Loman, S., Vatland, C., Strickland-Cohen, K., Horner, R., & Walker, H. (2010). *Promoting self-determination: A practice guide.* National Training Initiative in Self-Determination, University of Missouri.

Marchant, G. J., Paulson, S. E., & Rothlisberg, B. A. (2001). Relations of middle school students' perceptions of family and school contexts with academic achievement. *Psychology in the Schools, 38*(6), 505–519.

Mazzotti, V. L., Rowe, D. A., Kwiatek, S., Voggt, A., Chang, W.-H., Fowler, C. H., Poppen, M., Sinclair, J., & Test, D. W. (2021). Secondary transition predictors of postschool success: An update to the research base. *Career Development and Transition for Exceptional Individuals, 44*(1), 47–64. https://doi. org/10.1177/2165143420959793

Mazzotti, V. L., Rowe, D. A., Sinclair, J., Poppen, M., Woods, W. E., & Shearer, M. L. (2016). Predictors of post-school success: A systematic review of NLTS2 secondary analyses. *Career Development and Transition for Exceptional Individuals, 39*(4), 196–215.

McConnell, A. E., Martin, J. E., Juan, C. Y., Hennessey, M. N., Terry, R. A., el-Kazimi, N. A., Pannells, T. C., & Willis, D. M. (2012). Identifying nonacademic behaviors associated with post-school employment and education. *Career Development and Transition for Exceptional Individuals, 36*(3), 174–187. https:/doi. org/10.1177/2165143412468147

Nario-Redmond, M., Noel, J., & Fern, E. (2013). Redefining disability, re-imagining the self: Disability identification predicts self-esteem and strategic responses

to stigma. *Self & Identity, 12*(5), 468–488. https://doi.org/10.1080/1529886
8.2012.681118

National Collaborative on Workforce and Disability for Youth. (2005). *The 411 on disability disclosure: A workbook for youth with disabilities.* Institute for Educational Leadership. http://depts.washington.edu/doitsum/mer2017/files/6_Monday/561_411_Disability_Disclosure_complete_FINAL-es.pdf

National Technical Assistance Center on Transition. (n.d.). *Student-led IEP resources.* https://transitionta.org/wp-content/uploads/docs/IEP_SDIEP.pdf

National Technical Assistance Center on Transition. (2017). *Using the self-directed IEP to teach student involvement in the IEP meeting.* U.S. Office of Special Education Programs. https://transitionta.org/system/files/resourcetrees/PD_SDIEP.pdf?file=1&type=node&id=195&force=

Ni, Y., Yan, R., & Pounder, D. (2018). Collective leadership: Principals' decision influence and the supportive or inhibiting decision influence of other stakeholders. *Educational Administration Quarterly, 54*(2), 216–248.

Pacheco, T. (2019). *A focus group analysis of interdisciplinary knowledge held by special education teachers and community rehabilitation service providers* (Master's thesis). https://digitalcommons.usu.edu/gradreports/1408

Raley, S. K., Burke, K. M., Hagiwara, M., Shogren, K. A., Wehmeyer, M. L., & Kurth, J. A. (2020). The self-determined learning model of instruction and students with extensive support needs in inclusive settings. *Intellectual and Developmental Disabilities, 58*(1), 82–90. https://doi.org/10.1352/1934-9556-58.1.82

Rowe, D. A., Alverson, C. Y., Unruh, D. K., Fowler, C. H., Kellems, R., & Test, D. W. (2015). A Delphi study to operationalize evidence-based predictors in secondary transition. *Career Development and Transition for Exceptional Individuals, 38*(2), 113–126.

Rowe, D. A., Mazzotti, V. L., Fowler, C. H., Test, D. W., Mitchell, V. J., Clark, K. A., Holzberg, D., Owens, T. L., Rusher, D., Seaman-Tullis, R. L., Gushanas C. M., Castle, H., Change, W.-H., Voggt, A., Kwiatek, S., & Dean, C. (2021). Updating the secondary transition research base: Evidence- and research-based practices in functional skills. *Career Development and Transition for Exceptional Individuals, 44*(1), 28–46.

Sanders, M. G., & Harvey, A. (2002). Beyond the school walls: A case study of principal leadership for school-community collaboration. *Teachers College Record, 104*(7), 1345–1368. https://doi.org/10.1111/1467-9620.00206

Scheef, A., & Mahfouz, J. (2020). Supporting the post-school goals of youth with disabilities through use of a transition coordinator. *Research in Educational Administration & Leadership, 5*(1), 43–69.

Shogren, K. A. (2013). *Self-determination and transition planning.* Brookes Publishing.

Shogren, K. A., Hicks, T. A., Burke, K. M., Antosh, A., LaPlante, T., & Anderson, M. H. (2020). Examining the impact of the SDLMI and Whose Future Is It? Over a two-year period with students with intellectual disability. *American Journal on Intellectual and Developmental Disabilities, 125*(3), 217–229. https://doi.org/10.1352/1944-7558-125.3.217

Shogren, K. A., Luckasson, R., & Schalock, R. L. (2014). The definition of "context" and its application in the field of intellectual disability. *Journal of Policy and Practice in Intellectual Disabilities, 11*(2), 109–116.

Shogren, K. A., Palmer, S. B., Wehmeyer, M. L., Williams-Diehm, K., & Little, T. D. (2012). Effect of intervention with the self-determined learning model of instruction on access and goal attainment. *Remedial and Special Education, 33*(5), 320–330.

Shogren, K. A., Wehmeyer, M. L., Palmer, S. B., Forber-Pratt, A. J., Little, T. J., & Lopez, S. (2015). Causal agency theory: Reconceptualizing a functional model of self-determination. *Education and Training in Autism and Developmental Disabilities, 50*(3), 251–263. https://doi.org/10.1007/978-94-024-1042-6_5

Shogren, K. A., Wehmeyer, M. L., Palmer, S. B., Rifenbark, G. G., & Little, T. D. (2015). Relationships between self-determination and postschool outcomes for youth with disabilities. *The Journal of Special Education, 48*(4), 256–267. https://doi.org/10.1177/0022466913489733

Southward, J. D., & Kyzar, K. (2017). Predictors of competitive employment for students with intellectual and/or developmental disabilities. *Education and Training in Autism and Developmental Disabilities, 52*(1), 26.

Sprunger, N. S., Harvey, M. W., & Quick, M. M. (2018). Special education transition predictors for post-school success: Findings from the field. *Preventing School Failure, 62*(2), 116–128.

Test, D. W., Mazzotti, V. L., Mustian, A. L., Fowler, C. H., Kortering, L., & Kohler, P. (2009). Evidence-based secondary transition predictors for improving postschool outcomes for students with disabilities. *Career Development and Transition for Exceptional Individuals, 32*(3), 160–181. https://doi.org/10.1177/0885728809346960

Trainor, A. A. (2008). Using cultural and social capital to improve postsecondary outcomes and expand transition models for youth with disabilities. *The Journal of Special Education, 42*(3), 148–162. https://doi.org/10.1177/0022466907313346

United Nations. (2006). *Convention on the rights of persons with disabilities and optional protocol.* United Nations.

Wagner, M., Newman, L., Cameto, R., Javitz, H., & Valdes, K. (2012). A national picture of parent and youth participation in IEP and transition planning meetings. *Journal of Disability Policy Studies, 23*(3), 140–155.

Wakeman, S. Y., Browder, D. M., Flowers, C., & Ahlgrim-Delzell, L. (2006). Principals' knowledge of fundamental and current issues in special education. *NASSP Bulletin, 90*(2), 153–174. https://doi.org/10.1177/0192636506288858

Warren, M. R., Hong, S., Rubin, C. L., & Uy, P. S. (2009). Beyond the bake sale: A community based relational approach to parent engagement in schools. *Teachers College Record, 111*, 2209–2254.

Wehmeyer, M. L. (2007). *Promoting self-determination in students with developmental disabilities.* Guilford Press.

Wehmeyer, M. L., Abery, B. H., Zhang, D., Ward, K., Willis, D., Hossain, W. A., Balcazar, F., Ball, A., Bacon, A., Calkins, C., Heller, T., Goode, T., Dias, R., Jesien, G. S., McVeigh, T., Nygren, M. A., Palmer, S. B., & Walker, H. M. (2011). Personal self-determination and moderating variables that impact efforts to promote self-determination. *Exceptionality, 19*, 19–30. https://doi.org/10.1080/09362835.2011.537225

Wehmeyer, M. L., Agran, M., & Hughes, C. (2000). A national survey of teachers' promotion of self-determination and student-directed learning. *The Journal of Special Education, 34,* 58–68. https://doi.org/10.1177/002246690003400201

Wehmeyer, M. L., Palmer, S. B., Shogren, K., Williams-Diehm, K., & Soukup, J. H. (2013). Establishing a causal relationship between intervention to promote self-determination and enhanced student self-determination. *The Journal of Special Education, 46*(4), 195–210.

Wehmeyer, M. L., Palmer, S. B., Soukup, J. H., Garner, N. W., & Lawrence, M. (2007). Self-determination and student transition planning knowledge and skills: Predicting involvement. *Exceptionality, 15*(1), 31–44.

Wehmeyer, M. L., & Shogren, K. A. (2017). Self-determination and choice. In N. N. Singh (Ed.), *Evidence-based practices in behavioral health* (pp. 561–584). Springer.

Wilt, C. L., & Morningstar, M. E. (2018). Parent engagement in the transition from school to adult life through culturally sustaining practices: A scoping review. *Intellectual and Developmental Disabilities, 56*(5), 307–320. https://doi.org/10.1352/1934-9556-56.5.307

Wolbring, G. (2008). The politics of ableism. *Development, 51*(2), 252–258.

Workforce Innovation and Opportunity Act of 2014, Pub. L. 113-128, 128 STAT 1632, §404. https://www.govinfo.gov/content/pkg/PLAW-113publ128/pdf/PLAW-113publ128.pdf

CHAPTER 24

# JOURNEY OF SELF-DETERMINATION FOR A WOMAN WITH EPILEPSY

**Bridget Green**
*Duquesne University*

## ABSTRACT

The diagnosis is not the starting point of a person's journey as a person with a disability. Often, a person faces many obstacles before receiving a diagnosis, which impact their abilities to advocate for their needs. This chapter will use a framework of self-determination to explore my journey as a woman with epilepsy. Through different important stages, I will explain how my disability impacted my ability to advocate for my needs, wants, and goals. I will also provide recommendations for education-related personnel to ensure students with disabilities receive individual opportunities to explore and identify their needs.

The diagnosis of a person's disability activates immediate and long-term processes that impact the emotional acceptance of an individual's new life (Smart, 2016). People without disabilities, including educators, may not listen to the voices of the disability community about how their experiences

*Who Decides?*, pages 593–621
Copyright © 2022 by Information Age Publishing
www.infoagepub.com
All rights of reproduction in any form reserved.

and relationship to the disability influenced their journeys to adulthood. Consequently, the absence of conscious listening deprives both the educators and the students with a disability of tools to enhance academic, social, and emotional growth and success. Thus, it is essential that people with disabilities are able to share their experiences with educators with the goal of enhanced social, emotional, and academic development. In this chapter, my journey as a woman with epilepsy, both educationally and emotionally, is shared with the reader in the context of the theory of self-determination.

Listening to one's personal journey can have multiple impacts and provide opportunities for others to increase their empathy. Palmer (2004) argued the importance of listening to a person's journey to ensure that adults do not force their beliefs and ideals on children. He further discussed the need to continually empower people to understand their role regarding the broader community, which could be lost as adults focus on their successes at the students' cost (Palmer, 2004). He also contended that ignoring the value of a person's experience overlooks the person's or group's humanity. Furthermore, he maintained that belittling a person's story minimizes their experiences, encouraging the broader population to view the minority group as merely a data point for decision-making while silencing the value of a personal story (Palmer, 2004).

An immediate need exists for educational decision makers in the K–12 school system, to understand how they can help or hinder the academic, emotional, and social growth of individuals with disabilities. The person's life journey can provide a person-centered approach to building rapport with education moving beyond a standards-based approach. Respecting the value of our students' stories can give education-related personnel opportunities to interrogate and improve their practice. When school personnel listen to their students' journeys with an end goal to understand and empower them, educators can also improve our practice through meaningful reflection. For example, "What does this person need to have equity in my school?" or "How have I generalized abilities that negatively impacted the normalcy of my students?" To answer these questions, educators and related personnel must be willing to listen to and have empathy for the journeys of our students, peers, and community members as they experience their challenges, barriers, and successes across different academic and community environments. Throughout my life I had many people listen to me to ensure they met the legal requirements to support my disability. However, I needed people to listen to my confusion and desperation and help me assign words to those feelings. This type of listening must be repetitive and provide opportunities for one person to discover their needs, strengths, and interests through safe and honest discourse. Further, this listening can include information from others regarding a person's ability so long as respect for the individual is at the center of the discussion.

My educational and emotional journey of self-determination as a woman with epilepsy changed as the symptoms of my disability changed. It is important to note that I view myself as disabled and a person with epilepsy. Some advocates prefer person-first language (i.e., woman with epilepsy) while others choose to identify first (e.g., disabled); I am both. In the advocacy world I am proudly disabled. In my academic role, I model person-first language to my students with the caveat that, at the end of the day, self-identity is the person's choice. For example, when educators work with a student who prefers to be called autistic rather than a student with autism, all school personnel should support the individual's choice of language around the disability identity. When and how a student requests to identify (e.g., disability first or person first) is a personal choice and should be treated as an initial step towards self-determination. In this chapter I discuss my journey as a woman with epilepsy so that educational personnel realize the importance of empathy and empowerment in interactions with students with a disability. Indeed, the kindness experienced in a school setting may be the only kindness the individual with a disability receives. The first section of this paper will introduce self-determination as it relates to people with disabilities. Then I will discuss my experience receiving a diagnosis and navigating high school. I will end the chapter discussing my transition into the collegiate environment.

## Self-Determination

Self-determination is a term that transcends a variety of educational fields. Self-determination theory provides insight to one's personality, and how internal and external motivation are used to motivate an individual to fulfill a need (Ryan & Deci, 2000). Furthermore, environmental conditions (e.g., transportation, interpreters, printed materials) or lack thereof, can impact a person's enthusiasm to complete a short or long-term goal. In the field of disability, self-determination provides individuals with opportunities to implement control over their decisions, lives, and requested supports and services (Ryan & Deci, 2000; Smart, 2016). Self-determination provides people with disabilities to make choices, identify and advocate for their needs, and request accessible and inclusive activities in their communities.

The definition of self-determination that I relate to is one that is found in special education, specifically the transition of students with disabilities to postsecondary environments. Self-determination is both "the attitudes which lead people to define goals for themselves and the ability to take the initiative to achieve those goals" (Ward, 1998, p. 2). These attitudes drive a person's self-understanding in the K–12 setting, and provide opportunities to voice interests, wants, and needs experienced by a person with a disability (Shogren

& Ward, 2018). Field et al. (1998) expanded the definition of self-determination to acknowledge the ability for an individual to develop "a combination of skills, knowledge, and beliefs that enable a person to engage in goal-directed, self-regulated, autonomous behavior" across a variety of environments (p. 2). As individuals begin to learn about practicing their self-determination skills, they should receive opportunities to request support within the school and community settings, ensuring that they receive meaningful accommodations and modifications provided under special education laws.

Ideally, self-determination would be taught throughout the K–12 school setting to ensure students with and without disabilities can advocate for their needs across various environments. Persons with disabilities must practice self-determination skills across a variety of settings, as no two environments may require the same skill (Field et al., 1998). For example, a student with a disability will need different accommodations in the classroom than on the soccer field. This student may have extra time on an exam in the classroom and require visuals cues (e.g., adapted playbook) on the field to remember plays.

Understanding the different needs for success and then voicing them demonstrates self-awareness and self-determination (Wehmeyer et al., 2000; Wehmeyer & Shalock, 2001). Research has demonstrated that opportunities to practice self-determination skills lead to increased postsecondary success (Field et al., 1998; Newman et al., 2011), academic performance (Raley et al., 2018), and attainment of post-school employment goals (Shogren et al., 2012). People with disabilities must receive adequate and meaningful opportunities to practice self-determination skills across environments to ensure present and future postsecondary successes.

The focus of self-determination for students with disabilities in our schools should embrace both postsecondary outcomes and success in day-to-day challenges. Self-determination for persons with a disability means that they can identify and voice their needs, attitudes, and desires across classrooms and communities (Field et al., 1998; Ward, 1998). In the field of transition, self-determination encompasses education, employment, and independent living-focused competencies across day-to-day as well as postsecondary environments. Both settings are not always the clear focus of educators of students with a disability. Currently, educators address self-determination of these students in the transition plan of an IEP, as required by the Individuals With Disabilities Education Act (IDEA, 2004). In the transition plan, there is a focus on annual goals that support postsecondary school outcomes, such as postsecondary education or career-related skills, and it is common for self-determination to be an annual goal (Test et al., 2009). Self-determination is practiced by students with disabilities in a measurable manner such as requesting an accommodation or asking a question relating to a classroom task. These opportunities are essential as they lay the foundation for postsecondary successes and, as well, nurture abilities to adapt to change. However, some self-determination skills are just as essential but not measurable (e.g., vocalizing "something is not right with me"). Effective self-determination skills are important for students in their adolescent years as they are also experiencing adolescent brain development and interests, emotions, and goals are changing (Giedd, 2015). Thus, annual IEP goals may not be sufficient to address the needs and abilities of persons with a disability. There is an immediate need for educators to encourage self-determination through attentive listening to personal experiences of growth and failures voiced by persons with disabilities. This knowledge will enrich individuals with disabilities throughout their educational and work experiences and provide pathways for education personnel to improve their practice and enhance their opportunities to build rapport with all students. For the remainder of this chapter, I will discuss how I navigated the development of my self-determination and self-knowledge throughout my journey of being diagnosed as a woman with epilepsy.

## THE DIAGNOSIS OF EPILEPSY

The first signs of my disability occurred when I was 13 years old as I was traveling for a chorus competition. It was April, and due to the lengthy travel time on a bus, I was sleep-deprived. I had to wake early and in a different time zone, which further impacted my ability to get a restful sleep. That morning, after a restless night's sleep, I fell to the ground. At this time, I had no idea that disruption of my sleep negatively impacted my day-to-day functioning.

To compensate for the lack of sleep the previous night, the chorus teacher recommended I sleep on the bus while the group traveled from the hotel to the competition. While thoughtful, it was not a helpful suggestion because I was bothered by the lamp posts which presented as flashing lights as the bus drove past them; each flicker caused parts of my face to twitch. I draped an item of clothing over my eyes to minimize interaction with my environment. The eye covering was a simple accommodation that enabled me to reduce the facial twitching and, in turn, the falls I was experiencing during the trip. Oftentimes, people with disabilities receive suggestions from people without disabilities under the disguise of healthy life choices and modifications. For example, it was once recommended that I could "fix" my epilepsy through yoga. Unfortunately, these quick and often costly fixes require people with disabilities to delay effective psychological and medicinal therapies and do not lessen the impact and severity of the underlying medical issues.

While I made minor accommodations to support my safety, I still did not understand what was wrong with me. When I returned home from the competition, I told the school nurse I collapsed to the floor during the choir trip. She dismissed the falls, and insinuated that I had an eating disorder, which I did not, since I had a low body mass index (BMI). During this period of my life, I was thin in part due to participating in year-round sports and in part normal adolescent growth. Without knowing the "why" behind my falls, it was hard to explain how I felt and to convince others that I was not myself. I experienced an onslaught of inappropriate inquiries as some adults questioned me because of how I looked (e.g., asked me if I was eating, how often I use the bathroom post meals) or queried whether I was simply seeking attention.

As the frequency of the falls increased, so did my family's and my need to understand what was wrong with me. I received a request from my middle school principal in the beginning of May of my eighth-grade year to give a tour for sixth-grade students; when I arrived at school, I collapsed. Simply, my muscles stopped contracting to support my body and I fell to the ground. Two peers picked me up, I then walked a few more steps and fell, hurting my ankle. After this incident, the school called my mother who came to pick me up.

My mother had called my pediatrician and he saw me right away. He stated that based on my symptoms a reasonable diagnosis was epilepsy, but he was unable to make a specific diagnosis as he was not a neurologist. Within a few days, my pediatrician was able to schedule for me to see a pediatric neurologist who ordered a set of diagnostic tests which came back inconclusive. The neurologist downplayed my experiences and attributed them to puberty; he hypothesized that I could be allergic to fluorescent lights since they were the common thread across my falls both at the hotel and at school. It was incredibly frustrating and angered me to know that my symptoms were being documented, but that my experience, fears, and concerns were ignored. It was as though my symptoms fit an all-inclusive box titled "teenage puberty" and due to its convenience, no further investigation was needed. Therefore, my personal experience was that my initial attempt to understand why I was falling received a vague and indifferent response from those who specialize in identifying these types of medical issues. In time, I found that this uncertainty or misdiagnosis is a common experience in the initial stages of receiving diagnosis by people with disabilities (Smart, 2016). While I was still new to the process of listening to my body, hearing the hypothesis that I was allergic to fluorescent light felt wrong to me. I participated in after-school swim practice, in a facility with florescent lights, and the lights there never caused me to have a reaction. In my gut I knew that it was much bigger than a reaction; I knew that something was wrong with me and I needed more answers.

My family and I decided to seek a second opinion and additional testing. By chance, my mother's colleague's wife was a pediatrician who worked closely with a pediatric neurologist. Using my social support network, only a few short weeks after my May fall, I was able to see a highly regarded pediatric neurologist. This pediatric neurologist ordered an electroencephalogram (EEG), a method to monitor brain waves using metal electrodes glued to my head (MayoClinic, n.d.), a procedure that required me to stay up all night before a series of tests in order to make a diagnosis. I was afraid to lose sleep due to my previous experience during the choir trip; however, I am fortunate that I had a friend who kept me up at night to ensure I was sleep deprived, but safe.

I did not make it through the full exam before the doctor diagnosed me as having juvenile myoclonic epilepsy (JME). This type of epilepsy has both tonic-clonic and absence seizures. He explained that each time I would "fall," I was having a seizure. After receiving the diagnosis, I was prescribed medication. I began a treatment plan that also included attention to lighting, adequate sleep, and stress management, which allowed me to understand myself and pave the way to becoming a self-determined adult with a disability.

The diagnosis and my family's support aided me personally in my acceptance of the disability, self-determination, and seeking help. Receiving the diagnosis provided me with the feeling that I no longer needed to prove that something was wrong with me (Smart, 2016). While some are against labeling, for me, receiving a diagnosis felt as though my reputation was cleared and I was able to prove to adults that I was not lying to obfuscate an eating disorder. After receiving my diagnosis, my mother said to me,

> You have two choices: you control the disability, or you let it control you. If you control it, you need to know there will be good and bad days, but your family will do whatever we can to help you. Or, you can let epilepsy control you. It is your choice.

Like many people with a disability diagnosis, I wanted to do whatever I could to control the change. I knew that I wanted to control my epilepsy and that I would never be "cured." I could, however, pay attention to environments that made me feel uneasy, ensure that I was receiving adequate sleep, and take my medication at the same time each day. Receiving the diagnosis of epilepsy gave me a reason to implement structure in my new identity and pay attention to my needs across environments.

The disability diagnosis provided me with relief that I finally knew the unknown (Smart, 2016), my need for daily structure and discipline, and the communication skills to advocate for myself. I am not sure I would have developed these skills early in my life without receiving the diagnosis. In applying the new regimen to my day-to-day life, I understood what I needed to do to achieve success, what I needed to address with others, and what I needed to avoid (e.g., staying up all night to study). Receiving the diagnosis became my armor in my battle to educate peers, parents, and school administration that I had a neurological disability that impacted the way my neurons communicated throughout my brain. Being diagnosed as disabled meant that I was not the "bad" or "apathetic student" teachers had branded me, but that my "daydreams" during class were in fact seizures. Receiving the label of epilepsy meant that I received protection under The Rehabilitation Act (1973) and the Americans With Disabilities Act as amended (2008). The diagnosis was my protective barrier that prevented peers' and educators' judgements from becoming my personal narrative. I realized that if I was not clear in what I was feeling or experiencing and how I believed it was negatively impacting my education, I would lose the ability to receive opportunities to have access to an appropriate education.

I became aware very early in the process of the importance of communicating my needs effectively with peers, teachers, and my parents if and when something was wrong with me. My communication took many forms, whether an illustration, a printout, or a clarification about what my disability was and was not. My pediatric neurologist used a drawing to assist my knowledge of my disability and my self-determination by explaining how my neurons misfire or inappropriately communicate with each other, which caused my seizures. See Figure 24.1 for the image. I was taught that in a normal brain, a neuron communicates from Point A in the brain to Point B. In my brain, the neurons can misfire causing a seizure, represented by the squiggly lines acting as a cluster or seizure activity. When I collapse and fall, daydream, or have a tonic-clonic seizure, it is because my neurons have misfired causing the cluster to occur.

During this period of time in my life, the visual acted as a physical accommodation helping me explain that I was having an absence seizure. The picture also aided me in vocalizing the harm the classroom environment could have on my brain. For example, if the lights were flickering in the classroom or a teacher turned the lights on and off as a form of classroom management, it would put me at risk for seizures. While the image did very little to assist me in advocating for my need for extra time on tests or for medication and for access to water during class, it did provide me the pathway to develop my self-determination skills. Receiving a diagnosis allowed

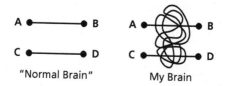

**Figure 24.1** My neural communication. *Note:* I recognize that there is no such thing as a "normal" brain, but this was how I was taught to differentiate the way my brain talked to itself.

me to be a student who no longer had to demonstrate to my teachers that something was wrong with me and who was not trying to be problematic or attention-seeking in their classes.

## Reflections for Education Personnel and the Period of Diagnosis

As school-related personnel, our day-to-day practice must respect the time and expertise needed for accurate diagnosis and have an understanding and respect for the student. There is no standard length for the diagnosis period. In fact, my diagnosis was unusually fast; from symptoms to diagnosis within 3 months. Depending on the disability, a diagnosis could be mislabeled or not be determined for years (Smart, 2016). As education related personnel, it is essential to understand how a misidentification may cause inadequate medicinal and educational interventions. Furthermore, labels can receive a negative connotation. There is an opportunity for the school personnel to change the negativity around labeling. When educators and related personnel view having a disability as a negative, that is modeled for our students and, in turn, that becomes their self-talk. My label of epilepsy became an opportunity to fight against those who imposed their beliefs on my character and my 13-year-old self. I often wonder if I had not received the diagnosis, how their words would have helped or hindered the development of my self-love.

It is important to remember that an educator's day-to-day language can shape the student's self-perception and also expectations within the individual with disability's larger social support network. This network provides us insight to the person's access to transportation, insurance, and access to care which are all factors involved in a person's journey of discerning the diagnosis of a disability. My social support network was fortunate to have connections within the medical community near a city with numerous nationally ranked hospitals. This network changes for families who live in small towns with no public transportation, one rural doctor, or that have poor in-network insurance coverage. The diagnosis process can take months or even years, and may impact how education personnel collaborate with the family to identify and understand the disability during this ambiguous time which can have a monumental impact on a person's life. During this period, the lack of diagnosis often impacts the student with a disability negatively in the classroom since they may not know what is wrong with them and, therefore, what self-advocacy and academic requests are needed. The opportunity for an accurate diagnosis may not be accessible due to family reasons, which is why education related personnel need to ensure that our day-to-day practice encourages us to listen, hear, and trust

602 · B. GREEN

our students. Our young people are watching our responses to disability and diversity and, as educators, it is one of many responsibilities we have to ensure that we are providing pathways to positive school experiences with empowering language.

### School Administrators

Seattle's Center for Ethical Leadership created innovative pathways to provide individuals the opportunity to engage meaningfully with one another. This center has called the process of producing these engagements, creating gracious spaces. When a leader creates a gracious space, there is intent to develop meaningful relationships with others with commitment and clearly defined expectations and shared goals (Hughes & Grace, 2010). These relationships challenge members to see beyond biases, preconceived notions, and personal fears to support personal and group growth. There is a goal for the leader to "invite the stranger to learn in public" (Center for Ethical Leadership, n.d., p. 1). When leadership allows strangers to learn in public, they are required to evaluate if and how they create a space and provide opportunities that value another person's abilities, needs, and voice. Further, it requires active listening and self-reflection on behalf of leadership to ensure that individuals have the opportunity to experience growth, empowerment, and community (Hughes & Grace, 2004).

Prior to my diagnosis, I do not believe I was given a gracious space to learn about my differences, abilities, and needs. I am fortunate to have had school leaders who reminded me about my academic and athletic abilities. During doctors' visits and trying to understand the cause of my behaviors, I yearned for someone at school to help me answer my lingering question of "Why is this happening?" When I was told, "Bridget, you have juvenile myoclonic epilepsy" the space I was offered at school changed. The visual I used to explain my seizures provided me with an opportunity for my teachers and I to understand epilepsy together and understand how it impacted my learning; this enabled us to address the issue together in a proactive manner. Before this point, I understood that I needed to sleep a certain amount of time each night to prevent unanticipated falls; however, it never occurred to me that the effect of lack of sleep was due to an underlying disability. Providing me with safe space to understand how my disability may impact my academic and social performances was essential to my growth, given that prior to the diagnosis I was viewed as a disengaged student.

School administrators leading personnel must be empathetic during this period and remember that our words matter. All people in our schools, including children and adults, will observe the interactions between teachers, administrators, and students and the perceived safety of educational and social spaces. Educators' words and behaviors can have an indelible impact on a student's self-determination and perceived safety for self-growth.

The comments that I heard by peers, teachers, and administrators planted seeds of doubt and inability and made me feel powerless in my life. It was as though comments from adults caused me to create weaknesses in my armor and lessened my confidence in my self-advocacy. I became self-conscious of my body and tried to always eat something around adults, to avoid the perceived eating disorder. I provided my coaches with a list of what I ate to satisfy my need to prove that I did not have an eating disorder so that I would be allowed to practice. I strictly followed the rules so that no one could say I was trying to gain attention; I was desperate to be a normal teenager. I was taught to listen to teachers and school leaders, as they were intended to be there to help me succeed in my education and personal growth. This life lesson collided with reality when I was on the receiving end of their preconceived notions about my health, abilities, and honesty.

Part of my journey in the diagnosis period was seeing how different doctors approached the diagnosis using varying criteria and truly understanding the value of a second opinion. The first neurologist I saw used a limited approach in collecting data and assessing what was wrong with me and what I needed. While the first opinion was not accurate, the second opinion was, and that persistence opened doors of understanding for me, my parents, peers, and teachers. When collaborating with families as they navigate academic changes juxtaposed with doctors' visits, recommend second, third, or even more opinions. The shared goal between school administration and families should be that the individual with a disability understands and can communicate their abilities, needs, and wants for achievement of success in education and community settings to the best of their ability. Encourage families to think about any possible social connections for emotional support, medical access, and educational advocacy to see if there are pathways for the added perspectives. In the field of education, assessments are informed by the information about the strengths, weaknesses, and budgetary abilities of our educational institutions. Meaningful listening moves beyond hearing students' requests during a classroom activity and invites and allows the student to be a stranger and learn *with* the teacher. Active listening should include acknowledging and evaluating other professionals' perspectives of disabilities, and how as educators we can effectively include students', families', and professionals' voices and recommendations during the diagnosis period to ensure students feel safe and supported in the academic environment.

A second opinion can often take time and require additional financial resources, which often leads to educational practitioners being inclined to go with the first diagnosis and unknowingly guide the student off the path of self-determination. This misdirection can occur when educational practitioners do not have accurate information about the disability or about the educational and social needs for the student with a disability. For example,

I was my own advocate while I traveled to the chorus competition. Yet, I could not explain what I needed and how I felt. I only vaguely verbalized my needs (e.g., I fell, I think something is off with me). For me, the second diagnosis put me on firmer ground of understanding what I needed for safety. Educators who respect the time and expertise needed for accurate diagnosis and who have an understanding and respect for the concerns of the student can contribute enormously to the development of self-determination. Some people with disabilities never receive a specific diagnosis. When the policy is only to provide an educational need after receiving a qualifying diagnosis and a person does not have a definitive diagnosis, the educational needs of the person may not be fully met. The diagnosis process provides a person with a disability with a starting point toward an understanding of the complexities of their disability and an appreciation of the needed accommodations to their learning and community environments based on their strengths and needs.

The absence, though, of a shared understanding among education personnel, family, and the student with a disability invites personal biases to enter, question the student's intention, and dissolves the gracious space. The personal perspectives of educators can limit the students' self-determination efforts and opportunities. For me, some thought that I was attempting to act out for attention. Others thought that I was purposefully being vague so I did not have to answer questions or take ownership of my actions. All of these ideas and comments collided with who I thought I was and what I thought I could accomplish. Educators must not openly assert power in ways that undermine the validity of a person's experience as they try to understand their relationship with the disability. Acknowledging our personal biases prevents us from vocalizing deficit-based language to the student. Understanding the power of our language as adults in the education setting can make or break our students' rapport with learning and exploring their needs. Focusing on only identifying students' needs without allowing them to explore and vocalize their strengths and wants hinder the development of independent living skills necessary for postsecondary success. School leadership, teachers, and related personnel must embed in positive, empowering language in their day-to-day practices to transform students' educational experiences to ensure students receive gracious space to grow.

## HIGH SCHOOL

There was a notable administrator during my initial diagnosis, who aided my self-understanding. In ninth grade, I started in a new school in the same district. My principal during ninth and 10th grades made a point to get to know me after hearing about my eighth-grade experience and reviewing my academic accommodations. Early in my ninth-grade year, he called me into the office to talk about my academic, professional, and personal goals, all of which were shortsighted. I was under the impression that he just wanted to help the disabled girl and provide a rather insubstantial conversation in his outreach to me. I did not realize at that time that he had an incredible ability to build rapport and create a gracious space which allowed me to talk around my disability since, at the time, I did not feel comfortable talking about it directly. For example, when we met to "catch-up" as he did with many of his students, he asked me what I wanted to be when I grew up. I told him I wanted to be a neurologist so that I could help young people like me. "Like you? A female?" he asked. He and I both knew what I meant, but he used those questions to assess my comfort with my epilepsy. When I refused to engage in disability-related topics, he reviewed my file with me. Each time he talked to me, his tone and choice of words reminded me that every issue we covered addressed my future. "You have a chance to take honors courses that would help you become a neurologist. I think that is a wonderful opportunity for you and you should take it. But what do you think? Do you want to take on the extra work?" He gave me a safe place to explore choices, acknowledge my uncertainty, and question his intention before making my final decision. These meetings became the sessions that enhanced my self-determination skills.

There was a norm that emerged as I talked with the principal, he was a person who used his power to value my voice. He did not use deficit-based language, and when I said "No" to his ideas, he respected my answer. He encouraged me to disagree with him, but always asked me to explain my rationale. Using this discourse, my principal focused each discussion on my wants and needs in ninth grade and my future. He made a point to discuss my postsecondary goals and eventually discussed how my plans needed to include protecting my disability because that was never going away. He was the first education-related adult to talk to me as though my disability would be my "plus one" on my life's journey. He never spoke to me as though I was only my disability. He made it clear that whether I wanted him there or not, he wanted to be part of the team that would help me control and manage my disability. While we did not interact each day, he paid attention to my classroom success and school activities. He stopped me in the hall to congratulate me on my personal best time in the pool, acceptance into the honors math program, and the growth of my voice as I began requesting my needed accommodations.

Throughout my ninth and 10th years, with my principal's constant communication and conversations, I slowly began conveying what I needed and expressing my disability beyond just the picture of "how my brain was communicating." My conversations moved from "I get hungry in the morning" to "I think my medication makes me hungry. How do I talk to the counselor about having a study hall in the morning so that I can eat and not feel sick?" Through these intentional check-ins and conversations, he did not try to be my friend but made an effort to teach me how to use my voice to protect myself and my dreams. I had many adults who solely listened with an intent to fix an immediate problem (e.g., I need more clarity on questions). My principal allowed me to see him as a stranger and respected the process to build mutual trust. He did not listen to fix, he listened to understand, empower, and see me. While he would sit and listen attentively with his hands on the table while we spoke, I learned later that he would make notes in my file after each meeting. These records provided him with the context for questions to address during our next meeting, and also used these emerging themes to navigate topics I wanted to understand and master. The way the principal listened helped develop my self-determination skills and encouraged me to use my voice to identify my abilities and needs across school and during extracurricular environments.

I switched schools the summer before my 11th-grade year, transferring to a private school whose principal had a child with epilepsy. The move to the new school was essential to me for a few reasons. When I attended public school, it was during a time when you could not have a disability and concurrently be enrolled in honors classes. At the time, the policy was that participation in honors class demonstrated that a person's disability was not hindering the learning process. This policy was changed when IDEA was amended in 2004 (IDEA, 2004). Therefore, I received a 504 plan in the public school. The 504 Plan under the Rehabilitation Act of 1973 provided reasonable accommodations and was helpful for me because I was allowed to receive extra time on tests and assignments. However, there were days when my medication impacted my ability to process information and there were no accommodations in my plan to address this. In my case, reasonable accommodations did not fully support my complex medical needs and impact of sleep or stress. While no piece of legislation can fully take that into account, we can begin asking questions of disability-related triggers in initial meetings with families to develop a truly supportive IEP, 504 Plan, or student service plan. The private school was not required to follow the IDEA or the Rehabilitation Act of 1973 because it did not receive federal funds; yet, the school provided accommodations to students with documented disabilities. In my particular case, the principal understood the impact the brain-based medication could have on a student's learning because of the direct impact epilepsy had on her family. As a team, led by my mom, my principal, and myself, we were able to design an education plan that modeled a 504 Plan and focused on the effects of my medication on learning, which in turn, positively impacted my academic success.

Overall, the transition to the private school went well. My 11th-grade year provided me with a deeper understanding of my needs. During this year, I learned the impact of my environment on my epilepsy. For example, I discovered that driving through back roads while the sun was shining through trees acted like a strobe light and caused me to have seizures in the car. I learned about a special diet that could lessen the tonic-clonic seizures and I tried to implement it at each meal. I found that stress was a huge trigger for my myoclonic twitches causing more frequent seizures and, when combined with a lack of sleep, could result in me being in bed for days on end. Finally, I developed a small support system of peers who encouraged me to be myself both in and out of the classroom.

Taking time to understand my epilepsy triggers, the physical and emotional effects of tonic-clonic seizures, and self-care to minimize stressors within my environments, were significant because each taught me a lesson about personal safety and the importance of discipline. At the new school, all my teachers knew about my disability but did not isolate me or impose beliefs about my epilepsy on my academic abilities or future goals. Furthermore, at that school you could be both honors and disabled, which was not a common view at the time. Not only did the principal set high expectations and more rigorous goals, but so did the secretary, counselor, and gym teacher who all provided me with space for my growth. With the transition to the new school, I began to enjoy learning again. Little did I know my senior year would test my emerging rapport with education.

## Senior Year

My senior year became one of the most impactful years of my life both as a person with a disability and as an advocate. On my 18th birthday, I attended school like any other day. During my second-period study hall, I was unable to lift my head off my desk. A peer purchased me crackers, which I ate, then felt incredibly dizzy. I crawled to the garbage can and vomited. I was escorted to the nurse's office and sent home. This began the complicated relationship between managing my epilepsy, responding to health concerns, and advocating for my safety.

After the study hall experience, I began to live for the day because each day could be vastly different. One day I would wake up and feel fine the whole day; these days gave me hope. There would also be days when I would wake up and ride to school and then be physically unable to move as I arrived. Some days I could walk, but it felt as though I lost my depth perception, and the world was an obstacle course. For example, if I had to cross the street during these days, I could not tell if a line on the road was a step or a flat surface. Other days I would have seizures and be resigned to bed for hours.

Upon discussion with my pediatric neurologist, I learned I could have painless migraines or a brain tumor and he advised that I receive magnetic resonance imaging (MRI) to see if any growths were causing my body to shut down slowly. Fortunately, the scan cleared me of any terminal brain-related issues. My pediatric neurologist increased my medication to control my seizures, but my health continued to decline. During the last month of my senior year, I experienced the loss of vision, vertigo, seizures, vomiting, and inability to reliably move my limbs which ultimately required me to use a wheelchair on some days. It is important to note that, for me, it was the uncertainty of my day-to-day and having so many unanswered questions, not the fact that I had a disability or used assistive technology that caused me frustration during this time. The only way I was told to cope with my new normal was with more medication.

The increase in medication negatively impacted my academic success. Looking back, I can see from formal and informal data how my attendance and cognitive ability decreased. I started my senior year with a 3.8 grade point average (GPA); at the end of the second semester, I had a 1.5 GPA. Informally, there would be times when I would need people to repeat themselves one or two times before I understood the purpose of the statement. Further, there seemed to be a disconnect between what I was trying to say and what I was producing in writing. It was as though I lost my ability to be intentional and clear in the conveyance of my words. All of this was hard to connect directly to epilepsy, as I did not know yet that there was a cause behind my failing health.

During this time, my self-determination changed from thinking about myself and my future education and employment goals to day-to-day survival. I could not care about college when, in the moment, I could not understand how I had just lost my vision during a 40-minute car ride. Furthermore, I again could not convey what was wrong with me in a way that made my experience believable. I knew something was not right, and I would tell my teachers or the nurse that I "felt funny" or "something is not right." I did not have the mental or emotional capacity to care about calculus while trying to convince a peer I could not stand up because I could not feel my legs. It was hard for me to worry about the SATs when I could not focus, the floor in front of me was blurry, and I struggled with day-to-day tasks such as using the restroom. Some days, my understanding of myself in relation to my environment was, "Please help me" or "Something is not right." It is important to note that these comments during the end of my senior year were examples of my self-determination expressed to others. These statements became how I tried to explain my needs, yet I could not apply accurate words. Unfortunately, my lack of knowledge about my underlying issue made these statements appear as excuses.

The simplicity of my statements veiled as requests for support, and my need for teachers and administrators to believe me to achieve academic success, was put to the test during finals my second-semester senior year.

Since I had missed quite a bit of school I had failed to turn in homework, missed deadlines for significant assignments, and barely met requirements for passing senior year. Reflecting back on this, I can understand why educators did not believe something was wrong. From an outside perspective, I again became perceived as an unreliable student, and my actions, they concluded, were either the result of senioritis or apathy; they were not linked to my disability. If teachers took time to talk to me and ask me why I was skipping school they would see that it was not because I did not want to come or I had other things to do (both can be examples of senioritis). If I had the space and opportunities to discuss my experiences without judgment, teachers would hear the fear that was beginning to cloud my thoughts and suppress my self-worth. I was afraid that all of the work I did to listen and understand what my body was telling me did not matter because my body and cognitive functions were declining, and at the time no medical doctor could tell me why. I was constantly thinking about what could go wrong and if I had a tomorrow to look forward to. I was desperate for anyone at the school to believe in me and remember the student I was just a year earlier.

The lack of faith surfaced during my final exam in AP Physics when I did not receive the extended time I was allocated in my accommodation and I ultimately failed the exam. My teacher implied that I would not do well on the exam with the extra time, so it did not matter if I received the accommodation or not. While I may not know the truth behind that belief, those words impacted my identity and worth as a person with a disability. It caused me to question my self-assessment of my needs and abilities and my ability to request appropriate accommodations and support. The implication of the words stated by the teacher still impacts me today. There are still days when I question if the accommodation would make a difference in the outcome.

As my senior year came to an end, and finals were over, my health continued to decline. My pediatric neurologist recommended that my parents no longer encourage me to attend college because it was not an option for my future. I received a recommendation that I should begin to look for community-based employment options. During this time, my verbal language was declining, and my mother became my advocate. I also started to lose friends and invitations to social activities with peers.

One activity that I was able to look forward to and attend with my peers was senior prom. Unfortunately, prom became a tainted memory for me that put my epilepsy at the center of my peer relationships. Not too long after I arrived with my friends, I had a seizure at prom. I believe this was in part due to the prom disc jockey (DJ) refusing to turn off the strobe lights, a known trigger for my seizures. I woke up with emergency medical technicians (EMTs), a priest, and my mother looking down at me. Typically, prom is a celebration of friends and the ending of high school. Yet, I only associate prom as an event where I could not communicate what was happening to me and what

I needed to be safe. Fortunately, a friend advocated the need to turn off all flashing and colored lights to further prevent putting my health at risk. It was essential to my safety that my friend acted as an advocate for me by reaching out to my family and administrators to ensure my safety.

Prom, plus more consistent seizures, reinforced the need to find new doctors to assess what was potentially wrong with me. My uncle used his social network and was able to find an adult neurologist who specialized in epilepsy and was willing to see me immediately. At the appointment, the doctor asked me to stand up from the wheelchair and walk towards him. My mother and father helped me stand, and I took one step and fell into the wall. This simple interaction, along with the data that my parents and I presented about my declining health, led the neurologist to conclude that my brain began rejecting my medication and responding to it as though it was poison to my body. Therefore, I was experiencing the side effects of the medication with greater intensity as my medication levels were increased. My body protected itself by shutting down areas impacted by my medication. The adult neurologist recommended a change of medication plan that slowly weaned me off the medication that was harming me and introduced a new prescription drug. Within two quite difficult months, I was off the initial medication and able to walk, talk, and resume my previous life. That fall, I attended my freshman year of college.

## Reflections for High School Educational Personnel

There is no handbook on how your life will play out as a person with a disability. You must learn from each experience, whether it was a success or failure. Educators need to be attentive to and supporting of the individual throughout high school, beyond getting good grades. There must be an effort to assure that education plans including IEPs, 504 Plans, and school-focused accommodations recognize that medications the individual uses to manage the disability may have significant side effects. While most such plans acknowledge the medication that is used, few list the potential side effects. This is essential because most students spend approximately 8 hours a day in school, and their medication can release over time. Teachers, aides, parents, and students with disabilities need to begin to collect data on how, if at all, medication impacts our students' learning. There needs to be intentional effort by the individuals with a disabilities social support network to understand how medication impacts their day. I recommend to my students who are on medication to document in calendars or journals how they are feeling each day. This small act encourages self-awareness to become part of one's daily routine. Educators need to communicate these observations with school-based teams and families to see if behaviors impacted by medication are being observed across multiple settings. Without constant and accessible communication between the family and appropriate school personnel, it is hard to guarantee that students transitioning to postsecondary environments are truly self-determined and ready to advocate for their needs. Further, what may be an appropriate medication for young people who have developing brains may not be an appropriate medicine after puberty. Therefore, it is important to have data to provide observed impacts of medication on academic, behavioral, emotional, and social abilities of the student.

Neuroscience teaches us that teenagers' knowledge of themselves change during adolescent development (Giedd, 2015). As stated above, our language influences the self-talk of our students which influences the safety of space for growth. It is essential that educators always remember that we do not know the whole story of our students and their experiences and, often, neither do they. This reinforces the importance to allow the student to understand themselves in a gracious space to gain self-determination skills. It is essential to provide students with opportunities to grow without our bias and deficit-based language. Educators may not appreciate how impactful our words can be during our students' most challenging times. I remember feeling constant need, almost obsession, to convince people I was not lazy, disinterested, or poor performing. I did not want it associated with my academic identity as a student or my personal character. The need to convince others to remove the negative language about me only enhanced the fear I was already experiencing due to my body shutting down. Educators must make a clear effort to permit individuals and peers to celebrate successes and strengths because we are called to stop the cycle of deficit speech and behavior and to embrace the day-to-day successes, no matter how small.

### School Administrators

Oftentimes, as an educator or administrator your hands are tied due to things beyond your control. These issues can include budget cuts, legislation, or politics that influence community decision-making. School administrators have the power to make significant social change in their schools. A simple, yet significant change, can be implementation of language and behavior to create gracious spaces (Hughes & Grace, 2004). If you recommend to your colleagues to remove deficit-based language while talking to one another, how will that transform trust in your school among your peers? As school leaders there is a need to be intentional about inviting students and colleagues to grow with you; it cannot be one sided. It is important to ask how leadership is encouraging implementation of the same ideas within their classrooms. School administrators have the unique opportunity to reinforce that all persons are valued at their school and pay attention to how leadership's actions help or hinder the school's progress towards its shared goals.

Students are watching what teachers and administrators say and whether actions are matching words. If there is a narrative that everyone has a voice that should be heard, yet those who speak out are silenced, our students know and will refrain from learning with leaders in public spaces. When school administrators support and value the voice of people with disabilities in your school, their colleagues and students will follow.

Inclusivity is essential for success. It must go beyond demonstrating how a student with a disability is in the least restrictive environment for the majority of the day. School personnel must make a thoughtful effort to engage all learners from all backgrounds. My experience at prom is not a story to give rationale to not have extracurricular activities. It should act as a reflective guide for school administration to encourage teachers to create a space where all students with or without disabilities have opportunities to assist in planning and think of creative and inclusive ways to allow all students to participate. While I was not the student who would partake in the prom planning committee because my health was of greater concern to me at the time, I do know that if my friend had been there, he would have recommended a reconsideration of strobe lights use. Instead of strobe lights, he could have suggested different color lights that stay on all night. Having voices of people with disabilities at the table or advocates who are aware of the needs of the members of their class, can prevent barriers and obstacles from arising that could stop the occurrence of the activity or hinder a group from attending. For example, if there are individuals with serious food allergies that their peers were aware of, advocates can ensure that food which might trigger a reaction not be offered at prom. School personnel need to trust that our students have the ability to ensure their peers are included in school-based activities, but it is up to school administrators to demonstrate they value students' ideas in the planning processes and there is a desire for accessibility. Allowing students to educate leadership on the needs of their peers so that everyone feels safe attending school-wide functions models meaningful inclusivity in the school and larger communities.

## COLLEGE

My initial time in college was clouded by my experiences in senior year when my new doctor had concluded that my body's response to the old medication had hindered my ability to learn. I felt as though I was normal because I was evaluating myself on daily life activities as defined by the Americans With Disabilities Act (ADA) before it was amended in 2008 (ADAAA, 2008). I was able to walk, eat, sleep, and talk without being interrupted by a seizure. To me, I was back to normal or pre-high school senior year behaviors because physically I felt normal again.

I had not, however, realized how the old medication had impacted my cognitive abilities. In my freshman year in college, I discerned that I now had academic needs of which I was initially unaware. It is easy to generalize that when the physical capacity of the person appears to be fully functional, so too are their cognitive abilities. That is how I viewed myself before college. I evaluated my physical ability only and ignored the impact that my senior year had had on my cognitive processing. While my body had reacted to medication as poison and the poisoning had stopped with the new medication, I had nevertheless failed to understand how other needs, such as my cognitive abilities, would emerge in the collegiate environment.

My freshman year of college was challenging academically and socially. I attended a 4-year, private college 6 hours away from my home. I did not receive any cognitive assessments in my transition into my first year in college; therefore, I did not know that my academic skills had diminished. I learned about my cognitive needs through classroom failures. Slowly, through unsatisfactory progress in classes, I realized that I had lost aspects of my spatial reasoning abilities, working and short-term memory, abstract thinking, and organizational skills. I needed much more than extended time on tests. I needed to relearn how to create outlines, write sentences and paragraphs, and critically analyze text. Working memory is essential for learning (Giedd, 2015). Essentially, I had to use my first semester freshman year to relearn how to study and how to process information. In short, my high school senior year experience had not only impacted my physical health, it had also impacted my working and short-term memory and I was not prepared for that important piece of the collegiate experience.

Another impact of my high school experience was my lack of emotional maturity. Whether it was the poison of the medication or the suppression of emotions just to survive, I soon learned that I was very reactionary to situations. I did not take time to think about an appropriate response to discourse or conflict. At college, while I was a member of the swim team, I realized that I envied my peers. Interestingly, my envy was not about their swimming talent but about their high school experiences. They were able to reflect on their high school training and senior activities. My senior year memories were merely snapshots, as though I was looking at photographs of my experience through swiss cheese. The frustration of being unable to remember and the lack of peer-related experiences that make high school memorable began to build. The anger built, and I needed an outlet. I spent my weekends looking for events to meet as many people as I could. I wanted to have friends.

I did not understand how my anger impacted my self-determination. My focus turned from day-to-day survival toward playing a continual game of catch-up. Academically, I needed to be able to compete against my peers within the classroom. The frustration increased when I tried to use the academic skills that I no longer had. Socially, I was trying to play catch-up and do everything that my peers did in high school in college. I wanted to be part of the swim team and have an engaging social life. Emotionally, I did not have the tools needed to manage my frustration of losing a significant period of my life.

I appreciated that I needed support but I did not understand how to obtain it. I did not understand the difference between advocacy in higher education and advocacy in high school. I needed a different set of skills. I was astounded that some of my professors did not seem to care about my disability. I only recall two professors who expressed an interest in knowing about my disability, needs, and signs I might have a seizure in their classrooms. Otherwise, I felt that the only thing professors cared about was the documentation they needed to follow. They did not see me as a person but a legal responsibility within their classrooms.

## Reflections for Higher Education Personnel

The transition to college by people with disabilities can be challenging. Approximately 11% of the freshman class have a documented disability (Newman et al., 2011). Many of these students disclose their disabilities to the school's disability support services. Depending on the institution, some professors receive documentation of the accommodations required to receive in their classes, other schools expect the student to provide the letter to the professor while requesting reasonable accommodations under the ADAAA.

There is a power imbalance created when the student is required to provide a letter of documentation and request accommodations from the professor. It is intimidating for any person to disclose their disability to a stranger, let alone a professor who has the power of grades or does not understand disabilities. A student does not know the professor's biases or what judgements the professor may make or questions the professor will ask, which can negatively impact a gracious space. From my experience, I was nervous about disclosing my epilepsy to faculty because I felt as though I needed to prove that I was otherwise qualified to be their student. Part of my need was due to the fact that my disability, while quite real, was not visible. A few professors questioned whether I even had a disability or offhandedly commented they knew nothing about epilepsy. Other professors responded that they were shocked I could even attend college. In addition to the imbalance of power, I had to be both an educator about my disability and an advocate for myself which is difficult while you are still learning about your needs and abilities.

Higher education personnel are often not adequately educated about disabilities and the impact they have on learning (Newman & Madaus,

2015). This disconnect, and the fact the student may not know they have the legal duty to self-advocate, can impact the individual's education. Further, there is a lack of understanding with education personnel that they have a legal responsibility to accommodate disabilities in accordance with the ADAAA and the requirements of the institution's disability services department. A breakdown in knowledge, advocacy, or implementation of reasonable accommodations can impact inclusion and success of the individual with a disability in higher education. There is an immediate need for professors who have students disclose their disabilities in one-on-one meetings, to take time to learn about the disability, to then ask specific questions about how the disability may impact the individual's performance within the classroom, and to implement the required accommodations. If professors take time to understand the impact of the disability on the person, students may feel safer within their classroom.

Of the two professors who empowered me, one reached out to me to encourage me to find my voice, which led to my academic pursuit. She knew I did not know what to major in and persuaded me to consider studying under her. She reminded me that I have a story that might guide me to my interest. She taught me how to communicate my needs without my emotions overpowering the conversations. This professor reminded me that writing is a skill that develops over time, and that no draft is ever the last draft. Finally, she offered to mentor me through my senior project. Through her leadership, I conducted a qualitative study to understand how colleges and universities accommodate and support students with disabilities. Because of her outreach, I had an opportunity to explore the disability community, collegiate experience, and preparedness of colleges to support students with disabilities, which eventually led me to my current position today.

The population of people with disabilities attending college is increasing (Newman et al., 2011). Higher education personnel cannot assume that all people with disabilities will disclose at college because some students with disabilities do not want to be associated with having a disability (Newman & Madaus, 2015). There is an immediate need to appreciate the avoidance of identity as a person with a disability that is due to a broader societal concept that, as a whole, expresses pity for people with disabilities (Smart, 2016). Furthermore, engagements with disability are often generalized, in that one's experience with one type of disability is translated to vastly different situations; however, that is a false assessment as one interaction with someone with a disability does not represent the whole disability community. Each person has their own experience and relationship with their disability, especially as it relates to education.

Higher education personnel must lead the change for inclusive practices where all students have a voice and opportunities to grow. Professors in particular must take time to learn how to make lessons accessible to all types of learners. For example, staring at a computer for long periods of time triggers my myoclonic twitches. COVID-19 transformed the delivery of collegiate coursework and many students did not have a choice, but were forced into taking completely online classes. In today's reality, we have to begin to inquire how online learning helps or hinders learning by people with disabilities. Higher education personnel must put forth the effort to ensure their activities are accessible, use language that does not isolate people with disabilities, and implement content that empowers all of their students' voices.

## Assistant Professor

My current position is an assistant professor in special education. My professional goal is to prepare teachers with and without disabilities to ensure they have the tools needed to educate and empower students with disabilities throughout all stages of their education. I chose a position that challenges my disability daily. I am open with my colleagues about my disability; however, I do not know if they fully understand me and my relationship with my disability. For example, stress can cause me to be resigned to bed for a day after a major deadline, and being in front of a computer for extended periods of time can trigger my epilepsy causing my myoclonic twitches to surface. I still face insecurities wondering if or how my myoclonic twitching during lectures might make my students feel, and if the sudden movements might negatively impact my student evaluations and their perceived safety. Some days I wonder if my peers understand that not saying much during a meeting might not be because I have nothing to say or I am indifferent on the outcome, but because my medication is causing intense brain fog and it takes the majority of my focus to just be present.

Paulo Freire (1970) wrote:

> No pedagogy which is truly liberating can remain distant from the oppressed by treating them as unfortunates and by presenting for their emulation models from among the oppressors. The oppressed must be their own example in the struggle for their redemption. (p. 54)

I work in a field where people would like to support individuals with disabilities in education. I often wonder why they have chosen this field as their vocation. I wonder if it is because of a child with a disability, a family member, or if there is an innate need to support individuals to succeed in life. These reasons can cause subconscious biases that impact liberation experienced by people with disabilities. It is essential that educators, with or without disabilities, actively work to interrogate their biases as they work with people with disabilities. If we truly support people with disabilities to experience success post-K–12 school settings, we must ask how we are including them in the narrative. Is academia listening to the disability community's recommendations regarding best practices? Are people with disabilities active in the program design as initial planners, or are they a secondary thought? I am constantly in a personal struggle to promote the successes of people with disabilities in education, while also meeting requirements of tenure. This internal battle causes me to think how to be intentional about my work and include people with disabilities in my research teams. Personally, it is challenging to sit in a field as a disabled person and listen to what we should do for the disability community without having the community engage with us and critique our research. As a disabled person, it can be tiring to work in the field where we let the majority speak and determine the educational pathways of the oppressed under the disguise of empowerment (Freire, 1970).

I still use the self-determination skills that I practiced with my high school principal today. For safety reasons, the first day of each class I disclose my epilepsy to my students. On my difficult or bad days, I sometimes walk my undergraduate and graduate students through how I am feeling and the ways I will accommodate the environment to successfully complete class. I open the floor for questions and discussion identifying how they can adapt their future classrooms to ensure student safety. It is important to me that we learn together. When I am tired or stressed and my myoclonic twitches surface and impede my speech, we discuss what is occurring, what I need to continue class, and if they need to process what they are observing. I believe that, and my students may disagree, the transparency regarding my needs enhances classroom community. I believe being a disabled professor in special education gives me a unique opportunity for my students. I challenge the biases and perceptions of my students both with and without disabilities who may have preconceived ideas about jobs outcomes for the disabled population. For my students with disabilities, I represent that opportunities exist beyond those presented in a 15-minute meeting with a medical doctor.

While I am unable to change the system, I am able to provide representation as a person with a disability. As I work with students in developing their language, I have the opportunity to bring in voices of the disability community. For example, I have speakers with disabilities, I assign popular podcasts that represent disability voices (e.g., Disability Visibility Podcast), and bring in prominent advocates' stories (e.g., Alice Wong, Vilissa Thompson, Imani Barbarin) to challenge our practice. I aim to model how to effectively bring a person's voice, fears, needs, and dreams into the classroom and research to promote inclusion. Furthermore, I challenge my students to listen to what various members of the disability community say about their abilities. For example, some people with autism view eye contact as a neurotypical need and should not be a social skill goal imposed on the autism community. I challenge my students to move beyond the textbook and listen to various groups within the disability community to influence and adjust their practices.

## CONCLUSION

The experience of diagnosis and being a person with a disability is individualized. The disability is not the only identity of the person, the individual must receive opportunities to understand who they are, accept what they believe, and identify what they need as they navigate experiences and environments. I am a daughter, wife, sister, mom, advocate, professor, and woman, as well as a person with epilepsy.

My audience determines which identity I will apply to my lens for critique. For example, during my work as an advocate for teaching families and children, many young people with epilepsy have asked me how I handle certain seizures or reactions to medications. I have yet to receive questions about college rankings or SATs. In this context, my lenses as a professor, wife, or daughter are not as important as my view as a person with epilepsy. These young people wanted tools to survive the day-to-day and sought validation of their experiences because they felt so different. Persons with a disability have their own stories, experiences, and fears and each one should be met on an individual case. There should be a focus to discuss the person beyond the label of their disability, but conversations must be had targeting how their needs impact their day-to-day quality of life. School personnel must create gracious spaces that help students with disabilities put words to their perspectives beyond "I do not understand" or "I feel funny." Each student is an individual and, while our students may have similar accommodations or modifications, each one deserves the opportunity to tell their experiences and stories and receive the gift of meaningful listening. This listening will look different based on the individual. Some will draw pictures, others write stories, and one might tell their story verbally. It is essential that we are aware and present when our students are trying to speak to us so that we can understand how to support their self-determination and self-advocacy skills. We cannot expect students will always communicate to us in our preferred method; we must be open to creating pathways and shared goals and receiving information in ways that encourage students to speak with us. Listening to our students is the initial step all educators must take prior to promoting self-determination.

During their educational experiences, all students will explore their self-determination abilities when discussing their strengths and needs, those who truly value their opinion, and who are willing to remind them of their talents and abilities. Educators and school leadership must set time to allow our students to explore all their identities and to learn how to communicate their needs and wants effectively. All students need to develop self-determination skills and multiple chances to practice these abilities across a variety of environments. Students with disabilities need opportunities to understand who they are beyond the label that provides accommodations and modifications. Education personnel can be the difference in students with disabilities lives by engaging in conversations where we listen and encourage both self-determination and self-advocacy, which are essential for their future successes in college, employment, and community life. School personnel must remind their students of the good and the bad in everyone's journey, but recognize that the bad in the journey can teach how to live meaningfully in the day-to-day.

We are all strangers trying to learn with one another. It is time we create intentional spaces where we can allow all members of society to take part in supporting the self-determination skills necessary for success. My journey was successful because I had many opportunities to practice my advocacy and many people who supported me. With chances to understand my needs, wants, preferences, and desires, along with the support of my family, friends, and doctors, I learned how to claim my voice and my place in society. As I understood my value as a human being was worthy of being heard, I began to love myself and be proud of my disability. My journey was not overnight; it took years. My experiences allow me to accept that, yes, I am different and that it is not something to make me feel less than a person without a disability. My journey allowed me to accept the good and bad parts myself, including the relationship with my epilepsy. These intricate pieces of my identity create an empathetic leader today who consistently works from a place of self-love, self-preservation, and loyalty to the spectrum of voices that are part of the disability community. My journey provided me with opportunities to control my disability to the best of my ability with people who listened with an open heart and a shared goal to encourage me to be self-determined so that I could achieve my goals. Finally, my story taught me that there is nothing wrong with embracing my disability, because it is my disability that provided me with pathways to understand myself and use my experiences to empower others to voice their strengths, needs, wants, and goals across various environments.

## AUTHOR NOTE

I have no known conflict of interest to disclose.

# REFERENCES

Americans With Disabilities Act of 1990. Pub. L. No. 101-336, 42 U.S.C. § 12101. https://www.govinfo.gov/content/pkg/STATUTE-104/pdf/STATUTE-104-Pg327.pdf

Center for Ethical Leadership. (n.d.). *What is gracious space?* Center for Ethical Leadership. https://www.ethicalleadership.org/uploads/2/6/2/6/26265761/gs_overview.pdf

Field, S., Martin, J., Miller, R., Ward, M., & Wehmeyer, M. (1998). Self-determination in career and transition programming: A position statement of the Council for Exceptional Children. *Career Development for Exceptional Individuals, 21,* 113–128. https://eric.ed.gov/?id=EJ579472

Freire, P. (1970). *Pedagogy of the oppressed.* Herder and Herder.

Giedd, J. N. (2015). A ripe time for adolescent research. *Journal of Research on Adolescence, 28*(1), 157–159. https://doi.org/10.1111/jora.12378

Hughes, P., & Grace, B. (2004). *Gracious space: Working better together* (2nd ed). Center for Ethical Leadership.

Individuals With Disabilities Education Act, 20 U.S.C. § 1400 § et seq. (2004). https://www.govinfo.gov/content/pkg/USCODE-2010-title20/pdf/USCODE-2010-title20-chap33-subchapI.pdf

MayoClinic. (n.d.). *Grand mal seizure.* https://www.mayoclinic.org/diseases-conditions/grand-mal-seizure/symptoms-causes/syc-20363458

Newman, L. A., & Madaus, J. W. (2015). Reported accommodations and supports provided to secondary and postsecondary students with disabilities: National perspective. *Career Development and Transition for Exceptional Individuals, 38,* 173–181. https://doi.org/10.1177/2165143413518235

Newman, L., Wagner, M., Knokey, A. M., Marder, C., Nagle, K., Shaver, D., Wei, X., Cameto, R., Contreras, E., Ferguson, K., Greene, S., & Schwarting, M. (2011). *The post-high school outcomes of young adults with disabilities up to 8 years after high school: A report from the National Longitudinal Transition Study-2* (NCSER 2011-3005). U.S. Department of Education. https://ies.ed.gov/ncser/pubs/20113005/pdf/20113005.pdf

Palmer, P. (2004). *A hidden wholeness: The journey toward an undivided life.* Jossey-Bass.

Raley, S. K., Shogren, K. A., & McDonald, A. (2018). Whole-class implementation of the self-determined model of instruction in inclusive high school mathematics classes. *Inclusion, 6*(3), 164–174. https://doi.org/10.1352/2326-6988-6.3.164

Ryan, R. M., & Deci, E. L. (2000). Self-determination theory and the facilitation of intrinsic motivation, social development, and well-being. *American Psychologist, 55*(1), 68–78. https://doi.org/10.1037/0003-066X.55.1.68

Shogren, K. A., Palmer, S. B., Wehmeyer, M. L., Williams-Diehm, K., & Little, T. D. (2012). Effect of intervention with the self-determined learning model of Instruction on access and goal attainment. *Remedial and Special Education, 33,* 320–330. https://doi.org/10.1177/0741932511410072

Shogren, K. A., & Ward, M. J. (2018). Promoting and enhancing self-determination to improve the post-school outcomes of people with disabilities. *Journal of Vocational Rehabilitation, 48,* 187–196. https://doi.org/10.3233/JVR-180935

Smart, J. (2016). *Disability, society, and the individual* (3rd ed.). Pro-Ed.

Test, D. W., Mazzotti, V. L., Mustian, A. L., Fowler, C. H., Kortering, L., & Kohler, P. (2009). Evidence-based secondary transition predictors for improving post-school outcomes for students with disabilities. *Career Development for Exceptional Individuals, 32,* 160–181. https://doi.org/10.1177/0885728809346960

The Rehabilitation Act 1973. Pub.L. 93-112, 87 Stat. 355, 29 U.S.C. § 793. https://www.govinfo.gov/content/pkg/COMPS-799/pdf/COMPS-799.pdf

Ward, M. J. (1988). The many facets of self-determination. *Transition Summary: National Center for Children and Youth with Disabilities, 5,* 2–3. https://eric.ed.gov/?id=ED305805

Wehmeyer, M. L., Palmer, S. B., Agran, M., Mithaug, D. E., & Martin, J. E. (2000). Promoting causal agency: The self-determined learning model of instruction. *Exceptional Children, 66,* 439–453. https://doi.org/10.1177/001440290006600401

Wehmeyer, M. L., & Schalock, R. L. (2001). Self-determination and quality of life: Implications for special education services and supports. *Focus on Exceptional Children, 33*(8), 1–16. https://kuscholarworks.ku.edu/handle/1808/8643.

# CHAPTER 25

# LEADERSHIP FOR INCLUSIVE EDUCATION IN BRAZIL

## Potential Contributions of Disability Studies to the Training of School Leaders and Teachers

**Cynthia Paes de Carvalho**
*Pontifícia Universidade Católica do Rio de Janeiro*

**Flávia Pedrosa de Camargo**
*Instituto Federal de Mato Grosso do Sul, IFMS*

**Mônica de Carvalho Magalhães Kassar**
*Universidade Federal de Mato Grosso do Sul, UFMS*

In this chapter, we present a case study of school leaders' implementation of inclusive education policies in a Brazilian municipality. The case study herein examines school leaders' perceptions of disability and how those perceptions may have influenced their approaches and implementations of inclusive education policies. We also highlight in-service training provided (or not provided) to educational leaders and school communities around implementing inclusive educational practices.

We first present a brief overview of how the Brazilian educational system is organized and outline educational policies aimed at providing more access and inclusion for students with disabilities. We then present a synthesis of literature before describing our methodological approach in the field of research and data analysis. After presenting results, we conclude with some final considerations about Brazilian educational leadership development and potential contributions of disability studies to the preparation of equity-focused leaders.

## OVERVIEW OF THE BRAZILIAN EDUCATIONAL SYSTEM

Although Brazil's 1934 constitution established mandatory schooling for children, only in the 1990s did attendance approach "universal" rates. Mandatory school attendance for children from 7 to 14 years of age was formalized by the 1988 constitution and reinforced when Brazil signed the Jomtien agreement (UNESCO, 1990). Two interconnected movements accompanied the "universalization" process: the progressive expansion of mandatory attendance ages and the introduction of more inclusive approaches to education. Currently, attendance is mandatory from age 4 to 17.

### Educational Governance in Brazil

The Brazilian education system is organized into two levels: basic education and higher education. The basic education system is further divided into three levels: early childhood for children 0 to 5, Elementary I for ages 6 to 10, Elementary II for 11 to 14, and high school for ages 15 to 17 (Kassar & Magario, 2017). The Brazilian educational landscape includes both public and private institutions. The 1988 federal constitution organizes the relationship between three governmental levels—federal, state, and municipal—for the implementation of educational policy (Constituição da República Federativa do Brasil, 1988). The public educational system as a whole (federal, state, and municipal) serves more than 81% of Brazilian basic education students (INEP, 2020). The Education Guidelines and Bases Law (Law no. 9.394/96; Brasil, 1996) structures the three sectors of public education (federal, state, and municipal) and establishes the Union (federal level) as responsible for ensuring "the coordination of the national educational policy, articulating the different levels and systems, and exercising a normative, redistributive and supplementary role in relation to other educational instances" (Law no. 9.394, 1996, s/p). Each state or municipality is able to define "the forms of collaboration in the provision of basic education, which must ensure proportional distribution of responsibilities according to the population to be served and the financial resources" (Law no. 9.394, 1996, s/p).

Some policies are proposed by the central (Union) level and diffused to the state and municipal educational systems (including programs and regulations originating in federal legislation or national decrees). States and municipalities are then encouraged to locally implement policies that employ the federal technical and financial resources necessary for the policy initiatives. Therefore, states and municipalities have a certain degree of decisional autonomy and can develop their own policies and programs, provided they possess sufficient resources and can align with general national policy guidelines, particularly those of Law 9.394/1996. This institutional structure forms the overarching system for serving students with disabilities.

## Students With Disabilities[1] and Inclusive Education Policy

The first special-needs schools in Brazil were built in the 1850s for blind and deaf students. More contemporary efforts began in 1950, as schools were built to support intellectually handicapped students. Most of the 1950s schools were created by philanthropic private initiatives to serve students with disabilities (SWD), while the Brazilian government mandated special classes at regular public schools. Until the beginning of the 2000s, the majority of Brazilian students with disabilities attended special needs schools and classes. In 1974, the first special education report published by the Brazilian Ministry of Education showed a total of 96,413 special education students: 36,986 (38%) of whom were in regular schools[2] and 59,427 (62%) were in special schools.

The first Brazilian Education Guidelines and Bases Law (Law 4024/1961) had emphasized the importance of enrolling "exceptional" students (the most commonly used contemporary descriptor) in regular schools. However, only after the federal government's dissemination of the "Inclusive Education: Right to Diversity" plan in 2003 did the system-wide construction of an *inclusive educational system* begin with increased federal technical and financial support. The inclusive educational system means that in Brazil: (a) schools cannot deny enrollment due to disability; (b) when feasible, all children must be educated in ordinary classes at regular schools; and (c) specialized educational assistance must be free and available whenever necessary (at all levels, stages, and modalities of education).

From 2003 to 2016, the implementation of the inclusive educational system framework was made possible through projects and programs specifically targeted at schools. It included a program for training principals and teachers to build inclusive educational systems (Ministry of Education, 2004). These programs were designed to provide "a specialized educational service" (Ministry of Education, 2007) with "equipment to improve accessibility" (Ministry of Education, 2013). In 2008, a new federal document called the "National Policy on Special Education, From the Perspective of Inclusive Education" (Ministry of Education, 2008) established direct actions to assist students with disabilities, decreeing that all children must be educated in ordinary classes in regular schools. It also emphasized that specialized educational assistance does not replace schooling in common classes.

Nevertheless, inclusive education is not a legal obligation in Brazil. There continue to exist special classes and schools across the country, where SWD are housed separately from other students. Of the three components mentioned previously (enrollment, education at ordinary classes at regular schools, and required specialized educational assistance free of charge), only the first became mandatory by law (Law n.13.146, 2015; Ministry of Foreign Affairs, 2009). The others are framed by decrees and guiding documents (Ministry of Education, 2004, 2007, 2008). Still, Brazilian regular schools, including the public schools, have received an increasing number of SWD and special needs students in ordinary classes, perhaps in response to the recent special education policies cited. Data from 2019 shows 1,090,805 (87%) of SWDs in regular classrooms and 160,162 (13%) in special classes or special schools (INEP, 2020). These numbers indicate growth, in both numerical and percentage terms, of SWD enrollment compared to 2014 data (10 years after the adoption of the inclusive education policy), when 698,768 (79%) special education students were registered in regular classrooms of regular schools, and 188,047 (21%) were in special classes or special schools (Kassar et al., 2018). This increase suggests enrollment effects from special education policies implemented after 2004.

In compliance with school universalization and school inclusion, Brazil has followed a perspective adopted in other countries by describing inclusive education as a "vector of social protection" (Ebersold et al., 2016, p. 10). Brazilian policy dictates that inclusive practices are a resource for social well-being and an element of economic development as well as a way of materializing human rights (Ebersold et al., 2016). From this point of view, inclusive practices are not a societal or policy burden on educators, nor should they be understood by practitioners as such. To this end, Brazil has constructed a legal framework that honors diversity and aims to eliminate many types of discrimination, including discrimination toward people with disabilities (Law n.13.146, 2015; Ministry of Foreign Affairs, 2009), as has been the case in other countries as well (Duncan et al., 2020).

## School Leadership and Implementation of Inclusive Education Policies in Brazil

In-service training had been offered to principals and teachers since 2003 as part of the effort to build an inclusive educational system (Ministry of Education, 2004), but the new effort demanded enormous commitment, understanding, and creativity from teaching staff and school leaders, the latter of whom were legally responsible for implementing inclusive practices. Many international (Day et al., 2016; DeMatthews et al., 2020; Leithwood et al., 2008; among others) and Brazilian researchers (Franco et al., 2007; Freitas et al., 2016; Oliveira & Paes de Carvalho, 2018) have shown the importance of quality principals on both student outcomes and the creation of inclusive and equitable schools.

There is, however, less consensus in the literature regarding the relevance of direct organizational intervention by school principals on the successful implementation of school inclusion policies (Waldron et al., 2011). A case study conducted in Brazilian schools has found that inclusive schools tend to be led in a more participative manner with more teacher and community input (Silva & Leme, 2009). More recent research has documented the importance of principals in developing an equitable school culture (Vioto & Vitaliano, 2019). Considering the centrality and relevance of school management for school success, we sought to study the school principal's professional training related to daily challenges, community concerns and policy implementation as it related to the creation of inclusive schools. The chapter aims, therefore, to address possible relationships between school principals' perceptions of disability and inclusion and their initial or in-service training in dialogue with disability studies through the concept of ableism, defined as the way in which people with disabilities are generally treated as incapable (Mello, 2016).

## LITERATURE REVIEW

Academic discussions on ableism begin with a critique of the common premise that people with disabilities have second-class status and are thought of as inferior by their peers without disabilities. This premise seems to lead to the generation of harmful attitudes and discriminatory behaviors based on disability, regardless of type (physical, intellectual, sensory...). As Campbell (2009) underlined, "Ableism is embedded *deeply* and *subliminally* within culture" (p. 22; emphasis added by authors). The hegemonic positioning of individuals considered "normal" in society tends to result in negative connotations for those outside socially established standards of normality. This starting point is important for understanding both the influence of societal perceptions on the implementation of inclusive school policies and the potential contributions disability studies (DS) can have for the training of school leaders who are effective and committed to equity and inclusion.

## School Leadership and Inclusive Education—A Brief Literature Review

Several international studies indicate that school principals have strong impacts on educational outcomes (Alves & Franco, 2008; Day et al., 2016, Leithwood et al., 2010; among others). Lima (2019) detailed the importance of principals in organizing and implementing educational policies, centering on quality communication with staff and the community, but also detailing the importance of operations management (spaces, resources, etc.). DeMatthews and colleagues (2020) further documented the importance of quality principals in the creation of inclusive schools, particularly through navigating the intersections of racism, ableism, and other forms of staff and student marginalization. The authors analyzed how principals face the multiple challenges of school inclusion, while acknowledging varied thematic perceptions the leaders possess. These perceptions, the authors found, have a sometimes inconsistent focus on either school effectiveness or social justice. They found that despite the significant expansion of school inclusion efforts, equal scholastic opportunities continue to be denied and that an inclusive administration needs to consider further how articulations and interactions of prejudice intersect with ableism to prevent effective school inclusion.

It should be noted that although a social model of disability—one that views disability as framed by social, historical, and cultural constructions—is increasingly used to support inclusive education around the globe, little articulation or reflection on inclusion policies or the analytical potential of DS exists in contemporary Brazil. DS emerged from the disability-rights activism of disabled people (Longmore, 1995) with the expectation of developing systems that bridge academic communities with communities of disabled people:

Disability studies' project is to weave disabled people back into the fabric of society, thread by thread, theory by theory. It aims to expose the ways that disability has been made exceptional and to work to naturalize disabled people—remake us as full citizens whose rights and privileges are intact, whose history and contributions are recorded, and whose often distorted representations in art, literature, film, theater, and other forms of artistic expression are fully analyzed. (Linton, 2005, p. 518)

DS treats disability as a phenomenon to study, seeking to understand how society builds mechanisms for classifying and ranking "impaired" individuals. DS helps to unveil values and make explicit the social constructions of disability by the hegemonic culture through utilizing a social model instead of a medical model, which defines disability as an individual problem to be treated and cured (Lacerda, 2006; Longmore, 1995). In this perspective, DS reframes the study of disability by naming it a social phenomenon, shifting the emphasis away from treatment or remediation towards social/cultural/political analysis and framing of disability. DS aims to disentangle impairments from the myth, ideology, and stigma that influence social interactions and policies, challenging the idea that economic and social status and assigned roles of people with disabilities are inevitable outcomes of their conditions (Longmore, 1995).

Another fundamental aspect of DS is the critique of ableism. Valle and Connor (2014) stated that conceptions of normal/abnormal in special education influence educators into regarding students as "adequate" or "inadequate." Educators' expectations seem to start from a "myth of homogeneity" and then move to classifying students according to their similarities. However, instead of conceiving of an "appropriate model" based on homogeneity, the authors argue for greater consideration of human diversity within educational contexts, even if doing so involves widespread and occasionally uncomfortable professional collaboration.

Students possess multiple intersecting forms of diversity, including but not limited to their ethnicity, socioeconomic class, family configuration, religion, culture, race, linguistic tradition, gender, and life experiences. SWDs are the same in this regard, and so these intersections must be considered when striving towards inclusive education (DeMatthews et al., 2020; Valle & Connor, 2014). In fact, as DeMatthews et al. (2020) describe, an inclusive administration at school is one that considers the intertwining of ableism with prejudice in relation to disability, racism, sexism, xenophobia, and socioeconomic origin, which influence school segregation.

School administrator capacity relates directly to teacher performance in areas of inclusive practices. Dias et al. (2015) highlighted democratic and participative administration practices, communication, and organization of spaces for discussion and reflection and sensitization of the school community for inclusive education as key components for creating an inclusive culture. In their research, principals and staff who support inclusive education understand the challenges and yet are able to continue the drive towards equitable practices.

Conceptions about SWD found in schools are also found in society at large. DS describes certain values as dominant and framing. DS emphasizes the social construction of disability by the dominant culture, thus contesting a medical model of disability which tends to define disability as a problem to be treated and cured. The medical model of disability contributes to the interpretation of social issues as the responsibility of the individual (Lacerda, 2006). In contrast, Ebersold (2005) stated that people with disabilities should be part of all spheres of society; the author defined a specific version of an "inclusive approach" (Ebersold, 2005, p. 43) that emphasized the potential of people with disabilities and not their difficulties.

The shift towards a more social and cultural model of disability has been strengthened by the growing movement of people with disabilities who advocate for themselves as they face structural and normative barriers within a variety of social institutions (Caldwell, 2011; Dowse, 2010). In opposition to the individual-centered view of disability, DS starts with the subjects' ability to contribute to society while avoiding "adapting" to unhelpful norms and standards. In the same direction, Ebersold (2005) stated that disability is too often associated with participatory restrictions based on inaccessibility imposed by society and stressed that this need for adaptation is not linked to the individual, but to social, political, and cultural norms and frames in society.

## METHODS

Our research took place in Corumbá, a municipality located in the Mato Grosso do Sul state on the border between Brazil, Bolivia, and Paraguay. Since 2003, Corumbá's schools have been implementing an inclusive education policy initiative. The area was chosen for this study due to the autonomy of the municipal government since the area is located more than 400 kilometers from other cities that offer special education services. This geographical location provided a unique context in which to study the implementation of inclusive practices based on local interpretations of national policy (Kassar et al., 2018). With 111,435 inhabitants (IBGE, 2020), Corumbá has 29,144 students enrolled in 49 public and private educational institutions (School Census, 2018). Approximately half of these students (14,754) attend elementary schools under municipal administration.

### Survey Research in Schools

Schools in Corumbá are located in both urban and rural areas. In 2017 and 2018 we conducted a survey with education professionals who worked in 16 of the total 24 urban schools. The 16 urban schools were selected because they offered Elementary I and II education, making them interesting sites to study implementation of inclusive education policies offered to SWD aged at least 6 to 14 (the other eight urban schools attended only preschool) for a longer period.

We gathered survey information about leadership training (initial and in-service), experiences and perceptions of disability, and involvement with inclusive policy implementation. Principals and coordinators of all 16 municipal urban schools received the questionnaires. While the schools had varied organizational structures, each had the following management structure: an administrative director, an assistant director, and up to three pedagogical coordinators (Municipal Secretary of Education, 2018). Principals and coordinators manage all the pedagogical activities in the school, including planning, organizing, monitoring and evaluation of all curriculum and instructional processes. According to data from the 2018 School Census, of the 257 students with disabilities enrolled in the 16 urban municipal schools, 13 were in preschool, 156 were attending the initial years of elementary school (Elementary I), 63 of them attended the final years of elementary school (Elementary II), 14 attended adult education for early years of elementary school, and 11 attended adult education for the final years of elementary school.

A second, additional phase of data collection involved conducting interviews at three of the urban municipal schools. Two of these schools were selected based on the enrollment of SWDs and survey response rates. An additional school had a long history of educating SWDs in the municipality and was therefore also included. Differentiation of organizational contexts played a role in selection, as two schools had resource rooms for specialized educational assistance and support professionals, while one did not. Table 25.1 synthesizes the information on students with and without disabilities in the three schools involved.

A second round of interviews was performed between June and September 2018. Eight coordinators and three school principals were interviewed in this phase of the study. The interviews were set as semi-structured and followed the same guide with all the participants. Thus, they were asked regarding their duties in the school, the relationships among the staff, whether they participated in a formal staff selection process and how it was

**TABLE 25.1  Total Quantity of Students and SWD per School Selected for the Second Line of Research**

| School Units | Number of Students | Number of SWD |
|---|---|---|
| School 1 | 1,153 | 35 |
| School 2 | 1,287 | 14 |
| School 3 | 739 | 35 |

*Source:* School Census 2018.

632 • C. P. de CARVALHO, F. P. de CAMARGO, and M. de C. M. KASSAR

carried out. The guide used for the interviews focused on the question of whether they considered their school inclusive and how the work was with SWDs. To maintain the participants' anonymity, numbers were attributed to them (i.e., Principal I, Coordinator I, Coordinator II).

Since the researcher who conducted the interviews had worked in the special education field before, the participants were familiar with the researcher. The working relationship between the researcher and interviewees might bring into question the reliability of the information collected, it also favored closeness with the interviewees that tended to ensure agreement about the contents and interpretations of the communication (Bourdieu, 1999, p. 610). Nonetheless, considering possible effects on the perceptions shared by the interviewees, on-site observation was conducted (on average 30 days *in loco* observation per school) as a complementary research strategy to triangulate and validate the information collected (through the survey and the interviews).

The interview analysis was inspired on the philosophy of language perspective (Bakhtin, 1981), valuing the interviews of the interviewees, implementing agents of the school inclusion policy, and their correlating perceptions on disability and the policy itself. The contributions of Valle and Connor (2014) were also important with regard to how the concept of normal/abnormal in special education influences teachers' perceptions of students with disabilities and their right to school education. The analysis of the collected material started by their organization into categories, from which we highlighted their conceptions about disability and inclusive education and their perceptions about the work conditions of the school units.

## FINDINGS

### Survey Results

Fourteen (14) principals and 20 coordinators responded to the survey, for a total of 34 school leaders. The majority were female (25) and 13 of the respondents were 40–49 years old. In total, 17 of the participants had a degree in pedagogy and 15 had degrees in other subjects. The great majority (27) had been teachers in basic education, and 18 had worked as teachers for 20 years or more. As for time in school administration, 17 had 5 years or less of experience, three had worked as a principal between 6 and 10 years, six for 11 years, three for 16 to 20, and three for more than 20 years.

Regarding experience in special education, 16 of the survey respondents reported not having any, 10 reported having over 3 years of experience, four between 1 and 3 years, and one did not answer. As for training in special education, 23 of the participants said they did not have any, eight said they had already participated in training in this area, and one did not respond. It appears that most principals and coordinators had not participated in any specific training related to special education for students with disabilities, although approximately half reported having more than 1 year of overall experience.

Most survey respondents (22) said they had received materials and information related to public policies aimed at SWD either from the municipal education department or directly from the Ministry of Education. However, 12 claimed to not have received the information they needed for their work, leading them to seek for the necessary knowledge to implement inclusive practices[3] by themselves. In fact, none of the principals and most of the coordinators who answered the survey had not participated in any training on this topic. In the interviews they said that the training sessions offered by the municipal secretary of education on inclusive education were attended only by the education professionals that worked with SWDs in the resource classes (when existing) and other special support professionals.

## Interviews

The interviewed educational leaders were first asked to describe the municipal education department's training regime, which usually started with each semester. The interviewees only mentioned in-service training targeted at improving the schools' Basic Education Development Index (IDEB), a Brazilian marker for education quality based on scholastic examination performance. Among the principals, priorities seemed to be strongly directed to their school's IDEB results, impacting decisions related to educational goals. The principals also mentioned the National Common Curricular Base, a guiding document for organizing Brazilian curriculum, in addition to discussions about school discipline and student behavior training.

Interviewees highlighted that professional training often involved a series of presentations from the municipal secretary to the principals, rather than any hands-on training. One principal stated that she had participated in just a single training course, because it was mandatory for leadership candidates. She desired more training and felt that the informational meetings were insufficient.

We interviewed principals regarding inclusion of SWD in regular education. We asked the school principals and coordinators if they believed their school was sufficiently inclusive and, while all answered yes, they typically justified their answer in the following manner: "Inclusive because ... it welcomes students that ... we have no problem ... enrolling students that have some kind of apparent disability. With a medical report, anyway" (Director II, School I). The coordinator of School II, for example, said that the school was inclusive because it offered broad services. However, she emphasized the importance of teacher work only in terms of welcoming students, omitting issues related to learning:

Our teachers are already... they already come with this vision that they have to welcome the student, that they have to include him in the pedagogical activities, no matter how needy he may be... of affection... he has to be welcomed, received in the classroom. (Coordinator I, School II)

Similarly, in School I:

So, I say this is more the *welcome* with which we receive these students, the question of the teachers, the question of the administrative staff. It's part of it, we've been receiving these special children for a long time, haven't we? [...] So we already have *all* this work, all this preparation. However difficult it may be... there is almost no training. [...] So we really go for what we like, for the vocation to work. (Coordinator II, School I, 2018, emphasis added, from the emphasis on discourse)

Regarding concerns about where and in what ways the school is inclusive, principals and coordinators mostly referred to SWD enrollment, narrowly linking aspects related to inclusion only to the reception of these students.

While enrolling SWD students in school served as a typical response, aspects related to learning were largely ignored. Some principals vacillated by claiming that SWD students cannot learn due to their disability. As an example, the coordinator of School III mentioned a student with intellectual disability by indicating that the ordinary school would not be an appropriate place for his education:

We have a problem with... a student... [...] he has been in second grade, for years, he is probably already 12 to 13, you know? [...] We have already asked parents to enroll him in the special school to receive more support.... (Coordinator I, School III, 2018)

These ableist perceptions often correlate to lowered educational goals for SWD populations. In the schools researched, SWDs were largely believed to be unable to master the standard curriculum. One principal expressed this:

Depending on the need, she (the child) progresses well or not. But a *minimum* step forward is a victory. In the eyes of many it may be little, but for that child to reach *that* level, it often required immense effort to succeed, and this has to be valued... in some way. (Principal I, School II, 2018)

Consequently, learning expectations for students seem to have been lowered. Schools offered a "delimited learning" as a predictive and naturalized way detailing student development, marked by limitations and disabilities. The coordinator of School I explained it this way:

We create a learning boundary because we know that he will not be the same as the others in the third year. We follow the content of the third year, but we limit the knowledge for him to learn by the end of the year. (Coordinator I, School I, 2018).

School I's coordinator described the reduction of school content as a way of making the curriculum more flexible for SWD students, especially a third grade individual:

> What does this student have to know to move forward? Do you have to know [to count] up to number 10? Up to number 20? Speaking Portuguese? Is there a need to know how to write one's full name? (Coordinator I, School I, 2018)

The interviews confirmed the existence of ableist thought, with coordinator discretion left to define "best" places for SWD to receive "adequate" educational care. The coordinator thought it best for this student to occupy a space with students "like him," directly contradicting inclusive education policy goals. Furthermore, this coordinator tended to blame the student, rather than the educators, for any learning gain failures.

The results of the survey showed that, although half of the school administration (principals and coordinators) claim to have more than 1 year of experience with SWDs, their initial and in-service training in the field of inclusive education is almost nonexistent. During the interviews, the ableist conceptions regarding the capabilities of people with disabilities were clearly dominant. Inclusion of students with disabilities was necessary for their socialization, without valuing their right and potential to learn. These views about disability are embedded within the history of special education in Brazil, based on ideas first related to segregation (until the mid-20th century), where most people with disabilities have received education in places apart from non-SWD students.

## DISCUSSION

Camargo (2017) stated that inclusion is a conceptual paradigm that applies to a wide variety of physical and symbolic spaces. All people should be able to participate effectively in inclusive contexts, as identity, difference, and diversity should represent social advantages that favor solidarity and collaborative relationships. Despite the existence of a policy designed to provide more inclusive education in Corumbá, our findings reveal limiting and harmful attitudes and behavior towards SWDs. The school leaders used deficit notions and did not often consider that SWDs have the ability to develop other skills not related to the limiting biological capacity ways of viewing them (not listening, not seeing, not walking, not fully exercising all mental or intellectual faculties, among others; Mello, 2016). According to Harpur (2009), such perceptions regarding the capacities of people with disabilities highlight the concept of ableism as a discriminatory behavior towards people with disabilities. The findings of the study challenge us to seek to understand how value judgments linked to the capabilities of individuals are present in society with their excluding effects (Martin, 2017).

Principals and coordinators seemed to believe inclusion of SWDs in schools to entail only socialization. The question of why students with disabilities attended school and did not learn did not occur in the interviews. However, the welcoming of SWD by the school and the professionals who work there was extolled, even though they did not feel prepared to teach these students. School leadership perceptions suggest that despite welcoming students with disabilities, the supposed inability of SWD to learn remained at the analytical forefront and leaders failed to appreciate SWD development potential. Confirming these expectations, Soares et al. (2010) observe that in Brazil most of the students with disabilities attending the regular schools repeat the same grade level several times and rarely complete their basic schooling.

It is important to consider the educational system context and especially the working conditions provided to these professionals. The majority of the school leaders who answered the survey did not have any training in special education. Coordinator II highlights that training opportunities that address the theme of special education are practically nonexistent at school. On the other hand, she insists that what motivates school professionals is "to like what they do," bringing to the individual level or personal reasons (be it principal, coordinator, or teacher) the responsibility to provide what they consider a good work—based on a personal commitment (Dias et al., 2015). As Pazey and Cole (2012) pointed out in other national contexts, despite the fact that principals and other members of school management teams face the challenge of implementing and administering inclusive schools, the discussion about SWD is rarely an integral part of their preservice or in-service training programs. In addition, as noted by Oliveira and colleagues (2020), in Brazil there are currently no national parameters describing school management teams' skills or competencies to guide preservice or in-service training and recruiting. The majority of the acting school leaders in Brazil take on the role counting only on their initial training in graduate teacher courses (Oliveira et al., 2020), that normally do not include training for educational administration.

The study or discussion about DS and the implementation of inclusive policies in schools is rare in their preservice training as teachers. This context severely limits the discussion on disability and inclusion policies, and issues related to SWD are generally delegated to the competence of specialists. This approach tends to remove responsibility from school leaders and stands in stark contrast with the perspective of equity and social justice in which inclusion is fundamental and is everyone's responsibility.

## Final Considerations

DS offers relevant support for the discussions regarding students with disabilities and management teams' perceptions of inclusive education (Omote, 2004). Nogueira (2012) highlighted the importance of investment in in-service training of professionals who work in the administration of education systems, emphasizing that educational leaders deal directly with public policies that favor school inclusion processes. Such professionals face daily challenges in organizing teacher training processes, and reorganizing or adapting school spaces and resources. However, there are few publications in Brazil that emphasize the need for training aimed at principals in the area of special education. Nogueira (2012) also pointed out the importance of academic research that addresses the professional development of public school principals in the area of special education. In the context of special education, knowledge ends up being constructed and acquired in the pedagogic practice itself whether in learning with peers, from a pedagogic support nucleus or from fellow students (Sousa, 2017).

This research points to the need to discuss the training of education professionals, particularly those who work as principals, pedagogic coordinators, administrators, or leaders. Thus, we assume the relevance of DS as an important knowledge field to sustain the implementation of consistent inclusive education policies in schools. DS brings an important intersectional identity lens as well. DeMatthews et al. (2020) argue that racism, ableism, and other identity markers articulate and reinforce each other and work in an interdependent and invisible way to support the idea of normality. This in turn contributes to segregation and intraschool inequality. Annamma and colleagues (2014) also argue that a multifaceted approach contributes to a greater understanding of the marginalizing conditions that affect Black students with disabilities, for example.

Regarding the behavior of principals, the analytical perspective advocated by DeMatthews and colleagues (2020) indicates that they often reinforce the status quo of segregation and marginalization. Thus, we propose the simultaneous, integrated, and historical critical consideration of the multiple social aspects of schooling and the identities of students and their families for a critical review of the principals' approach to school inclusive improvement and their initial and in-service training.

Finally, the articulation of DS with the critical race theory (DisCrit) proposed by DeMatthews et al. (2020) exposes how labels have many meanings for students of different races, genders, social conditions, and disabilities, challenging the school management team to combat and overcome all forms of exclusion, marginalization, and injustice. While the literature on school leadership provides important clues about effective practices for principals to improve student outcomes, they are not necessarily intersectional or mindful of the multiple forms of oppression that perpetuate inequalities and segregation in public schools. Thus the DisCrit perspective on school leadership can provide clues as to how principals can increase their schools' potential to work collaboratively, question beliefs on unique identities, reflect on how labels work within schools, and recognize that culture and school practices must change to address deeply rooted institutional racism and ableism (DeMatthews et al., 2020, p. 11).

Training opportunities for school leaders that contemplate DS can be fundamental to providing academic support to develop ideas that consider human diversity as a starting point to understand teaching and learning processes and, above all, for the deconstruction of ideas that link disability to incapacity. Actions in this direction for initial and in-service training could favor both the inclusion of students with disabilities in school and the improvement of the quality of schooling for all students. This discussion is even more urgent and important in Brazil, since the Ministry of Education is proposing a national matrix of competencies focusing on school principals and planning to develop similar guidelines for other professionals that compose the management team—as pedagogical coordinators. The central government perspective is to promote and support public basic education systems (federal, state, and municipal) as well as universities and other training institutions for education professionals to implement common patterns for school leaders' preservice and in-service training in the coming years. This study intends to contribute to the necessary discussion in the higher education sector about the professional development of inclusive and effective school leaders. We consider that the contribution of DS can broaden the training horizons of education professionals, school managers in particular, toward the promotion of a more inclusive education for all.

## NOTES

1. Following the International Convention on the Right of Persons With Disabilities, promulgated in Brazil in 2008, that chose the term "person with disabilities," in this work chose to use the term students with disabilities (SWD).
2. 1974 was the year of the first enrollment survey of special education students held in Brazil and, in this document, there is no distinction, in regular schools, as to whether students were enrolled in common or special classes.
3. It was questioned whether they received training material with information regarding the inclusive policies implemented by the federal government.

# REFERENCES

Alves, M. T. G., & Franco, C. (2008). A pesquisa em eficácia escolar no Brasil: Evidências sobre o efeito das escolas e fatores associados à eficácia escolar [Research on school effectiveness in Brazil: Evidence on the school effects and factors associated with school effectiveness]. In N. Brooke & J. F Soares (Eds.), *Pesquisa em eficácia escolar: Origem e trajetórias.* Belo Horizonte: UFMG.482-500.

Annamma, S., Morrison, D., & Jackson, D. (2014). Disproportionality fills in the gaps: Connections between achievement, discipline and special education in the school-to-prison pipeline. *Berkeley Review of Education,* 5(1), 53–87. https://doi.org/10.5070/B85110003

Bakhtin, M. (1981) *Marxismo e Filosofia da Linguagem* [Marxism and the philosophy of language]. Hucitec.

Bourdieu, P. (1999). *The weight of the world: Social suffering in contemporary society.* Polity Press.

Caldwell, J. (2011). Disability identity of leaders in the self-advocacy movement. *Journal of Intellectual & Developmental Disability,* 49(5), 315–326. https://doi .org/10.1352/1934-9556-49.5.315

Camargo, E. P. D. (2017). Inclusão social, educação inclusiva e educação especial: enlaces e desenlaces [Social inclusion, inclusive education and special education: Connections and disconnections]. *Ciência & Educação (Bauru),* 23(1), 1–6. https://doi.org/10.1590/1516-731320170010001

Campbell, F. K. (2009). Disability harms: Exploring internalized Ableism. In E. Kendall & C.A. Marshall (Eds.), *Disabilities: Insights from across fields and around the world* (pp. 19–33). Greenwood Publishing Group.

*Constituição da República Federativa do Brasil de 1988* (1988). http://www.planalto .gov.br/ccivil_03/constituicao/constituicao.htm

Day, C., Gu, Q., & Sammons, P. (2016). The impact of leadership on student outcomes: How successful school leaders use transformational and instructional Strategies to Make a Difference. *Educational Administration Quarterly,* 52(2), 221–258. https://doi.org/10.1177/0013161X15616863

DeMatthews, D. E., Serafini, A., &Watson, T. N. (2020). Leading inclusive schools: Principal perceptions, practices, and challenges to meaningful change. *Educational Administration Quarterly,* 57(1), 3–48. https://doi.org/10.1177/ 0013161X20913897

Dias, M. A. L., Rosa, S. C., & Andrade, P. F. (2015). Os professores e a educação inclusiva: identificação dos fatores necessários à sua implementação [Teachers and inclusive education: identifying factors required for its implementation]. *Psicologia USP,* 26(3), 453–463. https://doi.org/10.1590/0103-656420140017

Dowse, L. (2010). Contesting practices, challenging codes: Self advocacy, disability politics and the social model. *Disability & Society,* 16(1), 123–141. https://doi. org/10.1080/713662036

Duncan, J., Punch, R., Gauntlett, M., & Talbot-Stokes, R. (2020). Missing the mark or scoring a goal? Achieving non-discrimination for students with disability in primary and secondary education in Australia: A scoping review. *Australian Journal of Education,* 64(1), 54–72. https://doi.org/10.1177/0004944119896816

Ebersold. S. (2005). L'inclusion: Du modèle médical au modèle managérial? [Inclusion, from a medical model to a managerial model?]. *Reliance, 2*(2), 43–50. https://doi.org/10.3917/reli.016.0043

Ebersold, S., Plaisance, E., & Zander, C. (2016). *Rapport de la Conférence de Comparaisons Internationales. École inclusive pour les élèves en situation de handicap: accessibilité, réussite scolaire et parcours individuels* [Report of the International Comparisons Conference. Inclusive school for students with disabilities: accessibility, academic success and individual pathways]. Conseil National d'Évaluation du Système Scolaire. http://www.cnesco.fr/wp-content/uploads/2015/12/rapport_handicap.pdf

Franco, C., Ortigão, I., Albernaz, A., Bonamino, A., Aguiar, G., Alves, F., & Sátyro, N. (2007). Qualidade e equidade em educação: reconsiderando o significado de "fatores intra-escolares" [Quality and equality in education: Reconsidering the meaning of "within-school factors"]. *Ensaio: Avaliação e Políticas Públicas em Educação, 15*(55), 277–298. https:/doi.org/10.1590/S0104-40362007000200007

Freitas, S. N., Teixeira, C. T., & Rech, A. J. (2016). Alunos com deficiência em situação de acolhimento institucional: Desafios para a gestão e a inclusão escolar [Students with disabilities in institutional care condition: Challenges for management and school inclusion]. *RIAEE – Revista Ibero-Americana de Estudos em Educação, (11)*4, 2104–2124. https://doi.org/10.21723/riaee.v11.n4.8214

Harpur, P. (2009). Sexism and racism, why not ableism? Calling for a cultural shift in the approach to disability discrimination. *Alternative Law Journal, 34(3)*, 163–167. https://doi.org/10.1177/1037969X0903400304

Instituto Brasileiro de Geografia e Estatística. (2020). *IBGE Cidades* [Brazilian national institute of geography and statistics—Cities]. Corumbá, Mato Grosso do Sul, Brasil. https://cidades.ibge.gov.br/brasil/ms/corumba/panoram

Instituto Nacional de Estudos e Pesquisas Educacionais Anísio Teixeira. (2018). *Microdados do Censo Escolar 2018*. [2018 School Census Dataset].

Instituto Nacional de Estudos e Pesquisas Educacionais Anísio Teixeira. (2020). *Sinopse Estatística da Educação Básica 2019* [Statistical synopsis of basic education 2019] [online]. http://portal.inep.gov.br/sinopses-estatisticas-da-educacao-basica

Kassar, M. C. M., & Magario, R. (2017). Brazil. In P. Wehmaeyer (Ed.), *The Praeger International handbook of special education: Volume 1: The Americas and Africa* (pp. 171–181). Praeger.

Kassar, M. C. M., Rebelo, A. S., Rondon, M. M., & Rocha Filho, J. F. (2018). Educação especial na perspectiva da educação inclusiva em um município de Mato Grosso do Sul [Special education in the inclusive education perspective in a municipality of Mato Grosso do Sul, Brazil]. *Cadernos CEDES, 38*(106), 299–313. https://doi.org/10.1590/CC0101-32622018199077

Lacerda, P. M. (2006). *De perto, ninguém é anormal: A construção discursiva de identidades, em narrativas de trajetórias escolares longas, de 'pessoas com deficiência'* [Close up, no one is abnormal: The discursive construction of identities of people with deficiency in extended educational trajectories]. Tese de Doutorado em Educação da Pontifícia Universidade Católica do Rio de Janeiro, Rio de Janeiro. https://doi.org/10.17771/PUCRio.acad.9611

Lei de Diretrizes e Bases da Educação Nacional n° 9.394/96. (1996). *Estabelece as diretrizes e bases da educação nacional* [Establishes the guidelines and bases of national education]. http://www.planalto.gov.br/ccivil_03/leis/l9394.htm

Lei n° 13.146, de 6 de julho de 2015, (2015). *Institui a Lei Brasileira de Inclusão da Pessoa com Deficiência* [Establishes the Brazilian Law of Inclusion of Person with Disabilities]. Estatuto da Pessoa com Deficiência. http://www.planalto.gov.br/ccivil_03/_ato2015-2018/2015/lei/l13146.htm

Leithwood, K., Harris, A., & Hopkins, D. (2008). Seven strong claims about successful school leadership. *School Leadership and Management, 28*(1), 27–42. https://doi.org/10.1080/13632430701800060

Leithwood, K., Patten, S., & Jantzi, D. (2010). Testing a conception of how school leadership influences student learning. *Educational Administration Quarterly, 46*(5), 671–706. https://doi.org/10.1177/0013161X10377347

Lima, N. M (2019). Diretores escolares: Burocratas de nível de rua ou médio escalão? *Revista Contemporânea de Educação, 14*(31), 84–103. https://doi.org/10.20500/rce.v14i31.25954

Linton, S. (2005). *What is disability studies?* (Conference on disability studies and the university). *PMLA,* 120(2), 518–522. https://doi.org/10.1632/S0030812900167823

Longmore, P. K. (1995). *The second phase: From disability rights to disability culture.* Independent Living Institute. https://www.independentliving.org/docs3/longm95.html

Martin, M. T. (2017). Capacitismo (Ableism). In R. L. Platero, M. Rosón, & Ortega, E. (Eds.), *Barbarismos queer y otras esdrújulas* [Queer Barbarisms and other Esdrújulas] (pp. 73–81). Edicions Bellaterra.

Mello, A. G. (2016). Deficiência, incapacidade e vulnerabilidade: do capacitismo ou a preeminência capacitista e biomédica do Comitê de Ética em Pesquisa da UFSC [Disability, inability and vulnerability: On ableism or the pre-eminence of ableist and biomedical approaches of the Human Subjects Ethics Committee of UFSC]. *Ciência & Saúde Coletiva, 21,* 3265–3276. https://doi.org/10.1590/1413-812320152110.07792016

Ministry of Education. (2004). *Programa Educação Inclusiva: Direito à Diversidade. Documento Orientador* [Inclusive education program: Right to diversity. Guiding document]. Secretaria de Educação Especial. http://portal.mec.gov.br/par/194-secretarias-112877938/secad-educacao-continuada-223369541/17434-programa-educacao-inclusiva-direito-a-diversidade-novo#:~:text=Objetivo%3A%20Apoiar%20a%20forma%C3%A7%C3%A3o%20de,educacionais%20em%20sistemas%20educacionais%20inclusivos

Ministry of Education. (2007). *Portaria normativa n°- 13, de 24 de abril de 2007. Dispõe sobre a criação do "Programa de Implantação de Salas de Recursos Multifuncionais"* [Normative Ordinance No. 13, of April 24, 2007. Provides for the creation of the "Program for the Implementation of Multifunctional Resource Rooms"]. http://portal.mec.gov.br/index.php?option=com_docman&view=download&alias=9935-portaria-13-24-abril-2007&Itemid=30192

Ministry of Education. (2008). *Política Nacional de Educação Especial na perspectiva da Educação Inclusiva* [National Special Education Policy from the perspective of

Inclusive education]. http://portal.mec.gov.br/arquivos/pdf/politicaeduce special.pdf

Ministry of Education. (2013). *Documento Orientador do Programa Escola Acessível* [Guiding Document of the Accessible School Program]. Secretaria de Educação Continuada, Alfabetização, Diversidade e Inclusão. http://portal.mec .gov.br/index.php?option=com_docman&view=download&alias=13290-doc -orient2013&Itemid=30192

Ministry of Foreign Affairs. (2009). *Decreto n° 6.949, de 25 de agosto de 2009*. Enacts the Convention on the Rights of Persons With Disabilities and Its Optional Protocol, signed in New York on the 30th March 2007. http://www.planalto .gov.br/ccivil_03/_ato2007-2010/2009/decreto/d6949.htm

Municipal Secretary of Education. (2018). Decreto 2.018 de 25 de julho de 2018. *Dispõe sobre a reordenação da tipologia das unidades escolares e dos centros de educação infantil da Rede Municipal de Ensino de Corumbá, e dá outras providências*. Corumbá. http://do.corumba.ms.gov.br/corumba/portal/visualizacoes/pdf/ 3147#/p:1/e:3147?find=Decreto%20n.%202018

Nogueira, J. O. (2012). *Formação continuada de gestores públicos de educação especial: constituindo caminhos* [Continuing training of public managers of special education: constituting paths]. Dissertação de Mestrado. Programa de Pós-graduação em Educação da Universidade Federal do Espírito Santo [Masters dissertation. Graduate program in Education at the Federal University of Espírito Santo]. Vitória, Brasil. http://repositorio.ufes.br/handle/10/6096

Oliveira, A. C. P., & Paes de Carvalho, C. (2018). Gestão escolar, liderança do diretor e resultados educacionais no Brasil [Public school management, leadership, and educational results in Brazil]. *Revista Brasileira de Educação, 23,* 1–18. https://doi.org/10.1590/S1413-24782018230015

Oliveira, A. C. P., Paes de Carvalho, C., & Brito, M. M. (2020). Gestão Escolar: Um olhar sobre a formação inicial dos diretores das escolas brasileiras [School management: A look at the initial training of brazilian public schools' principals]. *Revista Brasileira de Política e Administração da Educação-Periódico científico editado pela ANPAE, 36*(2), 473–496. https://doi.org/10.21573/vol36n22020.99857

Omote, S. (2004). Estigma no tempo da inclusão [Stigma in the time of inclusion]. *Revista Brasileira de Educação Especial, 10*(3), 287–308.

Pazey B. L., & Cole, H. A. (2012). The role of special education training in the development of educational leadership programs socially just leaders: Building an equity consciousness in educational leadership programs. *Educational Administration Quarterly, 49*(2), 243–271. https://doi.org/10.1177/0013161X12463934

Silva, C. L., & Leme, M. I. (2009). O papel do diretor escolar na implantação de uma cultura educacional inclusiva. *Psicologia, Ciência e Profissão, 29*(3), 494–511. https://doi.org/10.1590/S1414-98932009000300006

Soares, T. M., Fernandes, N. S., Ferraz, M. S. B., & Riani, J. L. (2010). A expectativa do professor e o desempenho dos alunos [Teacher's expectation and students' performance]. *Psicologia: Teoria e Pesquisa, 26*(1), 157–170. https:// doi.org/10.1590/S0102-37722010000100018

Sousa, K. C. (2017). *A formação docente para a educação especial e a prática profissional do professor* [Teacher training for special education and the teacher's professional practice]. Dissertação de Mestrado, Universidade do Porto, Porto, Brasil.

https://bdigital.ufp.pt/bitstream/10284/6041/4/DM_Kelly%20de%20 Sousa.pdf

UNESCO. (1990). *Final report: World Conference on Education for All: Meeting basic learning needs Jomtien, Thailand.* https://unesdoc.unesco.org/ark:/48223/ pf0000097551

Valle, J. W., & Connor, D. J. (2014). *Ressignificando a deficiência: Da abordagem social às práticas inclusivas na escola* [Rethinking disability: A disability studies approach to inclusive practices]. AMGH.

Vioto, J. R. B., & Vitaliano, C. R. (2019). O papel da gestão pedagógica frente ao processo de inclusão dos alunos com necessidades educacionais especiais [The role of the pedagogical management in the process of inclusion of students with special educational needs]. *Dialogia, 33,* 47–59. https://doi.org/ 10.5585/dialogia.N33.13671

Waldron, N. L., McLeskey, J., & Redd, L. (2011). Setting the direction: The role of the principal in developing an effective, inclusive school. *Journal of Special Education Leadership, 24*(2), 51–60. https://education.ufl.edu/disability -policy-practice/files/2012/05/Waldron-et-al-JSEL-2011-Principal-copy-4.pdf

CHAPTER 26

# REMEMBERING WHAT MATTERS MOST

## A Framework to Build Social Justice Leaders and Transform Schools Into Inclusive Spaces

**Georgina E. Wilson**
*Central Michigan University*

**Regina R. Umpstead**
*Central Michigan University*

### ABSTRACT

This theoretical article proposes a framework to support leaders in building the mindset and practices to create equitable learning environments for all students, especially those with disabilities. Our approach uses servant leadership, social justice leadership, and transformative leadership frameworks, and the literature related to disability studies and intersectionality to create a new framework for school leaders with three pillars: care, connection, and collaboration. The leadership literature shows promising results for students when

*Who Decides?*, pages 645–674
Copyright © 2022 by Information Age Publishing
www.infoagepub.com
All rights of reproduction in any form reserved.

leaders and teachers cultivate caring, connected, and collaborative schools in partnership with the community.

Public schools have been an essential part of society in the United States since the common school movement in the mid-19th century. These universal schools were designed to bring together rich and poor students for high-quality education as the "great equalizer of the conditions of men" (Mann, 1848, para. 9). Common schools would accomplish our nation's ideal of equality by promoting the general intelligence of all to support our republican form of government and new opportunities for all in our economy (Mann, 1848). American's hope in the power of public schools was high, even as educational reformers did not necessarily agree upon the same vision of equal educational opportunity for all children (Church & Sedlak, 1976).

Yet, schools operate within the larger political and economic systems in our society, and our nation's ideals are steeped in the culture in which we live (Labaree, 1997; Mann,1848).

Even Mann's work reflected the bias of the time as he contrasted the education of the Native Americans to the more "civilized" educational system he was proposing; and without this education, he predicted that society would fall into "barbarism" (Mann, 1848, paras. 11–12). Similarly, Katz (1976) noted class and racial bias at play during the late 19th century when the systems of public schools were established by the affluent, whose children benefited from them, while the promise of social mobility for all was never realized for the children of poor and minority families. More recently, Labaree (1997) described our nation's inability to reach its educational ideals as a political problem in which we fight over which of the conflicting goals of our educational system to pursue. The current educational outcomes are a result of the goal of social mobility (promoting individual student interests) overtaking the pursuits of social efficiency (preparing future workers) and democratic equality (preparing future citizens). As in the past, our nation's current political, economic, and cultural context values certain individuals over others, a familiar situation that results in offering the members of valued groups a better education than the members of the less valued ones. The individuals with the most power retain it for themselves and their children.

The vision of education as a unifying force has only been partially realized as our public schools continue to strive to prepare all American youth for adulthood. In fact, an analysis of the laws creating public schools, adopted by state legislatures in the common school era, suggests they are intended to prepare current students for their future lives in three ways: (a) to be "adults who possess a basic understanding of the world, who are capable and self-aware, and who interact with others in a complex and rapidly changing society," (b) "workers who compete for and perform in their future career pursuits," and (c) "participants in the American political system" (Umpstead, 2007, pp. 306–308).

Schools have historically served students with varying quality and care levels, leading to many students' marginalization. While no longer considered uncivilized (Mann, 1848), non-White students, non-male students, English language learners, students in poverty, and students identified as having emotional, behavioral, medical, learning, or cognitive disabilities are considered *others* (Kanter, 2011). The marginalization of minority groups shares common roots (Willie & Willie, 2005) with an inferiority paradigm (Zion & Blanchett, 2011). More recently, scholars have noted a problem for male students based on the feminization of education (Mulvey, 2010). Limited empirical evidence currently exists on this claim (Verniers et al., 2016). Conversations about the emasculation of Black boys in schools continue (Lindsay, 2018) and should be explored empirically.

One example of an othered population are students with disabilities (McKinney & Lowenhaupt, 2013). In considering the way American culture and educational systems fail to value those who have been othered (Pearson et al., 2016), our work suggests that this understanding of disability has led to significant flaws in the development and delivery of educational services for students. Students' needs have received inadequate attention in crucial areas such as curriculum development and delivery, social-emotional support, and discipline. The medical model of disability (a deficit-based model) justified the undervaluing and exclusion of individuals with disabilities in the United States for the first half of the 20th century. Even though disability studies as a reconceptualization of disability as a normal part of life began to offer educators a new lens to examine their practices to better support students with disabilities in the 1960s and 1970s (Pearson et al., 2016), our work suggests that this understanding of disability as a social construct has not yet fully taken hold.

The underservice of students has led scholars and practitioners to call for social justice in schools that starts with paying attention to "the experiences of marginalized groups and inequities in educational opportunities and outcomes" to ultimately end these practices (Furman, 2012, p. 194). Although many scholars have acknowledged the problem of underserving the needs of certain students in our educational system, and some have offered suggestions for correcting it within educational leadership preparation programs, there are limited solutions that specifically address school leaders' behaviors in the field. Even when these frameworks exist, they do not address serving students' whole identities, including the intersectionality of students who are minoritized, especially students who have disabilities. We suggest that a transformation of mindsets in school leaders and educators will lead to a reconceptualization and reconstruction of educational practices and environments. Through continually recurring critical self-reflection, framing, building equity literacy, and engaging in discourse amongst each other and the community, school leaders and teachers will interrupt their deficit mindset and biased practices that marginalize and minoritize students and deepen their relationship and appreciation with and for the community. The ultimate outcome of changing the ways of knowing, being, and doing of school leaders and educators will transform schools into co-constructed environments where the communal wealth and contribution is acknowledged and valued. In these environments, students are accommodated and invited to contribute and actualize as school community members.

In this chapter, we look holistically at equity and inclusion reform efforts meant to positively affect marginalized students and then specifically at the experiences of students with disabilities in schools. The framework proposed here is unique, because it integrates theory and practice to accomplish sustainable change in the educational system by encouraging school culture and climate that is welcoming and supportive through the transformation of leader and teacher mindsets. Ultimately, this work relies on important theoretical foundations, core research, and key educational leadership practices. We drew from various leadership theories for the heart of the framework (Brown, 2004; Cambron-McCabe & McCarthy, 2005; Furman, 2012; Gooden & Dantley, 2019; Kose, 2009; Poekert et al., 2020). We then added the disability studies lens to address students with disabilities' specific needs and an intersectionality lens to present a new perspective on challenging and changing our current educational environments to be truly inclusive for all students, especially students with disabilities (McKinney & Lowenhaupt, 2013). Thus, our framework takes an inclusive mindset approach using an equity lens that builds leadership practices to support and cultivate learning in caring, connected, and collaborative environments.

## OUR FRAMEWORK

The theoretical framework aims to create three pillars of transformation for principals and teachers (see Figure 26.1). The first pillar, care, seeks to transform the leader and teacher mindsets. The second pillar, connection, seeks to establish relationships with students and the community for the leaders and teachers to grow in appreciation, and empathy. The third pillar, collaboration, seeks to reconcile the practices of the principal and teachers to the needs, values, and hopes of the community enabling a co-construction of vision and goals for the school. Through critical reflection, leaders will work to change their ways of knowing, doing, and being, while building the skills to guide the transformation of teachers through their own critical

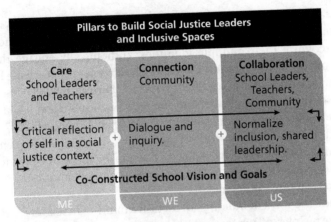

**Figure 26.1** Conceptual model: Pillar for building inclusive mindset in leaders and teachers. *Note:* This model shows how the pillars flow and support one another, while addressing different focus and keeping the community centered.

reflection process. Principals and teachers will act to construct new ways of knowing, being, and doing the business of learning.

We see the me, we, us model for organizational well-being working from the foundation of several pillars of scholarship: social justice, transformative and servant leadership, DisCrit, and intersectionality literature (Jarden & Jarden, 2017). Additionally, the principles of leadership for professional learning towards educational equity, constructed by Poekert et al.'s (2020) systematic literature review on professional learning and educational equity, guides work in which the leaders, teachers, and community will engage.

We use a well-being model to help us construct our framework and highlight the integrated nature of the work. In the me, we, us model the distinct levels of assessment and intervention are defined and organized at the employee level—me; the group level—we; and the organizational level—us (Jarden & Jarden, 2017). The model communicates the interconnectedness of each level, and how the engagement and success of one level affects the engagement and success of another. The model, intended for use by organizations seeking to increase well-being, when applied to our framework, defines where the work is focused.

The theoretical foundation for our framework is informed by two leadership theories—transformative and social justice—that seek to include and advocate for marginalized populations of students through critique and disruption. Transformative leadership builds from transformative teaching and learning (Shields, 2010). It calls on leaders to critique and disrupt the existing practices of organizations that are detrimental to the people served by the organization (Cooper, 2009) and offers a more inclusive, equitable, and democratic conception of education (Shields, 2010). Likewise, social justice leadership calls for a fundamental transformation of the systems of education that marginalize groups to students into spaces that value all students, recognize their multiple identities, authentically engage the community, and promote equitable educational outcomes for everyone in a balanced way (DeMatthews et al., 2020; Rodela & Bertrand, 2018).

We also utilize servant leadership theory, which calls upon leaders to be of service to the employees they supervise and lead (Greenleaf, 1977/2002). Many of the major practices of a servant leader, such as listening, empathy, and healing, will be essential skills to develop in the school leaders and teacher to ensure the work in the connection and collaboration pillar results in the intended outcomes.

To guide the work of building an inclusive mindset in leaders and teachers, the principles of professional learning towards education equity are used. In their systematic literature review, Poekert et al. (2020) sought to identify themes that would inform professional learning to help attend to the ever-growing inequities in school settings. They identified five themes to inform and guide professional learning for district leadership and teachers: (a) critical framing of issues towards social justice; (b) dialogue and inquiry; (c) learning and identity development; (d) context, resources, and motivations; and (e) normalizing inclusion and shared leadership (Poekert et al., 2020).

## OUR WHY: SUPPORTING DIVERSE LEARNERS

School leaders play an essential role in establishing effective school cultures (Cruz-Gonzalez et al., 2019; Deal & Peterson, 2016). Educational leadership scholars for social justice have stressed the essential role school leaders play in ensuring the academic success for all students, regardless of race, ethnicity, gender, ability, sexual orientation, age, language, religion, or socioeconomic status (Brooks et al., 2007; Brown, 2004; Cambron-McCabe & McCarthy, 2005; Frattura & Capper, 2007; Marshall & Oliva, 2010, McKenzie et al., 2008; Theoharis, 2007). Additionally, culturally responsive leadership influences academic achievement and students' engagement within the school environment (Banks & Banks, 2004).

On the basis of underlying organizational assumptions, institutions frequently and unknowingly engage in unintentional discrimination and oppression (Constantine & Sue, 2005). If schools are to evolve, the traditional organizational structure of schools must be transformed to reflect a new set of assumptions that epitomizes social justice (Cambron-McCabe & McCarthy, 2005).

## Representation

Our country's students are becoming increasingly diverse, yet this diversity is not reflected in our teaching force. According to the National Center for Education Statistics (NCES) 2017–2020 data, 48% of public-school students identify as ethnicities or races other than White. More specifically, 27% identify as Hispanic, 15% Black, 6% as Asian, 3.6% as two or more races, 1% as American Indian/Native American, and 0.4% as Hawaiian/Pacific Islander. NCES also reported only 20% of the teaching force identifies as a race or ethnicity other than White. Of these non-White teachers, 8.8% identify as Hispanic, 6.7% as Black, 2.3% as Asian, 1.4% as two or more races, 0.4% as American Indian/Native American, and 0.2% as Hawaiian/Pacific Islander. Likewise, only 22% of principals identify as an ethnicity or race other than White. More specifically, 8.2% identify as Hispanic, 10.6% as Black, 1.4% as Asian, 1.1% as two or more races, 0.7% as American Indian/Native American, and 0.2% Hawaiian/Pacific Islander. The disparities in representation and shifts in the American population only serve to perpetuate the inequities previously discussed in this chapter and will increase the divide in schools between the student population and that of teachers and principals in American public schools (Cooper, 2009).

Representation related to ethnicity and race between leaders, teachers, and students is important and diversifying the racial and ethnic makeup of staff in U.S. schools is necessary (Milner & Howard, 2013) as students need leaders who are prepared to be cultural change agents (Cooper, 2009). When teachers of color are in classrooms, they serve as role models for all students, subtly yet profoundly shaping students' values and academic performance (Villegas et al., 2012). For students of color, having teachers of color in classrooms increases the likelihood of connection and understanding of the students' lived experiences (Villegas et al., 2012). The commonality of cultural and societal lived experiences between teachers and students of color give teachers credibility that can impact academic engagement (Cherng & Halpin, 2016; Villegas et al., 2012). Discourse surrounding the need for racial representation in school staff often fail to consider the intersection of other identities.

Without an explicit focus on social justice, school leaders continue implementing systems that marginalize students. When White school leaders do not attend to their own biases, they inadvertently reproduce racial oppression (Khalifa et al., 2016) and undermine reform work related to advocacy and activism for students who are systemically marginalized. Additionally, a leader's inability to address intersectionality of a student's identities, specifically the intersection of race, gender, sexual orientation, and disability, equally undermines reform and advocacy work (McKinney & Lowenhaupt, 2013). Social justice reform cannot be realized in schools where students with disabilities are routinely, and by practice, segregated and pulled out from classrooms or receive a separate learning experience (Theoharis, 2007).

## Student Achievement and Opportunity

The achievement and opportunity gaps have served as significant drivers of social justice and equity work (Cambron-McCabe & McCarthy, 2005; Capper & Young, 2014; Furman, 2012; McKenzie et al., 2008).

The gaps are now so pronounced, according to the National Center for Education Statistics (2020), that throughout elementary and secondary school, Blacks scored lower, overall, on mathematics and reading test scores than Whites. These gaps continue in higher education with disparities being present in college attendance and completion, between Black and White young adults. A recent report found that Black men had the lowest college completion rates at four year institutions of only 40%, in contrast to an overall graduation rate of 62.4% (Shapiro et al., 2017). While there is significant literature exploring what researchers have termed the achievement gap between racial groups in the United States, others point to systemic racism in naming it the opportunity gap (Welner & Carter, 2013). We work from this perspective to highlight the disparity found in academic research in relation to race. Against the backdrop of the demographic shifts occurring in the U.S. school system, a call for greater attention to schools' need to provide culturally relevant teaching to close the achievement gap has been made (Griner & Stewart, 2013; Scott, 2000). Although academic gaps are prevalent, the statistics represent an outcome. To explain a possible root cause of the achievement gap, and to focus on equity, a discussion on the opportunity gap is critical.

It is difficult to statistically quantify the opportunity gap in the same manner as the achievement gap. The opportunity gap addresses equitable access and moves the focus from the student deficiencies to societal, school, and community conditions for creating difference in educational outcomes for students (Welner & Carter, 2013). For example, the concern that students attending "nonperforming" schools and living in urban and impoverished settings are not able to access the same opportunities as those living in higher socioeconomic communities and attending high performing schools demonstrates an "opportunity gap" (Miretzky et al., 2016). A lot can be learned about a leader's paradigm according to the gap they choose to highlight—achievement or opportunity. Those who seek to address the opportunity gap often seek to increase access and programming to support the students; those who focus on achievement statistics alone often view the academic outcomes as a lack of effort by the student or a deficiency in what the student brings from home according to a readiness perspective (Flores & Gunzenhauser, 2018).

Cambron-McCabe and McCarthy (2005) asked the field to consider, "What skills leaders need to engage the school and the community in confronting social justice issues?" (p. 211). In addition, they asked educational leaders to consider, "How do we avoid the trap of confusing gains in test scores with substantive educational improvement" (p. 211). To answer these questions, educational leadership must engage in critical discourse that is significantly different from past leadership preparation. A crucial part of a leader's role is to maintain high expectations for student outcomes (McKinney & Lowenhaupt, 2013). Regardless of how it is measured, student learning and achievement must remain at the heart of social justice work (Capper & Young, 2014).

## RESPONSIVE FRAMEWORKS

Existing frameworks such as culturally responsive leadership and inclusive leadership are being utilized in schools to create more inclusivity, close opportunity gaps, and consider the needs of the historically marginalized populations of students. These frameworks often call for leaders to challenge their mindsets and expand their awareness related to the experiences of their students, which may differ from their own and encourage leaders to change marginalizing traditions, policies, and perceptions that perpetuate the status quo in schools (Cambron-McCabe & McCarthy, 2005) and interrupt the behaviors of educators that continue to exclude and other students (Hernandez & Fraynd, 2014; Khalifa et al., 2016). To begin this work, leaders must be conscious that schools are still functioning in a way that systemically marginalizes student populations, so that students are positioned as either normal or others (McKenzie et al., 2008; McKinney & Lowenhaupt, 2013). Although a broad range of students may experience positive results from school leaders' intentional actions, the frameworks define and target specific student populations and often do not explicitly attend to the intersection of multiple marginalized statuses. School leaders need to disrupt social contexts related to bias from their mindsets.

### Culturally Responsive Leadership

Culturally responsive pedagogy is a way for educators to attend to the cultural needs and contexts of students and the community (Ylimaki & Jacobson, 2013). It is an important aspect of building inclusive school environments and improving academic outcomes for marginalized students. Its first application in schools was focused on classroom practices controlled by the teacher. As it has grown and made impacts, the tenets of culturally responsive pedagogy are being applied to educational leadership.

In their literature review, Khalifa et al. (2016) sought to identify educational leaders' behaviors in relation to leadership, social justice, and culturally relevant schooling literature. The review resulted in five strands of culturally responsive school leadership behaviors: (a) critical self-awareness, (b) culturally responsive curricula, (c) teacher preparation, (d) culturally responsive and inclusive school environments, and (e) engaging students and parents in community contexts. Khalifa et al. (2016) distinguished culturally responsive pedagogy/teaching and leadership behaviors to frame their discussion in leadership behaviors specific to school leaders and leadership literature.

Johnson (2007) reanalyzed data from the U.S. case study of schools in the International Successful School Principal Project (ISSPP) through a lens of culturally responsive leadership. The practices Johnson identified as culturally responsive included affirming students' home cultures, increasing parent and community involvement in poor and culturally diverse neighborhoods, and advocating for change in the larger community. Johnson (2007) primarily focused on how school leaders included history, values, and cultural knowledge of students' communities into the school curriculum and how they worked to develop critical consciousness among both students and faculty to challenge inequities in larger society. In Johnson's findings, it was evident that the principals engaged in practices that created a welcoming environment for students and parents. Additionally, the interactions were student- and parent-centered. However, there were minimal examples of the inclusion of a student's home culture or sources of knowledge being utilized in the day-to-day curriculum.

## Inclusive Leadership

Even though much progress has been made towards greater acceptance and inclusion of individuals with disabilities in U.S. society, much work remains to be done. Traditional concepts of leadership do not easily support inclusion (Ryan, 2006). Ryan's (2006) inclusive leadership framework notes that to be successful, leaders must reject hierarchical views of leadership as these reinforce unequal social norms and instead embrace more collective forms of leadership. Key practices to accomplish this work are "advocating for inclusion, educating participants, developing critical consciousness, nurturing dialogue, emphasizing student learning and classroom practice, adopting inclusive decision- and policy-making strategies, and incorporating whole school approaches" (Ryan, 2006, p. 9).

Inclusion helps change social constructions of normalcy and difference. McKinney and Lowenhaupt (2013) explain that meaningful inclusion implies that inclusion applies not only to students with disabilities, but to all people in a school community and to all situations and issues that touch the lives of students and educators. While such a definition of inclusion flows from a Disability Studies orientation, inclusion is *not* a special education, or disability issue. (p. 321)

Yet, inclusive approaches have been identified by some schools as inadequate to address the educational needs of students with disabilities (Kauffman & Bader, 2014). Hornby (2015) proposed a theory of inclusive special education that integrates inclusive education and special education by considering students' right to be included in the general classroom environment while also receiving appropriate educational and related services, things that may be provided in resource or other specialized spaces for students with disabilities. Inclusive special education recognizes that the goals of education for students with disabilities are broader than purely academic ones since they also include life, vocational, and social skills to allow individuals to live happy, productive adult lives. It also provides students with curriculum that meets their individualized needs.

Students with disabilities have faced significant discrimination in our educational system. The general policies and laws that govern our nation were made without consideration for individuals with disabilities (Scotch, 2001). Moreover, the medical model of disability, which sees individuals as having a medical condition that needs to be treated, was widely adopted as the policy lens for many years and served to foster prejudice and discrimination against individuals considered to have a disabling condition (Dirth & Branscombe, 2017). During the first half of the 20th century, children with disabilities were not only separated from general education students but many were denied an education altogether (Ferri & Connor, 2005).

Although the disability rights movement or series of "interconnected projects" was barely visible before the 1970s (Bagenstos, 2009, p. 12), the U.S. Congress adopted Title V of the Rehabilitation Act of 1972 and passed the Education for All Handicapped Children Act in 1975 (now known as the Individuals With Disabilities Education Act; Bagenstos, 2009; Scotch, 2001). The movement embraced the social model of disability that explains any difficulty an individual with a disability has is not an inherent trait of that individual but instead is due to the interaction of a person's characteristics with barriers and constraints society imposes on that individual that limit their ability to fully participate in society (Bagenstos, 2009; Dirth & Branscombe, 2017). The reform legislation of the 1970s, culminating in the enactment of the Americans With Disabilities Act of 1990, a major victory for the movement, reflected a general societal acceptance of this view (Bagenstos, 2009). Thus, disability was seen as a social issue, not a personal issue, and civil rights legislation was designed to eliminate attitudes and practices that excluded people (Bagenstos, 2009; Scotch, 2001).

Even though much progress has been made towards greater acceptance and inclusion of individuals with disabilities in U.S. society, much work remains to be done, especially when conceptualizing PK–12 schools as inclusive spaces. Traditional concepts of leadership do not easily support inclusion (Ryan, 2006). McKinney and Lowenhaupt (2013) stated: "Meaningful inclusion implies that inclusion applies not only to students with disabilities, but to all people in a school community and to all situations and issues that touch the lives of students and educators" (p. 321).

## TRANSFORMATIVE/ACTIVIST PARADIGMS INFORMING FRAMEWORKS

Many reform efforts designed to include and meet the needs of marginalized student populations have been created, utilized, and have positively impacted schools. Advocates for improving education for students of color, students with disabilities, and English learners drew inspiration from *Brown v. Board of Education of Topeka* (1954; Willie & Willie, 2005). Although positive impacts exist, the far-reaching, systemic overhaul needed to close the gaps in access and outcomes in schools has not yet occurred. School leadership is a key element to the lasting impact of the efforts (see Table 26.1). Social justice leadership promotes both inclusion and activism (Cambron-McCabe & McCarthy, 2005; McKenzie et al., 2008). To address the needs of students with disabilities, it is important to incorporate a disability studies' perspective into this work, so that existing definitions of normalcy around disability are problematized (McKinney & Lowenhaupt, 2013).

We believe inequities occur because the current culture, policy, and practice throughout our education system has been constructed for and by the majority (Khalifa et al., 2019). More specifically, schools function in a culture that normalizes and values male, heterosexual, cis-gendered, able, White, English-speaking, native-born American students and views other students as inferior (Zion & Blanchett, 2011). The existence of the normative culture creates a lack of social cohesion in school communities, where all other forms of culture and experience are judged in comparison to the norm; and students valued in the normative culture have little responsibility to the community (Khalifa et al., 2019; Yosso, 2005).

School leadership is a key element to the lasting impact of the efforts. Social justice leadership promotes both inclusion and activism (Cambron-McCabe & McCarthy, 2005; McKenzie et al., 2008). In order to educate all students equitably, it is critical for those in power to create learning environments that explicitly include the students' needs, values, experiences, and histories. Most of the models used currently in educational leadership preparation programs neglect to adequately train or prepare school leaders

**TABLE 26.1  Organizational Framework for Building Inclusive Mindset in Leaders and Teachers**

| Pillars | | Mindset | Learning Principles | Theories/Lenses |
|---|---|---|---|---|
| Care (Me) | Leaders | Critical self-reflection<br>• Identity<br>• Leadership | Critically framing of issues towards social justice.<br><br>Learning and identity development. | Transformative Leadership<br>Social Justice Leadership<br>Intersectionality<br>• DisCrit |
| | Teachers | Critical self-reflection<br>• Identity<br>• Practice | | |
| Connection (We) | Teachers<br>Leaders | Disruption<br>• Deficit<br>  Thinking | Dialogue and enquiry.<br><br>Normalizing inclusion and shared leadership | Social Justice Leadership<br>Servant Leadership |
| | Community | Trust building cultural capital | | |
| Collaboration (Us) | Teachers<br>Leaders<br>Community | Co-construction<br>• Belief<br>• Value<br>• Vision | Dialogue and enquiry.<br><br>Normalizing inclusion and shared leadership. | Social Justice Leadership<br>Servant Leadership |

*Note:* This is a table that demonstrates the organization of the pillars, the strategy used to engage in the work, the principles and model used to frame, and the theories used to inform.

for this work. Too many programs primarily focus on a knowledge-based approach to training and development without real strategies to foster meaningful change within school leaders and the schools they serve (Brown, 2004; Gooden & Dantley, 2019). To address the needs of students with disabilities, it is important to incorporate a disability studies' perspective into this work, so that existing definitions of normalcy around disability are problematized (McKinney & Lowenhaupt, 2013), as the goals of the disability rights movement have not yet been achieved (Feischer & Zames, 2011). Here we review the key leadership theories that inform our framework.

## Social Justice Leadership

Although differences in social justice practices in education continue, its underlying principles are based on moral values such as justice, respect, care, and equity. Social justice leadership centers around an ultimate concern for ending marginalization. In schools, principals make issues of race, class, gender, disability, sexual orientation, and other historically and currently marginalizing contexts in the United States central to their advocacy, leadership, practice, and vision. A social justice perspective puts forth the notion that educational leaders cannot separate the job's daily realities as principal and the activist work of social justice (DeMatthews, 2015; Gooden & Dantley, 2019; Theoharis, 2007). Theoharis (2007) found that social justice leadership was enacted in four ways by principals: (a) raising student achievement, (b) improving school structures, (c) recentering and enhancing staff capacity, and (d) strengthening school culture and community. Additionally, the social justice principals developed strategies to sustain their impacts for the marginalized populations.

DeMatthews et al. (2020) describe a school where social justice had taken hold as follows:

> A socially just and inclusive school is one that does not only emphasize academic achievement or prioritizes academic achievement as an all for nothing trade-off other important aspects of the school community, such as authentic family engagement, recognition of multiple student identities, the social and emotional development of students, and an inclusive and welcoming environment that values all people. (p. 10)

Many scholars have advanced social justice leadership models or frameworks to accomplish the work of eliminating educational inequity and establishing socially just schools (Brown, 2004; Furman, 2012; Gooden & Dantley, 2019; Kose, 2009; Poekert et al., 2020). The majority of the frameworks focus on principal preparation programs (Brown, 2004; Furman, 2012; Gooden & Dantley, 2019; McKenzie et al., 2008). Others situate the school leader's role in the process of developing social justice in school environments (Kose, 2009; Poekert et al., 2020). Although many frameworks mention students with disabilities, only a few explicitly attend to their unique needs (McKinney & Lowenhaupt, 2013). Recently, the DisCrit literature has provided a new critical framework for school leaders to scrutinize their current leadership practices with students where both race and ability are relevant (DeMatthews, 2020; DeMatthews et al., 2020).

### Principal Preparation Programs

Scholars have focused most of their attention on developing socially just leaders at the principal preparation program level. This is the place where scholars have the most influence and where they are able to shape leaders' beliefs and actions prior to principals serving in that official role. We highlight four frameworks to show the development of thinking in this field around critical pedagogy and discuss the contributions of two other authors in this field.

In depth discussions of educational leadership programs making social justice a top priority for their students occurred in the 2000s. McKenzie et al. (2008) recommended that principal preparation programs train students who have three key characteristics: (a) strong commitment to social justice or equity or, at least, an already existing tendency to question social inequities; (b) good teaching and a strong understanding of teaching and learning; and (c) a demonstrated inclination toward leadership as a teacher leader (p. 119). Cambron-McCabe and McCarthy (2005) advocated for both structural program changes (such as adopting a better recruitment process for applicants and revising curriculum) and also for a shift in the general understanding of the principal's role from principals as the chief administrator to a leader for social justice who participated in critical discourse and engaged in fieldwork (Cambron-McCabe & McCarthy, 2005). Brown (2004) asked leadership programs to adopt a process-oriented pedagogical framework to create schools that valued rather than marginalized students. This work acknowledged that traditional models of leadership preparation were not up to the task and that most college faculty were not trained nor prepared to do this work. Brown's (2004) framework utilized adult learning theory, transformative learning theory, and critical social theory to provide educational leadership candidates opportunities for critical reflection, rational discourse with colleagues, and action through policy praxis to allow for them to make connections between their learning and the social context in which they worked ultimately allowing them to make social change (Brown, 2004).

Furman (2012) placed social justice leadership as a praxis—focused on reflection by the future leader and action towards building skills and knowledge—at the center of their conceptual framework to be a leader for social justice. They expanded the understanding of praxis by explaining that social justice leaders must develop the capacity to engage in this work in five critical dimensions: personal, interpersonal, communal, systemic, and ecological. Ultimately, social justice leadership is action-oriented and transformative; committed and persistent; inclusive and democratic; relational and caring, reflective, and oriented toward a socially just pedagogy. Leadership programs must support the development of these skills in principals (Furman, 2012).

Because significant inequities continue to exist over 60 years after separate educational systems for Black and White children were declared inherently unequal in *Brown v. Board of Education* (1954), Gooden and Dantley (2019) stressed the importance of race in their leadership preparation conceptual framework. They focused on the need of more critically interrogating racial and cultural differences that lead to inequities among students though self-reflecting leadership, grounding in critical theory, challenging prophetic voice, linking theory to practice (praxis), and including race language.

### Leaders in Schools

Two social justice leadership frameworks stand out as making important contributions to training leaders in the field. Providing support for current principals is essential to accomplishing this work. Kose (2009) developed a framework of the principal's role in professional development for social justice based on the case studies of three Midwestern principals working towards social justice. The framework names five transformative roles for principals (transformative visionary, transformative learning leader, transformative structural leader, transformative cultural leader, and transformative political leader) as they promote teacher professional learning to enhance their subject matter expertise and their social identity development. When principals serve in these roles, they help create the right conditions for socially just organizational learning, socially just teaching, and socially just student learning (Kose, 2009).

Poekert et al. (2020) conducted a systematic review of the research on educational leadership, professional learning, and educational equity and identified five nascent principles of leadership for professional learning towards educational equity. These principles are: (a) context, resources, and motivation; (b) normalizing inclusion and shared leadership; (c) learning and identity development; (d) dialogue and enquiry; and (e) critical framing of issues toward social justice (Poekert et al., 2020). We have incorporated these principles into our framework.

### Transformative Leadership Theory

As culturally responsive school leadership builds from culturally responsive pedagogy, transformative leadership theory was developed from transformative teaching and learning (Shields, 2010). Transformative leadership is often confused with transformational leadership, although it is distinctly different. Transformational leadership works to reform and transform the organization (Bass, 1985), whereas transformative leadership critiques and disrupts the existing practices of the organizations that are detrimental to the people served by the organization (Cooper, 2009). There have been many discussions about transformative leadership, and Shields (2010) sought to further develop the theory of transformative leadership and connect it to school leaders' work and spotlight its potential in practice to offer a more inclusive, equitable, and democratic conception of education.

Shields (2010) felt that the core characteristics of transformative leadership were promise, liberation, hope, empowerment, activism, risk, social justice, courage, and revolution. These characteristics inform the seven major elements of a transformative leader's practice, which include:

- critique and promise,
- an attempt to effect both deep and equitable change,
- engagement in the deconstruction and reconstruction of knowledge frameworks that generate inequity,

- an acknowledgement of power and privilege,
- emphasis on both individual achievement and the public good,
- a focus on liberation, democracy, equity, and justice, and
- the presence of moral courage and activism activities.

These characteristics link education and educational leadership within the broader social context. Transformative leaders critique inequitable practices, and they offer the promise of greater individual achievement and a better life lived in common with others. Transformative leadership theory is related to critical theories of race and gender, cultural and social reproduction, and social justice leadership, yet it is grounded in the concepts of critique and possibility. An activist agenda, transformative leadership combines a rights-based theory that every individual is entitled to be treated with dignity, respect, and absolute regard with a social justice theory of ethics that takes these rights to a societal level (Shields, 2010).

In this framework, Cooper (2009) considered how principals can serve as transformative leaders for social justice in the schools and communities they serve. Cooper relied on Cornel West's cultural politics theories to inform the discussion and define the "cultural work" leaders should participate in to address inequity, cross sociocultural boundaries, and foster inclusion (p. 698). Cooper stated:

> A cultural worker in educational leadership is an educator who validates and draws on critical, multicultural, and interdisciplinary knowledge. They recognize and cultivate cultural capital among culturally and linguistically diverse students and families, forge a collaborative relationship with school community members and share leadership while forming alliances with those who hold a similar vision of equity and inclusion. (p. 718)

Engaging in cultural work offers school leaders, educators, and the community opportunities to build inclusive and integrated learning environments (Cooper, 2009).

### Servant Leadership

In servant leadership theory, the servant leader assumes the position of servant in their relationships with fellow workers (Greenleaf, 1977/2002). A servant leader's motivation is to serve the needs of others and is not centered on self-interest (Russell & Stone, 2002). Those who are led by servant leaders are likely to become servants themselves (Greenleaf, 1977/2002). Russell and Stone (2002) completed a review of the literature on servant leadership, since, at the time, the leadership theory lacked support from published empirical research. Any evidence to support the theory was philosophical and anecdotal. Russell and Stone (2002) sought to develop a researchable theory by categorizing and appraising servant leadership attributes to provide the foundation for the practical application of servant leadership and for future research.

Initially, Greenleaf (1977/2002) identified 10 major attributes to servant leadership, which included listening, empathy, healing, awareness, persuasion, conceptualization, foresight, stewardship, commitment to people's growth, and building community and nine *functional attributes*, which included vision, honesty, integrity, trust, service, modeling, pioneering, appreciation of others, and empowerment. Additionally, Greenleaf identified the accompanying attributes of communication, credibility, competence, stewardship, visibility, influence, persuasion, listening, encouragement, teaching, and delegations (1977/2002). It is important to remember that accompanying attributes are not secondary and may even be prerequisite (Russell & Stone, 2002).

A more contemporary view of servant leadership, in the form of a conceptual model, was shared by van Dierendonck (2011). The model is an attempt to resolve confusion in the literature of what servant leadership is and to highlight the important aspects of the theoretical framework. van Dierendonck (2011) collapsed servant leadership attributes even further by identifying six key characteristics which give a good indication of what followers of servant leaders experience. The characteristics are empowering and developing people, humility, authenticity, interpersonal acceptance, providing direction, and stewardship.

## Consideration of the Individual

### Intersectionality

Schools engage in the practice of subgrouping students by their marginalized status to understand and attend to the gaps in achievement and access. This grouping in schools is a dissection of the students. It exacerbates the existing disconnect between students and educators as the students are often discussed and educated based on the needs of their subgroup. This practice reinforces the deficit mindset of educators and strips the student of their place as an individual that deserves to be accommodated and included. Educational leaders that include intersectionality in critique of existing policies, practices, and structures mitigate the dissection that occurs in schools based on the valued normative culture (Agosto & Roland, 2018).

Intersectionality, a term Kimberlé Crenshaw (1991) coined in her work examining how women of color, particularly Black women, experience employment discrimination and violence, explained how individuals who occupy multiple marginalized identities can be silenced by intersectional forms of oppression. This framework can help educators attend to the whole student by first acknowledging and understanding the intersectional identities that impact a student's educational experience and outcomes.

Hernández-Saca et al. (2018) conducted a review of education research examining how the social construction of identity intersects with disability and affects young adults' experiences. Hernández-Saca et al. found key dimensions of the dominant discourse around the intersections of disability and race, gender, sexual orientation, class, and language. In addition, they concluded that youth and young adults with dis/abilities need to make sense of what it means to be labeled with special education categories and at their intersections. An additional finding focused on the interaction between the structural and the personal level of intersectionality. These authors also exposed how oppression is rooted in the social construction of the intersection of the youth and young adult identities that they experienced. They argued that disability experience and identity can no longer be considered separate from other socially constructed intersectional identities. The continued omission by scholars perpetuates historical impacts, such as disproportionate placement of marginalized students and the high number of special education labels (Hernández-Saca et al., 2018).

### The DisCrit Lens

DisCrit connects critical race theory (CRT) and disability studies to provide a lens to allow scholars and practitioners to consider situations where the intertwined nature of an individual's race and ability are important (Annamma et al., 2013) and may make them subject to multiple oppressions (Annamma & Handy, 2020). DisCrit is intersectional, acknowledging that both racism and ableism promote whiteness and ability as "normal," while also working to change this view (DeMatthews, 2020; DeMatthews et al., 2020, p. 33). It has been applied to school leadership practice to create inclusive schools (DeMatthews, 2020). It is also useful to examine the ways in which "racism, ableism, and other forms of discrimination influence the organized routines, structures, and processes within schools" (DeMattews et al., 2020, p. 8). DeMatthews (2020) identified the following critical actions principals should take to build school capacity through intersectional leadership: (a) rejecting notions of normalcy, (b) problematizing singular identities, (c) applying an interdisciplinary lens, and (d) engaging in activism and resistance. DeMatthews et al.'s (2020) study on successful inclusive schools found that using both an intersectional and an improvement-focused leadership approach worked best.

# THE PILLARS OF OUR FRAMEWORK

## Mindset of Educators

School leaders are key players in the educational environment as they lead schools' efforts to educate our children and support the community. Additionally, they are often the only voice heard (Rodela & Bertrand, 2018). Thus, leaders should be willing to question the status quo and be equity-minded if they are to engage in social justice leadership (Lac & Cumings Mansfield, 2018; McKenzie et al., 2008). A principal's professional identity is influenced by personal factors, such as race and gender, the school's culture, and the surrounding community's context. This information should be kept in mind when designing professional development and training activities to support leaders' strong professional identity in order for them to adopt the best practices for their schools (Cruz-González et al., 2019).

As school leaders aim to interrogate their biases—often in schools and communities where they are privileged by identities their students do not hold—it is imperative that they are supported by leader preparation programs and ongoing training dedicated to justice (Gooden & Dantley, 2019; Lac & Cumings Mansfield, 2018; Rodela & Bertrand, 2018). Additionally, school leader preparation and professional learning opportunities should guide leaders to develop culturally responsive skills and knowledge and the ability to assess school-wide cultural competence (Bustamante et al., 2009). School leaders often struggle with identifying and promoting inclusive practices in schools, particularly when underlying norms and assumptions that reinforce inequitable practices are deeply embedded in a school's culture and reinforced by societal expectations and power differences (Bustamante et al., 2009). When an educational leader is unaware of their personal biases and lacking cultural awareness, they may implicitly choose to maintain the status quo of inequitable practices (Bustamante et al., 2009).

Theoharis (2007) identifies several ways leaders' deficit thinking can negatively impact their efforts to lead equitably. They posit that leaders can do harm in their tendency to erase issues of race, deny racism, and work from a deficit mindset. Equally detrimental to students is the leader's non-attention to the barriers that negatively impact students, their families, and the communities in which they live (Theoharis, 2007). When a leader engages in the transformative leadership practice of promise, they make a commitment to lead in an equitable manner; and when they incorporate critique, the leader's intentionality in critiquing personal perceptions and leadership practices to meet the promise (Shields, 2010). The transformative leadership practices of critique and promise allows leaders to consistently use these skills to foster growth in themselves and the organization they lead in an equitable and just manner (Shields, 2010). Also, servant leaders' identified attributes would be helpful for education leaders to practice when leading reform efforts related to equity and inclusion. In servant leadership, meaningful dialogue is a way to engage in an exchange of perspectives that can lead to the development of self in relation to others and elicit empathy, critical in social justice work (Ferch, 2020).

## Pillar of Care—Me

Guided by the work of Poekert et al. (2020), we establish the first pillar using the principles of social justice, learning, and identity development, focusing first on building inclusive mindsets in school staff. By design, school leaders will first engage in the mindset work and then lead teachers through the same process. We believe the process will build an inclusive mindset in the leader and support the acquisition of leadership identity, including skills and knowledge essential to guide teachers through building inclusive mindsets and creating inclusive school communities.

For leaders to effectively work towards transformative social justice, they will need to understand and counteract the inequities in their schools. Leaders will only be able to identify disparities and solutions after first working on themselves—doing the inner work of critiquing, uncovering, and attending to their own biased viewpoints (Cooper, 2009; Dantley & Green, 2015; Poekert et al., 2020; Shields, 2010). The critical self-reflection and framing create an opportunity for principals and building leaders to effectively mediate reforms and understand how their mindset and cultural background influences their decisions and—most importantly—learn to recognize and understand how these institutional powers favor some groups to the detriment of others (Cooper, 2009; Furman, 2012; Poekert et al., 2020). Putting into action the commitment for self-development and personal transformation must be ongoing to create the skills, awareness, and knowledge necessary for school leaders to engage and begin to reimagine the alternative to the current school environment (Dantley & Green, 2015; Furman, 2012; Khalifa et al., 2016).

Leaders who work to develop reflective habits using the context of social justice can build from reflective habits for instructional leadership; one example of an instructional leadership practice that can be used as a tool for critical reflection is action research (Cornito & Caingcoy, 2020). Action research can be as beneficial during the critical work of addressing bias and developing cultural consciousness as it is during school improvement. When utilizing action research as a tool for critical reflection, specifically when focusing learning around identity and history, leaders seek to learn about marginalized students and communities, examine the students' lived experiences and the societal constructs that historically and presently impact that lived experience, analyze how the intersection of marginalized and minorities' statuses affect students, and critique their lived experiences, cultural background, and leadership practices that have affected students (Poekert et al., 2020). In helping leaders acknowledge, unlearn, and learn again, the leader will cultivate an inclusive mindset in themselves and establish a process of self-reflection to employ while sustaining and building upon their learning.

For teachers, constructing inclusive mindsets is about building communal accountability for organizational choices related to integrating social justice practices into classrooms and the school community. The leader, having done their self-reflection, can now facilitate social identity development in teachers and inspire, mobilize, and guide teachers to deconstruct perceptions and other mental barriers and fears that keep school community members from connecting (Cooper, 2009; Poekert et al., 2020).

The personal nature of action research allows each teacher to perform critical self-reflection according to their level of knowledge and self-awareness. This process equips teachers to dismantle the barriers that keep them from establishing psychologically safe environments for students and building connections in those safe spaces. While guiding teachers through the process of framing, self-reflection, developing racial literacy, and learning about historical and societal contexts that impact the students and communities they serve. This pillar strengthens the leaders as they attend to the teacher's individual and collective capacity to engage in critical social justice work (Cooper, 2009; Furman, 2012; Kose, 2009; Poekert et al., 2020; Theoharis, 2007). Framing can help teachers engage with equity work on a deeper level and creates a long-lasting change in perspective (Poekert et al., 2020). Through the pillar's learning discourse, leaders and teachers develop interpersonal and intrapersonal skills and strategies to enhance their social-emotional competencies to engage in activism within the school effectively (Berkovich, 2014; Furman, 2012). Additionally, the discourse is used as a data source to challenge established practices and attitudes while promoting dialogue and reflection in safe spaces (Poekert et al., 2020). When leaders create opportunities for teachers to work with colleagues on a mutual task collaboratively and reflectively, it inspires professional growth, communal accountability, and shared leadership amongst the teachers and principals related to organizational choices, which challenge the norms and assumptions that often reinforce inequitable practices embedded in a school's culture (Bustamante, 2009; Cornito & Caingcoy, 2020; Causton-Theoharis & Theoharis, 2008; Poekert et al., 2020).

## Pillar of Connection—We

The Pillar of Connection creates the opportunity for school leaders and teachers to take their learning from the pillar of care and apply it forward. Teachers and building leaders apply their learning as they engage in a process of assessment, critique, and vision development. During this process teachers are engaged in dialogue with community members, assessing and critiquing the school culture, and creating an equity-centered vision for the school that includes assets, resources, and responsibilities (Furman, 2012; Green, 2018), and engage in dialogue with the community. The pillar is guided by the Poekert et al. (2020) principles of dialogue, inquiry, and normalizing inclusion and shared leadership. The activities work to develop teachers' and leaders' ability and further their openness to engage the community in discourse and create relationship building and collaboration opportunities.

Educators for social justice and equity must be committed to lifelong learning and growth, related to eliminating prejudice and oppression by increasing awareness, facilitating change, and building connected and collaborative communities (Brown, 2004). Dialogue is essential in this process, as dialogical practices provide bridges that bring together different communities in ways that enable them to overcome barriers (Furman, 2012). Building leaders need to facilitate dialogue that demonstrates shared responsibility, equity of voice, critical listening, curiosity, affirmation, and the consistent challenging of implicit assumptions (Poekert, et al., 2020). These activities disrupt the deficit mindset that educators often have, giving them new, more equitable perspectives rooted in cultural wealth (Yosso, 2005). In this pillar, teachers and leaders use a non-bureaucratic communication strategy with the aims of learning what is important to parents—what do they want schools to be like (Khalifa et al., 2019)? What are the issues important to them (Fenton et al., 2017)?

The goal of this pillar can be met through the leaders and teachers engaging in listening sessions, as described by Jiménez-Castellanos et al. (2019), where they asked students, parents, and community members to participate in meetings to build connection and relationships. At those meetings, participants were asked to introduce themselves, to share experiences in the neighborhood and school community, to share any challenges they have faced, and what their goals are for the children/themselves, and what kind of school community they wanted to create. To ensure the listening sessions are inclusive, they should be conducted in multiple languages. The summaries of the listening sessions should be utilized further by building leaders and teachers to develop a deeper understanding of the community they serve and their lived experiences.

Also foundational to this strategy is ensuring the community is visible and welcome in the school setting; one way of accomplishing visibility is by consistently inviting the community's parents and elders to share cultural experiences and their ways of knowing with the students (Ishimaru, 2018; Khalifa et al., 2019). Another strategy to accomplish parent and community visibility is by inviting parents and community members to facilitate professional learning for teachers, serve as guides and helpers in lunchrooms, hallways, and before and after-school (Ishimaru, 2018; Mayfield & Garrison-Wade, 2015).

## Pillar of Collaboration—Us

The pillar of collaboration is also guided by dialogue and inquiry principles and normalizing inclusion and shared leadership. As a foundation to establish a co-construction practice with the community, teachers and school principals must cultivate a deep and relational connection to the community and its communal wealth (i.e., knowledge, expectations, experiences, resources, and rituals; Furman, 2012; Jiménez-Castellanos et al., 2016; Khalifa et al., 2019; Yosso, 2005). Educators collaborate with parents to critique policies and systems that harm students in order to develop whole-school approaches to more equitable systems (Furman, 2012; Khalifa et al., 2019; Yosso, 2005). The structures should engage parents and communities in a way that allows them to access, value, transit, and experience their capital wealth (Fernández & Paredes Scribner, 2018) to drive the decision-making related to the school's vision and the outcomes that measure success for their children.

The critique results will inform the opportunities where the co-construction and reconstruction begin with the community to improve school-community outcomes (Fenton et al., 2017; Green, 2018). This pillar requires school leaders to replace their deficit mindset with one that is inclusive. School leaders will also reconstruct the school's normative cultural capital (Theoharis, 2007; Yosso, 2005) to recognize the community's communal wealth.

Leaders can acknowledge community strengths by bringing the knowledge and stories from the community into school contexts (Furman, 2012; Yosso, 2005). As school leaders center communal wealth they demonstrate their commitment to equity to the communities they serve. This shift can make space for difficult dialogue about race, culture, class, language, and inequality with their staff and families, leading to additional decision-making that is rooted in equity and cultural responsiveness (Cooper, 2009; Fernández & Paredes Scribner, 2018; Ishimaru & Takahashi, 2017). Co-construction happens when parents and community members are consistently present where decisions are being made.

## CONCLUSION

In conclusion, the framework sets out to create an inclusive learning environment for all students where the school's vision, beliefs, and values can be co-constructed with teachers, principals, students, parents, and the community. Co-construction gives ownership and value to the communities that are typically viewed through a deficit lens and relegated to engagement as a school guest rather than contributors of knowledge, perspectives, and expertise of their children. By building the habits of critique and self-reflection in school leaders and teachers, they become equipped with a process of continual growth and improvement related to equity and social justice. Likewise, by disrupting deficit mindsets and biases and replacing them with a perspective of community value, appreciation, and equity, educators will elevate the students, parents, and the community to experts and resources, thus interrupting the normalized and othering structures in schools.

## AUTHOR NOTE

We have no known conflict of interest to disclose.

## REFERENCES

Agosto, V., & Roland, E. (2018). Intersectionality and educational leadership: A critical review. *Review of Research in Education, 42*(1), 255–285.

Annamma, S. A., Connor, D., & Ferri, B. (2013). Dis/ability critical race studies (DisCrit): Theorizing at the intersections of race and dis/ability. *Race Ethnicity and Education, 16*(1), 1–31. https://doi.org/10.1080/13613324.2012.730511

Annamma, S. A., & Handy, T. (2020). Sharpening justice through DisCrit: A conceptual analysis of education. *Educational Researcher, 50*(1), 1–10. https://doi.org/10.3102/0013189X20953838

Bagenstos, S. R. (2009). *Law and the contradictions of the disability rights movement.* Yale College.

Banks, J. A., & Banks, C. A. M. (2004). *Multicultural education: Issues and perspectives.* Jossey-Bass.

Bass, B. (1985). *Leadership and performance beyond expectations/Bernard M. Bass.* Free Press, Collier Macmillan.

Berkovich, I. (2014). A socio-ecological framework of social justice leadership in education. *Journal of educational administration , 52*(3), 282–309.

Brooks, J. S., Jean-Marie, G., Normore, A. H., & Hodgins, D. W. (2007). Distributed leadership for social justice: Exploring how influence and equity are stretched over an urban high school. *Journal of School Leadership, 17*(4), 378–408.

Brown, K. M. (2004). Leadership for social justice and equity: Weaving a transformative framework and pedagogy. *Educational Administration Quarterly, 40*(1), 77–108.

Brown v. Board of Education of Topeka, 347 U.S. 483 (1954). https://supreme .justia.com/cases/federal/us/347/483/

Bustamante, R. M., Nelson, J. A., & Onwuegbuzie, A. J. (2009). Assessing schoolwide competence: Implications for school leadership preparation. *Educational Administration Quarterly, 45*(5). https://doi.org/10.1177/0013161X09347277

Cambron-McCabe, N., & McCarthy, M. M. (2005). Educating school leaders for social justice. *Educational Policy, 19*(1), 201–222.

Capper, C., & Young, M. (2014). Ironies and limitations of educational leadership for social justice: A call to social justice leaders. *Theory Into Practice, 53*(2), 156–164.

Causton-Theoharis, J., & Theoharis, G. (2008). Creating inclusive schools for all students. *School Administrator, 65*(8), 24–25.

Cherng, H. Y. S., & Halpin, P. F. (2016). The importance of minority teachers: Student perceptions of minority versus White teachers. *Educational Researcher, 45*(7), 407–420.

Church, R. L., & Sedlak, M. W. (1976). *Education in the United States: An interpretive history/Robert L. Church and Michael W. Sedlak.* Free Press.

Constantine, M. G., & Sue, D. W. (Eds.). (2005). *Strategies for building multicultural competence in mental health and educational settings.* John Wiley & Sons.

Cooper, C. W. (2009). Performing cultural work in demographically changing schools: Implications for expanding transformative leadership frameworks. *Educational Administration Quarterly, 45*(5), 694–724.

Cornito, C. M., & Caingcoy, M. E. (2020). Reflective habits of the mind: A systematic literature review. *International Journal of Research Publication and Reviews, 1*(3), 13–19.

Crenshaw, K. (1991). Mapping the margins: Identity politics, intersectionality, and violence against women. *Stanford Law Review, 43*(6), 1241–1299.

Cruz-González, C., Segovia, J. D., & Rodrigues, C. L. (2019). School principals and leadership identity: A thematic exploration of the literature. *Educational Research, 61*(3), 319–336.

Dantley, M. E., & Green, T. L. (2015). Problematizing notions of leadership for social justice: Reclaiming social justice through a discourse of accountability and a radical, prophetic, and historical imagination. *Journal of School Leadership, 25*(5), 820–837.

Deal, T. E., & Peterson, K. D. (2016). *Shaping school culture* (3rd ed.). John Wiley & Sons.

DeMatthews, D. (2015). Making sense of social justice leadership: A case study of a principal's experiences to create a more inclusive school. *Leadership and Policy in Schools, 14*(2), 139–166.

DeMatthews, D. (2020). Addressing racism and ableism in schools: A DisCrit leadership framework for principals. *The Clearing House: A Journal of Educational Strategies, Issues and Ideas, 93*(1), 27–34.

DeMatthews, D. E., Serafini, A., & Watson, T. N. (2020). Leading inclusive schools: Principal perceptions, practices, and challenges to meaningful change.

*Educational Administration Quarterly, 57*(1). https://doi.org/10.1177/001316 1X20913897

Dirth, T. P., & Branscombe, N. R. (2017). Disability models affect disability policy support. *Journal of Social Issues, 73*(2), 413–442.

Fenton, P., Ocasio-Stoutenburg, L., & Harry, B. (2017). The power of parent engagement: Sociocultural considerations in the quest for equity. *Theory Into Practice, 56*(3), 214–225.

Ferch, S. R. (2020). Servant-leadership, forgiveness, and social justice. In J. Song, D. Q. Tran, S. R. Ferch, & L. C. Spears (Eds.), *Servant-Leadership and Forgiveness: How Leaders Help Heal the Heart of the World* (pp. 119–132). SUNY Press.

Fernández, E., & Paredes Scribner, S. M. (2018). "Venimos para que se oiga la voz": Activating community cultural wealth as parental educational leadership. *Journal of Research on Leadership Education, 13*(1), 59–78.

Ferri, B. A., & Connor, D. J. (2005). Tools of exclusion: Race, disability, and resegregated education. *Teachers College Record, 107*(3), 453–474.

Fleischer, D. Z., & Zames, F. (2011). *The disability rights movement: From charity to confrontation.* Temple University Press.

Flores, O. J., & Gunzenhauser, M. G. (2018). Justice in the gaps: School leader dispositions and the use of data to address the opportunity gap. *Urban Education 56*(2) 261–288.

Frattura, E. M., & Capper, C. A. (2007). *Leading for social justice: Transforming schools for all learners.* Corwin Press.

Furman, G. (2012). Social justice leadership as praxis: Developing capacities through preparation programs. *Educational Administration Quarterly, 48*(2), 191–229.

Gooden, M. A., & Dantley, M. (2019). Centering race in a framework for leadership preparation. *Journal of Research on Leadership Education, 7*(2), 237–253.

Green, T. L. (2018). Enriching educational leadership through community equity literacy: A conceptual Foundation. *Leadership and Policy in Schools, 17*(4), 487–515.

Greenleaf, R. K. (2002). *Servant-leadership: A journey into the nature of legitimate power and greatness.* Paulist Press. (Original work published 1977)

Griner, A. C., & Stewart, M. L. (2013). Addressing the achievement gap and disproportionality through the use of culturally responsive teaching practices. *Urban Education, 48*(4), 585–621. https://doi.org/10.1177/0042085912456847

Hernandez, F., & Fraynd, D. J. (2014). Leadership's role in inclusive LGBTQ-supportive schools. *Theory Into Practice, 53*(2), 115–122.

Hernández-Saca, D. I., Gutmann Kahn, L., & Cannon, M. A. (2018). Intersectionality dis/ability research: How dis/ability research in education engages intersectionality to uncover the multidimensional construction of dis/abled experiences. *Review of Research in Education, 42*(1), 286–311.

Hornby, G. (2015). Inclusive special education: Development of a new theory for the education of students with special educational needs and disabilities. *British Journal of Special Education, 42*(3), 234–256.

Ishimaru, A. M. (2018). Re-imagining turnaround: Families and communities leading educational justice. *Journal of Educational Administration, 56*(5), 546–561. https://doi.org/10.1108/JEA-01-2018-0013

Ishimaru, A. M., & Takahashi, S. (2017). Disrupting racialized institutional scripts: Toward parent–teacher transformative agency for educational justice. *Peabody Journal of Education, 92*(3), 343–362.

Jarden, A., & Jarden, R. (2017). Positive psychological assessment for the workplace. In L. G. Oades, M. F. Steger, A. Delle Fave, & J. Passmore (Eds.), *The Wiley-Blackwell handbook of the psychology of positivity and strengths-based approaches at work* (pp. 415–437). Wiley.

Jiménez-Castellanos, O., Ochoa, A. M., & Olivos, E. M. (2019). Operationalizing transformative parent engagement in Latino school communities: A case study. *Journal of Latino/Latin American Studies, 8*(1), 93–107.

Johnson, L. (2007). Rethinking successful school leadership in challenging US schools: Culturally responsive practices in school–community relationships. *International Studies in Educational Administration, 35*(3). https://www.academia.edu/30747586/Rethinking_successful_school_leadership_in_challenging_U_S_schools_Culturally_responsive_practices_in_school_community_relationships

Kanter, A. S. (2011). The law: What's disability studies got to do with it or an introduction to disability legal studies. *Columbia Human Rights Law Review, 42*(2), 402–479.

Katz, P. A. (1976). *Towards the elimination of racism.* Pergamon Press.

Kauffman, J. M., & Bader, J. (2014). Instruction, not inclusion should be the central issue in special education: An alternative view from the USA. *Journal of International Special Needs Education, 17*(1), 13–20.

Khalifa, M. A., Gooden, M. A., & Davis, J. E. (2016). Culturally responsive school leadership: A synthesis of the literature. *Review of Educational Research, 86*(4), 1272–1311.

Khalifa, M. A., Khalil, D., Marsh, T. E. J., & Halloran, C. (2019). Toward an indigenous, decolonizing school leadership: A literature review. *Educational Administration Quarterly, 55*(4), 571–614.

Kose, B. W. (2009). The principal's role in professional development for social justice: An empirically-based transformative framework. *Urban Education, 44*(6), 268–663.

Labaree, D. F. (1997). Public goods, private goods: The American struggle over educational goals. *American Educational Research Journal, 34*(1), 39–81.

Lac, V. T., & Cumings Mansfield, K. (2018). What do students have to do with educational leadership? Making a case for centering student voice. *Journal of Research on Leadership Education, 13*(1), 38–58.

Lindsay, K. (2018). *In a classroom of their own: The intersection of race and feminist politics in all-Black male schools.* University of Illinois Press.

Mann, H. (1848). Report no. 12 of the Massachusetts school board. In L. A. Cremin (Ed.), *The republic and the school: Horace Mann on the education of free men* (pp. 79–80). Teachers College Press.

Marshall, C., & Oliva, M. (2010). Building the capacities of social justice leaders. In *Leadership for social justice: Making revolutions in education* (2nd ed., pp. 1–15). Pearson.

Mayfield, V. M., & Garrison-Wade, D. (2015). Culturally responsive practices as whole school reform. *Journal of Instructional Pedagogies, 16.* https://eric.ed .gov/?id=EJ1069396

McKenzie, K., Christman, D., Hernandez, F., Fierro, E., Capper, C., Dantley, M., Gonzalez, M., Cambron-Mccabe, N., & Scheurich, J. (2008). From the field: A proposal for educating leaders for social justice. *Educational Administration Quarterly, 44*(1), 111–138.

McKinney, S. A., & Lowenhaupt, R. (2013). New directions for socially just educational leadership: Lessons from disability studies. In L. C. Tillman & J. J. Scheurich (Eds.), *Handbook of research on educational leadership for equity and diversity* (pp. 309–326). Taylor & Francis.

Milner, H. R., IV, & Howard, T. C. (2013). Counter-narrative as method: Race, policy and research for teacher education. *Race Ethnicity and Education, 16*(4), 536–561.

Miretzky, D., Chennault, R. E., & Fraynd, D. J. (2016). Closing an opportunity gap: How a modest program made a difference. *Education and Urban Society, 48*(1), 48–76.

Mulvey, J. (2010). The feminization of schools. *The Education Digest, 75*(8), 35–38.

National Center for Educational Statistics. (2020). *Fast facts: Back to school statistics.* https://nces.ed.gov/fastfacts.asp?id=372

Pearson, H, Cosier, M., Kim, J. J., Gomez, A. M., Hines, C., McKee, A. A., & Ruiz, L. Z. (2016). The impact of disability studies curriculum on education professionals' perspectives and practice: Implications for education, social justice, and social change. *Disability Studies Quarterly, 36*(2). https://doi.org/10.18061/ DSQ.V36I2.4406

Poekert, P. E., Swaffield, S., Demir, E. K., & Wright, S. A. (2020). Leadership for professional learning towards educational equity: A systemic literature review. *Professional Development in Education, 46*(4), 541–562. https://doi.org/10.108 0/19415257.2020.1787209

Rodela, K. C., & Bertrand, M. (2018). Rethinking educational leadership in the margins: Youth, parent, and community leadership for equity and social justice. *Journal of Research on Leadership Education, 13*(1), 3–9. https://doi .org/10.1177/1942775117751306

Russell, R. F., & Stone, A. G. (2002). A review of servant leadership attributes: Developing a practical model. *Leadership & Organization Development Journal, 23*(3), 145. https://doi.org/10.1108/01437730210424

Ryan, J. (2006). Inclusive leadership and social justice for schools. *Leadership and Policy in Schools, 5*, 3–17. https://doi.org/10.1080/15700760500483995

Scotch, R. K. (2001). American disability policy in the twentieth century. In P. K. Longmore & L. Umansky (Eds.), *The new disability history: American perspectives* (pp. 375–392). New York University Press.

Scott, G. J. (2000). Equal educational opportunity and the significance of circumstantial knowledge. *Education Economics, 8*(3), 197–208.

Shapiro, D., Dundar, A., Huie, F., Wakhungu, P., Yan, X., Nathan, A., & Hwang, Y. A. (2017, April 26). *Completing college: A national view of student attainment rates by race and ethnicity—Fall 2010 Cohort* (Signature Report No. 12b). National Student

Clearinghouse Center. https://nscresearchcenter.org/signaturereport12 -supplement-2/

Shields, C. M. (2010). Transformative leadership: Working for equity in diverse contexts. *Educational Administration Quarterly, 46*(4), 558–589.

Taylor, E. (2006). A critical race analysis of the achievement gap in the United States: Politics, reality, and hope. *Leadership and Policy in Schools, 5*(1), 71–87.

Theoharis, G. (2007). Social justice educational leaders and resistance: Toward a theory of social justice leadership. *Educational Administration Quarterly, 43*(2), 221–258.

Umpstead, R. (2007). Determining adequacy: How courts are redefining state responsibility for educational finance, goals and accountability. *Brigham Young University Education & Law Journal, 2007*, 281–320.

van Dierendonck, D. (2011). Servant leadership: A review and synthesis. *Journal of management, 37*(4), 1228–1261.

Verniers, C., Martinot, D., & Dompnier, B. (2016). The feminization of school hypothesis called into question among junior and high school students. *The British Journal of Educational Psychology, 86*, 369–381.

Villegas, A. M., Strom, K., & Lucas, T. (2012). Closing the racial/ethnic gap between students of color and their teachers: An elusive goal. *Equity & Excellence in Education, 45*(2), 283–301.

Welner, K. G., & Carter, P. L. (2013). Achievement gaps arise from opportunity gaps. *Closing the opportunity gap: What America must do to give every child an even chance, 1*(10). https://doi.org/10.1093/acprof:oso/9780199982981.003.0001

Willie, C. V., & Willie, S. S. (2005). Black, White, and Brown: The transformation of public education in America. *Teachers College Record, 107*(3), 475–495.

Ylimaki, R., & Jacobson, S. (2013). School leadership practice and preparation: Comparative perspectives on organizational learning (OL), instructional leadership (IL), and culturally responsive practices (CRP). *Journal of Educational Administration, 51*(1), 6–23.

Yosso, T. J. (2005). Whose culture has capital? A critical race theory discussion of community cultural wealth. *Race, ethnicity, and education, 8*(1), 69–91.

Zion, S. D., & Blanchett, W. (2011). [Re] conceptualizing inclusion: Can critical race theory and interest convergence be utilized to achieve inclusion and equity for African American students? *Teachers College Record, 113*(10), 2186–2205.

CHAPTER 27

# UNCOVERING DISTRICT AND CAMPUS LEADERS' PRACTICES AROUND SPECIAL EDUCATION

## Preparing Aspiring Leaders to Advocate for and Address the Needs of Special Education Students and Stakeholders

**Irma L. Almager**
*Texas Tech University*

**Fernando Valle**
*Texas Tech University*

## ABSTRACT

This case study presents the findings of three aspiring leaders in a 15-month principal preparation residency program and their experiences observing, leading, and implementing special education best practices in rural, suburban, and urban school districts and school settings. The aspiring leaders engaged with district leaders and campus principal mentors on daily practices, policy and law implementation, and the monitoring of progress of services provided to students in special education. Interview and study findings revealed inconsistencies between district special education expectations and campus implementation. The findings exposed an absence of school leaders formally leading special education meetings, while aspiring leaders learned to engage in deeper advocacy and engagement with special education students and teachers. This study provides implications for school districts, schools, and principal preparation programs to provide the important training support for aspiring and current leaders to effectively lead the inclusive work involved with special education.

Aspiring school principals should have depth of knowledge and competencies to lead the instruction, services, and social-emotional well-being of all students in their schools. Over 7 years of university-to-district partnerships in Texas, the authors have realigned the principal preparation course curriculum to address gaps discovered through graduate student residency experiences. They now include a strong focus on instruction, law, policy, and advocacy for students with disabilities who are served through special education services. This chapter captures the experiences of aspiring school principals in a job-embedded principal preparation residency program as they learned to collaborate with multiple stakeholders and learned to identify and address equity issues in special education. The aspiring principals-in-residence worked in real time with mentor principals and with faculty coaches in the field learning to lead curricula; they grew into practicing social justice leaders who advocated for all students in their schools, especially students under the umbrella of special education.

## STATEMENT OF THE PROBLEM

Recent literature (Christensen et al., 2013; Pazey & Cole, 2013; Pazey & Combes, 2020) has consistently attested to the need for developing the advocacy capacity of future special education social justice leaders and their knowledge and skills as instructional leaders for minoritized and marginalized school populations. Catering for the diversity and abilities of all learners has become crucial in preparing students for participation in a global society (Owen & Davis, 2011). Additionally, the role of the principal has changed from being the school disciplinarian and supervisor of the building and physical plant, to one of instructional leader responsible for implementing the Individuals With Disabilities Education Act (IDEA, 2004) and the Every Student Succeeds Act (ESSA, 2015; DiPaola & Walther-Thomas, 2003; Roberts & Guerra, 2017). School principals have a vital role in the education and lives of special needs students (Hoppey & McLeskey, 2013; Roberts & Guerra, 2017).

However, principals do not always have the necessary knowledge and skills, including understanding of best practices, to meet the needs of special education students they serve. This study aimed to add to the body of knowledge by immersing aspiring principals in year long special education leadership experiences and collaboration with layers of district and campus stakeholders. The authors attest that effective school leaders and educators are those who can foster a collective commitment to collaboration, provide professional learning experiences to increase team members' collaborative skills, and create schedules that support different forms of ongoing meeting collaboration (e.g., individualized education program [IEP] teams, co-teachers, teachers–families, teachers–paraprofessionals).

## RELEVANT LITERATURE

Campus administrators are asked to lead, understand, and make decisions in many areas concerning the process of schooling. They are accountable for instructional growth and equitable schooling of all school populations. Most schools have been doing an adequate job of providing a quality education for White middle-class students, but this has not been the case for students of color, especially those living in poverty (McKenzie & Scheurich, 2004). When schools or districts show success gaps, it means that they are not serving all groups of children equally well; this requires a closer look at issues of equity, inclusion, and opportunity (O'Hara et al., 2016). *Addressing Success Gaps* (O'Hara et al., 2016) focuses on addressing the impact of success gaps (i.e., differences or gaps in a variety of educational factors and outcomes that affect the likelihood of educational success for some groups of children compared to their peers). Research indicates that the achievement of PreK–12 children with disabilities, and that of their general education peers, is tightly linked (Hehir et al., 2012; Malmgren et al., 2005; O'Hara et al., 2016). Children who are members of racial, ethnic, economic, or linguistic minorities have barriers, and if they are identified as children with disabilities or English language learners, they should have maximum appropriate opportunities to benefit from evidence-based instruction within the general education setting (O'Hara et al., 2016).

It is the role of the culturally responsive instructional leader in rural, suburban, and urban school settings to serve the educational needs of all students through collaboration with communities and valuing stakeholders (Khalifa, 2020). The awareness of special education must now accompany instructional equity action in schools to move beyond low expectations for minoritized racial groups. The drive for principals and teachers to successfully lead instruction and school reforms to educate all student populations equitably continues to be at the forefront of measurable outcomes. Taylor (2018) reported that according to the 2014 Americans With Disabilities Report by the U.S. Census Bureau, approximately 13% of the U.S. population has some form of disability. Substantial progress has been made since the original passage of IDEA in 1975, and today, about 95% of students with disabilities are educated in regular public schools, with most placed in a general education classroom for at least 80% of the school day (U.S. Department of Education, 2017). Zhang et al. (2014) attest that the overall picture of minority representation in special education has not changed significantly and remains the same as it was a decade ago (Zhang et al., 2014). The recognition of structural inequalities in society along racial, gender, socioeconomic, and identity lines has translated into a discussion that the education system actually presents an opportunity gap that leads to unequal outcomes, such as achievement gaps (Ladson-Billings, 2013). In attempting to understand the achievement gap from the perspective of inequality, Reardon et al. (2016) conducted a multifactor analysis study which found that segregation (defined as areas where more Black students attend higher poverty schools than White students) resulted in greater achievement gaps. Within the instructional areas of classroom and school inclusion are law and policy which weigh heavily on decision-making by school leaders and educator stakeholders.

The implementation of special education continues to be an intimidating, litigious, and underfunded area for schools. It is impossible for school administrators to ignore the pressures and responsibilities of facilitating special education programs within their schools (Pazey & Cole, 2013). Pazey and Cole (2013) further cite that much of the legal pressure imposed by sweeping federal legislation comes with underfunding, since the introduction of special education in the mid-1970s, while the number of students with disabilities being served in public schools has nearly doubled over that time. A research study conducted by Davidson and Algozzine (2002) examined the perception and level of knowledge of special education law among 120 beginning school administrators. They found that most respondents believed they had insufficient knowledge of special education law and expressed a need for additional preparation in special education law (Davidson & Algozzine, 2002). The field of educational leadership continues to challenge principal preparation programs to prepare future social justice and equity-driven leaders to have the required training in special education law (Christensen et al., 2013; Roberts & Guerra, 2017; Schulze & Boscardin, 2018).

The required training involves knowledge and experiences with special education including the implementation of federal, state, and local law and policy to serve individuals with disabilities and their families. Under the

IDEA (2004), schools are required to provide a free and appropriate public education (FAPE) to students with disabilities regardless of costs. Congress reauthorized IDEA (2004) through Public Law 114-95. ESSA (2015) added that disability is a natural part of the human experience and in no way diminishes the right of individuals to participate in or contribute to society. Improving educational results for children with disabilities is an essential element of our national policy of ensuring equality of opportunity, full participation, independent living, and economic self-sufficiency for individuals with disabilities.

Accountability in special education continues to present one of the major instructional challenges facing school leaders in this era of high stakes testing (ESSA, 2015). DiPaola and Walther-Thomas (2003) argue that schools must provide students with disabilities appropriate access to the general curriculum and effective instructional support and closely monitor student progress demonstrated through participation in assessment efforts. Research suggests that the principal's role is pivotal in the special education process; however, few school leaders are prepared for this responsibility (DiPaola & Walther-Thomas, 2003). There is an overarching fear of accountability which often results in making uninformed decisions in the special education arena. Because of this lack of knowledge, many principals defer the instructional decision-making process to individuals they feel have a broader understanding of laws, policies, and best practices surrounding special education, some of which include special education teachers, diagnosticians, counselors, and central office directors.

Inclusive education, according to Carter and Abawi (2018), is an increasingly contentious term that challenges educators and education systems. In the 21st century, however, concerns have shifted toward improving the preparation of educational leaders who need to know more about supporting students with disabilities and other diverse learners (U.S. Department of Education, 2010). DeMatthews et al. (2020) investigated the preparation and leadership experiences of six principals who successfully created inclusive schools in one midsized school district with identified beliefs, values, and mind-sets critical to inclusive school support of students with disabilities. To address the misconceptions and lack of understanding of administrators, DeMatthews et al. (2020) argue that aspiring administrators require leadership preparation programs to address special education knowledge and skill gaps during coursework.

Supporting this knowledge base also requires that university faculty guide aspiring leaders through the misconceptions concerning the level of knowledge of special education leadership in the field. In addition, the absence of general training about this historically underserved population adds a social justice issue that is rarely discussed through a special education lens. To truly develop social justice leaders, issues concerning this underserved population must be addressed. Theoharis (2007) specifically addresses special education issues within the social justice practice of school leaders; his position is that social justice leadership entails making "issues of race, class, gender, disability, sexual orientation, and other historically and currently marginalizing conditions in the United States central to their [school leaders] advocacy, leadership, practice, and vision" (p. 223). He argues that the elimination of marginalization requires a practice of inclusive school practices and that inclusion itself is about social justice.

## METHODS

This descriptive qualitative case study explores the experiences of three aspiring principal residents in decision-making and authentic experiences in special education leadership and how they advanced inclusion and advocated for equitable education for all students. A case study approach was selected to narrow the focus, embrace the learning context, and provide opportunity to seek in-depth analysis of specific participants-in-residence within their unique school settings (Creswell & Poth, 2016). It aimed to identify to what extent aspiring school principals-in-residence engaged in appropriately guided and modeled special education leadership and instruction to constitute instructional and social justice leadership. The research questions guiding this case study included: (a) "What were the most difficult areas to lead the learning and advocate for special education students?"; (b) "What interventions were you able to implement and lead to advocate for and support the instruction of your selected special education student?"; and (c) "Describe the collaborative work engaged with stakeholders both at the campus and district levels."

The experiences of the aspiring leaders-in-residence in schools were gathered through participant interviews, targeted coursework goals, artifacts, and principal preparation coursework assignments covering one academic year of learning and supporting the special education process through the lens of a selected student. To understand the school equity and the instruction and support decisions for their assigned special education students, the principals-in-residence engaged in conducting strategic leadership equity audits for special education in public schools through: (a) framing equity to drive equitable instruction for special education students and uncover inequities around their instruction and social emotional well-being; (b) developing an inclusive systematic instructional framework where curriculum, student engagement with educators, and engaging faculty and staff to address the learning needs of the student with disabilities was utilized; and (c) designing and implementing instructional interventions with specific goals and action plans to improve the educational outcomes and access of students.

## Case Study Context: Aspiring School Leaders in Residence Complete Equity Audits

The aspiring leaders-in-residence in the university-to-district partnership moved to their assigned campuses in the early summer to complete a principal residency over 15 months. Residents began the program by conducting an equity audit of the entire school using state and district data from the previous year. Collaborating with a newly assigned campus mentor principal, instructional action plans were designed and set to improve the instructional coaching of selected teachers and selected student populations in the school across the residence experience. The residents collaborated with the mentor principal using equity audit data to select teachers to grow and support through instructional coaching. The collaboration continues with aspiring leaders' selection of highly at-risk students who are identified and served as English language learners and students being served under special education. The teachers and students become part of the six high need projects selected to follow, learn, monitor, and support throughout the year.

## Case Study Context: Learning to Lead With a Social Justice Lens

Aspiring principal residents collected, disaggregated, and analyzed all campus student data, including special education data searching for inequities based on processes developed by Skrla et al. (2009) to assess equity in schools. Using the social justice lens, residents analyzed data to uncover, understand, and challenge inequities that are internal to schools and districts in three areas—teacher quality, educational programs, and student achievement (Skrla et al. 2009). In most of the assigned partner schools who house an aspiring school leader-in-residence, the special education student group is either one of the lowest or the lowest-scoring demographic as revealed in the equity audit.

Based on this knowledge, the residents selected a highly at-risk special education student to advocate for over the entire school year. Learning to utilize their instructional and social justice leader lenses, residents examined the role gender and ethnicity played in academic outcomes of this school population. The intervention planning and work continues by preparing specific, measurable, attainable, relevant, and time-based (SMART) yearly and quarterly goals to address any learning, attendance, services, and/or discipline issues. This is achieved by collaborating with all stakeholders who had contact with the student receiving special education services. Aspiring school leaders also created four specific interventions per quarterly goal following the Texas Education Agency's (2018) effective schools framework (ESF) procedures for planning and progress monitoring. The ESF's goal is to provide a clear vision for what districts and schools across the state do to ensure an excellent education for all Texas students.

## Case Study Context: Campus and District Leadership Interviews Over Special Education

To ensure that aspiring principal residents build program and campus foundational knowledge, the assignment to have in-depth interviews with their mentor principal included multiple areas of instructional leadership and special education. Through this initial interview, residents were able to gauge principal mentors' knowledge, skill, and mindset levels concerning all student populations.

Next, the residents interviewed each of their district's professionals responsible for leading and implementing aspects of the special education program. Through this second interview residents discovered the districts' expectations for the school leaders' knowledge and skills across special education. Through interviews and collaboration work with school stakeholders, residents began to uncover discrepancies between the districts' expectations for school leaders and the campus administrators' understanding and implementation of that expectation. The principals-in-residence analyzed the responses during the school and district leader interviews, and then observed and documented verbal conversations in individual education plan (IEP) meeting discussions and decisions; they used special education student data to process decision-making and the impact of the educational outcomes for this underserved population.

## Case Study Context: Harnessing Special Education Law and Policy

Following the proper procedures for federal, state, and local law and policy, the residents learned to advocate for their selected special education student by researching the student's entire cumulative record over the education career including academic, attendance, and discipline history. They requested permission for advocacy and access from parents and attended all school admit, review, and dismissal (ARD) meetings concerning the student. In addition, the residents learned and applied specific special education law in real time with teachers and school leaders through focused course work to develop special education knowledge and skills.

## FINDINGS

To illustrate the findings of this case study, the authors selected the experiences of three aspiring principal residents who demonstrated a proficiency to articulate field experiences through submitted written assignments. These participants were from urban, suburban, and rural school district contexts; they learned to navigate leadership, decision-making, and act as social justice leaders as they advocated to address the needs of their special education student.

It is important to acknowledge that all 15 residents were assigned the same curricular work and were tasked to select the same type of projects for advocacy and special education learning tasks. Additionally, it is important to note that the principal mentors and district professionals working with the aspiring principals in residence had various levels of special education knowledge, skills, and mindsets. Based on these contexts and parameters, the faculty support, focus, and individual coaching plan for each resident is unique and contextual. Students submitted written class assignments which were analyzed using NVivo. The findings are organized and presented based on the study questions and the following emerging themes: (a) district decisions regarding accessing special education and the difficulty for principal residents to advocate and lead learning, (b) special education program equity in practice and obstacles for implementing appropriate instruction and interventions, and (c) learning to lead and serve the needs of special education students through collaborative work with stakeholders.

## District Decision-Making and Special Education Access

Every year the principal preparation program-in-residence partners with school district leaders who have various degrees of expertise and depth of knowledge of special education. The request for residents to access special education data in rural districts usually came with no reservation or issues. The rural district was open to the idea of leading and learning through advocacy. In contrast, the resident from the suburban district had several minor issues, including clearance for administrator level data access. The suburban district guided the requested parental notification and permission process to allow the resident access to selected student data including access to classroom observations and stakeholder meetings and conversations. The urban district, however, had stricter protocols for special education access and initially denied the university-to-district partnership request for data access needed to advocate for student and special education processes. The contested request was based on the district's definition of personnel who were considered as those in the "needs to know" group. Based on their normal decision-making protocols, their discussion and opinions framed special education access to only those affiliated with the student. These affiliates were the campus administrators, classroom teacher/s, instructional coaches, special education teachers, diagnosticians, counselors, and central office program staff. Based on the district definition, practice, and protocols, our aspiring principals-in-residence did not fall into any of the provided categories.

Creating a dialogue with the district's special education personnel allowed the principal residents to be seen as those who did have an educational impact on students. The discourse requesting data access for residents provided an opportunity for the university educational leadership faculty team to bring different district department leaders together to make decisions concerning the access to data and special education programming. Once everyone was on the same page, the issue was resolved. Bringing the special education and leadership departments in this urban district together was eye-opening for both university faculty and district leaders. Regrettably, this exposed the nuances of larger district central administration departments and their staff operating in silos. The impact of this real time curriculum work unlocked university-to-district dialogue and collaboration needed to grow aspiring special education leaders. Keys to the process were to implement equity data decision-making, support the district and campuses to meet student outcomes, and create bridges of collaborative practice. Each district partner addressed the resident's request for access to special education student data based on established district norms and protocols. District partners framed special education law and policy based on the depth of knowledge, expertise, mindset, and experiences of their personnel.

## Special Education Programs and Equity in Practice

As aspiring principal residents studied IDEA and sought out special education best practices through real time program coursework in their assigned schools, equitable instructional leadership mindset and skills grew. As their skills improved, they were able to implement and discuss the expectations for special education students in their new schools. In the interview with district level leaders covering the special education program, aspiring leaders in residence learned what the district expectation was for campus administrators. Based on this newly acquired special education leader knowledge, their observations of school leaders' practices around special education steered them to document what was observed and experienced versus the best practices they were learning to implement. Participating in campus leadership meetings, observing classrooms, examining the instruction designed to serve special education students, along with curricular and service conversations with teachers, the residents began to experience discrepancies between the district leaders' expectations for implementation and what was happening on their respective campuses. The aspiring school leaders were experiencing the gray areas of schooling, campus norms, and what faculty coaches framed as "policy versus practice."

All three selected residents reported special education program academic gaps and inequities based on a three-pronged residency program curricular approach: utilizing campus equity audit data and teacher, student, and program findings; assessing campus teacher and leadership understanding of special education programming and implementation of IEP; and decision-making in committee meetings. Aspiring leaders-in-residence reported that observations and decisions made on campus often contradicted district special education expectations. The real-time experiences and contradictions in district versus campus decision-making were vivid examples of policy interpretation and consideration that were not always implemented and practiced. For example, all three residents reported that their principal mentors or assistant principals did not lead IEP meetings. The meetings to determine progress and services were led by the assessment individual and or district diagnostician. Additionally, in each of their projects, all major instructional decision-making was made by the assessment diagnostician. The aspiring leaders-in-residence came to understand that on their assigned campus, the administrator's role was to agree with the diagnostician's directives and sign in agreement in IEP and program meetings. Two aspiring leaders-in-residence who were in rural and urban districts found that administrators who did attend special education meetings were not versed or clear on the proper meeting protocols and procedures. The campus leadership defaulted the process to the diagnosticians who led the entire IEP and instructional support meetings.

The learning for aspiring school leaders-in-residence was to assess special education practice versus policy in three ways. First, they were to monitor and respect IDEA and ESSA policies ensuring that there is an understanding between district interpretations and expectations and campus norms and unmonitored practices. Second, they were to learn the transfer and implementation of IEP accommodations and make recommendations in the classroom to serve the needs of students. Third, they were to understand district expectations, observe campus leadership, use equity data, and filter student services and needs while observing classroom practices which exposed classroom, grade level, and department norms on campus on the ways student IEPs were implemented (or ignored, as in the case described above).

Understanding the political tensions and dynamics of district to campus level leadership is important when communicating in-house policy discrepancies and practices. The opportunity to engage in deep instructional practice and decision-making around special education for aspiring leaders in this case study exposed ignored practices, hidden norms, and silencing stakeholders as uncontested practices. As future social justice and special education school leaders, it is crucial to learn law and policy and the leader's legal and ethical responsibility for equitable inclusivity for all students, especially those identified as special education. The data, meetings, and inequitable experiences in classrooms by the aspiring leaders-in-residence, their newly formed IEP meeting leadership and implementation awareness, and campus layers of implementation findings around policy to practice in this section align with arguments Theoharis (2007) posed on the elimination of marginalization: it necessitates a practice of inclusive school practices, where inclusion itself is about social justice.

## Learning to Lead and Serve the Needs of Special Education Students

After the aspiring leaders-in-residence collaborated with the principal mentors to select highly at-risk special education students to serve and advocate for during the academic year, the preparation program curriculum provided opportunities to schedule interviews with selected students and teachers to provide deep rich data and a portraiture to begin to know and understand the students. During the interviews, the aspiring leaders-in-residence introduced themselves and explained the "special educational interest" they would be taking with the student in a selected content area. It was during these advocacy conversations and interview questions to personally know the student, where topics including grades, attendance, and/or discipline issues provided the inequitable and rich experiential data around school spaces where a social justice leadership lens also came into action. Together they set staggered goals in a supportive and collaborative meeting setting so as not to push too much during the initial meeting. An intentional schedule for special meetings times was created for authentic engagement, interactions, and rapport building with the students being served.

All three aspiring leaders found their "special" student projects had attendance issues because they did not like school. Regardless of grade level, the selected students in special education did not feel successful and avoided school when possible. One student stated, "I don't think anyone cares if I'm here or not so why come?" Another student said, "I get tired of not understanding the work so I try to miss that class when I can." Since the reason for missing was usually academic frustration and failure, each of the three aspiring leaders-in-residence began to address the identified issues in the classroom by collaborating with and bringing together all stakeholders on campus who impacted their students' learning. Through this collaborative assessment process toward a deeper inquiry on the knowledge of students, all parties began to discuss the support and work regarding student needs. In a campus collaborative effort, all stakeholders were included in creating and writing out the SMART goals which would be monitored and adjusted throughout the year to support the students' academic outcomes and success.

Throughout the academic year the aspiring leaders-in-residence visited the classroom for observations and student progress monitoring. They planned with the teacher/s to ensure each student's academic, attendance, and discipline needs were effectively being served and met. The residents also met with the student during scheduled times and continued to build and sustain rapport for overall school success. One student had academic success in elementary but had regressed significantly in middle school in all content areas. Two of the other students being advocated for had never passed any content area in the state assessments. This relationship building was crucial to each student's connectedness with school and goal setting for continued success that academic year.

During these scheduled advocacy visits, all three residents informed their students on improvements they were making based on academic and other forms of data. As a result, each selected student attended school more often, worked on creating fewer interruptions and not being sent to the office. They were all proud to have positive feedback and ongoing improved academic data. Additionally, parent feedback reported their children's change in attitude toward school and willingness to go to school. For these three students, the continued collaboration and advocacy into the spring semester showed growth improvements in quarterly goals and academic data including performance on the state test. The advocacy and personalized meetings made an impact in student outcomes as it was reported that stakeholders' attitudes and mindset toward SMART goals also positively improved, as all three students' academic data showed progress.

Through consistent progress monitoring and scheduled times to talk, it was evident that the aspiring school leaders-in-residence were impacting student outcomes and demonstrated success with their special education projects. The residents reported on students' feedback, where they told them having someone constantly monitoring their class work, attendance, and discipline helped them want to work harder. One student stated, "No one has ever paid attention to what I do. It was hard to have you on my case all the time, but I like it. It helped me work harder." A resident shared in a shaky voice, "My student cried when I told her she passed her math test because she had never passed anything. She couldn't believe it!"

Overall, the learning for aspiring leaders-in-residence was to help teachers uncover what was keeping students from succeeding in school. The students needed the individual academic attention as described in their IEPs and reacted with indifference and disconnect to what they perceived as uncaring teachers in an uncaring school environment. Teachers have multiple instructional responsibilities to serve the needs of students. Quiet students and those being served by special education services can easily become invisible, especially in schools with larger classroom and school populations. The preparation program's real time instruction utilized a project—a micro approach—within a larger organization structured setting. This deeper dive into the needs and implementation of student support impacted the knowledge, skills, and aspiring leader mindset to learn school leadership for a "macro school impact," leading with an equity-driven decision-making focus and social justice leadership advocacy. Progress monitoring and collaboration produced improved teaching and learning which overflowed in the classrooms being monitored. As teachers improved their instructional delivery for one special education student, the micro to macro approach was experienced over the course of the academic year as the delivery and change positively impacted the outcome for other students in the classroom.

# IMPLICATIONS

School leaders, such as principals and assistant principals, face situations and decisions involving students with special education needs daily (Sider et al., 2017). This case study presented the interactions, observations, and experiences of aspiring school leaders-in-residence across rural, suburban, and urban school settings. They learned to lead, serve, and implement special education to meet student and teacher needs while completing a 15-month principal residency program. Findings of the study are aligned to Cameron's (2016) assertions which argue that (aspiring administrators) found special education leadership practices were often based on a school leader's past experiences with—and perceptions of—effective practices.

Aspiring and current administrators must also have the mindset necessary to be effective and ethical education leaders for all students. *All* includes a mindset of social justice leadership practice to provide the IEP implementation and close progress monitoring of teachers' instruction to serve students, and the collaboration with educators who are important stakeholders in special education programs. To prepare aspiring leaders to understand and know what it means to truly meet all student needs, the depth of learning and authentic experiences must begin during principal preparation coursework, continue, and grow in depth and scope during internship opportunities, and collaborate with current leadership to forge experiences across the school year to assess the impact of leadership and services implemented.

## Implications for School Districts

For school district leadership and district level departments, the findings of this case study reveal that messages and visioning provided by district personnel for policy expectations were not always properly implemented and monitored, and therefore were realigned with normed practices in schools. It is important for district departments and district leaders to implement systems of progress monitoring and lead the monitoring of discrepancies around policy to practice ensuring policy compliance for all special education students. The responsibilities for district leadership personnel are vast: leading programming, implementing curriculum, supporting and leading campuses, and providing professional development to campus and district staff. To ensure that systemic inequities are addressed across districts and campuses, quarterly monitoring of processes and implementation protocols as teams can be a proactive measure which can temper the litigious scenarios that arise from district to campus disconnects.

As aspiring leaders-in-residence observed in their school placements, campus administrators did not lead and direct the instructional outcomes of the IEP meetings in their schools. Since aspiring or current leaders understand that special education law is one of the most litigated educational laws (Strader, 2007), appropriate preparation for the leader's role during these meetings is crucial for students, families, and the school district. The fact remains, even with the most judicious decision-making by the diagnostician in all major special education decisions, the principal is the leader, the head of the school and can still be liable for the lack of implementation on campus. The systematic training of all leaders in the district to effectively lead special education meetings and collaborate with stakeholders will support the skills and competencies needed to facilitate and gain assertiveness when leading and making decisions concerning special education students.

## Implications for Schools

There is a disconnect between educational policy, research-based practices, and the implementation of these policies and practices in the work that school leaders do in supporting students with special education needs in their school environments (Jahnukainen, 2015). As the creators and supporters of a campus culture and climate conducive to both adult and student learning, school principals must develop the skills to effectively lead the protocols and procedures for IEP meetings, and have clear and deep understanding of monitoring IEP implementation in the classrooms to ensure law and policy compliance in their schools.

Taking personal responsibility for continued instructional leadership knowledge is the responsibility of district and campus leaders to ensure alignment and collaboration to effectively lead and support the implementation of best practices crucial for ensuring instructional equity for all students. District and campus politics are real and can be disruptive to the learning process especially around the work of planning and implementing services for students. We strongly suggest that current and future principals proactively seek knowledge and training to lead special education meetings, instructional, and assert their leadership roles during IEP and student support meetings.

## Implications for Principal Preparation Programs

The knowledge and alignment of federal, state, and district policy expectations for campus leaders impacts the modeled learning for aspiring leaders. This aligned learning provides the authentic best practice experiences to make and lead important decisions, use data to drive equity, and promote true advocacy based on student needs during meetings. Ensuring that principal preparation programs align curriculum and theory to current best practices is crucial to assisting district and campus leaders who are building solid instructional leadership pipelines. Coursework blended with real-world in-residence experiences provided authentic and real-time learning opportunities for our aspiring leaders. Providing this environment required engaged scholarship and partnerships to reframe the traditional internship learning space and cultivate accurate special education experiences. It provided competency-based student learning outcomes that ensure graduating aspiring leaders are ready to advocate for and lead our most underserved populations, including those identified as special education.

As the pendulum swings in higher education on hiring trends and principal preparation program needs, the successful setting requires that faculty and clinical instructors who are leading the charge in certification have recent experience in PK–12 public education. Additionally, having faculty who have former campus leadership experience in leading schools assists in the complexities of successfully navigating districts and schools with practical, nuanced, and contextual differences. Faculty in principal preparation programs who are well-versed in theory and practice provide realistic opportunities that are twofold. First, aspiring leaders must successfully demonstrate mastery of the state's principal certification competencies and standards. Second, an authentic and realistic experience leading special education meetings and monitoring IEP implementation provides the reality of needed school leadership. Principal preparation programs are crucial to special education leadership and to the social justice readiness for advocacy.

## CONCLUSION

This study uncovered the special education experiences of aspiring leaders-in-residence as they engaged with school leaders and education stakeholders to gain awareness, implement best practices, and experience the complex challenges that special education leaders face every day in public schools advocating for the most marginalized populations. The challenge persists as there is a continued dearth of research on how to adequately prepare a special education leader. The "why" and the need also persist, as our schools need and deserve leaders who can successfully create and lead high-performing inclusive schools for students with disabilities.

School principals are expected to have the depth of knowledge and skills to lead diverse and multiple populations with a wide variety of academic, language, and specialized needs in schools, including those in special education. However, few leaders have knowledge of the curricular and pedagogical needs of the students in their schools and find themselves deferring this work to others. Through the job-embedded residency, the aspiring school leaders uncovered practices, some outside of policy, that have become part of their practice when addressing the needs for special education students and their teachers. To address the gap, faculty involved in this study provided students in university-to-district partnerships residency experiences with consistent opportunities to learn to lead by requiring prepared interventions and action plans with teachers to improve the educational outcomes of identified special education students in their districts.

## REFERENCES

Cameron, D. L. (2016). Too much or not enough? An examination of Special Education provision and school district leaders' perceptions of current needs and common approaches. *British Journal of Special Education, 43*(1), 22–38.

Carter, S., & Abawi, L. A. (2018). Leadership, inclusion, and quality education for all. *Australasian Journal of Special and Inclusive Education, 42*(1), 49–64.

Christensen, J., Siegel Robertson, J., Williamson, R., & Hunter, W. C. (2013). Preparing educational leaders for special education success: Principals' perspective. *The Researcher, 25*(1), 94–107.

Creswell, J. W., & Poth, C. N. (2016). *Qualitative inquiry and research design: Choosing among five approaches.* SAGE Publications.

Davidson, D. N., & Algozzine, B. (2002). Administrators' perceptions of special education law. *Journal of Special Education Leadership, 15*(2), 43–48.

DeMatthews, D. E., Kotok, S., & Serafini, A. (2020). Leadership preparation for special education and inclusive schools: Beliefs and recommendations from successful principals. *Journal of Research on Leadership Education, 15*(4), 303–329.

DiPaola, M. F., & Walther-Thomas, C. (2003). *Principals and special education: The critical role of school leaders.* Prepared for the Center on Personnel Studies in Special Education and the National Clearinghouse for Professions in Special Education. Arlington, VA.

Every Student Succeeds Act of 2015, Pub. L. No. 114-95 § 114 Stat. 1177 (2015–2016). https://www.congress.gov/114/plaws/publ95/PLAW-114publ95.pdf

Hehir, T., Grindal, T., & Eidelman, H. (2012). *Review of special education in the Commonwealth of Massachusetts.* Thomas Hehir and Associates.

Hoppey, D., & McLeskey, J. (2013). A case study of principal leadership in an effective inclusive school. *Journal of Special Education, 46*(4), 245–256.

Individuals With Disabilities Education Act, 20 U.S.C. § 1400 (2004). https://www.govinfo.gov/app/details/USCODE-2011-title20/USCODE-2011-title20-chap33-subchapI-sec1400

Jahnukainen, M. (2015). Inclusion, integration, or what? A comparative study of the school principals' perceptions of inclusive and special education in Finland and in Alberta, Canada. *Disability & Society, 30*(1), 59–72.

Khalifa, M. (2020). *Culturally responsive school leadership.* Harvard Education Press.

Ladson-Billings, G. (2013). Lack of achievement or loss of opportunity. *Closing the opportunity gap: What America must do to give every child an even chance, 11,* 11–22.

Malmgren, K. W., McLaughlin, M. J., & Nolet, V. (2005). Accounting for the performance of students with disabilities on statewide assessments. *The Journal of Special Education, 39*(2), 86–96.

McKenzie, K. B., & Scheurich, J. J. (2004). Equity traps: A useful construct for preparing principals to lead schools that are successful with racially diverse students. *Educational Administration Quarterly, 40*(5), 601–632.

O'Hara, N., Munk, T. E., Reedy, K., & D'Agord, C. (2016). *Equity, inclusion, and opportunity: Addressing success gaps* [White paper]. Version 3.0. IDEA Data Center.

Owen, S., & Davis, G. (2011). Catering for student diversity: Building academic skills in graduate attributes learning and assessment opportunities through collaborative work. *Journal of University Teaching & Learning Practice, 8*(2), 1–11.

Pazey, B. L., & Cole, H. A. (2013). The role of special education training in the development of socially just leaders: Building an equity consciousness in educational leadership programs. *Educational Administration Quarterly, 49*(2), 243–271.

Pazey, B., & Combes, B. (2020). *Principals' and school leaders' roles in inclusive education.* Oxford University Press. https://doi.org/10.1093/acrefore/9780190264093.013.1215

Reardon, S. F., Kalogrides, D., & Shores, K. (2016). *The geography of racial/ethnic test score gaps* (Center for Education Policy Analysis Working Paper No. 16-10). Stanford Center for Education Policy Analysis.

Roberts, M. B., & Guerra, F. R. (2017). Principals' perceptions of their knowledge in special education. *Current Issues in Education, 20*(1). https://eric.ed.gov/?id=EJ1137948

Schulze, R., & Boscardin, M. L. (2018). Leadership perceptions of principals with and without Special Education backgrounds. *Journal of school Leadership, 28*(1), 4–30.

Sider, S., Maich, K., & Morvan, J. (2017). School principals and students with Special Education needs: Leading inclusive schools. *Canadian Journal of Education/Revue canadienne de l'éducation, 40*(2), 1–31.

Skrla, L., McKenzie, K. B., & Scheurich, J. J. (2009). *Using equity audits to create equitable and excellent schools.* Corwin.

Strader, D. L. (2007). *Law and ethics in educational leadership.* Pearson.

Taylor, D. M. (2018). *Americans with disabilities: 2014: Household Economic Studies* (Report Number P70-152). U.S. Census Bureau. https://www.census.gov/content/dam/Census/library/publications/2018/demo/p70-152.pdf

Theoharis, G. (2007). Social justice educational leaders and resistance: Toward a theory of social justice leadership. *Educational Administration Quarterly, 43*(2), 221–258.

Texas Education Agency. (2018). *Effective school's framework.* https://tea.texas.gov/sites/default/files/effective-schools-framework-2021overview-22.pdf

U.S. Department of Education. (2010). *A blueprint for reform: The reauthorization of the elementary and secondary education act.* Office of Planning, Evaluation and Policy Development. https://www.ets.org/s/education_topics/ESEA_Blueprint.pdf

U.S. Department of Education. (2017). *39th annual report to Congress on the implementation of the Individuals With Disabilities Education Act, 2017.* https://sites.ed.gov/idea/2017-annual-report-to-congress-on-the-individuals-with-disabilities-education-act/

Zhang, D., Katsiyannis, A., Ju, S., & Roberts, E. (2014). Minority representation in special education: 5-year trends. *Journal of Child and Family Studies, 23*(1), 118–127.

# SECTION VI

## AFTERWORD

In the concluding chapter, Danzig, Black, and O'Brien continue the effort to build community by sharing additional experiences with dis/ability and highlighting issues that are raised by the various chapter authors and woven across the volume. The Afterword continues the effort to craft a narrative that connects examples of the ways dis/ability is experienced with the conceptual and research literature findings.

# CHAPTER 28

# AFTERWORD

## Scratch a Theory and Find a Personal Story: Navigating Dis/Abilities at Home, School, and Work

**Arnold B. Danzig**
*San José State University*

**William R. Black**
*University of South Florida*

**Catherine O'Brien**
*Gallaudet University*

> *Neither the life of an individual nor the history of a society can be understood without understanding both.*
>
> —C. Wright Mills, *The Sociological Imagination*, p. 3

The contributions in this volume of the Research and Theory in Educational Administration book series push the field of educational leadership toward embracing a wide array of intersecting new engagements that collectively inform teaching, learning, and research with dis/ability in educational

*Who Decides?*, pages 697–713
Copyright © 2022 by Information Age Publishing
www.infoagepub.com

leadership. And as we conclude the volume, we circle back to a stance that Bornstein and Manaseri highlight in their chapter: Schools prioritize normalcy as an essential way of knowing. Ableism is embedded in unexamined assumptions of school structures and school talk in ways that continually construct hierarchical and marginalizing systems. In this chapter, we restate these themes one last time, add to our own narratives, and weave the story of *Who Decides? Power, Dis/ability, and Educational Leadership.*

## SOURCES FOR AND IMPORTANCE OF CONFLICT IN EDUCATIONAL LEADERSHIP AND DIS/ABILITY STUDIES

In order to deconstruct and ultimately improve the many of the processes and practices described in the preceding chapters, we argue that conflict is inevitable. Rather than viewing schools in Weberian notions of bureaucracy and organizational hierarchy, the importance of conflict needs to be recognized and even embraced in leadership research, theory, preparation, and practice. Exploring conflict, between recipients and providers, among parents, teachers, and administrators, within and between organizations, is not new. There is rich literature, over many decades and across multiple disciplines—research by educators, historians, sociologists, organizational theorists, that has explored conflicts: conflict between people and policy, conflict between and among the providers of services and recipients of services (Coles, 1989; Dreeben, 2002; Eccles & Harold, 1993; Epstein, 1984, 1986; Finkelstein, 1989; Heymann, 1995; Katz, 1975, 2001; Schultz, 1973; Tyack, 1974; Waller, 1976). There has also been significant research literature on potential solutions and promising practices (Apple, 1999; Crowson & Boyd, 1993; Davies, 2001; Danzig, 2003, 2012; Danzig & Harris, 1996; Gaitan, 2004; Gonzalez et al., 2005; Harvard Family Research Project, 2008; Hiatt-Michael, 2004; Lareau, 1989; Valdés, 1996; Willis, 1978; Yossi, 2005). More recently, U.S. Department of Education's Office of Special Education Programs (OSEP) such as the National Center on Intensive Intervention which provides resources to state and local leaders, educators, coaches, higher education faculty and parents to support the implementation of intensive interventions in reading, math, and behavior for students with severe and persistent learning and/or behavioral needs. As pointed out in the chapter by Yoon, the programs have costs and side effects.

The experiences and frameworks explored in this volume update the multiple contexts that people bring to their experiences with schools, with a new focus on dis/abilities and fresh stories of experience; it presents important new sources for understanding conflict among people within specific settings, among end-users, and among the service providers themselves. These newer perspectives build on and highlight the importance of race, class, gender, language, culture, social/historical narrative, ableism, audism, the meaning of ability and dis/ability, and the intersections among these dynamics in and across educational and other organizational settings.

Conflict is important for understanding whose interests are prioritized, who benefits (or not), how people engage with others, and how people engage with systems (Apple, 1999; Gaitan, 2004; Gonzalez et al., 2005; Lareau, 1989; Valdés, 1996; Vickers, 1995; Willis, 1978; Yossi, 2005). Clearly, no single best way exists for serving all families and children. Good practices for one child or family might not yield the same benefits or positive outcomes for a different individual or family. In our experience, however, conflict is often viewed as a negative. This volume, however, proposes that the combination of narratives, conceptual frameworks, and empirical data provides insights into the meaning and importance of conflict in understanding *Who Decides?* Taken as a whole, it points to the ongoing experiences and needs of actual people and the ways to improve individual systems' responses to these needs.

## Benefits, Costs, and Side Effects of Conflict

Acknowledging the significance of conflict involves considering benefits, costs, and side effects involved in accessing services and getting needed help. Parents and end users learn to weigh the potential benefits that come from receiving services (educational, medical, social) with the stigma associated with a label that makes children eligible for services but that can stay with the child long past their days at school. One response by education systems has been to reduce the stigma of labeling by anticipating challenges and design learning and behavioral interventions sooner rather than later, to mitigate more serious problems before they happen. But as Yoon (in this volume) and others (e.g., Berliner & Glass, 2014; Zhao, 2018) point out, system responses have side effects, unanticipated negative effects. Teachers and administrators heightened concerns with behavioral and academic learning can easily slip into added scrutiny of talk and for other behaviors. The consequences of this added attention, especially for children of color, has often been detrimental, reducing potential benefits that special education placement in school offers. We are not arguing against school services for those identified with a dis/ability; rather, the benefits and costs must include consideration of side effects, stigma, labels, peer groups, expectations, aspirations, exclusions, and normalization of what is considered "abled." As it now stands, those identified with dis/abilities, as well as those that provide for educational, medical, social, and community services are often forced to weigh the benefits (e.g., inclusion) against the context-specific quality of the experience. The calculations that children, parents, and professionals use to weigh the various factors, circumstances, contexts of dis/ability, or specifics of what different settings have to offer, are often very different. Danzig's experiences as a White middle-class college professor with a profoundly dis/abled daughter are similar to and different from the needs, expectations, and experiences of other parents and children. For Danzig, the need for safety trumped other concerns, educational or social. Understanding conflict involves theorizing on education and dis/ability with attention paid not only to the dis/ability, but also to how race, class, gender, culture, and other factors contribute to the overall environment in which services are experienced at home, in school, and in the workplace (Danzig, 1994, 2003, 2012; Ferguson & Asch, 1989; Yossi, 2005).

Class and race within the systems that serve people identified with dis/abilities are a continuing source of conflict. In education systems, the reality is that the teachers, administrators, counselors, therapists, social workers, speech pathologists, and other professionals that serve the children are mostly White and middle class in perspective. At the same time, the children in today's schools are more diverse, which is also true of those identified with dis/abilities. The descriptions of how dis/ability is experienced, which are presented in this volume, are filled with examples of how cultural assumptions, classroom norms, and school structures contribute to practices that marginalize based on race, class, gender, and dis/ablity. The hope is that insights and nuances that result from describing conflicts in detail will result in new approaches to and new policies around dis/ability.

## Conflict, Communication, and Advocacy: The Language of Professionalism and Compliance

It is clear from reading *Who Decides?* that the language of professionalism itself leads to conflict by distancing the recipients of service from those that provide service. Professional discourse often limits the ability of students and parents, patients or clients, to articulate what they need and what will be most beneficial (Bledstein, 1976). Professional discourse gives higher status to the knowledge that is represented as neutral and seemingly objective. Too often, those with specialized knowledge are invited to provide their evaluations and feedback in technical ways, largely free from interruptions and exceptions. On the other hand, the talk that comes from parents, students, and teachers is more often interrupted, questions asked requiring clarification and requests for explanation of meaning (Annamama, 2018; Mehan, 1983; Turnbull & Turnbull, 1985). The discourse described in these chapters is very much centered around communication and miscommunication among participants and stakeholders.

Whose voices are heard and who has priority over the decisions that are made, that is, current placements and future directions, are inherently political questions that raise questions concerning who has the power to decide. The "best interests" of the child and family are typically referenced in the professional discourse on dis/ability. It is important, however, that the consideration of best interests include not only the voices of the people identified with a dis/ability but that these concerns be afforded greater priority (perhaps, the highest priority) in the mix of considerations and decisions. Conflicts become more visible in the episodes that consider the decision-making authority of administrators, the responsibility for costs and paying for services, and the concerns of parents/children. To better understand these conflicts, research in educational leadership should draw from communication studies and discourse analysis. In this regard, the volume provides fresh examples of the communication and miscommunication among parents and professionals, children and adults, teachers and administrators, those identified with dis/abilities and those who provide the services.

To illustrate how parents communicate the needs of their child and the miscommunications that often result, Danzig draws from his experiences on the mismatch among specific requests for assistance, what was actually provided, and the results of these decisions. The examples highlight how conflict is experienced and its importance to achieving short- and long-term outcomes. In some ways, these examples illustrate the Rolling Stones song "You Can't Always Get What You Want," but with a new ending... "You Get What Others Decide You Need."

- **Preschool Feeding Program.** Parents felt that a half-day preschool program would not only benefit their 4-year-old child's social needs, but also mother's need for respite and time to participate in the lives of her other children. Since feeding the child every meal took 1 to 2 hours, the mother also requested that the lunch meal be given at school, as part of the child's education. Spending more than 6 hours a day hand feeding Sidney was extremely wearing on her energy, and her request was to be relieved for one of the feedings so she could keep up her strength. A private Montessori preschool agreed to enroll daughter and manage her program and feeding if the state would pay for an aide to accompany and feed her at school.
  - *Services Provided.* State agency denied her request and recommended alternative placement in an integrated preschool housed at the university where dad worked; the program met for 2 hours per day, with no feeding program.
  - *Short-Term Result.* School agreed to provide "educational services," but would not agree to feed in the classroom at the integrated preschool. In the parents' view, the teacher "didn't want to get the carpet dirty." An aide to feed the child was hired separately but had limited training and no supervision. Lunch feedings for Sidney were unsuccessful, with lunches coming home uneaten and the mother being required to feed the child again.

- *Long-Term Result.* Public school special education teacher heard about the need and advocated for accepting Sidney into her kindergarten class 1 year ahead of schedule. The public school class included feeding with an aide provided. Sidney successfully joined her class.

- **Placement in Private School.** In neighborhood elementary school, Sidney was physically dropped on her face (no protective reflexes) on two separate occasions. The first time, she was left unattended on a bench after a diaper change; the second instance, an ambulatory child climbed on her wheelchair and tipped it over. Parents argued that school was neither prepared nor equipped to care for Sidney's safety needs, and requested placement in a nearby private school that served children with severe and profound disabilities.
  - *Services Provided.* Public school special education director argued that district's program was "defendable." Parents filed formal grievance and threatened litigation.
  - *Short-Term Result.* School district agreed to private school placement for 2 years only. Two years elapsed and the public-school system then denied support for private school placement.
  - *Long-Term Result.* With help from an outside advocate, Sidney was able to stay in a private school setting for the remainder of her days in school.

- **Residential Care in Nursing Home.** Danzig accepted a new position in another state and tried to bring Sidney to a residential care setting in a new state of his employment.
  - *Services Provided.* State offered residential care for Sidney in a group home, with six ambulatory men.
  - *Short-Term Result.* Parents declined state placement recommendation. Parents found a nearby nursing home willing to accept Sidney but the state refused payment. Parents negotiated with insurance for a private pay option. State pressured the nursing home to reverse the decision to accept Sidney as client. A second nursing home was found that was willing to accept Sidney but required a federal authorization number, needed by all clients in nursing homes. The state refused to do the required assessment to obtain a federal client number, thereby preventing her placement. Sidney separated from her parents.
  - *Long-Term Result.* Parents hired an attorney and sued the state. It took the better part of a year but a court case was decided in Sidney's favor, assessment was completed. Sidney was then reunited with her family in a new city/state. Nursing home was located only a few blocks from the house where the rest of the family lived. Sidney attended the same public school as her two

younger sisters and they interacted with her on a daily basis. Sidney had many *grandmothers* "oohing and aahing" over her at the nursing home as well as daily contact with family.

Reflecting on these conflicts, Danzig recalls the frustrations of meeting with people from different organizations and agencies as well as the need for legal assistance to challenge conventional authorities and decision makers. In Danzig's view, there were some people who just didn't get "it," and others that did get "it," however he defines "it." In the thousands of interactions around dis/ability, Danzig as well as the other authors in this volume came into contact with many great people who were kind, thoughtful, and helpful. There were others who were less caring, more bureaucratic; and in a few instances, there were mean-spiritedness and even incompetent people. It is not Danzig's intention to blame others or to see Sidney (or her family) as victims. Instead, the focus is on the nature of these conflicts and challenges of asking for help. Conflict is often about the power to decide; it necessarily involves deeper understanding of the basis for conflict and how formal (legal) authority as well as informal authority (moral authority) are involved in negotiating for services, especially requests that don't match providers' philosophy, values, orientations, or resources. Unpacking the sources of conflict and miscommunications, which are part of the lived experiences of people identified as dis/abled, is needed to inform these systems and the people that lead them. Some people are more willing to engage in conflict to achieve sought after outcomes than others; it is also apparent that some people are more knowledgeable of how schools and provider systems work. Both attributes are needed, however, and those with less knowledge or are less willing to engage in conflict are hindered in their efforts to bring about needed change.

## Conflict, Communication, and Advocacy: Considering Constrained Notions in a Professional Organization

As illustrated in this volume, the field of educational administration has developed and engaged a broad strand of research and preparation practices that engage issues of social justice, equity, and diversity in the last 30 years. Advocacy for equity-oriented research and preparation practice has been central to the work of one of the oldest professional organizations related to the research on and preparation of school leadership is the University Council for Educational Administration (UCEA) as well as many UCEA affiliated scholars and institutions (e.g., Khalifa et al., 2016; Marshall & Oliva, 2010; Murphy, 2002; Reedy, 2017). As a leading organization in educational leadership, UCEA sets an important tone and vision for research in educational leadership and the preparation of school leaders. On its website, UCEA positions itself as "a community of learners that values diversity, equity, and social justice in all educational organizations" (University Council for Educational Administration, n.d., para. 1). Furthermore, over the last 2 decades UCEA's commitments to diversity, equity, and social justice have been operationalized in multiple initiatives. For example, UCEA has sponsored a Center for Educational Leadership and Social Justice and the Jackson Scholars program. UCEA developed and promulgated modules around engaging racism and social justice issues, as well as promoted a range of publications with editorial teams that provide outlets for research around issues of equity and social justice. This commitment is clearly represented in the organizing themes of recent UCEA conventions, including the last three meetings: Mission Critical: Revolutionizing the Future Through Equitable Educational Leadership, Research, and Practice (2018); Where Y'at: Validating Subaltern Forms of Leadership and Learning With/in and Outside of Schools (2019); and Re/Building Home: Coloniality, Belonging, and Educational Leadership (2020). As a member of the UCEA executive committee and president of the organization for 1 year, Black has a personal connection to UCEA as an institution.

**Equity and the presentation of dis/ability on the UCEA website and in the UCEA Review.**   In an effort to examine dis/ability as it was positioned within a pantheon of commitments to equity within UCEA, Capel and Black (2019) analyzed the ways language was linked to advocacy and compliance. In particular they conducted a systematic qualitative content analysis (Krippendorff, 2003) of how the terms "disability," "special education," and "inclusion" were invoked in two extensively accessed UCEA materials: (a) the UCEA website and (b) the last 10 years of the *UCEA Review*. In total, they reviewed a total of 67 links on UCEA's website and 30 issues of the *UCEA Review*.

**Findings.**   Capel and Black's findings suggest that despite clear and consistent commitments to equity and diversity, dis/ability was framed in particularly limited ways in two major communication platforms. The language invoked was more reminiscent of compliance often seen in professional stances in educational leadership rather than language of advocacy and communication. The content analysis reveals a constrained discourse that suggests that in many ways dis/ability is invisible. In contrast, while scanning the website and the *UCEA Review* we found a significant set of resources and language around race, racism, diversity, and equity. Without centering dis/ability in educational organizations, rather than serving as an add on, might the field. perpetuate the normalized views that only some identities belong under the drive towards inclusive and equitable practices.

To support their findings, Capel and Black (2019) reported that the following terms were mentioned 74 times within the website: special education, 38 times; inclusion, 25 times; and disability, 11 times. In terms of the UCEA Review, these terms were mentioned 386 times: special education, 168 times; inclusion, 139 times; and disability, 79 times. Within the website content, 5% out of the total mentions of the three terms were located on citations: special education, 5.3% (2/38); inclusion, 8% (2/25); and disabilities, 0% (0/11). Within the *UCEA Review* content, 8.8% out of the total mentions of the three terms were located on individual and/or organization biographical information: special education, 3% (5/168); inclusion, 15% (21/139); and disability, 10% (8/79).

Interestingly, within the website content, 69% out of the total mentions of the three terms were not located in primary text, but in citations: special education, 87% (33/38); inclus[ion/ive], 64% (16/25); and disabilit[y/ies], 18% (2/11). Within the *UCEA Review* content, 17.1% out of the total mentions of the three terms were located in citations: special education, 5% (8/168); inclus[ion/ive], 39% (54/139); and disabilit[y/ies], 5% (4/79). Across both sources, Capel and Balck (2019) looked at intersectional language as well as critical disability studies perspectives that engage intersectional identities. They found the following: special education and race, 5 times; inclusion and race, 1 time; disability and race, 5 times; special education and ELL, 1 time; and disability and ELL, 8 times. When they then looked at the instances where the word "inclusive" appeared, they found it to be an ambiguous "umbrella" term that covered many marginalized identities without including either an operational definition or a focus on dis/ability. Some examples from recent UCEA presentations include: "UCEA is an organization dedicated to inclusive practices that act in the best interests of all children" and "What we are doing is not only being inclusive and giving everybody a voice, but everybody then can take the lead on unpacking different areas that really need to be addressed" (Capel & Black, 2019, n.p.).

The point to highlight is that even within the leading organization that prepares researchers, informs policy makers, and helps define the field of educational leadership, dis/ability is often considered separately from discussions that consider equity, inclusiveness, and social justice. Separating the concern for dis/ability from these other concerns of educational leadership fragments the field; as a result, meaningful connections between theory and practice, between educational leadership and dis/ability studies, are lost.

## Dilemmas Faced Negotiating and Experiencing Dis/ability Services

When the priorities and concerns of the recipients of services (or their family members) are less valued, the risk is that the parents and children are seen as lacking; they lack understanding of how the system works or they are unrealistic in their expectations for what the provider systems can actually do. In some of the examples presented, parents are accused of child abuse by allowing their child to miss school to participate in more personal and family oriented events or by keeping children at home for safety reasons (especially relevant considering COVID-19 concerns today). More recently, there has been a greater appreciation that parents already participate in school at a number of levels, from basic parenting, communicating with teachers and administrators, volunteering, supporting a home learning environment, formally participating in school governance by serving on committees, informally volunteering and supporting class-based activities (Epstein et al., 1997). And many more parents have "opted out" by homeschooling their children. When parent involvement is viewed as lacking, however, the system responds in different ways. In some cases, a child's needs are overlooked or ignored, as the demands of other parents or concerns take priority...the squeaky wheels get oiled. In other cases, the perceived absence of involvement results in teachers, administrators, or providers rushing to the rescue, providing what they considered to be the best course of action, separate from what parents think or do. Highly engaged parents risk alienating the professionals that work with them and their child. Popular literature even characterizes some parents as being too involved in the lives of their children (e.g., helicopter parents who hover over their children; lawnmower parents that mow down obstacles placed in the path of their children). Involved parents also risk being accused of distrusting the professional judgment of the people who provide services and getting in the way of teachers and other administrators trying to do their jobs. One the one hand, expecting professionals to do their work risks being seen as uncaring and uninvolved; on the other hand, parents that strongly advocate for their child risk being seen as aggressive, unrealistic, and "in denial." Advocates and policy makers must also balance the idealism of pushing against perceived injustice with a more pragmatic approach needed to negotiate services within and across organizations.

The above dilemma is only a sample of the many possible interpretations of the advocacy situations. Describing the conflicts experienced related to dis/ability is a (necessary) first step. Understanding the multiple contexts/perspectives embedded in these conflicts moves readers further down the path of knowing what to do. Determining what is needed to make things better and then implementing the changes comes next. Assessing impacts, outcomes, and side effects completes the cycle, followed by starting over again. From the descriptions in this volume, there is no single route that emerges for parents or educators to follow. Individual circumstances and "road" conditions dictate the routes to follow. According to Furman (2012), the routes to be covered span multiple dimensions—the personal, interpersonal, communal, systemic, ecological and praxis, and they imply action and reflection across multiple dimensions (Furman, 2012).

It is the view of the co-editors that personal experience with dis/ability is an important source of expertise. O'Brien deeply understands and appreciates the challenges faced by a Deaf person, growing up, in school, and now as a college professor at Gallaudet. Like most parents, Danzig and Black see themselves as experts on their own children. From her birth, Danzig learned to access his daughter's strengths and weaknesses, in places and in ways that may not be available at school. He also holds a different time frame for consideration of his child's needs, knowing that he would have the responsibility for his child's care long past any particular teacher, classroom, school, or system. However, the kinds of service deemed as necessary and the decisions to provide services ultimately resided with the providers. What counts as dis/ability, the definitions of the conditions that determine eligibility for services—educational, social, and medical—these conditions are defined by providers. The system, made up of the individual practitioners, in schools, agencies, institutions, makes the determination of what is really needed and how to budget for payment of services deemed as "required." Ultimate decision-making authority is given to the gatekeepers and payers of last resort. Inevitably, the result is conflict.

## Conflicts Over Cultural and Organizational Norms: Parenting, Time, Resource Priorities

New and conflicting views on the importance of parenting abound in the world. A critical role of parents in impacting their children's social and academic achievement is often cited by researchers and used as a rationale to prioritize the importance of parental involvement in schools. In retrospect, Danzig sometimes wonders how important parents really are in determining school (and life) outcomes. Danzig's four children (3 girls and 1 boy) have all had very different experiences (successes and failures) at school, though all have had the same parents, largely in the same social and economic circumstances. This realization suggests the need for less blaming (and perhaps less crediting) of parents for social and educational outcomes and more understanding of the mechanisms by which school and societal structures intersect with how dis/ability is experienced at home, in school, and in the workplace.

### Conflict Over Time

COVID-19 has made more visible the many challenges experienced by parents, now faced with the new constraints and responsibilities of having their children at home and not in school. In Danzig's experience as a parent, time was always a concern: Time to eat, time to get dressed, time to get to school, time to get to work, time to get to the doctor's office, time to get therapy, respite time, free time. Black similarly mentions time, time to spend with son, time for meetings, time to spend with grandparents and family. The increased time demands required for routine practices and needed care adds stress (distress) to the people and the systems that provide for education and care related services. Providers often rely on the family as a resource, as parents and family members supplement the time that is needed by service providers to do their jobs. Lack of time stresses health and adds to chronic fatigue. Time spent illustrates how adults balance competing demands of self, career, and family. Time conflicts illustrate whose time is valued and who has the power to make decisions over time.

### Conflicts Over Resources

Costs are less often discussed or referenced as the determining factor of what services should be provided or not. Reality, however, is that money affects how dis/ability is defined, and which services are prioritized and provided, and which are denied. Conflicts are exacerbated by institutional authorities that maintain that "publicly provided and paid for services are only required to provide the 'minimum' or standard level of services to all eligible clients." For parents and those impacted by the services, there is greater need to customize services based on particular circumstances and needs. Developing customized models that combine public and private resources has been difficult if not impossible to put into practice. The kinds of financial, organizational, and institutional analysis needed to accomplish better outcomes is at very early stages. The economics of education as well as public administration provide needed research for understanding revenues and resources in schools, how they are allocated, and strategies to address issues related to equity and fairness.

### Inter-Organizational Conflict

Another source of conflict comes from the fact that schooling and educational services are often separated from the organizations that consider the medical, social, legal, respite, and other service needs. This results in fragmentation by: (a) isolating problems rather than considering a more holistic view of well-being, (b) labeling of children in order to qualify for services, (c) ignoring benefit, costs, and side effects (i.e., stigmatization, tracking, placements, and quality). Fragmentation and separation result in systems failure: failure to bring the needed resources to bear on the challenges faced, failure to navigate the inter-organization connections that are needed to provide and pay for services, failure to see the whole child within a larger context of family and community.

## LEADERSHIP PREPARATION AND ITS IMPLICATIONS: EXTENDING TRANSDISCIPLINARITY COMMUNITIES

Johansson (2006) argues in *The Medici Effect* that game-changing innovations (step-changes) become possible when ideas and talented people from different fields come together. For Johansson, the Medici effect illustrates the power of intersectional ideas, which combine concepts from multiple fields (p. 40). These intersectional innovations are "surprising and fascinating, take leaps in new directions, open up entirely new fields, and can affect the world in unprecedented ways" (p. 43). The ability to combine divergent ideas and concepts in the pursuit of new solutions is key to understanding innovation.

The authors and chapters in this volume illustrate that the concern with power, dis/ability, and educational leadership also draws from many fields of inquiry. The research on dis/ability and school leadership is transdisciplinary; it crosses interdisciplinary bridges to understand problems and point to solutions. A few of the fields of inquiry and bridges to be crossed include:

- school–community relationships
- disability studies
- critical theories
- economics of education, school finance
- education policy and political influence
- intersectionality
- diversity and disability
- race and disability
- communication studies
- organizational leadership
- leadership theory
- identity theory
- systems theory

At its core, this volume illustrates how these interdisciplinary bridges are part of the study of educational leadership. The narratives, empirical studies, and conceptual frameworks presented on dis/ability are fundamental to understanding leadership practice and draw from these multiple fields and intellectual pursuits. Our hope is that this volume provides an inkling of the wide range of disciplines which have something to offer the study of educational administration, school leadership, and the connections to dis/ability studies.

In retrospect, we also see the benefits of reading this volume differently from what we have learned individually or collectively through managing dis/abilities on a day-to-day basis. An essential first step requires understanding how dis/ability is experienced by the individuals, families, and professionals impacted or in service. While the narratives of identity and experience are a crucial part of the knowledge and learning needed to improve the quality of services, they are not enough. The systems themselves need to be studied, described, and improved. New conceptualizations are needed to recognize the complexity of dis/ability and its meaning in contemporary culture and the service professions. As Anderson (1990) reminded the field of educational leadership over 30 years ago:

When social constructions are so tightly legitimated that certain questions are unaskable and certain phenomena remain unobservable, how does the researcher gain access to these nonissues and non-events? What makes this problem even more intractable is the fact that researchers in the field of educational administration are generally uninterested themselves in asking research questions that challenge the legitimating myths that mask the social reproduction of structural inequality. (p. 42)

The field has shifted since that time, yet dis/ability and power have not been deeply examined in educational administration. The analytic stances revealed in this volume informs new possibilities for supporting more equitable scholarship and practice, as well as examining possible ways research reinscribes notions of normalcy that reinforce dis/ability as independent identities. By contrast, dis/ability is incredibly generative as a subject identity that resides with other identities, for example, dis/ability and race, dis/ability and gender, dis/ability and sexual identity, dis/ability and class, dis/ability and nation, dis/ability and educational leadership, and dis/ability and advocacy. The intersection of disabilities provides a useful centering-rather than marginalizing theoretical space to engage educational leadership research and practice. Yet, even as the volume chapters and narratives focus on subject identity, normalization, and micropolitical negotiations (little "p" policies and practices), volume chapters also suggest that changes in big "P" educational policies are needed to shape the local, state, and federal systems that provide material services and accountability.

## CONCLUSION: BUILDING NEEDED ROADMAPS FOR NAVIGATING DIS/ABILITY

The knowledge and perspectives of users and providers are necessary; they are needed to navigate the many connections among organizations (public, private, nonprofit) that provide educational, medical, legal, social, workplace, and community services to the people identified as dis/abled. For a roadmap to be user-friendly, it includes best routes and alternative routes to follow; it needs to include the organizational equivalents of congestion, accidents, potholes, and road barriers. A map might also anticipate the need for new intersections, connections, and roads to meet traffic demands. A *Field of Dreams* metaphor implies that if we "build it, they will come." From the chapters presented in this volume, new and reimagined educational and other services are required. The roadmaps for building and navigating these systems are built on the strengths and limitations of people and institutions, which in turn requires an understanding of how services are experienced by those identified with dis/abilities. In this sense, we hope that this volume provides a map for some of this territory and some relief to the challenges faced by those navigating schools and beyond.

Collectively, the authors in this volume are part of a larger community of people who are learning and have learned from their experiences with dis/ability. Within this system, the people identified as dis/abled have changed our lives; they are the geniuses that help us find solutions. Their importance is found not only in their actions, but in the deeds of those that they have influenced. We have come to realize that we learn from the most vulnerable amongst us. We hope that the values embedded in this volume are driven by the motivation to make our learning explicit, and we hope that it will also contribute to building a better long term future—for all.

## REFERENCES

Annamma, S. A. (2018). *The pedagogy of patholization: Dis/abled girls of color in the school-prison nexus.* Routledge.

Apple, M. (1999). What counts as legitimate knowledge? The social production and use of reviews. *Review of Educational Research, 69*(4), 343–346. https://doi.org/10.3102/00346543069004343

Berliner, D., & Glass, G. V (Eds.). (2014). *50 myths and lies that threaten America's public schools: The real crisis in education.* Teachers College Press.

Bledstein, B. (1976). *The culture of professionalism: The middle class and the development of higher education.* Norton.

Capel, J., & Black, W. (2018, November). *How we engage DisCrit tenets to contribute to UCEA's vision for equity-oriented leadership?* Ignite session presented at the annual convention of the University Council for Educational Administration, Houston, TX.

Coles, R. (1989). *The call of stories: Teaching and the moral imagination.* Houghton Mifflin Company.

Crowson, R. L., & Boyd, W. L. (1993). Coordinated services for children: Designing arks for storms and seas unknown. *American Journal of Education, 101*(2), 140–179. https://doi.org/10.1086/444037

Danzig, A. (1994). Parents versus professionals: Social class and services to children and families. *People and Education: The Human Side of Schools, 2*(3), 296–319.

Danzig, A. (2003). Schooling as an embedded institution: Challenges to parent–school–community connections. *Journal of School Public Relations, 24*(2), 124–141.

Danzig, A. (2012). Don't ask, don't tell, don't pay: Services for children with severe and chronic disabilities. In M. Strax, C. Strax, & B. Cooper (Eds.), *Kids in the middle: The micro politics of special education* (pp. 123–140). Rowman & Littlefield.

Danzig, A., Borman, K., Jones, B., & Wright, W. (Eds.). (2007). *Learner centered leadership: Research, policy, and practice.* Lawrence Erlbaum Associates.

Danzig, A., & Harris, K. (1996). Building competence by writing and reflecting on stories of practice. *Journal of Educational and Psychological Consultation, 7*(2), 14–30.

Davies, D. (2001). Family participation in decision making and advocacy. In D. Hiatt-Michael (Ed), *Promising practices for family involvement in schools* (pp. 107–151). Information Age Publishing.

Dreeben, R. (2002). *On what is learned in school.* Percheron Press/Addison-Wesley. (Original work published in 1968)

Eccles, J., & Harold, R. (1993). Parent–school involvement during the early adolescent years. *Teachers College Record, 94,* 568–587.

Epstein, J. (1984). School policy and parent involvement: Research results. *Educational Horizons, 62,* 70–72.

Epstein, J. (1986). Parents' reactions to teacher practices of parent involvement. *The Elementary School Journal, 86,* 277–294.

Epstein, J. L., Coates, L., Salinas, K. C., Sanders, M. G., & Simon, B. S. (1997). *School, family, and community partnerships: Your handbook for action.* Corwin Press.

Ferguson, P., & Asch, A. (1989). Lessons from life: Personal and parental perspectives on school, childhood, and disability. In D. Biklen, D. Ferguson, & A. Ford (Eds.), *Schooling and disability: Eighty-eighth yearbook of the National Society for the Study of Education* (pp. 108–140). University of Chicago.

Finkelstein, B. (1989). *Governing the young. Teacher behavior in the popular primary schools in 19th-century United States.* Falmer.

Furman, G. (2012). Social justice leadership as praxis: Developing capacities through preparation programs. *Education Administration Quarterly, 48*(2), 191–229. https://doi.org/10.1177/0013161X11427394

Gaitan, C. D. (2004) *Involving Latino families in schools: Raising student achievement through home–school partnerships.* Corwin Press.

Gonzalez, N., Moll, L. C., & Amanti, C. (2005). *Funds of knowledge: Theorizing practice in households, communities, and classrooms.* Lawrence Erlbaum Associates.

Harvard Family Research Project. (2008, Spring). *The evaluation exchange, XVI*(1&2), 1–40. Harvard Graduate School of Education.

Heymann, J. (1995). *Equal partners: A physician's call for a new spirit of medicine.* Little, Brown & Company.

Hiatt-Michael, D. (2004). *Promising practices to families of children with special needs.* Information Age Publishing.

Johansson, F. (2006). *The Medici effect: What elephants and epidemics can teach us about innovation.* Harvard Business School Press.

Khalifa, M. A., Gooden, M. A., & Davis, J. E. (2016). Culturally responsive school leadership: A synthesis of the literature. *Review of Educational Research, 86*(4), 1272–1311.

Katz, M. (1975). *Class, bureaucracy, and schools: The illusion of educational change in America.* Praeger.

Katz, M. (2001). *The irony of early school reform* (2nd ed.). Teachers College Press.

Krippendorff, K. (2003). *Content analysis: An introduction to its methodology* (2nd ed.). Sage.

Lareau, A. (1989). *Home advantage: Social class and parental intervention in elementary school.* Taylor & Francis.

Marshall, C., & Oliva, M. (2010). *Leadership for social justice: Making revolutions in education* (2nd ed.). Pearson.

Mehan, H. (1983). The role of language and the language of role in institutional decision making. *Language and Society 12*, 187–211.

Murphy, J. (Ed.) (2002). *The educational leadership challenge: Redefining leadership for the 21st century.* University of Chicago Press.

Reedy, M. (2017). What can you do when racism comes to town? UCEA Quality Leadership Matters Blog, August 14, 2017. http://www.ucea.org/2017/08/14/can-racism-comes-town/

Schultz, S. (1973). *The culture factory: Boston public schools, 1789–1860.* Oxford University.

Turnbull, H. R., & Turnbull, A. (1985). *Parents speak out: Then and now.* Charles E. Merrill.

Tyack, D. (1974). *The one best system: A history of American urban education.* Harvard University.

University Council for Educational Administration. (n.d.). *Vision, goals, and values.* http://www.ucea.org/2013/11/07/vision-goals-values/

Valdés, G. (1996). *Con respeto: Bridging the distances between culturally diverse families and schools: An ethnographic portrait.* Teachers College Press.

Vickers, G. (1995). *The art of judgment.* SAGE Publications.

Waller, W. (1976). *The sociology of teaching.* John Wiley & Sons. (Original work published in 1932).

Willis, P. (1978). *Learning to labor: How working class kids get working class jobs.* Routledge.

Yossi, T. J. (2005). Whose culture has capital? A critical race theory discussion of community cultural wealth. *Race Ethnicity and Education 8*(1), 69–91. https://doi.org/10.1080/1361332052000341006

Zhao, Y. (2018). *What works may hurt.* Teachers College Press.

# ABOUT THE EDITORS

**Catherine A. O'Brien** is an associate professor and Deaf scholar at Gallaudet University in Washington, DC. She began her career as a science, special education, and physical education teacher. She has a total of 15 years of K–12 teaching experience including serving 2 years as an assistant school principal. She received her doctoral degree in 2011 in educational leadership and policy analysis from the University of Missouri—Columbia. In 2012, the American Education Research Association, Division A, selected her dissertation as the Dissertation of the Year for her study, *The Influence of Deaf Culture on School Culture and Leadership: A Case Study*. In 2011, she began her higher education career at Gallaudet University in 2011 with her first 2 years as the first I. King Jordan chair fellow. In 2017, she was awarded the Graduate Faculty of the Year Award. Her research interests include studying schools and programs that serve d/Deaf students. Her leadership research centers on school culture, culturally relevant leadership, principal preparation, Deaf culture, Deaf education, special education, social justice, and improving educational outcomes for Deaf children. She is currently working with a faculty committee and university administration developing a doctoral educational leadership program at Gallaudet University.

**William R. (Bill) Black** is a professor in educational leadership and policy studies at the University of South Florida. Bill has served as program coordinator and PI of multiple federal and state personnel preparation grants as well as Art4All Florida, a statewide organization for the arts for all. He is interested in investigating educational leadership program characteristics

*Who Decides?*, pages 715–716
Copyright © 2022 by Information Age Publishing
www.infoagepub.com
All rights of reproduction in any form reserved.

and graduate outcomes and strives to develop collaborative means to evaluate university-based leadership preparation. His research also includes conceptualizing preparation for inclusive and equitable educational leadership practice and examining ways in which educational policies are articulated and implemented in schools—particularly in relationship to dis/ability and bilingual/bicultural communities. He currently serves as president of the University Council for Educational Administration.

**Arnold B. Danzig** is professor of educational leadership and education policy at San José State University. He is the founding director and now core faculty member in the EdD program in educational leadership. He is also professor emeritus at Arizona State University, where he served in multiple leadership positions including division director and associate dean in the Mary Lou Fulton Teachers College, and associate director of the school public affairs. His research and teaching focus on educational leadership. His research uses qualitative, narrative, and descriptive methods to better understand leadership preparation, professional development, and practice, and focuses attention on inclusion, equity, and human concerns in education and schooling. He has authored, edited, and co-edited books, chapters, journal volumes, and journal articles on education leadership and policy during a career that includes K–12, government, and higher education leadership and service.

# ABOUT THE CONTRIBUTORS

**Irma L. Almager** is an associate professor in the educational leadership program at Texas Tech University. Irma's main focus is the academic achievement of poor students and those of color through the development of culturally responsive leaders who are instructionally strong. Irma has 15 years of experience in public school as a classroom teacher and campus principal.

**Abdullah Alofi** is currently working in Saudi Arabia's education ministry. A Lamar University alumni, Dr. Alofi is multilingual and works as an ally in the Saudi Deaf community.

**Edward H. Bart IV** is a Deaf scholar with over 15 years of experience in public education, working in Deaf education and general education. Currently he is the World Languages department lead in a Texas high school and is completing his doctorate in Deaf studies and Deaf education at Lamar University. His research interests include Deaf representation in popular culture and media, and American Sign Language literature.

**Pam Bishop** is professor of educational leadership in the faculty of education at Western University in Ontario, Canada. Her earlier appointments were at University of Calgary and University of Tasmania. Pam was previously a teacher and principal in Australia.

**William R. Black** is professor of educational leadership and policy studies at the University of South Florida. He is currently the co-editor (with Arnold Danzig) of the IAP book series Research and Theory in Educational Admin-

*Who Decides?*, pages 717–725
Copyright © 2022 by Information Age Publishing
www.infoagepub.com

istration and previously served as the co-editor of the *Journal of Cases in Educational Leadership*. His research interests are characterized by two arenas of activity: leadership preparation, partnerships, and pathways; and policy implementation and educational politics in diverse contexts.

**Samuel Bland** is a teacher in a self-contained special education (SDC) classroom in a middle school setting in California. He identifies as African American or Black with a learning disability. He has been working in the education field for close to 10 years.

**Corina Borri-Anadon** teaches in the Education Department at the University of Quebec in Trois-Rivières. She's a regular member of the Laboratoire International Sur l'Inclusion Scolaire (www.lisis.org) and co-director of the Laboratoire Éducation et Diversité en Région (uqtr.ca/ledir). Her academic work focuses on three main axes: ethno-cultural, linguistic, and religious diversity in training school personnel, inclusion-exclusion issues in special education and paramedical personnel practices in schools.

**Joshua Bornstein** is presently assistant professor and director of the Educational Leadership at Fairleigh Dickinson University. Dr. Bornstein has served as teacher, union leader, principal, staff developer, and school board member. He has worked in urban, rural, and suburban communities in Maryland, New Jersey, and New York. His research and writing are on inclusive educational leadership that eliminates race, class, gender, disability, and first language as predictors of student success.

**Denia G. Bradshaw** is an educator, professional flutist, disability and performing arts advocate, and a universal design for learning (UDL) researcher and facilitator. Currently, she is working with students, faculty, and staff, under the leadership of the department chair, in managing the music department at California State University, Los Angeles. Her work has appeared in the *Journal for Higher Education Theory and Practice*, and she has presented on her research at the American Educational Research Association, the California chapter of the National Association for Multicultural Education, and the California Association for Postsecondary Education and Disability. Dr. Bradshaw holds a bachelor's degree and master of music from California State University Northridge, and a doctorate in educational leadership from California State University, Los Angeles.

**Melissa Brideau** is a PhD student at Western University in the Faculty of Education in London, Ontario, Canada. Melissa previously graduated from Kings University College at Western University with both a master's and a bachelor's degree in social work. She has worked for several years as a disability advocate helping individuals with diverse needs access crucial supports and services to increase their independence/improve health and well-being.

**Tya Collins** is a PhD candidate in the Department of Administration and Foundations of Education at the Université de Montréal. Her thesis focuses on the experiences of Black students in special education. As a former special education teacher and administrator, some of her research interests include racism, ableism, professional practices, collective trauma, ethics of care, and social justice in education, as they relate to blackness.

**Monica de Carvalho Magalhaes Kassar** is a senior researcher at the Federal University of Mato Grosso do Sul, where she works in the postgraduate program in education—social education. She has a doctorate in education from the UNICAMP (Brazil) with postdoctoral internships from universities in Spain, Brazil, and Portugal.

**Robert Cooper** is an associate professor of education at the UCLA Graduate School of Education and Information Studies and serves as co-faculty director of the UCLA Principal Leadership Institute. The overarching focus of Professor Cooper's research activities over the past two decades has been on issues of educational access, equity, and segregation in America's public schooling system. His research and scholarship are conceptually and analytically linked to his interests in public policy, in that he seeks to identify effective policies and practices that lead to both excellence and equity in urban schools serving large numbers of poor and minority youth.

**Michelle L. Damiani** is an assistant professor of inclusive education at Rowan University. She received her PhD in special education and certificate of advanced study in disability studies from Syracuse University. Formerly, she was a public school elementary special education teacher and a new teacher mentor. In her research, she uses a disability studies in education framework to explore disability as an aspect of diversity in the teacher workforce that contributes to understanding school structures, pedagogical approaches, and inclusive practices. She is also engaged in research and systemic change initiatives around developing sustainable inclusive education practices in national and international contexts.

**Arnold B. Danzig** is professor of educational leadership and education policy and founding director of the EdD program in educational leadership at San José State University. He is professor emeritus at Arizona State University and served in multiple leadership positions including division director and associate dean in the Mary Lou Fulton Teachers College, and associate director of the School Public Affairs at Arizona State University. He has authored, edited, and co-edited books, chapters, journal volumes, and journal articles on school leadership and education policy during his career in higher education. Dr. Danzig holds a PhD with a focus on education policy, planning and administration from the University of Maryland, College Park. He is also a fellow with the National Education Policy Center.

**Natalie J. Delgado** is a Deaf Latinx ASL user, and English and Spanish speaker born to hearing parents. Delgado is the director of outreach at a residential school for the Deaf and has worked in Deaf education for over 11 years. Delgado's research interests include Deaf Latinx people, early childhood/early intervention, identity, and language development.

**Joanna Marina Gaeta** is a middle school special education teacher who identifies as Mexican. She is working towards her masters in special education researching the effects of discipline disparities on male minority students with disabilities.

**JPB Gerald** is an EdD student at the City University of New York—Hunter College whose research focuses on the intersection of language teaching, racism, and whiteness. He also teaches classes on decentering Whiteness and lives with his wife, son, and dog.

**Bridget Green** is an assistant professor of special education in the Department of Counseling, Psychology, and Special Education at Duquesne University. Her research focuses on understanding the needs of students who have disabilities transitioning into college and employment, transition assessment, and developing best practices to ensure students with and without disabilities have access to meaningful career-based assessments in the general education classroom. Other interests include disability rights, accessibility for all, and self-advocacy for the disability community.

**Ashley Greene** is an assistant professor in the Department of Deaf Studies and Deaf Education at Lamar University. She has over 10 years of experience working in the K–12 setting. Her recent research has focused on bimodal bilingualism and the evaluation of deaf children's language development.

**Molly Greer** is from Kentucky where she was a functional academics teacher for 5 years before moving to Florida to pursue her PhD. Molly holds a bachelor's degree in moderate to severe disabilities and elementary education, she also earned a Master's of Divinity in family ministry. Molly's mission is to prepare teachers and inform policy makers on how to merge learning sciences and mathematical practices to effectively increase educational outcomes for students with exceptionalities.

**Mayumi Hagiwara** is an assistant professor in the Extensive Support Needs (moderate/severe disabilities) Program in the Department of Special Education. Before joining the faculty at SFSU, she was a postdoctoral researcher at University of Kansas, focusing on promoting self-determination and inclusive community participation for people with extensive support needs. Her primary teaching responsibilities include courses in instruction of students with extensive support needs and transition planning. Her research interests focus on inclusive education, self-determination, family–school partnerships, transition planning, and inclusive adult outcomes for people with extensive support needs.

**Christine Hancock**, PhD, is an assistant professor of early childhood special education at Wayne State University. Her scholarship focuses on fostering equitable interactions between families and professionals that result in meaningful and mutual decisions.

**Angela Passero Jones** is an assistant professor at the University of Wisconsin—Eau Claire in the Department of Special Education and Inclusive Practices where she teaches in the Unified Early Childhood Program. Her research interests are situated across early childhood education and special education policy with a focus on how policies are operationalized across educational contexts to support, challenge, or mediate social oppression.

**Roderick Jones** is an assistant professor in the Department of Special Education and Inclusive Practices at the University of Wisconsin-Eau Claire. His research interests include special education law and policy, leadership mentoring, and leadership hiring and selection practices.

**Saili S. Kulkarni** is an assistant professor of special education at San Jose State University. Her research seeks to understand the beliefs of special education teachers of color and examines the intersections of race and disability across teacher education. Her work also looks at exclusionary discipline disparities for young children of color with disabilities.

**Gloshanda Lawyer** (she/ella) is a community-based disability justice and language justice practitioner with an emphasis in abolition and making social justice spaces more accessible. She also does research at the community, national and international levels on social justice, colonization, Deaf education and Deaf studies with emphasis on analyzing systems of power, and multilingualism for Deaf, DeafBlind, DeafDisabled and hard of hearing populations.

**Marie-Odile Magnan** is an associate professor in the faculty of education at the Université de Montréal. Her research focuses on educational inequalities from primary schools to postsecondary education, as reported by youths, and on the equity practices of teachers and other staff involved in education. She has produced the documentary "En route vers l'équité" (On the Road to Equity), documenting the inclusive leadership of school principals.

**Julia Mahfouz** is an assistant professor in the School of Education and Human Development at the University of Colorado Denver. Her research explores the social, emotional, and cultural dynamics of educational settings. Her work seeks to deepen our understanding of social-emotional learning (SEL) and mindfulness through lenses of intervention implementation, school improvement efforts, and preparation of school leaders.

**Holly Manaseri** is an associate specialist at the Center on Disability Studies in the College of Education at the University of Hawaii at Manoa where she teaches courses in the graduate disability studies program. She received her PhD in the cultural foundations of education from Syracuse University, with a specialization is disability studies. Holly is a former teacher, school administrator, and professor of both teacher preparation and school leadership preparation where her work has focused on creating inclusive and caring classrooms.

**Erica McFadden** serves as the executive director of the Arizona Developmental Disabilities Planning Council. McFadden has more than 20 years of experience working in the aging and disability communities. Her research focuses on addressing disability policy issues in Arizona and nationally.

**Nikki Murdick** is a professor emerita in special education at Saint Louis University. Her research focus is focused on issues related to disability and inclusion in school and society. She has published and presented on this topic nationally and internationally.

**Brande Otis** is a PhD student at the University of California, Los Angeles. She received her MA and EdS in school and educational psychology and worked with young learners with disabilities. Currently she pursues research at the intersection of Blackness, disability, and family engagement, and is interested in pursuing qualitative research methodologies that draw from and highlight Black epistemologies.

**Cynthia Paes de Carvalho** is a professor and researcher in the Department of Education at Pontifícia Universidade Católica do Rio de Janeiro/PUC-Rio since 2008. She earned her PhD in Education PUC-Rio in 2004. Since 2010 she has coordinated the research group GESQ—Gestão e Qualidade da Educação/PUC-Rio and supervises postgraduate students (MA and PhD) on school management, sociology, and politics of education.

**Flavia Pedrosa de Camargo** has a PhD in education (2019) from the Pontifical Catholic University of Rio de Janeiro (PUC-Rio) and a Master in Education (2011) from the Federal University of Mato Grosso do Sul (UFMS). She serves as a psychologist at the Federal Institute of Mato Grosso do Sul (IFMS) Campus Corumbá, where she is a researcher of special education with emphasis on public policies. She additionally serves as a member of the research group Education Management and Quality (GESQ) from PUC-Rio.

**Adam Rea** teaches history at Polk State College in Florida. He has a PhD in educational leadership from the University of South Florida and has published work on educational law and educational policy implementation. He is currently working on a comparative historical analysis of the 1960s and the 2020s regarding civil rights and education.

**Andrew Scheef** is an assistant professor of special education at the University of Idaho (Moscow, ID) and has extensive experience teaching in public schools. Dr. Scheef's research interests focus on supporting post-school transition for students with disabilities.

**Marrok Sedgwick** is a multiply-disabled activist, educator, and award-winning documentary filmmaker. His film practice borrows from ethnographic and experimental traditions to tell stories that push for a more just society. He is currently working towards a PhD in learning sciences, where he studies how youth with intellectual and/or developmental disabilities learn.

**Sarah Semon** earned her PhD in curriculum and instruction in special education from the University of South Florida. She is a visiting instructor of special education in the Department of Teaching and Learning at USF and has over 20 years of experience teaching in K–12 and higher education settings. Sarah has dedicated her career to improving inclusive education services for diverse learners.

**Regina Umpstead** is a professor of educational leadership at Central Michigan University. Her research interests explore the law and policy dimensions of PK–12 education issues. She is passionate about diversity, equity, and inclusion as a means to respect the dignity and worth of individuals within the education system.

**Fernando Valle** is professor and chair in the College of Education at Texas Tech University where his research in leadership preparation encompasses addressing the development of leadership pipelines and ongoing inequities driving problems of practice in schools and districts. He currently leads and trains leadership teams for K–12, classroom, school, and district improvement. Dr. Valle works with TTU leadership faculty in district to university partnership efforts across the state to grow and graduate job ready principals through residency preparation.

**Sofia Vergara** has been a Spanish educator/cofounder Bridges to Inclusion for the last 15 years and served as curriculum coordinator for the Spanish division of her department. She is an alumnus of the school and decided to go back and work there after graduating from UC Berkeley with a degree in political science and minors in both Spanish and disability studies. She also earned a master's degree in secondary education and doctorate degree in educational leadership for social justice both from Loyola Marymount University, Los Angeles. In 2017, Sofia was asked to join LMU's School of Education as a lecturer where she has taught undergraduate and graduate courses. In 2020, Sofia and a colleague co-founded Bridges to Inclusion, a company providing training and support to educational institutions, organizations, families, and individuals with disabilities.

**Catherine Kramarczuk Voulgarides** is assistant professor of special education at the City University of New York—Hunter College. She received her PhD from New York University in sociology of education. She examines how equity, access, and opportunity are constructed in policy and law and how the socio-cultural contexts of schools relate to equity.

**Julie Whitaker** is an educator and disability advocate. She has worked to promote the rights of individuals with disabilities as a teacher, state disability program specialist, and, most recently, as a research and outreach coordinator at an institute dedicated to autism research and public health.

**Gina Wilson** is an assistant professor in the Department of Educational Leadership, working with aspiring school and district leaders at Central Michigan University (CMU). Additionally, she serves as the program director for the Master of Arts in Educational Leadership and the Specialist in Education degree programs. Before joining CMU, she served as a public school educator for 20 years as a teacher, coordinator, and administrator.

**Jodi Wood** is completing her 16th year at Saint Louis University where her expertise is in education. Her practice areas are curriculum and instruction, professional development and teacher evaluation. Her research interests include curriculum, early childhood, and universal instructional design

**S. J. Wright** is an assistant professor at Rochester Institute of Technology, and the director of the Deaf MetaLiteracy Lab, housed within the National Technical Institute for the Deaf. He began his career in adult education for DeafDisabled learners, while finding a passion for research that encompasses three broad domains of literacy: health literacy, cultural literacy, and digital literacy as it coexists with the lives of Deaf, DeafBlind, DeafDisabled, and

Hard of Hearing individuals. His work also encompasses Critical Theory as it pertains to the intersectionality of Deaf individuals, particularly that of Deaf Critical Theory and the cross-pollination of Disability Studies along with legal frameworks that shape much of his interpretations of Critical Theory.

**Irene H. Yoon** (she/her) is associate professor of educational leadership and policy at the University of Utah. Her research examines the construction of equitable and inclusive school cultures and learning environments with particular attention to intersections of race, gender, disability, and social class. Her work has used critical approaches to whiteness in teaching and teacher communities, temporality in school improvement, haunting and transgenerational trauma, and qualitative methodologies.

Printed in the USA
CPSIA information can be obtained
at www.ICGtesting.com
LVHW020204191223
766776LV00003B/22